Imagining Mary

Imagining Mary breaks new ground in the long tradition of Christian mariology. The book is an interdisciplinary investigation of some of the many Marys, East and West, from the New Testament Mary of Nazareth down to Our Lady of the Good Death in the twentieth century. In *Imagining Mary*, Professor Rancour-Laferriere examines the mother of God in her multireligious and pan-historical context.

The book is a scholarly study, but it is written in a clear, straightforward style and will be comprehensible to an educated – and, above all, intellectually curious – general audience. It will appeal to anyone who has ever wondered, for example, about the flimsy scriptural basis of many beliefs about Mary; or the tendency of many mariologists to depict Mary as an incestuous "bride of Christ"; or the theological notion of Mary's "loving consent" to her son's crucifixion; or the idea that Mary was a "priest" officiating at the sacrifice of her son; or the unfortunate association of Mary with Christian anti-Semitism; or the curious appeal of Mary to the terminally ill; and so on. Special attention is given to the psychology of representations of Mary, such as: the psychological basis for promoting Mary to the status of a "goddess"; the psychology of Mary's compassion for her son at the foot of the cross; and the psychological conflict in Mary's personal relationship with her son Jesus.

These topics are admittedly diverse, but they all have long been on the minds of mariologists. The author takes a questioning approach to received wisdom about marian themes – including the assumption that one has to be a theist in order to understand the great appeal of Mary down the centuries. Indeed, *Imagining Mary* may be regarded as a first step in the direction of an atheist mariology.

Daniel Rancour-Laferriere was born and was baptized into the Roman Catholic Church in 1943, grew up a devout Catholic, and served as president of his Newman Club in college. Since receiving a PhD in Slavic Languages and Literatures from Brown University in 1972, Rancour-Laferriere has published numerous scholarly articles, as well as a dozen books, including *The Slave Soul of Russia* (1995), *Tolstoy on the Couch* (1998), *Tolstoy's Quest for God* (2007), and *The Sign of the Cross* (2011). As Emeritus Professor at the University of California, Davis, Rancour-Laferriere continues his psychological research on Christian themes.

Imagining Mary

A Psychoanalytic Perspective on Devotion to the Virgin Mother of God

Daniel Rancour-Laferriere

Routledge
Taylor & Francis Group
NEW YORK AND LONDON

First published 2018
by Routledge
711 Third Avenue, New York, NY 10017

and by Routledge
2 Park Square, Milton Park, Abingdon, Oxon, OX14 4RN

Routledge is an imprint of the Taylor & Francis Group, an informa business

Library of Congress Cataloging-in-Publication Data
Names: Rancour-Laferriere, Daniel, author.
Title: Imagining Mary : a psychoanalytic perspective on devotion to the Virgin Mother of God / Daniel Rancour-Laferriere.
Description: 1 [edition]. | New York : Routledge, 2017. | Includes bibliographical references and index.
Identifiers: LCCN 2017029616| ISBN 9781412865067 (hb : alk. paper) | ISBN 9781315121550 (eb : alk. paper)
Subjects: LCSH: Mary, Blessed Virgin, Saint.
Classification: LCC BT603 .R36 2017 | DDC 232.91—dc23
LC record available at https://lccn.loc.gov/2017029616

ISBN: 978-1-4128-6506-7 (hbk)
ISBN: 978-1-315-12155-0 (ebk)

Typeset in Bembo
by Swales & Willis Ltd, Exeter, Devon, UK

Contents

Figures

Preface

There is a vast scholarly literature on Mary the mother of Jesus. No one scholar can presume to "cover" the topic of mariology. This is remarkable in view of the fact that so very little (and much of that historically unreliable) is said about the mother of Jesus in the New Testament.

So, why a new book on Mary? One answer is that psychological aspects of Mary have, in the past, been neglected. Or, to be more precise, psychoanalytic studies of *how Mary is represented* in a wide variety of cultural artifacts, in addition to the Bible – theological treatises, passion plays, poetry, iconography, papal bulls, ritual practices, and so on – have been lacking.

Of particular interest in this book are representations of Mary's relationship with her son Jesus. Here are some examples. In viewing images of Mary breastfeeding her infant child, we are inevitably reminded of who that child will grow up to be. When we hear the famous medieval hymn *Stabat Mater*, we are given an opportunity to empathize with Mary as she responds with great pain to the agonies her divine son is voluntarily enduring on the cross. In some theological treatises from the early modern period, we are told that Mary actually offers up her son as a sacrifice at Golgotha. In the twentieth century, an infallible papal statement informs us that Mary now resides in heaven because (in part) her son called her to join him there in an act of gratitude for her having once agreed to be his mother.

All of these situations stage Mary's relationship with her son in a certain way. They represent the desires and fears of individual viewers, listeners, and readers. They become more comprehensible in the light of psychoanalysis.

Another answer to the question of why there needs to be another book on Mary is more personal in nature. I was born and raised in a Roman Catholic family, and I was a devout believer until my early twenties. It is my religious background which makes me deeply sympathetic to veneration of the mother of God. However, I am now an atheist. Ordinarily, this would not be mentioned in a scholarly work about Mary. But the scholarly aim in this case is objectivity – psychological objectivity in particular – and that aim, in my opinion, excludes any religious credulity on the part of the scholar. Many of the conclusions drawn in this book follow from explicitly stated atheist premises and could not have been reached otherwise.

Many scholars in the field of religious studies – and even some theologians – are silent atheists. This phenomenon is quite understandable, but it hinders scholarly and theological research. As I am in the fortunate position of no longer having employment-related obligations, I am not required to keep silent. An atheist mariologist is also a mariologist. The chapters of this book may be regarded as preliminary steps toward an atheist mariology.

There is an old adage about Mary often attributed to Saint Bernard of Clairvaux: *De Maria numquam satis* ("Never Enough of Mary"). This is a favorite saying among mariophile theologians and scholars, who seem never to be satisfied by what has already been said about the mother of Christ. I hope to show that, indeed, altogether too much has been left unsaid about Mary.

*

In the five years of writing this book, I have had numerous occasions to be grateful. First to hear me out was always my wife, the artist Barbara Milman. Others who made valuable comments or provided useful materials include: Mebrahtu Aregai, Mario Beer, Benjamin Beit-Hallahmi, Michael K. Bourke, William Craft Brumfield, the late Donald Capps, Alicja Coe, Joanne Feit Diehl, Sue Easton, Paul Elovitz, Sean Griffin, Mitchell Hall, Priscilla Hunt, Paul Jacobs, Asher Jason, Claire Kahane, German Kidane, Roman Kurowski, Theresa Laferriere, Valerii Leibin, Burton Melnick, David Mermin, Dorothy Mermin, Abraham Negash, Leonard Pitt, Livia Rosman, Richard Rosman, Naomi Seidman, Julie de Sherbinin, Stephen J. Shoemaker, David Traill, and Annette Volfing. At a late stage, an anonymous reader provided some very helpful and useful comments on the manuscript.

I have profited from participation in the PSYART listserve (moderated by Professor Norman Holland of the University of Florida), and particularly from contributions to threads on marian themes by: Carole Brooks-Platt, Terry Burridge, Don Carveth, William Conger, Vito Evola, Dianne Hunter, Maria Kardaun, Louis Lagana, Norman Rosenblood, Lew Schwartz, Mary Scriver, Richard Allen Shoaf, Yves Thoret, David Topper, Ellen Trezevant, Francina Valk, and Meg Williams. I have also learned much in some lively exchanges with participants on the SEELANGS listserve for Slavists, especially from contributors to threads on marian prayers, terminology, iconography, and sophiology, including: Kenneth R. Allan, Yuliya I. Ballou, John Barnstead, Tom Beyer, David Borgmeyer, Wayles Browne, Ralph M. Cleminson, Luciano Di Cocco, June P. Farris, Anna Frajlich-Zajac, Philippe Frison, Genevra Gerhart, Stuart H. Goldberg, George J. Gutsche, Maria Hatjigeorgiou, Brian Hayden, Alina Israeli, Michael R. Katz, Eugenia Kelbert, Daria Kirjanov, Alina W. Klin, Svitlana Malykhina, Robert Orr,

Tom Rowley, Will Ryan, Irina G. Stakhanova, Christine Worobec, and Jan Zielinski.

Antiquarian bookseller Michael Hackenberg was most helpful in spotting and/or tracking down mariological titles for me. As always, the staff of the University of California Libraries (including the friendly people at UC Berkeley Interlibrary Services) provided indispensable research materials. I was also able to consult the rather extensive collection of marian titles in the Library of the Graduate Theological Union in Berkeley. Much appreciated is the warm hospitality and conviviality of the French Hotel Café in Berkeley.

Translations are mine, except where otherwise indicated. All quotations from the Bible in English are from the New Revised Standard Version unless otherwise indicated.

Daniel Rancour-Laferriere
June 15, 2016
El Cerrito, California

1 Introduction

From a Humble Mother of Nazareth to "Our Lady of Everywhere"

Mary in Scripture

Mary's son Jesus is the most important figure in canonical Christian scripture, and Christian believers would eventually come to accept him as their God. Mary herself is a different matter altogether. She has a minimal role to play in the New Testament, even if she is the mother of the Messiah (that is, the Christ). She conceives and gives birth to her child only in Matthew and Luke, with the author of Luke's gospel paying additional attention to the circumstances of the conception as well as to some aspects of Mary's involvement in the development of the child. Mary appears rarely during the ministry of the adult Jesus in any of the gospels, and her silent presence at her son's cross is registered only in John. After Jesus dies, Mary has no further contact with her son, despite his alleged resurrection from the dead. Mary then makes just one (again, silent) appearance at the beginning of the Acts of the Apostles, a work believed to be a continuation of the gospel of Luke. By this time, Mary's son had already "ascended" into heaven. After that comes total silence about Mary. The other authors of what remains of the canonical New Testament do not mention her by name.

One might therefore be inclined to ask: if the crucifixion of Jesus is the most important event in Christian scripture, and if the cross is the chief symbol of Christianity,[1] then why is there any need to speculate on the relevance of Mary to this event and this symbol? Such a question would seem particularly obvious to most Protestants and to other Christians who do not believe Mary is of any special importance for the Christian faith, and who are for the most part not relevant for this book. The question is also obvious to historians, for there is so very little historically reliable information to go on.

There is, however, much more to Christian belief systems than what is presented in canonical scripture. The relentless post-biblical growth of marian narratives, doctrines, poetry, drama, music, visual imagery, political discourse, pilgrimage sites, and so on, makes it obvious that Mary is important – for many Christians, even more important than her son.

Questers of the "historical Jesus" are already familiar with the problems of insufficient, inconsistent, and outright fabricated accounts in the New Testament. Some of these accounts involve the mother of Jesus as well, in particular the so-called infancy narratives early in Luke and Matthew. For example, the genealogies of Mary's husband Joseph, given by Luke and Matthew, cannot be reconciled with one another.[2] Or, Luke tells a story (2:1–7) about a journey made by Mary and Joseph from Nazareth to Bethlehem in order to register in what would have been the *wrong* city for a Roman imperial census, which, in any case, did *not* take place at the time indicated.[3] Matthew too (2:1–13) places Mary and Joseph in Bethlehem for the birth of the future Messiah – but only because this was supposedly prophesied in Micah 5:2. The subsequent flight into Egypt, the slaughter of the innocents, and the move to Nazareth (Matthew 2:14–23) are also attempts by Matthew to *historicize* Old Testament prophecies, so that New Testament scholar Gerd Lüdemann concludes that the "historical content" of the second chapter of Matthew is "nil."[4] Even a strongly mariophile church Father such as Maximos the Confessor (d. ca.662) admits that there are problems with the historical veracity of some passages in the infancy narratives and attempts (unsuccessfully) to solve them.[5] It comes as no surprise that the group of historical scholars known as the Jesus Seminar concluded that, "there is very little in the two infancy narratives that reflects historical reminiscence."[6] Any quest for the "historical Mary" would appear to be doomed from the start.

It is generally agreed among historians, however, that there did exist a man from the Galilean village of Nazareth named Jesus (*Iēsous* in the Greek original of the New Testament, *Yeshua* in Hebrew), who was crucified on the outskirts of Jerusalem in approximately 30 CE.[7] This Jesus was a Jew, and he must have had a biological mother who was also Jewish.[8] Indeed, all four canonical gospels, as well as Acts, allude to the "mother" of Jesus. Although the name of this "mother" is not always mentioned when she makes an appearance, and although she is not named at all in John's gospel, it is reasonably certain from the 18 times she is named in the other (synoptic) gospels and the one time in Acts[9] that her name was Mary (*Mariam* [or *Maria*] in Greek, *Miryam* in Hebrew).[10] Mary's son Jesus, by contrast, is named 913 times in the New Testament.[11]

Mary, then, is historically real, if infrequently mentioned by name and included in few events that have historical credibility. Mary was no more a docetist phantom than was Jesus himself – who was real enough to die and who, therefore, must have been sufficiently real to be born, as Tertullian (d. ca.220) insisted in his polemic *De Carne Christi*.[12] If Jesus was "born of a woman," as Paul says (Galatians 4:4), then both Jesus and this "woman," Mary, are historically real.

Early Elaboration

Mary's son led the way. Marian narratives and imagery could not be enabled until ideas about her son became thoroughly unmoored from reality in the minds of his increasingly populous followers. After the crucifixion, there were sightings of Jesus by some who had been emotionally attached to him, and who had not had an opportunity to complete the mourning process that normally leads to acceptance, rather than denial, of the death of a loved one (apparitions of the newly departed are a commonplace of bereavement).[13] In this case, the lost object was also a charismatic religious leader. Word spread of the "resurrection" of Jesus from the dead, and increasingly grand, idealizing theological constructs deriving from what Jesus had preached would eventually come to be the church's "christology." Jesus the Messiah/Christ was made flesh through the action of the Holy Spirit within Mary's virginal womb, and evidence of Jesus' pre-existing divine identity could be found in some writings, which were to become the New Testament.[14] Orthodox Christians were expected to believe that Christ was essentially one with God the Father, according to conclusions reached at the Council of Nicaea in 325. By the Council of Chalcedon in 451, a definitive doctrine about the person of Christ was achieved.[15]

Of course, this oversimplifies the early historical development of beliefs about the death and resurrection of Jesus Christ, God's incarnation in his person, his place in the holy trinity, and the two distinct yet inseparable natures – perfectly human and perfectly divine – of Jesus Christ. But, our primary concern here is with beliefs about Christ's mother Mary.

If Jesus Christ was indeed God as well as a human being, then what was believed to be the status of his mother? Was she the one who gave birth to the man (*anthrōpotokos*), to the Messiah/Christ (*christotokos*), or to God himself (*theotokos*)? The most contentious and effective voice in this matter was patriarch Cyril of Alexandria (d. 444), who, in 429, expressed his indignation about the teachings of Nestorius (then patriarch of Constantinople): "I was completely amazed that certain people should be in any doubt as to whether the holy virgin ought to be called the *Theotokos* or not. For if our Lord Jesus Christ is God, then how is the holy virgin who bore him not the *Theotokos*?"[16] Because of Cyril's untiring efforts at the Council of Ephesus in 431 (and with the support of his fellow mariophiles there and at Chalcedon in 451), Mary was officially recognized as what might variously and clumsily be translated into English as the "Birthgiver of God," or the "Godbearer," or the "Godbirther" (Greek *Theotokos*, roughly equivalent to the Latin *Dei Genitrix/Genetrix* or *Deipara*).[17] As for the more personalized notion "Mother of God" (Greek *Mētēr theou*, Latin *mater Dei*), it had been sporadically utilized before Ephesus, but was slower to gain acceptance in the Greek East than in the Latin West.[18]

The male Christian leaders who ratified the *theotokos* designation were painfully aware of pagan polytheism, with its various gods and goddesses. Unlike pagans, they believed in a god named Jesus Christ, and there were no Christian goddesses. With time, of course, there would be at least one: the Blessed Virgin Mary, Queen of Heaven, and Mother of All. Ephesus was just the first, halting step in Mary's extraordinary transformation into Christianity's own goddess.

Just what a "goddess" is (or was in the fifth century) is a matter of debate. If one presumes to "know" that Christianity is a monotheistic religion, then of course Mary cannot possibly be a goddess, for she is just the humble Saint Mary. If, however, one keeps an open mind about this, and especially if one notices that many mariophiles seem actually to *worship* Mary as if she were the equal of – or even greater than – her divine son, then it has to be admitted that Mary is, for these people, a goddess.[19] But, for other mariophiles who seem only to be *venerating* Mary, for example by praying that she *intercede* with her son regarding some personal matter, Mary might not appear to be a goddess at all. Worship of Mary goes under the derogatory term "mariolatry," whereas veneration of Mary is – and has long been – the theologically acceptable level of devotion to Mary, at least within the contexts of Roman Catholicism and Eastern Orthodoxy.

Whatever the cognitive structure and affective intensity of the attachment to Mary, it is clear that the attachment is to a *mother figure*, that is, to the mother of Christ. Indeed, for most religions that hold a female figure of any kind in high esteem, that figure is usually a mother.[20] In the case of Mary, however, there is also the question of *whose* mother she is. It is not enough to confirm the fact that she was the mother of the Christian savior, Jesus Christ. For those who have worshiped or venerated her, she has also been their own mother, or at least the mother of others besides the historical Jesus. In ancient and medieval Latin prayers, poems, and hymns, for example, Mary was called "our mother [*mater nostra*]," "my mother [*mater mea*]," "mother of orphans [*mater orphanorum*]," "mother of the poor [*mater pauperum*]," "mother of the faithful [*mater credentium*]," and so on.[21] Aelred of Rievaulx (d. 1167) went so far as to declare of Mary that, "she is our mother much more than our mother according to the flesh [*Ideo magis nobis mater quam mater carnis nostrae*]."[22]

The use of maternal metaphors for Mary makes sense from a psychological viewpoint. A mature adult who is no longer literally dependent on his or her own real mother may need a metaphorical "mother" from time to time. Devout mariophiles probably need such metaphors more often. All human beings in all cultures and in all historical periods have had personal experience of a real mother (or a designated mother-substitute) in early ontogeny, so that everyone has a concept of a mother. Given that dependence on one's mother normally begins nine months before birth and continues for years, as physical and psychological independence are only gradually achieved at best, then it is not surprising that adult experience of culturally designated mother images can have a profoundly emotional resonance.

Not everyone who has grown up Christian has been exposed to the same representations of Mary. At various times and in various places in the history of Christianity, there have been various special titles under which the mother of Christ could be venerated or worshipped. For example, while I was growing up in a large French-Canadian (but mostly English-speaking) Catholic family in the middle of the twentieth century, "the Blessed Virgin Mary"

("BVM") was the title of choice. As it happens, this particular expression is not an explicit maternal metaphor, but we were well aware of others such as "Mother of Christ," "Holy Mother of God," "Mother of the Church," "Mother of good counsel," and so on (from the Litany of Loreto),[23] and, in any case, we learned at an early point that "Mary" was the mother of the child "Jesus" in the Christmas carols we sang.

In many parts of the world, during certain historical periods, altogether different choices (than Mary) have been available as metaphorical mothers. For example, in many places, there have been the local pagan goddesses. Pagans, like everyone else, have had personal experience of a real mother. Pagans and Christians, moreover, have often lived in close physical proximity. For example, any woman who worshipped Isis – mother of Horus – in late antique Egypt was at some level re-imagining experience of her real mother, just as any woman who worshipped Mary in the same late antique Egypt was re-imagining experience of *her* real mother.

The universal core experience of having been mothered helps to explain why it is possible for one maternal metaphor to replace (or to exist in syncretistic overlap with) another such metaphor. In ancient Rus', for example, the Mother of God (*Bogoroditsa*, a calque on the Greek *Theotokos*)[24] arrived from Byzantium in the tenth century and began to provide some of the same maternal amenities that the pagan mother earth (later known as "Mother Moist Earth" [*mat' syra zemlia*]) was providing.[25] Even in the late pre-Soviet period, Russian peasants would still sometimes refer to the Mother of God as "Earth" (*zemlia*) and, conversely, they would sometimes refer to Earth as "Mother of God" (*Bogoroditsa*).[26] This replaceability or interchangeability of metaphorical mothers was made possible by the ontogenetic past of the individuals involved, that is, by personal childhood experience of the real mother in those particular adult individuals who were choosing to worship one or other – pagan or Christian – maternal deity. Even without the help of psychology, the Russian folk themselves understood perfectly well that a third party – one's real mother – had to be involved, as in this passage from a spiritual song collected in the middle of the nineteenth century:

> *Первая мать – Пресвятая Богородица;*
> *Вторая мать – сыра земля;*
> *Третия мать – кая скорбь приняла.*
> The first mother is the Most Holy Mother of God;
> The second mother is Moist Earth;
> The third mother is the one who took on pain [i.e., in childbirth].[27]

From a religious (Russian Orthodox) viewpoint, the Mother of God was certainly 'number one,' as indicated here. From a historical viewpoint, however, this ditty is wrong. Moist Earth was first, not second, for this pagan metaphor (among others) was revered in Rus' before Christianity officially arrived there in the tenth century. From a psychological viewpoint, however, neither the Mother of God nor Moist Earth was primary. One's own mother was (and still is) 'number one' in Russia (as elsewhere), for she was the first human being an individual interacted with from the moment of conception, and for quite some time after birth the preponderance of interaction was with this particular, literal mother. Both "Moist Earth" and the "Mother of God" were derivative. They were maternal metaphors imagined relatively late in childhood development – if at all, depending on the individual's sociocultural environment within Russia.

Purist Christian authorities have sometimes not been too pleased with the interchangeability or syncretism of any pagan maternal metaphor with their own maternal metaphor, that is, Mary the mother of Christ. Alluding to the old cult of Cybele in a homily on the feast of Mary's dormition, John of Damascus (d. ca.750) declared, "we do not bring flutes and revelers, or join in revels like those that are said to be celebrated for the mother of the so-called gods."[28] Here it is understood that Cybele the mother of the gods is inferior to Mary the Mother of God. In sixteenth-century New Spain (Mexico), a Franciscan priest complained that devotees of Tonantzin (any Aztec goddess specifically in her maternal aspect) were coming from afar to worship *their* goddess at the Christian church of Our Lady of Guadalupe at Tepeyac. Here, Mary Our Lady of Guadalupe surpasses the Aztec Tonantzin.[29]

"New Mother-Goddess of the Christians"

The fact that the male God of the council participants at Ephesus in 431 had two natures, divine and human, led to the question (among many others) of where the human element might have come from. It could not have derived from the heavenly Father, who was divine, so it must have originated in the female human being who gave birth to Christ, hence the term *theotokos*. As Stephen Benko explains: "'*Theo-tokos*' unites the idea of God ('*theo*') with the ideal of human birth ('*-tokos*') and thus presents the Christian idea of the incarnation in a well balanced way." The term *theotokos* was not supposed to confer any "privileges" upon Mary, for it was the carefully formulated expression of "faith about the person of Jesus Christ."[30] In other words, the issue that gave rise to the term was not supposed to be a matter of what would come to be known as mariology, but of christology.

Yet, mariology happened. It was what Vasiliki Limberis terms the "logical result" of the aggressive christological stance that Cyril took against his rival Nestorius.[31] There is also reason to believe that an incipient popular devotion to Mary[32] and an intrinsic, nonderivative mariological component in Cyril's christology[33] both played important roles in the christological debates at Ephesus.

Still, on the surface at least, the term *theotokos* did seem to consign Mary to the shadows, where her seemingly surrogate motherhood would not have to distract attention from the grandeur of her divine son. Mary gave birth to the child Jesus in normal fashion, but the conception of that child had not exactly been normal, insofar as God the Father appeared to "rent" Mary's womb for his own purposes – that is, to sacrifice his child for the salvation of humankind.

Since Ephesus, Mary has gone on to become a *grande dame* in her own right, and today's mariophiles do not think in terms of maternal surrogation. For example, devotional writer Jon M. Sweeney declares, "The Virgin Mary was not a surrogate mother. It was her egg that produced the child, making her the genetic mother." Regardless of the official belief that Jesus had no *human* father, Mary was the *human* mother of "the zygote that became Jesus."[34] As the human mother of a human being who also happened to be a divine being, Mary deserved and still deserves an extra measure of respect. That is not "mariolatry." It is just a commonsense conclusion that ordinary Christian believers have often drawn.

Of course, Sweeney's biological concepts – "egg," "genetic mother," and "zygote" – are modern, empirically based scientific concepts. They were certainly unknown to the authors of the New Testament infancy narratives in the first century, as well as to theologians and ordinary believers in the fifth century. There is also the little problem that a "zygote" is by definition a *fertilized* egg, as well as the problem that a parthenogenetically produced Jesus – that is, an offspring produced without fertilization by a male gamete bearing a Y chromosome – would have two X chromosomes and would therefore have to be female (XX), not male (XY), making Jesus a girl at birth.

But, from the viewpoint of the psychology of a widely held religious belief – both in the first century and in the twenty-first – these empirical matters may be regarded as irrelevant. To borrow the announcing angel Gabriel's utterance of a conventional sentiment from the Hebrew Bible,[35] "nothing will be impossible with God" (Luke 1:37). So, Sweeney's point about "the zygote that became Jesus" is well taken. One does not have to be a believer to understand that his point is correct in spirit, even if technically false. It is a way of representing what many believers have long believed, even if the belief in question is a biological impossibility and is therefore a fiction.[36]

For the atheist, a temporary suspension of disbelief is essential for understanding religious belief. One has to put oneself in the position of a believer. When the oxymoronic single word "virginmother" (*parthenomētōr*) is utilized by Greek patristic writers, it has to be taken seriously.[37] The scholar has to "get into the spirit" of denying a mother's sexuality before it is even possible to understand why such a denial would be psychologically necessary. Even if believers know that, under normal circumstances, a mother cannot also be a virgin, some empathy is required of the scholar who would understand why, when believers assert that a mother can indeed be a virgin, that mother is always and only Mary: *Tu sola mater virgo es*.[38] Mary must be accepted as the ideal "virgin mother" of Jesus by anyone who would understand the importance of Mary in the history of Christianity. Disbelief has to be suspended at least temporarily. This is like paying *due scholarly respect* to ancient pagan goddesses no one believes in any more.

The comparison is not accidental. In a brief 1911 paper, Freud characterizes Mary as "the new mother-goddess of the Christians."[39] The old mother-goddess in this instance is Artemis, whose cult was (and still is) thought by historians to have been particularly strong in ancient Ephesus.[40] Freud writes: "With its concourse of priests, magicians and pilgrims, and with its shops in which amulets, mementoes and oblations were offered for sale, the commercial metropolis of Ephesus might be compared to a modern Lourdes."[41] Freud does not mention the council of 431, but he does speak of biblical and apocryphal accounts about "Mary" and "the virgin" in the same even, noncommittal fashion as he does about "Artemis" and "Diana." We know that Freud was an atheist, but, in most contexts (including this one), he hardly needs to say so. To his reader he extends the courtesy of suspending disbelief. At the same time, however, Freud politely makes his point that Mary is a "mother-goddess," and he reinforces this point by naming the goddess in question both "Mary" and "the virgin" – much as pagans could apply either the name "Artemis" or "Diana" to their goddess, depending on context.

Mariophile scholars have sometimes felt a need to deal with the pagan–Christian interface that surfaced at Ephesus in 431 (and, of course, in other early Christian contexts as well). John McGuckin writes:

> It cannot be incidentally insignificant that when the bishops emerged from what was already called the "Mary Church"[42] at the docks in Ephesus, and which was an extensive basilica, having accepted that it was legitimate to designate Mary as *Theotokos*, they were escorted home by women bearing lighted torches. Now, significant men retiring to their lodges late at night would surely command a lighted torch in their retinue, but this large procession of women bearing the lighted *lampada*s, that Cyril of Alexandria so delights in telling his readers was a sign of devotion they had to the Virgin Mary, was actually an inescapable symbol of women associated with the Isis–Artemis cult. Women bearing lighted torches were an integral part of her processional ritual.

McGuckin believes that there is no solid evidence that the crowd of women was even Christian, or exclusively Christian, for:

> the crowd could as easily have been a gathering of Artemisian devotees, or pagan women mixed in with Christians, among whom the Artemisians were celebrating the welcome advent of a large group of high-ranking visitors to their town, as well as their belief that the Christians had appeared to them finally to be making some ground in allowing what they themselves had long claimed anyway – that

> Mary, the recent Christian "goddess," was yet another form of the Isis *polynomos* whom they worshipped. Such syncretic blurring of the boundaries was absolutely typical of the Isiac–Artemisian traditions; just as it was *not* absolutely typical of the Christians.[43]

With the passage of centuries, Mary would become thoroughly as *polynomos* as any non-Christian "goddess" ever was, as we will see. But, behind the eventual multiplicity of Mary's names, there would always be the one historically real human being – Mary – of the canonical New Testament. In this respect, Mary does differ from the pagan goddesses. To my knowledge, it has never been claimed that there was a real, flesh and blood woman named Isis to whom the goddess of this name can be traced. The same goes for various other pagan goddesses, named Artemis, Diana, Demeter, Cybele, Astarte, Juno, Athena, Rhea, Vesta, and so on.[44]

Mary's Virginity and Her Son's Paternity

Mary was a twelve-year-old[45] Jewish virgin (*parthenos* – Matthew 1:23; Luke 1:27)[46] when she managed to get pregnant without losing her virginity. How this could have happened remains problematical for many biblical scholars, theologians, religious historians, ordinary clergy, and lay believers to this day. The infancy narratives in Luke and Matthew refer, not to a biological father, but to a divine agent as the initiator of Mary's pregnancy. Many early Christians may not have been familiar with these narratives, however. The gospels of Mark and John, the epistles attributed to Paul, and the early non-scriptural *Epistle of Barnabas* and the *Shepherd* of Hermas make no clear reference to a virginal conception of Jesus.[47]

What believers in the virginal conception of Jesus rely upon is chiefly this: the angel Gabriel appears before Mary and declares to her (among other things) that, "you will conceive in your womb and bear a son, and you will name him Jesus." In response to Mary's objection, "How can this be, since I do not know a man?," the angel responds: "The Holy Spirit will come upon you, and the power of the Most High will overshadow you; therefore the child to be born will be holy; he will be called Son of God" (Luke 1:31, 34–35). In Matthew, an unsuspecting Joseph discovers that his betrothed is pregnant, but an angel informs him in a dream that she is with child "from the Holy Spirit" (1:20). In both of the infancy narratives, Mary later gives birth to Jesus in Bethlehem (Matthew 2:1–11; Luke 2:4–20). Whether it was she who gave birth to the "brothers" and "sisters" of Jesus referred to elsewhere in the gospels (e.g., Mark 3:32, 6:3; Luke 8:19–20; John 2:12, 7:3–10) – that is, whether they were full siblings, half-siblings, cousins, or others – is an issue still debated by some theologians.[48]

As depicted in the infancy narratives, the conception of Jesus has traditionally been understood as virginal, and the title "Virgin" has been applied to Mary in various sectors of Christianity to this day.[49] Jesus was believed (and by many still is believed) to be without an earthly father. His father, like his kingdom, was "not from this world" (John 18:36). His father was God the Father in heaven, working through the agency of the Holy Spirit. For believers, whatever it was that happened to Mary when she became pregnant and gave birth to Jesus had to be some kind of miracle, for it contradicted known reproductive processes. The marvel of this contradiction is expressed well in the famous (probably fifth-century) Akathistos hymn, where Mary is hailed as "you who bring opposites together," "you who unite virginity and childbirth," and "bridal chamber of a seedless marriage."[50] Repeatedly, this hymn rings forth with the refrain: "Hail, bride unwedded [*numfē anumfeute*]!"[51]

As for the husband named Joseph, in scripture it is asserted that he accepted a degree of paternal responsibility for the sake of propriety (he is the legal *patēr* at Luke 2:48, and the adult Jesus is referred to as the son of Joseph [Luke 3:23, 4:22; John 6:42]). Curiously, no genealogy of Mary is provided, but Joseph's descent from King David is emphasized by the genealogies of those very gospel writers (Matthew and Luke) who, despite leaving an impression that the conception of Jesus was virginal, evidently accepted the ancient Jewish idea that the promised Messiah (in Greek, the Christ) would have to be a descendant of David.[52]

More curious still is the fact that, in the adult Jesus' own home territory, he is referred to as "the son of Mary" (Mark 6:3) by people who cannot have been unaware of how serious were the implications of calling a man after his mother. This hint at illegitimate origin in the earliest of the gospels has been obvious to some religious scholars.[53] Mark, of course, has nothing explicit to say about the conception and birth of Jesus, and does not even mention Joseph, but Matthew's gospel more than makes up for this lacuna. The locals in Nazareth/Capernaum seem to think just what Matthew's kinder and gentler Joseph had originally thought when he discovered that his betrothed was already pregnant: "being a righteous man and unwilling to expose her [Mary] to public disgrace, [he] planned to dismiss [divorce] her quietly" (Matthew 1:19). Fortunately, Joseph was dissuaded from carrying out this plan by an angel of the Lord who appeared to him in a dream. To judge from his *initial response*, however, Joseph had already concluded that a sexual irregularity of some kind had made it impossible for Mary to be his wife, for he had understood that his betrothed was pregnant and no longer a virgin.

It would appear, then, that the virgin birthers – to coin a term – are challenged, not only by biological science, but here and there by scripture as well. Those scholars who do reject the possibility of virgin birth – theists and atheists alike, some feminists, some scholars who quest for the "historical Jesus," such as the majority of members of the Jesus Seminar, and various others – have suggested that the father of Jesus was human. Perhaps the biological father of Jesus was in fact Joseph, the man who would become Mary's husband. But, perhaps the father was someone else, for many hypotheses about possible rape, seduction, adultery, incest, and mixed marriage have been explored, or at least mentioned.[54]

Widely studied is the idea that Jesus was illegitimately fathered by a certain non-Jew Panthera (Pandera), for sources such as the medieval Jewish *Toledot Yeshu*, passages dating to the fourth century in the (Babylonian) Talmud, and the second-century pagan anti-Christian Celsus (as reported in Origen's third-century *Contra Celsum*) make this claim.[55] Also relevant to the fathering of Jesus is the recent de-mythologization of the Matthean figure of Joseph by Donald Capps, who argues that, although Joseph did go on to marry an already pregnant Mary because he had no choice in the matter, he then failed actually to adopt Jesus, so that Mary's first-born child turned out to be illegitimate anyway in the eyes of his peasant family and community.[56]

Neither Mary nor Joseph plays much of a role in the gospel drama overall, but Mary is important enough, not only to conceive and give birth to Jesus (and very possibly some siblings or half-siblings), but also to make occasional appearances during his ministry, and to appear at the redemptive climax, which is the crucifixion of her son (John 19:25–27), as well as once more after the crucifixion (Acts 1:14). As for Joseph, he makes no appearance once the ministry of Jesus has begun. Jesus himself does not explicitly refer to Joseph.[57] However, he does refer quite often to a heavenly Father (*patēr*), and, in one particularly emotional prayer in the garden of Gethsemane, this Father is invoked by means of the Aramaic *abba* (Mark 14:36).[58] Indeed, the heavenly Father – as opposed to an earthly father – is the *only* father to whom Jesus ever refers as his own.

The absence of the merely human Joseph is quite convenient for an itinerant preacher who teaches his followers to pray to "Our Father in heaven," or who says that he has come "to set a man against his father," or who directs his followers to "call no one your father on earth, for you have one Father – the one in heaven" (Matthew 6:9, 10:35, 23:9).[59] Such passages are meant to glorify God the Father at the explicit or implicit expense of earthly fathers, but they might also have offended Joseph – had this "father" been around to hear them, and assuming he had been much more attached to his son and concerned about finding a place for him in the earthly world than is indicated anywhere in the New Testament.

Jesus glorifies not only his heavenly Father. He is perceived by others as glorifying himself. This is evident in the incident in John's gospel where Jesus works a miracle in Jerusalem on the Sabbath, thereby angering "the Jews," who want to kill him "because he was not only breaking the Sabbath, but was also calling God his own Father, thereby making himself equal to God" (John 5:18). Elsewhere in John, it is obvious that Jesus does in fact consider himself to be the equal of God: "The Father and I are one" (10:30); "Whoever has seen me has seen the Father" (14:9). Theologically speaking, Jesus may be laying a claim to divine identity. Psychoanalytically speaking, Jesus may be grandiose. Also, both may be true.

Whatever the case, these statements by Jesus may be interpreted as a response (defensive in nature) to the illegitimacy or perceived fatherlessness of a human being in the social world he inhabited. As various scholars have demonstrated, Jesus was bereft of basic social identity within a society built around extended patriarchal households.[60] The ministry of Jesus can be understood as a systematic endeavor to establish for himself (and for his followers) a substitute family, that is, a metaphorical family headed by God the Father (see below, pp. 133–136).

Practicing what their charismatic Jesus preached, early Christians became accustomed to praying to Jesus' heavenly God the Father themselves, and worshipping Jesus as the rightful "son" of this God. It is true that Jewish tradition had long before fostered the practice of designating all male Israelites as "sons of God," but, with time, this metaphor had become increasingly restricted to the holy among them, and eventually to the expected royal Messiah. The characterization of Mary's future child as "son of God" in the Lucan infancy narrative (1:35) and elsewhere in the New Testament therefore carries special weight.[61] In addition, any familiarity early Christians (especially Gentiles and Hellenized Jews) might have had with contemporary Roman imperial theology, which featured a designation "son of God" (Latin *Divi filius*, Greek *Theou huios*) for the emperor himself, would have led to a natural association with – or even a stimulus for – worshipping their own "son of God."[62]

Mary's Virginity and Her Incestuous Relations in the Light of Psychoanalysis

It could be argued that any given individual pagan goddess – such as Artemis, or Diana, or Isis – was not both a virgin[63] and a mother, as Mary was claimed to be. A few other pagan goddesses, however, come closer to fitting the bill in this respect. What happens to Mary in the gospels of Matthew and Luke resembles what happened to Danae in Greek mythology – a parallel that was noted already by the scoffing Jew Trypho in a second-century dialogue concocted by the Christian apologist Justin: "in the fables of those who are called Greeks, it is written that Perseus was begotten of Danae, who was a virgin; he who was called among them Zeus having descended on her in the form of a golden shower."[64] There is also the virginal conception of Rome's founders, Romulus and Remus, who, according to some accounts, were born of the Vestal virgin R(h)ea Silvia after she had been violated by a spectre of the god (*tou daimonos eidōlon*) Mars.[65] Another pagan figure who may also be mentioned in this connection is the great celestial goddess Virgo (Astraea), as she appears in *Eclogue IV* of the Roman poet Virgil (ca.40 BCE), and who was even believed by some early Christians to be a prefiguration of Mary.[66]

Apart from pagan influence, there were also numerous Jewish prefigurations of Mary, as we will see. However, in properly Jewish religious traditions around the time of Jesus, the combination of direct divine intervention with *virginal* conception was apparently unheard of.[67] This may mean that the idea of a virgin mother of Jesus reflects pagan rather than Jewish influence. Or it may not.

The question of how – or even whether – historical "influence" determined beliefs about Mary's supposed virginity does not really have to be settled here. More directly relevant to such beliefs is their psychoanalytic meaning.[68] A young woman's virginity was (and still is) an important psychological concern across cultures (not just in Mediterranean cultures, with their paired values of honor and shame).[69] Previous psychoanalytic studies have viewed Mary's virginity essentially as a repudiation of some aspect of Oedipal ideation. For example, the late folklorist Alan Dundes wrote: "A son who is born of a virgin can deny that his father ever had sexual access to his mother."[70] That son would originally be Jesus, and later would be any male mariophile identifying with Jesus. To quote my own paraphrase of Michael P. Carroll's pioneering psychoanalytic study of the cult of the Virgin Mary in the West, any distancing of Mary from sexuality is:

> a way for the worshipper to deal with an old Oedipal desire to sexually possess the opposite-sex parent. By attributing virginity to the maternal figure of Mary, a man can repudiate his archaic wish for sexual relations with his mother. Similarly, by attributing virginity to the daughterly figure of Mary (who avoids sexual relations with God the Father), a woman can repudiate her wish for sexual relations with her father.[71]

Generally speaking, then, the attribution of virginity to Mary is a complex of interrelated denials: (1) Mary and her son Jesus *did not* have an incestuous relationship; (2) God the Father above and his daughterly Mary here below *did not* have an incestuous relationship; and (3) by identification with the same-sex deity, both male and female mariophiles *did not* have an incestuous relationship with the opposite sex parent. These denials of incest are by definition denials of Oedipal fantasizing. They have appealed to Christians down the centuries and across cultures, for Oedipal desire at some stage(s) in individual ontogeny is probably a cross-cultural universal.[72]

The association of incest or Oedipal desire with a supposedly virginal Mary may seem quite unnecessary, even bizarre. Yet, mariologists know that "bride" is a topos, that is, a commonplace designation, for Mary, and that Mary's "bridegroom" is her son Christ. These designations are based on a perceived linkage of Mary and Christ to that collection of erotic love songs known as the Song of Songs (or Song of Solomon) in the Hebrew Bible.[73]

There is, for example, the joyful declaration "Blessed is the Babe whose mother was / bride of the Holy One" in a hymn penned by Ephrem the Syrian (d. 373).[74] There is also the repeated paradoxical characterization of Mary as "bride unwedded [*numfē anumfeute*]" in the traditional Byzantine

Akathistos hymn (and to whom, we may ask rhetorically, was this "bride" NOT wedded?).[75] In the Byzantine liturgy, "bride of God" (*Theonumfos*) is one of the most frequent designations for Mary.[76] In various hymns to Mary in the medieval West, we hear a forthright "bride of Christ [*sponsa Christi*]," or even "mother and bride of Christ [*Christi mater et sponsa*]."[77] Here, the idea of mother–son incest is explicit and Oedipal, with no apparent denial.

The "bride" topos and associated nuptial images ("bridegroom," "marriage-chamber," "kisses") are also salient in some mariological commentaries on the Song of Songs and in liturgical texts for marian feasts, especially the Assumption.[78] For example, in his *Commentaria in Cantica Canticorum*, Philip of Harvengt (d. 1183) has Mary quoting a famous pleonasm from the Song of Songs, "Let him kiss me with the kisses of his mouth!" (*Osculetur me osculo oris sui* – Song 1:2). Philip goes on:

> The virgin wants that in her womb [*in suo utero*] the harmony of God and humanity might be restored, and that this harmony so restored might be strengthened by an unbreakable contract (*foedere*), in such a way that he who was God and the Son of God the Father might become, through a new and wonderful birth, the bridegroom and son of the mother (*sponsus et filius . . . matris*). He is to become a bridegroom, joining himself to the virgin by a certain conjugal contract, pausing in his marriage-chamber, peace having been effected with a nuptial kiss [*in ejus pausans thalamo pace facta osculo nuptiali*].[79]

Medievalist Rachel Fulton offers a personal response to what she has translated here:

> Now, I would hope that even those of us already all too familiar with such erotic images from our reading of later-medieval mystical treatises . . . might still find this image – of the Son *arranging for his marriage to his mother in her womb* – at the very least momentarily shocking, if not (as Philip seems to have intended it to be), simultaneously titillating, provocative, and yet somehow faintly repulsive (much like the Incarnation itself).[80]

Fulton is writing a scholarly study of the marian commentary on the Song of Songs by Philip of Harvengt. Yet, her vocabulary – "momentarily shocking," "simultaneously titillating," "faintly repulsive" – would also be a cross-culturally normal emotional response to the idea of mother–son incest. Indeed, it *is* a response to the idea of mother–son incest, which is to say that Philip successfully conveyed precisely this idea without having bothered to deny it.

Psychoanalytically stated, when the adult Christ weds his maternal bride, he becomes what Martin S. Bergmann terms an "oedipal victor."[81] In the visual arts, this victory is often represented as the coronation or the

Figure 1.1 Mary and Christ enthroned in the apse mosaic of Santa Maria in Trastevere (mid-twelfth century), Rome (Verdon 2005, 37, fig. 31).

queenship of Mary. For example, a mosaic image (Figure 1.1) of Mary and Christ enthroned in the apse of Santa Maria in Trastevere (mid-twelfth century) in Rome shows Christ with his right arm thrown over the shoulder of his already crowned mother, while she displays a scroll with the words, "O that his left hand were under my head, and that his right hand embraced me!" (Song of Songs 2:6, 8:3). Bergmann writes, "We are asked to accept this erotic verse as appropriate to a relationship between the divine mother and her divine son."[82]

In fact, in some contexts, we are asked to accept more than mother–son incest. If we are familiar with the theologically correct view that the Father and the Son are one, then we have the added complication of father–daughter incest. For example, in the *Sigillum Beatae Mariae* by Honorius of Autun (early twelfth century), God the Father speaks to Mary with these words: "Your lips distill nectar, my bride [*Favus distillans labia tua, sponsa* – Song 4:11]," and Honorius explains, "He calls her bride because she bore the Son to him [*ei Filium generavit*]."[83] Moreover, in addition to father–daughter incest, brother–sister incest has to be reckoned with as well, as when, in the same work, Christ speaks about Mary, saying, "A garden locked is my sister, my bride [*Hortus conclusus, soror mea, sponsa* – Song 4:12]" – to which the author adds: "She was a garden of herbs and trees, that is, she was full of virtues; she remained closed in giving birth, sealed with the Holy Spirit. *A garden locked* because after birth, the seal of her virginity [*virginitatis signaculum*] was not opened."[84]

In the *Sigillum*, it would seem that Mary can be as incestuous as she pleases, so long as she retains the "seal of her virginity." Such medieval texts could be (and have been) very kindly characterized as mystical, or allegorical, or paradoxical, or miraculous. In fact, they are just as incoherent as the underlying idea of the virgin birth of Christ, based as it is on denial of Mary's incestuous union with God the Father. Such texts depend, moreover, on the reader's ability to disregard the idea of the sexual abuse of Mary by the men within her theologized "family."[85] It was not enough that Mary give birth to the savior of humankind while retaining her virginity. She also had to sleep around with members of the Trinity – also while retaining her virginity.

One way to tone down the absurdity and the sexual victimization inherent in marian nuptial imagery was to shift attention away from Mary. One could, for example, revert to a more traditional kind of "bride" for Christ, namely, an abstract but personified *Ecclesia* (decades after penning the *Sigillum*, the mature Honorius wrote his *Expositio in Cantica Canticorum* in this vein).[86] Another way was actually to emphasize the absurdities of Mary's trinitarian polyandry in a playful fashion, as did Dante when having Saint Bernard address *Vergine madre, figlia del tuo figlio* at the beginning of the last Canto of *Paradiso*,[87] and as did others before him in passages such as this one from a thirteenth-century hymn, quoted and translated by Barbara Newman:

> *Tui patris tu, Maria,*
> *Mater es et filia.*
> You, Mary, are your father's
> mother, and his daughter.

In such "riddling stanzas," Mary managed to be what Newman terms "bride of the God who is at once her father, son, and brother."[88] The one condition was that Mary remain chaste, a virgin. There was a Trinity of adult male sexual partners for a young "bride" named Mary, but no sex.

This was a comic fantasy, perhaps. But it was comic only in the sense of comic relief from something terrible that one must not know, something dubbed "the incest wound" by psychologist Christine A. Courtois, or a variety of "soul murder" by psychoanalyst Leonard Shengold.[89] Any mariologist brave enough to read the case histories of real people who have actually had experience of incest will soon lose any appetite for linking the Song of Songs to Mary.

Of course, the documentation of actual cases of incest in pre-modern times is nothing like what modern clinical psychologists have been able to obtain. Nevertheless, in the medieval West for example, there did exist prohibitions against incest, which would already indicate that there was a problem. Indeed, by the beginning of the thirteenth century, the prohibitions had been extended by so many degrees of familial relationship that, "most people living in small communities could not legally marry anyone they knew."[90] Yet the court records of cases of incest within the nuclear family are very few. Elizabeth Archibald writes: "It seems likely that cases of this kind of incest very rarely came to court, but were handled largely in the confessional – or else ignored."[91] Experienced clinicians today are quite familiar with the tendency of incest victims to ignore (or attempt to ignore) what they have experienced. That first line of defense usually fails, however. Sadly, the list of potential pathological conditions linked to the experience of incest is long and variegated.[92]

A glance at the relevant entries in Tubach's *Index Exemplorum* demonstrates that, despite the scanty court records, and without any assistance of modern psychology, the medieval imagination was perfectly able to conjure up lurid tales of nuclear family incest:

> 2731 *Incest, father with daughter.* I. A girl sins with her father and then kills both her parents. She dies of contrition and is saved.
>
> 2732 *Incest, father with daughter.* II. A man and his wife had a beautiful daughter. After his wife's death the man committed incest with the daughter.
>
> 2733 *Incest, mother and son.* I. A mother dies of fright when she learns that she is about to commit incest with her son.
>
> 2734 *Incest, mother and son.* II. When a son refuses to make love to his lustful mother, she accuses him before a court of having done so. St. Andrew's prayers cause a thunderbolt to strike her dead.[93]

Exempla were didactic, illustrating official Church views. Archibald writes: "The literature of the period . . . suggests that incest occurred quite frequently. If it had been extremely rare, it would have been bad propaganda for the Church to make a showpiece of the contrition of incestuous sinners."[94]

Given the existence of such a showpiece, it is difficult to fathom the motivation of those mariophile poets, hymnographers, and artists who arranged for Mary actually to wed her trinitarian kin, or of those theologians who wrote mystical–allegorical marian commentaries on the Song of Songs. Perhaps religious poets and theologians were very isolated from the reality of incest, much as clinical psychologists themselves were quite isolated from this reality before the arrival of Freud and the psychoanalytic movement he created. On the other hand, the childhood experiences of those poets and theologians who were preoccupied with incestuous imagery would (where the data are available) be worth closer examination by medievalists and might contain previously unnoticed incidents relating to incest. The widespread representation of Mary as the "bride" of her earthly son (and/or her heavenly Father) could not have emerged from a psychological vacuum.

Mary's Post-Scriptural Grandeur

In the New Testament, Mary is a simple peasant woman from Galilee. She receives little attention from the authors of what would someday become holy writ. Other authors, however, felt obliged to praise her to the skies.

Even before the Council of Ephesus Mary had gained a special kind of prominence within certain sectors of Christianity. Ephrem the Syrian, for example, drew some rather creative parallels between Mary and God himself. In his fourth hymn on the nativity – here translated from the Syriac by Kathleen E. McVey – Ephrem offers paradoxes such as these:

> By power from Him [God] Mary's womb became able
> to bear the One who bears all.
> From the great treasury of all creation
> Mary gave to Him everything that she gave.
> She gave Him milk from what He made exist.
> She gave Him food from what He had created.
> He gave milk to Mary as God.
> In turn, He was given suck by her as human (182–185).[95]

Although these paradoxes possess an unquestionable literary appeal, it is clear that the parallels upon which they are based do not imply an equality of Mary with God: what Mary is capable of is determined "By power from Him." He is the creator; she is a creature (albeit a very special creature in her role of incarnating the creator). Mary is great, but she is not the greatest.

Subsequent development of Ephrem's paradoxical approach by other authors would come closer to the brink of outright logical contradiction. In the Greek Akathistos hymn, for example, Mary is assigned strikingly paradoxical properties that, for true mariophiles, are just part of "the mystery or miracle involved in the Incarnation."[96] Close examination shows, however, that some of these properties make Mary greater even than God. Two – here translated by Leena Mari Peltomaa – are of particular importance:

> Hail, since you bear [carry] him who bears [carries] all. (1:13)
> Hail, container of the uncontainable God. (15:6)[97]

If God "bears all," but another bears this very God, then it follows that this other bears all – and then some – and is therefore greater in a certain sense than is the 'all-bearing' God.[98] Similarly, if God is uncontainable (*achōrētou*), he must be everywhere: that is, he is a pantheistic God; but anyone or anyplace (*chōra*) large enough to contain this God is by definition greater even than this "everywhere."[99] In the second (and perhaps also the first) of these paradoxical lines, it is the womb of Mary that is understood to accomplish the task of bearing or containing something, for Mary is hailed as "womb [*gastēr*] of the divine Incarnation" in 1:15 of the Akathistos.[100]

Proclus of Constantinople had asked rhetorically, in his famous homily delivered in Constantinople in 430: "Who ever saw, who ever heard, of God dwelling without restriction in a woman's womb? Heaven itself cannot contain him, and yet a womb did not constrict him."[101] Here too a woman's womb (*gastēr*; also Luke 1:31) contains the uncontainable God. That is the "mystery," and it was declared official church doctrine at Ephesus in 431 when Mary was designated *Theotokos*, the one from whose womb was born God.

It has often been said that the utilization of the term *Theotokos* for Mary did not entail the attribution of any special personal properties to her. Even if that were true, believing Christians hardly felt restricted by the logical limitations (or lack thereof) of a theological term. There was an irresistible inclination to aggrandize the mother of one's savior.

For mariophiles, Saint Mary is unquestionably the greatest of the saints. No other saint was ever in the position of being able to refuse an offer from God to mother a son (she accepted). No other saint has ever achieved the seemingly oxymoronic status of "virgin mother" (even "perpetual virgin" after having given birth – see note 46, pp. 83–85). In the Eastern Orthodox liturgy, the choir praises Mary as "more honourable than the Cherubim, and beyond compare more glorious than the Seraphim."[102] In Roman Catholic missals, Mary is elevated "above the choirs of angels" on the feast of her Assumption into heaven.[103]

John of Damascus wrote of Mary in the eight century: "she is truly, after God, the holiest of all beings."[104] According to Saint Anselm of Canterbury (d. 1109), "nothing but God is greater than Mary."[105]

If Jesus is the Lord (*Dominus*), Mary has customarily been referred to as Lady (*Domina*) – a term with royal overtones – in the Roman Catholic world. In a wide variety of texts – East and West – Mary is represented as "Queen" (Russian *Tsaritsa*, Polish *Królowa*, Greek *Basilissa*, Latin *Regina*, French *Reine*, and so on) – primarily by virtue of her double linkage of literal maternity and (supposedly metaphorical) marriage to "Christ the King." According to Catholic mariologist Gabriel-Mary Roschini, "Mary is the true Mother and the veritable Spouse of the King of Kings,"[106] as the God she gave birth to was the same God who brought about – with her consent – the conception of her son Jesus.

Numerous images from the history of Christian art represent a majestic Mary seated upon a throne (sometimes with the Christ child on her lap, sometimes alongside an enthroned adult Christ) and/or wearing a crown or in the process of being crowned as queen.[107] Some of the coronation imagery involves all three persons of the holy trinity and thereby suggests that Mary might even be part of a divine quaternity.[108]

Queen Mary has been known to boss around her king. Giovanni Miegge writes, "In Mary humanity governs the Kingdom of Heaven and even gives orders to the Omnipotent."[109] Hilda Graef gathers evidence for belief in Mary's own omnipotence among such theologians as Richard of St. Laurent (d. after 1245), Jean-Jacques Olier (d. 1657), and Alphonsus of Liguori (1696–1787).[110] The last of these wrote:

> Since the Mother . . . should have the same power as the Son, rightly has Jesus, who is omnipotent, made Mary also omnipotent; though, of course, it is always true that where the Son is omnipotent by nature, the Mother is only so by grace. But that she is so is evident from the fact, that whatever the Mother asks for, the Son never denies her.[111]

Here, maternal omnipotence depends on filial omnipotence. In effect, there is a one-way transfer of omnipotence from divine son to mother. One may question whether what the mother obtains is "omnipotence" at all, after such a transfer. In any case, the underlying psychological reality is this: *I* get what *I* want because *my* mother of God wants it for *me*. This narcissistic core of requests for marian intercession is often obscured by the narcissist's seeming preoccupation with the grandeur of Mary – including the attribution of "omnipotence" to her.

Many Marys

Mary has been and continues to be many things to many people(s). Beginning at least as early as in the original Greek Akathistos in the East, and continuing in various works in both the East and in the medieval West, Mary acquired countless salutations, honorific titles, poetic epithets, hyperbolic expressions, biblical typologies, tutelary titles, and other kinds of formulaic name.[112]

The abundance of names persists even today. Some cultures stress a particular property of Mary in naming her, so that a multiplicity of cultures means a multiplicity of her names. For example, in Orthodox Russia, the emphasis is placed on her maternal aspect (*Bogoroditsa*, *Bogomater'*), and, in Roman Catholic Poland, there is a similarly maternal emphasis (*Matka Boska*). But, in Orthodox Greece, the customary designation idealizes her holiness (*Panagia*, i.e., "All Holy"). In the West, generally, some variety of "virgin" has been particularly common (e.g., in English, *Blessed Virgin Mary*; in Mexican Spanish, *la Virgen de Guadalupe*; in German, *die Jungfrau Maria*; in French, *la Sainte Vierge*; and so on). Neither motherhood nor virginity has to be mentioned, however – for example, the perfectly standard French *Notre Dame* or the Italian *Madonna*. There is also the simple word "Mary" (or the linguistic equivalent), which is appropriate in a wide variety of contexts, ranging from private prayer and public choral music to theology and scholarly analysis. Even within a single language such as English, the number of general terms for the mother of Jesus can be substantial: the Blessed Virgin Mary, the Virgin Mary, Holy Mary, the Virgin, Our Lady, the Mother of God, the Most Holy Mother, and so on.

Mary has been drawn into the discourse of those who wage war and otherwise engage in politics. This too has contributed to the proliferation of Mary's names. Once Constantine had prevailed at the battle of Milvian Bridge in 312 under the sign of the cross, and once this Christian sign had become a signifier of Roman imperial power,[113] then related signs – including visual images of the mother of the one yet to be crucified – could be utilized for political purposes. Not only was the cross (*stauros*) of Christ deemed to be victory-making (*Nikopoios*),[114] but an image of the *Theotokos* in frontal pose, together with the frontal Christ child held directly before her and (sometimes) enclosed in a medallion, might also be deemed *Nikopoios*.[115] And, as it happens, roughly that same configuration also acquired other names, such as *Blachernitissa* (of the Blachernai monastery), or *Platytera* (wider [than the heavens]), or *Episkepsis* (protection/visitation), depending on the historical context.[116] In other words, Mary's names multiplied even as the names of marian icons multiplied – a fact of particular relevance to the Eastern Orthodox faithful, who have traditionally reverenced their marian icons with prostrations, kisses, and speech (including prayers and hymns), as if these objects were the real Mary.

Christian cities (and their surroundings) East and West were drawn to Mary. She protected and defended their residents. In the early seventh century, Constantinople was dubbed *Theotokoupolis* ("City of the *Theotokos*").[117] In the West, a fine example is Siena, where, from the thirteenth century, Mary was recognized as protector and defender, *avvocata di nostra città*.[118]

Of course, Mary was capable of doing more for political entities than just defend them. She was known to go on the offensive as well, facilitating both conquests of territory and conversions to Christianity. Not for nothing was she called *La Conquistadora* on the Iberian peninsula, as well as in the Spanish New World (New Spain), as Amy G. Remensnyder has thoroughly demonstrated in a recent study.[119]

Bissera V. Pentcheva observes that it was in Byzantium that a "powerful link between Marian devotion and the idea of empire became established and from which it then spread to the rest of the medieval world."[120] In the Russian empire, that link has been powerful indeed. Elsewhere, I have summarized a pious compilation of religious stories (*skazaniia*) concerning the power of certain marian icons in Russia:

> These icons have often been brought right out onto the field of battle, or soldiers have venerated these icons before going out to fight. Thus the city of Novgorod was supposedly protected by an icon of the Mother of God from an attack by the Suzdalians and their allies in 1140. An icon of the Assumption of the Mother of God helped defeat the Tatars on the field of Kulikovo in 1380. Tsar Fedor Ivanovich was

> assisted by an icon of the Don Mother of God in fending off Crimean Tatars from Moscow in 1591. The Poles were driven out of Moscow during the "Time of Troubles" early in the seventeenth century, and in memory of this victory the Kazan Mother of God is honored every year on 22 October. Later, in the seventeenth century, the Turks were driven back from lands south of Kiev with the help of a local icon of the Mother of God. The Napoleonic invasion of Russia in 1812 was a failure, in part, through the assistance of the Smolensk Hodegetria.[121]

If, as mentioned earlier, the individual who honors Mary with great praise is motivated by personal issues in the realm of narcissism, the citizen who is gratified by Mary's seeming ability to protect one's empire from enemies is imbued with something that may be termed the narcissism of empire.[122] For example, many Orthodox Russian nationalists have believed (and some to this day believe) that Mary makes Russia her "home" (*dom Bogoroditsy*).[123] When Mary defends Russia and the Russians, she is defending her own territory. A militarized marian icon helps bolster the self-esteem and promote the self-satisfaction of individual Russian nationalists. Russians who think this way are locked within their own specifically Russian imperial–national worldview. They cannot understand that Mary has other places to be, other people to protect. If it were possible to subtract their narcissistic preoccupation, Russian nationalists would notice that Mary is in fact what George H. Tavard has called "Our Lady of Everywhere."[124]

In a book on the Catholic theology of nationality, Dorian Llywelyn includes a chapter titled "Our Lady of All Nations."[125] Llywelyn believes that the widely prevalent, yet very particularistic, marian patronages – the "Vladimir Mother of God," "Our Lady of the Philippines," "Our Lady, Queen of Ireland," "Queen of Poland," "Queen of New Spain," and many others – are category markers separating "us" from "them": that is, they delineate one's own national group from the "out-group," which does not benefit from the protective relationship with Mary.[126] This would be a statement about the social psychology of certain large groups. As it happens, however, the "out-group" itself is in many cases also under the protection of Mary, which is to say that Mary's "children" quarrel with one another, even slaughter one another in warfare, so that Mary, by definition, sometimes fails to "protect" them.

Russia and France, for example, have fought wars against one another – with occasionally interesting results in the realm of marian imagery. In their book *Under the Heel of Mary*, Nicholas Perry and Loreto Echeverría write in passing about the Crimean war of 1853–1856:

> "Our Lady of France", a colossus fashioned from the molten steel of 213 captured Russian cannons, was entrusted to the Bishop of Le Puy on imperial orders. Standing on a globe, the statue is crowned with stars and bears the inscription "Salve Regina!" The serpent under her heel measures seventeen metres.[127]

Much more could be said about these topics. However, imperial, national, and ethnic issues will not be a major concern of this book. Religion will be – primarily Christianity, but also Judaism to some extent. This makes it somewhat easier to utilize the simplest possible name for the most important woman in the history of Christianity. When not quoting others who designate her differently or when not scrutinizing some specifically named role of hers, I will continue to call her Mary. Her many formulaic designations come from many cultures and many historical periods. But, behind them all is Mary, the mother of Jesus.

*

There is precious little detail about Mary the mother of Jesus in scripture, and post-scriptural elaboration on her life was slow in coming. But, by the fifth century, she was already being represented by some as a kind of goddess. For many of her devotees, Mary was a mother and a virgin (simultaneously). As if this were not enough of a cognitive clash, she also became the "bride" of her divine son, so that near-conscious fantasies of Oedipal sexuality (mother–son incest) became an integral part of the mariophile imagination. Despite these psychologically problematical phenomena, Mary's grandeur increased in the medieval period and reached a level where she was even deemed "omnipotent" by some, and a military "conquerer" by others. In the modern period, Mary retains much of her earlier grandeur in both the Catholic West and the Orthodox East. At the same time, Mary possesses many other specific qualities, besides grandeur, among mariophiles. Thousands of special titles have been lavished upon Mary from all corners of the Christian world. Mary has been – and continues to be – many things to many people (or peoples – ethnic groups, nation-states, and empires).

Notes

1 Rancour-Laferriere 2011, and the abundant literature cited there.
2 For example: Brown 1993 (1977), 57–94, 587–589; Meier 1991, 238, n. 47; Vermes 2006, 18–38.
3 See, for example: Crossan 1991, 371–372; Bovon 2002, 83–85 (with detailed bibliography).
4 Lüdemann 1998 (1997), 86.
5 Maximus the Confessor 2012, 61–91 (with notes to the text by Stephen J. Shoemaker).
6 Funk and the Jesus Seminar 1998, 499. See also Vermes 2006 for a detailed and entertaining investigation of the historical context and historical improbability of what is presented in the nativity stories.
7 For example: Crossan 1991; Meier 1991; Sanders 1993.
8 Modern Jewish scholars have sometimes devoted serious scholarly attention to Mary: for example: Ben-Chorin 1971, 1983 (an extract translated from the 1971 book); Flusser 1986 (1985); Neusner 2001 (1991), 117–129; Rubin 2009; Kessler 2011; and others. Some Christian scholars have also directed their

attention to the specifically "Jewish Mary": for example: Buby 1994–1996, vol. 2; Johnson 2003, esp. 162–184; Athans 2013.

9 Matthew 1:16, 18, 20; 2:11; 13:55; Mark 6:3; Luke 1:27, 30, 34, 38, 39, 41, 46, 56; 2:5, 16, 19, 34; Acts 1:14.

10 Schneider 1991 (1981)a, 387–388.

11 Schneider 1991 (1981)b, 181.

12 *Ante-Nicene Fathers* 2004 (1885–1887), vol. 3, 521–542.

13 See: Lüdemann 1995; 2004; Allison 2005, 204–207, 242 ff., 269–299, 364–375; Rancour-Laferriere 2008; 2011, 121–138. Although Dale C. Allison Jr. prefers to believe that Jesus rose from the dead, he provides very clear and thorough comments on the psychological studies of bereavement and, following the line of thinking initiated by Gerd Lüdemann, he makes a strong argument for the relevance of bereavement studies to understanding what the disciples accomplished after Jesus died (2005, 364–375).

14 For one of the many detailed analyses available, see: Dunn 1996 (1989).

15 For a concise history of the doctrine of the trinity in the early Church, see: Dünzl 2007 (2006). For a very readable recent study, see: Jenkins 2010.

16 "Cyril's Letter to the Monks of Egypt," as translated in: McGuckin 2004 (1994), 247. I have twice replaced McGuckin's rendition "Mother of God" with Cyril's original *Theotokos* in this passage. See: Cyril of Alexandria 1859, col. 13a.

17 For examples of utilization of some (grammatical) form of the original Greek *theotokos* at Ephesus and at Chalcedon, see: Tanner, ed. 1990, vol. I, 44, 47, 58, 59, 70, 71, 84, 86. The term had been used occasionally before Ephesus (McGuckin 2008, 9 ff.). Indeed, the very first recorded prayer to Mary, written in Greek on a fragment of papyrus dating to the third or fourth century – addresses her with the vocative *THEOTOKE*. See: the entry "Sub tuum, the," in O'Carroll 2000 (1982), 336 (with bibliography); Maas-Ewerd 1994 (with bibliography). Today, this Greek term is best understood to mean simply "Mother of God" (Maria Hatjigeorgiou, posting to SEELANGS listserve, February 16, 2014).

18 There is a vast literature on matters relating to both "*Theotokos*" and "Mother of God." See, for example: Miegge 1955, 53–67; Lampe, ed. 1961, under the entries *theotokos* (639–641) and *mētēr* (868); O'Carroll 2000 (1982), under the entries "Theotokos, God-Bearer" (342–343) and "Mother of God" (257–259); Kalavrezou 1990; Benko 2004 (1993), 245–262; Limberis 1994; Pelikan 1996, 55–65; Peltomaa 2001, 135–139; Wright 2004; Price 2007; McGuckin 2008; Atanassova 2008; Jenkins 2010, 131–167, 209–210; Reynolds 2012–, 9–49. For an informative study of the Christological controversy from which the designation "*Theotokos*" emerged, see: McGuckin 2004 (1994). A cogent argument that the famous Akathistos hymn to Mary as *Theotokos* reflects the triumphant christology proclaimed at Ephesus and was probably composed between the councils of Ephesus and Chalcedon is offered by Peltomaa (2001).

19 For two fine introductions to the "goddess" issue, see: Miegge 1955, 68–82; Benko 2004 (1993). Brian K. Reynolds grants that Mary achieved "an exalted place . . . in the Christian hierarchy," and adds: "This did not mean that she had become a goddess, however, at least in the official teaching of the Church, if only for the simple reason that she had to be fully human for the Word [Christ] to take his humanity from her, but it did lead to an increasingly fervent and elaborate cult which sometimes spilled over into Mariolatry and threatened to overshadow Christ himself" (Reynolds 2012–, 5). In other words, Mary has been at least an unofficial "goddess" according to this Catholic scholar.

20 For some of the psychoanalytic studies of "mother worship" in various cultures, see: Beit-Hallahmi 1996, 161–163.

21 See the entry *mater* in Meersseman's mariological glossary (1958–1960, vol. 2, 329–331) and in Barré's marian lexicon (1963, 335).

22 Aelred of Rievaulx 1989, 186 (translated by Bynum 1982, 137). In Orthodox Russia, there is a widespread attitude that Mary the Mother of God is one's own mother, one's *rodnaia mat'*, one's *matushka* (see: Rancour-Laferriere 2001, 66–67, and the literature cited there).

23 Keller, ed. 2013, 225.

24 Fasmer 1986–1987 (1950–1958), vol. I, 183. Today, the Russian term *Bogoroditsa* (like the Greek *Theotokos*) is best rendered as "Mother of God" in everyday English (Ralph M. Cleminson, posting to SEELANGS listserve, February 15, 2014).

25 For a review of some of the literature on this topic, see: Rancour-Laferriere 2005, 256–260 (from which some of the observations about the Russian *Bogoroditsa* made here are adapted). S. Smirnov (1914, 262) notes that there is no *direct* historical evidence that the pagan ancestors of the Russians worshipped the Earth as a deity, but presents a substantial body of indirect evidence for this thesis (262–283).

26 Uspenskii 1996–1997, vol. 2, 93.

27 Quoted in: Fedotov 1991 (1935), 78; Uspenskii 1996–1997, vol. 2, 85.

28 John of Damascus 1998b, 219. Cf. Borgeaud 2004 (1996), 130.

29 Ruether 2005, 209. See also Carroll (1986, 182–194) for evidence that the Guadalupe story "arose as part of the effort to Indianize the shrine dedicated to Our Lady of Guadalupe at Tepeyac, and that it was constructed simply by Indianizing the original Guadalupe legend" (187), i.e., by Indianizing the fourteenth-century legend, which led to construction of the shrine dedicated to Our Lady of Guadalupe in the Estremadura region of Spain (see also: Poole 1995, 73–75, 216).

30 Benko 2004 (1993), 257.

31 Limberis 1994, 109.

32 Shoemaker 2008.

33 Atanassova 2008.

34 Sweeney 2006, 17.

35 Bovon 2002, 53

36 More precisely stated: the virginal conception of Jesus is so improbable that it would have to have been a miracle in order to be believed. As the *Christian* geneticist Professor R. J. Berry states, "there is no certain record of parthenogenesis in humans, nor of a male being conceived without fertilisation by a Y-bearing sperm" (1996, 108). Even with parthenogenetic replication of an ovum, there would have to be some additional way in which a virginally conceived Jesus would have developed the XY chromosome complement of a male, e. g., Mary was herself chromosomally XY, with reversible androgen resistance, was capable of producing an ovum, and happened to possess a uterus (107–108). Berry grants that the probability of this and of his other theoretical proposals being true is vanishingly small, yet insists that, "if God is a God of miracles, the credibility or probability of any particular miracle should be wholly irrelevant" (108). I agree that this generalization would have to be true, if and only if its premises (God exists, and God is a God of miracles) were true.

37 For example, in writings by Athanasius of Alexandria (d. 373), Cyril of Alexandria (d. 444), Modestus of Jerusalem (d. 634), and Sophronius of Jerusalem (d. 638). See: Lampe 1961, 1037.

38 From a tenth-century hymn from Moissac (Meersseman 1958–1960, vol. 1, 155). Compare lines from an early English carol to the Virgin by James Ryman, ca. 1492: "Moder and mayde in one persone / Was nevir none but thou allone" (Greene, ed. 1977 [1935], 128).

39 Freud 1958 (1911), 343.

40 Trebilco 1994, 302–357.

41 Freud 1958 (1911), 342.

42 Some scholars cite the existence of a church already bearing Mary's name in Ephesus in 431 as one piece of evidence for the hypothesis about a tradition that Mary had lived in Ephesus after the crucifixion, and had died there (for example: De la Potterie 1985–1991, 220). Others do not find adequate historical evidence for this tradition (for example: Shoemaker 2004, 74–76). The "Ephesus tradition" does live on in the last pages of the novella *The Testament of Mary*, where Mary rejects the gospel message of her Christian minders and whispers prayers to "the great goddess Artemis" (Tóibín 2012, 80).

43 McGuckin 2008, 13–14 (cf. Benko 2004 [1993], 256–257). In section 53 of his tract on Isis and Osiris, Plutarch writes that Isis "by most people has been called by countless names [*muriōnumos*]" (Plutarch 1936, 128–129). Appearing to Lucius, the hero of *Metamorphoses* by Apuleius, Isis declares: "My divinity is one, worshipped by all the world under different forms, with various rites, and by manifold names [*nomine multiiugo*]" (Apuleius 1989, vol. 2, 244–245). The title of the aforementioned paper by Freud – "Great is Diana of the Ephesians" – illustrates an aspect of the naming problem. It is an indirect reference – via the title of a poem by Goethe – to Acts 19:34, where a crowd of pagans in Ephesus harass Paul, the great missionary to the Gentiles. They shout repeatedly at him, "Great is Artemis of the Ephesians!" In Ephesus itself, it seems, Artemis (Greek), not Diana (Roman) was the genuine article. Not that Paul was preaching Diana, nor was he preaching Artemis. He was getting into trouble because he was preaching Christ. Yet it is interesting that the polynomy of Artemis is bolstered by some simply by virtue of her being viewed through Roman imperial eyes. The New Testament, after all, was written in Greek.

44 Some women from imperial Roman royal families were deified, and therefore constitute a curious exception to this generalization. For example, in his *Roman History* (60.5) Dio Cassius reports that Livia Drusilla (d. 29 CE, wife of the emperor Augustus) was not deified until her grandson Claudius became emperor (Dio Cassius 1924, 379). Emperor Caligula's recently (38 CE) deceased favorite sister Drusilla (daughter of Germanicus) was given a lavish funeral and was declared to be a goddess with the name Panthea. Dio Cassius (*Roman History* 59.11) writes sarcastically that "a certain Livius Geminius, a senator, declared on oath, invoking destruction upon himself and his children if he spoke falsely, that he had seen her [Panthea] ascending to heaven and holding converse with the gods; and he called all the other gods and Panthea herself to witness" (Dio Cassius 1924, 295; cf. Suetonius [*Lives of the Caesars* 4.24] 1998, 453–455). Women who were deified received the title of *Diva*, but not *Dea* (as did men the title *Divus*, but not *Deus*). Hence, Livia Drusilla became Diva Augusta, Caligula's sister became Diva Drusilla (apparently "Panthea" fell by the wayside), Emperor Trajan's sister Marciana (d. 112 CE) became Diva Marciana Augusta, Empress Faustina Maior (who in 140 CE predeceased the husband and

emperor who would become Divus Antoninus Pius) became Diva Faustina Maior, and so on. For a highly readable treatment of emperor and empress worship in relation to Roman religion, see: Gradel 2002. For a relief panel depicting the apotheosis – basically, the ascension – of the late Empress Sabina (d. 136 CE) on her way to becoming Diva Sabina, see: Gradel 2002, 306, fig. 12.2. I mention the term "ascension" here because the apotheoses of the various Roman *divae* resemble aspects of marian ascension imagery and might well be worth investigating. Generally speaking, however, it is obvious that the women who became *divae* were never to become as important to Roman pagans as Mary became to Christians. Freud's Mary, "the new mother-goddess of the Christians," would become someone more in the order of a *dea*, not a *diva*, if only because of the eternal predestination attributed to her as recently as Vatican II (*Lumen Gentium*). I am grateful to Maria Kardaun for providing the information and references on Caligula's sister Drusilla in a posting to the PsyArt listserv (September 24, 2013).

45 See Bovon (2002, 49) for information on traditional Jewish marriage practices at the time. The demographic analysis by Bas van Os, however, points to a different conclusion: "Jesus was her [Mary's] firstborn when she was between 15 and 20 years old" (Van Os 2011, 49).

46 The problem with the Greek term *parthenos* is this: Matthew 1:23 alludes to Isaiah 7:14 ("A virgin will conceive and bear a son"), where the Septuagint (widely used by hellenized Jews) has *parthenos*, but the Hebrew Bible has *'almah* ("a young woman"). See: "The Virgin Birth" (sidebar essay), *The Jewish Annotated New Testament* (2011), p. 4; Vermes 2006, 52–75. For some of the background issues and bibliography, see: Brown 1993 (1977), 143–164, 697–712. A straightforward explanation in layman's terms is offered by Ehrman 2014, 242–243. Basically, by the time we get to Matthew's first-century utilization of the Septuagint's Old-Greek *parthenos*, the Greek word had gone from sometimes meaning "virgin" to always meaning "virgin."

47 See, for example: von Campenhausen 1964 (1962), 10–24.

48 For a concise overview, see: Johnson 2003, 195–199.

49 For a historical overview of belief in Mary's virginal conception (which gives no serious consideration to disbelief), see the entry "Virginity of Mary" in: O'Carroll 2000 (1982), 357–361. O'Carroll, a well known mariologist, is a believer who begins his brief survey with the words, "Mary of Nazareth conceived her son Jesus while remaining a virgin" (357). By contrast, Raymond E. Brown, a respected Roman Catholic exegetical scholar, concludes that the historicity of Mary's virginal conception cannot be established "on exegetical grounds alone" (1993 [1977], 698). For the record, Brown's book is marked with the *Nihil Obstat* and *Imprimatur*, whereas O'Carroll's is not. However, O'Carroll's book is a better reflection of traditional mariophile attitudes than is Brown's.

50 Peltomaa 2001, 13, 17.

51 Peltomaa 2001, 2, 4, 6, 8, etc.

52 Peter Schäfer (2007, 21) notes that, "only under this premise, that Joseph was his [Jesus'] real father, does the emphasis put on his geneology make sense."

53 Schaberg 2006 (1987), 141–145; Lüdemann 1998 (1997), 53–55; Van Aarde 1997, 466; 2001, 74. Brown (1993 [1977], 534–542, 706–708) believes that there is not enough evidence to support the charge of illegitimacy.

54 See Capps (2000, 129–163) for a fascinating survey and synthesis of some of the literature on this topic, including especially: Schaberg 2006 (1987) and

Van Aarde 1997. Other relevant studies in this area include: Meier 1991, 222–229; Lüdemann 1998 (1997); Schaberg 2005 (1997); Funk and the Jesus Seminar 1998, 504–506; Van Aarde 2001; Crossan 2005 (2003); Vermes 2006, 53–75.

55 See: Celsus 1987, 57; Schaberg 2006 (1987), 145–156; Schäfer 2007, 19–21, 56–57, 60–61, 97–98, 133–134, 138–139; Rubin 2009, 57–59. For interesting recent studies on the complex prehistory of the *Toledot Yeshu*, see: Schäfer et al., eds. 2011.

56 Capps 2002a, 392–393. For context and elaboration, see "The Hidden Years: The Fatherhood Question," in: Capps 2000, 129–163. See also: Van Aarde 1997, 2001.

57 The gospel verse in which Jesus comes closest to mentioning Joseph is Luke 2:49, where the adolescent boy has just been found by his parents in the temple and says to them, "Why were you searching for me? Did you not know that I must be in my Father's house?" The "Father" in this instance is not Joseph, but God the Father. However, the repeated plural forms (*ezēteite*, *ēdeite*) point to Joseph and Mary. This is the closest Jesus ever comes to acknowledging the paternal figure of Joseph, but that is not close enough, and can hardly be compared with Jesus' close contact with God the Father.

58 On the importance of God as a father (the Father) to both Jesus and to his followers, see, for example: Vermes 1993, 152–183; Van Os 2011, 102–123. Paul too (Romans 8:14–17; Galatians 4:4–7) utilizes the Aramaic term *abba* in reference to God as an adoptive father of "children of God."

59 The last quotation is an admonition against using "Father" as an honorific.

60 See: Capps 2000, 129–163; Van Aarde 2001.

61 Vermes 2006, 45–46, 150–151.

62 See, among others: Collins 1999; Crossan and Reed 2004, 10–12, 88, 91, 137, 204–205, 235–236, 242; Peppard 2011.

63 In the ordinary sense of *virginitas ante partum*.

64 *Ante-Nicene Fathers* (2004, vol. 1, 231); cf. Dundes 1980, 225; Beit-Hallahmi 2010, 162.

65 For example: *The Roman Antiquities* (I. 77, 2) of Dionysius of Halicarnassus (1937, 256–257).

66 Virgil 1999, 48–53; cf. Bovon 2002, 45; Benko 2004 (1993), 113–115. Some of the enormous literature on the potential influence (either direct, or via Judaism) of pagan goddesses on the formation of the Christian image of the Virgin Mary includes: Daniélou 1949; Miegge 1955, 68–82; Benko 2004 (1993); Maunder 2008, 26–28; McGuckin 2008.

67 See, for example: Crossan 2005 (2003).

68 Some psychoanalytic work has in fact already been done on the widespread belief that Mary was a virgin mother. In addition, numerous (and highly diverse) psychological studies relating to Mary have appeared since the invention of psychoanalysis. See, for example: Jones 1964 (1914); Arlow 1964; Dundes 1980 (239; 256 ff.); Carroll 1986, 1989, 1992, 1996; Hood et al 1991; Bergmann 1992, 149–163; Capps 2000, 129–163; Beattie 2002 (1999); Rancour-Laferriere 2001, 2005, 2014; Grünbaum 2010 (1993), 29–32; Beit-Hallahmi 2010; Boss 2000, 22, 156–211, 214–216; Waller 2011.

69 Rancour-Laferriere 1992 (1985), 178–191. On the importance of honor and shame in cultures of the Mediterranean area, see: Gilmore, ed. 1987.

70 Dundes 1980, 239 (cf. 256 ff.).

71 Rancour-Laferriere 2005, 254, loosely paraphrasing Carroll 1986, 49–61, on the strong Mary cult in southern Italy and Spain.

72 See the index entry on "Oedipal matters" in Rancour-Laferriere 1992 (1985), 466.
73 See the entries "Song of Songs" and "Spouse of God (Bride of God), Mary as" in: O'Carroll 2000 (1982), 327–328, 333–334.
74 Ephrem the Syrian 1989, 122. Ephrem was apparently the first to call Mary the bride of Christ (O'Carroll 2000 [1982], 133).
75 Peltomaa 2001, 2, 4, 6, 8, etc.
76 Ledit 1976, 180–193.
77 Meersseman 1958–1960, vol. II, 134, 172, 209, 214, 216, 219, 234, 238.
78 See: Rubin 2009, 139–143, 158–161, 164–165, and the abundant literature cited there. There is also an extensive iconography of the "coronation of the Virgin" which unites Mary (or the Church) as *Sponsa* with Christ as her *Sponsus* (e.g., Verdier 1980, ch. 5, 81 ff.).
79 Philip of Harvengt 1855, col. 192, as translated by Fulton 2002, 356–357.
80 Fulton 2002, 357. See also Graef (2009 [1963–1965], 199–200), who writes of the "eroticism" and "sensuousness" of Philip's marian commentary on the Song of Songs.
81 Bergmann 1992, 158.
82 Bergmann 1992, 158–159.
83 Honorius Augustodunensis 1854, 507D; 1991, 67 (translation modified, DRL).
84 Honorius Augustodunensis 1854, 507D; 1991, 68 (translation modified, DRL).
85 Barbara Newman speaks of "the late medieval tendency to represent the Trinity itself as a family, with Mary its honorary female member" (2003, 247).
86 For a very useful historical overview of the relationship of "The Church and Our Lady," see: De Lubac 1986 (1953), 314–379.
87 Dante Alighieri 1939, 478.
88 Newman 2003, 250 (cf. Meersseman 1958–1960, vol. I, 188 [No. 36, stanza 16]). For more examples of playfulness of this kind, see: Woolf 1968, 131–134; Philippart 1996, 581–585; Archibald 2001, 238–240. Ronig (1974) laces his discourse with these offensive wordplays.
89 Courtois 2010; Shengold 1989, esp. 155–180.
90 Archibald 2001, 41.
91 Archibald 2001, 46.
92 Among the many psychological effects of the experience of incest that may persist in adulthood are: self-estrangement, emotional deadness, dissociation, depression, suicidal thinking, shame, guilt, hypervigilance, anxiety attacks, sleep disturbance and nightmares, psychosomatic symptoms, difficulties in intimate relationships, alcohol (and other drug) abuse, and others. For a comprehensive clinical study, see: Courtois 2010.
93 Tubach 1981 (1969), 215. Archibald points out that Tubach's survey is not complete (2001, 134, n. 64; 194, n. 5).
94 Archibald 2001, 231.
95 Ephrem the Syrian 1989, 102 (and see Kathleen McVey's comments in her Introduction to this work, 33–34).
96 Peltomaa 2001, 182.
97 Peltomaa 2001, 5, 13. The line 15:6 may be read as an allusion to the words of King Solomon, who, having just finished the construction of his huge temple in Jerusalem, prays: "But will God indeed dwell on the earth? Even heaven and the highest heaven cannot contain you, much less this house that I have built" (1 Kings 8:27).
98 Cf. later utilization of the same paradox in a sermon attributed to John of Damascus and in a homily by Emperor Leo VI (Maguire 1981, 55). There is

also an apocryphal gospel of uncertain date (the Gospel of Bartholomew, or the Questions of Bartholomew), in which the apostles ask Mary to explain "how you bore him who cannot be carried" (Elliott 1993, 658; Schneemelcher, ed. 1991–1992, vol. I, 543). Also important outside the Western context is the related paradox in the Russian/Slavonic *akafisty*: *raduisia, iako nosishi Nosiashchago vsia* (*Akafistnik* 2000, 57). In the medieval West, we find, e.g., *Ave, que portas portantem omnia, Omnia portanta portans, Portat portantem omnia*, etc. (Meersseman 1958–1960, vol. I, 104, 131, 154; vol. II, 49, 220, 238).

99 This aggrandizing paradox persists in Russia (*Raduisia, Boga nevmestimago vmestilishche* [*Akafistnik* 2000, 62]) and in the medieval West (*Ave, dei incapabilis regio* [Meersseman 1958–1960, vol. I, 118]).

100 Peltomaa 2001, 143, 182–183.

101 Constas 2003, 138–139; cf. also 200–201, 226–227; and Peltomaa 2001, 112, 182.

102 From the Divine Liturgy of Saint John Chrysostom in, for example: Hapgood 1922, 108 (English); Kallis 2000, 139 (Church Slavonic: *Chestnĕishouiu kherouvim", i slavnĕishouiu bez" sravneniia serafim"*; Greek: *Tēn timiōteran tōn cheroubim kai endoksoteran asugkritōs tōn serafim*).

103 *The Liber usualis* 1952, 1600–1601, 1607 (*Super choros Angelorum ad caelestia regna*); Socias 2011, 1899 (*Maria, quae hodie exaltata es super choros Angelorum*).

104 John of Damascus 1998b, 220.

105 Anselm of Canterbury 1973, 120.

106 Roschini 1949, 617. Some idea of the great heterogeneity of meanings manifested in devotional, liturgical, theological, doctrinal, iconographic, political, and other representations of Mary as "queen" in various time periods and branches of Christianity may be gathered from: Roschini 1949; Carroll 1955, 45–50; Miegge 1955, 68–82; Schmidt 1957; numerous papal statements catalogued under the entry "Mary's Queenship and Glory" in the analytical index of *Papal Teachings: Our Lady* 1961, 533–538; Van Os 1970; Ledit 1976, 241–252 (in Eastern Orthodox liturgy); Verdier 1980; the entry "Queenship, Mary's" in O'Carroll 2000 (1982), 301–302; Fastenrath and Tschochner 1991; Benko 2004 (1993), 216–228; Sri 2005; Boss 2007a, 156–166.

107 Kondakov 1998 (1914–1915), vol. I, figs. 24, 93, 95, 97, 98, 101, 122–126, 139–148, 155, 159–161, 180–182, 184, 186, 193, 195, 199, 202–207, 212, 213; vol. II, figs. 30, 59, 60, 149, 160, 179, 182, 183, 185–187, 192, 195, 196, 197–199, 201, 202, 207, 208, 215, 220, 225, 228–232, 234, 235, 236, 239, 240–243; Lasareff 1938, figs. 2, 10, 25–35, 37, 38, 41–49; Garrison 1949, nos. 1–42, 175–203, 207, 208, 210–237, 248–253, 281, 282, 291, 291A, 306–310, 325–327, 333–336; Küppers, ed. 1974, figs. 1–8, 12, 14, 16, 18–20, 22, 23, 25–34, 36, 37, 42, 52, 57, 59–61, 71–74, 76, 114, 354, 355, 358, 359, 378; Purtle 1982, figs. 33, 47, 48, 50, 52, 53, 68, 76, 77; *Biblia pauperum* 1987, signature ·q· (with extensive commentary and bibliography, 119, 148); Gregori 1994, figs. 6, 7, 8, 9, 10, 11, 20, 21, 25, 36, 44, 79, 82, 102, 124, 127, 132, 141, 142, 156, 400; Langener 1996, Part II, figs. 8, 10–14; Lifshits and Lukashov 2000, cat nos 49, 50, 58, 72, 81, 86; Vassilaki, ed. 2000, cat nos 1, 3, 19, 28, 68; figs. 12, 30, 45, 46, 47, 48, 51, 52, 53, 54, 61, 62, 72, 73, 107, 188, 223, 224, 228, 247, 254, 256, 381; Schiller 1966–1991, vol. 4,2, figs. 411, 413–415, 417, 420, 438–440, 453, 454, 459, 463, 613, 617–619, 626, 627, 632, 633, 635, 638, 639, 647, 670, 676, 679, 713, 714, 730–750, 772, 773, 780, 792, 794, 797, 799, 803, 805, 807, 810, 811, 815, 817–820, 824–826, 831–833. Insofar as the *Sedes Sapientiae* images involve an enthroned (and sometimes crowned) Mary in majesty, most of the many plates in Forsyth (1972) would have to be included here.

108 Newman 2003, 247, 254–261, and figs. 6.2, 6.3, 6.4.
109 Miegge 1955, 184.
110 Graef 2009 (1963–1965), 212–213, 307, 337.
111 Alphonsus de Liguori 2012 (1977), 153.
112 See, for example: Peltomaa 2001; Meersseman 1958–1960 (2 vols, especially vol. I, 94–98, and his *Mariologisches Glossarium* in vol. II, 276–387); Pelikan 1971–1989, vol. 3, 161 ff.
113 Rancour-Laferriere 2011, 15–17, 139–171.
114 For example: Rancour-Laferriere 2011, 139 (n. 6).
115 N. P. Ševčenko 1991c.
116 See: N. P. Ševčenko 1991d; Baltoyanni 2000, 140; Pentcheva 2006, 174–175, 179, fig 116.
117 Mango 2000;
118 See: Norman 1999, 251, index entries, "Virgin . . . as advocate, defender, governor, protector of Siena," "as patron saint of Siena," "as queen of Siena;" Rubin 2009, 300.
119 Remensnyder 2014.
120 Pentcheva 2006, 2.
121 Rancour-Laferriere 2005, 262–263; cf. *Skazaniia o zemnoi zhizni presviatoi Bogoroditsy* n. d. (reprint of 1904 edition), 241–260. See also: Shevzov 2004, 244–257 (on stories of marian icons as protectors of the "chosen" Russian people); Shevzov 2007 (on stories of the Kazan icon, "the most widely publicly revered of Russia's twenty-eight nationally recognized miracle-working icons of the Mother of God" [63], and "a sacred national symbol" [84]).
122 Rancour-Laferriere 2000, 157–176.
123 Riabov 2001, 114–120; Rancour-Laferriere 2005, 265–268.
124 Tavard 1996, 248.
125 Llywelyn 2010, 225–275. Curiously enough, there is a specifically Dutch cult of "Our Lady of All Nations" (*de Vrouwe van alle Volkeren*) that originated in a long series of apparitions and "messages" to a woman in Amsterdam named Ida Peerdeman, starting in 1945. By now, this cult has achieved international status, having attracted a large following and propagated branches in various parts of the world. Among the several controversial ideas advocated by members of the cult is the establishment of a new marian dogma, which includes the notion that Mary is the coredeemer of humankind along with her son (Laurentin and Sbalchiero, eds. 2007, 79–84; Margry 2009; Maunder 2016, 114–121; see below, pp. 268–272, on the issue of Mary's coredemption).
126 Llywelyn 2010, 241.
127 Perry and Echeverría 1988, 109 (cf. Rancour-Laferriere 2005, 268). For images of the statue *Notre-Dame de France* in Le Puy-en-Velay, see: https://commons.wikimedia.org/wiki/Category:Statue_de_Notre-Dame_de_France_(Le_Puy-en-Velay)?uselang=fr (accessed 7 July 2015).

2 Mary and the Foolishness of Wisdom

Appropriating the Old Testament Figure of Wisdom

A particularly revealing incursion of Mary into the category of the divine comes up in mariophile discourse about the ancient figure of divine Wisdom. Among the so-called Wisdom books of the Christian Old Testament is the apocryphal Ecclesiasticus (also termed Sirach). One chapter of this work contains a poem in praise of Wisdom, which is personified as a woman: *hokhma* in Hebrew, *sophia* in Greek, *sapientia* in Latin – all feminine nouns. Wisdom praises herself, and she speaks about her creator: "Before the ages, in the beginning, he created me, and for all the ages I shall not cease to be" (24:9 [= Vulgate 24:14]). Similarly, in another of the Wisdom books, Proverbs (of Solomon), we read: "The Lord created me at the beginning of his work, the first of his acts of long ago" (8:22). Although these originally pre-Christian, Hebrew texts could not possibly have referred to a certain Jewish woman of the future who lived in a humble Galilean village, some Christian mariophiles have acted as if that were nonetheless the case. In other words, they have seen fit to expropriate Wisdom for their own use.

For example, in various Catholic liturgical texts for marian feast days, one or the other of the above-cited verses has in the past been given as part of the lection. Thus, in a tenth-century mass honoring the *birth of Mary*, one of the readings included Proverbs 8:22, and the gospel reading for the same mass was the genealogy of Jesus, which immediately precedes the narration of *the birth of Jesus* in Matthew (1:1 ff.). This suggested, not only an equation of Mary with the ancient Hebrew figure of Wisdom personified, but also an affirmation that Mary, like her son, somehow pre-existed the fleshly human being, or was as much predestined for her role as he was for his. After all, the prologue to John's gospel refers to Jesus the Word in the following terms: "In the beginning was the Word, and the Word was with God" (1:1), and it was only later that this Word "became flesh" (1:14). Sarah Jane Boss comments:

> As Christ was present from eternity, and in the fullness of time became flesh in his mother's womb, so Mary was in some manner present from the foundations of the world, and likewise was born when the time was right for her part in the fulfilment of God's plan.[1]

Boss notes that it became the norm for Proverbs 8:22–31 to be read at masses for the feasts celebrating Mary's birth and Mary's conception, and that these readings probably contributed to the establishment of the doctrine of the immaculate conception.[2]

Given these earlier developments, it is not surprising that members of the clergy would take similar liberties in our time. There is, for example, the church censor who pronounced a *Nihil obstat* in permitting publication of a book in 1943 titled *EGO SAPIENTIA . . . La sagesse qui est Marie.*[3] Or, there is the Dominican Aegidius Doolan, who contributed a paper *about Mary* titled "Ab Aeterno Ordinata Sum" to the mariological congress held in Rome in 1950. Doolan justifies his approach: "quite deliberately, the Church, notably in the Office of the Immaculate Conception, applies what is said in inspired Scripture of the conception of the Word to the conception of the Mother of the Word." He concludes his presentation with "Our Lady" speaking some phrases about her immaculate conception. They are cribbed from the discourse of Wisdom speaking Latin in Proverbs (8:22–24) and include the phrase, "When there were no depths I was brought forth [ego iam *concepta* eram]."[4]

I find Proverbs 8:22 still being quoted in the mass for the feast of the Immaculate Conception (December 8) in my tattered daily missal from the 1950s.[5] As a devout teenager in those days, however, I did not really comprehend what "immaculate conception" meant, much less who a person named "Wisdom" was. I did somehow gain the impression that the Blessed Virgin Mary was a sort of ethereal and perfect goddess who, like the god named Jesus Christ, was always "up there," had always existed, and would always exist. The visits of these two divine persons to planet Earth had been temporary. After participating briefly in the misery of life here below, they cleared out. The rest of us would have to wait until judgment day.

Technically speaking, that impression was incorrect: both Jesus and Mary had gone up into heaven, but only the former was returning there and was God eternal (and many other things as well that Mary would never achieve in the context of Roman Catholicism). I should have remembered that there was a difference between "Ascension [of Jesus] Day" and the feast of the "Assumption of Mary."

The same old missal contains another marian item that is also relevant to the figure of Wisdom. It is the so-called Litany of Loreto, which probably originated in the twelfth century as an independent work, and was formally approved by Pope Sixtus V in 1587. It includes this verse:

> *Sedes sapientiae, ora pro nobis.*
> Seat of wisdom, pray for us.[6]

When we came to this part of the litany in our recitation, the believer I once was felt a vague glow of gratitude, for I understood that someone "wise" was being called upon to arrange things for the best on our behalf. As most of the verses in the litany both praised Mary and requested her intercession, I must have guessed that Mary was this "Seat of wisdom."

In scholarly retrospect, the famous marian epithet *Sedes Sapientiae*[7] makes more sense than *Sapientia* alone for those theologically mature Christians who do not wish to elevate Mary entirely to the status of a pre-existing deity. Rather, they venerate her as the physical site where the pre-existing Sophia–Logos was made incarnate, or as the human vessel from whom this deity emerged in the person of the Christ child who took his *seat* upon his now royal mother's lap. Hence, the litany's request, "Seat of wisdom, pray for us," should be understood to mean: "Mother of Wisdom, please intercede for us with your divine child, who is the person named Wisdom."[8]

Related to the "Seat of Wisdom" is the royal "Throne of Wisdom." Mary's child was Christ the King, and any king needs a throne. There is already a suggestion of enthronement in the first Greek Akathistos (1:12), which represents Mary herself as the throne of Christ the King, *Basileōs kathedra.*[9] Furthermore, if Christ the King was to become Wisdom, what better prefiguration of his throne might be appropriated from the Old Testament than the throne of the proverbially *wise* King Solomon? Hence, there developed a marian tradition that looked tendentiously back at Solomon's gold and ivory throne (1 Kings 10:18–20).[10] For example, in an edition of the late medieval *Mirror of Human Salvation* (*Speculum humanae salvationis*), we find: "The throne of the true Solomon [*Thronus veri Salomonis*] is the Most Blessed Virgin Mary in whom resided Jesus Christ, true Wisdom [*vera Sophia*]."[11]

Byzantine images of the Christ child seated on the lap of a majestic Mary started to appear after the Council of Ephesus, and enthroned mother and Christ child images eventually became common throughout Christendom.[12] In parts of medieval Europe, there developed an abundance of artifacts (most notably Romanesque wood statues) depicting what art historians customarily term *Sedes Sapientiae.*[13] An example is the famous Black Madonna of Montserrat, the *Patrona de Catalunya*, in northeastern Spain.[14] This statue is the heart of a pilgrimage site, and it continues to be an object of devout veneration in the twenty-first century. On a spring day in 2011, I observed a long, slow-moving line of pilgrims approaching this object in order to touch it and to pray before it with servile gestures of reverence. As far as I could determine, the object of their veneration was Mary, not the child Christ seated on her lap.

The Roman Catholic West has hardly been alone in surreptitiously utilizing the title of Wisdom for marian purposes. In Orthodox Russia, for example, there is a rich tradition that links Mary to Wisdom as personified in the Old Testament. Not that this linkage is any stronger in official liturgical or festal practice than it is (or was) in the West, nor is it particularly evident even within the abundant iconography of Mary in Russia/Rus', which provides relatively few examples linking Mary to Wisdom or equating the two figures in some fashion.[15] But, the connection (and sometimes the equation) is a very important theme in Russian religious philosophy, particularly in a field that Russian scholars are accustomed to calling *sofiologiia*.[16] Pavel Florensky (1882–1937) and Sergii Bulgakov (1871–1944) may be briefly commented on as examples.

Florensky not only waxes eloquent on the purity and grandeur of Mary in the context of an essay titled "Sophia,"[17] but goes so far as to suggest that this Sophia or Wisdom is a fourth hypostasis of God.[18] Is Florensky suggesting that the trinitarian God of Christianity is really a quaternity, or is his sophianic Mary only playing a previously unimagined supporting role? Either way, we have something quite subjective and creative, and possibly heretical as well. We also have grist for the psychoanalytic mill – but no more than would be had regarding the other, more orthodox beliefs of Russian Orthodoxy.

As for Bulgakov, his sophiology is both more cautious and more radical. Mary participates [*prichastna*], if only by the grace of God, in the life of the triune God.[19] It cannot be said that Mary *is* God, according to Bulgakov, but her divinization or deification (*obozhenie*) cannot be questioned either, for after her death God saw fit to resurrect her and to take her up, body and soul, into the heavens, where she sits forever with her resurrected God the Son at the right hand of God the Father.[20] This is a theologically correct application of the Eastern Orthodox notion of post-resurrection *theōsis* to one who is believed to be an already-resurrected individual, and is similar in some respects to what would become the Roman Catholic dogma of Mary's Assumption (below, pp. 56–57). But Bulgakov moves Mary a bit further along the trajectory of deification by (1) proposing that she is the "perfect manifestation" of the Holy Spirit and (2) adding the element of sophianization, for Mary is also "the personal manifestation of the Wisdom of God, of Sophia."[21] Again, we have here something quite subjective and creative, and in some respects definitely heretical.[22]

And scripture? Simply put: if we trust that Russian sophiology – the closest thing to Roman Catholic mariology in Eastern Orthodoxy – refers to anything that can be found out about Mary (as opposed to her son) in the Christian New Testament – then our trust will be misplaced.

In fact, Mary is *never* represented as Wisdom in the New Testament – which is not surprising, given that she is hardly represented there at all in comparison with her illustrious son. Even if it can plausibly be argued that the historical *provenience* of some representations of Mary lie in the imperfectly remembered person of Wisdom, who was "a fundamental figure in the ancient faith of Jerusalem" before she was "banished from the Jerusalem Temple in the seventh century BCE,"[23] this does not mean that Mary is represented as Wisdom in the canonical New Testament.

The Representation of Christ as Wisdom

Christ is represented as Wisdom in the New Testament. The parallel of pre-existing God the Word (Logos) in the first chapter of John's gospel with pre-existing Wisdom (Sophia) in earlier (or even contemporary) Jewish writings in Greek is acknowledged by scholars of the New Testament. Compare, for example, John 1:1–2:

> In the beginning was the Word, and the Word was with God.

with The Wisdom of Solomon 9:9:

> With you [God] is wisdom, she who knows your works and was present when you made the world.[24]

Barbara Newman writes that, "John's revered prologue is a virtual Sophia-hymn in honor of Jesus, and would have been recognized as such by its original audience."[25] Of course, John's is the latest of the four canonical gospels, and it cannot be claimed that before John a clear "Wisdom–Logos christology" (James D. G. Dunn) had been articulated.[26] But, it is worth noting that, already with Paul, the earliest New Testament author and "the first great Christian theologian,"[27] references to Wisdom are made. Paul not only applies traditional Wisdom imagery to Christ (e.g., "the firstborn of all creation" – Colossians 1:15), but also explicitly declares that the crucified Christ is "the power of God and the wisdom of God [*theou sofian*]" (1 Corinthians 1:24), and that Christ "became for us wisdom from God [*sofia hēmin apo theou*]" (30).[28] There is also some less explicit evidence that Christ is a Wisdom figure in the synoptic gospels, especially Matthew.[29]

Various grounds for interpreting Christ as Wisdom are surveyed by Elisabeth Schüssler Fiorenza, who, however, is disappointed with the findings. Even if a rich, hellenized Jewish Wisdom tradition (including elements of the Egyptian Isis cult) was flourishing before the advent of someone whom Schüssler Fiorenza calls "Miriam's child," and even if fragments of this tradition can be detected on the margins of early Christianity, Christ himself turned out to be "Sophia's prophet" at best. One problem, from the viewpoint of Schüssler Fiorenza's feminist theology, is "the overwhelming androcentric shape and kyriocentric framework of the texts that speak of Divine Wisdom."[30] Another problem is that Jesus not only seemed to be a beneficent male "Lord," but that he also drew crowds by prophesying on behalf of the poor and the oppressed of Israel, and consequently was subjected to the violence of crucifixion by the authorities governing in Jerusalem. He was the messenger who was killed for his "sophialogical" message.[31]

But, can the messenger be so easily separated from the message? And, would a pre-Christian Sophia even have preached such a message? What Jesus was preaching was provocative and highly dangerous. This human being accomplished (or, more precisely, he is represented as having accomplished) a personal goal that matched the divine purpose for which Christian theologians would later claim he was predestined: he got himself crucified.

On several occasions, Jesus is recorded as predicting his own demise[32] and, after his final provocation (the so-called "cleansing of the Temple"),[33] he got what he was looking for, namely, the painful and humiliating agony of dying on a cross. The canonical gospels clearly depict Jesus' grandiosity and his psychological need to be humiliated and to suffer, as I have demonstrated elsewhere.[34]

Whereas the person of Wisdom in parts of the *Old* Testament and in other Wisdom writings was no masochist, Jesus the Christ of the *New* Testament was the model masochist for all who wished to follow in his steps: "If any want to become my followers, let them deny themselves and take up their cross daily and follow me" (Luke 9:23; cf. Mark 8:34; Matthew 16:24). If the hubris of such a call does not sound like a claim to divine authority and identity, then much else in the gospels – especially John's – should convince us – for example, "The Father and I are one" (10:30); or, "Very truly, I tell you, before Abraham was, *I am*" (8:58). We cannot avoid the conclusion that this Jesus is someone under the sway of grandiose thinking, that is, someone who thinks he is God, or someone who is in very close communication with God.

After John's famous opening hymn alluding to Wisdom, Jesus quickly emerges as God's own victim, that is, "the Lamb of God who takes away the sin of the world" (John 1:29). Said lamb is sacrificial, and is in need of a cross upon which to be sacrificed. So, he goes about the business of preaching, predicting, and provoking, until finally, one day, he manages to die on the cross at the very time that Passover lambs are being slaughtered not far away, in the Temple courtyard.[35] By his self-sacrifice on the cross, Jesus the Lamb of God "takes away the sin of the world."

Anyone who ever sang (or heard sung) that part of the old Tridentine mass right after the fraction of the host will remember the plaintive melody of a prayer addressed to John's sacrificial lamb: *Agnus Dei, qui tollis peccata mundi: miserere nobis.*[36] After singing such words, we would consume the eucharistic host, that is, the "Lamb of God," which had long since replaced (superseded) the Jewish Passover lamb.[37]

Paul, who, decades before John, was already thinking of his Christian Messiah as "our paschal lamb" (1 Corinthians 5:7), was willing to borrow "Wisdom language"[38] to characterize the sacrificial death of Christ on the cross. The aforementioned words to the fractious brethren in Corinth about "the wisdom of God" should be quoted in their full context:

> For the message about the cross is foolishness to those who are perishing, but to us who are being saved it is the power of God. For it is written, "I will destroy the wisdom of the wise, and the discernment of the discerning I will thwart" [cf. Isaiah 29:14]. Where is the one who is wise? Where is the scribe? Where is the debater of this age? Has not God made foolish the wisdom of the world? For since, in the wisdom of God, the world did not know God through wisdom, God

> decided, through the foolishness of our proclamation, to save those who believe. For Jews demand signs and Greeks desire wisdom, but we proclaim Christ crucified, a stumbling block to Jews and foolishness to Gentiles, but to those who are the called, both Jews and Greeks, Christ the power of God and the wisdom of God. For God's foolishness is wiser than human wisdom, and God's weakness is stronger than human strength.
>
> (1 Corinthians 1:20–25)

Here, we see that Paul's thinking about "the power of God and the *wisdom* of God" occurs specifically in the context of rationalizing Christ's violent death. Paul presents "the message about the cross [*ho logos gar ho tou staurou*]" as a proclamation of the equivalence of "Christ crucified [*Christon estaurōmenon*]" with "the wisdom of God" (or later, in verse 30 of the same chapter, with "wisdom from God").

Joseph A. Fitzmyer, in his Anchor Yale Bible volume on First Corinthians, writes: "This formulation, 'Christ crucified,' supplies the key to Pauline theology, because from it Paul develops *all* his other doctrinal and ethical teaching, for Christ crucified is for Paul the criterion and norm of *all* Christian thought and conduct."[39] Regardless of whether one believes that "Christ crucified" is "foolishness" or is "the wisdom of God," the main point is that Paul's idea of a messiah, Paul's Christ – was a crucified messiah. Or: Paul's idea of wisdom was wisdom personified, and wisdom personified was Christ crucified.

Nowhere in the Hebrew Bible is "the wisdom of God" revealed in a voluntary act of being crucified. Nor is the person of "Wisdom" there ever associated with such a repugnant act. Crucifixion was a degrading punishment: "Anyone hung on a tree is under God's curse" (Deuteronomy 21:23). Paul paraphrases these words in a letter to the Galatians (3:13), understanding them to refer to crucifixion, the capital punishment of choice in his Roman imperial context.[40] The very idea of a crucified Messiah (Paul's "Christ crucified") was – and continued to be in Paul's day – a "stumbling block" (*skandalon*) for Jews, as Paul recognizes at 1 Corinthians 1:23. Paul also utilizes this Greek word *skandalon* in connection with the crucifixion elsewhere, as when he speaks of "the offense [*skandalon*] of the cross" (Galatians 5:11), or when he alludes to Isaiah (28:16) in Romans 9:32–33: "They [Israel] have stumbled over the stumbling stone, as it is written, 'See, I am laying in Zion a stone that will make people stumble, a rock that will make them fall [*petran skandalou*], and whoever believes in him will not be put to shame'" (Romans 9:32–33).[41]

According to Paul, what for Jews is scandal, for Gentiles is foolishness. Christ on the cross seems to have displayed "God's foolishness." But paradoxically, he writes, God's was a foolishness "wiser than human wisdom" (1 Corinthians 1:25). Such a formulation is rhetorically more elaborate and psychologically more defensive than the formulation of the previous verses

(23–24), where "Christ crucified" is simply "the wisdom of God." But, either way, from a clinical viewpoint, Paul is saying that God's idea of wisdom (or of the person of Wisdom) was the grandiose masochism of Christ (or Christ the Grandiose Masochist, in person).

To judge from the clearest indications of wisdom (Wisdom) in the New Testament, then, they point to Jesus, not to Mary. In particular, they point to Jesus' self-sacrificial goal orientation. "Miriam's child" (Schüssler Fiorenza) was an adult who did not need to consult his mother on the matter of getting himself crucified. He, not his mother, was Wisdom in the Pauline sense. He arranged the Passion by himself and for himself, apparently under the grandiose impression that his was an act performed under the supervision of God the Father and – according to many subsequent theologies – on behalf of all humankind. Any pre-crucifixion consultations between mother and son are post-biblical. The earthly mother of Jesus also could conceivably have looked on with great sorrow and loud lamentations as her son was dying on the cross, for this would be expected of a normal mother anywhere. Yet, of the four canonical gospels, only John places Mary at the scene (19:25–27), where, however, she remains silent.

Mary's Unbelief, According to Origen

Some scholars have pointed to the righteous old man Simeon, who, on the occasion of the baby Jesus' so-called "presentation in the temple,"[42] turns to Mary and prophesizes: "This child is destined for the falling and the rising of many in Israel, and to be a sign that will be opposed so that the inner thoughts of many will be revealed – and a sword will pierce your own soul too" (Luke 2:34–35). The "sword" in this somewhat mysterious passage has been interpreted in a variety of ways, most notably as a "sword of compassion" that would later pierce the *Mater dolorosa* at her son's Passion.[43] But, another meaning, at once more ancient and more relevant to Paul's ideas about "Christ [the Messiah] crucified" – is Origen's notion that the sword that would pierce the soul of Mary during the Passion would be a "sword of unbelief."

According to Origen, Mary was just as dubious as the apostles themselves when it came time for her son actually to be crucified. In a third-century homily, Origen comments on a declaration made by Jesus in Mark (14:27; parallel passage in Matthew 26:31):

> The Lord himself said, "All of you will be scandalized [as in the Vulgate version of Mark, *scandalizabimini*, but in Matthew, *scandalum patiemini in me*; cf. Greek original of both, *skandalisthēsesthe*; "You will all become deserters" – NRSV; "You will all lose faith" – Jerusalem Bible; "All ye shall be offended because of me" – King James Version] tonight." Therefore everyone was scandalized, so that Peter himself, head of the apostles, denied Jesus three times. What! Are we to suppose that, when

> the apostles were scandalized, the Lord's Mother was exempt from scandal [*a scandalo . . . immunis*]? If she did not suffer scandal [*scandalum*] during the Lord's Passion, then Jesus did not die for her sins. If, however, "all have sinned and fall short of the glory of God, if all have been justified and redeemed by his grace" [Romans 3:23–24] – then surely Mary as well was at that time scandalized [*scandalizata est*]. And this is what Simeon prophesized, "and thy own soul . . . shall the sword" of unbelief [*infidelitatis gladius*] "pierce," and thou shalt be stabbed with the spear of doubt [*ambiguitatis mucrone ferieris*], and thy thoughts shall tear thee asunder [*lacerabunt*], when thou shalt see him whom thou hadst heard to be the Son of God, and knew to have been begotten by no seed of man, crucified and dying, and subject to human torments, and at last with tears complaining and saying, "Father, if it be possible, let this chalice pass from me" [Matthew 26:39]. And thus will your soul be pierced by a sword.[44]

Origen's Mary has not experienced just a momentary shadow of doubt here. There is something much larger, something "scandalous." The pointed reference to Romans actually makes Mary a sinner. Origen may be trying to show that Mary, like everyone else, was in need of redemption.[45] Perhaps that is so, but – in her own mind – Mary of Origen also questions who her son thinks he is in a much more serious fashion than do her son's disciples (including Peter, who would not have known and understood Mary's son as well as Mary herself did). The pileup of violent imagery directed against Mary – piercing, stabbing, tearing her – is so graphic that the reader must imagine Mary undergoing a deeply painful internal conflict. The "sword" of Simeon inflicts serious psychological wounds.

Yet why exactly does Origen utilize a vocabulary of "scandal" to explain the "sword" of Simeon? If the "sword" has a scriptural subtext, then so must the "scandal." This brings us back to Paul. What Origen (and quite a few others after him)[46] have thought about Mary having doubts about her son – that is, being "scandalized" – is precisely an affirmation of Paul's position (1 Corinthians 1:23–24) concerning the "scandal" of a crucified Messiah: "we proclaim Christ [Messiah] crucified, a stumbling block [*skandalon*] to Jews," but for Christian believers, "Christ the power of God and the wisdom of God." If Mary was a Jew, then it follows that the idea of a crucified Messiah had to be for her a "scandal." Mary would have been "scandalized" because her son's crucifixion meant that he was not the Messiah after all.

To paraphrase Origen's view, Mary failed to see either the power or the wisdom (much less the Pauline "wisdom of God") in her son's crucifixion. She was taking a Jewish point of view on the matter. Of course, the apostles were also Jewish and were also "scandalized." But, Origen hints that, in the case of Mary, some additional element was possibly contributing to her doubtful state of mind. He writes that Mary sees on the cross "him whom thou hadst heard to be the Son of God, and knew to have been begotten by no seed of man." And how had Mary first learned about these things, if not from Luke's announcing angel?

> The angel said to her, "Do not be afraid, Mary, for you have found favor with God. And now, you will conceive in your womb and bear a son, and you will name him Jesus. He will be great, and will be called the son of the Most High, and the Lord God will give to him the throne of his ancestor David. He will reign over the house of Jacob forever, and of his kingdom there will be no end."
>
> (Luke 1:30–33)

> The angel said to her, "The Holy Spirit will come upon you, and the power of the Most High will overshadow you; therefore the child to be born will be holy; he will be called Son of God."
>
> (Luke 1:35)

At the time, Mary had taken these words quite seriously, to judge from the high expectations she expressed at the beginning of the so-called Magnificat:

> And Mary said, "My soul magnifies the Lord, and my spirit rejoices in God my Savior, for he has looked with favor on the lowliness of his servant. Surely, from now on all generations will call me blessed; for the Mighty One has done great things for me, and holy is his name."
>
> (Luke 1:46–49)

It would seem, then, that Mary had been tricked by the announcing angel, Gabriel (this theme will be picked up by subsequent writers, as we will see). Mary had not agreed to give birth to the "Son of God" in order to see him crucified. As a future mother, she had been led to believe that her son was going to be a winner, not a loser (if she was a normal mother, she would of course also have been deeply concerned about her son's welfare, regardless of whether he was a winner or a loser). Origen does not quite say so explicitly, but, for Mary, the disappointment on Golgotha is not only the "scandal" of a crucified messiah, but also the broken promise received at the annunciation. There is no indication in the canonical New Testament that Mary ever overcame what must have been a double disappointment. Whether on Golgotha (John 19:25–27) or in the upper room afterwards (Acts 1:14), Mary is silent.

Mary the Mother of Wisdom

Regardless of whether Mary believed or disbelieved in what Christians would later claim to be an essential part of her son's identity, Mary was the mother of her son. Mary was not Wisdom, but the mother of Wisdom.

When, in post-scriptural representations of the passion, Christ is brought into contact with Mary, Christ is sometimes represented in explicitly sapiential terms. An early example of this is provided by Romanos the Melodist (d. ca.560). In his famous hymn about Mary conversing with her son just prior to his crucifixion, Romanos draws a parallel between the suffering and the wisdom of Christ. Addressing the "Son of the Virgin, God of the Virgin," the poet-composer declares, in the last stanza: "yours is the suffering, yours the depth of wisdom [*son to pathos, son to bathos tēs sofias*]."[47] Mary herself displays no such "depth of wisdom" in this composition, however. She is a normal, sensible mother who is upset – to put it mildly – about the suffering that her son is bringing upon himself.

In the earliest *Life of the Virgin* (seventh century), by Maximos the Confessor, Christ on the cross speaks his final words to Mary and John, entrusting them to one another as mother and son (cf. John 19:26–27). The author, however, writes, not "Jesus" and not "Christ," but that "Wisdom herself opened her sweet mouth"[48] to accomplish this task. That is, the man voluntarily suffering and about to die on the cross was "Wisdom herself." This is both a personification of wisdom and an interrogation of the gender of Christ. As for Mary – "the mother of the Word, the mother of Wisdom"[49] – she stood by and watched her son as he voluntarily suffered before her eyes. When the son finally gives up his spirit, Maximos marvels at the compassionate mother's strength:

> How did the immaculate mother endure the pain? How did she not give up her spirit as well? But it is clear that the grace and power of the crucified Lord sustained her. He gave up his spirit himself as he saw it was necessary, but his power sustained the soul of his mother so that she was [as] invested in every action as he was himself.[50]

Much could be said about such a pious meditation. At the very least, it is clear that a close bond unites "the mother of Wisdom" with "Wisdom herself," that is, the mother of the grandiose masochist with the masochist himself (herself?). Nevertheless, the two persons remain objectively distinct from one another, for it is Christ on the cross who is Wisdom, while the mother of Wisdom looks on with compassion.

In the medieval West, wisdom (Wisdom) was linked to Mary as well as to Christ. Barbara Newman has studied these linkages in some detail.[51] She observes that, when the linkage is to Mary, Mary tends to be divinized (cf. the example from the marian liturgy, above, p. 32). When the linkage is to Christ, the result tends to be a feminized Christ. This latter category is relevant to Christ's passion and to the Pauline sense of wisdom as Christ crucified.

For example, a French manuscript of Henry Suso's widely read *Horologium Sapientiae* (*Horloge de Sapience*, mid-fifteenth century) contains several illustrations of Dame Sapience with cruciferous nimbus – a thinly veiled allusion

Figure 2.1 *Majestas Sapientiae. Horloge de Sapience* (detail), mid-fifteenth century. Brussels, Bibliothèque royale ms. IV, III, f. 13r (Monks 1990, 135).

to the crucifixion of Christ. One of the illustrations shows Dame Sapience together with a suffering Christ carrying his cross, and *each* of these personages is adorned with a cruciferous nimbus.[52] Mary is entirely absent from the picture. Another illustration (the first in the manuscript) is titled *Majestas Sapientiae* and shows the goddess seated upon a throne of majesty (see Figure 2.1, detail). Again, this goddess has Christ's cruciferous nimbus. She also holds "the traditional attributes of Christ in majesty: an open book in her right hand, an orb in her left."[53] According to the medieval commentator, she is "Lady Wisdom [*dame Sapience*] in the form and likeness of a woman, signifying Jesus our Savior, who is called the power and wisdom of God the Father (1 Cor. 1.24)."[54] Wisdom is indeed a lady here, and the lady is not Mary, but Mary's son. Perhaps Paul would have rolled his eyes at such a transgendered Christ, but Paul's own words[55] are being quoted, which is to say that Lady Wisdom is a personification of wisdom in the Pauline sense of "Christ crucified."

In Russian Orthodox iconography, Wisdom is rarely represented as Paul's "Christ crucified." From among the various allegorical image types representing Wisdom, however, there is one that does include a crucifix, the so-called *Sofiia Krestnaia* ("Wisdom of the Cross"). This type dates to the seventeenth or perhaps the sixteenth century.[56] Here, the vertical pillar of the cross upon which Christ hangs is also the central pillar of seven pillars that support a baldachin overhead – an allusion to the personified Wisdom figure of Proverbs 9:1: "Wisdom has built her house, she has hewn her seven pillars." Numerous angels and saints of various categories (including Mary and John the Baptizer in their standard deesis configuration) are included in this elaborate picture, but the crucified Christ literally occupies center stage, and the rest is mostly esoteric clutter. It is curious that the central crucifix bearing Christ (with the lance wound in his right side) emerges from the top of an *altar* under the baldachin, suggesting eucharistic reenactment of Christ's voluntary sacrifice on the cross.[57]

One more historical example of Wisdom in the Pauline sense may be taken from the writings of the great mariophile Saint Louis-Marie Grignion de Montfort (1673–1716). According to Montfort, Christ is "Wisdom incarnate [*la Sagesse incarnée*],"[58] and this is *because of* the scandalous suffering, humiliation, and death that Christ welcomed on his cross:

> But O wonder! He perceives [*Elle voit*] something which is a source of scandal and horror to Jews and an object of foolishness to pagans [1 Corinthians 1:23]. He sees [*elle voit*] a piece of vile and contemptible wood which is used to humiliate and torture the most wicked and the most wretched of men, called a gibbet, a gallows, a cross. It is upon this cross that he casts his eyes [*elle jette les yeux*]; he [*elle*] takes his delight in it; he [*elle*] cherishes it more than all that is great and resplendent in heaven and on earth. He decides that that will be the instrument of his conquests, the adornment of his royal state. He will make it the wealth and joy of his empire, the friend and spouse of his heart. O the depths of the wisdom and knowledge of God! [Romans 11:33][59]

Here again is an interesting incongruity of gender between Wisdom the woman and Christ the man, which, however, the translator has attempted to erase.[60] Behind the incongruity is the same old core issue of Christ's grandiose masochism, for the cross is something to take delight in, something to be cherished, something that is grander than anything on earth or in heaven – regardless of whether the one to be crucified is a woman or a man. Montfort may "genderize" the grandiose masochism, much as Maximos the Confessor and the illustrated Henry Suso did, but he does so without forgetting Paul's equation of *la sagesse de Dieu* with *Christ crucifié*. Masochism trumps gender.[61]

These examples of post-scriptural representation of what Paul said about the "wisdom" of "Christ crucified" demonstrate that it has been possible to understand what Paul really meant and, more broadly, to understand what his Christ was up to when he provoked the authorities into crucifying him. Such examples, however, are exceptional. More often one finds that wisdom is an attribute of Mary, or is personified as Mary (when not personified as a separate deity altogether). This may be explained in part by the availability and attraction of Jewish Wisdom writings to mariophiles down the centuries. Equally important, however, was the psychological need to avoid confronting the "wisdom" of Christ's own motivation leading up to his being crucified.

Some Russian icons of Sophia the Wisdom of God (*Sofiia Premudrost' Bozhiia*), for example, appear to represent what Russians term the Mother of God (*Bogomater'*) – that is, Mary instead of her son.[62] Such icons not only fail to respect the boundary between mother and son, they have no basis in New Testament scripture. Some other Wisdom icons do signify Christ crucified, and are therefore scripturally valid. But they do so in a complicated allegorical manner, as when Christ/Sophia appears as an androgynous figure, with the wings of an angel, and is seated in resplendent garments upon a backless throne – rather than nailed naked to a cross.[63] That leaves only the *Sofiia krestnaia* type, which, as noted above, is quite rare.

Of course, there do exist countless images graphically depicting the crucifixion of Christ – in Russia and in many other parts of the world as well. These were (and still are) presented *as such* to the Christian faithful. Christ on the cross has been understood as a male victim persecuted for the message of love that he preached, or as a lamb sacrificed in ransom for the sins of all humankind, or as an exemplary martyr to be imitated. It is difficult not to experience horror at the sight of one's God being treated so badly, when what he was doing was "saving" all of us – myself once included. There is a sense of relief at having a fall guy take the pain and humiliation, and a powerful sympathy for him wells up spontaneously. In such a situation, with its traumatizing potential, little room is left for rational thinking.

It is one thing, however, to contemplate "The Crucifixion" of one's God *as such*. It is quite another to contemplate the very same image (or narration) under a different title – "The Wisdom of God." Suddenly, there *is* room for rational thinking. Questions are permitted. Why does a male God have to be feminised?[64] Where, exactly, is the "wisdom" in such suffering and shame? Why worship this seemingly *un*wise and foolish God?

Paul's flimsy rhetoric is the questioner's only recourse: "God's foolishness is wiser than human wisdom" (1 Corinthians 1:25). But that is to state that God is a woman and a fool, and that humans are too stupid to understand. No wonder, then, that Christ on the cross has not often been advertised as Wisdom. Better to look for the person of Wisdom in Christ when he is a man preaching some "wise" parable and not busy getting himself crucified; or to find the person of Wisdom in the woman who is Christ's mother, rather than Christ crucified; or to venerate this mother as the one at least temporarily capable of containing the "uncontainable" God, as the Akathist affirms – and remain a believer. This solution both suits the mariophile's overall affection for the mother over the son and relieves anxiety about the son's strangely masochistic inclinations.

Containing Wisdom

Christians have often resorted to the notion of Mary as some kind of "container" of her son. Greek patristic writers ransacked the Old Testament for such images, such as these from a homily by Andrew of Crete (d. 740): "bridal chamber," "house of God," "[second] tabernacle," "enclosed garden," "golden jar [of manna]," "Ark [of the covenant]," "[sealed] spring," and so on.[65] Such "containers" would also become marian commonplaces in the religious discourse of the Catholic West. Today, the website for the International Marian Research Institute at the University of Dayton lists 183 titles for Mary under the heading "Vessel or Tabernacle," such as: "Blest chalice," "House built by Wisdom," "Living tabernacle of Eternal Wisdom," "Pure paten," "Temple of God," "The new Jerusalem," and "The temple of Incarnate Wisdom."[66]

In the medieval West, there were special physical repositories, such as the tabernacle, the aumbry, the pyx, and the tower (*turris*), which acquired marian significance in part by virtue of what they contained: the consecrated eucharistic host.[67] It is important to note that, by the thirteenth century, the priest's ritual utterance consecrating the host was increasingly understood to transform it into the sacrificial body of Christ – that is, Wisdom in the Pauline sense (see below, pp. 107–108, on transubstantiation). Late in the thirteenth century, William Durand related the generally acknowledged marian significance of these containers:

> the case [*capsa*] in which the consecrated hosts are preserved signifies the body of the glorious Virgin [*corpus Virginis gloriose*], about whom is spoken in the Psalm, *Ascend, O Lord, to your rest, You and the ark of your sanctification* [Ps 131:8]. The case is sometimes made of wood; sometimes of white ivory; sometimes of silver; sometimes of gold; sometimes of crystal; and according to these diverse varieties and properties the different graces of the Body of Christ [*corporis Christi*] itself are expressed.[68]

Another container for the consecrated host was the monstrance, including a so-called "Platytera monstrance" from about 1651, which was literally crafted in the shape of Mary's openable body, and featured a transparent circular chamber for displaying the host.[69]

There also exist images that display Christ (literally, not eucharistically) within Mary's upper body. Best known in the East are the Byzantine *Platytera* ("Wider than [the heavens]") and the Russian *Znamenie* ("Sign"). Christ is always a child in these images.[70]

Figure 2.2 Opening Virgin (*Vierge ouvrante*) from Morlaix, Brittany, ca.1400, closed (Radler 1990, fig. 54).

Starting approximately in the late twelfth century in the West, a daring new version of Mary the "container" emerges. It takes the form of a devotional sculpture that scholars have termed "opening Virgin" (French *Vierge ouvrante*, German *Schreinmadonna* – see Figures 2.2 and 2.3). Here, a pair of doors on the front of Mary's body opened up to reveal (in the majority of the surviving figures)[71] a sculptural representation of the Trinity known as the Mercy-Seat Trinity or Throne of Grace (*Gnadenstuhl*). The latter is by itself a rather striking – some would say grotesque – configuration of the three persons in one God: an enthroned God the Father holds his Son the crucified Christ from behind, while God the Holy Spirit in the form of a dove hovers somewhere in the vicinity.[72] All of this trinitarian apparatus is somehow made to fit into the body of a mere creature named Mary.

The Akathistos paradox – "container of the uncontainable God" – comes to mind, except that the God in this case is represented specifically as the

Figure 2.3 Same Opening Virgin, open (Radler 1990, fig. 58).

Trinity. Some found such an image disturbing. In a Christmas sermon of 1396, Jean Gerson spoke about his experience of seeing a Mercy-Seat Trinity inside one of these statues, as if the "whole Trinity [*toute la Trinité*]" could take on "human flesh [*cher humainne*]" within Mary's body. Gerson could find neither beauty nor devotional appeal in such an object, and believed that it could also lead to "error" and "irreverence [*indevocion*]."[73]

For Gerson (and for Pope Benedict XIV, some three and one-half centuries later),[74] the opening Virgin was a theologically incorrect image. The Mercy-Seat Trinity by itself was acceptable, as was the idea of God the Son's incarnation within the human body of Mary. But, of course, the Father and the Holy Ghost were not separately incarnated there – or anywhere else for that matter. As Jan Hallebeek has observed, the opening Virgin "could easily create the false impression that the entire Trinity was incarnate."[75]

On the other hand, the Trinity *was* also a unity. As François Boespflug notes in his analysis of the theology of opening Virgins, the Trinity was in part the unity of Father and Son, as in John's gospel: "Those who love me will keep my word, and my Father will love them, and we will come to them and make our home with them" (14:23; nor should we forget the more direct assertion of 10:30, "The Father and I are one"). Boespflug also cites a passage from the Profession of Faith of the Eleventh Synod of Toledo (in the year 675): "we believe that the Father and the Son and the Holy Spirit are one substance; we do not, however, say that the Virgin Mary gave birth to the unity of this Trinity, but only to the Son."[76]

That Mary's body should temporarily house the Trinity was actually taken for granted in some quarters. Best known is a passage from the famous sequence *Salve, mater salvatoris* by Adam of St. Victor (d. ca.1192):

Salve, mater pietatis
Et totius trinitatis
Nobile triclinium,
Verbi tamen incarnati
Speciale maiestati
Praeparans hospitium.
Hail, dear mother so devoted,
noble banqueting-hall
of the whole Trinity;
you prepared a special lodging
for the majesty so glorious
of the Word which was made flesh.[77]

This sequence was sung on the feast of the Nativity of the Virgin Mary (September 8). Mary was represented as a special lodging place for the Trinity in various other Latin hymns as well. The epithets *trinitatis triclinium, trinitatis arca, trinitatis templum*, and so on, appear in Meersseman's mariological glossary.[78] Also, in some vernaculars, Mary housed the Trinity, as in a fifteenth-century French prayer to Mary (*vous estes la chambre de toute la Trinité*),[79] or in an English carol on the annunciation of the same century:

The Holy Goost in the shall light,
And thurgh his working thou shalt be
Moder of God in persones thre.[80]

Numerous available texts such as these demonstrate that it was not always controversial to write, speak, or sing about the presence of the Trinity in Mary's body.[81]

The problem with the opening Virgin was perhaps, not so much the idea that it contained the Trinity, but that it contained the Trinity in a certain visual configuration, namely the Mercy-Seat Trinity. This visible image of the three persons of the one Trinity leaves the impression that all three had taken on flesh and had interacted with one another as persons are normally expected to interact with one another. But, the key interaction of the three persons of the Trinity from the viewpoint of human salvation was to arrange for God the Son to sacrifice himself on a cross, and, in order for that arrangement to be carried out, a fourth person's – Mary's – body was required. To suggest, however, that this salvific arrangement was already being brought to completion *within Mary's body*, before she could even bring her child to term, was bizarre. Why the hurry? In historical reality, Mary's son did not provoke the authorities to crucify him until about thirty years after he was born. So, the opening Virgin not only contained all three persons of the Trinity, it collapsed into one time and place the essential, predestined steps taken by the triune God to save fallen humankind. The opening Virgin might have been a correct theological schematization of the redemption, but it seemed to inflate Mary's role by literally making her the largest element in the schema. Did this image not make Mary too grand, even divine, even the fourth person of a divine quaternity?

Yet, even the excessive aggrandizement of Mary in the opening Virgin does not go far enough to explain the oddity of this religious artifact. What was *called* the Trinity was not the only significant entity *seen* in Mary's body. For, in addition to the Father, Son, and Holy Spirit, viewers beheld the holy cross upon which the Son was *already* suffering and dying. *That* was too much. It is as if Mary's son had been pre-crucified, or test-crucified, within her body. This was to represent Pauline Wisdom ("Christ crucified" – 1 Corinthians 1:23) in such a way as to make it appear to be an attribute of Mary, when Paul had only intended that it be an attribute of the adult Christ.

Worse, displaying the crucified Christ within Mary's body also seemed to make Mary guilty by association of the crime of killing her son on the cross. A pregnant Mary could only recently have pronounced her *Fiat* to the angel Gabriel. Was that *Fiat* then an authorization of her son's crucifixion? If we are to judge by actually opening the opening virgin, we will see Wisdom no longer contained but plainly visible, and we will not be able to avoid the inference that Mary pondered much more in her heart than is indicated by scripture. But that is getting ahead of an unbearably sad story.

*

In the medieval West, some mariophile theologians appropriated the female figure of Wisdom from the Old Testament in order to represent Mary as near-divine. In more recent times, Russian Orthodox Sophiologists did the same thing. This practice contradicted Paul's clear identification of Wisdom with the crucified Christ in the New Testament. Mary herself, as represented by some early Christian thinkers such as Origen, was "scandalized" by the Pauline Wisdom of her son's voluntary crucifixion. Other Christian thinkers, such as Maximos the Confessor, represented Mary as understanding and accepting the idea that her dying son on the cross was "Wisdom herself." Such understanding has been rather uncommon, however, in most manifestations of the mariophile mind, including in marian iconography, both East and West. More acceptable is verbal and visual imagery that represents Mary as "containing" Wisdom – much as Mary's body "contained the uncontainable God," to quote the Greek Akathistos.

Notes

1 Boss 2007a, 170. Cf. Catta 1961, 695–696, 802–803; Duffy 1988, 210; Newman 2003, 197–199.
2 The immaculate conception is the idea that Mary was free from original sin from the first moment of her conception. The idea was made dogma by Pius IX in the bull *Ineffabilis Deus* issued in 1854.
3 De Koninck 1943.
4 Doolan 1952, 22, 26.
5 Lefebvre 1956, 597; cf. *Liber Usualis*, 1317. I have not been able to find Proverbs 8:22 quoted for the feast of the Immaculate Conception in any (non-reprint) missals published since Vatican II, the ecumenical council that concluded in 1965. Two recent bilingual publications that follow the *Editio Typica* of the 1961 *Breviarium Romanum* continue to tie Wisdom passages to Mary, namely: *The Little Office of the Blessed Virgin Mary* (Keller, ed. [?], 2013, e.g., 61, 128 [Ecclesiasticus 24:14]); and the *Roman Breviary* (Newton and Durham, eds. 2013, e.g., vol. I, 956 [Proverbs 8:18–25], 971, 972, 978, 981, 983 [Ecclesiasticus 24:14], 1657, 1659 [Proverbs 8:22–24]).
6 Lefebvre 1956, 1117; *Liber Usualis*, 1858; Socias 2011, 2414. On medieval litanies to Mary, including the historical background of the Litany of Loreto, see: Meersseman 1958–1960, vol. II, 44–76, 214–256; Dürig 1992.
7 For textual variants of the expression *Sedes Sapientiae* contributing to its reconstruction, see: Meersseman 1958–1960, vol. II, 228 (item 28).
8 Among the many modern sources about Mary as the Seat of Wisdom (or, as often happens, Mary as Wisdom itself/herself) in Catholic tradition, see also: Bouyer 1965 (1957); Catta 1961; the entry, "Wisdom, Seat of" in O'Carroll 2000 (1982), 368–369.
9 Peltomaa 2001, 4; cf. Catta 1961, 732; Proclus of Constantinople in Constas 2003, 138–139, 230–231.
10 See especially the lengthy entry in the *Marienlexikon* (Lechner 1994a).
11 Lutz and Perdrizet 1907–1909, vol. 1, 21 (quoted also by: Forsyth 1972, 27; Lane 1984, 36, n. 6).
12 For some of these images, see above, n. 107, p. 30. On the iconography of Mary enthroned, see: Kirschbaum and Braunfels, eds. 1968–1976, vol. 3, under "Maria, Marienbild," cols. 157–158, 162–165, 182–184. See also Chapter 1 of Lane (1984, 13–39) for analysis of various images of Mary enthroned and of related texts.
13 See especially Forsyth 1972.
14 Carreres 1988, 53–66 (devotional material); Altés et al. 2003 (scholarly studies). See also: Forsyth 1972, 143, n. 10.
15 In Eastern Orthodox practice, if the Annunciation (a *marian* feast) falls on a Saturday, Sunday or during Easter Week, Proverbs 8:22–30 (a *wisdom* passage) is read (Ralph M. Cleminson, personal communication, February 14, 2011; cf. also Hapgood 1922, 201; Mother Mary and Kallistos Ware 1969, 441). Titular feasts of some of the *Sophia* cathedrals in Russia (e.g., in Novgorod, Vologda, Tobol'sk, Moscow) were celebrated on August 15, i.e., the feast of the Dormition/Assumption of *Mary*, and the titular feast of the Sophia cathedral in Kiev was celebrated on September 8, the feast of the nativity of *Mary* (Fiene 1989, 452, and the literature cited there). For the ordinary Russian Orthodox believer, it would come as no surprise that the standard devotional compendium of Russian icons of *Mary* contains two entries on *Sofiia – Premudrost' Bozhiia* (Snessoreva 1999 [1898], 270–271, 307–309). Donald Fiene's conclusion about the ambiguities

of Divine Sophia imagery in Russia is to the point: "Though church doctrine insisted always on interpreting *any* image of Wisdom as Christ or the Logos, the actual iconography (or the feast day associated with it) often seemed to the naïve viewer to signify a female figure, the Bogomater' [Mother of God] in particular" (1989, 475).

16 For a compact summary, see: Averintsev 2001, 163. For a broad overview with bibliography, see: Kozyrev 1995. Among the many scholarly studies in English are: Meyendorff 1987; Richard F. Gustafson's Introduction to Florensky 1997 (1914), ix–xxiii; Valliere 2000 (see index entries under "Sophia" and "Sophiology"); Kornblatt 2009; Hunt 2009.

17 Florensky 1997 (1914), 256–267.

18 Florensky 1997 (1914), 235 ff.

19 Bulgakov 1927, 133.

20 Bulgakov 1927, 124–137.

21 Bulgakov 1927, 138 (cf. 191). This is toned down slightly in a later work, *Agnets Bozhii* (*The Lamb of God*), where Bulgakov states that, although both Christ and Mary may be called Sophia, they are Sophia "in different senses." Thus, whereas Christ is "the hypostasis of the Heavenly Sophia and of the creaturely Sophia," Mary is the "creaturely hypostasis of the creaturely Sophia" (Bulgakov 2008 [1933], 203).

22 As a reward for the sophiology developed in his Parisian exile, Father Bulgakov was attacked as a heretic by Russian Orthodox Church officials (both in the Soviet Union and in the West). See: Valliere 2000, 287–289.

23 Barker 2010, 112, 123; cf. Barker 2011.

24 See: Dunn 1996 (1989), 164.

25 Newman 2003, 192. For detailed textual analyses, see: Brown 1966–1970, vol. I, cxxii–cxxv, and vol. II, 521–523; Dunn 1996 (1989), 239–245; Scott 1992, 94–115; Witherington 1994, 282–289.

26 Dunn 1996 (1989), 258.

27 Dunn 1996 (1989), xiv.

28 For detailed analyses of Christ as Wisdom in passages from Paul, see: Dunn 1996 (1989), 176–196; Witherington 1994, 295–333.

29 Witherington 1994, 211–236, 341–368.

30 Schüssler Fiorenza 1994, 133.

31 Schüssler Fiorenza 1994, 142–143.

32 Matthew 16:21, 17:22, 20:18–19; Mark 9:31, 10:33–34; Luke 9:44, 18:31–33.

33 Mark 11:15–19; Matthew 21:12–16; Luke 19:45–48; John 2:14–17.

34 Rancour-Laferriere 2011, 21–85.

35 See the discussion of this remarkable coincidence of timing, unique to John's gospel, in: Vermes 2000, 36–37.

36 Lefebvre 1956, 560.

37 See: Denzinger 2012, 418 (No. 1743).

38 Dunn 1996 (1989), 176 ff.

39 Fitzmyer 2008, 160 (emphasis added).

40 Paul was probably interpreting the "tree" on which an already executed religious criminal was hung (the original meaning behind Deuteronomy 21:23) as a "cross" because this interpretation was current among Hellenistic Jews of his time. See: Thornton 1972. For a much more detailed account of the background to Paul's interpretation of Deuteronomy 21:22–23, see: Chapman 2010 (2008), 241–251.

41 Apart from the letters of Paul, there is abundant documentary evidence that, in antiquity, Jews regarded crucifixion with horror, humiliation, and shame

(among other attitudes), as they, as a people, had been subjected to individual and mass crucifixions by outside occupiers (or their Jewish quislings) in Judaea. See: Hengel 1977 (1976), 84–90. In a very detailed historical study that can hardly be summarized here, Chapman 2010 (2008) finds that, "there were many reasons for a Jewish person to have disputed the church's claim that Jesus was the crucified messiah" (260). Among these reasons were: an association of the crucifixion of Jesus with the annual celebration of the crucifixion of Haman, enemy of the Jews (festival of Purim); the Jewish practice of hanging some blasphemers and magicians; the widespread practice of crucifying brigands; and other matters related to crucifixion. Of course, Jews may well have wished to continue practicing their own religion instead of Christianity for positive reasons as well, which had nothing to do with crucifixion.

42 In this scene, Luke (2:22–38) conflates the originally distinct Jewish customs of presentation (consecration) of a child to the Lord with purification of the mother after birth (Brown 1993 [1977], 447–451). On related Christian feasts and liturgical observances, see the entries "Candlemas," "Circumcision, Feast of the," "Presentation of Christ in the Temple," "Purification of the BVM" in: Cross and Livingstone, eds. 1997, 275, 354, 1323, 1350. In the Orthodox East, the relevant feast is termed Meeting (Greek *hupapantē*, Russian *sretenie*). See: Azarov 2002, 638. For a valuable historical study of Candlemas and related feasts (including Roman pagan antecedents), see: MacGregor 2008.

43 For a valuable overview of theological hypotheses about Simeon's sword, see: Brown 1993 (1977), 460–466, 687–688. See also: the entry "Sword of Simeon" in O'Carroll 2000 (1982), 387; Fulton 2002, 534, n. 9. The predominant interpretation of the sword of Simeon in the medieval West would become Mary's compassion for her dying son (*gladius compassionis*, a term first utilized by Peter Damian – see: Laurentin 1991 [1968], 110, n. 16).

44 Here, I modify O'Carroll's (2000 [1982], 275) translation of the crucial passage (Latin version – only fragments of the Greek original survive) from Origen's seventeenth homily on Luke (Origène 1998 [1962], 256–259). See also: Miegge 1955, 108; Brown 1993 (1977), 460; O'Carroll 2000 (1982), 274–275 (with extensive bibliography); Buby 1981–1982, 88–97.

45 As Brian K. Reynolds suggests, Origen's "intent here is not to assail the holiness of the Virgin but to ensure that the principle of Christ's universal redemption is upheld" (Reynolds 2012–, 249).

46 Other church fathers who thought that the sword of Simeon might refer to Mary's doubts at the foot of the cross include Basil the Great (Buby 1981–1982, 88–97; Gambero 1999 [1991], 148–149; Keeler 2003, 260–261), Amphilochius of Iconium (Gambero 1999 [1991], 168–169), Cyril of Alexandria (Gambero 1999 [1991], 246), Romanos the Melodist (Gambero 1999 [1991], 332), and Maximus the Confessor (2012, 81). With time, starting with Odo of Ourscamp (d. 1171), and followed by several other authorities, Mary would be represented as the *only* one who *kept* her faith in the divinity of her son during the three days of his death, the *triduum mortis* (Laurentin 1952–1953, vol I, 138–139; Laurentin 1991 [1968], 111–112, n. 18).

47 Maas and Trypanis 1963, 148; translation by Alexiou 2002 (1974), 154–155.

48 Maximus the Confessor 2012, 109.

49 Maximus the Confessor 2012, 113. Compare Bernard of Clairvaux, who praises Mary by declaring her to be "the mother of Wisdom himself" (Bernard of Clairvaux and Amadeus of Lausanne 1979, 45).

50 Maximus the Confessor 2012, 111.

51 Newman 2003, 190–244.

52 Monks 1990, 151, "Sapientia and the Disciple Behold Christ Carrying the Cross." The illustration is also reproduced by Newman 2003, 219, fig. 5.8.

53 Newman 2003, 212.

54 As translated by Newman 2003, 213.

55 A caveat: Paul's words are slightly mangled, for Paul does not characterize "Christ crucified" as (what might be translated as) "the power and wisdom of God *the father*" in either the Greek original or the Vulgate Latin, but as (what is correctly translated from the original as) "the power of God and the wisdom of God" (NRSV, 1 Corinthians 1, 24). By gratuitously bringing "God the father" into the picture, the French commentator is deflecting attention away from Christ's own grandiose masochism and toward sadistic aggression by "God the father." The commentator's *sapience de Dieu le pere* (Newman 2003, 380, n. 75) is possibly influenced here by the much-loved anonymous fourteenth-century Latin hymn beginning with the words "Patris sapientia, veritas divina" (Dreves and Blume 1909, vol. 2, 69), and customarily used in Hours of the Cross.

56 On this image type, see: Florensky 1997 (1914), 272–274; Fiene 1989, 468–469 (and fig. 7); Lifshits and Lukashov 2000, cat. no. 47 (with commentary by I. Sosnovtseva).

57 A variant of the "Wisdom of the Cross" type may be seen on a fresco of the Yaroslavl Church of St. John Chrysostom. Florensky refers to an inscription on the cross there that reads "Holy Communion and the Fourth Council" (1997 [1914], 272). This must be a reference to the Fourth Lateran Council of 1215, which affirmed the "transubstantiation" of the eucharistic bread and wine into the body and blood of Christ (see below, pp. 107–108).

58 See especially De Montfort 1966, 214–216, as translated in De Montfort 1988, 112–114. Here, it is worth mentioning the opening lines of a prayer in Old French that deals with the Passion: *Jesus, divine sapience / Et second en la trinité* . . . (Sonet 1956, 174, no. 965; cf. nos 976, 1510).

59 De Montfort 1966, 181–182, as translated in De Montfort 1988, 95.

60 The English sentences beginning with the phrases "He decides . . ." and "He will make . . ." further distort the French, for such phrases are absent in the French original.

61 Fastiggi (2007, 295) notes "the theme of humility or self-debasement" in another aspect of the works of Montfort. As for Montfort's personal life, the signs of moral masochism are everywhere. For example: in seminary, Montfort deliberately deprived himself of sleep, heat, and food and practiced various forms of corporal penance, and as a result he had to be hospitalized on one occasion (Pérouas 1982 [1973], 34); as a young priest, Montfort was only at home missionizing among the poor, sharing their "meager fare," sleeping "on straw," and taking care of "the most repulsive cases" (46); on numerous occasions, Montfort antagonized church superiors and others with his excessive religious zeal, provoking punishments, condemnations, and humiliations, but often his response was one of sincere masochistic gratitude, as when he wrote in a letter, "Let them calumniate me, let them mock me, let them tear my reputation to threads, let them throw me into prison. How precious are these gifts!" (57). As Pérouas shows, there was some attenuation of the masochism in the final years, when Montfort became preoccupied with developing followers who would succeed him (78–92).

62 Fiene 1989, 475–476.

63 Fiene 1989, 457 ff. ("Novgorod Angel-of-the-Lord type").

64 This is not the same as the question, Why does one's God have to be male?

65 Andrew of Crete 2008, 127–132.
66 On the web at http://campus.udayton.edu/mary/resources/titles/HailMary.html (accessed June 6, 2015).
67 See: Hirn 1957 (1909), 162–164, 321; Vloberg 1946, 285–286 (on what he terms *Vierge-tabernacle*); Lane 1984, 13, 30 (fig. 20, sacrament house in the shape of a tower), 32, 33 (figs. 22, 23 – aumbries); Bynum 1987, 81, 335 (nn. 56–59), 268, 409 (nn. 37–40); Van Ausdall 2012, 605–615.
68 Durand 2007, 39; Durand 1995, 42 (I, 3, 25).
69 Weis 1985, 133, fig. 116. On monstrances, see: Vloberg 1946, 286–287, 290; Vetter 1958–1959, 52, figs. 20, 21; Lechner 1981, 149–154, figs. 247–256; Lechner 1993b.
70 The two image types mentioned have been given different names by different authorities, a problem that need not be explored here. Also, the view of the Christ child within Mary's body may be interpreted instead as a clipeus attached to (or a medallion hovering in front of) Mary's body. For some of these images that feature "The Mother of God with the Immanuel [Emmanuel]," see: Onasch and Schnieper 1997 (1995), 158–159.
71 In a minority (14 of the 43) Opening Virgins catalogued by Radler (1990), Mary's body opens up to reveal scenes from Mary's and/or her son's life, in most cases including the crucifixion.
72 Some of the relevant bibliography: Baumer 1977 (a pioneering work published within a mariological context); Radler 1990 (an art historical dissertation, with a valuable catalogue and photographs of 43 surviving figures); Boespflug 1984, 280–285 (on the 1745 condemnation of opening Virgins by Pope Benedict XIV in his bull *Sollicitudini Nostrae*); Lechner 1994b; Newman 2003, 269–72, 283–284 (interdisciplinary considerations of "the sheer, goddess-like grandeur and autonomy of the *Vierge ouvrante*"); Ruether 2005, 155 (and fig. 31); Rimmele 2006; Hallebeek 2007, 363–364; Bynum 2011, 83–89 (and fig. 26).
73 Gerson 1960–1973, vol. 7, 963.
74 Paragraph 27 of the 1745 bull *Sollicitudini Nostrae* (for the Latin text of this document with French translation, see: Boespflug 1984, 21–59).
75 Hallebeek 2007, 363. In another sermon of the same year (May 28, 1396), Gerson had contemplated the idea of Mary as a temple (*temple sacré*) for the Trinity, but there he had placed special emphasis on the incarnation of the Son of God in this temple (Gerson 1960–1973, vol. 7, 672; cf. Hallebeek 2007, 364).
76 Denzinger 2012, 186 (no. 535). Cf. Boespflug 1984, 283.
77 Dreves and Blume 1909, vol. I, 269, as translated in Walsh, ed., 2012, 323 (with modifications in accordance with Newman 2003, 271).
78 Meersseman 1958–1960, vol. II, 377–378.
79 Quoted from the prayer of a Frenchwoman by Baumer 1977, 251 (cf. Newman 2003, 272, 395, n. 77).
80 Greene, ed. 1977 (1935), 158 (no. 248 – by the Franciscan James Ryman, ca.1492).
81 See also: Wittkemper 1967, 1448–1449 (numerous examples of Mary as *Tempel, Wohnung, Ruhelager* for the Trinity; also cited by Boespflug 1984, 283, n. 68).

3 Mary Dies and Goes to Heaven

Pope Pius XII Makes an Infallible Pronouncement

The most important measure mariophiles took in transforming Mary from an ordinary human being into a powerful deity was to deny the fact of her death. This was accomplished by having Mary follow in the footsteps of her divine son, who – believers asserted – had already risen from the dead and had ascended into heaven to live eternally with the Father.

Consider, for example, what Pope Pius XII proclaimed in his Apostolic Constitution of 1950 titled *Munificentissimus Deus*, on the dogma of the assumption (*Assumptio*) of Mary into heaven. This document is noteworthy, not only because it aggrandizes Mary enormously, for Mary had long been aggrandized in many ways – including informal recognition of her assumption into heaven since late antiquity. What is new is the unique status of this document in the history of the Roman Catholic Church: it is the "one papal document [that] has explicitly fulfilled the *ex cathedra* conditions of infallibility" since the doctrine of infallibility itself was proclaimed in 1870.[1]

According to *Munificentissimus Deus*, Jesus was essentially fatherless in the flesh, the only source of his physical body being his mother Mary's physical body. But, his body rose from the dead and entered the state of eternal glory appropriate to God, and Pius XII, along with his numerous supporters, wanted the Catholic faithful to understand why *her body too* – not just her soul – also deserved to be taken up into such a state: "it seems impossible to think of her, the one who conceived Christ, brought Him forth, nursed Him with her milk, held Him in her arms, and clasped Him to her breast [*peperit, suo lacte aluit, eumque inter ulnas habuit pectorique obstrinxit suo*], as being apart from Him in body, even though not in soul, after his earthly life."[2]

These sentiments of the twentieth-century pope are essentially the same as those that had been expressed by various theologians in centuries past. For example, Patriarch Germanos of Constantinople (d. ca.742) attributed the following words of invitation to Mary's son:

> Come eagerly to the one whom you brought into the world. I want to make you happy, as a son should do – to pay you the pension due a mother's womb, to recompense you for feeding me milk [*apodounai soi ta tēs mētrikēs koilias enoikia, tēs galaktotrofias ton misthon*], to reward you for your nurture, to give your maternal love its full return.[3]

Both Pius XII and Germanos view gestation, childbirth, and breastfeeding, not only as essential manifestations of maternal love, but also as processes whereby Mary provided Jesus with the entirety of his physical body. Conversely, both view the assumption of Mary's body into heaven as Christ's way of providing Mary with a physical body, one that – like his – was incorruptible and would live in glory forever. Mary's acquisition of a now "glorified" body was an appropriate act of reciprocation on her son's part – although it was an act that was "fitting" for other reasons as well. In the papal bull, Pius XII considers such factors as: Mary's immaculate conception, rendering her free of original sin; her virginity before, during, and after giving birth to her only child, Jesus; her status as the mother of a child who was obliged to "honor" her in accordance with God's law – that is, the fourth commandment; and various other matters.[4] In short, to quote a theologian-contemporary of the pope, Mary deserved to receive "all that she is and has" as a result of her following through on her consent to be the human mother of God, for that consent was the height of motherly love: "Mary would give to Christ all that a mother gives her child: something of her own substance, the benefit of her motherly care, the gentleness of her affections: *cum lacte praebens oscula*."[5]

Catholic theologians still do not agree on whether Mary actually died or not before she was assumed bodily into heaven by her divine son (Pius XII is careful not to commit himself – one way or the other – on this issue). If Mary did not die, she would be unlike her son in one important respect, for Jesus died on a cross. Even if Mary did not die, however, it could be argued that she would have "paid her debt to death" and would have been "configured to Jesus crucified by her dolorous compassion at the foot of the cross," to quote Martin Jugie, who served on the committee of theological experts assisting the pope in formulating *Munificentissimus Deus*.[6]

Of course, the historical Mary, like her historical son, died and remained dead. From a psychoanalytic perspective, any affirmation of their postmortem lives constitutes denial of their deaths. Mary and Jesus were mortals, like the rest of us. That is the truth of Ash Wednesday: "Remember, man, you are dust, and to dust you shall return."[7] But, denial of death is an essential feature of Christianity, especially in its Roman Catholic and Eastern Orthodox variants, and especially when it comes to the two deities.[8]

In scripture, it is affirmed that Jesus died, but this acknowledgment of reality is also retracted with affirmations of his resurrection and ascension into heaven. Thus, denial of the death of the chief deity remains in place, that is, in scripture and in the minds of those who believe scripture.[9]

The case of Mary is more complicated. Many centuries would pass before the highest ecclesiastical personage of the Roman Church, speaking *ex cathedra*, dared to make an "infallible" denial of Mary's death. For Pius XII to avoid saying whether Mary died or not is irrelevant, as a denial of her death is built into the logic of declaring that she was assumed up into heaven, body and soul (*corpore et anima*). What else could have been left to be rescued from the jaws of death?

When he was about to be crucified, Jesus declared to his disciples, "I am leaving the world and am going to the Father" (John 16:28). What happened after that delusional declaration is the death of Jesus on the cross – in the presence of his mother Mary (John 19:25–30). What happened to Mary, on the other hand, is that she went nowhere in particular (she makes only a cameo appearance in Acts 1:14). When, where, and under what circumstances Mary died is unknown. The silence of scripture is deafening. Before Pius XII spoke, mariophile theologians down the centuries have acted as if Mary had said something like, "I am leaving the world and am going to the Son, who is with his Father," when, in fact, Mary said nothing of the kind.

Not to be deterred, advocates for the assumption of Mary kept coming up with arguments based on entitlement. Mary deserved to follow her son to heaven because it was *she* who bestowed upon a deity emptied of his divinity (*kenōsis*) the entirety of his body, a body that enabled him to pass as a human being among other human beings. Ironically, the very flesh that this son received from his mother was, like all flesh, obliged also to die. So, die Jesus did, on a cross retroactively repurposed for the forgiveness of the sins of all humankind.

But then, Jesus also rose from the dead, teaching by example that there would be no death (1 Corinthians 15:54). And, who should be called *first* to follow that marvelous resurrection of the son's body, if not the mother who was its sole source?

And so, Mary rose in glory and found her seat – as Pius XII infallibly declares – "at the right hand of her Son, the immortal King of the Ages."[10]

In the Roman Catholic West Mary Was Assumed into Heaven

What Pius XII proclaimed in 1950 required considerable effort and initiative on his part, but his conclusions were not substantially different from what both the Roman Catholic and the Eastern Orthodox faithful had already believed for many centuries. The Protestant reaction to the papal bull, on the other hand, was negative. As Jaroslav Pelikan writes, to elevate some pious marian traditions to "the status of an official doctrine, binding on the entire church *de fide* and laying claim to the same authority as the doctrine of the Trinity, seemed to be completely presumptuous and utterly without biblical warrant."[11]

Diverse traditions about what happened to Mary after she died had emerged by the fifth century (with some evidence available already from the fourth century). As Stephen J. Shoemaker summarizes in his magisterial analysis of the ancient narratives in many languages about this phenomenon:

> Although all the narratives conclude with Mary's transfer to the garden of Paradise, some versions describe Mary's bodily resurrection in Paradise, while other narratives report only the transfer of Mary's lifeless body to Paradise, where it remains separate from her soul.[12]

By the eighth century, a celebratory theology of Mary's dormition (her "falling asleep," Greek *Koimēsis*) was being formulated in the East, most notably by the church fathers Germanos of Constantinople and John of Damascus.[13] Both are quoted in support of promulgation of the dogma of the assumption in *Munificentissimus Deus*.[14]

For many centuries, in the Latin West, there was considerable reluctance or hesitation about accepting the idea of Mary's bodily assumption.[15] But, starting late in the eleventh century, a strong interest in this topic emerged. Various theologians (Pseudo-Augustine,[16] Philip of Harvengt [d. 1183], Arnold of Bonneval [d. after 1156], Amadeus of Lausanne [d. 1159], Alain of Lille [d 1202], Peter Abelard [d. 1142], William of Newburgh [d. ca.1199], and Guibert of Nogent [d. 1124], among others) argued that Mary's flesh had not rotted in the grave, but had been resurrected incorrupt.[17] In the bull of 1950, Pius XII quotes one of these theologians, Amadeus of Lausanne, who speaks of Mary as the perfectly self-sacrificing mother who deserved her assumption into heaven:

> She alone merited to conceive the true God of true God, whom as a virgin, she brought forth, to whom as a virgin she gave milk, fondling Him in her lap, and in all things she waited upon Him with loving care.

Here, Mary is giving her all to Jesus – conceiving him (*concipere*), gestating him (implicitly), giving birth to him (*peperit*), breastfeeding him (*lactavit*), fondling him (*fovens*), and waiting upon him with loving care (*in omnibus almo ministravit obsequio*).[18] Having done these things for a God whose body would not rot in the grave, the mother of this God should also not have to be food for worms. Indeed, says Amadeus, "it is wrong to believe that her body has seen corruption [*neque enim credi fas est corpus eius vidisse corruptionem*]"[19] – precisely the words of Pius XII in *Munificentissimus Deus* (but, strangely, without quotation marks).[20]

In essence, for Mary to give her all to Jesus was to enable his incarnation, that is, his complete enfleshment. What Jesus received from his mother was, at the very least, her flesh. It was believed that there was no human father (Mary's virginity), and in any case it was also believed that the initiative for the incarnation was taken by God the Father, who, however, was not a fleshly being. What Jesus was *in the flesh*, therefore, was originally Mary's flesh. This had already been affirmed many times over in both Greek and Latin patristic writings.[21] As the influential Pseudo-Augustine later put it, "The flesh of Jesus is the flesh of Mary [*Caro enim Jesu caro est Mariae*]."[22] Earlier, the real Augustine had written: *de carne Mariae carnem accepit.*[23]

Any discussion of whether or not Mary was going to be "assumed" up into heaven *in the flesh* turned on her role in the very "en-flesh-ment" of Jesus. As Rachel Fulton observes, what was at stake was:

> the very reality of the Incarnation, particularly the reality of the flesh that Christ had assumed (*assumpsit*) from his Mother – Mary having been both the sole source of the matter from which that flesh was formed (as per [then] standard scientific theories of physiological generation) and, as his only human parent, the sole source of his humanity.[24]

A certain lexical coincidence facilitated this discussion. The belief that Jesus "assumed" his flesh from Mary is closely linked to the belief that Mary was "assumed" bodily into heaven. Two rather different images come to mind in connection with the use of the same Latin verb, *assumere*, here. What goes on in the womb and at the breast of Mary is far humbler in scale than what goes on in the wide heavens. But, the difference is partially overcome by the lexical sameness, which is to say that the doctrine of Mary's assumption was to some extent facilitated by the Latin lexicon (to my knowledge, this particular linguistic facilitation is uniquely Latin[ate], and does not occur in, say, Greek or Church Slavonic). Alain of Lille quotes Pseudo-Augustine as saying, "We believe that not only the flesh which Christ assumed [*carnem quam Christus assumpsit*], but also the flesh from which he assumed flesh [*carnem de qua assumpsit*], to have been assumed into heaven [*esse assumptam in coelum*]."[25] The play of polyptoton here subtly boosts the credibility of Mary having been assumed up into heaven.

In any case, given the "concarnality"[26] of Christ and his mother, and given the belief that Christ had already ascended (been "assumed") into heaven, then it was fitting to believe that Mary too had ascended (been "assumed") into heaven.

Assumptionist thinking focuses on the physical Mary (Mary's sinless soul having already been saved). Ultimately, this is because the incarnation of God in the person of Mary's human son was also a decidedly physical process. The incarnation initiates the process whereby it is later possible to deduce (primarily from the virginal conception) that Mary's flesh was "concarnal" with her son's flesh. Or, Mary's body was "one body" or "concorporeal" with the body of her son – to translate a Greek term from an earlier encomium on Mary's dormition attributed to Modestus of Jerusalem (d. 634):[27]

> Hail, holy Mother of God! The King of glory, the Lord Jesus chose you to be his spiritual kingdom on earth, and through you he has bestowed on us his heavenly kingdom; there he has ordained that you became one body [*sussōmon*] with him in incorruption.[28]

> Because she [Mary] is the glorious mother of Christ, our God and Savior, who bestows life and immortality, she was raised to life by him, con-corporeal [*sussōmos*] in incorruption for all ages with him. He raised her from the grave and took her to himself, in a way known only to him.[29]

The term used here in reference to the concorporeality of Mary and Jesus apparently does not come up again in other Greek texts on the assumption. But, the notion of concorporeality is an explicit (or at least implicit) argument in many theological tracts defending Mary's bodily assumption into heaven. Hilda Graef detects the argument from concorporeality in writers as various as, for example: Theoteknos of Livias (d. late sixth century?), Cosmas Vestitor (d. mid-eighth century), Pseudo-Augustine, Guibert of Nogent, Abelard, Philip of Harvengt, and Albertus Magnus (d. 1280).[30]

Practically speaking, arguments from concorporeality are difficult to disentangle from arguments from concarnality, the difference being a matter of emphasis. For example, in one sermon, Cosmas Vestitor, as translated by Graef, writes that "the same *flesh* she gave to Christ, this Christ has made alive," whereas, in another sermon, he has Christ say, "my own living *body* taken from her has been restored to me."[31] In his chapter on Mary's assumption, Reynolds utilizes the terms "con-carnality" and "con-corporeality" in roughly equivalent fashion.[32]

Much of what has been written on Mary's assumption utilizes the bridal imagery of the Song of Songs in representing the physical basis of the relationship between Mary and her son. The problematical nature of this first category of images has been discussed above (pp. 12–18). A second category utilizes instead imagery relating to the physical basis of the incarnation, such as the virginal conception, the womb that carried the precious cargo, the birth of the child, the breastfeeding of the child, and so on. There is some overlap of these two categories. Both utilize images of physical oneness (concarnality or concorporeality) uniting Mary and her son. Both, of course, utilize imagery in the service of denying the death of Mary in order to affirm her bodily assumption into heaven. Both categories also deny sexual activity of any kind: in the first category, the bride is not literally a bride, but a metaphor; in the second, the conception is literally virginal.

Peter Comestor (d. 1178) expresses an interesting preference for the second category in his writing about Mary's bodily assumption: "Man and woman are two in the one flesh, but even more clearly are mother and child of the one flesh [*vir et uxor duo sunt in carne una; expressius autem mater et filius una sunt caro*]."[33] From the viewpoint of physical anthropology, Comestor is quite right, as one's mother is a consanguine relative, whereas a spouse in marriage is ordinarily only an affine relative. Indeed, to some extent, the bond of spousal attachment is even *derivative* of early mother–child interaction, as interdisciplinary thinkers from a variety of fields have observed.[34]

This too suggests that the "one flesh" argument for Mary's bodily assumption is stronger when based on the mother–child relationship than on a bride–groom relationship.

In the Orthodox East Mary's Dormition Culminated in Her Deification

In the East, there is a beautifully standardized image for representing Mary's falling asleep in death (Greek *koimēsis*, Russian *uspenie*). The recently deceased Mary is shown lying upon a funeral bier surrounded by the (sometimes downcast) apostles, and with an angel (or angels) overhead reaching down to take Mary upward. The already resurrected Christ, majestic in his erect frontal pose with cruciferous nimbus, stands behind the bier and above his mother's body. He has just lifted up his mother's soul in the form of a (usually) swaddled child toward heaven, where it will be received in advance of her resurrected adult body (see Figure 3.1).[35]

Figure 3.1 Dormition of the Virgin, mosaic, Church of Matorana, Palermo (Maguire 1981, fig. 65).

Henry Maguire has demonstrated that this visual standard, which originated in tenth-century Byzantium, reflects a special association of the dormition of Mary with the nativity/infancy of Jesus, an association that had already been made by such writers as John of Damascus, Germanos of Constantinople, John Kyriotes, and others (Germanos has already been quoted above). An "epigram" (Maguire) from the tenth-century poet John Kyriotes in which Christ addresses his recently deceased mother is anatomically explicit: "formerly, Virgin, you embraced me in your arms; I sucked the mother's milk from your [nipple] [*Thēlēs de sēs espasa mētrikon gala*]. Now I myself, having embraced your spirit, send your body to the place of delight."[36] Further reinforcing the linkage of Mary's dormition (in standardized Eastern images) with the nativity/infancy are (1) inevitable structural similarities between images of Christ holding the personified "soul" of his recently deceased mother in his arms and images of Mary holding her newborn child in her arms, and (2) the specifically architectural aspect of juxtapositions of the dormition with the nativity.

The second of these categories is subtle and entails artistic execution on a grander scale. For example, mid-twelfth-century frescoes of the dormition and the nativity, with Mary's soul and the Christ child similarly swaddled, are placed in corresponding positions on either side of the apse on the east wall of a church in the Mirož Monastery of Pskov in Rus'.[37] With an abundance of such iconographic evidence, Maguire convinces us that "the icon of Mary's reception into heaven became a reflecting mirror of her son's reception onto earth."[38]

Such mirror reflection is not without theological and, ultimately, psychological significance. Just as the mother had once held and nursed the Christ child in her arms, now Christ reciprocates by holding his mother as a babe in arms. This role reversal suggests a certain equivalence between Mary's previous mothering of her son, God incarnate, and God the resurrected son's present 'mothering' of the soul of his still carnal mother. The role reversal also suggests equivalent results: if Mary mothered a child who would later die and then rise from the dead and ascend into heaven as God, so God would condescend to 'mother' a dead woman, who would then also arise and ascend into heaven as a now-divine being.

But how is this possible? The end result would appear to be two different, coexisting deities in the heavens above. Yet, there is an asymmetry here as well. The son is God himself, and had been such from the beginning of time. The mother, on the other hand, came into existence later and – only after her (albeit predestined) task had been completed – was deified. In other words, there are two deities, but only the son is *the* deity, the pre-existing filial component of the pre-existing triune God.

A major strand of Eastern Orthodox theology teaches that, after the general resurrection from the dead of all humans who have ever lived, the just will be picked out and will be reunited with their immortal souls to produce deities. What Christ had accomplished was to open up an opportunity for mere mortals to "become participants of the divine nature" (2 Peter 1:4). This opportunity, which would come to fruition in some eschatological future, is termed "deification" (translation of the Greek *theōsis*; cf. Russian *obozhenie*). Proponents of the notion like to quote a saying from the fourth-century church father Athanasius, Bishop of Alexandria: "He [God] was made man that we might be made God [*Autos gar enēnthrōpēsen, hina hēmeis theopoiēthōmen*]."[39] Various other church fathers, including Irenaeus of Lyons, Gregory of Nazianzus, Gregory of Nyssa, and Maximus the Confessor, also expressed essentially the same idea.[40]

Related notions about Christian believers taking on divine attributes have been given serious attention (not only by Eastern Orthodox theologians) in more recent times as well.[41] There are considerable complexities of historical development, as well as a variety of terminological muddles in this area, but it is clear that theological claims about any human being(s) literally *becoming* the deity – *the* deity – are avoided. Theological correctness – whatever that might be for the individual theologian – is always an issue, and is generally maintained when the matter of deification is considered in any depth.

In the case of Mary, who did not have to wait until the final judgment to rise from the dead and be judged, *deification has already been accomplished.* This is not altogether explicit in the Roman Catholic notion of Mary's assumption into heaven, but Mary's deified status is quite explicit in Eastern Orthodoxy. Here, for example, are passages from a Greek service on the Feast of the Dormition (August 15): "Thy death, O pure Virgin, was a crossing into a better and eternal life. It translated thee, O undefiled, from this mortal life to that which knows no end and is indeed divine [*pros theian ontōs*]" (Mattins, Canticle Four, Irmos of First Canon); "The whole world was amazed at thy divine glory [*epi tē theia doxē*]" (Canticle Five, Irmos of Second Canon).[42]

Russian Orthodox theologians have been particularly keen on asserting Mary's deified status. As Mary was the chief human instrument in making God into a human being, it is appropriate that she be the first human being to have become a deity in the sense of undergoing the process of deification. Vladimir Lossky writes that the "final vocation" of all of us "is already realized in one human person – Mary the Mother of God: She who gave life to the Son of God has received from her Son the fulness of the Divine Life."[43] Or: Mary is "the sole human person deified."[44] Other leading Russian Orthodox theologians hold the same view – for example, Sergii Bulgakov, who asserts that the resurrected Mary is already a "perfectly and completely deified creature" (*sovershenno i do kontsa obozhennaia tvar'*), and Leonid Uspenskii, who speaks simply of Mary's "deification" (*obozhenie*).[45]

But She Will Never Leave Us

Further exploration of the theological complexities of Mary's postmortem life is not necessary at this point. For most believers, it has been enough both to deny that Mary died and to imagine that she is still alive and available as a mother to them. It does not matter whether Mary's special postmortem maternity was achieved by assumption, or dormition, or theosis, or some other theological construct or combination of constructs. What matters at a psychological level is that Mary never dies, never departs, and, hence, never ceases mothering all of those who need her. To quote Russian Orthodox believers who repeatedly chant these words to Mary in an akathist hymn:

> Rejoice, O Joyful One, Who in Thy Dormition
> hast not forsaken us [*nas ne ostavliaiushchaia*]!"[46]

Always able to turn to a mother within who never left them in the external world, believers do not have to experience the terrible anxiety of separation from her (such as befalls a child who unexpectedly loses sight of the mother).[47] The voice of faith whispers: she will never leave us.

These minimal existential properties – Mary's bodily immortality and her uninterrupted availability to all of the faithful – have no basis in scripture. They have been essential, however, in paving the way for Mary's seemingly unlimited aggrandizement in theology and popular devotional practices, and in facilitating apparitions of Mary to deluded individuals and crowds.

*

In 1950, Pope Pius XII issued an "infallible" statement about the "assumption" of Mary into heaven, where she is seated "at the right hand of her Son." The pope's statement was a denial of death – Mary's death. In the Orthodox East, this denial is called the "deification" of Mary. In both the East and the West, a major theological justification for awarding such death-defying status to Mary is the idea that Mary and her son Jesus shared the very same flesh (there being no flesh from an earthly father, only from the virginal earthly mother, Mary). Mary deserved to relocate body and soul into heaven, just as her "con-carnate" son had risen from the dead and ascended body and soul into heaven. Not only theologians but also ordinary mariophile believers deny Mary's death. After having died, Mary is still alive for them, she has not forsaken them, and she is always available as a maternal figure in their times of need.

Notes

1 Perreau-Saussine 2012 (2011), 65; cf. Denzinger 2012, 616 (nos. 3073–3074), 808 (nos. 3900–3904).
2 *Papal Teachings: Our Lady* 1961, 317; *Acta Apostolicae Sedis* (vol. 42, p. 768).
3 Germanos of Constantinople 1998, 171; 1860a, col. 361.
4 Elsewhere, I have suggested that Pius XII also had a specific personal motive for proclaiming the dogma of the assumption. See: Rancour-Laferriere 2014.
5 Bonnefoy 1957, 163.

6 Jugie 1949, 623; cf. O'Carroll 2000 (1982), 210, 260. Jugie made a detailed examination of the question of whether Mary died or not in his treatise of 1944 (503–582).

7 *Memento, homo, quia pulvis es, et in pulverem reverteris*. See: *The Liber usualis* 1952, 525 (based on Genesis 3:19).

8 Denial of death will be most evident in representations of the confrontations that take place between Mary and her son at Golgotha, as we will see.

9 For a detailed psychoanalytic study of the alleged resurrection of Jesus, see: Rancour-Laferriere 2011, 121–138.

10 *Papal Teachings: Our Lady* 1961, 318.

11 Pelikan 1996, 205.

12 Shoemaker 2004, 282; cf. also Shoemaker 2008. Important earlier studies include: Mimouni 1995; Van Esbroeck 1995; Wenger 1955; Jugie 1944. On the dormition/assumption in the Eastern Orthodox liturgy, see: Ledit 1976, 221–238. For a useful overview of the development of narrative traditions and theologies concerning the dormition/assumption of Mary up until the late medieval period, as well as generous selections of primary texts in English translation, see: Reynolds 2012–, 293–329.

13 See: Daley 1998, 153–239; Burghardt 1957, 84–91.

14 *Papal Teachings: Our Lady* 1961, 309–310.

15 Reynolds 2012–, 308–316.

16 This particular Pseudo-Augustine was perhaps a disciple of St. Anselm, writing at the beginning of the twelfth century. See the entry "Pseudo-Augustine" in: O'Carroll 2000 (1982), 299.

17 Fulton 2002, esp. 383–397, 456–464; Reynolds 2012–, 316 ff. Conspicuously absent from the list of supporters of Mary's bodily assumption is the mellifluous doctor, Bernard of Clairvaux (d. 1153). Although Bernard wrote four sermons on the feast of the Assumption, Graef finds that he "never affirmed that he believed Mary to be in heaven with her body." See: Graef 2009 (1963–1965), 185; cf. Fulton 2002, 407–408.

18 *Papal Teachings: Our Lady* 1961, 312; *Acta Apostolicae Sedis* (vol. 42, p. 764); Amadeus of Lausanne 1960, 182–184.

19 Amadeus of Lausanne 1960, 202.

20 *Acta Apostolicae Sedis* (vol. 42, p. 763); *Papal Teachings: Our Lady* 1961, 312; Amadeus of Lausanne 1960, 202 (n. 1).

21 See the lengthy index entry *Christi caro, caro Mariae* in Casagrande 1974, p. 1993.

22 As quoted by Fulton 2002, 392, from Pseudo-Augustine 1845, col. 1145.

23 Augustine of Hippo 1845b, col. 1264 (cf. Perillo 2007, 226, n. 10).

24 Fulton 2002, 394. On medieval scientific theories of human reproduction, see: Bynum 1987, 265–266, 407 (n. 8). As Bynum points out, "Christ (who had no human father) had to be seen as taking his flesh from Mary" (265), and this was true regardless of which medieval theory of human reproduction was held. Indeed, it has to be true to this day for anyone who believes in the virginal conception of Jesus.

25 Alain of Lille 1855, col. 64, as translated by Fulton 2002, 393. Which "Pseudo-Augustine" is being quoted by Alain of Lille here is not clear.

26 See Reynolds (2012–, 298) on "the principle of con-carnality."

27 The work was probably composed by an unknown author "just prior to the great flowering of homiletic reflections on the feast [of the Dormition] in the first half of the eighth century" (Daley 1998, 15).

28 Modestus of Jerusalem 1860, col. 3301B; 1998, 95.

29 Modestus of Jerusalem 1860, col. 3312B; 1998, 100 (translation modified in accordance with Graef 2009 [1963–1965], 107 [and see also 471, n. 23]; cf. also Lampe 1961, 1348, the entry *sussōmos* B3; Reynolds 2012–, 300–301).

30 Graef 2009 (1963–1965), 105, 145, 174–175, 177, 183, 200, 219, resp.

31 Graef 2009 (1963–1965), 145 (emphasis added).

32 Reynolds 2012–, 293–329.

33 Peter Comestor (Hildebertus Cenomanensi) 1854, col. 630, as translated by Reynolds 2012–, 322.

34 Rancour-Laferriere 1992 (1985), 168–177, 196–199.

35 Only the main actions and chief personages in the cast of characters are included in this schematic description of the standard Eastern Orthodox dormition icon. For an assortment of examples from different time periods and locales, see: Onasch 1961, figs. 14, 88–90, 103, 116; Schiller 1966–1991, vol. 4,2, figs. 587–593, 601–603, 651–654, 656; Maguire 1981, figs. 49, 52–57, 59, 60, 62, 64, 65, 67; Ouspensky and Lossky 1982, 215; Lazarev 1994 (1983), figs. 7, 32, 67, 116; Evans and Wixom, eds. 1997, 112, and cat. nos 95, 101, 102, 309, 312; Onasch and Schnieper 1997 (1995), 66, 152, 153; Lifshits and Lukashov 2000, cat. nos 56, 73, 109, 135; Vassilaki, ed. 2000, 132 (fig. 78), 157 (plate 97), 173 (fig. 112), 187 (fig. 123); Rancour-Laferriere 2005, fig. 23.

As for images of the Assumption of Mary in the West, there is much more variety and a wide range of complexity – from a simple ascension of Mary with few other figures to a baroque assemblage of many interacting characters facilitating the progress of Mary upward toward the throne upon which she will be seated as her son crowns her. See, for example: Schiller 1966–1991, vol. 4,2, 83–154 (includes discussion of imagery from the East as well, with figures beginning from fig. 587); Verdier 1980; Schmitt 2006.

36 Quoted and translated (with slight modification – DR-L) by Maguire 1981, 60; 128, n. 36.

37 Maguire 1981, 66–67, and figs. 67, 68.

38 Maguire 1981, 68.

39 From the tract "On the Incarnation of the Word" in *Nicene and Post-Nicene Fathers* (second series) 2004, vol. 4, 65; Athanase d'Alexandrie 1973, 458.

40 Pelikan 1971–1989, vol. I, 155, 206, 216, 344–345; Lossky 1985 (1967), 97–110; Clendenin 2003 (1994), 117–137; and especially the massive scholarly treatise subtitled "Christian deification from its birth as a metaphor to its maturity as a spiritual doctrine" by Russell 2004.

41 Lossky 1985 (1967), 97–110; Rancour-Laferriere 2005, 219–221, 274–275; Constable 1995, 150–156, 160, 165, 167; Finlan and Kharlamov, eds. 2006.

42 Mother Mary and Kallistos Ware 1969, 517, 518 (*Mēnaion tou Augoustou* 1982, 151, 152).

43 Lossky 1985 (1967), 224.

44 Lossky in: Ouspensky and Lossky 1982, 76.

45 Bulgakov 1927, 128; Uspenskii 1989, 28.

46 *Book of Akathists* 1994, 137; *Akafisty Presviatoi Bogoroditse* 1999, 233. On the early narrations of Mary's dormition as one means of helping individual Christians deal with the fear of death, see: Daley 2001.

47 Cf. Rancour-Laferriere 2001, 69; 2005, 84–87 (Russian), 250–253 (English, and the literature cited there). On the theory of separation anxiety, see: Freud 1959 (1926), 169–170. See also: Bowlby 1973, as well as the literature cited under the entry "Separation anxiety" in Akhtar 2009, 262.

4 Daughter Zion, Mother Church

The Protoevangelium

Even professional theologians and Bible scholars who recognize how little in the canonical Bible is said of Mary do manage, nevertheless, to find much. What Christians term the Old Testament seems to be filled with foreshadowing references to Mary. For example, after Eve and Adam (in that order) have sinned through disobedience in the Garden of Eden, God himself speaks to the serpent/tempter about a "woman" who (or whose offspring) will allegedly defeat the offspring of the serpent:

> I will put enmity between you and the woman, and between your offspring and hers; he will strike your head, and you will strike his heel.
> (Genesis 3:15)

This passage is known among marian specialists as the Protoevangelium or Protogospel, that is, the prototype of the good news of the gospel. It has been considered by many Christian theologians – especially those influenced by the Latin Vulgate or the Greek Septuagint translations of the Hebrew – as an early prediction of Mary's victory (via her son) over the devil.[1] Indeed, for mariologists, it is the most important prediction. The Protoevangelium is referred to more often in Hubert du Manoir's eight-volume encyclopedia *Maria* (1949–1971) than any other verse in the Old Testament.[2] The leading twentieth-century Catholic mariologist René Laurentin concludes that the author of Genesis was envisaging "the messianic descendant and the woman who was to be his mother," and Laurentin then names Mary as this mother.[3]

In a mariological correlate of the Protoevangelium, Mary is prefigured by Eve. Mary is the "New Eve," or, technically speaking, the "antitype" of Eve, who was the original, prefigurative "type."[4] This has been so ever since the early patristic period, as when, in the second century, Irenaeus of Lyons (the "father of Mariology") summarized his theory of the necessary "recapitulation" of Eve in Mary: "the knot of Eve's disobedience was loosed by the obedience of Mary."[5] In the twenty-first century, a popular Catholic reference work still sees fit to devote a column to Mary as "The New Eve," and refers to Genesis 3:15 as supporting evidence.[6]

The reach of the Protoevangelium is extended by many mariophile theologians, not only to gospel reports and various epistles of the New Testament, but also to that nearly impenetrable dream salad known as Revelation (chapter 12), with its "woman clothed with the sun" (= Mary, or the church personified as Mary) who gives birth to a child (= Christ) and is attacked by a dragon (= the serpent).[7] In the iconographic realm, this idea is not merely expressed by means of an image of Mary in the sky radiating tongues of fire or blades of light, as in the many pictures of the Virgin of Guadalupe,[8] but it is elaborated upon in some of the images that show Mary treading upon a serpent,[9] or even the Christ child in her arms poking at or stabbing the serpent with his elongated, spear-like cross (the baroque *Maria de Victoria*).[10] There are also gentler and less apocalyptic images of the Protoevangelium – for example, those that show the mother Mary covering (protecting) one of the Christ child's feet and, in an Eastern Orthodox variant, the Christ child covering (protecting) the heel of his other foot as well from the serpent's presumed future strike.[11] There is also Jan Gossaert's composition (ca.1527) that shows an agitated Christ child gazing at an invented inscription, "Jesus, the seed of the woman, has bruised the head of the serpent."[12]

Needless to say, no prefiguration of Miriam and her son Yeshua (i.e., Mary and her son Jesus) in the New Testament has been detected by Jewish interpreters of 1 Moses 3:15 (i.e., Genesis 3:15). Nor has any corresponding Jewish iconography on this theme developed. There is no entry for "Protoevangelium" in the *Encyclopedia Judaica*, whereas there is an entry under that title in the *New Catholic Encyclopedia*.[13] Today's standard Jewish Publication Society translation of the Hebrew Tanakh is at variance with the NRSV translation quoted above, for it provides a collective "they" rather than an individual, messianic "he" striking the head of the serpent.[14] This is because the Hebrew *zerah* refers to coming generations of "offspring," not to an individual descendant – as is recognized by some Christian theologians as well.[15]

The Protoevangelium was created by Christian believers. It is a theological belief construct with its own psychological appeal. As I am concerned here with the psychology of what (at least some) Christians *believe* or have in the past *believed* about Mary, the Protoevangelium will have to be kept in mind, in case it becomes relevant for psychological analysis. This means it will be relevant to psychological consideration of any beliefs about Christianity replacing or superseding Judaism.

Supersessionism

The Protoevangelium (and associated concepts) is testimony to Christian creativity. Somewhat less creative is the straightforward appropriation of concepts and images from the Hebrew Bible in Christian theological treatises, commentaries, liturgical texts, devotional prayers and practices, hymnody, drama, and the visual arts. Representations of Mary are particularly famous for such appropriation. Mary's Christian representations include: tree of life, fountain of life, mother of the living, bride, throne of Solomon, tower of David, house of God, gate of heaven, closed garden, burning bush, jar of manna, rod of Aaron, root of Jesse, Gideon's fleece, morning star, Jacob's ladder, wisdom (or Wisdom), promised land, daughter Zion, Noah's ark, Ark of the Covenant, and so on. A complete list of such items would be very long indeed, and would have to be divided up into various sub-lists, depending upon which geographical areas, historical periods, or branches of Christianity are involved.

Some of these items have been appropriated from the Hebrew Bible in passing exercises of aesthetic license. As such, they seem to be harmlessly pleasurable or educational facilitators of faith. For example, "morning star" and "closed garden" are the familiar topoi of religious poetry and hymns. A few present real conceptual difficulties – for example, "Wisdom," which has been applied both to Mary and to her son, as we have seen.

Unfortunately, when these images are applied comparatively to Mary, that is, when they are considered with respect to their *non-marian* usages in the original Jewish sources, they have the potential to demean. It must not be forgotten that the Hebrew Bible has its own metaphors, meanings, and values, and that these were not created for the sake of the future Christian New Testament. Indeed, an entry in the authoritative *Lexikon für Theologie und Kirche* characterizes the typological utilization of imagery (not only marian) from the Hebrew Bible as a problematical factor in Jewish–Christian relations.[16] Recognition of this problem has been one of the positive effects of Vatican II.

The problem is that typology fosters ideas about Christianity superseding Judaism. *Supersessionism* may be defined as follows: "the traditional Christian belief that since Christ's coming the Church has taken the place of the Jewish people as God's chosen community, and that God's covenant with the Jews is now over and done."[17] The recent pope, Benedict XVI, provides some examples of this, even after Vatican II. He writes: "Jesus sits on the cathedra of Moses." Assuming that only one person can sit on such a "cathedra" at a time, then Jesus has superseded Moses. Or: "the Sermon on the Mount is the new Torah brought by Jesus."[18] This "new Torah" brought by the "new Moses" is understood to be the true Torah – the larger, "universal" Torah, as the pope says, which implicitly subsumes – supersedes – the old, the false, or at best the narrowly ethnonational Torah of the Jews.

When it comes to Christian views of Mary, supersessionist attitudes are rampant. Here, I will examine how three particular images from the Old Testament (ultimately, from the Hebrew Bible) – Daughter Zion, Ark of the Covenant, and Burning Bush – have been utilized by mariophiles in supersessionist fashion. The upshot of this process has been both to devalue the Jewish sources of such imagery and to encourage Christians to believe that Mary was a Christian.

Daughter Zion

As recently as 1980, the influential German theologian Hans Urs von Balthasar (1905–1988) made Mary the pivot of Christian supersessionism. This self-identified "slavewoman of the Lord" (Luke 1:38) gave her consent to being impregnated by God at the annunciation. Balthasar writes:

> Her Yes to the angel recapitulated (while raising to a new level) the whole Abrahamic faith of the Old Testament, together with the hope that it entails. It thereby signaled the incorporation of the Old Testament into the New, of Judaism into the Church.[19]

Such a view of Mary is supersessionist in the extreme. Not only has the Christian Church superseded Judaism here, it has swallowed it whole, cannibalized it. The humble Mary's "Yes" could not possibly have been such a monstrous crime.

"Mary's faith," according to von Balthasar, should be recognized as "the *final* fruit of the Old Covenant."[20] Or, as mariologist René Laurentin blithely declares, "Mary appears at the *culmination* of the chosen people's history."[21] Of course, there is nothing new in the idea that Judaism had essentially been transformed into a corpse after the birth of Christianity (e.g., Luther, Schleiermacher),[22] and so anti-Judaic overtones in the Christian theology of Mary should come as no surprise either.

Contributing to the same volume with von Balthasar, the recent pope – Benedict XVI, at that time Cardinal Josef Ratzinger – offered the reader a slightly less aggressive Mary, one who merely sets in motion the establishment of the "New Covenant": "Just as Abraham's faith was the beginning of the Old Covenant, Mary's faith, enacted in the scene of the Annunciation [Luke 1:26–38], is the inauguration of the New."[23] In another work, however, Ratzinger goes further, claiming that an actual erasure of boundaries between the two "Covenants" is accomplished by Mary:

> In the address of the angel, the underlying motif in the Lucan portrait of Mary surfaces: she is in person the true Zion, toward whom hopes have yearned throughout all the devastations of history. She *is* the true Israel in whom Old and New Covenant, Israel and Church, are indivisibly one.[24]

It is difficult to imagine how any religious Jew could acknowledge the possibility that the "Old Covenant" and the "New Covenant" might become "indivisibly one" – and this quite apart from the offensive potential of Ratzinger's terms "*true* Zion" and "*true* Israel" for Jews, religious and secular alike. Is the Jews' own Zion, however conceptualized, a *false* Zion? Is the post-Holocaust state of Israel – or any other Jewish conception of Israel – a *false* Israel? But this matter is hardly new either, having been studied by, among others, Marcel Simon in his pioneering work *Verus Israel*.[25] It is improbable that the widely read scholar Josef Ratzinger somehow overlooked books published by his scholarly predecessors. It is quite likely, however, that Ratzinger has simply disregarded the vast literature on the "historical Jesus," that is, the Jewish Jesus.

In addition to appropriating "Zion" and "Israel" for their own purposes, some Christian theologians and scholars (both Protestant and Catholic) have taken the traditional Jewish notion "Daughter Zion" (Septuagint Greek *thugatēr Siōn*, often translated "Daughter of Zion") and applied it specifically to Mary. In the Old Testament, this poetic expression referred to Jerusalem, or to the people of Israel generally (e.g., Isaiah 1:8; 37:22; 62:11; Jeremiah 6:2; 6:23; Lamentations 4:22; Zephaniah 3:14). In the New Testament, Mary is never explicitly referred to as Daughter Zion, but there are passages there that seem to some to invite such an interpretation. Most frequently mentioned is the announcing angel's salutation to Mary, "Rejoice [*Chaire*], favored one! The Lord is with you" (Luke 1:28). These words are said to reflect the way Daughter Zion is addressed in some Old Testament (Septuagint) sources, such as: "Rejoice [*Chaire*], O daughter Zion; shout, O daughter Israel! Cheer and exult with all your heart, O daughter Israel!" (Zephaniah 3:14).[26]

In fact, Christian theologians and scholars do not agree on whether Mary is represented as Daughter Zion, even in the rich infancy narrative of Luke.[27] The term Daughter Zion is applied to *Jerusalem* when Jesus enters that city on a donkey (Matthew 21:5; John 12:15), but the term is never applied to Mary. Yet, at the Second Vatican Council of 1962–1965 (Vatican II), as recorded in a document generally known as *Lumen Gentium* (chapter 8), it was decided that Mary was indeed still "the exalted daughter of Sion," the one through whom "the new economy is begun."[28] And, as if to add a measure of papal authority to the counciliar declaration, the 1987 encyclical *Redemptoris Mater* by Pope John Paul II repeatedly calls Mary "daughter of Sion."[29]

Marian organizations, too, continue to propagate a supersessionist version of Daughter Zion. In 2003, the French Society of Marian Studies published its annual volume, the topic this time around being *Marie, fille d'Israël, fille de Sion*.[30] Although some contributors to the volume are concerned primarily with the matter of Mary's Jewish identity or with the ways in which she truly reflects Jewish themes from the Hebrew Bible, others strike traditional supersessionist chords with titles such as: "In Mary, Zion Becomes Mother of the New Creation Inaugurated by the Christ"; "Mary is 'All of Israel' in Person, and as a Person"; "Mary, 'Daughter of Zion' in the Liturgy."[31]

For educated Christians, the identification of Mary as Daughter Zion is firm enough to be targeted with irony. In 2001, Johannes Heil and Rainer Kampling published a volume the title of which ends with a poignant question mark: *Maria – Tochter Sion?*[32] Below this title, on the cover of the volume, is a reproduction of a Strasbourg woodcut from about 1515 showing a group of Jews who attack an image of Mary holding the Christ child in her arms. One of the Jews, dressed in garments decorated with fake Hebrew letters, stabs the image with a lance, and it bleeds (narrative and visual representations of marian images being stabbed or otherwise desecrated by Jews are not uncommon in the history of Christianity).[33] The image is obviously anti-Jewish and is in keeping with the stated goal of the volume, namely, to discuss openly the connection between the historically real Christian hatred of Jews and mariology and marian devotion.[34]

The message actually conveyed by the cover image, however, is more subtle. Can Christians who regard Mary as Daughter Zion honestly welcome the hateful, anti-Jewish story told by this image? Either the Christians' Blessed Virgin Mary *is* Jewish (and their idea that Mary's fellow Jews would assault her image is meaningless), or, Mary is really Christian (and their idea that a Jew would assault Mary's image is paranoid). Actually, the meaninglessness of the first alternative suggests that the second alternative is true – that is, Mary is not really Jewish but Christian, and Christians *imagine* that is why Jews are attacking her image.

The idea of Mary as Daughter Zion bears a certain resemblance to the conversions of Jewish synagogues into marian chapels that took place in medieval Europe. Such transformations were associated with genocidal pogroms against Jews. Mitchell B. Merback writes:

> For every city purified of unbelievers [i.e., Jews], another victory was won by the militant Virgin, whose own [imagined] persecution at the hands of the Jews at the Crucifixion made her their natural sworn enemy. Numerous municipalities within the Holy Roman Empire saw the transformation of their Jewish quarters and the conversion of synagogues into Marian chapels.[35]

The marian title Daughter Zion is a semiotic expropriation of a Jewish title. A marian chapel built on the site of a synagogue is both a physical and a semiotic expropriation of a Jewish place of worship. One does not have to be a theist to understand that both of these phenomena are morally questionable. If, however, I could apply late-medieval Roman Catholic terminology about degrees of sinfulness to these two kinds of expropriation, I would say this: unrepentant propagators of the marian title Daughter Zion are guilty of a venial sin for which they need to spend some time burning in purgatory; unrepentant participants in the conversion of synagogues into marian chapels, on the other hand, are guilty of a mortal sin for which they must burn in the fires of hell for all eternity.

Ark of the Covenant

Another epithet for Mary with supersessionist potential is "Ark of the Covenant," or simply "Ark." In the Hebrew Bible, this term originally referred to the wood and gold chest that contained the "tables of the covenant," which was eventually installed in the inner sanctuary of the First – Solomonic – Temple, and which was considered to be a place where God himself might dwell in glory.[36] Many Christians came to believe, however, that the object in question was a prefiguration of Mary. For example, in the eighth century, John of Damascus preached a sermon in which he apostrophized the recently deceased Mary with the words, "The company of Apostles lift you up on their shoulders, the true ark [*tēn alēthē kibōton*] of the Lord God, as once the priests lifted up the typological ark [*tēn tupikēn kibōton*] that pointed the way to you."[37] In the West, starting from at least the twelfth century, various hymns, prayers, and litanies invoked Mary in terms of the ark (*arca foederis, arca testamenti, arca testamenti novi*).[38] An edition of the illustrated late-medieval *Mirror of Human Salvation* (*Speculum humanae salvationis*) contains an image with the caption, "The ark of the Covenant [*archa testamenti*] signifies Mary."[39] In an old standard of marian devotion, the so-called Litany of Loreto, Mary was (and still is) addressed personally with the request, "Ark of the covenant [*Foederis arca*], pray for us."[40]

This typologizing approach to the Ark of the Covenant persists at more complex, theological levels of discourse. Many marian specialists believe that the ancient sacred object is a type for Mary, and is alluded to, for example, in the words of the angel Gabriel to Mary explaining how she would conceive: "The Holy Spirit will come upon you, and the power of the Most High will *overshadow* you" (Luke 1:35; emphasis added). There are passages in the Old Testament where some form of divine presence *casts a shadow* over the Israelites, as, for example, when the "cloud of the Lord" repeatedly covered the meeting tent with its Tabernacle in the wilderness (Exodus 40:34–35; Numbers 9:15 ff.). Again, as with the Daughter Zion tag for Mary, Christian theologians disagree on whether there is actually a scriptural connection, or multiple connections, to the Old Testament.[41] Fuzzier analogies have also been made: for example, if the "old" covenant was contained by the Ark of the Covenant, the one who would bring a "new" covenant was at least implicitly contained within the body of Mary for at least nine months; or, if the Lord rose up *with the ark* and went to a resting place at Zion (Psalms 132:8–13), so also Mary was raised up bodily and taken along to her final resting place in Heaven, as Pope Pius XII, acknowledging previous theological studies, proclaimed in his 1950 Apostolic Constitution on the Assumption, *Munificentissimus Deus*.[42] In any case, ever since patristic times, tradition decrees that these and other connections and prefigurations do exist, and "Ark of the Covenant" therefore remains a commonplace designation for Mary.[43]

Before he became Pope Benedict XVI, Cardinal Josef Ratzinger wrote: "Mary herself thus becomes the true Ark of the Covenant in Israel, so that the symbol of the Ark gathers an incredibly realistic force."[44] "Realistic," indeed, is that "true" Ark of the Covenant. But what, we may ask, would an Ark with *un*realistic force be, or what would an *un*true Ark be – if not the Jewish Ark of the Covenant? Would it have been too much to ask for a greater sensitivity to pernicious supersessionism from a Catholic theologian who grew up in Nazi Germany?

Burning Bush

One of the most bizarre of the images appropriated for Mary is the "Burning Bush." This appropriation was apparently thought up by Gregory of Nyssa in the fourth century. According to Gregory, the bush at Sinai, which was on fire but remained unconsumed while speaking to Moses (Exodus 3:1 ff.), not only constituted a theophany of its own, but was a foreshadowing of something equally momentous to come: "What was prefigured at that time in the flame of the bush was openly manifested in the mystery of the Virgin, once an intermediate space of time had passed." Gregory goes on to say, "As on the mountain the bush burned but was not consumed, so the Virgin gave birth to the light and was not corrupted." By "not corrupted," Gregory means, not only the absence of sexual intercourse, but also the continued intactness of Mary's hymen after childbirth: "For it is the same woman who is presented as mother and as virgin, for just as her virginity posed no obstacle to her giving birth, neither did her childbearing destroy her virginity."[45] This notion was part of the already existing "perpetual virginity" fantasy about Mary.[46]

Ideas centering on the type of the burning bush might easily be dismissed as preposterous but harmless symptoms of patristic devotional enthusiasm from a distant era. However, the burning bush was not forgotten, and its marian significance has been elaborated upon in different parts of the Christian world over the centuries.[47] Some of the consequences are far from harmless.

For one thing, the field of prefigurative signification expands, so that the burning bush comes to be seen as a foreshadowing, not only of Mary's virginity, but also of Mary herself, together with her divine son who is destined to be crucified. Here is an example from the late medieval *Speculum humanae salvationis*:

> The bush withstood the fire and did not loose its verdure. Mary conceived a Son but did not lose her virginity. The Lord himself inhabited that burning bush [*habitavit in illo rubo ardente*], and the same God dwelt in the impregnated womb of Mary. He descended into the burning bush for the liberation of the Jews, and he descended into Mary for our redemption.[48]

What accomplished the foreordained plan of "our redemption" was the execution of Mary's son on a cross. In the illustration meant to accompany this text, the bush is occupied by God, whose head is adorned with a *cruci*-ferous nimbus signifying *cruci*fixion.[49] Likewise for the figure of God in the burning bush image of the somewhat earlier medieval *Biblia pauperum*.[50]

Some variants of the burning bush image display Mary herself in the bush. There are also variations in the manner of representing Moses. In some of the images, such as a thirteenth-century ikon from Sinai, or a fifteenth-century triptych by Nicolas Froment in Aix-en-Provence Cathedral, the great Jewish patriarch appears down on the ground while reverentially removing his sandal(s) before the mother and Christ child in the burning bush.[51] A fifteenth-century sculpture of Mary with the Christ child in the Hôpital de Tonnerre (Yonne) includes the burning bush together with a miniature Moses on his knees at Mary's feet.[52] In this case, Moses has two horns.[53] The Jew is literally diminished and demonized.

The burning bush type becomes theologically complex in the Orthodox lands of Rus', starting in the sixteenth century. New foreshadowings of Mary are incorporated, and Mary herself gains greater prominence. Moses is relegated to the upper left-hand corner of the picture, and, as Christina Tzvetkova-Ivanova observes, there is a preference for an image of Moses kneeling before Mary, as opposed to a Moses who merely removes his sandals.[54] Most recently, in Russia, many of the Burning Bush ikons do not even show the original witness of the burning bush at all, and Mary and her child are placed front and center, surrounded by angels and other figures in a blaze of light. This is clear from various published nineteenth- and twentieth-century devotional compendia of Russian ikons.[55] Moses has thus evolved from a kneeling person to a non-person, and what remains is a fused mother-and-child replacement deity. What began as wishful patristic foolishness has become demeaning anti-Judaism as well.

The notion of Mary as the burning bush beheld by Moses continues to be affirmed by some rituals and by some theologians in modern times, especially in the Eastern Orthodox world. The *Festal Menaion* includes canticles sung on the feast of the annunciation (March 25) praising Mary as the burning bush.[56] In 1927, Russian Orthodox theologian Sergii Bulgakov published his book *The Burning Bush* (*Kupina neopalimaia*). Although better known for his version of Russian sophiology, Bulgakov does not hesitate to make grandiose claims about the relevance of the burning bush (with its accompanying angel of the Lord) to the New Testament as well. He writes that, "the Burning Bush . . . is consistently explained by the Church as an image of the Blessed Virgin."[57] The appearance of God to Moses on Mount Horeb initiates a "new epoch of divine worship." This epoch "opens with a vision of the Mother of God in the Bush and closes exhaustively with her earthly presence through which the incarnation is accomplished."[58] Bulgakov attempts to characterize the "sophiophany" experienced by Moses in the following terms:

> On the one hand the Burning Bush itself, the bush engulfed in flames, the bush afire yet unconsumed, the "holy ground" (Exodus 3:5) [occupied by the bush] – is the Mother of God as she was overshadowed by

> the Holy Spirit; on the other hand, the angel of the Lord in the flame of fire in that thorn bush (3:2) is "God [himself] calling to Moses out of the bush" (3:4), the Son of God in the process of being incarnated. This vision is thus a tabernacular icon of the Mother of God [*senovniaia Bogomaterniaia ikona*] beheld by the prophet Moses, an image of the divine incarnation in which God's flame penetrates and deifies created being without consuming it.[59]

I have attempted to render Bulgakov's churchy Russian in all of its density, but what he writes is clearly supersessionist, and has no basis whatsoever in scripture. It is one thing to claim that the God of two Abrahamic religions, Judaism and Christianity, is the same God. After all, both Moses and Jesus supposedly communicated directly with that God. But, it is quite something else to assert that the burning bush is merely a way of envisaging a future woman, Mary, the mother of Jesus. Here, Bulgakov does not advance beyond traditional Christian appropriation of the burning bush – indeed, an ongoing appropriation in post-Soviet Russia, where devotional texts revive hackneyed phrases about the burning bush being "one of the Old Testament prototypes [*odnim iz vetkhozavetnykh proobrazov*] pointing to the Mother of God."[60]

Mother Church

Of the three supersessionist titles for Mary examined above, Daughter Zion was in part a kinship term that had previously been applied to the ancestral religious group, the people of Israel. The rhetorical effect of the term was to personify Israel. In some books of what Christians would come to term the New Testament, such personifications were normal: "virgin Israel" (Jeremiah 18:13, 31:4), "the virgin daughter – My people" (Jeremiah 14:17), "the virgin daughter Judah" (Lamentations 1:15), "mother Zion" (*Mētēr Siōn*, Psalm 86:5 [Septuagint]), and "Zion, the mother of us all" (2 Esdras 10:7).[61]

Perhaps vaguely aware of this ancestral practice, Christians started personifying *their* religious collective.[62] Among the Greeks she was Mother Church (*Mētēr Ekklēsia*), as when Origen wrote that, "God is silent over us when we rail at a brother and give scandal to a son of our Mother the Church [*kata tou huiou tēs Mētros hēmōn Ekklēsias*]."[63] In his *Paedagogus*, Clement of Alexandria (d. ca.215) idealized interactions between the Mother Church and her members, that is, her "children": "The Mother [*Hē Mētēr*] draws the children to herself; and we seek our Mother, the Church [*tēn Mētera, tēn Ekklēsian*]."[64]

At an early stage of Christian Latinity, Tertullian wrote about "mother . . . Church" (*mater . . . Ecclesia*) or even "our lady mother the Church" (*Domina mater ecclesia*).[65] Saint Cyprian of Carthage (d. 258) repeatedly utilized the maternal metaphor for the church and famously applied the metaphor when warning the baptized that, "you cannot have God for your Father if you no longer have the Church for your mother [*Habere iam non potest Deum patrem qui ecclesiam non habet matrem*]."[66] With Augustine, the metaphor is often extended by means of bodily imagery, so that the baptismal font becomes the uterus (*uterus*) from which are born members of Mother Church,[67] or the Old and New Testaments become her two breasts at which members feed (*et ubera ejus duo Testamenta Scripturarum divinarum*).[68]

What the term "Mother Church" accomplished was to provide a convenient password, as it were, for an individual Christian indirectly to access personal memories, feelings, and issues concerning his or her real mother, and to utilize these accessed materials in a way that assisted the individual Christian to imagine their large community of Christians in a constructive, nonthreatening fashion. For each Christian who utilized the term "Mother Church," the configuration of relevant psychological factors was no doubt different. On the other hand, the appeal of the term itself certainly had something to do with the experience of being mothered (or of being a mother) – otherwise the reference to a mother in the term Mother Church would have been pointless.

As Mother Church was being established as a psychologically real "mother" by patristic writers, there was also a felt need to relate this "mother" to the other prominent maternal figure in the Christian pantheon – that is, Mary the Mother of God. The result was another instance of typology (but not a supersessionist typology that straddled the boundary between Old and New Testaments). Mary became the type of Mother Church. The "full doctrine" (as O'Carroll says) of this typology was achieved by Saint Augustine:

> Consider how the Church is the bride [*coniux*] of Christ, a thing that is clear. What will be more difficult to understand, yet is true, she is the mother of Christ. The Virgin Mary went before her as her type [*typo*]. Whence I ask you is Mary the mother of Christ if not because she gave birth [*peperit*] to the members of Christ? You, to whom I speak, are the members of Christ; who has given birth to you? I hear the voice of your heart: Mother Church [*Mater Ecclesia*]. This Mother is honoured, similar to Mary, she brings forth, yet is a virgin [*Mater ista sancta, honorata, Mariae similis, et parit et virgo est*].[69]

The reasoning behind such a typology seems a bit complicated, strained even (not least because of the disturbing oedipal incest theme that it incorporates – see above, pp. 12–18 – and that may have been a serious psychological issue for Augustine).

Once established, however, the typology flourished.[70] And it flourished without any supersessionist detraction of value from images in the Hebrew Bible. In the twentieth century, the typology was reiterated at Vatican II, with the virgin-mother oxymoron being retained as a key component of the Mother Church's imitation of Mary the mother of Christ: "in the mystery of the church, which is also rightly called mother and virgin [*mater . . . et virgo*], the blessed virgin Mary has taken precedence, providing in a pre-eminent and singular manner the exemplar both as virgin and as mother." Further on in *Lumen Gentium*, it is stated:

> The church, contemplating her [Mary's] hidden holiness and imitating her love, and faithfully carrying out the will of the Father, by faithfully accepting the word of God also becomes a mother [*et ipsa fit mater*]: for by preaching and baptism it brings forth to new and immortal life children conceived of the holy Spirit and born of God. The church is also a virgin [*Et ipsa est virgo*] who keeps integral and pure the faith she has given to her spouse [Christ]; and in imitation of the mother of its Lord, by the power of the holy Spirit, it preserves virginally intact its faith, solid its hope and sincere its love.[71]

Here, Mary the real mother of Christ remains the Augustinian type of the metaphorical mother, that is, the personified mother, the Mother Church. From *Lumen Gentium* it is difficult to decide, however, which of the two mothers is supposed to be primary – Mary, or the church.

The issue is not new. In many of the patristic writings, Mary was the Church, and the Church was Mary. There was a certain fluidity of the boundaries, or a functional equivalence between the two.[72] Also, in medieval iconography of the crucifixion, there was some confusion as to who was supposed to be catching the blood spurting from Christ's side – Mary, who stood below the cross, or a figure labeled Ecclesia catching the blood in a chalice (see below, 112, 263–264). In the modern period, we find the equivalence expressed by many Catholic mariophiles, as when Paul Claudel (1868–1955) wrote, "For me, the Holy Virgin Mary is the same thing as the Holy Church, and I have never learned to distinguish the one from the other."[73]

Among the myriad reasons why Mary can represent the church, according to the late Henri de Lubac, was her unwavering faith:

> If it is true that the Church is founded on faith in her [the Church's] Lord, [then] during the Passion, our Lady, through the strength of her faith, sustained and carried the whole edifice of the Church, like a frame built of wood that cannot decay; when she stood before the Cross, it was the whole Church who stood there in her; on the evening of Good Friday, when the faith of all the others had been at least darkened, she alone constituted, through her ever-unshaken faith, the Church of Jesus; and in the long Saturday vigil, when Christ slept in the sepulcher, the whole life of the Mystical Body withdrew, taking refuge in her as in its heart.[74]

De Lubac knows that these assertions have no basis in scripture, for they are only matters of tradition (duly documented in his footnotes).[75]

Such assertions are also at variance with the idea that Mary had serious doubts about the divinity of her son (Origen and others, above, pp. 39–41). But, for De Lubac and for others in this tradition, Mary alone kept the faith and stood for the Church at its bleakest hour. Around what De Lubac terms Mary's "long Saturday vigil," there is in fact a considerable body of folklore, devotions, and a liturgy of "the Saturday of Our Lady."[76] My daily missal from the 1950s contains a section titled, "Masses of the Blessed Virgin Mary on Saturdays."[77]

Perhaps the idea that Mary was a faithful Saturday believer survived as long as it did because mariophiles cannot imagine the idea of a mother as anything other than faithfully devoted to her child, and such total devotion is probably a wishful memory of the quality of the early, pre-oedipal mother–child relationship. To give up the Saturday idea may have seemed like abandoning or even casting aspersions on the notion of a mother's faithful devotion to her child.

However, Saturday also happens to be the Jewish Sabbath. Consecrating Saturday to Mary made her a faithful "Christian" on the very day she normally should have been observing the one holiday explicitly mandated in the Ten Commandments: "Remember the sabbath day, and keep it holy" (Exodus 20:8). Would faith in her scandalously crucified son have been an appropriate way for Mary to keep the Jewish Sabbath holy? The question will be a painful one for any mariophile who truly understands that Mary was a Jew.

*

Here, I offer a critique of Christian supersessionism as it is manifested in the tendency of mariologists to appropriate from the Hebrew Bible such images as "Daughter Zion," "Ark of the Covenant," and "Burning Bush." This appropriation of images devalues their original Jewish source, where they had and still have their own meaning, which has nothing to do with Christianity. The historical Mary was a Jew, not a Christian. Medieval folklore about Jews attacking visual images of Mary added an element of paranoia to the already hostile supersessionism. The physical conversion of synagogues into marian chapels (and concommitant pogroms against Jews) leaves no doubt about the extreme anti-Jewish hatred that has existed in the minds of some mariophiles.

Notes

1 Patristic authors who dealt with Genesis 3:15 include Cyprian of Carthage, Ephrem the Syrian, Epiphanius of Salamis, Leo the Great, and Isidore of Seville (Gambero 1999 [1991], 93, 117, 129, 307, 378). Of course, Justin Martyr and Irenaeus of Lyons would have to be included here, if only implicitly by virtue of their exposition of the Eve–Mary parallel, but also explicitly (*Ante-Nicene*

Fathers 2004 (1885–1887), vol. I, 250, 548). Not all the church Fathers, however, offered a marian exegesis of Genesis 3:15 (for example, Ambrose, Augustine, Cyril of Jerusalem, Cyril of Alexandria, and others). When the cult of Mary as "Mediatrix" began to flourish in the Latin West in the eleventh and twelfth centuries, theologians (such as Fulbert of Chartres and Bernard of Clairvaux) became more inclined to see Mary as the one who would crush the head of the serpent/tempter. For some informative scholarly studies, see: Robert 1949, 34–36; Panella 1967; the entry "Woman in Genesis 3:15" in O'Carroll 2000 (1982), 370–373; Pelikan 1971–1989, vol. 3, 165–166; Buby 1994–1996, vol. 2, 124–135.

In 1854, Pope Pius IX affirmed that Mary was foretold by God in Genesis 3:15 (the Bull *Ineffabilis Deus*, in *Papal Teachings: Our Lady* 1961, 72, 75). In 1950, Pope Pius XII referred to the Protoevangelium as one form of evidence for establishing the dogma of Mary's Assumption into heaven (the Bull *Munificentissimus Deus*, in *Papal Teachings: Our Lady* 1961, 317–318). The participants in Vatican II (1962–1965) re-affirmed belief in the relevance of Genesis 3:15 by saying that Mary "is already prophetically foreshadowed in that victory over the serpent which was promised to our first parents after their fall into sin" (Abbott 1966, 87). The pre-Vatican II *Liber Usualis* quotes Genesis 3:15 on the feast of the Immaculate Conception (December 8, p. 1315). A post-Vatican II Roman Catholic missal features a reading from Genesis (which includes 3:15), also on the feast of the Immaculate Conception (Socias 2011, 2013–2014; cf. also pp. 2438–2439 for the Novena to the Immaculate Conception).

Numerous recent theological studies continue to read Genesis 3:15 in marian terms. For example, Bastero (2006 [1995], 65) includes Genesis 3:15 among the "Old Testament texts that definitely have a Mariological meaning" and concludes his analysis by saying that, "Mary, without excluding Eve, is the Woman of the proto-Gospel" (69). Sri (2005, 66) argues that Eve initiates the tradition of the "queen-mother figure" in Genesis 3:15, and that, "Mary, the mother of the Davidic King *par excellence* in the New Testament" could be understood in the light of this tradition. Hauke (2007, 28) asserts, as have many others (cf. Brown et al. 1978, 189, n. 423), that the fact that Jesus addresses his mother exclusively as "woman" in John's gospel (2:4, 19:26) is an obvious reflection of the "woman" in the Protoevangelium.

2 See the index of passages from scripture in du Manoir 1949–1971, vol. 8, 101.

3 Laurentin 1991 (1968), 274.

4 See, for example: Avril Henry's valuable introduction to biblical typology in her commentary on the *Biblia pauperum* 1987, 4–18 (and specifically p. 50 on the Eve–Mary pair); Peltomaa 2001, 35, 128–134; Steenberg 2004, 130 ff.

5 Irenaeus, *Adversus haereses* (3:22), in *Ante-Nicene Fathers* 2004 (1885–1887), vol. 1, 455. See also: Justin's *Dialogue with Trypho* (100), in the same volume (249), as well as brief summaries of the patristic context in: Daniélou 1950, 32–34, and Altaner 1960 (1958), 156–157; useful scholarly overviews on the parallelism of Eve and Mary in Burghardt 1955, 110–117, and Benko 2004 (1993), 235–245; the extensive patristic quotations and commentaries indicated in the index under "Eve–Mary parallel" in Gambero 1999 (1991), 425; and a detailed study of the iconographic manifestations of the Eve–Mary "antithesis" by Guldan 1966. The Eve–Mary connection was reaffirmed at Vatican II (Tanner, ed. 1990, vol. II, 893). An excellent scholarly analysis of the role of Mary as "Co-recapitulator" of Eve (in coordination with Jesus as recapitulator of Adam [1 Corinthians 15:21–22, 45; Romans 5:17–19]) in the writings of Irenaeus is offered by Steenberg (2004).

6 Hahn 2009, 587.

7 See: Gambero 1999 (1991), 126; Laurentin 1991 (1968), 41–45; Feuillet 1981, 30–46; the entry "Woman in Revelation 12," in O'Carroll 2000 (1982), 376–377; Ratzinger in Ratzinger and von Balthasar 2005 (1997), 51–53. In the last citation, here Ratzinger writes in support of the opinion expressed by Pope John Paul II in section 24 of his 1987 encyclical *Redemptoris Mater*: "In this way, she who as the one 'full of grace' was brought into the mystery of Christ in order to be his Mother and thus the Holy Mother of God, through the Church remains in that mystery as '*the woman*' spoken of by the Book of Genesis (3:15) at the beginning and by the *Apocalypse* (12:1) at the end of the history of salvation" (*Mary in the Church* 2003, 114).

8 See, for example, the profusely illustrated celebratory compendium *Felicidad de México* (Zerón-Medina 1995). On the connection between the miraculous image of the Guadalupe Virgin and the woman of the Apocalypse, see: Brading 2001, 54–75.

9 Guldan 1966, figs. 107, 108, 113, 115, 116, 119, 121–126, 133, 135, 136, 171–173, 176, 177, 179, 180, 183–185, 189, 190, 192; Essen 1968, cat. nos 128, 153, 154, 168, 169; Schiller 1966–1991, vol. 4,2, figs. 774, 780, 784–786, 791, 831; Küppers, ed. 1974, 178, 179, 184, 188, 372.

10 Guldan 1966, fig. 118; Essen 1968, cat. No. 159; Schiller 1966–1991, vol. 4,2, fig. 787; Lechner 1997, 157 (and illustration, p. 142).

11 Lifshits and Lukashov 2000, cat. no. 27 (*Bogomater' Smolenskaia Shuiskaia*, late seventeenth century), with instructive commentary by G. Sidorenko, p. 108.

12 MVLIERIS SEMEN IHS. SERPENTIS CAPVT CONTRIVIT. See: Acres 2006, 246 (fig. 5).

13 Namely, Panella 1967.

14 *The Jewish Study Bible*, 2004, 17.

15 For example, Westermann 1986, vol. I, 42.

16 Entry "Typologie" by Christoph Dohmen and Erwin Dirscherl in Kasper 1993–2001, vol. 10, 321–323.

17 Soulen 2005, 413.

18 Ratzinger 2007, 66, 68, 122.

19 Foreword to Ratzinger and von Balthasar 2005 (1997), 9.

20 Von Balthasar in Ratzinger and von Balthasar 2005 (1997), 143 (emphasis added).

21 Laurentin 1991 (1968), 48 (emphasis added).

22 For example: Chidester 2000, 493–494.

23 Ratzinger and von Balthasar 2005 (1997), 49. Ratzinger is commenting on the encyclical *Redemptoris Mater* (14) of Pope John Paul II (see: *Mary in the Church* 2003, 103).

24 Ratzinger 1983 (1977), 43.

25 Simon 1986 (1964); cf. Ben-Chorin 1971, 202.

26 I have modified the NRSV translations somewhat to show where *chaire* ("rejoice") appears in both the Septuagint text and in Luke's Greek. See: Lyonnet 1939, 131–133; Hebert 1950, 404; Laurentin 1991 (1968), 24–26.

27 For example: Brown 1993 (1977), 323–325 vs. Laurentin 1991 (1968), 24–26, and McHugh 1975, 40–42, where the issue is the similarity of a portion of the annunciation in Luke 1:28–33 to the prophet's message to Israel personified in Zephaniah 3:14–17. See the entry "Daughter of Zion" in O'Carroll 2000 (1982), 116–117, for a compact overview. A collaborative assessment of the issue by Protestant and Roman Catholic scholars (Brown et al. 1978, 128–132) finds no credible evidence that Luke understood Mary to symbolize Daughter Zion.

28 Tanner, ed. 1990, vol. II, 893.
29 *Mary in the Church* 2003, 95, 99, 131, etc.
30 Longère, ed. 2003.
31 Titles by Michel-Marie de Goedt (85–95), Marie-Thérèse Huguet (110–129), and Ignacio M. Calabuig Adàn (133–167), resp., in Longère, ed. 2003.
32 Heil and Kampling, eds. 2001.
33 See, for example: Worrell 1923, 370–371 (a Coptic sermon attributed to Theophilus of Alexandria has an ikon of Mary bleed after a Jew smashes it to pieces); Khitrowo 1966 (1889), 87, 163 (visitors to Constantinople from Rus' report on images of Mary there which had allegedly been stabbed by a Jew); Galavaris 1959 (eleventh- to thirteenth-century Byzantine lead seals of the Mother of God "stabbed with a knife" are based on stories about a Mother of God icon in the Hagia Sophia "stabbed" by a Jew); Weber 2001, 90–91, fig. 14 (a fifteenth-century legend about a marian image [*Pietà*] nestled in a beech tree at the Maria Buchen pilgrimage site which starts screaming after being stabbed by a Jew; cf. also Weber 2008, 359, 362–363, figs. 6, 7a, 7b, 8).
34 Heil and Kampling, eds. 2001, 9–12.
35 Merback 2012, 206–207 (cf. 222–224, 270–277, 327 [n. 21, for some of the literature in this area]).
36 Grintz 1972.
37 John of Damascus 1988 (498), as translated in John of Damascus 1998a (197–198). Some components of the Ark of the Covenant prefiguration may be detected in the fifth-century Akathistos hymn to Mary, such as tabernacle (*skēnē*), holy of holies (*hagia hagiōn*), and ark (*kibōtos*) – see Peltomaa 2001, 201. Michel van Esbroeck (2005, 68) concludes that "the Virgin as the Ark of the Covenant was introduced into the liturgy of the Dormition and became deeply rooted in the religious politics of the Byzantine Empire in the fifth and sixth centuries."
38 See entries in the *Mariologisches Glossarium* in: Meersseman 1958–1960, vol. II, 281 (under *arca*).
39 *The Mirror of Salvation* 2002, 36 (fig. 38); cf. Lutz and Perdrizet 1907–1909, vol. 1, 22 (where the text has *arca*, not *archa*).
40 Lefebvre 1956, 1117; *Liber Usualis*, 1858; Socias 2011, 2414.
41 For example: Brown 1993 (1977), 327–328, 344–345 vs. Laurentin 1991 (1968), 27–30. The Protestant–Catholic collaborative referred to in n. 27 above finds no convincing reason to believe that Luke was linking Mary to the Ark of the Covenant (Brown et al. 1978, 132–134).
42 *Papal Teachings: Our Lady* 1961, 311, 313 (cf. O'Carroll 2000 [1982], 50).
43 For overviews, see: Schildenberger 1967; the entry "Ark of the Covenant" in O'Carroll 2000 (1982), 49–51. For some iconographic examples, see: Kessler 2000, 31–34.
44 Ratzinger in Ratzinger and von Balthasar 2005 (1997), 65. Cf. the reference to Mary as "the true Ark of the Covenant and true Temple of God" in the 1974 apostolic exhortation *Marialis Cultus* (6) by Pope Paul VI (*Mary in the Church* 2003, 58).
45 Gambero 1999 (1991), 155; cf. also Proclus of Constantinople in: Constas 2003, 136–137. As Constas points out (150), the marian typology of the burning bush was "employed by virtually all factions in the christological controversy," including Cyril of Alexandria and Nestorius.
46 The idea of Mary's continuing virginity even after giving birth to Jesus – i.e., not only *ante partum*, but also *in partu* and *post partum* – has been a standard of marian devotion and theology in many strands of Christianity. The idea implies both

the retention of the hymen during the process of giving birth to Jesus, as well as continued heterosexual abstinence after Jesus is born. The belief in Mary's perpetual virginity goes back in part to the second-century Greek Infancy Gospel of James ("Protevangelium of James," chs. 19–20 [Elliott 1993, 64–65; Schneemelcher, ed. 1991–1992, I, 434–435], where a certain Salome performs a digital examination of Mary right after the birth of Jesus and confirms that she is still a virgin). The idea spread in the Latin West with the help of the sixth–seventh-century Gospel of Pseudo-Matthew (ch. 13 [Elliott 1993, 93–94]) and the mid-thirteenth-century *Golden Legend* (de Voragine 1993 (1850), vol. 1, 38). But, Mary's perpetual virginity is not affirmed in canonical scripture. It is defended by patristic writers (the Cappadocian Fathers, Epiphanius, Ambrose, Augustine, among others). By the time of the Second Ecumenical Council of Constantinople in 553, Mary is referred to as *semper virgo / aeiparthenos* on multiple occasions (see Tanner, ed. 1990, vol. I, 113, 114, 116, 121). The earliest *Life of the Virgin* (seventh century) by Maximos the Confessor affirms that Mary possessed "the grace of perpetual virginity" (as translated from the Old Georgian by Shoemaker 2005, 445). In the medieval Roman mass, some variation on *semper virgo Maria* was customarily intoned from about the tenth century on (e.g., Young 1962 [1933], vol. 1, 22, 32, 35, 39). Some popular medieval plays (for example, one of the N-Town plays) featured a *post-partum* vaginal examination of Mary by midwives (Waller 2011, 76–79).

A particularly clever theological simile, which was widespread in the medieval West (and possibly originated with St. Athanasius, d. 373), compares Mary (or her womb) with a glass window through which God as a ray of light was able both to enter and to exit without doing damage (note that Mary "gave birth to the light" in the characterization of her as the burning bush by Gregory of Nyssa), thereby leaving Mary a virgin both *ante partum* and *post partum*. The key text, attributed to Bernard of Clairvaux but not verified in critical editions, is: *Sicut splendor solis vitrum absque laesione perfundit et penetrat eiusque soliditatem insensibili subtilitate pertraicit nec cum ingreditur, violat nec, cum egreditur, dissipat: sic Dei verbum, splendor Patris, virginum habitaculum adiit et inde clauso utero prodiit*. See: Salzer 1893, 71–74; Hirn 1957 (1909), 343–349; Meiss 1945 (examples from the visual arts as well as theology); Greene, ed. 1977 (1935), 33, 34, 45, 128, 131, 135 (examples from early English carols).

Religious Muslims hold Mary in high regard (a Sura of the Qu'ran is devoted to Maryam). Many Muslims have believed that Mary was a virgin before and during the process of giving birth to Jesus. However, they have not accepted the idea of her *post-partum* virginity. Occasionally, this difference has provoked a hostile response from the Christian side. In a conversation with Ignatius of Loyola around 1522, a Mudejar man insisted that Mary did not remain chaste after giving birth to Jesus. As Amy G. Remensnyder puts it, "only divine intervention stopped Loyola from stabbing the man to death to avenge this insult to Mary's honor" (Remensnyder 2014, 166).

Reformers such as Luther, Calvin, Zwingli, Cranmer, and Bullinger were still willing to accept Mary's "ever virgin" status. As recently as Vatican II (1962–1965), Mary is also referred to as "ever virgin," first when the canon from the then-current *Roman Missal* is quoted, and second when "eastern Christians" are praised for their devotion to "the ever virgin mother of God" (Tanner, ed. 1990, vol. II, 892, 898). In the latest edition of *The Little Office of the Blessed Virgin Mary* the unconsumed bush (*Rubum . . . incombustum*) seen by Moses signifies Mary's virginity preserved (Keller, ed. 2013, 108, 110, 119, 124), and the phrase *semper virgo* is repeatedly applied to Mary (Keller, ed. 2013, passim). The current *Catechism of the Catholic Church* (2000 [1997], nos. 499–501, 510) still affirms the perpetual virginity of Mary. Eastern Orthodox Christians today venerate an "ever virgin" Mary, although ordinary mariophiles in the largest branch of Orthodoxy by far, the Russian Orthodox Church (Moscow Patriarchate), value Mary much more as a mother than as a virgin, and they are not even likely to understand the term *prisnodeva* ("ever virgin"), which is utilized in a few prayers (Rancour-Laferriere 2005, 255).

For some of the massive scholarly literature on Mary's perpetual virginity, see: Jouassard 1949; Miegge 1955, 36–52; Tappolet 1962, 49–54, 170–173, 240–249; Laurentin 1991 (1968), 316–334; Laurentin 2009, 174–181, 219–223; Casagrande 1974, 1996–1997 (lengthy index entries under *Maria Virgo ante partum, in partu,* and *post partum,* as well as *Maria semper virgo*); Ledit 1976, 167–179 (in the Byzantine liturgy); Avril Henry's rich commentary to signature b of *Biblia pauperum* 1987, 51; Clayton 1990, 3–6, 12; Neyrey 1990 (71 ff. on "Childbirth Yet Abiding Physical Virginity" as evidence for Mary's identity as a "Mediterranean maid"); Graef 2009 (1963–1965, subject index under "Virginity, perpetual"); the entries "Virginity of Mary" and "Virginity in Partu" in O'Carroll 2000 (1982), 357–362, with extensive bibliographies; Brown 2008 (1988), 352–356; Ziegenaus 1991; Van der Horst 2005 (1994–1995), 62–66; Lüdemann 1998 (1997), 7–14, 135–137; Peltomaa 2001, 127–128; Kreitzer 2004, 134–135; Rancour-Laferriere 2005, 253–256; Zervos 2005; Williams 2007, 250–251; Elliott 2008, 63–64; McGuckin 2011 (2008), 214–217; Reynolds 2012–, 51–106 (passim).

47 See: *Mariologisches Glossarium* in Meersseman 1958–1960, vol. II, 361 (under the entry *rubus*); Smith 1968; Schildenberger 1989 (overview of exegesis and patristics with bibliography); Bobkov and Shevtsov 1996, fig. 77 (with commentary, 167–171); Kessler 2000, 5–6, 47–48, 51 (fig. 2.16); Tzvetkova-Ivanova 2000 (an examination of texts and images relating to the burning bush from early patristic times down to the late medieval ikons and Church Slavonic texts of Orthodox Rus'); Collins 2006 (on images going back to the ninth–tenth centuries that express the exegetical background to the Burning Bush as a type for Mary); Price 2007, 68–69 (Mary as the burning bush in the writings of Severus of Antioch).

48 Prose rendition of: Lutz and Perdrizet 1907–1909, vol. 1, 17.

49 Lutz and Perdrizet 1907–1909, vol. 2, Tafel 13 (to go with text on Tafel 14).

50 *Biblia pauperum* 1987, signature b (and see p. 32 on the relationship between the *Biblia pauperum* and the *Speculum humanae salvationis*).

51 Nelson and Collins, eds. 2006, cat. no. 56 (cf. cat. nos. 58, 59, and figs. 85, 88, 95, 125); Vetter 1967, 1432, and plate 65.

52 Vloberg 1954, 280.

53 When Moses came down from Sinai with the tablets of the law, his face was radiant with light (the Vulgate says that Moses *ignorabat quod* ***cornuta*** *esset facies sua ex consortio sermonis Dei* (Exodus 34:29). Jerome's utilization of *cornuta* here for Hebrew *karan* had unfortunate consequences, as noted in a comment on the passage in *The Jewish Study Bible* (2004, 191): *karan* is from *keren* ("horn"), "in the sense of projection, emanation"; "In the Vulgate, Jerome, in an over-etymological translation, rendered 'was horned,' although he knew from the Septuagint that the meaning was figurative. Nevertheless, his translation led to the image of Moses with horns in medieval and Renaissance art (see esp. Michelangelo's Moses), and eventually, coupled with the notion of Satan's horns, to the anti-Semitic belief that Jews have horns."

Already in John's gospel (8:44), certain Jews are said to descend from the Devil. Later, in predominantly Christian Europe, Jews were commonly believed to be in league with the Devil, and were sometimes depicted as horned creatures in medieval (and later) imagery (e.g., Trachtenberg 1983 [1943], 44–46; Mellinkoff 1970, figs. 123, 124, 126–128). As a result, images of a horned Moses were probably understood by the uneducated masses to be derogatory (see: Mellinkoff 1970, 135–137). Note, moreover, that all images of a horned Moses in the presence of the burning bush (more examples: Mellinkoff 1970, figs. 60, 62, 78) are anachronisms, for Moses brought down the tablets from Sinai *after* the encounter with the burning bush (for further examples of anachronistic use of a horned Moses, see: Avril Henry's magisterial commentary to the *Biblia pauperum* 1987 (134, note f 9; 147, note p 8). Further images of a horned Moses may be found in: Schiller 1966–1991, vol. 4,1, figs. 279, 280, 281, 285, 295.

54 Tzvetkova-Ivanova 2000, 21; Lifshits and Lukashov 2000, cat. no. 43.

55 Poselianin 1911, 564–566; Dorenskaia 1999, 130–135; Snessoreva 1999 (1898), 305–307.

56 Mother Mary and Kallistos Ware 1969, 451, 458.

57 Bulgakov 1927, 218.

58 Bulgakov 1927, 222.

59 Bulgakov 1927, 220.

60 Pankeev, ed. 2001, 132.

61 Cf. Benko 2004 (1993), 243–244.

62 Of course, personification of large groups is a general psychological phenomenon. Some examples: Fatherland (German *Vaterland*), Mother Russia (*Rossiia-mat'*), Mothers of the Plaza de Mayo (Spanish *Asociación Madres de Plaza de Mayo*), Uncle Sam (American government), Muslim Brotherhood, Daughters of the American Revolution, Sisters of Mercy, Sons of Liberty, Daughters of the Heart of Jesus, etc.

63 Plumpe 1943, 76.

64 Plumpe 1943, 64.

65 The first quotation is from *Liber de Oratione*: Tertullian 1844, col. 1154. The second is from *Ad Martyras* (as quoted by Benko 2004 [1993], 232).

66 Cyprian 1971, 66–67.

67 De Lubac 1982 (1971), 52.

68 Augustine of Hippo 1841c, col. 1998 (cf. O'Donnell 1996, under the entry "Mother, Church as," 312). Other useful sources on the maternal metaphor of the church include: Plumpe 1943; De Lubac 1986 (1953), 236–278; De Lubac 1982 (1971); Benko 2004 (1993), 229–234.

69 Morin, ed. 1930, 163, as translated by O'Carroll 2000 (1982), 347.

70 At the same time, it was *un*common for Christian thinkers to interpret Mary as a type or figure of the "synagogue." On this topic, see: Benko 2004 (1993), 241–243 (on Tertullian and Hilary of Poitiers); Gambero 1999 (1991), 367 (on Gregory the Great); Graef 2009 (1963–1965), 201 (on Alain of Lille).

71 Tanner 1990, vol. 2, 896.

72 Cf. Congar 1954, 28 ff. For more on the parallelism of Mary with, or as the type (prototype, figure) of *Ecclesia*, see: Coathalem 1954 (1939); Congar 1954, 6–22; Semmelroth 1963 (1950); De Lubac 1986 (1953), 314–379; Thurian 1968, 255–267; Von Balthasar in Ratzinger and von Balthasar 2005 (1997), 125–144; the entry "Type of the Church," in O'Carroll 2000 (1982), 346–348; Benko 2004 (1993), 234–245; O'Donnell 1996, 292–293, and 294, notes 15–18 (numerous patristic sources).

73 As quoted in: De Lubac 1986 (1953), 338, n. 125 (cf. Laurentin 1952–1953, vol. 1, 655–656 for more examples, including Claudel on p. 656, n. 22).
74 De Lubac 1986 (1953), 338–339.
75 De Lubac 1986 (1953), 339, notes 128, 129.
76 Gougaud 1925, 65–73; index entry "Samedi (dévotion du)," in Du Manoir, ed. 1949–1971, vol. 8, 183; Congar 1950; Rosso 1986; Buono 1997.
77 Lefebvre 1956, 1043–1049.

5 Class Considerations

Mary, Voluntary "Slavewoman of the Lord"

One particularly important categorization of Mary taken from the Hebrew Bible has to do with her socioeconomic origin. It is generally acknowledged that Mary came from that class of lowly and oppressed people of Israel who had long been deprived of economic necessities and social justice and who, in biblical Hebrew, are called *'anawim*. Mary's perceived predecessor Hannah, for example, was one of these. Hannah had sung out words to the effect that the Lord "makes poor and makes rich; he brings low, he also exalts. He raises up the poor from the dust; he lifts the needy from the ash heap, to make them sit with princes and inherit a seat of honor" (1 Samuel 2:7–8). Unlike, say, the Ark of the Covenant or the Burning Bush, there is nothing uniquely Jewish about this category of traditionally poor and downtrodden people. Therefore, no supersessionist meaning need be read into the words of the famous Magnificat, where Mary declares that God her Savior "has looked with favor" on her "lowliness," and that the "Mighty One" has, among other things, "brought down the powerful from their thrones, and lifted up the lowly; he has filled the hungry with good things, and sent the rich away empty" (Luke 1:48, 52–53).[1] Mary is like Hannah here, but Mary does not supersede Hannah; she is not a new and better Hannah. Mary simply rejoices in a fashion appropriate to her own Jewish cultural context, and yet that context will be recognizable to anyone at the bottom (or who has done time at the bottom) of the socioeconomic ladder anywhere.

Mary is one of the *'anawim*. But, although she is at home among the poor and oppressed of Israel, it has to be said that her reaction to God's plan is rather classy. She gives a careful and considered response to Luke's announcing angel.[2] Perhaps there is even some deliberate hesitation and delay on her part – famously exaggerated in a homily by Bernard of Clairvaux (1090–1153): "The angel is waiting for your reply"; "Give your answer quickly, my Virgin"; "Only say the word and receive the Word: give your's and conceive God's"; "Why do you delay?" – and so on.[3] It is only when the angel informs Mary that her hitherto barren relative, the aging Elizabeth, has recently conceived that she understands that a miracle has been reported to her, for the angel ends by saying, "nothing will be impossible with God" (1:36–37.)

That breaks the logjam. Mary immediately consents,[4] saying to the angel: "Here am I, the slavewoman of the Lord [*Idou hē doulē kuriou*]; let it be with me according to your word" (1:38). Ten verses later, in the Magnificat (1:48), Mary again identifies herself as the Lord's "slavewoman": "for he has looked with favor on the lowliness of his slavewoman [*epi tēn tapeinōsin tēs doulēs autou*]." Here I have altered the NRSV translation of both instances of *doulē* to read "slavewoman" – the felicitous translation offered by Marianne Sawicki – as "[female] slave" is the literal meaning of the Greek word.[5]

Twice, then, Mary refers to herself as a slavewoman in the opening chapter of Luke's gospel. This does not mean that Mary has literally become a slavewoman. Rather, Mary uses the word "slavewoman" metaphorically, as an expression of her affirmative submission to the divine plan that the angel presented to her. There is no scriptural indication that Mary was *literally* anyone's "slavewoman." She was a free woman, albeit poor, and theoretically she was free to decline so bizarre a proposition from the Lucan angel (or at least she could have declined, until theologians came along and declared that Mary was "predestined from eternity" to be the mother of Christ[6] – it being understood that a person's freedom of choice and that person's predestination to make one specific choice cannot be reconciled).

Like his mother Mary, Christ was also a volunteer slave, for he "emptied himself" of his divinity and arrived on earth in the *form* of a slave (*morphēn doulou*), as Paul writes in Philippians (2:7).[7] Like Mary when she was confronted with making a choice by the announcing angel, Christ, when agonizing in Gethsemane, had to make a choice whether or not to accept the will of God the Father (*abba*) that he martyr himself.[8] Both Mary and her son are represented in canonical scripture as free, adult personal agents when they made decisions that changed history. Both were in a position to say *no* – Mary at Luke 1:38, Jesus at Mark 14:36 (cf. Luke 22:42 ff.; Matthew 26:39 ff.). But they each submitted, or, as Josef Ratzinger writes, there was "a unison of these Yesses."[9] Mary's "Yes," moreover, was primary, for it came first, and there would have been no Jesus to say "Yes" in Gethsemane without it[10] (unless both "Yesses" were predestined, in which case temporal sequence ought to have been irrelevant).

No Feminist, No Liberationist

Mary's low social station – but not necessarily her submissiveness – has made her popular among many Christians on the left to this day. Consider, for example, the appeal of Mary to poor and vulnerable women. Elizabeth A. Johnson writes that, "In Latin America, women in situations of poverty and violence pioneer the insight that Maria was like them, a poor woman of the people." This gendered parallel is striking:

> A villager who lived her trust in God in the midst of hard daily labor, she [Mary] knows their struggle and their pain. A widow who survived the violent public execution of her son, she is a companion on women's shared Calvary. As one lilting hymn sings, "she is our *compañera*." And it is to *this* woman that God has done great things [Luke 1:49]. Honoring her puts one in solidarity with God's own option for the poor,[11] and with the poorest of the poor, colonialized women in violent situations, most of all.[12]

Certainly, there is comfort to be gained from such solidarity. But, it comes at a price. As it entails belief, it does *not* entail any resistance or protest against the exploitative socioeconomic situation in which poor Latinas find themselves. Mary herself, after all, accepted her lot. As we have seen, she regarded herself as a "slavewoman" of the male Lord, who, she proclaims, "has looked with favor on the lowliness of his slavewoman" (Luke 1:48). Because the "Mighty One" did "great things" for her, Mary could predict that, "from now on all generations will call me blessed" (1:49). Clearly, this woman was no feminist. In what was the longest single utterance by any woman in the entire New Testament (Luke 1:46–55), Mary was hiding behind the skirts of her patron, the Lord God.

Johnson acknowledges the fact that "devotion to Mary has not liberated Hispanic women from sexual or economic oppression."[13] If anything, devotion to Mary has only fostered a stance of *marianismo*, which Johnson calls "the flip side of men's *machismo*.[14] According to Evelyn P. Stevens, *marianismo* is "the cult of feminine spiritual superiority, which teaches that women are semi-divine, morally superior to and spiritually stronger than men."[15] Latin American women who live in accordance with this cult may appear to be strong women, and may themselves feel empowered by their *marianismo*. But, spiritual strength has its drawbacks. It is based on humility, a self-sacrificing attitude, submissiveness to men, and other features that give at least the impression that these women are enslaved to their men ("husbands, sons, fathers, brothers," writes Stevens).[16]

There is also the appeal of Mary to poor and oppressed people generally, not only to poor and oppressed women. For example, Mary has enjoyed considerable popularity among both the men and the women who constitute the oppressed poor majorities in Latin American countries. Mary's relevance to such people has been proclaimed by practitioners of so-called *liberation theology* – for example, Franciscan priest Leonardo Boff:

> We in Latin America live a life characterized by injustice and oppression. The vast majority of our sisters and brothers are affected by it. The cries of our poverty-stricken people rise to the heart of our God, pleading for dignity, basic human rights, equal societal relationships, and the means for the most effective possible societal participation on

> the part of all. A tiny elite, possessed of a monopoly over the power, knowledge, and wealth needed to dictate the universal destiny, are in a position to confiscate the lives of whole peoples and appropriate them for their own sole advantage. They institutionalize Christianity itself, with all its symbols and concepts, and reduce it to the service of their selfish cause.[17]

Boff goes on to characterize the exploitation of the poor as "internal colonialism" and to mock the "wicked, iniquitous 'progress,' built on the blood of millions of brothers and sisters." What happens in Latin America is "contrary to God's plan for history." Activists there rightly call for "liberation," and this is where "Mary's prophetic hymn" – the Magnificat – becomes relevant:

> Mary does not simply open her ears to the message of the Most High. She has one ear open completely to God, and the other open completely to the cries of the oppressed Jewish people. She is the woman of true fidelity, a fidelity equal to that of all of the great prophets. All prophets, along with their fidelity to God, demonstrate an equal fidelity to an afflicted people. Loyalty to the one is loyalty to the other. Anyone deaf to the cries of the poor is also mute before God. But Mary raises her voice and speaks out. She praises God, and she intercedes for the people. She praises God's mercy, and begs his liberation of the lowly and the starving.[18]

Here, however, Boff oversteps scriptural limits. Mary does indeed praise God in her Magnificat, but it is not true that she "intercedes for the people," nor is it true that Mary "begs" God's "liberation of the lowly and the starving." Boff cannot cite verses in the Magnificat (or anywhere else in the infancy narratives) to support these claims.

Having studied the larger Lucan text of which the Magnificat is a part, mariologist Michael O'Carroll admits that "Luke's infancy narrative does not refer explicitly to any intercession by Mary."[19] Indeed, why would a young peasant woman, who has just been handed the unheard-of opportunity to give birth to the "Son of God," seek additional favors for her own class of people, the poor and downtrodden of Israel? It was one thing for Mary to have praised God's justice and mercy and to have acknowledged God's gracious inclination to "lift up" the lowly – herself included. It would have been quite another thing for Mary explicitly to request further, wider assistance from God.

Mary makes no explicit intercession with her son in the synoptics. In the infancy narratives, she is mostly preoccupied with matters relating to her child. After the child grows up, there is very little interaction with him. In John's gospel, however, Mary does make a statement to her now adult son which is an implicit request for a miracle:

> There was a wedding in Cana of Galilee, and the mother of Jesus was there. Jesus and his disciples had also been invited to the wedding. When the wine gave out, the mother of Jesus said to him, "They have no wine." And Jesus said to her, "Woman, what concern is that to you and to me? My hour has not yet come." His mother said to the servants, "Do whatever he tells you."
>
> (John 2:1–5)

At Jesus's command, the servants fill six large stone jars with water. The chief steward then tastes the water and discovers that it is wine. A miracle has been performed by Mary's son. Despite his harsh words to his mother, she has persisted with her request, and the request has been granted. It appears that Mary has effectively interceded with her son on behalf of the poor peasant family in Cana who had arranged the wedding. Elizabeth A. Johnson writes:

> Feminist reflection espies here the kind of woman whose movements typically run counter to the expectations of idealized femininity. Far from silent, she speaks; far from passive, she acts; far from receptive to the orders of the male, she goes counter to his wishes, finally bringing him along with her; far from yielding to a grievous situation, she takes charge of it, organizing matters to bring about benefit to those in need, including herself.[20]

I doubt that Mary can be viewed as an intercessor (much less a feminist) on the basis of this one explicit intercession she made with her son in the entire New Testament. In John's gospel, in particular, the figure of Mary is barely visible in the long shadow of her narcissistically preoccupied son.

Imagining Mary's Intercession on Behalf of the Poor and the Oppressed

On the other hand, the tenuous biblical evidence has hardly precluded *belief* in Mary's ability effectively to intercede with her divine son, for mariophiles have been praying to Mary for many centuries. Here, an axiom applies: *Lex orandi, lex credendi* ("The law of prayer is the law of belief").[21] The practical "reality" of Mary's intercessory power among those who pray to her has to be respected by anyone who would understand the mariophile mind.

There have been countless occasions in the history of Christianity where Mary has been thought to intercede on behalf of Christians. At least since the prayer *Sub tuum praesidium* (an early Greek version of which goes back to the third or fourth century, and which is recited in the *Little Office of the Blessed Virgin Mary* to this day), intercession has been an ingredient of the cult of Mary. The Latin version is ordinarily translated as follows:

> We fly to thy patronage, O holy Mother of God, despise not our petitions in our necessities, but deliver us from all danger, O ever glorious and blessed Virgin.[22]

The best known prayer to Mary today is of course the "Hail Mary" (*Ave Maria*), with its concluding request for her intercession:

> Holy Mary,
> mother of God,
> pray for us sinners,
> Now and at the hour of our death.
> Amen.[23]

Liberation theologian Boff probably had the Roman Catholic predisposition to pray to Mary – not scripture – in mind when he wrote that Mary "intercedes for the people," or that Mary "begs his [God's] liberation of the lowly and the starving." He might have been thinking about certain patristic writings, theological tracts, liturgical practices, devotional traditions, visual images, conciliar statements, and so on,[24] all of which have contributed to the idea that Mary intercedes with God her son on behalf of Christians.

In many Christian cultures, Mary has long been represented as an intercessor for the poor and the oppressed. This is evident, for example, in such medieval Latin epithets for Mary as *egentium victuaria* (sustenance of the needy), *mater pauperum* (mother of the poor), *pauperum refugium* (refuge of the poor), *solatium pauperum* (comfort of the poor), *salus humilium* (deliverance of the lowly), *spes gentis egentis* (hope of needy people), and so on.[25] Among Mary's many titles in German is *Mutter der Armen* (Mother of the Poor).[26] French has *Vierge des Pauvres* (Virgin of the Poor), the designation Mary gave for herself when she appeared to the girl Mariette Béco in 1933 at what is now a marian shrine in Banneux (Belgium),[27] and a designation that has been rendered in Polish as *Matka Boża Ubogich* (Mother of God of the poor ones).[28] In Spanish, there is *Maria Madre des los Pobres* (Maria, Mother of the Poor) – as in the name of a church congregation on the outskirts of San Salvador, in El Salvador.[29]

In some languages, there may be no generally known title or epithet that marks Mary as being someone to whom the poor and the needy can turn. But, in traditional Christian contexts, other relevant titles or epithets will always be available, and will suffice. For example, the Russian archpriest Viacheslav Vinnikov characterizes those who come to pray specifically to the icon *Vsekh skorbiashchikh Radost'* (Joy of All Who Sorrow) as follows:

> But we have consolation in our sorrows, illnesses, and disasters, for She [Mary, the Joy of All Who Sorrow] stands in the midst of those who sorrow, and all of them – the cold, the hungry, the ill-clad, the

> barefoot, and the naked – gather round Her like little children . . . If She is with us, with those who sorrow and who are unfortunate, then hope and faith that we will be helped enters into our hearts.[30]

Here, it is clear that the epithet "All Who Sorrow" includes the sorrowing poor and needy, and it is clear that a sympathetic Mary provides comfort to them.

Similarly, Italian immigrants who lived in the poor urban neighborhood of Harlem in New York City venerated a sympathetic Mary in the form of the *Madonna del Carmine* (Our Lady of Mount Carmel) on 115th Street. They brought their troubles to her – including their poverty or their unemployment. Robert A. Orsi writes that, "the Madonna was . . . asked to heal the inner hurts associated with work, such as the anxiety of unemployment and the preoccupations of poverty." Orsi relates a specific incident:

> In 1946, a woman wrote in to the church: "Two months ago my husband was laid off after having worked in the same place for nine years. I was so worried I didn't know what to do." Turning to the Madonna in her distress, she made a novena and happily she was able to report that her husband got his job back.[31]

From this woman's viewpoint, her special devotion to the Madonna in the form of a novena pulled her husband (and probably other family members) from the brink of poverty.

Like Mother, Like Son

Gustavo Gutiérrez is a liberation theologian who approaches the emotionally charged issue of poverty while paying hardly any attention to Mary. How is this possible? Gutiérrez does adduce a mass of scriptural evidence to support his contention that, "in the Bible poverty is a scandalous condition inimical to human dignity and therefore contrary to the will of God."[32] The prophets, for example, condemned poverty, as well as those who keep the poor in poverty and those who create a new poor. Concrete measures are prescribed (especially in the books of Exodus, Deuteronomy, and Leviticus) for preventing poverty and helping those who are poor, exploited, and enslaved. Gutiérrez observes that, "when just treatment is asked for the poor, the slaves, and the aliens, it is recalled that Israel also was alien and enslaved in Egypt."[33]

The picture is complicated, however, by a "second line of thinking," that is, a second form of poverty, which theologians term "spiritual poverty." Whereas literal, material poverty is an evil to be combatted, "spiritual poverty" is a state of mind, "a precondition for approaching God." Gutiérrez quotes the Lord speaking in Isaiah (66:2), translated here as: "The man I look to is a man down-trodden and distressed, one who reveres my words." He quotes Zephaniah as well, for example, "Seek the Lord, all in the land who live humbly by its laws, seek righteousness, seek a humble heart" (2:3). Matthew's version of the first beatitude also fits here: "Blessed are the poor in spirit [*hoi ptōchoi tō pneumati*], for theirs is the kingdom of heaven" (5:3). According to Guttiérrez, "The poverty which is called 'blessed' in Matt[hew] . . . is spiritual poverty as understood since the time of Zephaniah: to be totally at the disposition of the Lord."[34]

As for Luke's simpler version of the first beatitude, "Blessed are you who are poor [*hoi ptōchoi*], for yours is the kingdom of God" (6:20), Gutiérrez grants that the poverty in this version is real, but insists that Christ is not really preaching resignation to such poverty, for that "would lead to the canonization of a social class,"[35] namely, the poor. Instead, Gutiérrez believes that Christ is speaking about the *onset* of the kingdom of God. The kingdom has already begun: "the elimination of the exploitation and poverty that prevent the poor from becoming fully human has begun."[36] Just when it was supposed to finish, if ever, is not made clear.[37] More important, it is not clear why Jesus is not just saying what he appears to be saying – namely, that the poor are "blessed" as they are – a reading that is consistent with his preaching and his practice of moral masochism elsewhere in the gospels.[38]

What does all this have to do with Mary? First of all, the Mary of the Magnificat is Luke's Mary, not Matthew's. Indeed, no gospel but Luke's has anything like the Magnificat. That makes it all the more obvious that Mary, when referring to the lowly (*tapeinous*) who are lifted up, means those who are living in a state of material poverty. This is the poverty of Luke's first beatitude, the grinding poverty that Gutiérrez grapples with in constructing his liberation theology.

Second, Gutiérrez does devote one paragraph to the Magnificat, reading its thanksgiving and joy in liberationist terms, and concluding:

> The future of history belongs to the poor and exploited. True liberation will be the work of the oppressed themselves: in them, the Lord saves history. The spirituality of liberation will have as its basis the spirituality of the *anawim*.[39]

Unfortunately, Mary is not mentioned by name in Gutiérrez's brief reading of the Magnificat. Gutiérrez is interested in classes of people, not individual people. Although he thinks that the Magnificat expresses the "spirituality of liberation,"[40] he does not follow up on what actually became of Mary. Had he done so, he would have found that Luke's Mary is no more "lifted up" from her lowly social station by the promise she received from the announcing angel than are Luke's "poor" generally, who *already* possess "the kingdom of God" by virtue of their very poverty. Once again, the Lucan beatitude is: "Blessed are you who are poor, for yours is the kingdom of God" (6:20).[41]

Further on in Luke, Jesus says: "The kingdom of God is not coming with things that can be observed; nor will they say, 'Look, here it is!' or

'There it is!' For, in fact, the kingdom of God is among you [*entos humōn*]" (17:20–21). In other words, "you" already have it, and "you" have no need to be liberated from your poverty and external oppression in order to have it. As Donald Capps comments, "Jesus' 'kingdom of God' . . . has no location and occurs without social reformist activities and blueprints."[42]

The son's "kingdom of God," like the mother's Magnificat, is devoid of liberationist meaning. Like mother, like son. Had Mary and Jesus ever engaged in a real conversation in the New Testament (they do not), there would have been at least this one topic for them to agree on. She was "slavewoman of the Lord," whereas he was the Lord himself. But, he had also emptied himself of his divine Lordship, taking the form of a "slave," as noted above. Hence, mother and son were both metaphorically enslaved, but neither expressed any real resistance on behalf of the poor and the oppressed, which such a metaphor might suggest today.

*

In scripture, Mary characterized herself as "slavewoman of the Lord" at the annunciation. These words hardly make Mary a feminist, nor do any of her actions in the New Testament. Nor would it be right to say that Mary agitated on behalf of the poor of Israel, despite her Magnificat, and despite the claims of some liberation theologians. Like her son, Mary was poor, but, also like her son, she did not resist the socioeconomic exploitation of poor peasants. In modern times, one of Mary's titles is "Mother of the Poor," but occasional requests by Mary that her divine son intervene on behalf of poor individuals do not constitute a rejection of the blessedness of being poor.

Notes

1 On the generally acknowledged indebtedness of the Magnificat to passages about the *'anawim* of Israel in the Hebrew Bible (including Hannah's song quoted here), see: Gelin 1964 (1953), 91–98; Laurentin 1991 (1968), 19–20; Gutiérrez 1988 (1971), 120, 162–173; Boff 1989 (1979), 194–201; Brown et al. 1978, 141–143; Brown 1993 (1977), 357–365, 647–650; Gebara and Bingemer 1989 (1987),167–171; Sawicki 1994, 95–118; Johnson 2003, 263–271.

2 Boss (2007a, 159) speaks of the "contingency of Mary's response."

3 Bernard of Clairvaux and Amadeus of Lausanne 1979, 53, 54.

4 See the entry (with bibliography) "Consent, Mary's, at the Annunciation" in: O'Carroll 2000 (1982), 106–107.

5 See: Sawicki 1994, 95–118, especially the brilliant hypothesis (p. 116) that an interested party made the legal argument that "Mary in prayerful petition invoked her rights as God's slavewoman under Exod. 21:10 as interpreted in 1 Sam. 1:11." Cf. also: Miller ed. 1994, 119; Funk and the Jesus Seminar 1998, 515, 517; Gaventa 2004, 24; Barnstone 2009, 331. The Arndt/Gingrich translation and adaptation of Bauer's standard dictionary offers "female slave, bondmaid" as the correct English translation for *doulē*, and cites one of the very phrases in

question here (from Luke 1:38). Under the corresponding entry for a generic slave (*doulos*) it is observed that "'servant' for 'slave' is largely confined to Biblical transl[ation]" (Bauer 1957 [1952], 204). Why this should be (or once was) so in English would be a worthy topic of investigation. It is worth noting that for Luke 1:38 the Vulgate offers *ancilla Domini*, and a check of some Bibles in other languages yields the following: French (La Ligue Biblique): *la servante du Seigneur*; Spanish (Reina Valera Revisada): *la sierva del Señor*; German (Gute Nachricht, literal rendition): *die Sklavin des Herrn*; and Russian (Synodal): *Raba Gospodnia*. Obviously, opinion is divided on whether or not to tone down the literal meaning of the Greek original.

6 Saint Augustine wrote that, when Christ recognized his mother at the foot of the cross, "he had always known her. Even before he was born of her, he knew his mother in her predestination. Before he, as God, created her from whom he would be created as man, he knew his mother" (Gambero 1999 [1991], 218–219). In one of his homilies on the dormition, John of Damascus apostrophized Mary with the words, "Hail, you who were predestined to be Mother of God!" (John of Damascus 1998c, 237). For an overview, see the entry "Predestination, Mary's" in: O'Carroll 2000 (1982), 291. For papal statements, see the analytical index entry "Predestination of the Mother of God" in: *Papal Teachings: Our Lady* 1961, 506–507; cf. Denzinger 2012, 573 (no. 2800), 809 (no. 3902). For Vatican II, see *Lumen Gentium*, pars. 56, 61, in: Tanner 1990, vol. 2, 893, 895. The most recent edition of the *Catechism of the Catholic Church* (2000 [1997], nos. 488–489) continues to teach Mary's predestination (specifically in conjunction with her "free cooperation").

7 Cf. Buby 1994–1996, vol. 1, 22.

8 See especially the section titled "The Annunciation and the Agony" in: Schaberg 2006 (1987), 120–122. Schaberg is primarily concerned with the illegitimacy of Jesus and rejects any idea of a suicidal element in Christ's death. But, her exploration of parallels between the annunciation and the agony in the garden is fruitful.

9 Ratzinger and von Balthasar 2005 (1997), 50. Ratzinger (49, following the lead of Pope John Paul II in section 13 of *Redemptoris Mater*) prefers to locate Christ's "Yes" in Hebrews 10:5–9, rather than in any specific gospel text. See: *Mary in the Church* 2003, 103; cf. also Bouyer 1965 (1957), 163; Gaventa 2002, 54.

10 Cf. von Balthasar in Ratzinger and von Balthasar 2005 (1997), 119.

11 On the tradition of God's preference or option for the poor – which has gained new visibility during the current pontificate of Francis – see, for example: Gutiérrez 1988 (1971), xxv–xxviii; the encyclical *Redemptoris Mater* (37.3–37.4) of Pope John Paul II 2001 (1996), p. 349.

12 Johnson 2003, 13.

13 Johnson 2003, 14.

14 Johnson 2003, 10.

15 Stevens 1973, 91.

16 Stevens 1973, 95. Latinas who would prefer to escape this metaphorical servitude are given an opportunity in the form of a how-to manual of psychotherapy titled *The Maria Paradox*, by Rosa Maria Gil and Carmen Inoa Vazquez (1996).

17 Boff 1989 (1979), 191.

18 Boff 1989 (1979), 191–192.

19 O'Carroll 2000 (1982), 186. Of course, O'Carroll does acknowledge the widespread and heterogeneous beliefs concerning Mary's intercessory power, including the belief that Mary implicitly intercedes here: "In the *Magnificat* . . . she typifies Israel in prayer, and Israel in prayer was given to intercession."

20 Johnson 2003, 289–290.
21 Bretzke 2013, 126–127.
22 O'Carroll 2000 (1982), 336; Keller, ed. 2013, 68, 69.
23 Ayo 1994, 210.
24 For an overview, see the entries "Advocate" and "Intercession, Mary's" in O'Carroll 2000 (1982), 5–6, 186–189, with extensive references. See also: Rancour-Laferriere 2005, 256–285; de Visscher 2007, 185–186; Price 2007, 69–72; Shoemaker 2007, 130–137. That Boff is aware of some of the scholarly research on marian intercession is evident from the notes to Chapter 12 of his book (1989 [1979], 272–274), as well as from the scholarly apparatus of his book on the *Ave Maria* (Boff 1982).
25 See these entries in the *Mariologisches Glossarium* of Meersseman 1958–1960, vol. 2, 303, 331, 345, 362, 370.
26 Beinert and Petri, eds. 1996–1997, index, vol. 2, 655.
27 Laurentin and Sbalchiero, eds. 2007, 113.
28 Thanks to a posting to the SEELANGS list by Jan Zielinski, November 11, 2014.
29 McElvaney 1998, 31.
30 Vinnikov 2000, 191; cf. Rancour-Laferriere 2005, 296.
31 Orsi 2010 (1985), 201–202.
32 Gutiérrez 1988 (1971), 165.
33 Gutiérrez 1988 (1971), 165–168 (here, 168).
34 Gutiérrez 1988 (1971), 169.
35 Gutiérrez 1988 (1971), 170.
36 Gutiérrez 1988 (1971), 171.
37 Having proposed two meanings of poverty in the Bible, Gutiérrez lays them aside and discusses his own ideas of "solidarity" and "protest" as bases upon which the modern church should preach its own "spiritual poverty" (171–173).
38 Rancour-Laferriere 2011, 21–85.
39 Gutiérrez 1988 (1971), 120.
40 Gutiérrez 1988 (1971), 120.
41 Compare what Montfort says about Matthew's version (5:3) of the same beatitude: "Our Lord does not merely promise the kingdom of heaven . . . but states that, because you are poor in spirit, you possess it now." See: De Montfort 1966, 717, as translated in De Montfort 1988, 432.
42 Capps 2000, 233. Capps argues that the historical Jesus "was neither an apocalypticist nor a social reformer but a peasant-style utopian without a social agenda"; Jesus belonged to a "prophetic tradition" of utopianists whose views were rooted in "a deep sense of fatalism as far as prospects for social reform are concerned" (Capps 2002a, 391, 441; for detailed analysis of the "utopian-melancholic personality" of Jesus, see: Capps 2000, 219–250). See also: Crossan 1994, 54–74 (proposes that the "present or sapiential Kingdom of God" was understood by the peasants Jesus spoke to as "a kingdom of nuisances and nobodies"); Vermes 2003 (1983), 33–35 (notes the similarity of the kingdom to the simple peasant society of Galilee, as well as the significant absence of thrones, courtiers, choirs, and other royal ingredients – even a king! – in the kingdom preached by Jesus the Jew); Dodd 1961 (argues that the kingdom preached by Jesus within history already constituted a realized eschatology); Miegge 1955, 34 (in a comparison of the Magnificat and the Beatitudes in Luke, asserts that "the true Church in any age" seeks "no other greatness than its need, its hunger and thirst").

6 The Eucharist as Maternalized Son of Mary

The Trees in the Garden of Eden

Arboreal imagery is part of an old and venerable tradition in the history of Christianity. Thomas Aquinas (d. 1274) characterized the crucifixion of Jesus as:

> especially suitable in order to atone for the sin of our first parent, which was the plucking of the apple from the forbidden tree [*pomum ligni vetiti*] against God's command. And so, to atone for that sin, it was fitting that Christ should suffer by being fastened to a tree [*ligno affigi*], as if restoring what Adam had purloined.[1]

Here, Aquinas was making Christ on the "tree" of the cross equivalent (by contrast) to an edible fruit on the "forbidden tree" in the Garden of Eden.

Various early Christian sources, including early church Fathers – Melito of Sardis, Justin Martyr, Irenaeus of Lyons, Clement of Alexandria, and Tertullian – had characterized the Roman cross upon which Jesus was executed as a "tree" (Greek *xulon*, Latin *lignum*).[2] St. Paul, paraphrasing Deuteronomy (21:23), referred to the cross of Christ as a "tree": "Christ redeemed us from the curse of the law by becoming a curse for us – for it is written, 'Cursed is everyone who hangs on a tree [*epi xulou*]'" (Galatians 3:13). Visual images of the crucifixion in which the cross is formed from the fork of a tree (*Astkreuz*), or has had its branches pruned from it, or sprouts flowers, leaves, or fruit would become rather common in the late-medieval West.[3]

In the Garden of Eden (Paradise) stood two trees that are named, and which would eventually attain prefigurative potential for Christians. The first is the "tree of life" (Genesis 2:9, 3:22). It appears to have been interpreted by some of the early church Fathers as a prefiguration of the "tree" upon which Christ died. For example, in Justin Martyr's *Dialogue with Trypho* (opening of ch. 86), we read:

> Learn that He who, as it is said in the Scriptures will come again in glory, after His crucifixion possessed a symbol of the tree of Life [*sumbolon tou xulou tēs zōēs*], which is said was planted in Paradise and (a symbol) of what happened to all the righteous.[4]

Clement of Alexandria, praising the simplicity of barbarians and nomads who supposedly did not live lives of luxury, is reminded of our vocation to imitate the naked Jesus carrying his cross: "Such the Lord calls us to be – naked of finery, naked of vanity, wrenched from our sins, bearing only the wood [tree] of life [*epiferomenos to xulon tēs zōēs*], aiming only at salvation."[5]

The second named tree in the Garden of Eden is, of course, "the tree of the knowledge of good and evil" (Genesis 2:9). It too has been understood as a prefiguration of the "tree" of the cross (technically speaking, it, like the tree of life, has been interpreted as the type for its antitype, the cross). Thus, when Eve and Adam tasted the forbidden fruit of the tree of the knowledge of good and evil, they committed an act of disobedience that condemned humankind to lives of misery ending in death (3:1–19), but Christ's submission to death on the tree of the cross supposedly saved us from that earlier condemnation. In *Against Heresies* (Book V, ch. 19), Irenaeus of Lyons refers to the "disobedience which had occurred in connection with a tree" – that is, the forbidden tree of the knowledge of good and evil – and asserts that this disobedience was "recapitulated" by Christ's obedience "upon a tree" (Latin, *in ligno*; Greek, *en tō xulō*). Such "recapitulation" (Latin, *recapitulatio*; Greek, *anakefalaiōsis*) did away with the deleterious effects of the original "disobedience." Christ's mother Mary also participated in the "recapitulation,"[6] for Irenaeus asserts that, whereas Eve "did disobey God" in the garden of Eden, Mary "was persuaded to be obedient to God," presumably at the annunciation: "And thus, as the human race fell into bondage to death by means of a virgin [Eve], so is it rescued by a virgin [Mary]; virginal disobedience having been balanced in the opposite scale by virginal obedience."[7]

With the passage of centuries, less care would be taken in distinguishing between the two named trees in the garden of Eden, as Christian theologians, preachers, poets, artists, and others represented the "tree" of the cross upon which Christ submitted himself to death.[8] As for Christ's mother, she too would often be characterized as some kind of "tree."

For example, according to Louis-Marie Grignion de Montfort, "Jesus is the fruit and product of Mary wherever he is present, be it in heaven, on earth, in our tabernacles or in our hearts. She alone is the *tree of life* and Jesus alone is the fruit of that tree."[9] In the early eighteenth century, Montfort was apparently being true to certain devotional ideas about an "arboreal" Mary already in existence, especially in medieval hymnography, as will be seen below. As for other genres, we find that Jean Gerson (1363–1429), in an Easter sermon, represents Mary as a fruit tree bearing the fruit of Christ: "we must also greatly praise the tree [*l'arbre*], it is the Virgin Mary, who has born this fruit by which we have been refreshed."[10] Bernard of Clairvaux

(1090–1153) preached an Advent sermon in which he apostrophized the virgin mother of God with the words, "O true tree of life [*vere lignum vitae*], the only one who was worthy of bearing the fruit of our salvation!"[11] In an eighth-century oration on the nativity of Mary attributed to John of Damascus, Mary is "like a tree of life [*hōs xulon zōēs*], which gave its fruit at the time predetermined by God, [fruit which is] the incarnate God, the eternal life of all things."[12] At least twice in Latin translations of works attributed to Ephrem the Syrian, *lignum vitae* is a title of Mary.[13]

There have also been arboreal representations of Mary in the visual arts. For example, a German woodcut titled *Arbor Virginis* from about 1470 shows Mary in an abbreviated genealogy, springing from her apocryphal parents Joachim and Anna below, and with her son Jesus crucified as a child upon the continuation of the tree-like vine emerging upward from her breast.[14] A painting titled "Dream of the Virgin" by Simone dei Crocefissi (d. 1399) shows Mary lying asleep on her back as a tree emerges upward from her lower chest area (this marian tree has stylized branches, leaves, as well as the crucified Christ).[15] Nicole Fallon describes a wall painting from about 1200 at Chapelle du Liget, Chemillé-sur-Indrois, which shows "a towering figure of Mary crowned by curving fronds of foliage, herself the tree from which the nimbus-crowned Christ Child springs, almost like a fruit."[16]

When viewing an image that seemed to be representing Mary as a tree (or when a part of her was represented as a tree), one was free to respond to either Mary's life-giving features (such as the upward growth of the trunk from within her body), or her death-dealing features (such as the death of her son high in the tree) – or both. But, when an arboreal *title* was applied to Mary, and when that title was not a specific kind of tree ("Olive Tree," "Cedar of Lebanon," "Cypress," "Plane Tree," "Palm," etc.), then that title was usually Tree of Life. I am not aware of the application of other standard arboreal titles – such as Tree of the Knowledge of Good and Evil, Tree of the Cross, or Tree of Death – to Mary. These titles all existed, but they would have been nonsensical (or possibly offensive) had they been applied to Mary.[17]

Besides, ever since Irenaeus, Mary had been regarded as the antitype of Eve (the New Eve), for she set in motion the repair of the damage caused by Eve when the latter sinned, along with Adam, beneath the Tree of the Knowledge of Good and Evil. Better to exclude any hint of "evil" (sin) from the image of Mary, and therefore best simply to think of her as the wonderful Tree of *Life*, for it was she who brought forth a son who, as Paul writes, redeemed us from both sin *and* death (1 Corinthians 15:22; Romans 5–6). Or, as Irenaeus had put it in the passage quoted above, by her obedience Mary "rescued" humankind from "bondage to death." Does this not make Mary the Tree of Life?

Yes, perhaps, but there was a problem with this hypothetical idealization. It put Mary in the somewhat awkward position of competing with (or being compared with) her son's cross, which for many, since Justin, had also acquired the moniker Tree of Life. Not Mary, but her son's cross was literally wood made from a tree. It was precisely the son's – not the mother's – voluntary death on the wood/tree of the cross that returned life to humankind.

Two Referents for the Title "Tree of Life"

There was, then, what may be termed a double referent problem with regard to the notion Tree of Life, and the problem persisted in both theological writings and in devotional texts.

Consider, for example, two very different medieval theologians. The first is Amadeus of Lausanne (1110–1159) who, in a homily in praise of Mary, compares her to "the tree planted in the midst of paradise [*arbor plantata in medio paradisi*]." This can only be the Tree of Life, for it "brings forth the fruit of salvation, the fruit of glory, the fruit of life, and he who eats of it will live forever [*fructum refert salutarem, fructum gloriae, fructum vitae, de quo qui ederit, vivet in aeternum*]."[18] This is a eucharistic formulation which makes it clear that the "fruit" that Mary produces is edible. On the one hand, such wording of the formulation harkens back to God's affirmation that fallen Adam might take fruit "from the tree of *life*, and eat, and *live* forever" (Genesis 3:22; cf. 2:9). On the other hand, the formulation is also a clear reference to the words of Mary's son, "Those who eat my flesh and drink my blood have eternal *life*" (John 6:54; cf. Matthew 26:26–28; Luke 22:19–20; 1 Corinthians 10:16). Thus, according to Amadeus, those who partake of the sacrament of the eucharist will have consumed the fruit (Christ) brought forth by the Tree of Life (Mary).

The second theologian is the Franciscan Saint Bonaventure (d. 1274), who imagines that the tree in his treatise titled *Lignum Vitae* is not Mary, but the tree of the cross upon which Christ died, thereby restoring life to those who believed. The image of Christ as the already commonplace "fruit" upon which the faithful feed is there, of course, and is explicitly linked to the "fruit" of which Elizabeth spoke shortly after the annunciation: "This is the Fruit born of the virginal womb, and ripened on the tree of the cross [*in ligno crucis*] to delectable maturity."[19] With this rhetorical sleight of hand – or arbitrary extension of a metaphor – the "fruit" is *transferred* by Bonaventure from Mary to the cross. Only there on the cross, after the transfer has taken place, is the fruit "ripened." That is, only on the cross – after Christ the fruit of Mary's womb has undergone the necessary humiliation, suffering, and death – does this fruit become available for eucharistic consumption by the faithful. Not Mary, but the cross is the Tree of Life in Bonaventure's treatise of that title.

Here, it is worth noting that numerous images illustrating Bonaventure's treatise – including the famous *Albero della Vita* (ca.1310–1315) of Pacino di Bonaguida in the Florence Accademia, as well as Taddeo Gaddi's *Arbor Vitae* (ca.1360) in Museo del Opera di Santa Croce, also in Florence – show

Christ crucified on a complex, 12-branched *Lignum Vitae*. In the various related images, the Tree of Life is clearly the tree of the cross, and Christ is the central, largest, and most significant "fruit" hanging from this tree.[20]

In the thinking of Bonaventure, one can begin to see a resolution of the double referent problem, for he is willing to trace the "fruit" hanging on the *Lignum Vitae* back to Mary by recognizing that it was precisely this same "fruit" that was praised in Luke's infancy narrative: "blessed is the fruit of your womb" (Luke 1:42). For Bonaventure, the difference between Mary and her son's cross is merely a matter of where their shared "fruit" came to be when it "ripened." Bonaventure implies that Mary is the chronologically more *distal* Tree of Life, whereas the cross is the more *proximate* Tree of Life upon which the paradoxically life-giving death of Mary's son actually occurs.

Of course, according to canonical scripture, neither Mary nor the cross ever evinced any awareness of a special "arboreal" status. When she gave her consent at the annunciation, Mary certainly did not think of herself as the Tree of Life, nor could she imagine that her "fruit" would end up hanging on another Tree of Life, namely, the "tree" of the cross. As for the cross itself, being an inanimate wooden object, it did not imagine anything at all about such a "fruit." Nevertheless, by the time "arboreal" imagery was being created and elaborated upon – theologians, devotional writers, poets, composers, visual artists, and others had long since moved beyond scriptural literalism.

Medieval Western hymnography offers interesting views of both the distal and proximate variants of the Tree of Life. For example, G. G. Meersseman gathered a large corpus of Latin hymnographic texts related to the famous Greek hymn praising Mary, the Akathistos. Among them, we find instances of the expression *lignum vite* (or variants thereof) referring to Mary, often in conjunction with the tree's fruit (*fructus*, Mary's son), which was produced in distal fashion for the salvation of the world:

Ave, porta paradysi,
Lignum vite quod amisi.
Per te michi iam dulcescit
Et salutis fructus crescit.[21]
Hail, gate of paradise,
Tree of life which I sent away [lost].
Through you the fruit of salvation
Now becomes sweet and ripe for me . . .
Ave, virgo, vite lignum,
Quod perenni laude dignum,
Salvo voto, quod vovisti,
Mundo fructum attulisti.[22]
Hail, virgin, tree of life,
Worthy of everlasting praise,
With sound affirmation you made your vow

And brought forth your fruit to the world.
Ave, celi lux Maria,
Lignum vite es, o pia,
Fructum dans credentium. . . .[23]
Hail, Mary light of heaven,
You are the tree of life, O holy one,
Yielding the fruit of believers. . . .

Also worthy of note are the opening lines of a work by an anonymous twelfth-century Cistercian from Hennegau, as quoted by Joseph Szövérffy in his study of medieval Marian hymnody:

Stella maris, lumen orbis,
fidei praeconium,
Lignum vitae, quae portasti
fructum salutiferum. . . .[24]
Star of the sea, light of the world,
proclamation of the faith,
Tree of life, who bore
the salubrious fruit. . . .

Such effusions about the distal Tree of Life did not preclude the composition of poetic works about the more proximate Tree of Life. For example, Heribert of Rothenburg (d. 1042), in a hymn on the so-called finding of the cross (*De Inventione Sanctae Crucis*) – hails the cross as:

Signum salutis, salus in periculis,
Vitale lignum, vitam portans omnium.[25]
Sign of salvation, safety in dangers,
Tree of life [living tree], bearing the life of all.

In a hymn on the same theme, Peter Abelard (d. 1143) addresses the cross as follows:

Tu lignum vitae,
In qua rex ipse
Conscendit, palma,
Ut fructu tui
Letalis pomi
Restauret damna.[26]
You are the tree of life,
Which the king himself
Ascended, a palm tree,
In order that, by means of the fruit
Of your lethal tree,
Losses be restored.

From *Le prosaire de la Sainte-Chapelle* (ca.1250), we find a work titled *De Cruce* that begins:

> *Salve crux arbor vite preclara.*
> *Xpî [Christi] vexillum thronus et ara.*[27]
> Hail, cross, splendid tree of life,
> Banner, throne, and altar of Christ.

In a prayer to the holy cross by Ulrich Stöcklin von Rottach (d. 1443) may be found:

> *Ave, admirabilis*
> *Crux et lignum vitae,*
> *Satanae terribilis,*
> *Nobis vero mite. . . .*[28]
> Hail, admirable cross
> And tree of life,
> For Satan terrible,
> For us, in truth, gentle. . . .

From an anonymous hymn of 1518:

> *O crux, quae est lignum vitae,*
> *In qua corpus Christi mite*
> *Perpendit nimis squalidum. . . .*[29]
> O cross, being the tree of life
> Upon which the gentle body of Christ
> Weighs – in squalor most extreme. . . .

In all these poetic works, *lignum vitae* (or a variant of this term) clearly refers to the cross of Christ, whereas, in the group of poems quoted previously, the same term referred to Mary the mother of Christ.

Given these two separate but equally praiseworthy referents for the Tree of Life in so many works, it was inevitable that sooner or later both referents would be explicitly juxtaposed in the same poetic text.

Searching for the Tree of Life: An Anonymous Medieval Poem

Lignum vitae quaerimus[30] is a masterpiece of poetic contemplation on a theological theme. The author of the work is unknown, although a case can be made for including the work in the corpus of poems written by Chancellor Philip of Paris (d. 1236).[31]

The poem begins with some indeterminate number of lost souls wandering about in search of the Tree of Life. Apparently, these seekers wish to regain life as it existed in Paradise before the Fall:

Lignum vitae quaerimus,
Qui vitam amisimus
Fructu ligni vetiti,

Nec inventum noverit,
Qui fructum non viderit
Adhaerentem stipiti.

Fructus, per quem vivitur,
Pendet, sicut creditur,
Virginis ad ubera,

Et ad crucem iterum
Inter viros scelerum
Passus quinque vulnera.

Hic virgo puerpera,
Hic crux salutifera,
Ambae ligna mystica;

Haec hysopus humilis,
Illa cedrus nobilis,
Utraque vivifica.

We are searching for the tree of life,
We who have abandoned life
[By eating] the forbidden fruit.

Whoever has not seen the fruit
Attached to the tree –
Has also not recognized the tree.

The fruit which gives us life
Hangs, so it is believed,
At the breast of the virgin,

And again [it hangs] on the cross
Between [two] criminals,
Having suffered five wounds.

Here – the child-bearing virgin;
There – the health-bringing cross.
And both of the trees are mystical [in nature].

Here – a humble hyssop;
There – a noble cedar tree.
And both are life-giving.

Already, it is clear that there is not a single Tree of Life, but two. This may be deduced by following the commonplace "fruit" image, which, by the fourth stanza (at the latest), is obviously the "fruit" of Mary's womb – that is, Christ. With graphic concision, the poet places Christ first at the breast of Mary, then on the cross between criminals – thereby hinting that there is some mysterious relationship between these two positions.

In both positions, Christ remains the one "fruit of life," albeit attached to "two manifestations" of the Tree of Life,[32] namely, the "noble cedar" and the "humble hyssop." These names are not accidental, but derive from an ancient characterization of the breadth of Solomon's wisdom in what Christians know as 1 Kings: "He [Solomon] would speak of trees, from the *cedar* that is in the Lebanon to the *hyssop* that grows in the wall" (4:33) – in other words, from the noblest woody plant to the humblest.[33] Our poet has chosen both of Solomon's botanical extremes to represent the Tree of Life.

The borrowing of Solomon's two extremes bears a certain resemblance to Bonaventure's hint at a solution to the problem of two referents – distal and proximate – for the Tree of Life (above, p. 103). To regain life as it existed before the Fall is as much about finding Christ hanging at the breast of his humble mother, the humble hyssop, as about finding him hanging on the noble cedar, the noble, life-giving cross. What Mary does is nurse the future victim; what the cross does is finally kill that victim, so that he, the victim himself, is available in historical memory to "nurse" the faithful back to eternal life.

The Eucharist in the Poem

From a psychoanalytic viewpoint, we may say that the poet/hymnist is comparing and contrasting two different *oral* concerns – that is, matters pertaining to the human oral cavity.[34] The first is primitive and infantile. For the Christ child to be hanging at the mother's breast means that this child is applying its mouth to the mother's breast in order to obtain milk, a form of nutrition absolutely essential for the child's survival. Here, the poet is assisted by already existing oral associations with the biblical hyssop, such as the instruction by Moses to dip a hyssop branch into the blood of the (*edible*) passover lamb (Exodus 12:22), or the sponge full of sour wine held to the *mouth* of a dying Jesus by means of a hyssop branch (John 19:29).

The second oral concern is eucharistic. For the adult Christ to be hanging on the cross means that he himself will eventually be offered to the faithful for oral consumption – not literal consumption of his bloodied body on the cross, but consumption of the communion host and wine. These two physical substances together constitute an edible metaphor of Christ crucified.

Of course, not all medieval Christian believers understood the eucharistic bread and wine in a merely metaphorical sense. In fact, there was a growing belief that the bread and wine were quite literally the body and blood of Christ.[35] At the Fourth Lateran Council in 1215, it was declared that the body and blood of Jesus Christ are "truly contained in the sacrament of the altar under the forms of bread and wine, the bread and wine having been changed in substance, by God's power, into his body and blood [*transsubstantiatis pane in corpus et vino in sanguinem potestate divina*]."[36] The eucharist was moving from mere commemoration of Christ's original sacrifice *in ara crucis*[37] to a literal repetition, or a reenactment, of that sacrifice at the church altar.

It is true that the literalist understanding of the sacrament at the heart of the mass did not receive formal definition and doctrinal endorsement until the Council of Trent (in the session of September 17, 1562).[38] However, elements of such an understanding were already in place much earlier, and at a high theological level. For example, not long before he died in 1274, the influential Thomas Aquinas completed his *Summa theologiae*, where (Part 3, Question 75, Article 4) he defended the notion of transubstantiation as a divinely powered "conversion" in which "the whole substance of the bread is converted into the whole substance of Christ's body, and the whole substance of the wine into the whole substance of Christ's blood."[39] Aquinas also affirmed that Christ is actually sacrificed in the celebration of the sacrament of the eucharist, just as Christ had been sacrificed on the cross (*Summa theologiae*, Part 3, Question 83, Article 1).[40]

Corpus Christi – with its associated popular prayers, hymns, processions, dramatic productions, and iconography – was established by Pope Urban IV as a feast in 1264. Private visions, popular beliefs, and visual depictions of a bleeding communion host, or the Christ child appearing in the host, or a bleeding adult Christ on the eucharistic altar were also manifestations of eucharistic literal-mindedness well before Trent. Such phenomena were not necessarily supposed to prove the theological correctness of transubstantiation or illustrate the real presence of Christ in the sacrament of the eucharist. They just happened within a *Zeitgeist* preoccupied with the eucharist. A theologically unsophisticated individual – for example, a child – was perfectly capable of "seeing" another child (Christ) being eaten by a priest at the altar (or so we are told by folkloric texts relating this event).[41]

There is an enormous literature on the importance of the eucharist in medieval theological debates, liturgical and devotional practices, religious art and music, folklore of ordinary believers, anti-Jewish pogroms, and so on.[42] All of these phenomena involved a literalist understanding of the eucharist to a greater or lesser extent. Although the literalist view was the theologically correct view of the eucharist for Roman Catholics until at least the late twentieth century, there have been serious questions raised about eucharistic literalism, especially since Vatican II.[43]

For purposes of understanding *Lignum vitae quaerimus* (and other marian texts to be examined in this book), I will continue to assume that the eucharist can be no more than a metaphor. Indeed, to acknowledge the essentially metaphorical quality of the eucharist makes it easier to understand why the underlying eucharistic orality is not hostile, or aggressive, or sadistic in nature. After all, one partakes of the eucharistic bread and wine out of love for one's divine savior. One "eats" Christ, but one does not kill him in the process.

Even if the recipient (communicant) absolutely insists on the "real presence" of Christ in the bread and wine, still, the eating and the drinking of what one believes to be Christ's "real" body and blood do not actually constitute an act of aggression. To receive holy communion is to express a profound love of the God one believes in, and to expect profoundest love in return. The proof of this is that the victim (the "host," from Latin *hostia*, "victim" or "sacrifice")[44] always comes back for more. Indeed, having received holy communion once, one is free to receive it again every day for the rest of one's life.

Lignum vitae quaerimus bears witness to the ontogenetic origin of the eucharistic metaphor. There would be no such metaphor if the infant Jesus had not first literally sucked milk from the breasts of his loving mother. Having done so, he would grow up and go on to become the Christ who – now metaphorically – would "feed" the faithful from the sacrificial cross. Repeatedly, our poet compares these two alternative forms of orality – one literal and primitive, the other metaphorical and theologically nuanced/advanced. This comparison gradually becomes the essence of the poem's overall structural binarity.

Further along in the poem, for example, the comparison is cast in "pastoral" terms:

Hic adhaerens pectori
Pascitur ab ubere;
Hic adfixus arbori
Pascit nos ex vulnere.
Crux ministrat pabula
Fructu nos reficiens;
Mater est praeambula
Fructum nobis nutriens.
Here – clinging to the breast
He is fed from the teat;
There – affixed to the tree
He feeds us from his wound.
The cross serves up food,
Refreshing us with its fruit;
The mother has gone before,
Suckling the fruit for us.

In the interpretation of Franz Ronig, the breastfeeding mother here acts as a kind of prototype (*objektives Vorbild*) of the cross from which, in turn, Christ will be made available to provide the faithful with eucharistic nourishment.[45] Stated in this way, the image of Mary breastfeeding her child is not only a necessary condition for, but also bears a certain resemblance to, the very image of the cross from which Christ feeds himself as eucharist to the faithful. Or, conversely, Christ's eucharistic "breastfeeding" of the faithful bears a certain resemblance to Mary's literal breastfeeding of the Christ child.

Then, in the next line, the poet lays an even heavier emphasis on the mother's role in the ontogeny of the eucharist:

> *Crux in loco pascuae*
> *Pascit nos praecipue;*
> *Sed virgo praecipua*
> *Pascit ipsa pascua.*
> In its green pasture[46]
> The cross feeds us in an extraordinary way;
> But the extraordinary virgin
> Herself feeds [us] like a green pasture.

Note the adversative *Sed* ("But"), which cuts off the second couplet from the first couplet of the quatrain. In effect, what the son accomplishes is quite special, *but*, what the mother accomplishes is very special too. Beth Williamson comments: "The paradox in the concept of Christ as the Bread of Life [John 6:35, 48] is that he who feeds everyone needs also to be fed by his mother." More important, the "concept of the Virgin as the provider of the Eucharist – not just its container but the actual source of the Eucharist – is at the heart of the interpretation of the image of the Virgin *Lactans*."[47]

Of course one may ask the corresponding question about who the "source" of the "source of the Eucharist" was, and then again ask who the "source" of that "source" was – and so on, backwards in time until (for theists) the answer has to be: God. For God is ultimately the creator, and Mary is but a creature. This is true, despite the correct theological view of the second person of the trinity as having taken his fleshly form exclusively from his mother Mary (there being no fleshly, i.e., no human, father).

Our poet, however, is satisfied to remain within the roughly synchronic framework of those who are seeking the Tree of Life, and suggests that a choice does not really have to be made between the two available candidates. Both are the right choice, for seekers will find that both – the person of the virgin mother, as well as the personified[48] cross – bear the edible, life-giving *fructus*. Better still, affirms the poet, if you prefer to choose one, you will obtain the other as well: *nemo consequitur / Unam sine alia*.

Both alternatives are connected to suffering. The cross is obviously an instrument designed to inflict great suffering on Mary's son. As for Mary herself, she suffers simply by virtue of her standing by the cross of her son, for our poet duly notes where Mary is likely to be if the seeker is to understand why Mary is pierced by a sword (*per matrem . . . Gladium transire*), that is, the sword that old man Simeon had foretold would pierce her soul (Luke 2:34–35). Here, however, we have not the "sword of unbelief," which Origen and some other Fathers had offered as an interpretation of Simeon's prophecy (above, pp. 39–41), but the widespread medieval symbol (often a visual image) of Mary's compassionate suffering at the foot of the cross:

> Referred to as the sword of sorrow (*gladius doloris*), Simeon's sword (*gladius Simeonis*), or the sword of compassion (*gladius compassionis*), this motif was interpreted by medieval commentators variously as a symbol of Mary's pain at the Passion, as the counterpart of the lance used to pierce Christ's side, and as the embodiment of Christ's pain shared by his mother. All views have in common the understanding of the sword as an expression of compassion, conveying the belief that Mary suffered her son's tortures with Him.[49]

It does not suffice for our poet, however, to deploy only the *gladius* topos, for it is followed by yet another image of the mother's victimization, namely, she is herself crucified along with her son:

> *Fili matris unice,*
> *Matris crucifixae,*
> *Nos de cruce respice*
> *Fili crucifixe.*
> O only son of a mother,
> Of a mother crucified,
> Look down at us from the cross,
> O Crucified son.

Yet, why does Christ's mother have to be pierced by the sword of Simeon *and* crucified on a cross? Is this not excessive?

Of course, there is no indication that Mary was *literally* pierced by Simeon's sword, or was *literally* nailed to a cross. The poet's audience already understood that Jesus *literally* died on a cross, as that death was reported in all the canonical gospels and was common knowledge among both the educated and the illiterate in medieval Europe. But, no audience of *Lignum vitae quaerimus* would have made an analogous presupposition regarding the mother of Jesus. So, assuming that the mother of Jesus loved and was attached to her son, the audience would have understood that the seeming violence suffered by her in this work was a metaphorical expression of her extreme psychical pain, or a depiction of the traumatization she experienced as her son was suffering and dying before her eyes. Like the eucharistic metaphor, the representation of Mary pierced or crucified was metaphorical.

Drinking the Blood of a Maternalized Christ

From a scriptural viewpoint, the eucharistic concerns of this particular poem are best understood in light of the one canonical gospel – John (19:25–27) – where Mary stands in silence by her son's cross. Our poet speaks of the son's five wounds (*quinque vulnera*), from one of which, as we saw earlier, he feeds the faithful: *Pascit nos ex vulnere*. Such vocabulary reveals that the poet is aware of the so-called "cult of the Five Wounds," also dependent on the gospel of John.[50] Only in John's gospel is a fifth wound inflicted (opened), and that by the thrust of a lance into the side of Mary's son (*sub* ***latere***). The Vulgate reads: *unus militum lancea* ***latus*** *eius aperuit et continuo exivit sanguis et aqua* (19:34). Blood flowing in this fashion from the body of Christ points back to earlier words in John's gospel: "Those who eat my flesh and drink my blood [*bibit meum sanguinem*] have eternal life, and I will raise them up on the last day" (6:54). These words state concisely the salvific consequences of consuming the nonliteral body and nonliteral blood of Christ – that is, of receiving the eucharistic sacrament.

From the cross, then, Mary's son feeds the faithful in a manner resembling the way Mary herself had breastfed him as a child (*ab ubere*), and from an area on his upper body (*ex vulnere*) roughly analogous to the place on his mother's body that nourished him with breast milk. This lends a certain maternal quality to the son's ministrations from the cross. At the same time, such "breastfeeding" by Christ is scripturally and theologically incorrect: how can an already dead – and not yet resurrected – Christ give suck? The fifth wound is inflicted only after Christ has given up the ghost (John 19:30) and hangs dead on the cross. The poet is rushing in with a premature denial of death before the theologically correct denial of death, which would come later, in Christ's resurrection from the dead (John 20:14 ff.).

But again, thank goodness for incorrectness – and for the gender-bending propensities of many medieval Christians. Representations of the crucified Christ as a mother were not uncommon in the medieval West.[51] This includes visual representations. For example, there are images of Christ giving birth to the Church personified as a woman (*Ecclesia*) from out of his right side as he hangs from the cross.[52] There are also pictures of the crucified Christ providing personified *Ecclesia* with the blood that spurts from his right side and into the chalice which she holds,[53] suggesting that Christ indirectly "breastfeeds" the faithful as a collective from a single eucharistic cup. Occasionally, it is Christ's mother, Mary herself, whose mantle and veil are splattered by her son's blood,[54] or who even catches her son's blood in a cup.[55] Some post-crucifixion images of a (theoretically already) dead Christ show him actively squirting blood from the fifth wound into a chalice for later oral consumption by the faithful.[56] In some late medieval images, there is an explicit parallelism drawn between Christ proffering his bleeding (right) side wound and Mary exposing her right breast.[57] Atop the cross in some medieval crucifixions is a nest of pelicans, with the mother pelican tearing at her own breast, so that blood drips down into the open mouths of her young nestlings.[58]

Most relevant to the poem under consideration (and particularly the line *Pascit nos ex vulnere* ["He feeds us from his wound"]) are textual representations of the crucified Christ feeding individuals directly from his wound/breast:

> While I was standing in prayer, Christ on the cross appeared more clearly to me while I was awake, that is to say, he gave me an even greater awareness of himself than before. He then called me to place my mouth to the wound in his side [*quod ego ponerem os meum in plagam lateris sui*]. It seemed to me that I saw and drank the blood, which was freshly flowing from his side [*quod ego viderem et biberem sanguinem eius fluentem recenter ex latere suo*]. His intention was to make me understand that by this blood he would cleanse me. And at this I began to experience a great joy, although when I thought about the passion I was still filled with sadness.[59]
>
> (Angela of Foligno, d. 1309)

> He [Christ] stretches out his hands to embrace us, bows down his head to kiss us, and opens his side to give us suck [*ad suggendum latus nobis aperit*]; and though it is blood that he offers us to suck, we believe that it is health-giving and sweeter than honey and the honey-comb [Psalm 18:11]. Do not wean me, good Jesus, from the breasts of thy consolation [Isaiah 66:11] as long as I live in this world, for all who suffer this abide in death, as thou thyself didst testify in the gospel saying: "unless you eat the flesh of the Son of man and drink his blood, you shall not have life in you" [John 6:53].[60]
>
> (The Monk of Farne, d. 1371)

> He [Christ] behaved like a mother with her favourite child. She will show it the breast, but hold it away from it until it cries; as soon as it begins to cry, she will laugh for a while and clasp it to her and, covering it with kisses, delightedly give it her full breast. So the Lord behaved with me. That day, He showed me His most sacred side from afar, and I cried from the intensity of my longing to put my lips to the sacred wound. After He had laughed for a little while at my tears – at least that is what He seemed to do – He came up to me, clasped my soul in His arms, and put my mouth to where His most sacred wound was, that is to say, the wound in His side.[61]

> We must attach ourselves to the breast of Christ crucified, which is the source of charity, and by means of that flesh we draw milk. The means is Christ's humanity which suffered pain, and we cannot without pain get that milk that comes from charity.[62]
>
> (Catherine of Siena, d. 1380)

Bynum notes that Catherine "repeatedly called Christ's [fifth] wound a breast."[63] Breast imagery was indeed a prominent feature of late medieval spirituality. For those mystics[64] who were invited – or who urged others – to apply their lips to the fifth wound – it would seem that the best breast was the wounded breast of Christ.

In relating such experiences, visionary mystics were probably assisted by the medieval philosophical–physiological concept of breast milk as a mother's "transmuted" or "processed" blood,[65] as they obtained the imagined blood from an area on Christ's body roughly corresponding to the location of a mother's breast. They were also very likely influenced by personal psychological issues revolving around orality, which are known today as eating disorders, and in particular the diagnostic category of anorexia nervosa.[66] Rudolph M. Bell has invented the apt expression "holy anorexia" to title his pioneering study of the extreme oral asceticism of Angela of Foligno, Catherine of Siena, Margaret of Cortona, and many other late medieval holy women of Italy.[67] The anorexia of these women, writes Bell, "came to be seen as part of a wider pattern of heroic, ascetic masochism amply justified in the literature of radical Christian religiosity."[68]

To receive blood from the wound of Christ was to receive an extraordinary form of oral gratification. By contrast, the miraculous feeding of loaves and fishes to the multitudes (Mark 6:30–44, 8:1–10; Matthew 14:13–21; Luke 9:12–17; John 6:1–14) was merely grand. Christ performed that miracle without victimizing himself. As the poet Richard Crashaw (1613? –1649) put it:

> See here an easie Feast that knowes no wound,
> That under Hungers Teeth will needs be sound . . .[69]

It should be kept in mind, however, that down the centuries Christ does not continue (literally) feeding loaves and fishes to the faithful. What he does – through the agency of priests – is continue (eucharistically) feeding his body and blood to the faithful.

When the author of *Lignum vitae quaerimus* speaks of Christ feeding us "from the wound," we gain some notion of Christ providing nourishment in the form of his blood, but the imagery is not nearly as graphic and as elaborate as that encountered in the analogous narrations of mystical experiences. Nevertheless, the overall semantic basis is the same: Christ is represented as a mother who feeds an infantilized believer, not at the breast, but at the wound in his side; and not milk, but blood. The wound and the blood remind us that an act of violence has been perpetrated against Christ. It is understood, however, that Christ was voluntarily wounded as part of the divine plan to redeem us (sinful humankind), and that we ourselves wounded him – and continue to wound him – by sinning. Christ was the supreme, nonresisting victim (cf. Matthew 5:38–41; Luke 6:28–29), and we should be grateful for the gruesome gift of his blood.

Not the Tree of Life, but Its Fruit

Lignum vitae quaerimus ends on an aesthetically satisfying and theologically upbeat note.

Just as Mary is not literally but only metaphorically crucified in the poet's imagination, as we have seen, so also her son does not literally but only metaphorically feed the faithful from his wound. In the historical reality outside the poem, by contrast, Mary literally breastfed her son, and her son was literally crucified. We may put it this way: the "crucified" Mary is to the crucified Christ what the "breastfeeding" Christ is to the breastfeeding Mary. Mother and son seem to be imitating one another. This adds a certain balance to the aesthetic impact of the poem.

Lignum vitae quaerimus is a poem that foregrounds the representation of Mary's son with images of orality. This son is a metaphorically edible being who is repeatedly characterized as a fruit. Like his mother, he is never referred to by name; only twice is he addressed as a son (the vocative *fili*), whereas six times he is designated (with some case form of) *fructus*. He both feeds (*pascitur*) from his mother's breast (two case variants of *uber*) and feeds (*pascit*) others from the fifth of his wounds while hanging already dead on the cross. Of course, how he came to be dead was and still is generally known: his death was a voluntary sacrifice – that is, a self-sacrifice upon the cross intended to save or to redeem all humankind. Here, the masochism of provoking one's own death is difficult to extricate from the grandiosity of imagining how enormously beneficial such a death would be to humanity. What is foregrounded by the poet, however, is neither the masochism nor the grandiosity of Mary's son, but the overall psychical issue of orality. Within the setting of the poem, the redemptive sufferings and death of one's God are finished, at least for the time being. Now, it is possible to enjoy the fruit of what has gone before.

In the poet's opinion, it does not matter what the term Tree of Life refers to. The important thing is that renewed life is obtained by oral incorporation of the tree's fruit, for the fruit is the same for either referent, namely, Christ himself:

> *Fructus o vivifice,*
> *Fructus ligni vitae,*
> *Nos te ipso refice,*
> *Nobis da frui te.*
> O life-giving fruit,
> Fruit of the Tree of Life,
> Refresh us with you yourself,
> Grant that we may delight in you.

With this final stanza, the poem implicitly comes back full circle to the initial statement of purpose: *Lignum vitae quaerimus*. As it happens, the original search was slightly misguided. Not the Tree of Life, but its life-giving fruit – *Fructus ligni vitae* – was being sought; not a tree, but the savior hanging either at his mother's breast or from the tree of the cross. To partake of such a fruit is to receive the ultimate oral gratification. Why that should be so, however, is never made clear by the poet. But the idea that the Christ child at the breast and the Christ adult on the cross are the same highly desirable fruit will have to be, well, sufficient food for thought until some serious psychoanalytic matters can first be raised.

*

In the medieval West, the title Tree of Life could refer either to Mary or to the cross on which her son died. The anonymous poem *Lignum vitae quaerimus* takes advantage of this double referentiality, positing the idea that the Tree of Life is *both* Mary's body and her son's cross, with the eucharistic "fruit" on both Trees being Mary's son. The importance of the edible "fruit" imagery is here explored in light of the medieval eucharistic debate over transubstantiation. Psychoanalytically speaking, both Mary and Jesus offer oral gratification, Mary normally to the infant at her breast, Jesus with masochistic grandiosity to the faithful from the "wound" in his side. Those who were searching for the Tree of Life at the beginning of the poem found something more important, namely, its life-giving fruit.

Notes

1 Thomas Aquinas 2012, vol. 19, 485.
2 See especially: Reijners 1965, 18–96.
3 Rancour-Laferriere 2011, 43 (with bibliography on the theme of the "tree of the cross" in n. 119, p.77).
4 As translated by Reijners 1965 (38 [Greek], 41 [English]).
5 *Ante-Nicene Fathers* 2004 (1885-1887), vol. 2, 277 (English); Lampe 1961, 596 (Greek).
6 See Steenberg (2004) for a detailed analysis of the meaning of this term.
7 *Ante-Nicene Fathers* 2004 (1885-1887), vol. 1, 547 (for the Latin and [supposed] Greek, see: Irénée de Lyon 1969, 248–251).
8 Rancour-Laferriere 2011, 43–44 (and the literature cited there).
9 De Montfort 1966, 205, as translated in De Montfort 1988, 107 (emphasis added).
10 As quoted and translated in: Ellington 2001, 139, n. 123.
11 Bernard of Clairvaux 2004a, 130.
12 John of Damascus 2008, 66; John of Damascus 1988, 179 (line 30).
13 Casagrande 1974, 237 (no. 346), 243 (no. 350). In authentic works by Ephrem, however, the Tree of Life is Christ hanging on the cross or the cross itself (Murray 2004 [1975], 126–130; see, for example, Ephrem the Syrian 1989, 297 [opening line of hymn no. 8 on virginity]). For some further textual examples of the representation of Mary as the Tree of Life, see: Salzer 1893, 6–7, 113, n. 6; Nitz 1992; and below, pp. 102–104.
14 Nitz 1988, 220 (cf. Vetter 1958–1959, 61, fig. 32).
15 Meiss 1936, fig. 31.
16 Fallon 2012, 104 (fig. 4.2).
17 Among the many hundreds of known titles for Mary in the lists that have been compiled by scholars, I have been able to find only one instance of *croix*, in the

list appended to Laurentin's magisterial study of the sacerdotal role of Mary. See: Laurentin 1952–1953, vol. II, 215 (referring to a passage in Pseudo-Epiphanius about Mary being the "cruciform throne" as she held the Christ child in her arms; cf. vol. I, 46–47).

18 Amadeus of Lausanne in: Bernard of Clairvaux and Amadeus of Lausanne 1979, 62 (English); Amadeus of Lausanne 1960, 56 (Latin). The influence of Bernard on Amadeus is palpable.

19 Bonaventure 1960, 99; 1868b, 68.

20 See: Revelation 22:2. For images and commentaries, see: Bonaventure 1968b, frontispiece; Saxl 1942, plates 27b, 28a, 28b; Ladis 1982, 171–179 (and color plate of Taddeo Gaddi's *Arbor Vitae*, p. 7); Offner and Boskovits 1987; O'Reilly 1992, 178–181; Hatfield 1990, 137–143; Boskovits and Tartuferi, eds., 2003, 199–205 (with extensive bibliography); Sciacca 2012 (on Pacino di Bonaguida and his workshop, with images and bibliography).

21 Meersseman 1958–1960, vol. II, 79 (twelfth century; cf. vol. I, 199, for a nearly identical fourteenth-century example).

22 Meersseman 1958–1960, vol. II, 17 (fourteenth century).

23 Meersseman 1958–1960, vol. II, 17 (fifteenth century). Cf. also: vol. II, 164 (*lignum vite complantatum rivis aquarum* – thirteenth century); 241 (*Arbor vitae fructifera* – fifteenth century).

24 Szövérffy 1985a, 242.

25 Dreves and Blume 1909, vol. I, 137.

26 Szövérffy 1976, 68–69 (cf. also 70).

27 Hesbert, ed. 1952, 215 (abbreviation, spelling, and punctuation as in the photocopied manuscript).

28 Dreves and Blume 1909, vol. I, 460.

29 As quoted from "O crux sancta et praeclara" by: Szövérffy 1966, 38.

30 For the text being utilized here, see: Dreves and Blume 1909, vol. II, 282–283.

31 Dronke 1987, 585.

32 Huot 1997, 163.

33 It may seem odd to think of the hyssop here as a "tree," but the Vulgate does have Solomon speaking *super lignis* in the passage quoted (and *peri tōn xulōn* in the Septuagint). As a matter of fact, the term "hyssop" has been understood to refer to a number of different plant species in the Bible (Moldenke and Moldenke 1986 [1952], 160–162). The passage in 1 Kings is unlikely to refer to what in English is normally meant by "hyssop," but it could refer to "caper" or "fig," i.e., "the only 'trees' commonly found clambering over walls" (ibid., 161). Our anonymous poet is wise to refer to both woody plants (*ambae ligna*) with the ambiguous noun *lignum* (either "wood" or "tree"), not *arbor* ("tree," here utilized only with reference to Christ on the cross: *Hic adfixus arbori*).

34 See the entry "orality" in: Moore and Fine, eds. 1990, 135–136.

35 The scriptural origin of the key expressions pronounced at the eucharistic altar is Christ's discourse at the so-called Last Supper: "While they were eating, Jesus took a loaf of bread, and after blessing it he broke it, gave it to the disciples, and said, 'Take, eat; this is my body [*hoc est corpus meum*, which renders the original Greek *touto estin to sōma mou*].' Then he took a cup, and after giving thanks he gave it to them, saying, 'Drink from it, all of you; for this is my blood [*hic est enim sanguis meus*, which renders the original Greek, *touto gar estin to haima mou*] of the covenant, which is poured out for many for the forgiveness of sins'" (Matthew 26:26–28). The eucharistic expressions (here in brackets) are to be found in corresponding passages in the other synoptic gospels (Mark 14:22; Luke 22:19),

and in Paul (1 Corinthians 11:23). That these expressions belong to a continuous tradition within the Roman rite going back at least to the late fourth century is clear from an excerpt from mass prayers that was written by Saint Ambrose (d. 397), which, as Joseph A. Jungmann points out, "differs very little from the respective prayers of the present Roman canon." See: Jungmann 1951 (1949), vol. 1, 52; cf. also vol. II, 194–201.

36 Tanner, ed. 1990, vol. 1, 230.

37 The phrase *ara crucis* was a liturgical commonplace. It appeared, for example, in William Durand's late-thirteenth-century *Rationale Divinorum Officiorum*: "The exterior altar is the altar of the cross [*ara crucis*]" (Durand 2007, 27; Durand 1995, 29 [I, 2, 3]). The term was also utilized in direct reference to the crucifixion, as when Durand speaks of Christ, "who chose to be immolated on the altar of the cross [*in ara crucis*] for the salvation of all people" (Durand 2007, 98; Durand 1995, 109 [I, 8, 24]).

38 The Council of Trent "declared the objective character of the Sacrifice of the Mass as something more than a mere reminder of the Sacrifice of the Cross or a mere Communion rite" (Jungmann 1951 [1949], vol. 1, 133). The counciliar text itself states: "In this divine sacrifice [*in divino hoc sacrificio*] that is celebrated in the Mass, the same Christ who offered himself once in a bloody manner (cf. Heb 9:14, 27f.) on the altar of the Cross [*in ara crucis*] is contained and is offered in an unbloody manner." The paragraph ends, "For, the victim [*hostia*] is one and the same: the same now offers himself through the ministry of priests who then offered himself on the Cross [*in cruce*]; only the manner of offering is different." The eucharistic doctrine is backed with several condemnatory canons, such as the following: "If anyone says that the sacrifice of the Mass [*Missae sacrificium*] is merely offering of praise and thanksgiving or that it is a simple commemoration of the sacrifice accomplished on the Cross [*aut nudam commemorationem sacrificii in cruce peracti*], but not a propitiatory sacrifice . . . let him be anathema." See: Denzinger 2012, 418 (no. 1743); 420 (no. 1753).

39 Thomas Aquinas 2012, vol. 20, 206 ("tota substantia panis convertitur in totam substantiam corporis Christi, et tota substantia vini in totam substantiam sanguinis Christi").

40 Thomas Aquinas 2012, vol. 20, 333–334.

41 Tubach 1981 (1969), No. 1001.

42 Among the many valuable sources on the eucharist in the medieval period, see, for example: Pelikan 1971–1989, vol. III, 184–204, vol. IV, 52–59; Macy 1984; Rubin 1991; Macy 1999; Rubin 2004 (1999); Price 2003; Bynum 2006; Bynum 2007; Levy et al., eds. 2012. Today, the doctrine of transubstantiation is still officially held by the Roman Catholic Church. See: *Catechism of the Catholic Church* 2000 (1997), 356 (no. 1413), 346–347 (nos. 1373–1377); Wills 2013, 54–55.

43 For example, was it right in the long run to view Christ's crucifixion or its supposed reenactment in the eucharist as sacrifice? The "true meaning of Christian sacrifice" – to quote the subtitle of an important book by Robert J. Daly (2009) – is a matter still being debated by believers.

44 *The Oxford English Dictionary* 1991, vol. VII, 417.

45 Ronig 1956, 367–369 (and fig. 1; see also: Ronig 1974, 207–212, and fig. 72). The prototypical significance of the mother's breastfeeding is emphasized, as Ronig shows, by the layout of a page from the *Vergier de soulas*, a medieval compilation of texts and illustrations in the Bibliothèque Nationale, Paris. The page includes the text of *Lignum vitae quaerimus* (together with its Old French translation), as well as various images of Mary with the Christ child and of the

crucifixion. A large, cross-shaped configuration of miniatures – including two of Mary breastfeeding – dominates the left side of the page. Directly opposite this on the right is a large crucifixion image. Sylvia Huot writes: "both the text and the layout of illustrations . . . reflect the deep-seated analogy between the Virgin and the Cross as bearers of Christ and instruments of salvation" (1997, 163–165, and illustration on p. 164). Indeed, this analogy is sufficiently "deep-seated" to *implicate* Mary in the crucifixion of her son (about which, later).

46 I have stayed close to the traditional English translation of Psalm 23:2 ("He makes me lie down in green pastures"), that is, the Vulgate Psalm 22:2 (*in loco pascuae ibi me conlocavit*).

47 Williamson 1998, 129 (referring to an identical stanza in another of the many variants of this sequence).

48 As in phrases in the poem where the word *crux* occurs as the subject of a verb that would normally refer to the action of a person, e.g., *Crux ministrat* or *Crux . . . pascit nos*.

49 Schuler 1992, 6.

50 See, for example: Gougaud 1925, 74–128; Dumoutet 1932, 27–40; Gray 1963. Of course, medieval vulnerophiles were not always particular about the number five (or fifth), nor were devotees of Christ necessarily concerned about Christ's wounds per se, for there was a general interest in the meanings and powers of Christ's *blood*, and this interest is evident from many sources, such as theology, the liturgy, devotional prayers, hymnography, amulets, folk tales, documented visions of mystics, various sorts of iconography, and so on. See especially: Bynum 2007.

51 See, for example: Bynum 1987, 165–180, 270–275; Bynum 1991, 93–108, 157–165.

52 Schiller 1966–1991, vol. IV, part 1, figs. 217, 218, 219, 220 – all characterized by Schiller as *Geburt der Ekklesia*, from various manuscripts of the *Bible moralisée* dating from the mid-thirteenth to the early fifteenth centuries (cf. also Bynum 1991, fig. 3.6).

53 Schiller 1966–1991, vol. I, fig. 15; vol. IV, part 1, figs. 100, 101, 104–106, 108–111, 227, 267 – images dating from tenth-century Byzantium to the late medieval West. Cf. also Bynum 1987, plate 12.

54 See especially: Hamburger 2011 (with many illustrations, rich bibliography).

55 Thérel 1979–1980, esp. fig. 3 (fragment of a cross, ca.1057), fig. 4 (Umbrian sacramentary, mid-twelfth century). Cf. Katzew 2011, fig. 124 (oil painting of 1753, from Santa Cruz, Tlaxcala, Mexico). Rubin points to examples in the visual arts of the resemblance of *ecclesia* to Mary, noting "the powerful and long-standing habit of identifying the church as Mary" (2009, 168; cf. Hamburger 2011, 11–13; above, n. 72, p. 86 (sources on theological manifestations of this habit).

56 This category includes variants of the so-called Man of Sorrows (*Imago Pietatis*) shooting his blood into a chalice (e.g., Bynum 1991, 207, fig. 6.5), or a semi-naked Christ upon an altar in some variants of the so-called Gregory Mass doing the same thing (e.g., Bynum 1991, 209, fig. 6.7).

57 Bynum 1987, 272, and figs. 28–30; Bynum 1991, 106, 113 (fig. 3.13), 115 (fig. 3.14), 208 (fig. 6.6), 209 (fig. 6.7), 340–341 (n. 71), 380 (n. 86); Williamson 2000; Newman 2003, 261–265. Some of these images involve a sort of "double intercession" (see below, pp. 269–270).

58 Schiller 1966–1991, vol. II, 148–149, and figs. 443, 445, 451, 489, 504. The self-wounding mother pelican is a traditional symbol of Christ. See: Lampen 1946; Anonymous 1971; Tubach 1981 (1969), nos. 631, 3657; Rubin 1991, 310–312.

59 Angela da Foligno 1985, 142–144, as translated in: Angela of Foligno 1993, 128 (cf. Bynum 1987, 141–144, and 362, n. 183).
60 Farmer 1957, 182, as translated in: The Monk of Farne 1961, 64–65 (quoted by Bynum 1982, 152).
61 Raymond of Capua 2011 (1960), 151–152 (cf. Bynum 1987, 173, and 375, n. 121).
62 As translated from the Italian by Bynum 1987, 173.
63 Bynum 1987, 178.
64 Other such mystics, in addition to the ones quoted here, include: Ida of Louvain, Christine Ebner, Lutgard of Aywières, Aldobrandesca of Siena, Gertrude of Helfta, Margaret of Cortona, and Osanna Andreassi. See: Gougaud 1925, 108, 125, n. 20; Bynum 1982, 151–154, 192; 1987, 142, 271 ff., 411, n. 62.
65 Quoting Bynum (1987, 270; 1982, 132). Bynum notes that already Clement of Alexandria (d. ca.215) wrote in his *Paedagogus* about the transformation of blood into milk that occurs in a mother's breasts during pregnancy and after childbirth. See: *Ante-Nicene Fathers* 2004 (1885–1887), vol. 2, 219. The best-known medieval source on this matter was probably *De proprietatibus rerum* (ca.1230) by the Franciscan Bartholomaeus Anglicus (d. ca.1291). He writes: "she [the mother] takes care of the infant; while it is still in the womb, it is fed with blood, but at birth, nature drives this blood into the breast, so that it is transformed into milk [*ut mutetur in lac*] in order to feed the child." See: Goodich 1975, 80, translating Bartholomaeus Anglicus 1964 (1601), 241 (cf. also 179–180, "De Mamilla").
66 American Psychiatric Association 2013, 338–345.
67 Bell 1985.
68 Bell 1985, 21. Subsequent scholarship shows that Bell's term "holy anorexia" is not historically or culturally inappropriate, for there is abundant cross-historical and cross-cultural evidence for anorexia nervosa: "What seems to unite fasting saints and women with AN [anorexia nervosa] is the paradox that the [self-] starvation is both deliberate and nonvolitional. That is, across historical contexts women deliberately refuse to eat food that they require for sustenance. Yet, they do not appear to be able to stop their pattern of food refusal in response to reward or punishment" (Keel and Klump 2003, 754).
69 Crashaw 1974 (1970), 15.

7 Mary's Dispute with Her Son's Cross

A Poem by Philip the Chancellor

Mary Lodges a Complaint with the Personified Cross

It may be asked why the distal versus proximate referents of the Tree of Life have thus far required such close examination. The referents, after all, may be stated directly and simply: Mary versus the cross of Christ. This simplicity, however, makes it difficult to understand the tension generated by what the referents cannot possibly – simultaneously – hold in common, namely, the fruit of the Tree of Life, which, if Mary, cannot conceive of handing over her fruit to the cross if she is a normal mother; and, if the wooden cross, does not conceive of anything, let alone the fruit that hangs from it, because it is an inanimate object. As long as interpreters understood the Tree of Life to refer to either one or the other of these incompatible referents, then the tension remained. Not until someone thought to join Mary and a personified cross together in some kind of dialogue was it possible to represent the tension in a simpler, more direct way (and even in many cases to dispense with any notion of the Tree of Life altogether).

This is what happened in the medieval poetic tradition about a dispute between Mary and a personified cross. Numerous works in a variety of West European languages – Latin, Italian, Old French, Anglo-Norman, Old Provençal, Middle English, Middle Dutch – were created on this theme.[1] Peter Yeager observes that the personified cross does not enter into dispute with any personage other than Mary.[2] This would seem to suggest that these two – as opposed to, say, the cross and one of the other Marys, or the cross and the devoted disciple John, or the cross and the Roman centurion – constitute the relevant twosome at odds with each other over possession of some particular entity.

The best known of the dispute poems is titled *Dialogus Virginis cum Cruce*, by Philip the Chancellor (who might also have been author of *Lignum vitae quaerimus*, as mentioned earlier).[3] As the title implies, the tree of the cross upon which Christ died is capable of having a conversation with Mary. This is not surprising, as personification of the cross has often occurred in the history of Christianity. The noncanonical *Gospel of Peter* and the Old English *Dream of the Rood* come to mind,[4] not to mention *Lignum vitae quaerimus*. What is new in the dispute poems is the introduction of Mary as an interlocutor in a specifically antagonistic relationship with the personified cross. For Mary herself to be questioning the role of the cross is a serious matter. In the very idea of such a confrontation lurks the specter of theological incorrectness: perhaps the crucifixion of Mary's son was not salvific, but meaningless.

Chancellor Philip's dispute poem begins with Mary addressing the cross directly by name – *Crux* – thereby instantly personifying it:

> *Crux, de te volo conqueri,*
> *Quid est, quod in te repperi*
> *Fructum tibi non debitum?*
> Cross! I wish to lodge a complaint with you.
> What is it that I have found upon you,
> This fruit which does not belong to you?

The personifying effect is maintained by Mary's continued utilization of familiar pronominal forms (*de te*, *in te*, *tibi*, etc.) to address the cross as her anger rises. Mary is mightily upset with this wooden object. How has it come into possession of the "fruit of [her] womb [*fructus uteri*]?" That "fruit" would be her son, of course, and it is clear that he already hangs upon the cross. Mary complains to the cross that her "fruit" gives life and owes nothing to death. Of what crime is this "fruit" guilty that it should be abused so, that it should be hanging there naked to die a death suitable for brigands and murderers?

The cross responds (also familiarly), admitting that it rejoices at having gained possession of Mary's fruit (*De tuo fructu gaudeo*) and accepting what Yeager terms "its role as a second mother."[5] The sweet fruit, however, receives nothing like normal mothering from the cross. The cross declares that the fruit was born for the world, not for Mary (*Dulcem fructum possideo, / Mundo, non tibi genitum*). The cross justifies its participation in the cruel treatment of Mary's son with a little lesson in the harsher aspects of Christian soteriology. In Adam life was ruined, and a "second" Adam – that is, Christ – was needed in order to restore life to humankind. Such restoration of *life* had to be accomplished in a paradoxical fashion – that is, by the *death* of Christ (cf. Romans 5:12–21; 1 Corinthians 15:20–22, 42–49).[6] The tree of the cross did not refuse to bear the sacrificial offering (*oblatum*) of Christ, the fruit of Mary's womb. On the contrary, this tree played its paradoxical role in countering the fatal effects of Adam's having consumed the forbidden fruit from another tree, the tree of knowledge (*Lignum ligno opposuit*). In its own way, the tree of the cross even managed to "preserve" the life of the victim nailed upon it:

> *A te mortalem habui,*
> *Immortalem restitui.*
> From you I held one mortal,
> And I returned him immortal.

This is cleverer than the simple denial of death ("Weep not") that Mary has everywhere been fated to hear.

One of the theological advantages of a dispute between Mary and the cross is that the son does not have to speak at all. In Philip's poem, neither Mary nor the cross speaks with Christ. They speak to each other, while Christ, the subject of their dispute, speaks not a word. He is the bone of contention, or the object of a custody dispute. His presence is implicit, and the more powerful for that. Silence is an even more eloquent expression of nonresistance to evil than the sermon that the son had preached on the mount (Matthew 5:38–41). It is the silence of the lamb.

The personified cross goes on to compare itself to a rod of elm wood, something that apparently was utilized at one time to support a grapevine.[7] Mary is the vine (*vitis*),[8] and her son is a specific kind of fruit, the grape (*uva*).[9] In what Huot terms an "allegory of sacramental wine,"[10] the cross suggests to Mary that it is appropriate for the grape to be crushed in a winepress (*torcular* – cf. Isaiah 63:2 ff.).[11] In effect, how can the sweet fruit of the vine be transformed into the true wine (*Vinum sincerum*) to be imbibed by the faithful except after the harsh pressure of a winepress?

The Cross Gets Overly Defensive

Now it is clear that the poet has added a eucharistic element to the dispute between Mary and the cross, and this element will become even starker by the end of the poem than it was in *Lignum vitae quaerimus*. For Philip to deal with the theme of the eucharist was appropriate at a time when eucharistic issues were being mooted in theological discourse and were becoming increasingly relevant in liturgical practice, popular belief, and the arts. Nevertheless, the cross, not a winepress, was the real instrument of Christ's crucifixion, and the cross in Philip's poem does not let the eucharistic issue hide the fact that it – the cross – takes pride in its own work. Mary may be credited with producing the long-awaited fruit, who is her son, but, in the end, people need look no further than the cross to find that fruit (*Extra me non inveniunt*). As Szövérffy comments in this context, "the way to Christ leads only through the cross."[12]

Indeed, the cross seems a bit miffed at all the devotional attention Mary is getting (*Filium a te postulant / Et ad me non respiciunt*). The fruit of Mary's womb has matured, after all. So people ought to suck (*Sugant de meo palmite*) what they thirst for from the fruit of the vine, which was originally hers, but which now hangs from the cross where it really – theologically – belongs. Here, the poet manages to restate the primacy of the cross, but he does so in terms of eucharistic orality: sucking the wine/blood of the crucified son.

Both the winepress and the cross, then, enable Philip to extend the oral metaphor of Mary's son as *fructus* to the most gruesome extent possible, that is, to liquefaction: Jesus becomes wine. In this double extension of a metaphor, Jesus twice comes to be represented as dead. But, again paradoxically, drinking him under the eucharistic species of wine returns life to the communicant. Note that literal blood has not yet even been mentioned in the poem, only wine – a substance that, unlike blood, gives life without taking life away from another human being when consumed orally.

In the final stanza of the poem, the personified cross – apparently dissatisfied with its two attempts to convey the salvific importance of the crucifixion in terms of eucharistic wine – abandons altogether the niceties of eucharistic language. Now we have a real body and real blood:

Respondeas hypocritis:
Filium meum quaeritis,
Quem cruci dudum tradidi,
Iam non pendet ad ubera,
Pendet in cruce verbera
Corporis monstrans lividi.
Eum in cruce quaerite,
Guttas cruentas bibite,
Aemulatores perfidi.
You [Mary] could respond to the hypocrites:
"You are seeking my son,
Whom I have just now handed over to the cross.
He no longer hangs at the breast,
He hangs on the cross,
Showing the livid traces of scourging on his body.
Seek him on the cross,
Drink the bloody drops,
You perfidious and envious enemies."

Utilizing a subjunctive construction (*Respondeas*) to put these words into Mary's mouth, the cross has given Mary an opportunity to blame someone else ("hypocrites") rather than the cross itself for her son's death. As a result, both Mary and the cross stand to gain some degree of relief from the tension of the dispute. This resolves, or at least brings to a credible end, the dispute between Mary and the cross.

When in Doubt, Blame the Jews

But, just whom is Mary being made to blame for her son's death? The first people to be named (by the cross) are "hypocrites." What this term may suggest is the famous diatribe against the "scribes and Pharisees, hypocrites" in Matthew 23. There, Jesus had expressed indignation against certain holier-than-thou sectarians of his time. But, it was a righteous indignation,[13] tempered by sadness at having to make negative judgments that did not reflect well on his own people: "Jerusalem, Jerusalem, the city that kills the prophets and stones those who are sent to it! How often have I desired to gather your children together as a hen gathers her brood under her wings, and you were not willing!" (23:37).

Some have construed Chapter 23 of Matthew as an expression of hatred toward Jews. However, a better candidate for incipient anti-Semitism in the gospel of Matthew is the passage where Pontius Pilate yields to the noisy crowd's demand that Jesus be crucified. This was a call for *blood*:

> So when Pilate saw that he could do nothing, but rather that a riot was beginning, he took some water and washed his hands before the crowd, saying, "I am innocent of this man's blood [*apo tou haimatos toutou / a sanguine iusti huius*]; see to it yourselves." Then the people as a whole answered, "His blood [*To haima autou / sanguis eius*] be on us and on our children!"
>
> (Matthew 27:24–25; cf. Acts 18:6; Greek original and Vulgate translation in brackets)

In Philip's time, this ancient blood curse against Jews still applied, as if many centuries had not passed since the crucifixion of Christ. In the *Glossa Ordinaria* (a standard compendium completed by the early thirteenth century), we find the following interpretation of the Jewish crowd's call for blood: "The curse [*imprecatio*] exists until this day, and the blood of Christ [*sanguis Christi*] is not removed from them [i.e., Jews]."[14]

By taking upon themselves the blood of Christ, then, Jews as a category had come to be seen as Christ-killers, the so-called deicide people. This paranoid fantasy facilitated the development of derivative paranoias in the popular Christian imagination, such as beliefs about Jews desecrating eucharistic hosts, or killing Christian children for ritualistic purposes – for example, to obtain blood as an ingredient for their Passover matzoh or wine.[15] Philip the Chancellor would certainly have been aware of the pervasive anti-Jewish prejudice in his own culture, although not all manifestations of this prejudice known to medieval specialists can be dated before Philip's death in 1236.

It is only toward the end of the last stanza of Philip's poem that blood makes an explicit appearance. Could a Jewish connection be coming to the surface here? Those who would imbibe drops of blood (*Guttas cruentas bibite*) from the body of Mary's son are ridiculed as *Aemulatores perfidi*. Here, the blood is blood, which is to say that it is not eucharistic, as it had been earlier in the poem.

The blood is also imbibed as drops, not as a flowing liquid. The idea of consuming *drops* of Christ's blood was already familiar before the thirteenth century, when Chancellor Philip composed his poem. The context was not necessarily anti-Jewish, however. Caroline Walker Bynum writes: "Explicit reference to drinking discrete drops of Christ's blood appeared quite early in the development of devotion to the humanity and passion of Jesus." Bynum quotes from a letter of Peter Damian, ca.1060, who describes having a vision of Christ on the cross: "with my mouth I eagerly tried to catch the dripping blood." Also quoted is an English monk from Evesham Abbey, who admits to having swallowed "one drop" of Christ's blood during a vision (late twelfth century).[16]

These examples suggest intense empathic devotion to the suffering Jesus, and the devotion is expressed in visions of reverent oral consumption of Jesus' blood. But, no antipathy to Jews is expressed. There is instead an identification with the voluntarily suffering and bleeding Jesus. The identification is signified by oral incorporation of some small, but synecdochal portion of Jesus. Identification of this kind was apparently therapeutic for individuals obsessed with issues of guilt and punishment for guilt, including masochistic self-punishment (Peter Damian was also known to practice self-flagellation).

It is as if I, guilty sinner that I am, and therefore deserving of punishment, were suffering and dying too, along with Jesus. But no, Jesus is doing this as a sacrifice *for me*. I do not need to be subjected to actual flagellation, crowning with thorns, or crucifixion. Jesus is the proxy for my masochism. An imagined drop or two of the blood from his total exsanguination will do. And these drops *are* imagined, not literal, for they only appear in visions, or they are conjured up somehow in the red wine of the eucharist. After all, the masochistic Jesus had already voluntarily shed his real, literal blood for us, "once for all" (Hebrews 9:26), many centuries ago.

The very last line of Philip's poem does not, however, refer to mystic devotees of the Passion, or to communicants of the eucharist. On the contrary, the line appears to be a hateful epithet referring to members of some non-Christian out-group. The *Aemulatores perfidi* who drink the literal blood of Jesus on the cross do not thirst for holiness. Rather, they are bloodthirsty. They participate in the killing of Christ. They must be Jews.[17]

When I first came to this last line of Philip's poem I remembered an old Good Friday prayer "for the conversion of the Jews" that we used to recite in English during the late 1950s, when the Tridentine rite was still in use: "Let us pray also for the faithless Jews."[18] I also remembered that the Latin word here for "faithless" could also be rendered as "perfidious," which seemed to have more negative and more clearly anti-Jewish connotations – that is, "disloyal" or "treacherous." Even "faithless" was simply false for those Jews who had their own "faith," which just happened not to be the Christian one. Still, I pushed these thoughts aside, for the poem seemed to be too sophisticated and too preoccupied with the theology of the eucharist to include an element of religious hatred.

I was wrong. The first impression was the right impression. The Latin original of that old Good Friday passage urges us to pray *pro perfidis Judaeis*. Further on, it is said that God does not exclude from his mercy "even . . . the faithless [i.e., perfidious] Jews" (*etiam judaicam perfidiam*), and that we pray for "the blindness of that people" (*pro illius populi obcaecatione*) to be overcome by the light of Christ.[19] Such expressions would have been in common usage among the educated clergy in Philip's time. More importantly, they were just as offensive to Jews in the thirteenth century as in the twentieth. They could not be meaningfully disentangled from a background of hostility toward Jews in the New Testament (e.g., the blood curse of Matthew 27:25), or from the already long *Adversus Judaeos* tradition, or from the Good Friday *Improperia* spoken by Christ on the cross against Jews, and so on. Any educated Christian capable of reading about Jewish *perfidia* in Philip's twelfth and thirteenth centuries would not have been ignorant of the religious hatred that lay in the shadows of that epithet.

For example, Peter of Blois (d. ca.1212) penned an anti-Jewish piece under the title *Contra perfidiam Iudeorum* in which he refers to the "treachery of Judah" and the "obstinacy of the Jews" who "harden themselves in their malice."[20] These hateful phrases express the very *perfidia* that Peter attributes to Jews. Further examples in this period may be culled from Shlomo Simonsohn's in-depth documentation of views expressed by the Apostolic See toward Jews. From the year 1199, we find Pope Innocent III issuing yet another revision of the old papal Bull *Sicut Iudaeis*, which in this case opens with words taking Jewish "perfidy" for granted: "Although the *perfidia* of the Jews is to be condemned in every way, since through them the truth of our faith is proved, they are not to be oppressed severely by the faithful."[21] (I quote this particular variant of the Bull because it is the one that would also appear in an influential legal compendium, the *Decretals* of 1234.) In 1199, Innocent writes that, "Jewish blindness [*populus Iudaice cecitatis*] . . . continues damnably in its contumacy,"[22] and, in 1205, he refers to *Judei perfidi*.[23] One canon of the Fourth Lateran Council of 1215 (which had been summoned by Innocent) links the increase of usury among the Jews to the growth of Jewish "perfidy" (*Iudaeorum perfidia inolescit*).[24] In 1220, Innocent's successor, Honorius III, offhandedly mouths the deicide charge in a letter, remarking that "the *perfidia* of the Jews condemned them to perpetual slavery because of the acclamation by which they wickedly called the blood of Christ [*Christi sanguinem*] upon themselves and their children."[25] Simonsohn observes that the successor of Honorius, Gregory IX, "also made extensive use of the term Jewish *perfidia*, particularly in his condemnation of Jewish Oral Law (the Talmud)."[26]

Such odious statements coming from literate, educated Christians make it clear that the application of *perfidia* (and its cognates) to Jews in the twelfth and thirteenth centuries was no less hateful at that time than it would be in 1928, when a group of clergy known as *Amici Israel* appealed to Pope Pius XI to reform the offensive Good Friday prayer, *pro perfidis Judaeis*. This request – along with related proposals on how the church ought to show more respect for Judaism and the Jews – was rejected, and the *Amici Israel* coalition was brutally suppressed.[27]

The idea that those *aemulatores* in the last line of Philip's poem might be Jewish because they are *perfidi* leads to another, at first glance more positive,

Jewish connection. I am thinking of Paul's ruminations about provoking non-Christian Jews ("Israel") to jealous emulation of Gentile Christians in Chapter 11 of Romans. There, it is understood that most of Paul's fellow Jews have rejected Christ, and that this is a very bad thing. But, it is not too late, for Paul writes (Vulgate in brackets): "have they stumbled so as to fall? By no means! But through their stumbling salvation has come to the Gentiles, so as to make Israel jealous [*ut illos aemulentur*]" (11). Or: "Now I am speaking to you Gentiles. Inasmuch then as I am an apostle to the Gentiles, I glorify my ministry in order to make my own people jealous [*si quo modo ad aemulandum provocem carnem meam*], and thus save some of them" (13–14). This view that at least some Jews might become jealous emulators of Christians and eventually convert to Christianity was a manifestation of Paul's optimism, even an expression of his affection for his "own people."

With the wisdom of hindsight, however, we understand that Paul's optimism was unwarranted. There was a parting of the ways – and worse. Anti-Jewish attitudes – including the deicide charge enshrined in the New Testament canon – were incorporated into the very foundations of Christianity.[28]

Whoever speaks those final words of Philip's poem is not being optimistic or friendly in the Pauline sense. Jews are not being invited to emulate Christians. It is too late for that. Rather, they are accused of *perfidious* envy. They show no interest in what had been praised earlier in the poem by the personified cross, namely, eucharistic, nonliteral consumption of the blood shed by the sacrificial victim. On the contrary, it is alleged that they drink the literal blood of that victim – a preposterous charge in light of the ancient taboo in Jewish Law against ingesting sacrificial blood,[29] but a charge that would become familiar in the so-called "blood libel" against Jews.[30] Philip's poem foreshadows what David Biale terms "the nexus between the Eucharist and blood libel."[31]

Skepticism about the Eucharist

There is a certain symmetry here. Philip's blood drinkers – but not his wine drinkers – are celebrating the death of the Christian God. Philip's wine drinkers – but not his blood drinkers – are celebrating the *redemptive, life-giving effects* of the death of that God. In other words, Jews are just being literalistic, whereas Christians are capable of metaphor. However, if Jews had been given an opportunity to speak in this work – and, by the end of the poem, Mary certainly does not count as a Jew for Philip – they would have noted the central problem of transubstantiation: those Christians do take that metaphor *literally*, don't they?

Some do indeed. By the middle of the thirteenth century, Jewish writers were beginning to deride Christian transubstantiation. Miri Rubin quotes a passage from the *Book of Joseph the Zealot* (*Sefer Yosef ha-mekaneh*) that concludes simply: "all this worship is a nonsense."[32] From the *Old Book of Contention* (*Nizzahon Vetus*) come some satirical jabs at words spoken by Jesus at the so-called last supper – words commonly understood by Christians to institute the eucharist. In Mark's variant, Jesus first gives bread to the disciples and says, "Take; this is my body," then hands them a cup of wine from which they all drink, and says, "This is my blood of the [new] covenant" (14:22–24):

> In what sense was it his [Jesus'] body that they ate and drank? Did he cut a piece off his body which he gave to them, or did his body first become bread and wine and he gave them pieces of it? Moreover, where did that body which they ate and drank descend? Did it go on its way separately or was it mixed up in the stomach with all the other food?[33]

These questions obviously lead downward in the direction of excrement. They are meant to provoke laughter or to offend, for they expose a particularly serious theological challenge to transubstantiation, namely, the obvious mutability of something supposed to be the body and blood of Christ after it has entered the human digestive tract.

For Christian theologians, the fate of transubstantiated bread (and wine) in the human gut was no joke. It was an embarrassing issue, and it had to be addressed. In his *Summa theologiae*, Aquinas was cautious, admitting that, when "the substance of the bread or wine" becomes "corrupted," then "Christ's body and blood do not remain under this sacrament [i.e., the eucharist]."[34] Other theologians did not hesitate to explore the digestive sequelae of transubstantiated matter (or offered differing interpretations altogether of the words of consecration spoken at the altar).[35] What really became of the "body and blood" in the human gut – not to mention the gut of the random church mouse that nibbled on communion bread? Christ himself had asked, "Do you not see that whatever goes into the mouth enters the stomach, and goes out into the sewer?" (Matthew 15:17). Could it be true that saints who lived for periods of time on nothing but the eucharist nevertheless defecated? The usual tactic employed for cutting off serious consideration of such questions among transubstantiationalist theologians was to accuse those who paid too much attention to them of an abominable heresy, that is, "stercoranism" (from *stercus*, meaning feces).[36]

Philip himself might have enjoyed the humor, for there is no indication that his poem was intended as a defense of transubstantiation. Of course, the topic of transubstantiation was in the air at the time. It was a growing feature of the theological Zeitgeist of Western Europe in the twelfth and thirteenth centuries, just as anti-Jewish sentiment was a growing feature. After all, both transubstantiation and *Iudaeorum perfidia* were affirmed at the Lateran council of 1215, and it is highly unlikely that Philip would have been ignorant of such developments. But, Philip's poem only exploits the eucharist as a metaphor, not as transubstantiation. The author utilizes eucharistic imagery –

more the wine than the host – as a pedagogical technique for explaining what Christ was supposed to have accomplished on the cross. The poem is set in the past, when the literal death on the cross occurred and the literal blood was shed, and when Mary and the personified cross could conceivably have had a conversation. But, the poem also looks forward to a future when eucharistic celebration of the death of Mary's son would be possible. Not until the very last stanza, when literal blood is mentioned in religiously hateful terms, does the ancient deicide charge come to the surface. The rhetorically elegant (but non-transubstantiationalist) theology of the eucharist in the main body of the poem is paramount, and the non-eucharistic last stanza is a harsh coda.

Mary Speaks Her Mind

The poem's coda, as I suggested above, is an attempt to bring closure to the dispute between Mary and the cross. But still, it grates. Given the loving words she spoke in defense of the fruit of her womb at the beginning of the poem, why would the bereaved Mary now speak impersonally about having "handed over" her son to the cross for victimization? Why would she make a mockery of having breastfed him in order to convey the idea that he is a grown man now, and that those who would feed on his blood will find him on the cross? For the victim's own mother to toss off a clever comparison[37] between her son once feeding at her breast and now feeding his killers from the cross seems grotesque. It is as if an abusive Mary had passed her son directly from her breast to the cross as a sacrificial offering.[38] The idea would seem preposterous, but the poet may have caught just a glimpse of Mary's sacerdotal potential here (see below, pp. 251–285).

Of course, the comparison between hanging at the breast and hanging on the cross is also made in *Lignum vitae quaerimus*, as we have seen. But there, the context and tone are different. No religious hatred is expressed. Neither Mary nor the cross speaks, and so there is also no opportunity for an emotionally charged dispute. Instead, the poem's lyric persona quietly develops a symmetrical, reasonably harmonious pairing of Mary (and Christ child) with the cross (and Christ adult). The eucharistic theology is perhaps a bit bland, but the final stanza is upbeat, emphasizing renewal of life through consumption of the eucharistic fruit.

In one important respect, the dispute poem is an advance over the theologically bland *Lignum vitae quaerimus*: Mary the woman speaks her mind. She is angry. There is more to her than the already traditional mariophile imagery of her breasts, or her humility, or the sword piercing her heart. She comes close to challenging theological correctness, but at the last moment she turns instead to a vilification of her son's alleged killers, rather than questioning the salvific meaning of his death. Other versions of Mary at the foot of the cross will not hesitate to do both, as we will see.

*

Philip's poem deals with three primary topics. First, there comes a stark picture of the crucifixion as seen by the traumatized mother of the victim. Then, the personified cross attempts to explain the blood shed by this victim in soothing eucharistic terms, that is, in terms of the wonderful wine that is not the literal blood of the victim. Finally, sensing that this explanation has failed to persuade the mother of the victim, the cross nudges the mother to turn her attention toward the putative victim*izers* – that is, the "perfidious and envious enemies" who drink the literal blood of the victim. Forgetting that she is a Jew, Mary goes along with this. Her concluding outburst is a thinly disguised expression of religious hatred that would come to be known as the blood libel against Jews.

Notes

1 See, for example: Yeager 1981; Fein 1998, 87–160.
2 Yeager 1981, 58.
3 The textual variant being utilized here is: Dreves and Blume 1909, vol. 1, 303–304. I wish to thank my colleague Professor David Traill of the University of California, Davis, for providing very helpful advice while I was analyzing this poem.
4 For some examples, see: Yeager 1981, 57–58; Rancour-Laferriere 2011, 21–23.
5 Yeager 1981, 61.
6 This paradox is a commonplace of the "dispute poems," where "Mary often refers to the Cross as an instrument of death, and the Cross often refers to itself as a sustainer of life" (Yeager 1981, 57). Indeed, the "paradox" of life-giving death on the cross lies at the heart of Christian belief in the resurrection of the dead, which began with the resurrection of Christ (Rancour-Laferriere 2011, 123–129, 137, n. 24).
7 According to Anderson 1981, p. LXXXI, n. 7.
8 On the long history of representing Mary as a grapevine, see: Thomas 1970.
9 In another work of Philip, Christ crucified is a cluster of grapes (*botrus*) propped on a stake (Dronke 1987, 575).
10 Huot 1997, 130.
11 For a general study of the linkage of wine-making imagery to representations of Christ, see: Thomas 1981 (1936); cf. also Vloberg 1946, 172–183; Rubin 1991, 312–314; Boespflug 2012, 403–435.
12 Szövérffy 1985b, 96; cf. Szövérffy 1985a, 83.
13 Cf. Allison 2001, 874–876, for an analysis by a modern Bible scholar.
14 *Glossa Ordinaria*, in *Patrologia Latina* 114, col. 174, under verse 25, as translated in: Ocker 1998, 165 (n. 30).
15 For an in-depth historical study of the Christ-killer motif in Christian antisemitism, see: Cohen 2007. For a briefer, psychologically oriented survey, see: Rancour-Laferriere 2011, 173–243.
16 Bynum 2007, 175.
17 In a series of footnotes, Gordon A. Anderson (1981, p. LXXXI, nn. 8–10) also concludes that those being castigated toward the end of Philip's poem are Jews. Anderson, however, is working from a slightly different manuscript than the one

upon which the Dreves and Blume edition is based, and his conclusion derives from material in the next-to-last stanza, not from the last stanza upon which my own conclusion is drawn. Unfortunately, Anderson cites no scholarly sources to document the assertions he makes: for example, "The Jews pinned all their hopes on the crucifixion" (n. 9).

18 Lefebvre 1956, 311 (cf. Rancour-Laferriere 2011, 260, n. 19).

19 Lefebvre 1956, 311; *Liber Usualis* (1952), 703.

20 As translated and quoted by: Abulafia 1998, 63.

21 Simonsohn 1988, 74 (no. 71), as translated by Simonsohn 1991, 18. On the complex history of *Sicut Judeis*, see: Grayzel 1991 (1962).

22 Simonsohn 1988, 77 (no. 73), as translated by Simonsohn 1991, 19.

23 Simonsohn 1988, 87 (no. 82).

24 Tanner, ed. 1990, vol. I, 265.

25 Simonsohn 1988, 108–109 (no. 105), as translated by Simonsohn 1991, 21–22.

26 Simonsohn 1991, 22. For further examples of the hostile application of *perfidia* (and its cognates) to Jews in the thirteenth century, see: Bestul 1996, 102–103.

27 For a revealing, in-depth analysis based on recent access to Vatican archives, see the chapter titled "Perfidious Jews?" in: Wolf 2010 (2008), 81–125.

28 Rancour-Laferriere 2011.

29 Leviticus 7:26–27. See the entry "Blood" in: Werblowsky and Wigoder, eds. 1997, 136.

30 "Blood libel" may be broadly defined as the false idea "that Jews need Christian blood for their rituals" (Biale 2007, 2).

31 Biale 2007, 111.

32 Rubin 2004 (1999), 95.

33 Rubin 2004 (1999), 94.

34 Thomas Aquinas 2012, vol. 20, 240 (Part 3, Question 77, Article 4).

35 For an insightful historical overview, see: Macy 1999, 81–120.

36 Macy 1999, 64–67; Price 2003, 21–22; Bynum 2007, 138.

37 From a linguistic viewpoint, the poet has constructed a grammatical parallelism between two prepositional phrases headed by the same verb, and has emphasized the parallelism by placing it at a line boundary, thereby creating an anadiplosis: *pendet ad ubera / Pendet in cruce.*

38 Huot draws a psychologically less specific (yet valid) conclusion from the parallel between Mary's son hanging at the breast and hanging on the cross: "The adversarial relation between Virgin and Cross has, by the end of the poem, become analogy and even metaphorical equivalence; the power of the poem lies in its ability to maintain the tension of this double focus" (1997, 130).

8 Back to Scripture

A Son's Grievance against Mary

Was Mary a Disciple?

In scripture, Mary's *Fiat*, her "Yes" to divine utilization of her metaphorically enslaved body (Luke 1:38), was an important milestone in her life. For many mariophile thinkers, it was also an important step in the development of Christian discipleship. For example, according to Pope Paul VI, in his apostolic exhortation *Marialis cultus*, Mary is "worthy of imitation because she was the first and most perfect of Christ's disciples." This pope's attitude reflects the thinking of many theologians and scholars.[1]

As a matter of fact, nowhere in the gospels is there any assertion that Mary was a disciple of Jesus. She has little role to play during the ministry of her son in any of the gospels. In Luke, the one gospel where she pronounces her *Fiat* to the announcing archangel, she is a no-show at the crucifixion. This is odd. Similarly, the insertion of Mary into the overall Lucan narrative only after she has missed her resurrected son's ascension into the heavens (Acts 1:14) – never to be mentioned in the New Testament again – seems rather lame. These are not good signs of discipleship.

The team of Protestant, Anglican, and Roman Catholic scholars who produced the study *Mary in the New Testament* concludes a chapter (on Luke–Acts) as follows:

> Mary's first response to the good news was: "Behold the handmaid of the Lord. Let it be to me according to your word." The real import of Acts 1:14 is to remind the reader that she had not changed her mind.[2]

If that is so, why were readers not "reminded" earlier, for example during the narration of her son's ministry, or in the depiction of the crucifixion? We are supposed to accept Mary's cameo appearance in Acts 1:14 as the one known scriptural confirmation of the *Fiat* spoken by a 12-year-old girl some three decades earlier.

Perhaps the dearth of evidence for Mary's discipleship should not be taken so seriously. For example, all of the apostles abandon Jesus before the crucifixion (in the synoptics). Should Mary be held to higher standards?

The case of Peter is famous, for three times in a row he denies having any knowledge of Jesus (Luke 22:54–62). But, there is plenty of evidence elsewhere in Luke–Acts that Peter and some of the others could be correctly characterized as disciples. This is not the case for Mary.

In the gospels generally, none of the disciples are targeted with the special kind of reserve – even hostility – that Jesus directs at his mother (and at members of his immediate family). This matter is familiar to biblical scholars, as when David Flusser writes of "an emotion-laden tension [which] seems to have arisen between Jesus and his family."[3] Here, it is the tension between Jesus and his mother that is of interest.

In Mark, who knows nothing of the pious infancy narratives of Luke and Matthew, Mary's interaction with the adult Jesus is almost nonexistent. Rather than join in with the followers of her son after he has grown up and begun his preaching, she senses that something is wrong with what he is doing. When she and other family members hear (or assert)[4] that Jesus "has gone out of his mind [*eksestē*]" (Mark 3:21),[5] they set out to fetch him before he gets into serious trouble. The setting, after all, is Roman-occupied Jewish territory. This Jesus fellow is attracting crowds, and he could be taken for some kind of revolutionary by the authorities. There is no indication that Mary and the other family members who come for him are seeking attention or adulation for themselves.[6] They are just concerned about the strange behavior of a member of their family, and they want to help. But, what they find upon arrival at the scene is a supremely confident cult leader who has, by now, become alienated from them:

> Then his mother and his brothers came; and standing outside, they sent to him and called him. A crowd was sitting around him; and they said to him, "Your mother and your brothers and sisters are outside, asking for you." And he replied, "Who are my mother and my brothers?" And looking at those who sat around him, he said, "Here are my mother and my brothers! Whoever does the will of God is my brother and sister and mother."
>
> (3:31–35)

End of story. The reader is left hanging, as are Mary and other family members. Neither in Mark nor in the parallel passages in Matthew (12:46–50) and Luke (8:19–21) does the narrative continue with some kind of resolution. Mary and the other family members have been snubbed (disowned even) by one of their own.[7] All three synoptics show "Christ's deliberate distancing from his mother."[8] It is no wonder that some defensive mariologists have dubbed such passages "antimariological."[9]

Yet, a point has been made: true disciples of Jesus constitute a more significant, if only metaphorical, "family" (an "eschatological family," say Brown et al.; a "replacement family," says Crossan; a "true family," says Buby, "fictive kinship," says Johnson; "household of God," says Moxnes;

"family of God," says Finlan; "fictive family of children of the Father," says Van Os, "true paternity of believers," says Dunnill, etc. etc.) than do real family members.[10] The religious collective being assembled by the charismatic cult leader from Nazareth is primary. The earthly one mothered by Miryam of Nazareth is decidedly secondary. One has to wonder why Jesus treats his mother this way. Hans Urs von Balthasar remarks: "when he [Jesus] refused to see his family when they came to visit him, describing those who heard his word in faith as his 'brother, and sister, and mother' (Mt 12:50), a sword must have pierced his Mother's heart."[11] The "sword" is, of course, a reference to the mysterious prophecy about what the future held for Mary in Luke (2:35). Here, it is Jesus himself who is wielding the sword.

The above-mentioned ecumenical group of Protestant and Roman Catholic theologians informs us that "the point of the passage [in Mark] is to define the eschatological family, not to exclude the physical family."[12] But, if this is so, why does Jesus not immediately issue a friendly invitation to his "physical family" to join? Indeed, why does Jesus *never*, in any of the gospels, invite his "physical family" to join? To judge from the harsh tone conveyed by the words of Jesus, Mary and other family members had already made it clear that they would decline any such hypothetical invitation. "Their unbelief," as Tertullian had opined at an early stage in the development of Christianity, was "evident."[13]

To bring up the old theme of whether Mary had doubts about what her son was preaching, and about who he was, is to raise the issue of orthodox Christian belief generally. All gospel passages that highlight the contrast between the metaphorical family being preached by Jesus and the biological family of Jesus (or biological families generally) invite the reader to notice the difference between believing and not believing. Those who already believe may not be put off by the occasionally harsh words Jesus has for family members. The metaphorical family is more important. But those who do not believe will repeatedly be astonished by this aspect of the Galilean preacher's personality.

Particularly astonishing are those utterances that reveal the preacher's grandiosity. His metaphorical family is not only headed up by a paternal God, but occasionally by the preacher – Jesus – himself: "Whoever loves father or mother more than me is not worthy of me" (Matthew 10:37).

More than whom? Not worthy of whom? – "More than *me*," "not worthy of *me*," he says. To coin a phrase, this man seems to think he is Jesus Christ.[14] But, why *should* Mary be the "disciple" of a son who insults ordinary mothers and fathers in this fashion? She is his mother, after all. This is stronger than the sassy adolescent outburst that the mother and the substitute father hear after they find their lost Jesus in the Temple: "Did you not know that I must be in my Father's house?" (Luke 2:49). The adult Jesus even obliges members of his metaphorical "family" to suffer to the point of death in their devotion to *him*: "whoever does not take up the cross and follow me is not worthy of me" (Matthew 10:38). As Luke tells it, people should be willing to join Jesus in his coming suicide:

> Now large crowds were traveling with him; and he turned and said to them, "Whoever comes to me and does not hate [*misei*] father and mother, wife and children, brothers and sisters, yes, and even life itself, cannot be my disciple. Whoever does not carry the cross and follow me cannot be my disciple."
>
> (Luke 14:25–27)

Perhaps there is an element of "Semitic exaggeration" in the idea of *hating* one's own family members.[15] But, hating "life itself?" Jesus did in fact provoke the authorities into crucifying him, and a true "disciple" was supposed to take up the cross and follow *him* in his masochistic behavior. If any members of Jesus' immediate family wanted to become "disciples," they too were hereby obliged to follow him on the path of self-destruction. This is a very strange obligation to place on one's own family members. Was Mary, like her son, supposed to get herself crucified? Anyone who wants to believe that Mary was a "disciple" of her son ought first to acknowledge the fact that this son harbored an implicit death wish against his mother.

Jesus Speaks to Mary from the Cross

It is only in John's gospel (19:25–27) that a member of Jesus' real, nonmetaphorical family shows up at the crucifixion. That member is Mary, of course, but there is no indication that she is at Golgotha with Jesus because she is his "disciple," nor is there any record of her later taking up a cross in order to become "worthy" of her son. Mary simply remains silent as she stands in the vicinity of the cross with the two other Marys and the so-called beloved disciple. In this gospel account, Mary the mother of Jesus is an observer, not a participant in her son's passion – contrary to the various theological, dramatic, artistic, literary, and liturgical representations of the passion that later were invented and continue to be invented in our own time. Although Mary had spoken to Jesus earlier in the same gospel in an attempt to intervene at the wedding in Cana ("They have no wine" – 2:3), here, at the foot of the cross, she is speechless, and her dying son does the talking. He says: "Woman, here is your son" (19:26), thereby entrusting his biological mother to the care of the beloved disciple who, in turn, is addressed with the words: "Here is your mother" (19:27).

From the cross, a dying Jesus *seems* to be playing the role of a dutiful son with a last request that his mother now be cared for by family members. When he turns to Mary, however, he gives no indication that he is speaking to a member of his immediate family, let alone his mother, for he addresses her coldly as "woman" (as he had done earlier in Cana as well). In addition, the man Mary is being turned over to is not even a member of the immediate family, but is someone special in Jesus' metaphorical family.

What Jesus really does, then, is push his mother into the clutches of that religiously constructed, metaphorical family that Mary had never much cared for. Spoken by her own son, this performative utterance from the cross is a harsh reproach to her as a real mother. She already understands that she is losing her real son, and that the substitute son (the beloved disciple) he is foisting on her is no son of hers. Might she also understand something else, then, something terribly important, which also has to do with the replacement of someone real by a substitute?

I am referring to the matter of the real, biological ("natural," "earthly") father of Jesus. This, of course, is another issue that turns on belief. For traditionalist believers, the only father of Jesus is the "Father" – that is, God the Father in heaven. For nonbelievers, on the other hand, the real father of Jesus, whoever he was, had to be the biological father. If Jesus truly was a human being, he has to have had a biological father as well as a biological mother. If Joseph was not the biological father (an idea that many Christian theologians accept, and countless believers take for granted), then some other human male was the father (a theologically incorrect idea, and a slur on Mary's reputation).

Jesus himself never acknowledged the existence of any biological father. The heavenly Father was the *only* father to whom Jesus ever referred as his own. Jesus preached a message of acknowledgment of this heavenly Father at the expense of real fathers, as we saw earlier in this book. This message could not have escaped the adult Mary's attention, and yet, she (the only one who could have known who Jesus' biological father was) showed no sign of embracing her son's message.

What the 12-year-old Mary had apparently believed was supposed to happen after her encounter with the announcing angel in Luke's gospel did not happen. The mature, adult Mary has a more sober, realistic view of the son promised her by the angel. The now-grown-up son shows signs of being "out of his mind" (Mark 3:21). From Mary's viewpoint, there is no evidence that the Lord God has given her son "the throne of his ancestor David," as promised in Luke (1:32). Instead, what Mary beholds before her eyes at Golgotha is her son crucified (John 19:25–27).

Origen and other theologians were probably right in asserting that Mary was "scandalized" by the crucifixion and did not believe her son was a messiah. Mary was in a position to believe even less, however, than the male theologians (including Origen) imagined. As the mother of Jesus, she knew better than they did about how Jesus came into the world, and what she knew was mundane: she had had sexual intercourse with a man and had become pregnant in the usual way. After giving birth to Jesus, she fell silent, never revealing (in canonical scripture) who the father of her son was. Who, indeed, was the real father? Joseph? A lover? A rapist? Not a proper son of Abraham? Many scenarios have been imagined. All of them dump Jesus into a situation of social fatherlessness.

Hanging on the cross in the last of the gospels, Jesus has one last opportunity to confront his mother over the issue of his illegitimate origin.

When he tells her, "Woman, here is your son" (19:26), he really seems to be saying: "You gave me a pretend father, I will give you a pretend son." Jesus the human being wants her to understand, at last, that it was insufficient for her to mother him biologically. He had always needed, in addition to a biological mother, a legitimate and nameable father. This he did not have, as is already evident from the 12-year-old Jesus' rhetorical question about an obligation to be "in my Father's house [*en tois tou patros mou*]" (Luke 2:49; cf. John 2:16) – words spoken in the Jerusalem Temple to Mary *and Joseph*, who had been searching for him when he was lost.[16] Such an utterance makes it clear that, even as a child, Jesus did not accept Joseph as a father and was dealing creatively with the issue of who his father was.

Perhaps, in the end, Mary understood that her son's last words to her constituted a final act of aggression against her. And retrospectively, perhaps, she understood what her 12-year-old child had said to her and her husband in the Temple. She probably also comprehended the stories that had gotten back to her about an adult son who was preaching a message of hostility toward family members.

One has to put oneself in Mary's shoes. The conflict with the son cannot be disregarded or explained away. A devoted, empathic mother would internalize such a conflict. We can imagine that the mourning process must have been truly wrenching for the scriptural mother of Jesus.

A Note on Retaining the Crucifixion Accounts

Here, it is worth pointing out that historical evidence for gospel depictions of the crucifixion is meager. The historical Jesus may have been alone as he was dying on the cross, and there may not even have been a trial before the crucifixion. The prominent historian John Dominic Crossan concludes, "I cannot find any detailed historical information about the crucifixion of Jesus" – the reason being that most of what has in the past been taken as "historical information" turns out to be "prophecy historicized rather than history recalled."[17] Like most scholars of the historical Jesus, Crossan does believe that Jesus existed and was crucified, and that the immediate reason was a historically likely incident, the so-called cleansing of the Temple. But, in Crossan's view, the authorities acted quickly and with "brutal offhandedness":

> The elimination of a dangerous peasant nuisance like Jesus need not have involved any official trials or even consultations between Temple and Roman authorities. It was, in my view, handled under general procedures for maintaining crowd control during Passover. If individuals cause serious trouble in the Temple, crucify them immediately as a warning.[18]

What Crossan's historical assessment implies with regard to John's report of Jesus speaking from the cross to Mary and the beloved disciple is clear:

the report had best be disregarded by anyone questing for the historical Jesus (or the historical Mary). Pastoral psychologist Donald Capps, who has reviewed the historical studies of Crossan and others, states that, "John's account of Jesus entrusting his mother to the beloved disciple at the cross [was] an artistic invention."[19]

Fair enough – provided one is attempting to understand Jesus and Mary, son and mother, two historically real persons from first-century Galilee. Capps has certainly engaged the research findings on the "Jesus of history" to a degree unmatched by any other psychological scholar before him. If, however, the goal is to understand how believers have responded or might respond to passages in their canonical New Testament, then the crucifixion narrations cannot be disregarded. The death of one's God at Golgotha is too important. The last words of Jesus to Mary stand as is.

*

There is no evidence in the gospels themselves that Mary was a "disciple" of her son. Mary resisted joining the "metaphorical family" that Jesus was organizing and that eventually would become the Church. Mary was aware of the fact that devaluation of one's own family was part of the message Jesus was preaching to his followers. From the cross, Jesus addressed his mother coldly as "woman" and turned her over to one of his disciples, pushing her into the clutches of his "metaphorical family." The son's last words to his mother also indicate anger over the uncertainty of his paternity.

Notes

1 *Mary in the Church* 2003, 74. Other supporters of Mary's early discipleship include: Beinert 1991, 481; Brown 1993 (1977), 316–319; Brown et al. 1978, esp. ch. 6, 105–177; Bearsley 1980; Feuillet 1981, 28–29; Fitzmyer 1989, 78; Talbert 2002, 25–28; Gaventa 2004, 22–23; McGuckin 2011 (2008), 210–211. The role of Saint Augustine in the study of Mary's faith and discipleship is important: Bearsley 1980, 479–482; O'Carroll 2000 (1982), 64–65. In the Orthodox East, notably in the earliest *Life of the Virgin* (seventh century) by Maximos the Confessor, Mary's discipleship is raised to the level of a leadership position among the female followers of Jesus before the crucifixion, and afterwards is further raised to the level of a leading authority in the early Christian church (Maximus the Confessor 2012, 96–148; cf. comments by Stephen J. Shoemaker in the Introduction to that volume, 22–35; also Shoemaker 2005).

2 Brown et al. 1978, 177.

3 Flusser 1991, 163.

4 According to the translation proposed by Johnson 2002, 33.

5 See: Bauer 1957 (1952), 276, where the translation is, "He has lost his senses."

6 Contra Finlan 2009, 64. In the *Summa Theologiae*, Aquinas noted Chrysostom's claim that the family members had come out of vainglory (Thomas Aquinas 1969, 21).

7 Here is how Schalom Ben-Chorin (1983 [1971], 14) characterizes the way Jesus treats his mother in this scene: "*But he disowns her.* And he does so in a way which is characteristic of a Jewish dialogue, and answers in the form of a question: 'Who is my mother?'" Cf. Ruether 1977, 37; Johnson 2003, 217.

8 Clayton 1990, 2.

9 Laurentin writes: "En ces dernières années, certains mariologues en étaient venus à qualifier ces versets 'd'antimariologiques'" (1965, 99).

10 Brown et al. 1978, 53; Crossan 1991, 299; Buby 1994–1996, vol. 1, 29; Johnson 2002, 36; Moxnes 2003, 157; Finlan 2009, xiv; Van Os 2011, 140; Dunnill 2013, 121. Some have asserted that the "brothers" and "sisters" are not full siblings of Jesus. But, if they are not the full siblings that they seem to be in a natural reading of the text, then the contrast between what is real and what is metaphorical in the religious message Jesus attempts to convey loses much of its didactic force. See especially: Miegge 1955, 36–43.

11 Von Balthasar 1992 (1978), 330.

12 Brown et al. 1978, 54.

13 In Chapter 7 of the tract *De Carne Christi*, as translated in *Ante-Nicene Fathers* 2004 (1885-1887), vol. 3, 528.

14 Cf. the nonpsychological analysis of "Jesus' own high self-awareness" by biblical scholar David Flusser (2001, 118).

15 Franklin 2001, 946; cf. Flusser 2001, 35, n. 37.

16 Cf. von Balthasar in: Ratzinger and von Balthasar 2005 (1997), 105.

17 Crossan 1996, 159.

18 Crossan 1996, 212.

19 Capps 2002b, 443. I have expressed agreement with Crossan's view (Rancour-Laferriere 2011, 179), and for this very reason I should have noted that the lack of reliable historical information about the crucifixion is the reason why Donald Capps (2000) had not included a study of the passion in his insightful psychological analysis of the historical Jesus (Rancour-Laferriere 2011, 80, n. 163).

9 Jesus at the Breast

A Recognizable Visual Image

Modern Christians have often lamented the commercialization of Christmas. The humble birth of the son of God is overshadowed by Santa Claus (originally Saint Nicholas of Myra), Christmas trees, and presents – the more (and the more expensive), the better. Of course, anyone's birthday is supposed to celebrate the entrance of a human being into the world, but in this case it was the Lord God himself who deigned to enter into the world as a human being. Today, we know what year it is by counting from the year the Lord was supposedly born (1 AD), thereby ushering in the common era (CE).

Christmas celebrates the birth of Jesus into the world, not the birthing process per se – that is, not the mother's labor and the physical exit from her body. That would be inappropriate in most cultural contexts. In the past, some theologians have seen fit to speculate about whether Mary's virginity was preserved when she gave birth, as noted above. There do exist images of Mary pregnant with her child (*Maria Gravida*).[1] Images of the "nativity" per se do not show Mary giving birth, but of Mary *having given birth*, often with the newborn infant – usually swaddled, sometimes naked – nearby. If Mary is performing some maternal function in this context, it is usually the breastfeeding of her child.

Above (ch. 6), I have commented on the significance of Mary breastfeeding her child in the context of a poem that represents the adult Christ himself as "feeding" the faithful from the wound in his side (*pascit nos ex vulnere*). As it turns out, there is also an abundance of both verbal and visual imagery that represents a breastfeeding Mary without any reference to her *adult* son. This is yet another indication of the extent to which Mary has become a goddess in her own right.

Having been born a human being of a human mother, Mary's child required nourishment. Images of this child nursing at Mary's breast have been a persistent feature of marian iconography. Very few of these images survive from late antiquity,[2] but, by the late medieval period, they had accumulated in considerable numbers. Caroline Walker Bynum writes of the "hundreds of medieval paintings" in the West in which "the Virgin offers her breast to the infant Christ."[3] In post-Reformation Protestant territories, the production and veneration of such imagery were not encouraged, of course, but, in the Catholic lands of Europe and the New World, as well as in the Orthodox East (which now included the rapidly expanding Russian Empire), images of Mary breastfeeding the child Jesus proliferated.[4] In our time, all historians of Christian art are likely to have viewed such images.

Some devout Christians today actually pray before these images, although this practice is more prevalent in some cultures than in others. For example, I have never observed Russian Orthodox believers pray before icons of Mary nursing her child, nor have Russians reported praying before such icons in interviews with me. Churchgoing Polish Catholics, on the other hand, often carry a small devotional image of this type of madonna in their missals, and such an image is also thought to be the most popular domestic religious decoration in Poland generally.[5]

Images of Mary breastfeeding the Christ child constitute a category that transcends (art-)historical, ethnic, national, denominational, and linguistic boundaries. It does not matter, for example, that this category is signified with a multitude of terms, depending not only on the language being utilized, but also on the situational context of linguistic practice. In ordinary English, for example, one may speak of Mary "nursing," "breastfeeding," "suckling," or "giving suck" to her child. A professional art historian or a theologian writing in English, on the other hand, may refer to an image of the *Virgo lactans*. *Maria lactans*, too, is customary in learned discourse. Both of these Latin terms are utilized by specialists when writing in a variety of languages – although less so when writing in those languages that have their own customary term: Greek *Galaktotrophousa*, Russian *Mlekopitatel'nitsa*, Italian *Madonna del Latte*, Spanish *Virgen de la Leche*, French *la Vierge allaitant*, German *die Milchnährende* or *stillende Muttergottes*, Polish *Matka Boska Karmiąca* or *Maryja Karmicielka*, and so on.

Despite the plethora of terms and the variety of cultural contexts, the biology is a constant. When we see an image of Mary breastfeeding her child, we do not have to ask what is going on. What we see is a nursing couple.[6] Mary is attending to her child in what is a normal, recognizable biological interaction essential for her child's early growth and development. It is assumed that the child is Jesus – not a sibling of Jesus, and certainly not the child of another woman. It is also assumed that the woman nursing the child is Mary, not a wet nurse.

To my knowledge, no religious (non-blasphemous) images of Jesus being *wet*-nursed or *bottle*-fed have been produced anywhere, including in any cultural contexts where wet-nursing (e.g., pre-Soviet Russian Orthodox gentry) or bottle-feeding (e.g., mid-twentieth-century Catholic North America) was customary. Christians everywhere have understood that, when it came to nourishing the divine infant Jesus, there was no substitute for Mary's own breasts.

Messy Taxonomies

This brings us to the more general problem of categorizing images of Mary with the Christ child. Of course, the majority of such images do not involve breastfeeding at all. Many images in this majority have proven difficult to categorize (and even the minority that include the nursing couple have proven difficult to classify). Scholars agree that there is a need for detailed consideration of the historical period, ethnolinguistic context, sectarian identity, sociopolitical movement, theological context, and so on, within which specific images of Mary and the Christ child originated and were utilized for devotional purposes by believers. In most cases, however, the original image from which a particular class of images might have arisen has been lost, and the context in which that original might have been created is unknown.

Still, there are troves of historical evidence, so that it is both possible and necessary to ask questions about the derivation and descent of images. For example: when and under what circumstances did images of Mary with the Christ child begin to fall into a category that Byzantine Greeks termed (and art historians still term) *Hodēgētria* ("She who shows the Way")? This designation derives from *Hodēgōn*, "of guides," the name of a monastery in Constantinople that housed monks who guided (showed the way for) blind pilgrims to a miraculous sight-restoring spring, and that kept the original (now lost) icon of this type. In other words, the designation was originally a toponym. But, it became more than that as well, for in the "typical" *Hodēgētria* image, Mary holds the Christ child on one arm, while gesturing with the other hand toward the child, who is himself the way ("I am the way" – John 14:6). Now we have, not just a toponym, but a certain configuration of the mother and child with its own theological meaning.

Enter a new and very different type that, however, is neither a toponym nor a theologically meaningful spatial configuration. That type was (and still is sometimes) called *Eleousa* – "Virgin of Tenderness/Mercy," "Compassionate One," "Loving-kindness." The new type did not displace the older one, but supplemented it. Yet, if the two types were different, as is sometimes claimed, how could it happen that a given image was sometimes understood as both *Hodēgētria* and *Eleousa*? And why, with time, was the title *Eleousa* (or its supposedly inadequate Russian translation, *Umilenie*) applied to many icons of very heterogeneous physical appearance, and originating from very different sites in what was once the Byzantine world?

I cannot even begin to address these sample questions about two major, overlapping types of image of Mary and the Christ child.[7] The point here is to indicate how complicated and difficult the taxonomic questions can be, and to show that some images of Mary with her child may legitimately have more than one name. Identifying icons is not the same as identifying birds. A Gyrfalcon can never be a Peregrine Falcon, but a *Hodēgētria* can sometimes be an *Eleousa*.

Figure 9.1 Madonna of Humility (detail), Andrea di Bartolo, ca.1400. Washington, DC, National Gallery (Williamson 2009, 157, fig. 36).

Even the apparently straightforward category of images that portray Mary breastfeeding the Christ child is not immune to this problem. Not all images that depict the divine nursing couple are termed *Maria lactans*. Consider, for example, the so-called Madonna of Humility, which was once believed to have originated in the Italian Trecento. What was sometimes termed *La Nostra Donna de Humilitate* showed the (usually) breastfeeding Mary seated in a lowly position on the ground (see Figure 9.1). Some of the images of this type also applied the symbols of the Woman of the Apocalypse to Mary (sun, moon, a crown of 12 stars). Occasionally, elements of annunciation imagery (a lily, an angel with scroll, etc.) were present, and sometimes there were other figures (the donor, various saints, multiple angels, flagellants, an adult Christ, and others). In fact, of the 25 illustrations explicitly labeled "Madonna of Humility" in the pioneering study on this subject by Millard Meiss, only 12 are images of Mary alone with the Christ child – that is, without the accessory figures.[8]

The Madonna of Humility is clearly a rather heterogeneous category. Nevertheless, the name of the category is significant. Meiss asserts that, "the humility of the Virgin resided primarily in the single fact that she was seated on the ground."[9] This taxonomic conclusion is bolstered by various kinds of evidence, such as the idea that the Latin word for "ground" or "earth" – that is, *humus* – is, according to theologian Isidore of Seville, the etymological root of *humilis*, meaning "humble": *humilis dicitur quasi humo acclinis*.[10]

Another component of significance, according to Meiss, is the presence of the nursing couple: in images of the Madonna of Humility, Mary "sits on the ground *nursing her Child* 'in public,' more like a simple housewife or a poor peasant than the Queen of Heaven."[11] In 20 out of the 25 figures (i.e., 80 percent) furnished by Meiss, Mary is breastfeeding her child.[12] Clearly, there is at least an affinity here with that supposedly different category that art historians term *Maria lactans*.[13]

Meiss believes that representations of Mary nursing the Christ child "showed that situation in which the Virgin was most concretely and intimately the mother of Christ," and consequently displayed "that character and power which arose from her motherhood, i.e. her role as *Maria mediatrix*, compassionate intercessor for humanity before the impartial justice of Christ or God the Father."[14]

In a book-length study of the Madonna of Humility, Beth Williamson takes issue with Meiss on a number of topics. She considers a wider geographic range of images (including Bohemia) than Meiss had in his shorter, Italo-centric investigation, and she pays closer attention to manuscripts of books of hours than Meiss had. Williamson also arrives at an altogether different conclusion regarding the "humility" epithet:

> it seems that the image now known as the Madonna of Humility might have become associated with the concept of the Virgin's humility not because of its seated posture . . . but as a result of its connections, in its original manuscript form, with the Annunciation.[15]

Meiss and Williamson approach the Madonna of Humility as a category in the history of art, not as a psychological category. Both understand, however, that humility is an important psychological attribute of Mary for the images in question. Both Meiss and Williamson refer to theological and devotional thinking about humility (including St. Bonaventure) leading up to the middle of the fourteenth century. Both consider the one gospel account of the annunciation, where Mary proclaims her lowly social status as *ancilla Domini* (Luke 1:38), and both refer to Mary's proclamation of the Lord's favorable attitude toward *humilitatem ancillae suae* in the subsequent Magnificat (1:48). For Williamson, however, Luke's infancy narrative carries greater weight in the art-historical argument than it does for Meiss.

Both Williamson and Meiss offer highly sophisticated art-historical accounts of the origin and development of a certain category of images that has come to be known as the Madonna of Humility. Yet educated, nonspecialist museum-goers today are very unlikely to be able to identify an image from this specific category, much less understand where the "humility" lies in such an image. On the other hand, medieval churchgoers and uneducated peasant believers would have had a good grasp of what the "humility" was about, for they were immersed in a religious culture filled with stories, rituals, holidays, prayers, music, and images that both directly and indirectly referred to the humble mother of their God. Moreover, the sight of a mother breastfeeding a child would have been commonplace for such people. Meiss alludes to humble nursing scenes, comparing the Madonna of Humility to "a simple housewife or a poor peasant" who happened to be breastfeeding a child "in public."[16] Here, Meiss makes an implicit assumption about social stratification: poor women or peasant women – that is, women of "humble" social station, not women from the gentry or from the urban merchant class – would have been the ones seen nursing an infant.

Rehabilitating Maternity with Images of Mary Breastfeeding Jesus

Meiss makes the correct assumption. But Williamson has the advantage of access to more recent sources. These deal with the social status of women who breastfed infants in the sociocultural milieu from which there emerged images of the Madonna of Humility, and within which there must have been some sort of response to such images. Williamson reviews the extensive historical literature on wet-nursing in medieval Europe (and in fourteenth–fifteenth-century Italy in particular).[17] Included in her survey is a study of childrearing practices from the ninth to the thirteenth centuries in the medieval West by Mary Martin McLaughlin, who mentions "representations of the *Virgo lactans*, the nursing mother of Christ," and who suggests that such representations reflect "the ideal maternal image" – that is, "the mother who nursed her own children."[18] Included as well in Williamson's survey is the book *Childhood in the Middle Ages* by Shulamith Shahar, who also points to Mary: "The art of the fourteenth to fifteenth centuries, particularly in Italy, repeatedly depicts the Holy Mother nursing her child – the ideal image for all mothers in this world."[19] By and large, the historical literature does support a key statement made by the Franciscan Bartholomaeus Anglicus in an "extremely popular"[20] treatise titled *De proprietatibus rerum* (ca.1230): "The infant raised on his mother's milk [*materno lacte nutritur*] is more praiseworthy than one raised on the milk of another."[21] In other words, maternal breastfeeding was the ideal.

As Williamson points out, Bartholomaeus "allows for the hiring of a wet-nurse if necessary."[22] But when, exactly, was this "necessary"? To be in a position to hire a wet nurse was an indicator of social standing. In Florence and the surrounding areas, for example, the man who hired a wet nurse (*balia*) for his wife had to have sufficient funds to pay for this service (and it was the men who took care of these matters). In her book *Women, Family, and Ritual in Renaissance Italy*, social historian Christiane Klapisch-Zuber writes that "paid breast feeding was a distinctive sign of the urban elites."[23] For example, between 1302 and 1399, almost all fathers (although the sample size is still small) who left a written financial record of putting a child out to nurse came from "prominent families." This changed with time. The records show that, after 1450, "half of the families concerned were of modest social rank."[24] Assuming that the other half of the families were of higher than "modest" social rank, and assuming that the records (*ricordanze*) were representative, Klapisch-Zuber can report that:

> in the large city of Florence, nursing by a salaried nurse or by a slave woman became the dominant practice, at least from the middle of the fifteenth century onward, even if we cannot for the moment trace the exact limits of the practice.[25]

The "limits" in question involve both class and geography:

> We would probably have to look to a still lower social level; in particular we would have to leave Florence and delve into the smaller towns of the territory that it administered to get back to a world in which the mother took on the function of nursing.[26]

In other words, Klapisch-Zuber is granting that lower-class urban mothers, together with mothers out in suburban towns and in the countryside, were still breastfeeding their own infants (and, in some cases, being paid to breastfeed the infants of "urban elites").

Here, it should be obvious that the hiring of a wet nurse by Florentines would hardly have been viewed by anyone as a manifestation of "humility":

> Paid breast feeding was a distinctive sign of the urban elites: it flattered the vanity of the husbands, to be sure, but it also enhanced the woman's status as a fertile and prolific wife.[27]

Nouns such as "elites," "vanity," and "status" would hardly belong in the same semantic field as "Madonna of Humility." Indeed, Klapisch-Zuber says as much when, in a reference to the early research of Meiss, she asks:

> When painters removed the Virgin of *humility* from her throne and placed her on a cushion on the ground, did they not do more to rehabilitate maternity and its *humble* nursing tasks than all the rehashed preachings of doctors and moralists who from antiquity had lauded the benefits of maternal nursing, or the reflections of a few humanists writing on conjugal relations and the role of the woman in marriage?[28]

Margaret Miles goes further, suggesting that some of the images in question were actually intended as religious propaganda:

> It is likely that the same clergymen who advocated maternal nursing in sermons also commissioned paintings to be placed in the public space of churches. Depictions of the nursing Virgin conveyed the same message carried in sermons, namely, that women should emulate the mother of Christ.[29]

Before a middle-class Florentine mother's eyes, then, was an implicit ideal: a humble mother nursing her *own* humble child. Such an image plainly contradicted what she herself was doing every time she gave birth to a child and farmed the child out to another woman for purposes of nursing. The image before her represented, moreover, not just any mother, and not just any child, but the mother of God, with God himself at the breast. The Florentine mother who viewed the Madonna of Humility (or, for that matter, any image of Mary breastfeeding her child) was confronted with one of the highest ideals imaginable within her own medieval religious context. Such an image might well have left her conscience-stricken.

If we take the *viewpoint of the child* who was handed over to a wet nurse, it should become even clearer why an image of the divine nursing couple might have disturbed the middle-class Florentine mother. According to James Bruce Ross, the infant was typically separated from the biological mother shortly after birth and taken to a wet nurse, who was "generally a peasant woman living at a distance, with whom the infant would presumably remain for about two years or until weaning was completed." In this setting, the child "became wholly dependent for food, care and affection upon [the] surrogate, and its return to its own mother was to a stranger in an alien home, to a person with whom no physical or emotional ties had ever been established."[30]

It is not that the wet-nursed child was deprived of interaction with some adult capable of "mothering" the child. That adult was the wet nurse herself, who by definition already had experience as a mother. The problem was, rather, that the child both lost this "mother" after having been wet-nursed *and* was obliged to accept a second – biological – mother, a stranger who could never be the "mother" the child had just lost. Having feasted in the arms of a wet nurse, and having slept in a cradle near her or even in her conjugal bed, the child was snatched away and returned to an unfamiliar biological mother (as well as an unfamiliar father and probably unfamiliar siblings and/or other unfamiliar relatives).

After such a shock to the child, it must have been difficult for both the child and the original, biological mother to establish a mutual attachment of trust and love. For her part, the biological mother must have sensed the problem, but it is not easy to imagine what initiative she could have taken after the fact of her child's having been wet-nursed – and weaned as well. Denial may have been the best solution, but denial would have been undone every time she beheld one of those paintings of the Christ child nursing at Mary's breast.

What about the motives of the artists themselves? In her book *The History of the Breast*, Marilyn Yalom writes:

> It is possible that those urban middle-class children who later became the painters and sculptors of the early Renaissance were marked with a longing for maternal intimacy that may have been denied them as babes. They may indeed have latched onto *Maria lactans* as a substitute mother, elevating nursing to a sacred level because they and their generation had missed it in real life.[31]

This is an interesting idea. The middle-class children may have "latched onto" a breastfeeding Mary because she, unlike their own mothers, breastfed her own child. Here, in my opinion, is yet another illustration of the tendency of mariophiles implicitly to hold their own mothers in contempt. In this case, however, the contempt was morally justified, and the compensatory idealization of Mary must have been very intense. Some of the resulting images of the divine nursing couple are superb.

Textual Representations of the Divine Nursing Couple

Ephrem the Syrian (d. 373) wrote of the Christ child in hymns composed in the eastern Aramaic dialect of Syriac: "He was lofty, but he sucked Mary's milk"; or, "He drank from your breast [*tdky*] visible milk."[32] Hymns from the Syriac churches repeatedly display a sense of wonder at the Virgin Mary's ability to breastfeed her divine child:

> In her hands she carries the Infant
> – and yet she sees virginity's seals on her body.
> Milk flows warm in her breasts,
> yet she has not stirred in her virginity.[33]
> A young girl provides milk, a virgin gives birth –
> who will not be amazed at this glorious mother
> who kneels down to give birth, who gives milk to her child,
> who resembles an ordinary mother in all these things?[34]
> Mary the faithful, blessed among women,
> proffered Him milk from her breasts though still a virgin.
> A marvel is this: who is capable to tell of how it took place?[35]

It would seem that a virgin breastfeeding her child is – in the Syriac context – quite as remarkable as a virgin giving birth to a child. Indeed, from a strictly biological viewpoint, only a woman who has recently given birth is normally capable of breastfeeding a child (hence the exploitative nature of wet-nursing, which requires that another child's mother be "borrowed" for the purpose).

In a Coptic homily attributed to Theophilus of Alexandria (d. 412), Mary is praised for breastfeeding "the Christ who nourisheth us all": "Blessed art thou, nourishing Him with thy chaste milk!"[36] Cyril of Alexandria wrote (in Greek) to Nestorius in 430:

> Even when he is seen as a baby in swaddling bands still at the breast [*en kolpō*] of the virgin who bore him, even so as God he filled the whole creation and was enthroned with his Father, because deity is without quantity or size and accepts no limitations.[37]

Cyril's assertion about the divine nursing couple is not merely a statement about the great promise or potential that the child Jesus will eventually bring to fruition. Rather, it is a theological formulation of the ability of the eternal God of the universe to manifest himself temporarily in the humble guise of a nursing child. In a Coptic encomium of Mary attributed to Cyril, this Christ child exhibits his dependence on his mother in rather graphic terms: "He lifted up His eyes to thy [Mary's] face. He stretched out His hand, He took thy breast, and He drew into His mouth the milk which was sweeter than manna." Then, "Having drunk from thy spotless breasts, He called thee 'My mother'."[38] Of course, this child, being God, was the one who filled Mary's breasts with milk in the first place: "He gave thee milk in thy breasts in the heavens."[39]

Enthusiasm about the divine nursing couple in an Egyptian context reflects the strength of traditional beliefs there about the goddess Isis (Aset). A typical Isiac narrative reports that Horus, the son of Isis, was not thriving in the arms of his wet nurse, and so Isis understood that she herself must nurse the child at her divine breast in order for him to survive and grow up to become a strong god. And so he did, becoming "the living symbol of divine power on earth."[40] Isis is, therefore, often pictured with Horus seated on her lap with his head near her exposed breast, or nursing at her breast. Such an image is termed *Isis lactans*. Much research has been conducted in this area.[41]

In the eighth century, Greek fathers wrote about the divine nursing couple. Patriarch Germanos of Constantinople has already been mentioned above. The great iconophile theologian John of Damascus praised Mary's breasts, utilizing explicit imagery that appealed to the emotions and the senses of his readers. In one of his homilies, he declares to Mary that, "milk from your breast[s] suckled God [*gala mastōn sou ethēlasen ho theos*] and your lips were united with the lips of God."[42] Or, he not only utilizes the standard marian hyperbole, "lap [*Gastēr*] inhabited by the uncontainable," but follows this with a reference to Mary's "breasts of milk [*mastoi galaktos*] by which God was nourished, the child Jesus."[43]

Explicitness of lactational imagery was a feature of theology, preaching, and devotions relating to Mary and her infant son in the Latin West as well.

In his Christmas sermons, for example, Saint Augustine liked to refer to breastfeeding: "Ruler of the stars, He nurses at his mother's bosom"; "she [Mary] gave milk to our bread."[44] In a famous sermon Augustine addresses Mary directly: "Give suck, mother, to the one who is our food [*Lacta, mater, cibum nostrum*]; give suck to the bread [*lacta panem*] which comes from heaven and is placed in a manger, like feed for pious beasts of burden."[45] Here, Mary literally provides herself (her milk) to her son, who will in turn provide himself (the eucharistic bread) to the faithful (see below, pp. 257–260, on the equivalence of the manger with the eucharistic altar). As Henri Barré demonstrates, some of Augustine's readers picked up on this oral imagery: that is, they plagiarized it, repeating it with variations in their homiletic writings – for example: *Lacta, Maria, Creatorem tuum; lacta panem coeli, pretium mundi;*[46] or, *Lacta, mater, Christum, et Dominum nostrum et cibum;*[47] or, *Lacta ergo, mater, cibum nostrum; lacta panem caelestem.*[48] The relevant parts of Mary's anatomy are quite naturally referred to as well, for example in the pseudo-Augustinian sermon *Legimus et fideliter retinemus . . .*: "Offer your breast to the one who licks it [*lambenti mamillam*]"; or, "May the infant be nourished with the milk of your breasts [*tuorum uberum*]."[49]

Augustine and some of his imitators who sermonized on the nativity theme expressed Mary's nursing of the Christ child in language suggestive of the eucharist (*lacta . . . cibum nostrum, lacta panem coeli*, etc.). The eucharistic sacrament, however, is based on the sacrifice of Mary's son on the cross. It is not surprising, therefore, to find passages where the image of Jesus at the breast is directly linked to images of the passion. An example is provided by another variant of the sermon *Legimus et fideliter retinemus . . .*, this one attributed to Faustus of Riez (d. ca.490):

> O Mary, nurse your creator, nurse the Bread of Heaven, nurse the ransom of the world, offer your breast to him to suckle so that through you [*pro te*] he may offer his cheek to those who strike (Lam. 3.30); yes, nurture your child with the milk of your breast so that through you [*pro te*] he may in the flower of his youth accept the drink of vinegar. Now give him your hands so that through you [*pro te*] his arms may afterwards be fixed on the Cross.[50]

A text such as this leaves the impression that Mary is breastfeeding the infant Jesus specifically to prepare him for his violent death on the cross (in canonical scripture, she does no such thing, of course). Centuries later, it would become possible to make comparisons between Jesus hanging at the breast and hanging on the cross, as we saw in the hymn *Lignum vitae quaerimus*, above. Still later, as we will find in certain papal statements from the nineteenth and twentieth centuries, Mary will seem to be "fattening up" her child for sacrificial slaughter on the cross.

Mary's *ubera* continued to receive devout attention well into the Middle Ages.[51] In the recitation of a litany, for example, the worshipper might express admiration of the breasts that nourished the child Jesus:

> *Laudo et adoro beata ubera tua, que lactaverunt salvatorem mundi.*[52]
> I praise and adore your blessed breasts, for they gave suck to the savior of the world.

Prayers of benediction directed at specific bodily organs of Mary could mix metaphors in interesting ways, as in this item from the fourteenth century:

> *Adoro et benedico fecundissima ubera tua botris assimilata, virtute celesti repleta, quibus dei filium pro nobis parvulum factum, a quo pascuntur omnia, lactasti. Ave, Maria.*[53]
>
> I adore and bless your most fruitful breasts, like unto clusters of grapes, replete with celestial virtue, and by means of which you breast-fed the son of God, who for us was made into a little child through whom all are fed. Ave, Maria.

These (and many more) examples illustrating the importance of breastfeeding imagery for literate mariophiles in the medieval West may be tracked down in the "Mariological Glossary" of G. G. Meersseman's classic study of medieval hymns, litanies, and prayers.[54]

Yrjö Hirn observes that, "the Church's poets unceasingly sang of 'Mariae matris mammulae'."[55] Lyric and musical genres were especially likely to contain expressions of admiration for Mary breastfeeding her child. Venantius Fortunatus had already apostrophized, in a rhyming couplet, the glorious woman who breastfeeds her own creator (*Qui te creavit provide, / Lactas sacrato ubere*), and this seemingly self-contradictory conceit would be repeated, for example, in a tenth-century Beneventan hymn that had Mary nursing God (*Lactavit propriis uberibus Deum*).[56] In a sequence by Peter the Venerable (d. 1156), on the other hand, Mary is simply the mother whose sweet breast poured holy cups of milk into the little mouth of Jesus (*praedulcis mamilla / Iesu infudit labiolis / Pia lactis pocula*).[57] As an expression of his need for Mary's intercession, Saint Anselm of Canterbury utilizes the imagery of breastfeeding a child:

> Who can more easily gain pardon for the accused
> by her intercession,
> than she who gave milk to him [*quam quae illum . . . lactavit*]
> who justly punishes or mercifully pardons all and each one?
>
> Mother of the life of my soul,
> nurse of the redeemer of my flesh,
> [the one] who gave suck *[lactatrix*] to the Savior of my whole being.[58]

There is truly an abundance of breastfeeding imagery in medieval Latin hymns to Mary, as is clear from the wide selection of such hymns quoted and discussed by Joseph Szövérffy.[59] Such imagery persists right down to the present day, as in this passage from the latest edition of the *Little Office of the Blessed Virgin Mary*:

Qui te creavit, parvulum
Lactente nutris ubere.[60]

Not only medieval Latin, but also the vernacular poetry, prayers, and hymns of the time about Mary feature images of breastfeeding the Christ child. In Old French, for example, we find this fourteenth–fifteenth-century "Oraison a Nostre Dame":

Douce mere vierge et poucelle
Qui de ta tres douce mamelle
Ton fils allectas doucement,
Fay si ma conscience belle
Que ma povre ame ne chancelle
Au jour de mon trepassement.[61]
Sweet virgin mother and maiden,
Who sweetly nursed your son
From your so sweet breast,
Make my conscience so beautiful/clear
That my poor soul will not stagger
On the day of my passing.

From a compendium of early English carols, there are these jolly sixteenth-century stanzas on the nativity:

When she her deare Sonne se,
She set him on her kne
And song, "'Hydder to me –'
Cum basse [kiss] *thy mother, deare."*
On her lap she him layde,
And with her pappe [breast] *he playde,*
And euer sang the mayde,
"Come basse thy mother, dere."[62]

There are also Italian *laude* in which Mary expresses the idea that she deserves to be granted requests made of her son because – among other things – she breastfed him. Here is a stanza associated with the *Bianchi* movement (cf. below, p. 186):

"O dolce Figliuol benedetto,
per lo latte che del mio petto
poppasti, ogni rio difetto
perdona lor con dolce amore".[63]
"O sweet, blessed son,
by the milk that you
sucked at my breast,
forgive them with sweet love their every fault."

In this case, the request is immediately granted by Mary's son.[64]

Medieval theologians also utilized lactational imagery in their nonpoetic works. Amadeus of Lausanne, for example, imagines that Mary hears these words from God: "See, I have entrusted to you my Son, committed to you my only Son. Fear not to suckle the one you have borne [*Noli timere lactare quem genuisti*]." Mary is happy to feed her son – God himself – at the breast, that is "to suckle a son who pours milk into the breasts [*lactare filium qui lac ipsis uberibus infudit*]."[65]

Bernard of Clairvaux, who had been a teacher of Amadeus, is the hero of a miracle legend that quite surpasses the theological clichés. In these narrations, Mary appears to Bernard, bares her breast, and feeds him with her milk. Marina Warner tells one version of the legend:

> Bernard was reciting the *Ave Maris Stella* before a statue of the Virgin in the Church of St. Vorles at Châtillon-sur-Seine, and when he came to the words *Monstra [te] esse matrem* (Show thyself a mother), the Virgin appeared before him and, pressing her breast, let three drops of milk fall onto his lips.[66]

There are many textual variants and visual images of Mary's favor to Bernard. The incident seems to have been the cause of his famous eloquence (he is *Doctor Mellifluus* in the Catholic tradition).[67]

What Would Jesus Say?

Jesus himself would not have approved of the abundant images of his mother breastfeeding him, nor would he have been pleased by the praise lavished upon his mother's body. This is evident from a key statement he makes in Luke's gospel. An anonymous woman in the crowd declares, "Blessed [*makaria*] is the womb [*hē koilia*] that bore you and the breasts [*mastoi*] that nursed you!" Jesus responds: "Blessed rather [*Menoun makarioi*] are those who hear the word of God and obey it!" (Luke 11:27–28).

Here, Jesus has *corrected* a well-intentioned compliment to his mother. What kind of response is this? Again, how one interprets such an utterance depends on whether or not one is a believer. If the beneficiary of a human mother's efforts at giving birth and breastfeeding a child is God, then it could be said that this divine beneficiary deftly "changes the subject,"[68] moving on to something more important, or that Jesus has "priorities," and that "like all others [disciples], Mary too must meet a criterion of discipleship."[69]

If, however, one does not believe such things, then what Jesus says has to be seen as part of his delusional, grandiose scheme to deliver "the word of God" to mere mortals who happen to have been born and happen to have been breastfed by their mothers. The response to the anonymous woman's compliment is inappropriate because Jesus is blinded by the idea of his origin in a higher kind of parenting – that is, his own direct link to God the Father. Indeed, he is so preoccupied by this matter that he never once in the New Testament has the *human* decency to address his mother with respect or affection. He does not understand that, as far as his attitude toward his earthly mother is concerned, he is an ungrateful wretch.

In Luke's gospel at least, one would have expected filial respect and gratitude, for it is precisely there that Elizabeth, a relative of the newly pregnant Mary, had called Mary "blessed [*makaria*]" (1:45) for believing that the words spoken to her by the angel of the Lord about the coming birth of Jesus would be fulfilled; and it is there that Jesus' mother had sung her Magnificat, with the words, "Surely, from now on all generations will call me blessed [*makariousin*]" (1:48); and, of course, it is there that the woman in the crowd had spoken of the blessedness of Mary's womb and breasts (11:27). Yet never once in any of the canonical gospels would Jesus himself ever condescend to call his mother "blessed."

Filial gratitude would have to wait until the development of traditions about Mary's dormition and assumption in the fourth or fifth centuries (at the earliest). For example, there is a Coptic dormition narrative in which Jesus comes to his mother's tomb to raise Mary from the dead and declares to her: "Blessed are thy breasts, O Mary My virgin mother, for thou didst nourish Me from them, and I am He that nourisheth all the creation." There is what appears to be grandiosity on the part of Jesus here, but the post-resurrection context of the narration justifies real grandeur, not delusional grandiosity, and there is real filial gratitude as well. Further on in the narration, there is even more gratitude expressed: "And our Saviour . . . said to us in His gentle voice, Behold My beloved mother. This is she whose virgin womb carried Me nine months, and I was three years also receiving suck from her breasts which were sweeter than honey."[70]

After reading such words, who would even want to remember what Luke's Jesus had said to that poor woman in the crowd? The proliferation of textual and visual representations of Mary's womb and breasts would eventually become the decisive testimony to their blessedness and would essentially erase the scriptural picture of Jesus' ingratitude.

*

An abundance of visual imagery representing the divine nursing couple has been produced in both the Roman Catholic West and the Orthodox East (but not so much in Protestant areas). The historical derivation and taxonomy of these images are not always clear, but the essential action depicted in all of them is obvious: Mary is breastfeeding her child. Some medieval sources indicate that this primal and intimate form of care of one's own child represents the maternal ideal, and some modern scholars rightly believe that visual images of Mary breastfeeding the Christ child shamed affluent mothers who could afford to farm out their newborn children to a wet nurse. There are also textual representations of Mary breastfeeding her child as far back as Greek and Latin patristic sources, and in poetry in many languages, beginning with the hymns of Ephrem the Syrian. Medieval Latin hymnography abounds with references to Mary breastfeeding her child, as does (increasingly) medieval poetry in the vernacular. To judge from a key passage in the gospel of Luke, however, Jesus would have disapproved of these many positive representations of Mary breastfeeding him.

Notes

1 See the dissertation by Lechner 1981.

2 The fresco depiction of a woman holding her naked child at the breast in the Roman catacomb of Priscilla was once thought to be, not only the oldest pictorial representation of Mary nursing the Christ child, but also the oldest pictorial representation of Mary with the Christ child. There is an enormous art-historical literature on this famous image, including: Wilpert 1903, vol. I, 172–175; vol. II, plates 21, 22; Meiss 1936, 454, n. 62, and fig. 23; Lasareff 1938, 27–28; Cutler 1987, 336; Gambero 1999 (1991), 84; Bisconti 1996; Parlby 2007, 117; 2008, 41–48; Spier 2007, 177–178. Henri Leclercq (1932, col. 1988) boldly asserted that the fresco dates to the second century, as did Nikodim Kondakov (1998 [1914–1915], vol. I, 20), Millard Meiss (1936, 454, n. 62), and Victor Lasareff (1938, 27). Unfortunately, recent research by Geri Parlby offers strong technical evidence for the conclusion that, "the fresco in the Catacomb of Priscilla may be nothing more than a poignant funerary portrait of a dead mother and child" (Parlby 2008, 48).

3 Bynum 1987, 271–272.

4 Here are just some of the images of Mary breastfeeding her child, or exposing and making available her breast to the child (but not to the adult Christ, so that "double intercession" imagery is here excluded). No conscious attempt has been made to limit the images in this list with respect to historical date of creation, geographical location, linguistic context, artistic quality, or Christian denomination: Kondakov 1911 (1910), figs. 21–31; Meiss 1936, figs. 1–2, 4–9, 11–14, 16–17, 19, 21–25; Mâle 1931, figs. 85–87; Sánchez Cantón 1948, plates 155, 231, 246, 255–258, 265; Meiss 1951, figs. 128, 129, 131–137, 140, 142–144, 146–148, 150, 152–157, 159; Southern 1953, plates I, IV; Ronig 1956, figs. 1, 2; Aurenhammer 1956, figs. 8, 9, 15, 23, 33; Guldan 1966, figs. 87, 103, 120, 148, 150; Schiller 1966–1991, vol. I, figs. 106, 179, 328, 332; vol. IV (part 2), figs. 418–420; Essen 1968, cat. nos. 28, 36, 72, 114, 125, 131, 134, 143, 144, 274, 253; Küppers, ed. 1974, figs. 43, 54, 83, 113, 125, 152, 155, 157, 161, 193b, 269, 356, 374; Warner 1983 (1976), figs. 3, 33, 34, 44; Lane 1984, figs. 1–4, 6, 16, 17, 19; Monks 1990, frontispiece, 188; Langener 1996, figs. 7–15; Onasch and Schnieper 1997 (1995), 173; Williamson 1998, figs. 1–5; Snessoreva 1999 (1898), 92, 282; Boss 2000, fig. 3; Vassilaki, ed. 2000, 143 (fig. 86), 215 (fig. 160), 238 (fig. 185), 431 (fig. 221), 442 (cat. no. 70); Uryga 2001, 155, 295; Vassilaki, ed. 2005, plates 1, 16; figs. 2.1, 2.2, 21.1, 23.1; Evans, ed. 2004, 357 (cat. no. 215), 468 (cat. no. 278), 554 (fig. 17.15), 570 (cat. no. 340), 572 (cat. nos. 341, 341.1), 581 (fig. 347.1); Boskovits and Tartuferi, eds. 2003, figs. 36, 59, 117; Berruti, ed. 2006, figures on pp. 11, 19, 28, 31, 35, 41, 56, 58, 59, 62, 64, 72, 74, 76, 80, 82–85, 91, 147, 151, 153, 155, 159; color plates on pp. 165, 167–182; Miles

2008, plates 1, 7, 9, 11; figs. 1, 8–11, 20; Williamson 2009, color plates I–VII; figs. 1, 11, 13–16, 18, 19, 23–25, 28, 32–40; Dückers and Priem, eds. 2009, cat. no. 100; Boskovits and Parenti, eds. 2010, figs. 2, 3, 76, 86 (and color plates II, III, XXVIII, XXXII); Sciacca, ed. 2012, 60 (fig. 12.1), 62 (fig. 13), 63 (fig. 1.19). For an annotated bibliography of the *Maria lactans* theme (with 64 black-and-white plates), see: Bonani and Bonani 1995. For an online image source (accompanied by the usual internet detritus;), see, for example: www.google.com/search?q=Virgo+lactans&client=firefox-a&hs=ZSt&rls=org.mozilla:en-US:official&tbm=isch&tbo=u&source=univ&sa=X&ei=5tHyUurUA6K6yQG1z4DgDA&ved=0CCkQsAQ&biw=1366&bih=634 (accessed February 2, 2015).

5 Uryga 2001, 295; conversation with Alicja Coe, February 1, 2014.

6 "Nursing couple" is a term in pediatrics and related fields commonly applied to the nursing mother–infant dyad. See: Middlemore 1953 (1941).

7 Important efforts to deal with these questions include: Tatić-Djurić 1976; Belting 1994 (1990), 281–296; Pentcheva 2006, 56–59, 109–136, 174–181.

8 See: Meiss 1951, figs. 128–144, 146–148, 150–154.

9 Meiss 1936, 435, n. 1 (reprinted in Meiss 1951, 132, n. 1).

10 As quoted in: Meiss 1936, 456 (reprinted in Meiss 1951, 149). Isidore's is a true etymology, not a folk etymology. See the entry *humus* in: de Vaan 2008, 292.

11 Meiss 1951, 151 (emphasis added).

12 See: Meiss 1951, figs. 128–144, 146–148, 150–154.

13 Compare images labeled *Madonna dell'Umiltà* in: Tartuferi and Parenti, eds. 2006, 100, 101, 104, 105, 146, 147, 159, 198, 199, 203, 220, 222, 237, 243. Of the total of 17 images so labeled, Mary is breastfeeding the Christ child in 10 of the images (59 percent).

14 Meiss 1951, 151.

15 Williamson 2009, 174.

16 Meiss 1951, 151.

17 Williamson 2009, 132–147.

18 McLaughlin 1974, 115.

19 Shahar 1990, 55–56.

20 Williamson 2009, 134, n. 8.

21 Goodich 1975, 80, translating Bartholomaeus Anglicus 1964 (1601), 241.

22 Williamson 2009, 146.

23 Klapisch-Zuber 1985, 159.

24 Klapisch-Zuber 1985, 134.

25 Klapisch-Zuber 1985, 135.

26 Klapisch-Zuber 1985, 134–135.

27 Klapisch-Zuber 1985, 159.

28 Klapisch-Zuber 1985, 328 (emphasis added).

29 Miles 2008, 39.

30 Ross 1974, 184–185.

31 Yalom 1997, 43.

32 Ephrem the Syrian 1989, 100, 371 (translator Kathleen E. McVey provides the transliterated Syriac word for "breast").

33 Brock, ed. 1994, 39.

34 Brock, ed. 1994, 41.

35 Brock, ed. 1994, 62 (for more examples, see his Index of Subjects, under "milk, Mary's").

36 Worrell 1923, 361; cf. Langener 1996, Part I, 240–241.

37 McGuckin 2004 (1994), 268 (English); Tanner, ed. 1990, vol. I, 51 (Greek).

38 Budge 1915, Part I (Coptic), 139–140; Part II (English), 717–718.
39 Budge 1915, Part I (Coptic), 141; Part II (English), 719. See the valuable commentary on these passages attributed to Cyril by Langener 1996, Part I, 349–350.
40 McGuckin 2008, 7–8.
41 For example: Lasareff 1938, 28–29; Müller 1963; Witt 1971, 269–281; Tran Tam Tinh 1973, 40–49; Benko 2004 (1993), 43–53; Langener 1996; Mathews and Muller 2005; Bolman 2005; McGuckin 2008; Rubin 2009, 63–66 (and sources cited there, p. 439, ns. 50–52, 57).
42 English translation by Tsironis (2011, 192) of John of Damascus (1988, 177, lines 28–29).
43 English translation by Tsironis (2011, 193) of John of Damascus (1988, 179–180, lines 42–43).
44 Augustine of Hippo 1952b, 85, 75.
45 From Augustine's Sermon 369. The "dubious" version in *Patrologia Latina* (vol. 39, cols. 1655–1657) is replaced by a critical edition of C. Lambot (1952). See: Augustine of Hippo 1952a, 109; quoted by Barré 1963, 23.
46 From a pseudo-Augustinian sermon, *Legimus et fideliter retinemus* . . . (Barré 1963, 23).
47 From a pseudo-Augustinian sermon, *Audistis, fratres, quaemadmodum* . . . (Barré 1963, 24).
48 From the sermon *Scientes, fratres dilectissimi, auctori nostro* . . . (Barré 1963, 41).
49 From a pseudo-Augustinian sermon, *Legimus et fideliter retinemus* . . . (Barré 1963, 23).
50 See: Faustus of Riez 1891, 231–232, here translated by Keeler 2003, 264 (with my modifications; Keeler seems to be rendering *pro te* as "through you" – rather than "for you" – on the assumption that Mary was already without sin of any kind, that is, immaculate). A very similar passage in another variant of *Legimus et fideliter retinemus* . . . is quoted by Barré (1963, 23).
51 For example: Barré 1963, 33, 41, 183, 221, 246, 276.
52 Meersseman 1958–1960, vol. 2, 231, line 40 (cf. 240, line 86, which is identical, but in a different type of litany).
53 Meersseman 1958–1960, vol. 2, 188.
54 See the entries *mammilla*, *uber*, *lac*, and *lactare* in the *Mariologisches Glossarium* of: Meersseman 1958–1960, vol. 2, 329, 378, 323–324, respectively.
55 Hirn 1957 (1909), 360.
56 Dreves and Blume 1909, vol. I, 41; Meersseman 1958–1960, vol. I, 151; Woolf 1968, 131. Cf. also Szövérffy 1985a, 148 (a versified liturgical Office "borrows" from Venantius: *Qui te creavit provide / Lactasti sacro ubere*).
57 Szövérffy 1985a, 47.
58 From the second and third of the works titled "Prayer to St. Mary," in: Anselm of Canterbury 1973, 110, 116; Anselm of Canterbury 1968 (1938–1961), vol. 2, 15, 19.
59 Szövérffy 1985a, 36, 54, 103, 148, 164, 202, 233, 236, 239, 248–249, 269, 271, 285, 326, 363, 370, 378. See also the generous selection of examples from hymnography in: Hirn 1957 (1909), 534–536 (ns. 22, 24, 31, 32, 41).
60 Keller, ed. 2013, 34, 88.
61 Sonet 1956, 87, no. 484; for further examples, see the entries numbered 564, 689–691, 725, 1085, 2145, 2154, 2155.
62 Greene, ed. 1977 (1935), 30–31 (no. 60). For further examples, see: 30 (no. 59.1), 33 (no. 64), 135–136 (no. 208), 144 (no. 230). More examples (all from the fourteenth century) are to be found in: Brown 1924, 56 (no. 41), 91 (no. 75), 235 (no. 132).

63 Toscani, ed. 1979.
64 Cf. Bornstein 1993, 135.
65 Translations in: Bernard of Clairvaux and Amadeus of Lausanne 1979, 95, 96; Latin originals in: Amadeus of Lausanne 1960, 130, 132 (in the second quotation I have corrected what is presumably a misspelling, *lectare*).
66 Warner 1983 (1976), 197–198.
67 Dupeux 1991, 166. On what is termed "the lactation of Saint Bernard," see: Dewez and Van Iterson 1956; Bynum 1987, 270; Dupeux 1991; Schreiner 2006 (1996), 189–192; Rubin 2009, 350–351. See also the category *Virgin, Blessed, breasts of*, in: Tubach 1981 (1969), no. 5109. Others besides Bernard (Saint John Chrysostom, Henry Suso, Alanus de Rupe, Saint Dominic, among others) also drank from the breast of Mary (see: Bynum 1987, 410, n. 56 on sources; Dupeux 1991, 169–170).
68 Balthasar in: Ratzinger and Balthasar 2005 (1997), 109.
69 Brown et al., 1978, 172.
70 Translated from a Bohairic version of a homily falsely attributed to Evodius of Rome. See: Robinson 1896, 61, 65. For a Sahidic version, see: Shoemaker 2004, esp. 399, 404, 405. On the textual variants of the Pseudo-Evodius homily, see: Shoemaker 2004, 60–62, 422.

10 Marian Laments and the Psychology of Compassion

Marian Lamentation in the Orthodox East

In a great variety of contexts, we find Mary lamenting the suffering, dying, and death of her son on the cross: in homilies, liturgical passages, passion plays, mystery plays, prose narrations of the passion, lyric poetry, hymns, and of course in stand-alone laments. Here, it would be impossible to examine the enormously diverse cultural and historical contexts in which Mary laments, nor would it even be possible for any one scholar to consider all of the languages from around the world in which she laments. Nevertheless, for purposes of studying the psychology of marian lamentation, it is useful to examine some representative passages, both from sources known earlier in the East as well as from later sources in the West.

Mary grieves in the apocryphal *Gospel of Nicodemus* (known also as *Acts of Pilate*), which was originally composed in Greek in the fourth century, was translated into most languages of the Mediterranean, and gave rise to diverse elaborations in medieval vernaculars.[1] The sixth-century poet-composer Romanos the Melodist produced many hymns, the so-called *kontakia*, which were sung on various occasions in the Byzantine church, and among these is a particularly well-known Good Friday *kontakion* on the theme of Mary's lament, which will be examined here. Other marian laments from the Orthodox East, such as the liturgical *Stavrotheotokia* (from the ninth century)[2] and the vernacular *Thrēnos Theotokou* (from a few centuries later),[3] seem to have been influenced by Romanos as well as by other genres, including a popular tradition of Christian oral lament.[4] The rather lyrical *Epitaphios Thrēnos* (since the fourteenth century) ties Mary's lamentation to the lost beauty of Christ and to personified nature's own suffering at the crucifixion.[5] Mention should also be made of that long and rambling dramatic collage of the Passion, the *Christos Paschōn* (attributed by some to Gregory of Nazianzus [d. 389/390]), which features a narcissistically disturbed, suicidal Mary who rants against the treacherous Jews for killing her son and for spreading shameful stories about her son's illegitimacy (i.e., her adultery).[6] Nor should we forget the earliest (seventh-century) *Life of the Virgin* by Maximos the Confessor, a prose work that survives in Old

Georgian translation, and that features some strong doses of "affective piety" in the passages about Mary at her son's cross.[7]

The Good Friday *kontakion* of Romanos is an early poetic masterpiece about the Passion, and it is worthy of psychological study. Margaret Alexiou calls it "one of the most exciting achievements of Byzantine literature."[8] Without wasting words, Romanos exposes the core of the relationship between Mary and her grandiose, masochistic son as the two converse before the crucifixion actually takes place. From within the poetic framework of strophic repetition,[9] we hear a distressed mother trying to reason with a son who gives the impression that he has more important things to worry about than his mother's coming sorrow. Repeatedly, at the end of each strophe, Mary affirms that Jesus is both "my son and my God [*ho huios kai theos mou*]." Yet she cannot seem to understand why he must die: "You are on your way, my child, to unjust slaughter . . ."; "Do not embrace death . . ."[10] But surely, he explains in response, she must know that he has to die, even unjustly, for otherwise: "How then shall I draw to life those in hell?"[11] It does not befit the "all-wise Maiden" to mourn. Indeed, she should set an example by rejoicing over the explicitly masochistic enterprise that her son has undertaken:

> "So do not weep [*mē oun klaiēs*], Mother. Rather cry out with joy,
> 'As he wills he accepts suffering,
> my son and my God!'"[12]

Mary's sensible retort to this is that her son, "Fashioner" of all things, has already performed many miracles, such as cleansing the leper, giving sight to the blind, and raising Lazarus from the dead. Why not, then, simply raise up dead Adam as well? Christ's lame reply is that poor Adam had become ill of his own volition, is now in danger down there in hell, and deserves mercy, so, again: "Do not weep then [*mē klausēs oun*], Mother." Eve too suffers illness with Adam in hell, and both together may now understand that they need to follow "the physician's order [*tou . . . iatrou paraggelian*]"[13] – which order apparently will have the effect of pardoning both Eve and Adam. But, at this point, an exasperated Mary reveals her greatest fear:

> If you suffer, if you die, will you return to me?
> If you treat Adam, and Eve along with him, shall I see you again?[14]

Mary's issue is clearly the impending loss of her dear son, and he reassures her almost in passing: "you will see me first on my coming from the tombs."[15] Christ's issue, on the other hand, is the redemptive suffering and death that he believes his heavenly Father has ordained for him. What Mary will eventually see after everything has happened is her child restored to her, albeit with "the marks [of nails] in my hands." Through his suffering, the son will have saved Mary's "forebears" who had fallen into the illness of sin. Like a "physician" (again *iatros*), Christ will have used his cross as a kind of homeopathic remedy, so that his mother will be able to boast: "By suffering he has abolished suffering."[16]

Toward the end of the *kontakion*, Mary is still in psychological pain. But, with her son's strong encouragement, she puts on a brave face and even volunteers to come watch him die. This will make it possible for Mary to be present – in silence – at the crucifixion, in accordance with scripture (John 19:25–30).[17] Jesus is her God, after all, not only her son, as she courageously (obsessively, defensively) affirms at the end of each strophe of the hymn. Mary knows her son's words, "I am the way, and the truth, and the life [*hē zōē*]" (John 14:6). In an effective grammatical turn toward the end of her very last utterance in the hymn, Mary forcefully declares that her son is life itself:

> "Moses said this to Israel,
> 'What you are going to see on the tree is life [*tēn zōēn*].'
> Life [*hē zōē*], what is it? It is
> My son and my God."[18]

For Mary, there *must* be a real probability of her son escaping death on the tree of the cross, and this escape would have to be his resurrection and his everlasting life.

The text's foregrounding of "life" goes well with the son's repeated admonition to his mother not to mourn – that is, to set aside her grief as inappropriate. We should keep in mind, however, that within this *kontakion* Mary is never confronted with the actual sight of her dead or dying son on the cross. That will come later, so for now (in the context of this particular work by Romanos), it is easier for her to fend off the onset of mourning.

A period of mourning ordinarily accomplishes the *acceptance* of the death of a loved one. Failure to mourn (refusal, inability to complete the mourning process, external interference), on the other hand, amounts to a denial of death.[19] In the Romanos *kontakion*, Mary is encouraged, even ordered, by her still living son not to mourn him.

Taking this command even further into the realm of unreality, some visual representations of the *already dead* Jesus in the world of Eastern Orthodoxy bear the title "Weep not for me, Mother." For example, a configuration of images of the Man of Sorrows (the dead Christ still in vertical position before burial), his mother Mary, and her son's cross on the walls of the prothesis of the Kovalevo Church of the Savior in Novgorod (1380) bears an inscription in Church Slavonic, *Ne rydai mene, Mati*.[20] The same expression is written on a late-eighteenth-century icon from north-central Russia: the icon depicts a somber Mary holding her recently deceased – but still upright – son as he is being lowered into a tomb in front of the cross.[21]

The expression (and/or some variant) also occurs in many Russian spiritual songs (*dukhovnye stikhi*) about the Passion gathered by folklorists and ethnographers in pre-Soviet times. In these instances, Jesus – either dead or still alive – is actually singing to Mary from the cross.[22]

To this day, the faithful hear an exhortation not to lament the death of Jesus in the Orthodox liturgy. We may read this exhortation in both the Greek Orthodox and the Russian Orthodox Holy Saturday service (heirmos of the ninth ode):

> Lament not for me, O Mother [Greek, *Mē epodurou mou mētēr*; Church Slavonic, *Ne rydai mene mati*], when thou beholdest in the tomb the Son whom, without seed, thou didst conceive in thy womb, for I shall rise again [Greek, *anastēsomai gar*; Church Slavonic, *vostanu bo*], and glorify myself; and in that I am God, I will raise in glory that hath no ending those who, with faith and love, do magnify thee.[23]

The connection between the admonition against mourning and resurrection from the dead could not be clearer.

Resurrection itself is the most explicitly corporealized way for Mary to deny the death of her divine son. In scripture, of course, Mary is not among those who see Jesus alive after his crucifixion (that is the privilege of another Mary). But, scriptural lacunae seldom inhibit the imagination of the mariophile, as we have seen repeatedly. In the late Byzantine *stavrotheotokia*, for example, Mary will sometimes affirm that she beholds her son on the cross, but then will deny that he is dead by utilizing the noun *anastasis* (or some cognate form) to signify his resurrection from the dead. One item in the Tillyard collection has Mary crying out that a "cruel sword" has pierced her "when I see thee dead [*nekron*], without breath and voiceless," but a few lines later she states: "But glorify me, thy mother, O Word of God, by thy Resurrection [*anastasei*]."[24] The singers of this song understand implicitly that Mary's request will be fulfilled, and that she will indeed see her son alive again, even though he has died.

In the West as well, Mary is in the habit of denying her son's death by affirming his resurrection. And, as in the Byzantine East, her grandiose son sometimes encourages her in her denial. For example, in an anonymous fourteenth-century English lyric, Jesus responds to his mother lamenting at the foot of the cross: "Mother, stop your weeping [*Moder, do wey thy wepinge*]. / I suffer death for mankind."[25] From another lyric, late in the same century, he admonishes her: "Stop now, mother, and no more weeping [*stynt now, modir, & wep no more*]."[26] This latter lyric may derive (in part) from a Latin original (questionably) attributed to Saint Bernard, with these words addressed to Mary: *desine flere et dolorem depone*.[27] Other standard expressions in Latin are *noli flere* and *noli plangere*, which are spoken to a lamenting Mary by her son in prose texts of the passion, as we will see.

Mary at Her Son's Passion in the West

From a historical viewpoint, what is curious about Mary's affective involvement in her son's passion in the West is the fact that it happens relatively late there. With some few exceptions, the Roman Catholic Mary is a rather austere and Stoic figure at the foot of the cross, over many centuries.[28] Perhaps lamentation was avoided out of respect for Mary's total silence in the single canonical gospel where she appears at the foot of the cross (John 19:25–27), and more generally out of a lingering awareness of the early Christian view that mourning the dead and the dying was unseemly and pagan, for, after all, there would be consolation in the general resurrection of the dead.[29] The fact that Saint Augustine largely refrained from considering the role of Mary at the crucifixion must have inhibited subsequent commentators in the West.[30] Perhaps also, the still relatively restrained ceremonies of the Roman liturgy for Holy Week sufficed. There do exist late antique *Threni* attributed by some to Ephrem the Syrian, but they are Latin translations of earlier texts (Greek, presumably, and ultimately Syriac).[31] It is also possible that a variety of laments were sung, but were simply not preserved in written form. Dronke is inclined to explain this as follows:

> In the West, the evidence for *planctus* of Mary is sparse before the twelfth century – not, I submit, because such laments did not exist, but because in their essential impulse and conception they were more at home in the non-literate world than in the clerical.[32]

I suppose there is something to be said for each of the various explanations that have been offered for the late appearance of written marian lamentation and related affective expression in the West. But, this historical question remains open. And, in any case, we are primarily concerned here with the psychology of some of the better-known representations of Mary's affective involvement in her son's passion – wherever and whenever these representations happen to have been preserved.

Detailed attention to the passion developed rapidly from the late eleventh and beginning of the twelfth century in the Latin West. Mary's active participation was an important catalyst for this growth. For one thing, narrations, dramas, and visual images of Mary's participation in her son's passion were filtering in from the East.[33] For another thing, the faithful were apparently now more comfortable ignoring (or were just ignorant of) scriptural signs of the tension between Mary and Jesus, and imagining instead that a strong and durable emotional bond of some kind existed between mother and son. The idea of such a bond would have enhanced the credibility of representations of Mary's non-biblical *compassion* for her son.

Compassion is more difficult to ignore, easier to identify with, than is raw, lonely suffering. The pain, shame, and death of the one who volunteered to be crucified are normally repellent to simple mortals, who are not so masochistically inclined. But, motherhood is another matter. Everyone has a mother, and most women everywhere become mothers. Maternal feelings are – and always have been – familiar to most people. Given a favorable historical moment, this familiarity enabled large numbers of medieval Christians in the West to identify with the suffering mother of their suffering and dying God. As J. A. W. Bennett observes: "It is this emotional identification with the Divine Mother at the foot of the Cross that gave impetus to the devotional tide which swept through [Western] Europe for two centuries."

Indeed, at a certain point, complains Bennett, "concern with the sorrows of the Virgin comes near to outweighing that for the sufferings of her son."[34] From a psychological viewpoint, the development of such an asymmetrical – seemingly theologically incorrect – situation makes sense, for, in principle, (1) Mary was free to be as sorrowful as she pleased as long as she did not die, and (2) under no self-imposed *obligation* to die, she was also in no danger of being confused with the one who thought he was – that is, her son, the grandiose masochist at the scene of the crucifixion. In other words, as long as Mary did *not* follow through on any (psychologically quite understandable) suicidal intentions at the foot of her son's cross (see below, 182), and as long as her son *did* follow through on *his* plan to suffer and die on the cross, then no affective excesses[35] on Mary's part would have been a threat to core Christian beliefs about the incarnation and the redemption.

It does not matter that in some of her laments Mary actually rues the day she gave her *fiat* to the announcing angel, as, at Golgotha, it was too late to undo the incarnation of Christ. Nor does it matter that Mary blames "the Jews" for her son's troubles, as this attitude harmonizes with the drift of John's gospel as well as with the blood curse in Matthew ("His blood be on us and on our children" – 27:25). It also does not matter that in some laments Mary confronts her son, asking him to explain what he thinks he is doing *to her*. Remarkable, indeed, is the psychological latitude permitted to Mary in the context of her son's passion.

Thomas H. Bestul has compiled a ("preliminary and provisional") catalogue of 41 medieval prose narratives of the passion, from before 1100 through the fifteenth century. Many of the items listed exist in more than one textually different manuscript – and in some cases in numerous textually different manuscripts. Most of the works listed have by now been published in some form, and many had also been translated already in the medieval period into one or more vernaculars from the original Latin. Excluded from Bestul's list are works of poetry, dramatic works, homilies, sermons, biblical commentaries, reports of visions, and some other items.[36] Even so, the corpus of devotional prose fiction on the passion catalogued by Bestful is large and is bound to include much material about Mary's role at Golgotha – too much, indeed, for any single medievalist yet to have mastered. The problems of dating, sequencing, and otherwise interrelating individual manuscripts may never be solved in some cases, and questions of authorship are still disputed. The significance of such issues should not be overestimated, however. As Bestul observes:

> It seems most useful to conceive of these Latin treatises on the Passion as the products of a productive and complex textual community built upon mutual relationship and interdependence in which many works reveal the textual traces of many other works, and in which the texts themselves are not static, but attributed to various authors, subject to revision, recension, and modification.[37]

For present purposes, an examination of marian lamentation as it occurs in two notable prose texts in Latin – without detailed consideration of authorship, and leaving aside the question of a possibly "definitive" textual variant – will have to suffice. Other items from Bestul's list will also be mentioned in connection with specific marian topics.

First Prose Text: *Meditationes vitae Christi*

The book *Meditations on the Life of Christ* (*Meditationes vitae Christi*), formerly attributed to Saint Bonaventure, was perhaps originally composed in the late thirteenth or early fourteenth century by the Franciscan John de Caulibus in the north of Italy. This popular devotional work, which exists in numerous manuscripts of varying length and which has been published in several languages, offers richly imagined material on Mary's involvement in the passion.

Shortly before he is arrested, Jesus predicts his death directly to his mother:

> Most beloved mother, the will of my Father is that I spend the Pasch there [in Jerusalem], for the time of redemption is coming. Now all the things said of me will be fulfilled, and they will do to me what they wish.

Naturally, this clearly stated masochistic intention elicits great distress in the mother, who knows that the authorities are trying to capture her son. She commences weeping and begs her son to refrain from carrying out the Father's plan. Surely there must be some other way for the Father to accomplish his goal. After all, in a stance of obedient questioning taken by figures as different as Romanos the Melodist and Bernard of Clairvaux,[38] as well as paraphrasing words from the annunciation (Luke 1:37), pseudo-Bonaventure's Mary points out: "If it please Him, He can provide for the redemption in a different way, without your death, for all things are possible with Him." Mary continues her weeping (along with Mary Magdalen), but Jesus is firm in his resolve – again, as in the Romanos *kontakion*, but now in Latin instead of Greek: "Do not cry [*Nolite flere*]."[39]

But why *not* cry, if a beloved son is volunteering to die? Pseudo-Bonaventure's Jesus explains: "You know that I am bound to obey the Father, but be surely confident that I shall soon return to you, and on the third day I shall rise safe and sound."[40] In other words, Jesus is going to die, but somehow he is also *not* going to die, for he denies the reality of his death and proffers a fantasy of his resurrection from the dead. His admonishment against crying *means* the denial of death.

Of course, Jesus does return from the dead later on in these *Meditationes* aimed at Christian believers. But, Mary does not think or behave in a manner consistent with his promise that he will. She disobeys her divine son's "Do not cry" by crying rivers of compassionate tears while he is suffering and dying on the cross, wishing even to die with him.[41] Mary grieves as she helps take the dead Jesus down from the cross, she assists tearfully in the preparation of his body for burial, and she helps carry the shrouded body to its tomb. Her only acknowledgment of what her son had said to her when predicting his death comes in a monologue she pronounces as she presses her cheek against her son's dead face:

> You abandoned yourself for love of mankind, whom you wished to redeem. Hard and exceedingly painful is this redemption, in which I rejoice for the sake of the salvation of man [*ista redemptio, de qua gaudeo propter salutem hominum*]. But in your sorrows and death I am much afflicted, for I know that you never sinned and that you are destroyed without cause in a bitter and disgraceful death. Therefore, my Son, our companionship is broken, and I must now be separated from you. I, your most sorrowful mother, shall bury you; but afterwards where shall I go?[42]

Perhaps Mary really does "rejoice" on behalf of humankind, but this nod to theological correctness comes in a narrative of otherwise unrelieved darkness and desolation. Still weeping, she clings to her son's body, speaks to it, and eventually has to be pulled away from it by her friends, so that a stone can be placed at the entrance of the tomb. She leaves with her fellow mourners – and there is no indication that she ever expects to see her son again.

The next morning, Mary is secluded in a little house with the disciples and a few other companions. With great shame, Peter tells the story of how he abandoned and denied Jesus just before the crucifixion. Other disciples also castigate themselves for having abandoned their sweet good Lord. Although Jesus had voluntarily died on his disciples just the day before – abandoned them – they are fixated on *their* abandonment of *him*. At precisely this point, Mary intervenes with a little sermon about her son's forgiving nature and even declares that he will return to them: "Do not doubt that He will be restored [*reconciliabitur*]."[43] Mary is not exuberant about this, but her tears have stopped flowing, and her sorrow seems remarkably attenuated.

The mourning process has come to a premature close, or has been interrupted. The narrator tells us that "the Lady [*Domina*] kept a tranquil and quiet mind, for she had the most certain hope of the Resurrection of her Son [*certissimam spem habebat de resurrectione filii sui*], and in her alone faith [*fides*] remained on this sabbath day."[44] Mary seems to have taken charge of both the people in her household and the thoughts in her mind. She is not the same Mary as the one who was in profound mourning on the previous day.

Her faith is rewarded on the next day. Mary prays to God for the return of her son, as Jesus had predicted that he would rise from the dead "on the third day" (cf. Matthew 27:63). She is slightly impatient: "What are you doing? What causes your delay?" As she prays, she is carried away with longing: "More than anything else I long to see you. Let your return console me, as your departure so saddened me. Come back then, my Beloved; come, Lord Jesus; come, my only hope; come to me, my Son" – whereupon Jesus appears, clothed in "the whitest garments."

Mary is astonished, confused, uncertain even that this is her son. Has her wishful denial of his death actually worked? She kneels to adore the glorious figure before her eyes. He speaks: "My sweetest mother, it is I. I have risen and am with you."[45] Mary gets up, embraces him tearfully, joyfully. He is alive, a physical but now slightly ethereal human being. Mary notes the scars on his hands, but her risen Christ explains that he no longer feels pain, or sorrow, or hardship of any kind.

Mary's undead son – this glowing zombie from the now empty tomb – has accomplished the redemption of humankind. Mother and son rejoice together. They will even have opportunities like this to converse again before the son finally ascends to his Father in the heavens. What the author of the *Meditationes* imagines here is all so very pleasant and edifying. The audience of this (and other such accounts on the same theme) is invited to disregard the fact that post-resurrection interactions between mother and son are never once mentioned in canonical scripture.

On the other hand, according to Maximus the Confessor, a "mother's witness" might have been deliberately avoided by gospel writers in order to lend greater credibility to their affirmation of Christ's resurrection.[46]

Second Prose Text: *Quis dabit*

Even more popular in its time was the *Lament of the Blessed Mary* (*Planctus beatae Mariae*), which used to be attributed to Bernard of Clairvaux under the title *Liber de passione Christi et doloribus et planctibus matris eius*. In all likelihood, however, it was originally penned as part of a larger tract on Mary early in the thirteenth century (before 1205) by the Cistercian Ogier of Locedio in northern Italy.[47] The extract circulated under a variety of titles and was translated into such contemporary vernaculars as French, Provençal, Italian, Anglo-Norman, and Dutch.[48] It is now commonly referred to by its incipit, *Quis dabit*.[49] Numerous manuscripts exist, especially from the fourteenth and fifteenth centuries. Here, I will rely on the bilingual edition supplied by Bestul on the basis of a fourteenth-century manuscript in the British Library.[50]

The narrator, who characterizes himself as a servant (*servulus*) of Mary, and who assumes that Mary has already been taken up into heaven, prays fervently to her, requesting that she help him meditate in sorrow on the horrors that befell her dear son. He begs her not only to tell him what happened at his passion, but also to weep again as she had wept then. Eventually, Mary responds to this seemingly bizarre request: "What you seek inspires compunction and is very sorrowful; but because I have been glorified, I cannot weep [*glorificata sum, flere non possum*]. You, however, write with tears those things which I have pondered with great pain."[51] What for Mary has become impossible, then, will have to be performed by the sympathetic narrator. That narrator, in turn, will be replaced later by an omniscient narrator who completes the psychologically challenging task of telling one of the most gruesome marian variants of the Passion story.

But, why is it not possible for Mary herself to weep? We are told that she has been "glorified," and the theological meaning of this term provides an explanation. By "glorified," the mother of Christ means that she has already risen from the dead, body and soul, and that in so doing she has already achieved the state of glory that lesser souls of the just will eventually attain only at the Last Judgment. In the present context, Mary is referring specifically to a component of post-resurrection glorification being promulgated by theologians around the time *Quis dabit* was composed, namely, impassibility (*impassibilitas*), which is the inability to suffer or to feel pain (recall Jesus' explanation to his mother of his own glorified post-resurrection state in the *Meditationes* just discussed above; both the *Meditationes* and *Quis dabit* reflect a developing medieval theology of the "glorified body").[52]

With alacrity, our servile narrator obeys his Lady's command to write down with tears those things about which she supposedly no longer sheds tears, but which nevertheless caused her to pour forth fountains of tears at the time it happened. She tells the narrator that she was indeed in Jerusalem to witness the torture of her son, the crowning with thorns, the spitting, the mockery, the carrying of the cross, the nailing of her son to the cross, and her son's slow dying before her eyes. She says that, at the time, she was so overwhelmed with sorrow that, at first, she could not speak. Only sighs, moans, and half-formed utterances issued from her lips. We as readers begin to wonder whether the now impassible Mary will even be able to remember – much less disclose to us – what must have been painfully lurid details.

Suddenly, Mary remembers: she had wished to *die with her son*. At this moment, her impassibility vanishes. She is back at the scene of a crime. There follows a long, rambling, and emotional lament. Portions of it are worth quoting and mining for their theological implications and psychological insights:

> O son, sole delight, singular joy, life of my soul and my entire solace, make me die now, who bore you for death [*fac vt ego ipsa nunc moriar, que te ad mortem genui*]. O son, recognize that I am weak, and hear my prayer. It is fitting for a son to hear his desolate mother. Hear me, I beg you. Take me up onto your cross, that those who live as one flesh and love each other with one love might perish in one death. O wicked Jews! O wretched Jews, do not spare me! Since you crucify my only child, crucify the mother, or kill me with some other kind of cruel death, so long as I might die together with my son. It is wrong for him to die alone. You deprive the world of its ray; you, Judea, deprive me of my son, my joy, my delight.[53]

These ravings manifest, at minimum, a mother's suicidal identification with her suicidal son. Perhaps there is an element of guilt in her death wish as well, for here, Mary reveals a "secret," namely, her foreknowledge of her son's preordained death: she had given birth to her son for the specific purpose of sacrificing him, of handing him over to death – *ad mortem* – and now she is facing an opportunity to be punished along with her son for such a heinous crime (see analysis of Mary's sacerdotal function below, pp. 251–285).

But no, better blame, not herself, but the "wicked Jews," the "wretched Jews," "Judea" itself, for the crucifixion of her divine son. This is the ancient charge of deicide against the Jews (e.g., Matthew 27:25), a paranoid construct that fit in well with the general anti-Jewish tenor of medieval Passion narrations.[54] Better also to enlist these very Jews for the accomplishment of her own suicide. Here, Mary is obviously confused about who is Jewish and who is not Jewish in this whole affair.

But, then, the Jewish mother of Jesus changes the subject again, deciding to blame her Jewish son for not helping her to kill herself, calling him "harsh" in his treatment of her. And, as if that is not enough, she goes off on a tangent about kinship terms (inspired in part by marian commentaries on the Song of Songs):

> O dear son, o kind child, have mercy on your mother; hear her prayers. Be no longer harsh [*durus*] to your mother, you who were always kind to everyone. Take up your mother with you on the cross, so I might live with you always after death. Nothing, indeed, is sweeter to me than to embrace you and die with you on the cross. And nothing, certainly, is more bitter than to live on after your death. O true child of God, you were my father, you were my mother, you were my bridegroom, you were my son, you were my everything. Now I am deprived of a father, bereft of a bridegroom, forsaken by a son. I have lost everything.[55]

Eventually, Jesus responds to this nonsense from the cross, commending John to his mother, and his mother to John (as in John 19:26–27). Jesus then gives her a little theological lecture, explaining her "secret" from his (God's) viewpoint and offering words of consolation that include the usual denials of death from this grandiose, about-to-be-dead man:

> You know that I have come for this; for this I have assumed flesh from you [*de te carnem assumpsi*], that through the gallows of the cross I might redeem mankind. How shall the Scriptures be fulfilled? You know that it is indeed necessary for me to suffer for the salvation of mankind. I will rise again on the third day, appearing openly to you and my disciples. Leave off sorrowing, put away grief [*Desine dolere, dolorem depone*], for I go to the father, I ascend to the glory of the father's majesty.
>
> Do not weep [*noli flere*], woman; do not lament [*noli plangere*], most beautiful mother. I will not desert you. I will not abandon you. I am with you, and I will be with you throughout all time.[56]

These and similar assurances from the cross have little effect. The "woman" (*mulier*) is not blind. She sees that her son is dying before her very eyes. Both she and the beloved disciple John continue crying. Mary's sorrow is greater, of course, and is the affective focus of *Quis dabit.* But her son has appointed John to the position of substitute son, and she will be needing him.

Finally, we are informed – now by an unnamed omniscient narrator, rather than the impassible Mary from the beginning of the narration – that Jesus has died: "The tongue cannot speak, nor the mind conceive, the extent of the sorrow which affected the pious innards of Mary." But the tongue and mind of the narrator nevertheless do proffer some of the customary passion imagery. The death of Jesus was "heavier for the soul of the mother than to die herself." Or, utilizing a commonplace contrast (below, p. 222), the narrator says to Mary: "You did not feel pain in bearing your son; you suffered a thousand times more in the dying of your son." Nor does the narrator neglect to mention the hackneyed prophecy of old man Simeon: "She felt the sword of sorrow which he had forseen."[57]

Mary's son is now dead, but his body remains high above her, on the cross. She resumes her lamentation: "O me! o me! Now return his lifeless body to me his wretched mother." Or: "Take him down, I ask. Return to me the livid body that he might be a comfort to me, even though dead." She wants her son *back* (*Reddite*), as if she had previously owned him. She goes around the cross and reaches up, attempting to embrace her son, "whom not long ago she had suckled with her living breast [*viuido vbere lactabat*]," says the narrator.[58] This fails. She tries repeatedly to raise herself high enough just to touch him, and fails. All she can do is kiss the blood running down the cross and kiss the ground moistened with her son's blood. In this most helpless and abject position, Mary is now smeared with the blood and gore of her dead son. The image, as Bestul puts it, is "most spectacular":

> O bloody [i.e., bloodied] virgin breast [*sanguens pectus virgineum*]! Her soul has dissolved, her rosy face grows pale, but grows red sprinkled

> with the precious gore [*cruore*] of her son. She touched the falling drops of blood with her sacred mouth.[59]

This second reference to the breast of Mary follows closely upon the one where she is said to have suckled her infant son not so long ago. But that breast of a now seemingly topless Mary is bloodied with her son's blood, and, when the body of her son is later brought down from the cross, she is bloodied further from handling it, so that, in a hyperbole reinforced by an untranslatable polyptoton, the narrator declares: "They saw . . . Mary completely bloodied with his [Christ's] gore [*Mariam totam suo cruentatam cruore*]." The imagery in this verbal text seems to be even more "graphic" than that in the many medieval pictures of Mary spattered by her son's blood as she stands at the foot of the cross.[60]

The noble Joseph of Arimathea and Nicodemus arrive, having obtained permission from Pilate to bury the dead Jesus. The body is taken down from the cross, and Mary falls upon it with kisses and embraces, "out of uncontrolled grief and immensity of love."[61] She cannot let go of the corpse: she keeps kissing her son's face, eyes, mouth. Nor can she cease lamenting:

> "What have you done, dearest son? Why did the Jews crucify you? What is the cause of your death? Did you commit a crime that you should be considered worthy of such a death? None, my son, none: but in this way you deigned to redeem your own, that you might leave an example for your posterity. I hold you dead in my bosom [*In gremio meo te mortuum teneo*]. Alas for me, most sad! Where is that indescribable joy that I had had at your birth?"[62]

Mary's loss is final – for her. There is no denial here that her son is dead. Her grief puts her on the road to acceptance, not denial, of his death. She can name the agents of her son's death: the Jews (*Iudei*), which is to say, again, that she makes the ordinary paranoid charge of deicide. She can pay lip service to the theologically correct doctrine of redemption (*tuos redimere*), which by definition requires the death of the one who performs the redemptive act. She also is reminded of the joy of giving birth to her son (and, earlier in the narrative, the joy of holding him close in order to nurse him), only because the one she is now holding close is dead (*mortuum*).

Here, as in various other segments of *Quis dabit*, Mary's words and behavior are perhaps excessive. In the intensity of her grieving, she seems overly emotional, mentally unbalanced, even out of control.[63] Her next move is particularly outrageous. As Joseph and Nicodemus are about to take the body of Jesus and place it in the grave, Mary resists. She keeps holding on to the body, begging them to let her hold her son a bit longer. In despair, she asks to be buried with him: "if you wish to place the son in the grave, bury the mother, now not a mother, with him, for why should I live after him?"[64] The men try to take the body forcibly, but she draws it closer still.

There follows an "unseemly tussle," as Bestul puts it.[65] But soon, the body of Mary's son is in the grave.

Mary continues sobbing inconsolably, and a weeping John comes to assist her. He helps her to stand. She is in such physical and psychological pain that she can barely walk, but, with the help of the "holy women," she is led to John's house in Jerusalem. There, the faithful and devoted John can now care for the exhausted mother of Jesus as if she were his own mother.

At this point, however, just as the *Quis dabit* is about to end, the omniscient narrator remarks, almost in passing: "Finally, when her son arose, she was unable to go to the tomb, enfeebled by great weakness in her limbs." This is odd. Coming as it does right after all the preceding pages of extreme lamentation, such a development is not credible. To those who have already seen her risen son, Mary can say: "Daughters of Jerusalem, tell my beloved that I am sick for love."[66] This paraphrase of a verse from the Song of Solomon (5:8) is also lame. Apparently, the author of this particular textual variant is trying to avoid giving a scripturally incorrect post-resurrection encounter between Mary and her son, and is attempting to restore the original narrator – that is, the impassive, "glorified" Mary. It might have been better to avoid mention of Christ's resurrection altogether, as in the variant printed by Marx.[67] Or, if Mary really is "unable" to go to the tomb, then the tomb could have come to Mary – which is what happens when, in the continuation of the longer work by Ogier of Locedio of which *Quis dabit* was once supposedly a part, the post-resurrection Jesus appears to his mother.[68]

The textual variant of *Quis dabit* utilized by Bestul is disturbingly effective, even if it is a bit clumsy in its final moments. On the whole, it is a daring and realistic depiction of a mother's traumatic loss and of the initiation of the mourning process following that loss.

Mary Laments in a Passion Play: *Planctus ante nescia*

Another approach to elaborating on Mary's emotions about her son's death was the passion play. Numerous texts from many areas of medieval Western[69] Europe have survived in which Mary is given the opportunity to express herself in this popular dramatic mode. Most important in this genre, for our purposes, are her laments, typically staged at the foot of the cross, or somewhere nearby after the body of Jesus has been taken down from the cross. There was considerable regional variation in the marian laments' length, number of times performed, language utilized, verse structure, and so on, in these plays.[70]

In the *Ludus de passione* added to the *Carmina Burana* manuscript collection not long after 1230, Mary becomes a leading dramatic character during the final act of her son's demise.[71] Once "the Jews" have demanded that Jesus be crucified, and Pilate has acquiesced by washing his hands ("I am innocent of this man's blood – this is your affair"), Jesus is led away to Golgotha. Behind Jesus – in what may be understood as a prelude to

Mary's later lamentation – comes a crowd of wailing women. Jesus turns around and says: "Daughters of Jerusalem, do not weep for me, but for yourselves!" This is a clear allusion to Luke (23:28–31; cf. 21:23–24; 19:41–44), where Jesus speaks to the weeping Jewish women about a catastrophe that will befall them after he is gone, a catastrophe that theologians and historians have generally understood to be the future destruction of Jerusalem by the Romans in 70 CE.[72] In both the gospel and the medieval passion play, the prophecy made by Jesus cannot be understood without an implicit understanding of the psychological appropriateness of mourning – in effect: "weep not for me, for I will rise from the dead; weep for yourselves, for you and your Jewish Jerusalem will be destroyed, and will *not* rise again."

Jesus is then hung upon the cross. Mary (accompanied by the beloved disciple John) approaches her dying son and commences a series of three heart-rending laments. At this point, there is no indication that Mary expects her son to rise from the dead. In her first lament (a unique composition in an old German vernacular), she declares how wretchedly unhappy she is over what has become of her wonderful, beautiful child. She calls for all who can see what is happening to take pity on the tormented, bloodied body of Jesus, and even begs to be killed in his place. Life would not be worth living for her without her little child (*chindel*). There is no sign (yet) that this *Mariam* (as she calls herself) is aware of any salvific consequences that the death of her son will have.

The two remaining laments are in Latin, and are of French origin. First, a tearful Mary turns to the crowd of weeping women (*ad mulieres flentes*), for they are fine sisters and mothers capable of sympathizing with her in her great misfortune. The sad spectacle of cross and lance has wounded her virgin mind. Blood runs from the thorns crowning the bowed head of her dear Jesus. Blood runs as well from the wounds in his hands and, from the gash in his side, it runs in a torrent. The mother grows faint. A metaphorical sword is piercing Mary herself as she watches her son suffer – the customary sword (*ille gladius*) that Simeon had spoken of when her child was an infant (Luke 2:35). Turning to John, she asks him to lament as well, but does not actually give him an opportunity to do so. Instead, she sings of her new role as his mother (John 19:26–27). Then comes the first indication in the play that she is aware of her son's messianic identity, for she proposes that their tears be offered up to the dying Christ (*Christo morienti*).

Finally, Mary sings the sequence *Planctus ante nescia*, a standard of marian lamentation probably composed in the middle of the twelfth century by Godfrey of Saint-Victor.[73] She begins with a concise declaration of her newly wretched state, followed by an equally concise accusation regarding the source of her suffering:

Planctus ante nescia
planctu lassor anxia,
crucior dolore:

orbat orbem radio,
me Iudea filio,
gaudio, dulcore.
I who knew no lament before,
anguished, am worn with lament,
agonized by pain:
Judaea robs the world
of its light, me of my son,
my joy, my sweetness.[74]

To hear Mary tell it, her son Jesus had been the one good thing in her life (*dulcor unice, / singulare gaudium*). But now, suddenly, this sweet and gentle child is hung up on nails by Jews, and blood flows from his body. No sooner, it seems, has the noble child been begotten in grand fashion than he is dying in a most abject way. From the annunciation to the crucifixion is but a step in Mary's selective memory. Someone must be at fault for such a terrible situation, and Mary – forgetting her own and her own son's religious identity – lashes out at the Jews. They are an "envious," "savage," "blind" people (*gens*). They brutalize her innocent son, spitting at him, crowning him with thorns, beating him with rods. Mary beseeches them to give her child back or, as in her first lament in the play, to let her die in his place. She even asks to be fastened to the cross together with her son (an "almost erotic death-wish," says Dronke).[75]

Mary then elaborates upon her hatred toward that evil people – the whole of *Iudea* ("Jewry" in one translation)[76] – which she imagines is killing her son. She prophesizes the horrible consequences of Pilate's releasing the Jewish insurrectionist Barabbas instead of the peace-loving Jesus:

. . . veniet seditio.
Famis, cedis, pestium
scies, docta pondere
Iesum tibi mortuum
Barrabamque vivere!
. . . turbulence will come.
You'll know, taught by the heaviness
of famine, slaughter, plagues,
that for you Jesus is dead
and that Barabbas lives![77]

What Jesus had hinted at in his own earlier words to the "daughters of Jerusalem," Mary here transforms into an explicit threat, namely, the utter devastation of Jerusalem by Roman imperial power.

Strictly speaking, a military rampage against the Jews could only have been a retaliatory, wishful fantasy in the mind of Mary at the time of her son's crucifixion, many centuries before this lament was composed. But, in the medieval historical context of the lament, that fantasy was plausible because of the already accomplished fact of the destruction of Jerusalem in 70 CE and could not but have elicited *Schadenfreude* from the target audience of ordinary Christians.

The Jewish scholar David Flusser, who recognizes that *Planctus ante nescia* is a "splendid poem [which] belongs among the highpoints of the Latin hymnody of the Middle Ages," is nevertheless offended by the fact that, in the work, "Mary blames the envious Jewish people for causing the death of Jesus." About the passage just quoted from this lament, Flusser expresses consternation over, not only its "threatening and aggressive attitude against an entire group of human beings," but also the attribution of such hateful sentiments to a Jewish woman:

> I personally do not wish to contribute to the evil in the world by an aggressive critique of this [Mary's] attitude. But I would like to mention one thing in all of this that does not please me, namely, that such a verse was placed in the mouth of a sorrowful and accusing Mary under the cross.[78]

It was bad enough to be blaming "an entire group of human beings" – that is, the Jews – for killing Jesus, for that was just the familiar anti-Semitic charge of deicide. For Flusser, it was particularly reprehensible for the composer of *Planctus ante nescia* to have forced the Jewish victim's "sorrowful, Jewish mother"[79] to recite the anti-Jewish deicidal script.

Such a script was hardly new, of course, as it originated in canonical Christian scripture, flourished in the *Adversus Judaeos* tradition, starting with various early church Fathers and continuing with medieval Catholic theologians and, later, Reformationists (notably, Martin Luther), and finally yielded its most horrific harvest in the twentieth-century Shoah/Holocaust of the Jews of Europe.[80] The anti-Jewish script was normal in marian laments of the Byzantine East, as in the *Christos Paschōn* attributed to Gregory of Nazianzus, in the *Life of the Virgin* by Maximos the Confessor (where Mary hurls out reproaches against the Jews for what they are doing to her son), as well as in three Greek variants of the apocryphal *Acts of Pilate*.[81] The flowering of marian laments and related discourse about Mary in the medieval West added yet other outlets for the expression of anti-Jewish sentiments. In addition to *Planctus ante nescia*, many variants of the *Quis dabit* narrative (Latin, as we have seen, as well as versions in vernacular languages), and Philip the Chancellor's *Dialogus Virginis cum Cruce* (above), I should also mention: medieval German passion plays;[82] various medieval English lyrics, carols, and passion plays;[83] the thirteenth-century Iberian *Cantigas de Santa María*;[84] and at least one marian lament in Old Polish.[85] In this list (cross-cultural, if incomplete), Jews are characterized as enemies of both Mary and her crucified son.

Planctus ante nescia concludes with a bit of proselytism. It is not too late for the wretched Jews to do penance (*age penitentiam*), to accept the love of Jesus, to fall into his embrace upon the cross. Addressing the "daughters of Zion," Mary sings:

Flete, Sion filie,
tante grate gratie:
iuvenis angustie
sibi sunt delicie
pro vestris offensis.
In amplexus ruite
dum pendet in stipite:
mutuis amplexibus
se parat amantibus
brachiis protensis
In hoc solo gaudeo,
quod pro vobis doleo.
vicem, queso, reddite:
matris damnum plangite.
Weep, daughters of Zion,
for such joyous grace:
the young man's pains
are his delights,
offered for your sins.
Rush into his embrace
as he hangs upon the beam:
he waits to share the embrace
of those who love him,
with arms wide open.
I rejoice only in this,
that I grieve on your behalf.
Make exchange, I beg you:
lament the mother's loss.[86]

Only this late in her lamentation does Mary acknowledge the fact that her gentle, guiltless son is a masochist, a young man whose "pains / are his delights." He does not *need* the tears of the "daughters of Zion." It is his mother Mary who needs them. In the very last line of her plaint, she thereby exposes its narcissistic core.

More important from a theological viewpoint is Mary's acknowledgment of the redemptive nature of her son's act. According to Dronke, Mary "comprehends the joy of the redemption."[87] She declares that her son's "pains" are "offered for your sins" – as if one man's sufferings on a Roman cross could somehow compensate for any guilt carried by others. Speaking in a condescendingly familiar manner (*tibi*) to the Jewish people (*Gens ceca, gens flebilis*), Mary represents this compensation as the "streams of fountains" of (implicit) blood shed by her son:

> *Quos fecisti, fontium*
> *prosint tibi flumina:*
> *sitim sedant omnium,*
> *cuncta lavant crimina.*
> Let the streams of fountains
> you [Jews] made flow now give you aid:
> they slake the thirst of everyone,
> they wash away all guilt.[88]

Here, Christ's blood is shed, not only for the detested Jews, but for all. Streams of his blood wash away all guilt (*cuncta . . . crimina*), slaking the thirst of all (*omnium*). That Jews would drink blood was of course unthinkable, but that medieval Christians drank Christ's blood under the eucharistic species of wine was commonplace.

By the end of *Planctus ante nescia*, Mary has bought into her son's grandiosity, that is, his delusions of grandeur. He is not only the Messiah, the Christ, he is also implicitly divine, for only a woman who thought that her son was God would be able to explain that his volunteering to undergo the torture of crucifixion constituted redemption for the sins of *others* – be they Jewish "daughters of Zion," or deicidal Jews generally, or members of the audience of this particular passion play – or all of humankind for that matter. Suffering there on his cross, Mary's son, "with arms wide open," welcomes *all* who will love and follow him. In this way, Mary consoles herself: her one dear son is dead, but in dying he opened the way to salvation for all. The death is not meaningless, for Mary achieves what Dronke terms "a *peripeteia*"[89] – however delusional it may be. She suffers involuntarily, without being quite the masochist her son is, but now she is just as deluded about her son's identity as he is. He seems to be God, and what he accomplishes on his cross is nothing less than redemption for the sins of everyone.

All of this may mitigate Mary's grief to some extent, and so may the wailing of the "daughters of Zion," if they will only wail for her. But, regardless, she loses her son. The loss is real. Her redemptive God is a dead God.

Mary Laments in an English Mystery Play: The N-Town *Crucifixion*

The tension between the need to mourn and the need for theological correctness is evident in almost all of the marian laments. In *Planctus ante nescia*, this tension seems to be resolved in a last-minute *peripeteia*. In other laments, the resolution can be messier, or nonexistent.

For example, one of the late-medieval English mystery plays, the N-Town *Crucifixion* (late fifteenth or early sixteenth century), features a Mary who is particularly resistant to acknowledging the redemptive force of her son's crucifixion.[90] There, Mary is shocked at the sight of her sweet son hanging on a cross in the company of thieves. Her heart is about to burst with sorrow, she expresses a wish to die herself – and then she swoons. The response from Jesus on the cross is to address his *Fadyr Almythy* in heaven with a request to *Forgyff these Jewys that don me wo!*, for they do not know what they are doing (cf. Luke 23:34), that is, they do not know that they are killing such an important personage. Three of the four Jews who had nailed Jesus to the cross – they are given numbers, not names – reply with mockery. One of the crucified thieves, however, asserts that Jesus is innocent of any crime, and that he is indeed *the Sone of God* – whereupon Jesus rewards him with the famous promise to meet him that same day in paradise (Luke 23:43).

Mary, meanwhile, has recovered from her swoon and notices that Jesus is conversing with people other than herself:

> *O, my sone, my sone, my derlyng dere!*
> *What? Have I defendyd* [offended] *thee?*
> *Thu hast spoke to alle tho that ben here,*
> *And not o word thu spekyst to me!*
> *To the Jewys thu are ful kende* [most kind];
> *Thu hast forgove al here mysdede* [their offenses].
> *And the thef thu hast in mende* [remembered] –
> *For onys haskyng mercy, hefne is his mede* [heaven is his reward]!

Perhaps Jesus should have paid more attention to his suffering mother. Her own words, however, are not exactly compassionate. Eventually, Jesus does respond to the narcissistically preoccupied *modyr* – although at first he can only bring himself to call her *woman* – and commends her to the care of his beloved disciple John (cf. John 19:26–27). He then reminds her that his *Fadyr of hefne* sent him on a mission to pay Adam's ransom, and that she – his merely human *modyr* – gave birth to him in order to facilitate the accomplishment of that grand mission. Why then, he asks, is she lamenting his painful death?

> *. . . for to suffre al this for man, I was born of thee,*
> *To the blys that man had lost, man agen to restore.*

Oblivious to what her son has just said, however, Mary rushes to the cross and embraces it, insisting that she too be hung upon it: *For ther he is, ther wold I be!* Mary clearly wishes to die. The gentle John intervenes, asking her to stop mourning (*now leve youre morning*), and she is taken away from the cross.[91]

After Jesus dies, Mary resumes her lamentations with even greater vehemence. John, not to be outdone, keeps interrupting her, attempting to console her, and even offering a theologically correct explanation of why she should instead be in a cheerful mood. For example:

> *He sufferyth deth for oure trespace,*
> *And thorwe* [through] *his deth, we shal have grace*
> *To dwelle with hym in hevyn* [heavenly] *place.*
> *Therfore, beth mery in hert* [be merry in heart].

To this, Mary responds:

> *A, dere frende, weel woot* [well know] *I this*
> *That he doth bye us to his blyss.*
> *But yitt* [yet] *of myrth evyrmor I mys* [lack]
> *Whan I se* [see] *this syght.*[92]

Dronke believes that this passage is "the nearest that the lamenting Mary of the English plays ever comes to admitting the truth of the Redemption – and still her human grief prevails over that truth." Dronke goes on to observe that Mary never acquiesces to the idea of her son's redemptive action – "truth" or not – in any of the four major cycles of English plays,[93] for, in all of them, "Mary's sorrowing remains unabated to the end." Even when (in the Towneley *Crucifixion* of about 1500) the dying Jesus himself tells her to cease weeping (*Sease of thi sorow and sighyng sere*), there is no indication that she complies, as Dronke notes. Theological explanation is of no use:

> *Therfor, moder, make none mowrnyng,*
> *Sen mankynde thrugh my dyyng*
> *May thus to blis be b[r]oght.*
> *Woman, wepe thou right noght.*[94]

Of course, all of the passion plays ever created in the Christian context have a theological message, but here in the English plays, according to Dronke, "we have a particularly forceful resurgence of the ancient non-theological traditions of women's laments."[95]

For Dronke to phrase this insight in historical terms is not to discount the psychological presupposition behind it. To mourn is human, and in any historical context it is utterly right and normal for a woman to mourn the passing of someone she loves. Mourning may be loud, communal, and musical – as in the "ancient non-theological traditions of women's laments." Or, it may be silent and intensely private, as so often happens in the secular West today. The historical and sociological manifestations of mourning are many, but the psychological reality is one thing: someone you love is lost forever.

Generally speaking, if the bits and pieces of correct theology are excluded from the depictions of Mary lamenting, it becomes clear that Mary herself is not particularly interested in the matter of pan-human redemption. She is interested in her son, and, if redemption contributes to the aggrandizement of her son, she occasionally displays some token acknowledgment, but also sometimes (at least since the Romanos *kontakion*) raises the question of why so grand a son could not find some *other* way to redeem sinful humankind than by volunteering to die on a cross. The fact that she so often laments (rather than keep the biblical silence) demonstrates that she does not have a welcoming attitude toward the death of her son. On the contrary, by lamenting, she resists it mightily. She sometimes offers her own suicide in its place (or in tandem with her son's death). She often heaps blame on the alleged perpetrators (always "the Jews"). She sometimes ignores or pays only token attention to those who attempt to intervene with explanations of the theological party line about Jesus' redemption of sinful humankind. She often disregards admonitions against mourning and, like her predecessor Rachel bewailing her children in the Hebrew Bible (Jeremiah 31:15), in Matthew (2:17–18), and even in some medieval laments where Rachel may be understood as a type prefiguring Mary[96] – she refuses to be consoled. The only thing that could make Mary cease grieving, as she herself states in her final lament at the tomb in the apocryphal *Gospel of Nicodemus / Acts of Pilate*, would be the resurrection of her son: "Who shall stay my tears, if not you yourself when you rise on the third day?"[97]

And so her weeping ceases in those works where she beholds her apparently risen son (as we found in the post-crucifixion appearance to Mary in the *Meditationes* and in a few other works – see below, p. 192, n. 46). These few instances of a delusional denial of death bring Mary's mourning to an abrupt, premature halt. Nothing else can do so, including any *promise* of resurrection made to her by Jesus or by John.[98] Mary simply mourns, for she has beheld her dead or dying son before her eyes. Seeing – not theology, not an unforeseeable future – is believing.

Mary was human after all. Even correct theology required a *human* mother of Jesus – that is, a being at least capable of grieving the death of a God made *human* through the agency of her body. Any other God would not die by definition, and therefore any other God would not need to be mourned.

Stabat mater: Mary's Compassion, Our Guilt

Mary's expression of a *wish* to die with her son on Golgotha is comprehensible to any audience, for her death would at least bring an end to her own unbearable suffering and would relieve her of the task of having to mourn her son's death. More importantly, Mary's wish to die also confirms the impression we have of her life as a mother. Her very identity is tied up with her child's very existence. If he ceases to exist, how can she continue to exist? Suicide becomes an option.

The motif of Mary wishing to die with her son (or even instead of him) on Golgotha is rather common in marian lamentation. It can be found in the apocryphal *Gospel of Nicodemus*.[99] It can be read in the earliest *Life of the Virgin* (seventh century) by Maximos the Confessor.[100] It is to be found in Byzantine Greek laments (such as the marian lament in the *Christos Paschōn*)[101] and in all of the relevant modern ballads in Greek ("Songs of Good Friday").[102] Also, in the spiritual songs (*dukhovnye stikhi*) of late imperial Russia, Mary expresses a death wish when she asks to be swallowed up by "mother moist earth,"[103] a phrase that, among its other meanings (above, p. 5), represents the personified place of the dead for Russian peasants.[104]

Mary's death wish occurs repeatedly in the medieval West, as we have already seen from a variety of examples – to which may be added the famous dramatic poem or *lauda*, *Donna de paradiso* by Jacopone da Todi (d. 1306),[105] the anonymous thirteenth-century *Vita rhythmica*,[106] some medieval English lyrics and carols,[107] as well as the prose narrative *Lamentacioun of Oure Lady*.[108]

There seem to be no instances, however, where Mary actually and unambiguously dies along with her son at Golgotha. At most, she begs to be hoisted up onto the cross with him, or she swoons, or she is spattered with his blood, or she feels the metaphorical sword of Simeon piercing her body as she wails with grief, or she is "crucified" metaphorically, and so on. Furthermore, no one in the vicinity seems inclined to kill Mary, so that the only way she would be able to die would be to kill herself.

Suicide would not work, however. The temporarily mortal God incarnate is free to die voluntarily on the cross, but his mortal mother is not free to commit suicide. Mary's death, unlike her son's, would be in vain, for it would have no redemptive or salvific effect for others. Mary is not God, or at least in the Golgotha time frame she is not yet the powerful post-Assumption deity she would later become for mariophile sectarians within the Christian world.

Mary's role, then, is to be *com*passionate as her son undergoes his *passion*. The advantage of this is to highlight her son's role. When, in a passion play for example, Mary endures along with her divine son something like the same horrible suffering he endures, she encourages a responsive audience to experience more fully the son's own suffering and dying on the cross. As a result, members of the audience (they know who they are) have an opportunity to feel guilty for the sins they have in the past committed against their God.

The experience of guilt is a necessary component of any meditation on what happened at Golgotha. Here, again, is a relevant passage from my old daily missal, in this case from the ritual procession of the Stations of the Cross:

> First Station. Jesus is condemned to death.
>
> Pilate dares to condemn the all-holy Savior to death. No, not Pilate; but my sins have condemned Jesus to be crucified. O Jesus, have mercy on me and remember Thou didst choose to die that I may have eternal life.

> Third station. Jesus falls the first time.
>
> Weakened by torments and by loss of blood, Jesus falls beneath His Cross. Alas! More truly was He crushed to earth by the number and enormity of my sins!
>
> Seventh station. Jesus falls a second time.
>
> My feeble resolutions, my oft-repeated sins have crushed Jesus to earth a second time.[109]

In my own experience, praying these words in silence on Good Friday had the effect of eliciting guilt feelings.

The son came to Golgotha to suffer and die on behalf of sinful humankind, whereas, in scripture (John 19:25–27), the mother only appeared there while this salvific act was in progress, and for no stated purpose. But, if a mother's suffering is more effective at inducing guilt feelings than a son's by itself, and if it can be agreed that a normal mother would certainly suffer grievously under such circumstances, then the creators of marian laments, passion plays, and the like must have thought that a didactic theological message could be transmitted. In effect: see how Mary weeps for her son, who is God himself suffering for us; understand how precious for us his suffering is; stop sinning, for it is our very own sins that make him suffer (as the Church teaches).[110] In a word, do penance.

The penitential result of marian compassion can be illustrated in a schematic way by a marian lament in vernacular German originating from Füssen in the first half of the fifteenth century. Peter Loewen has published and translated selected stanzas from the manuscript containing the *Füssener Marienklage*. At the end of the drama, Mary interprets for the audience the terrible suffering she has been enduring:

> Alas, me, so poor a woman,
> indeed I saw his pure body
> so horribly colored;
> this you should all consider well.
> I saw him standing on the cross
> and three nails go through him –
> through his hands and feet.
> Alas, poor sinners, repent [*su^{e}nder bo^{e}z*]!
> He has, through the pain of sin,
> suffered death upon the cross
> with scourging and with a spear;
> sinners, sin no more![111]

Loewen comments: "Here, the Virgin Mary beseeches her audience . . . to consider her witness of the Crucifixion, particularly these heartrending details of human agony, and to repent."[112] In other words, to the extent that

Mary expresses credible compassion for her dying son, and thereby induces our own compassion both for her and for him, then we have been put in a position to feel guilt – for, again, it is *our sins* that have caused the crucifixion of Mary's son. In the end, our compassion for the compassionate Mary should lead to our own repentance. We can be truly contrite when at last we understand that we ourselves have caused the son's horrible sufferings, which we now behold through the mother's eyes.

A more familiar and perhaps more convincing example of how Mary's sorrows at Golgotha can induce our own sorrow is offered by some opening stanzas of the famous hymn *Stabat mater dolorosa* (often attributed to Jacopone da Todi). This hymn, "a supreme achievement of Franciscan and, indeed, of the religious verse of the Middle Ages,"[113] was still being sung on September 15 in my own experience of the Tridentine rite.[114] With its rocking, insistently trochaic rhythm, the work draws us deeply into the mother's keening:

Stabat mater dolorosa
Iuxta crucem lacrimosa,
Dum pendebat filius;
Cuius animam gementem,
Contristantem et dolentem
Pertransivit gladius.
O quam tristis et afflicta
Fuit illa benedicta
Mater unigeniti!
Quae maerebat et dolebat,
Et tremebat, dum videbat
Nati poenas incliti.
Quis est homo, qui non fleret,
Matrem Christi si videret
In tanto supplicio?
Quis non posset contristari,
Piam matrem contemplari
Dolentem cum filio?
At the Cross her station keeping,
Stood the mournful Mother weeping,
Close to Jesus to the last.
Through her heart, his sorrow sharing,
All his bitter anguish bearing,
Now at length the sword had passed.
Oh, how sad and sore distress'd
Was that Mother highly blest
Of the sole-begotten One!
Christ above in torment hangs;
She beneath beholds the pangs

Of her dying glorious Son.
Is there one who would not weep
Whelm'd in miseries so deep
Christ's dear Mother to behold?
Can the human heart refrain
From partaking in her pain,
In that Mother's pain untold?

This is not merely a call to empathize nonjudgmentally with another person's suffering. It is an appeal to *sympathize*, to take judgmental *pity*[115] on this poor woman who is in extreme psychological pain. What is happening to her son on the cross should not be happening. There is something morally wrong with what Mary is obliged to endure, and with what her son has obliged himself to endure. And it is wrong because of *me*. I am responsible, I have sinned, and this would not be happening if I (as well as the poem's persona, and we human beings generally) had not sinned:

Sancta mater, istud agas,
Crucifixi fige plagas
Cordi meo valide,
Tui nati vulnerati,
Tam dignati pro me pati,
Poenas mecum divide.[116]
Holy Mother! Pierce me through;
In my heart each wound renew
Of my Saviour crucified:
Let me share with thee His pain,
Who for all my sins was slain,
Who for me in torments died.[117]

Edward Caswall's lexicon is not quite right, but his rhythm and rhyme are both right and effective, and he captures the penitential theme.

Like the mother, I too am encouraged to suffer because of the son's sufferings. I too should be subjected to the same pains or punishments (*poenas*) that the mother endures. That is repentance. I am repentant, contrite, heartbroken. I recognize and reject sins that I have committed in the past.

Surely, everyone has sinned. Who has not felt guilt or remorse over some action that has hurt another human being? And who has not felt a need to repair harm that we (you, I) have done, to make amends, to find forgiveness, to make some kind of reparation? Even if a religious vocabulary of "sin" and "repentance" is not used, everyone understands this intuitively.[118] Except for the occasional psychopath, everyone has a conscience, and everyone is capable of experiencing this kind of guilt.

In the case at hand, I (along with the poem's speaking persona) feel guilty and repent because the victim's *mother* moves me to do so. I want to make some kind of reparation even to her, not only to her son, the immediate cause of her woes. Either way (or both ways), I am conscience-stricken, not beaten up internally by some harsh superego. The ontogenetic basis of conscience, according to Donald L. Carveth and some of his psychoanalytic predecessors, is identification with a nurturer (usually the mother) in one's past.[119] As I read or listen to *Stabat mater*, I am not identifying masochistically with a paternal aggressor who once punished me. I am instead identifying with a *maternal* figure who once watched over me with loving, depressive concern, who long ago showed me the difference between right and wrong, and who now, in the person of the *mother* of Jesus in *Stabat mater*, is suffering wrongfully because of what her son is doing to himself.

If we accept the traditional Christian premises that Mary's son is God, and that he volunteers to suffer and die on the cross out of a loving concern *for us*, then we will not think to ask why he does such a thing to his poor mother. It is Mary to whom we are drawn. Mary's suffering is subjectively identical to her son's suffering. It is a perfectly realized sympathy, or compassion. In this Mary is represented as the ideal of motherhood. Our natural response is to take Mary for who she is in the context of *Stabat mater*, and to experience with her the terrible sword that pierces her breast.

Mary is a mother; she is, indeed, the ideal mother. Her son may be the perfect fool, but she is his mother nonetheless. It may be difficult to feel compassion for the perfect fool. Only the perfect fool's perfect mother can do that. But that alone also suffices to make us compassionate.

Of course, if suffering with Mary is what it takes to make us compassionate towards Mary's son Christ as well, then so be it, for there does have to be an element of theological relevance in this work.[120] But, the affective magnet of the work is the *mater dolorosa*, and it is she who, for the duration of our perception of – and meditation upon – the work, personifies conscience itself for us, provoking our repentance and our wish somehow to bring her suffering to an end.

In 1399, thousands of white-robed penitents (*Bianchi*) marched out on the roads and in various cities in northern and central Italy for a period of nine days. They were doing this because (so the story goes) Mary had miraculously appeared to a certain peasant and told him that her son was displeased by the sinfulness of humankind and was planning to destroy the world. The only way to avoid this catastrophe, she said, was for people to don white robes and go out barefoot in processions while beating themselves, crying out for mercy and peace, repenting of their sins, forgiving one another – and singing *Stabat mater* and other hymns. Many witnesses in fact heard *Stabat mater* being sung by those marching in the processions.[121] Those who sang the hymn were perhaps frightened by the rather "un-Christian" threat made by Mary's son to destroy the world. More importantly, they understood the call to repent in the marian hymn. Their marching was itself repentance. It was also concrete testimony to the moral greatness, to the call of conscience, in the hymn that they sang as they marched.

Reproaching Gabriel

Occasionally, one has to wonder whether compassion for the mother of Jesus is called for. Perhaps anger would be the more appropriate response.

As we have seen, at the beginning of Luke's gospel, Mary is led to believe that a marvelous future is in store for her child. No Christian theologian that I am aware of has paid much attention to the discrepancy between Mary's great expectations and the horrific death of Jesus toward the end of the same gospel. Nor have theologians seriously considered the question of why Mary was not present at her son's crucifixion in the only gospel to have both an annunciation and a magnificat.

These lacunae were filled by various apocrypha and other imaginative writings that brought Mary to the scene of her son's death and permitted her to impeach the honesty of Luke's announcing angel. In Greek recensions of the *Gospel of Nicodemus* (*Acts of Pilate*), for example, Mary remembers Gabriel in the midst of bursts of lamentation:

> Alas, alas! My so sweet son, light of my eyes, ruler of the world.
> Alas, alas! How can I bear it when I behold you hanging on a cross?
> Alas, alas! What has become of the good news from Gabriel [*tou Gabriēl ta euaggelia*]?[122]

Or:

> Oh Gabriel, where are you that I should have gotten mixed up with you?
> What has become of the "*Ave*"["*Chaire*"] which you spoke to me?
> How does it happen that you did not speak to me [*pōs ouk eipes moi*] from the first about the boundless sufferings of my so sweet and so dear son, and about the unjust death of my only-begotten son?[123]

These are sensible questions (in the second passage, I quote only the first three of six). Mary is literally questioning the credibility and the authority of God's own messenger at the beginning of Luke's gospel. And, if the messenger is not credible, is not the messianic identity of Mary's son also cast into doubt?

Yes, perhaps. But this apocryphal Mary of the *Gospel of Nicodemus* is not the creation of a theologian. This Mary is not, for example, the theological Mary of Origen's homily, who, like the apostles, is "scandalized" and who is stabbed by the "sword of unbelief," as we saw earlier. Here, in a work of fiction, Mary actually speaks, and with vehemence. She addresses (the memory of) Gabriel in the midst of a trauma in progress. She is carried away by her pain. Later, before Jesus dies, she redirects her anger at the "iniquitous Jews [*hoi paranomoi Ioudaioi*]"[124] for having delivered her dear son to a bitter death, and she stops referring to Gabriel. In desperation, she grasps at straws.

There is a category of early English lyrics in which Mary attempts to soothe her baby Jesus with a lullaby, only to hear him deliver a speech to her about his future suffering and death on the cross. Amy N. Vines characterizes this sudden turn of events as "a kind of second Annunciation" that gives Mary "the information that Gabriel omitted: he [Jesus] will be martyred." Such new information has the potential to traumatize Mary.[125] Furthermore, it is not as if some outside oracle such as Gabriel has just spoken, for this time around the future victim himself speaks. Mary has no choice but to begin the grieving process decades before the actual crucifixion. In one case, she speaks of Gabriel with implicit *anger*,[126] for the announcing angel had misled her at the annunciation:

> "*When gabrell cnellyd* [kneeled] *before my face,*
> *And sayd 'heylle lady full of grace',*
> *He neuer told me nooþing of þis.*"[127]

More explicit is the reproach directed at Gabriel in another early English work, the prose narrative of the passion *Lamentacioun of Oure Lady*:

> "*O angel Gabriel, where is nowe the begynnynge of þy gretynge? Where is now þat same blisse that þou behete* [promised] *me? Where is now þat same holsomenes of grace þat þou behete me? O Gabriel, why woldest þou scorne with me, most vnworthiest of al modres?*"[128]

Why, in other words, had the future mother been treated with covert disdain and derision? Here, Mary understands that her pain was inflicted by a sadist.

Another example of Mary's reproach comes from a lament in Old Polish:

> "O, angel Gabriel,
> Where is this great joy of yours [*Gdzie jest ono twe wesele*],
> Of which you had promised me so much,
> Saying: 'Virgin, you are full of grace!'?"[129]

Utterances such as these are, of course, fictional. But they are not improbable. Taken collectively, they rebuke sacerdotalist theologians who like to read Mary's *fiat* as an assent to the torture and killing of her son. This fictional Mary understands better than do theologians what it means to take on the task of mothering a child.

This Mary did not understand Gabriel, however. Counting on Mary's humility and avid generosity, Gabriel took advantage of her. But, Gabriel was only the messenger. It was God who took advantage of Mary.[130] This was a manipulative, even sadistic, God. Our compassion is spontaneous and natural in such cases, but it is a theologically incorrect compassion, for it directs our attention to God's guilt, not our own guilt. It angers us; it does not humble us.

A reproachful Mary is not the Mary of *Stabat mater* – who speaks not a word, much less raises any embarrassing objections to what her son is doing to himself at Golgotha. Yet, even in contexts where it is clear that Mary does recognize her son's masochism, she does not openly reproach him for it, or at least does not explicitly reject its supposed theological basis. We saw, for example, that the Mary of *Planctus ante nescia* understands that her son's pains are his *delicie* offered up for the sins of the daughters of Jerusalem, but still, she does not reproach him for taking the pleasure of redeeming others (and she blames the Jews for killing him). Sometimes also, as we have seen, Mary takes a stance of polite questioning of her son's oddly self-destructive actions, as in the Romanos *kontakion*, or in Pseudo-Bonaventure's *Meditationes vitae Christi*, but then she seems to back off.[131] Even in those English mystery plays where Mary's grief is so powerful that it appears to prevail over what Dronke terms "the truth of the Redemption" (above, p. 180), Mary nevertheless does not explicitly refute that "truth." The life of Mary's flesh-and-blood son is obviously a higher "truth" for her or, as Sarah McNamer puts it, in the laments Mary's "locus of value is the body of the one who has been nurtured."[132] As a consequence, Mary has no interest in making anything that resembles a theological refutation within the horrifying context of Golgotha.

*

Mary's compassion for Jesus before, during, and after his suffering and death on the cross may be heard in numerous and varied laments. In the Byzantine world, the Good Friday *kontakion* of Romanos the Melodist eloquently expresses Mary's anxiety over what her son is about to do to himself, yet he insists that he will rise from the dead. In the later Greek and Russian Orthodox Holy Saturday liturgies, Mary hears her son urging her to deny his death even when she beholds him dead in the tomb.

The medieval West saw a surge in the production of liturgical texts, homilies, prose narrations, poetry, passion plays, mystery plays, and other genres that foreground Mary's participation in her son's passion. In some of these works, Mary's lamentation gets quite complex and emotionally extreme. Sometimes, Mary expresses a wish to die herself, but she never commits suicide (historical accuracy and theological correctness permit only her son the grandiose masochist to do that). In the Latin prose work *Quis dabit*, Mary rants against the "wicked Jews" for what they are doing to her son, asking that they crucify her in his place. In the famous lament *Planctus ante nescia*, anti-Jewish sentiments are again prominent, with Mary urging the "daughters of Zion" to repent and to accept Jesus. The hymn *Stabat mater dolorosa* urges us all to participate in Mary's compassion, to feel the enormity of our sins, which have brought Mary's son *and* Mary to Golgotha. The religious vocabulary of sinfulness is quite appropriate here, for it is a way to express the guilt feelings – sometimes in the sense of a punishing superego but primarily in the sense of a nurturing conscience – experienced by believers.

There also exist some texts in which Mary gets angry at someone besides the Jews. An example is the early English *Lamentacioun of Oure Lady*, in which Mary reproaches the angel Gabriel for tricking her into having to be the compassionate mother of a crucified God. Such works direct attention to God's guilt, not the guilt of believers. Mary accuses God himself of doing her wrong in at least one of these works, thereby suggesting that her pain was inflicted by a sadistic God.

Notes

1 Gounelle 2008, 7–8 (Mary laments in medieval Greek variants that fall under Gounelle's Greek recension M, formerly C. von Tischendorf's Greek recension B).
2 Tillyard 1949, 163–208.
3 Zoras 1956, 60–62.
4 Alexiou 1975, 116–118, 129 ff.; Alexiou 2002 (1974), 62–64, 142–144.
5 Alexiou 2002 (1974), 65–68.
6 Gregory of Nazianzus 1969; Rosemary Woolf dubs this work an "imitation Greek drama" (1968, 247); see also the comments by Alexiou 2002 (1974), 64 ff.
7 See especially: Maximus the Confessor 2012, 101–118; Shoemaker 2011a.
8 Alexiou 1975, 113.
9 For a structural analysis, see: Alexiou 2002 (1974), 142–144.
10 Maas and Trypanis, eds. 1963, 143, 145, as translated by Ephrem Lash in Romanos the Melodist 1995, 144, 146.
11 Maas and Trypanis, eds. 1963, 143; Romanos the Melodist 1995, 144.
12 Maas and Trypanis, eds. 1963, 144; Romanos the Melodist 1995, 145. This admonition against mourning is possibly an echo of Luke 23:28, where Jesus turns to the weeping women who follow him to his crucifixion and declares: "Daughters of Jerusalem, do not weep for me." See: Dobrov 1994, 393.
13 Maas and Trypanis, eds. 1963, 146; Romanos the Melodist 1995, 147.
14 Maas and Trypanis, eds. 1963, 146; Romanos the Melodist 1995, 147.
15 Maas and Trypanis, eds. 1963, 146; Romanos the Melodist 1995, 148.
16 Maas and Trypanis, eds. 1963, 147; Romanos the Melodist 1995, 148. Compare Dobrov (1994, 393), who speaks of Christ's salvific mission in this passage as "a curious homeopathic surgery."
17 See Reynolds (2012–, 254) on this "clever device" that enables Romanos "to avoid contradicting the evidence of the gospel of John."
18 Maas and Trypanis, eds. 1963, 148; Romanos the Melodist 1995, 149 (here modified in an attempt to capture Romanos's utilization of an anadiplosis together with a polyptoton in the Greek).
19 From the large psychoanalytic literature on mourning, it is worth mentioning: Freud 1957 (1917); Klein 1994 (1940); the entry "Mourning" in Moore and Fine, eds. 1990, 122–123 (with bibliography).
20 Pallas 1965, 230; Lifshits 1987, 504.
21 Tradigo 2006 (2004), 234. Cf. a similar icon from Moscow dating from the second half of the sixteenth century in: Lifshits and Lukashov 2000, cat. no. 13.
22 Bezsonov 1861–1864, vol. 2, part 4: 188 (*Ne rydai, o Mati moia*), 189 (*Ne plach', o Mat' moia*), 195 (*Ne plach' ty, Matushka Bozh'ia Mariia*), 205 (*Ei, ne plach', ne trat' svoei krasoty!*), etc.

23 Hapgood, 1922, pp. 222, 224; *Triōdion katanuktikon* 1983, p. 483; *Triod' postnaia* 1992, vol. 2, p. upe. The passage quoted here is part of a conversation between Jesus and his mother in a hymn composed by Kosmas of Jerusalem (d. ca.760). See: Nikolakopoulos 1991.

24 Tillyard 1949, no. 16, p. 186, as translated on p. xvi.

25 Davies, ed. 1964, 86 (no. 24), quoted and translated in de Visscher 2007, 185.

26 Brown, ed. 1924, 228.

27 See: Brown, ed. 1924, 285, n. 128.

28 For example: Wechssler 1893, 11; Young 1962 (1933), vol. 1, 493–495; Bestul 1996, 112; Ellington 2001, 81; Fulton 2002, 205 ff.

29 Hence, Saint Ambrose's famous reminder that Mary stood – not wept – at the foot of the cross in John's gospel (*Stantem illam lego, flentem non lego* – see: Ambrose of Milan 1845, par. 39, col. 1371). On the early Christian view of death, which derived from the belief that Christ had already risen from the dead and that all others who had died would follow (1 Thessalonians 4:13–14), see, for example: Favez 1937; Scourfield 1993; Woolf 1968, 240; Rancour-Laferriere 2011, 133–134. In the medieval West, various theologians and preachers criticized "excessive" mourning by parents of recently deceased children (Shahar 1990, 149–155). It is curious that Mary does not weep over her dying son in the very same gospel where Jesus *does* weep over the recently deceased Lazarus (John 11:35; see especially the analysis in a medieval context by Fulton 2002, 417–428). The fact that the biblical Mary did not weep as she stood by her son's cross could be taken to mean that she had already converted to the "Christian" belief in eternal life (denial of death) preached by her son. The fact that she does weep in so many of the post-scriptural texts and images suggests otherwise – namely, that Christians eventually preferred to see in Mary a normal (i.e., a sorrowful, compassionate) mother who would weep upon the death of her son, and perhaps also a skeptical human being who doubts the feasibility of anyone – including even her son – rising from the dead.

30 Reynolds 2012–, 264–266.

31 Dronke 1992, 470; cf. Brock 1993.

32 Dronke 1992, 476. Here, it is worth noting (with McNamer 2010, 158) that woman's lament is a "cross-cultural genre and anthropological event."

33 See, for example: Shoemaker 2011a.

34 Bennett 1982, 35, 59.

35 For a review of some of the literature on the emotionalism of marian laments in the late medieval period in the West, see: McNamer 2010, 155–159.

36 Bestul 1996, 186–192.

37 Bestul 1996, 51.

38 On Romanos, see above. On Bernard of Clairvaux and other medieval Western writers (including our pseudo-Bonaventure) who politely questioned the need for Christ's sacrificial death – especially the need for Christ to shed sacrificial blood – see: Bynum 2007, 230 ff.

39 Ragusa and Green, eds., trans. 1961, 308–309. Passages inserted here in Latin are from the *Meditationes vitae Christi* originally attributed to Bonaventure (here: Bonaventure 1868a, 596). The Bonaventure edition of what originally might have been *Meditaciones vite Christi* is chosen here because it is the one "most frequently quoted by current scholars" (M. Stallings-Taney in de Cavlibvs 1997, x, n. 6), and because it probably is closer to what literate believers have been reading during the centuries since the Tuscan Franciscan penned his original in an Italianized Latin. Bestul lists the work as item # 21 in his catalogue (1996, 189).

40 Ragusa and Green, eds., trans. 1961, 309.
41 Ragusa and Green, eds., trans. 1961, 335–340.
42 Ragusa and Green, eds., trans. 1961, 344; Bonaventure 1868a, 610.
43 Ragusa and Green, eds., trans. 1961, 348; Bonaventure 1868a, 612.
44 Ragusa and Green, eds., trans. 1961, 349; Bonaventure 1868a, 612.
45 Ragusa and Green, eds., trans. 1961, 359–360.
46 Maximus the Confessor 2012, 119–120. In passing, the *Meditations* narrator states: "For how He appeared to His mother is not mentioned anywhere, but is piously believed" (Ragusa and Green, eds., trans. 1961, 373; cf. Wechssler 1893, 28). Jesus also makes a post-resurrection appearance (or appearances) to his mother in various other works in the history of Christianity, such as: the apocryphal Coptic (so-called) *Gospel of Gamaliel* (O'Carroll 2000 [1982], 41; Elliott 1993, 163); the earliest *Life of the Virgin* by Maximos the Confessor and derivative works by George of Nicomedia, John the Geometer, and Symeon Metaphrastes (see Shoemaker 2005, 452, 459, 462, 464, on Mary's actually witnessing her son's resurrection in works by these authors; Maximus the Confessor 2012, 119–120); in various prayers and hymns in the medieval West, e.g. the salutation, *Ave, que filium dei resurgentem a mortuis vidisti* (Meersseman 1958–1960, vol. II, 163); shortly after the *Quis dabit* within Ogier of Locedio's homily *In Praise of God's Holy Mother* (2006, 160, 162); *The Golden Legend* (de Voragine 1993 [1850], vol. 1, 221–222); and at least once in the English mystery plays (*N-Town Plays* 2007, 286–287; more examples from other dramatic works from other parts of Europe are listed in: Muir 1995, 257, n. 77). In parts of southern Italy, an elaborate meeting (*incontro*) is staged on Easter Sunday between a statue of Mary (*Addolorata*) and a statue of the resurrected Christ (Carroll 1996, 98–100). For some visual representations of a post-resurrection appearance of Christ to his mother, see: Grimoüard de Saint-Laurent 1872–1875, vol. IV, 388–391; Guldan 1966, figs. 160–163 (and discussion, 144–148); Monks 1990, 189.
47 Barré 1952.
48 Bestul 1996, 139.
49 *Quis dabit capiti meo et oculis meis imbrem lacrimarum* ("Who will give a stream of tears to my head and eyes" (cf. the Vulgate Jeremiah 9.1: *Quis dabit capiti meo aquam et oculis meis fontem lacrimarum*).
50 Bestul 1996, 165–185; cf. 188 (item 12).
51 Bestul 1996, 168–169.
52 On the notion of a "glorified body," which is grounded ultimately in 1 Corinthians (ch. 15) and which by the early thirteenth century was being characterized in terms of the "dowries" (*dotes*) – including *impassibilitas* – that such a body receives from its beatified soul at the end of time, see: Corcoran 1967; and especially Bynum 1995, 100, 121–137, 172, 235–236 (with rich bibliography).
53 Bestul 1996, 171–172, 172–173.
54 On the deicide charge and its persistence in the history of Christianity, see: Cohen 2007; Rancour-Laferriere 2011. On the anti-Judaism of medieval passion narratives, see: Bestul 1996, 69–110.
55 Bestul 1996, 172–173.
56 Bestul 1996, 172–175.
57 Bestul 1996, 176–177.
58 Bestul 1996, 176–179.
59 Bestul 1996, 134, 178–179.
60 See: Hamburger 2011.
61 Bestul 1996, 179–180.

62 Bestul 1996, 180–181.
63 See Bestul's discussion of this issue (1996, 128–134).
64 Bestul 1996, 182–183.
65 Bestul 1996, 131.
66 Bestul 1996, 184–185.
67 Marx 1994, 129.
68 For example: Ogier of Locedio 2006, 160.
69 Alexiou (1975, 134) observes that the passion play was "essentially a western phenomenon."
70 Muir 1995, 253, n. 52.
71 For the text being utilized here, see: Dronke, ed., trans. 1994, 198–235 (and informative comments, 185–197). See also these useful studies: Young 1962 (1933), vol. 1, 518 ff.; Szövérffy 1985a, 72–77; Stevens 1986, 130–138; Dronke 1992, 457–489; Boynton 2004, 328–333.
72 For example: Brown 1994, vol. 2, 920–932; Franklin 2001, 957.
73 Young 1962 (1933), vol. 1, 496 ff.; Dronke 1992, 464; Bernt 1993.
74 Dronke, ed., trans. 1994, 230–231.
75 Dronke 1992, 466.
76 Stevens 1986, 134.
77 Dronke, ed., trans. 1994, 232–233.
78 Flusser 1986 (1985), 13–14.
79 Flusser 1986 (1985), 15.
80 Rancour-Laferriere 2011, 173–243, with bibliography.
81 Alexiou 1975, 123, 125; Maximus the Confessor 2012, 107 ff.; Shoemaker 2011b, 60. In one variant (M3) of the *Gospel of Nicodemus* (*Acts of Pilate*), the lamenting Mary accuses the ungrateful Jews of wanting to nail Jesus to the cross (Gounelle 2008, 233); in three (M1, M2, and M3), she cries out that the Jews have delivered him up to a bitter (and dishonorable – M3) death (Gounelle 2008, 240–241).
82 For example, in a fifteenth-century lament from St. Gall, Mary cries, *Owe hertötet ist din zarter lip / von der bösen Juden kip* ("O, woe! Your tender body has been done in / by the obstinacy of the evil Jews"). As quoted by Schreiner 2006 (1996), 439 (I wish to thank Livia Rosman for assistance with the translation, June 15, 2015). See also: Frey 2001.
83 Woolf 1968, 249 (an example from John of Grimstone's preaching-book), 260 (from the lament *Listyns, lordyngus, to my tale*); Greene, ed. 1977 (1935), 104–114 (early English carols of the passion, nos. 158 ["wykyd Jewes"], 162 ["fals Jewes"], 171 ["The Jues me bet"], etc.), the N-Town *Crucifixion* (in *The N-Town Plays* 2007, 268–270).
84 In one of the *cantigas*, a farmer invokes Mary, "the Mother of Him Whom the Jews had killed on the cross" (as quoted by Rubin 2009, 239; cf. Remensnyder 2014, 133–139).
85 Czarnowus 2010, 147 ("When I see an infidel Jew / As he beats, tortures my dear Son.").
86 Dronke, ed., trans. 1994, 232–233 (modified).
87 Dronke, ed., trans. 1994, 191.
88 Dronke, ed., trans. 1994, 232–233.
89 Dronke 1992, 466; Dronke, ed., trans. 1994, 191.
90 *The N-Town Plays* 2007, 266–273.
91 *The N-Town Plays* 2007, 268–270.
92 *The N-Town Plays* 2007, 272.

93 That is, the play cycles of York, Chester, Towneley, and N-Town (the latter "an incomplete, eclectic, regional [East Anglian?] anthology," say the editors of the 2007 edition (p. 18).
94 *The Towneley Plays* 1994, vol. 1, 302; Dronke 1992, 489.
95 Dronke 1992, 489.
96 Boynton 2004, 322–327.
97 Translation by Alexiou 1975, 126; cf. Gounelle 2008, 268–269 (M1, M2, and M3 are identical at this point).
98 In the Digby mystery *The Burial of Christ*, John reminds a lamenting Mary that her son shall rise from the dead, and Mary even appears to agree (*I knaw it well*), but is so overcome by what *the Iues so vnkind* have done to her son that she carries on lamenting at great length (Furnivall 1965 [1882], 189–199).
99 Gounelle 2008, 238–239 (variants M2 and M3; cf. p. 94; Alexiou 1975, 126).
100 Maximus the Confessor 2012, 109; Shoemaker 2011a, 581, 583.
101 Alexiou 1975, 123; Alexiou 2002 (1974), 64–65.
102 Alexiou 1975, 136.
103 Fedotov 1991 (1935), 50 (the line, *Uvy, mat', syra zemlia, voz'mi menia k sebe*).
104 Rancour-Laferriere 1995, 74–75.
105 The poem ends with an image of mother and son, "Embracing each other and their common cross" (Jacopone da Todi 1982, 280). For pungent comments, see: Dronke 1996 (1968), 61–62.
106 Reynolds 2012–, 282 ("I will go and die with my beloved Son").
107 Woolf 1968, 249–250 (three examples from John of Grimestone's preaching-book), 258 (from a manuscript with the title *a tretys to lerne to wepe*); Davies, ed. 1964, 119, no. 44 (the line, *So lat us deiyen bothen isame*; cf. also Brown 1924, 81, no. 60); Greene, ed., 1977 (1935), 107 (no. 158, *Why mygh[t] I not with my Son dye?*).
108 Towl 2010, 253 (*. . . son, dey þou nat without þy modyre . . . let vs . . . dey togidderes*).
109 Lefebvre 1956, 1121–1122. I have cited this same passage in: Rancour-Laferriere 2011, 111.
110 On Christian masochism by proxy, see: Rancour-Laferriere 2011, 109 ff.
111 Loewen 2008, 338.
112 Loewen 2008, 326.
113 Raby 1953 (1927), 440.
114 Lefebvre 1956, 867–868, under feast of "The Seven Sorrows of the Blessed Virgin Mary." Cf. Socias 2011, 1934–1936, under "Our Lady of Sorrows."
115 See the entry "Empathy" in: Moore and Fine, eds. 1990, 67; Carveth 2013, 71–72.
116 Dreves and Blume 1909, vol. I, 392.
117 Caswall 1884 (1849), 138–140.
118 Cf. Carveth 2013, 36.
119 Carveth 2013, especially 60–82, and the literature cited there.
120 See: Duffy 1988, 215–216.
121 For a detailed historical study, see: Bornstein 1993.
122 Gounelle 2008, 231 (M3).
123 Gounelle 2008, 237 (M3). Mary's invocation of Gabriel does not occur in the variant M1, and in M2 it is more fully developed (Mary suffers more) than in M3.
124 Gounelle 2008, 240–241 (M1, M2, M3).
125 Vines 2010, 202.
126 Vines 2010, 218.
127 Brown 1939, 2.

128 As quoted by Towl 2010, 258.
129 As quoted by Czarnowus 2010, 147; cf. 137.
130 Mary does accuse God the Father of doing her wrong in *Lamentacioun of Oure Lady*. See: McNamer 2010, 162–163.
131 Cf. Bynum 2007, 230 ff.
132 McNamer 2010, 162.

11 Time Future, Time Past

Improper Annunciations

All indications from the infancy narratives of Luke and Matthew are that Mary knew nothing about the way her son would die. But that has not prevented speculation on the theme of Mary's proleptic knowledge of Christ's passion. The visual arts offer an especially suggestive trove in this area.

There is a category of annunciation imagery in which an already fully formed and naked Christ child, having emerged from God the Father, is seen moving downward from the heavens toward his future mother, Mary. David M. Robb, in his 1936 study of late medieval annunciation iconography, offered some striking examples of this, including a subcategory of works in which *the Christ child is already bearing his cross as he approaches Mary.* This same subcategory would be discussed and illustrated with a variety of images three decades later, by Gertrud Schiller, in the first volume of her encyclopedic survey of Christian iconography.[1]

We find, for example, a fresco (ca.1300) from Santa Maria in Trastevere in Rome that shows the Christ child following the (more customary) dove (the Holy Spirit) downward along a trajectory from God the Father in the upper right and toward Mary in the center left of the image.[2] Lorenzo Veneziano's painting in Venice (1371) has the Christ child with his cross seeming to hesitate in the arms of the Father, as the dove descends straight down toward the head of Mary.[3] Meister Bertram's Grabow altarpiece (1383) in Hamburg has God the Father releasing the dove, followed by the Christ child bearing a cross – both in the direction of Mary's head.[4] In the center panel of the magnificent Mérode Altarpiece (ca.1425), probably by Robert Campin, the cross-bearing Christ child flies down through the air directly behind the head of the archangel Gabriel and toward Mary (see Figure 11.1).[5] An annunciation from the Church of the Madeleine in Aix-en-Provence (ca.1443) shows the Christ child high above the head of the archangel, but it is clear that this child is proceeding down along a path of light emanating from God the Father in the upper left of this panel painting, and toward the head of Mary.[6]

There are other annunciation images in this same subcategory, and there are related (mostly devotional) images that may not be annunciations,

Figure 11.1 Robert Campin, Mérode Altarpiece, center panel (detail), Metropolitan Museum of Art (Cloisters), New York (Lane 1984, 40, fig. 25).

technically speaking, but that plainly show Mary in a receptive attitude as her cross-bearing infant approaches her from above. For example, the title page (by Erhard Altdorfer) of Martin Luther's New Testament of 1533 shows Mary welcoming the Christ child, who – as Jennifer O'Reilly writes – "streams earthwards . . . in a burst of light and glory already bearing his cross."[7] A woodcut (*Holzepitaph*) in Breslau (?1558) shows Mary overshadowed by the Holy Spirit as she looks up in pious expectation at her naked son, who, cross on his back, is flying down toward her and away from God the Father at the top center of the image.[8] In another late medieval image, the Christ child is seen carrying his cross from the Father "down the shaft of light leading to Mary," to quote Avril Henry's commentary to an edition of the *Biblia pauperum* (ca.1460).[9]

In all such images, Mary gives no indication that she wishes to turn away the Christ child who is flying down toward her. On the contrary, it appears that she has given, or is about to give, her assent to what God is sending her way – namely, a child who will grow up to be tortured and killed upon a cross. Of course, the canonical infancy narratives make no reference to a cross for the baby Jesus. Indeed, the angel Gabriel arrives only with a request that Mary agree to conceive through the agency of the Holy Spirit (Luke 1:35), not that she adopt an already existing child bearing a cross. With good reason, it was declared by the fathers gathered at the Council of Ephesus in 431 that Christ the "Word of God," for the sake of human salvation, "took flesh from the holy virgin [*carnem de Virgine suscipiens*] and made it his own."[10] Any images that suggested otherwise – that is, that Christ was already a fully (or even partially) formed, physical human person before being conceived in Mary's womb – were wrong. Commenting, for example, about the numerous artistic representations of a toddler-Christ swooping downward from the heavens toward the virgin Mary, in his *Guide de l'art chrétien* (1872–1875), Henri-Julien Grimoüard explains: "The Son of God, in becoming incarnate, did not come to live in this virginal womb with a fully formed body, for after all his body was formed from the most pure blood of Mary."[11]

The chief psychological implication of Mary welcoming an infant or toddler Christ who already bears his cross is this: she is agreeing to mother a child whose life she already knows will come to a violent end. She, like the viewer, cannot but notice that this child comes down from the Father with cross preinstalled. This is more than theological incorrectness (although it is that). It is also an expression of the mother's proleptic knowledge and tacit acceptance of God's plot to kill God her son.

Of course, God the absent Father in the faraway heavens had already long ago ordained this sacrificial fate for his son. Indeed, the correct view is that the son already existed before Mary gave birth to him. In the "Definition of the Faith" issued by the Council of Chalcedon in 451, "our Lord Jesus Christ" is characterized as "begotten before the ages [*ante saecula*] from the Father as regards his divinity, and in the last days [*in novissimis autem diebus*] the same for us and for our salvation from Mary, the virgin God-bearer, as regards his humanity."[12] From this, it would appear that Christ was really born twice, the first "birth" having been what might be termed the couvade of God.[13] But, of course, the earthly Mary could not have been acquainted with her son until he was born the second time, in the flesh, so that she could not possibly have seen him descending earthward already bearing his cross. Hence, the images considered here are improper allegations of Mary's prolepsis. Nevertheless, viewers of such images do come away with an impression that Mary knew how her son was going to die.

Bilateral Icons, Diptychs, and the Passion Madonna

More subtle indications of Mary's advance awareness of what will happen to her infant son are communicated by certain bilateral icons from the Eastern Orthodox world. On these icons, one side depicts mother and child in some

Figure 11.2 Double-sided icon, Mary holding her child in *Hodēgētria* fashion, front side. Byzantine, late twelfth century. Byzantine Museum, Kastoria, Greece (Evans and Wixom, eds. 1997, 126, fig. 72).

configuration, and the other side shows the crucifixion or images closely connected to the crucifixion. A well-known example is an icon of the passion from Kastoria, Greece, dating from the late twelfth century (see Figures 11.2 and 11.3). On one side is a visibly anxious, frowning Mary holding her child in *Hodēgētria* fashion; on the other is a dead Christ represented as the Man of Sorrows (*Akra Tapeinosis*), with his cross in the background.[14] It is difficult to avoid the impression that, as Annemarie Weyl Carr states, "the frown serves to link obverse and reverse of the panel, as the Virgin in cradling her child looks forward to his – and her own – Passion."[15] In other words, it is difficult for the viewer to resist a proleptic reading of the pair of images. The two sides also represent the crucifixion, insofar as Christ – both as child and as adult – is shown with the customary cruciferous nimbus. Some damage at the base of the icon suggests that it was attached to a pole, so that it could be carried in procession and viewed from both sides. It was

Figure 11.3 Same double-sided icon, dead Christ represented as the Man of Sorrows (*Akra Tapeinosis*), back side (Evans and Wixom, eds. 1997, 126, fig. 72).

very likely utilized as such for Good Friday services.[16] It is known that these double-sided icons were incorporated into church ritual, as when the choir addressed such an icon while singing Mary's lament over her dead son.[17] The icons constituted a "visual counterpart"[18] to the so-called *stavrotheotokia* and other hymns on the theme of Mary's lamentation. It is worth noting that these icons are not connected with the annunciation in any way, so that there is no question of applying Mary's *fiat* to the proleptic knowledge represented here (unlike the images analyzed in the previous section).

Numerous bilateral icons clearly connecting the death of Christ on the cross with Mary holding the Christ child in her arms have survived. They include: a processional *Hodēgētria* from the third quarter of the thirteenth century with a crucifixion scene on the reverse;[19] an early-fourteenth-century *Hodēgētria* with a crucifixion scene on the reverse;[20]

a processional *Hodēgētria* from the second half of the fourteenth century with a *Hetoimasia* image (i.e., an apocalyptic throne, including in this case the cross and the other instruments of torture) on the reverse;[21] a fifteenth-century *Glykophilousa* with a crucifixion scene on the reverse;[22] and a late-sixteenth-century processional *Hodēgētria* with the Man of Sorrows and his cross on the reverse.[23]

The most famous of such bilateral marian icons is, of course, the Vladimir Mother of God (*Bogomater' Vladimirskaia*), probably created in Constantinople in the first third of the twelfth century and now housed in the museum–chapel of the Tretyakov Galery in Moscow. Mary's somber face is pressed close to the face of her child, in the configuration generally known as the *Eleousa* type (Russian *Umilenie*). The obviously affectionate child is trying to get his mother's attention as she gazes sadly out into space, in the sure knowledge that her son must be sacrificed. On the reverse is the toolkit that will be used for that sacrifice (*orudiia strastei*, i.e., the cross, lance, sponge, crown of thorns, nails),[24] which is the concrete evidence for Mary's prolepsis. The Vladimir icon also happens to be the palladium of Russia, and it has a long history of popular veneration as well as scholarly interpretation. As a result, this bilateral icon reveals much about the beliefs of Russian Orthodox Christians regarding the relationship of Mary to her son's crucifixion. Elsewhere, I have offered considerably more detailed comments on this image.[25]

Another means for pairing an image of Mary and the Christ child with an image of (or an image suggesting) the adult Christ crucified is the diptych. This method is more direct than that of the bilateral icon, for the viewer has the opportunity to see both images at the same time. As Demetrios I. Pallas observes, diptychs of specifically this kind become abundant in the West starting from the middle of the thirteenth century.[26] Edward B. Garrison's illustrated index of Italian Romanesque panel painting offers many examples of such pairings,[27] to which may be added: an early fourteenth-century north French ivory diptych with the Adoration of the Magi on the left and a crucifixion with Mary and John at the foot of the cross on the right; an early fifteenth-century Westphalian diptych that is irresistably proleptic, as Mary and the Christ *child* in the *Hortus Conclusus* (Song of Solomon 4:12) on the left side are paired with a remarkably *child-like* Christ hanging from his cross on the right.[28]

There is a small category of diptychs in which Mary and her child are paired with the mercy-seat Trinity.[29] The idea of placing one enthroned parent (God the Father, holding his crucified adult son) beside the other enthroned parent (Mary the mother, holding her baby) suggests that a pact has been made between the royal parents to put off their abuse of the child until he has grown up. The only image that makes Mary more complicitous in the abuse of her son is the opening Virgin (*Vierge ouvrante*, above pp. 47–48), where Christ is crucified right inside her body, before he even has an opportunity to be born.

Figure 11.4 *Panagia Arakiotissa*, late-twelfth-century fresco (detail), Lagoudera, Cyprus (Pentcheva 2006, fig. 70).

The so-called Passion Madonna or Virgin of the Passion (Greek *Panagia tou Pathous*, Russian *Strastnaia*) is also relevant here. It is a type that harkens back to a late-twelfth-century fresco of Mary and her child, the *Panagia Arakiotissa* in Lagoudera, Cyprus (Figure 11.4). The image shows a little boy bearing a cruciform nimbus in Mary's arms, his right arm raised in "a gesture of instruction" as he looks up at his mother's face, and he "appears to be teaching [her] the meaning of the Passion," according to Hans Belting.[30] Mary's somber eyes, in turn, are directed further upward, and we see from this just what she is learning from her son: approaching from the upper right is an angel carrying a cross, and from the upper left another angel approaches carrying a spear. These are instruments of the Passion, here functioning in proleptic reference to the violent death of Jesus already sensed by Mary's somber eyes. Another hint at what the future holds for Mary's son is his semi-recumbent pose, which in Greek is termed *anapesōn*, designating images of Christ sleeping the so-called sleep of death before his resurrection.[31]

What eventually came to be known as the Passion Madonna (in a Roman Catholic context – Our Lady of Perpetual Help) differs from the bilateral images and the diptychs in one important respect: the basis of Mary's prolepsis is represented within a single, enclosed space of mother and child (*qua* child). In the upper corners of this space, angels approach bearing instruments of the passion. These horrifying objects catch the attention of the mother–child dyad in the center. The child appears to be frightened, while a gloomy mother typically holds his hands in a comforting gesture.

Russian art scholar Nikodim P. Kondakov[32] sees a relationship between the Passion Madonna (*Strastnaia*) and the *Eleousa* based on a proposed sequence of the two categories as they occur in the Greco-Italian early Renaissance. First, the Christ child of the Passion Madonna sees the persecutory angels approaching from above, jumps up in fright to be comforted by his mother, but loses his sandals in the process (one image shows a sandal dangling precariously;[33] another shows the sandal already falling[34]). Meantime, the mother too has seen the cause of the child's fright and has herself become upset, for she has understood that the approaching angels signify the future suffering in store for her son. As Simeon had prophesized, a sword has now already pierced her soul. So, she bends her head in sorrow. Seeing the anguish on his mother's face, the child in turn tries to comfort *her*, pressing his cheek against hers and/or putting his arm(s) around her neck. Now, subtract the persecutory angels and leave the child barefoot altogether and, according to Kondakov, you have the basic *Eleousa* type: a tender mother closely holding (and being held close by) her anxious child.

Kondakov's proposal may or may not work as a particular segment of art history,[35] but he does discern the real psychological similarity between the Passion Madonna and the *Eleousa*. In both there is a future danger to the child, and in both a response to the danger is indicated. In the Passion Madonna, both child and mother are responding – the child with fear, and the mother with a comforting gesture and an often sad and anxious countenance. In the *Eleousa*, the future danger is not explicitly represented, but viewers may find it elsewhere – for example, on the back of the image (bilateral versions), or in their own personal bank of cultural knowledge (biblical accounts of the passion, liturgical practices, etc.). Viewers of a given token of the *Eleousa* may also read the danger directly from the mother's countenance, and they may read many other things there as well. There is always more room for both projections and conjectures about the mother's psychological state in the finest examples of the *Eleousa*. In all examples, the mother's proleptic knowledge of her son's crucifixion is a given, but, in a work such as the Vladimir Mother of God, for instance, other ways in which she responded to that terrible knowledge are perhaps yet to be found by insatiable mariophile scholars: *De Maria numquam satis.*

Textual Representation of Mary's Proleptic Knowledge

Visual images are not the only means of representing Mary's proleptic knowledge. There are also written texts that convey the same idea, sometimes rather bluntly. This can be illustrated by examples from three very different religious cultures.

The first example is from the early Orthodox East. In the last three strophes of a sixth-century *kontakion* on the nativity by Romanos the Melodist, Mary approaches her child in the crib and asks him what, exactly, he plans to accomplish on behalf of humankind. The infant responds:

> "The one to whom thou dost give milk [*su galoucheis*], others will cause to drink gall [*potisousi cholēn*].
> The one whom thou dost call life [*hon zōēn*], thou shalt see hanging on a cross [*en staurō*],
> And thou shalt weep for him as dead [*dakruseis hōs thanonta*]; but thou shalt greet me risen [*aspasē me anastanta*],
> Mary, full of grace."

Here, Mary's proleptic knowledge is acquired directly from her infant son's improbable omniscience about his own future (plus his incredible ability to articulate what he knows about that future), so that Mary herself is left with little initiative in the matter. At first, it would seem that all Mary can do is wait patiently until, as her son says, she sees him "hanging on a cross" and, as he adds, "of my own will." However, in this particular *kontakion* (as in the one discussed earlier in this book), Mary does have an opportunity to respond to the bad news about her son's masochistic intentions. She sighs a deep sigh, and says:

> "O fruit of my womb [cf. Luke 1:42], do not let the lawless crush Thee;
> I caused Thee to burst into life, let me not see Thy destruction."

But, in the usual admonition against mourning, her son replies:

> "Cease, mother, lamenting [*Pausai, mēter, klaiousa*] for things which thou dost not understand."

This condescending invitation to join the son in his denial of his own death then takes the form of a promise of resurrection after just three days of "sleep" in the tomb. In other words, as Mary's grandiose son puts it, "thou shalt see me risen." The dutiful mother appears to accept this promise at face value, for she already believes that her son is truly grand (not merely grandiose or delusional). As she had declared to him in the first strophe of the *kontakion*, "Thou art my God." What difference could it possibly make if her "God" is a masochist who does volunteer to be crucified? If he is God, he will survive. As for Mary, she learns from her son that, because of these things, she has been empowered to rule as a sort of queen (*ek toutōn basileuson*) – that is, as the deified mother who will be in a position to intercede with her divine son on behalf of sinners who cry out to her.[36]

Mary is pleased with this, and she immediately goes off to Adam and Eve to bring them the good news – which is to say that she believes it herself. She tells the world's first sinners to be patient and (implicitly) to wait for the salvific effects of her son's future death and resurrection. Mary's powerful post-crucifixion role of intercessor has thus been represented by Romanos as a sort of balm soothing the pain of proleptic knowledge.

Another example comes from early English poetry. In a "Nativity lament"[37] from the middle of the fourteenth century, Mary is victimized by proleptic knowledge. As the baby Jesus tries to educate his mother about the horrors that will befall him toward the end of his life, he says, among other things, that:

> *'Samfuly for i sal deyȝe* [shall die],
> *Hangende on þe rode* [on the cross/rood],
> *For mannis* [man's] *ransoun sal i payȝe* [pay]
> *Myn owen herte blode.'*

Understandably, Mary is upset:

> *'Allas! sone,' seyde þat may* [maid],
> *'Siþen* [since] *þat it is so,*
> *Worto sal i biden þat day* [Why must I live to see that day]
> *To beren* [bear] *þe to þis wo* [woe]?'[38]

Just as she had once believed the announcing angel, so now Mary seems to believe her apparently prescient child, who offers a fuller version of God's plan. As Amy N. Vines comments, "Gabriel seems deliberately to have left her in the dark."[39] If there was joy before, now Mary is in despair, almost suicidal, over what the future holds. The child Jesus tries to reassure her, cheerfully promising to come back to life after he dies, make his way up to his heavenly father, and, in the end, take Mary herself up into heaven to be with him (*to ben with me, moder, in blis*).

Fine words these are from God the infant son. But, there is no response from his *swete moder*, nor is there any indication to the reader of what the response might be. As it turns out, the poem's lyric persona[40] has only seen and heard this dialogue between Mary and the infant Jesus in a dream-like meditation on one Christmas day, and the meditation has now come to an end.[41] We know that Mary had been deeply disturbed by the acquisition of proleptic knowledge of her son's cruel death, but we are left hanging as to how (or even whether) Mary might go on living until her son is crucified.[42]

The third example comes from late imperial Russia. In folklore collected since the middle of the nineteenth century, there is a motif known as the "Dream of the Mother of God" (*Son Bogoroditsy*), where Mary sees her son's life and passion unfolding before her very eyes.[43] In one such dream, for example, Mary sees a cross by the Jordan river, and, on that "holy cross," her "child" (*chado*) hangs, nailed to it by his hands and feet.[44] In another dream, Mary sees her child covered in blood "on that holy cypress tree [*na tom sviatom dreve kiparise*]."[45] Most of the dreams in this category are interrupted at some point by Jesus himself, who says that he already knows what the dream is about, and that he will indeed be crucified someday. Mary usually does not take this very well. In the text last mentioned, for example, she bursts into tears:

For whom are you abandoning me [*pokidaesh' menia*], my child?
In whose care are you leaving me, the Virgin?

This is a mother who is not so much concerned about her son's future suffering and death (compassion), as she is about being left alone and abandoned, with no one to pay attention to her own needs (narcissism). Jesus therefore replies that he is leaving her in the good hands of his "friend" John, and that in any case he, Jesus, will rise from the dead on the third day. And, as if that denial of death were not enough, he then promises to descend from the heavens when (implicitly) Mary herself dies, so that he may pluck her soul out of her body in order to pass it up to the angels in heaven (*Ia Sam iz tebia, mati, dushu vynu* – precisely as depicted in Orthodox icons of the dormition), and so that he may put her relics (*moshchi*) in a shroud (*plashchenitsu*) and bury them together with the saints, the cherubim, and the seraphim. In closing, Mary's son adds to this farrago of folk theology some lines that play on the Russian passion for icons (I translate as literally as possible in order to make plain what for some readers may be a rather exotic terminology):

I will write [*napishu*] your countenance [*lik*] upon an icon [*na ikonu*],
I will place your image [*obraz*] on the altar,
And people will pray to God to you *[budut na tebia Bogu molit'sia]*,
And they, mother, will keep you in their memory [*budut . . . pominati*],
And me, Christ, they will praise [*proslavliati*]![46]

Thus is Mary glorified alongside her illustrious son. Psychoanalytically speaking, Mary receives a large dose of narcissistic supplies that are supposed to ease the heavy blow of what she has learned about her son's future. The supplies are properly termed narcissistic in this case because of Mary's narcissistic response to the terrible things that will happen to her son. The response is not about what will happen to the son, but about how the mother's needs will be catered to. It is difficult to feel compassion for this version of Mary.

The foregoing examples constitute a small sample of a large category. They show that Mary's proleptic knowledge of her son's fate may be represented, not only in images, as we have seen earlier, but also in texts. In all three textual examples, Mary receives this knowledge in rather detailed form: in two cases (the Greek *kontakion* and the medieval English lyric), from the Christ child himself, and, in the last case (the Russian interrupted dream), from both her own dream and from Christ.[47] In all cases, Mary is upset, although for different reasons in each case. It is as if Mary had no choice but to be present at a dress rehearsal of her son's horrible death. Readers of these texts already know the script, just as viewers of, say, a gloomy *Eleousa* already understand why there is a shadow of foreboding in Mary's facial expression.

Anamnesis

Mary does not only see her future. She remembers time past, she reminisces. Prolepsis has a counterpart in anamnesis.

Scholars have often pointed to the backward turning of the clock in marian lamentation. Early in the twentieth century, Wilhelm Pinder was a pioneer in this area. Pinder surveyed the literary-devotional background to the development of the Pietà (*Vesperbild*) in fourteenth-century German lands and found a range of relevant maternal imagery. For example, the lamenting Mary may wish merely to get *back* the body of her sweet son so that she may gain some comfort in hugging and kissing her child again – as in these lines from the sequence *Planctus ante nescia*:

> *Reddite moestissimae*
> *Corpus vel exanime,*
> *Ut sic minoratus*
> *Crescat cruciatus*
> *Osculis amplexibus.*
> In my utmost sorrow, give me back
> the body, even without life,
> that so the torment
> may grow less
> through kissing, through embracing.[48]

This wish is actually fulfilled in *Quis dabit*, as we have seen, and elsewhere as well: for example, in Henry Suso's *Little Book of Eternal Wisdom* (*Büchlein der ewigen Weisheit*, probably written in the late 1320s). There, Mary receives her son from the cross, whereupon she presses him to her motherly heart, kisses his wounds, holds him in her lap, and looks at him – as if not quite believing that her baby is dead. Pinder quotes Suso: "I took my tender Son on my lap [*Ich nam min zartes kint uf min schoze*], and looked at Him. He was dead, but I gazed at Him ever and anon, although He had neither feeling nor voice!"[49] Mary is in an early stage of acceptance of her child's death. She sees what is real, but there is anamnesis as well.

In the anglophone world, there were interesting dramatic and textual representations of Mary's anamnesis, as when the aggressively lamenting mother of the Digby *Burial of Christ* (late fifteenth century) holds the body of Jesus on her lap and repeatedly, in different parts of the play selected and quoted continuously here, returns to the memory of breastfeeding him:

> *When ye war born, of me, a mayde myld,*
> *I sange lullay to bringe you on slepe:*
> *Now is my songe, alese, ales, my child!*
> *Yit suffer me to hold yow her on my lape,*

Which sumtym gafe you mylk of my pape.
The modere, with the child desires for to reste;
Remembere myn awn son / þat ȝe sowket my breste!
When ye sowkid my brest / your body was hole & sound.
Alese! In euery place Now se I many wound![50]

And so on. In her great sorrow, Mary cannot cease thinking of her dead son as a little child. Jesus is infantilized in death.

Mary's anamnesis is also evident in some iconographic representations of her mourning. Erwin Panofsky, without being as specific as his contemporary Pinder, notes a certain formal similarity between Pietà images and representations of the Madonna with child.[51] Hanns Swarzenski believes that the Pietà naturally "crystallized out" of the Madonna (with child) image, for the lamenting Mary with her dead son on her lap or on her knee is again holding him the way she did in his early childhood, and this is particularly evident in those variants of the Pietà where Mary's son is reduced to childlike proportions.[52] Émile Mâle also notes the reduction of the dead son's size on Mary's lap (*ce corps est à peine plus grand que celui d'un enfant*) in some medieval illustrated manuscripts.[53]

J. H. Emminghaus, in an iconographic classification of the Pietà images, includes the *Vesperbild mit kindhaft kleinem Christus* as one of its seven major types.[54] Having emerged around the middle of the fourteenth century, this type, according to Emminghaus, essentially reduces the figure of Christ – iconographically – to one of the attributes of his sorrowing mother. Psychologically speaking, the recently deceased adult is eclipsed by the anamnestic component of the mother's grieving. The mother's denial of her son's death takes the form of wishing to have him alive again, specifically as she remembers his being alive when he was a small child.

A remarkable fourteenth-century pair of images from southeastern Germany shows, not only the crowned Mary holding her miniaturized child in the form of the Man of Sorrows in her arms, but also an uncrowned Mary right next to her(self), holding the infant Christ child in her arms.[55]

A substantial sample of Pietà images gathered by Joanna E. Ziegler[56] includes many in which the figure of the recently deceased adult Christ is reduced in size – that is, 'juvenalized' or even 'infantilized' with respect to his adult mother. The sample itself is well defined insofar as the images in question are associated specifically with the Beguines of the southern Low Countries (roughly, today's Belgium), from about 1300 to 1600. In examining Ziegler's photographs, I find (admittedly as subjective impressions) that 43 of the total of 97 – that is, 44.3 percent of the unrepeated Pietà images that are clear enough for purposes of discerning relative body size – display a Christ figure who is *childishly small in his mother's arms*.[57] Perhaps it is useful to have this quantitative evidence for what many art historians have long thought obvious.

Figure 11.5 *Thrēnos* fresco (detail), 1164, Saint Panteleimon Church, Nerezi, Macedonia (Belting 1980, fig. 1).

Miniaturization is not the only way to suggest that the dead Christ was once Mary's baby. There is, for example, a powerful twelfth-century *Thrēnos* fresco at Saint Panteleimon church in Nerezi, Macedonia, in which a large, dead Christ is stretched out before his mother as she embraces him, presses her cheek against his face, and cries with obvious intensity (see Figure 11.5).[58] Ioli Kalavrezou writes of this image:

> She kneels on the ground and, *opening her legs* holds her Son's body to rest on her lap. . . . Visually this composition is the most explicit of her maternal passion for her dead Son. On the one hand it makes a direct reference to his birth, and on the other, through her passionate *embrace around his body and the tender pressing of her cheek against his*, it reminds us of her icons where she lovingly cuddles the Christ child.[59]

The viewer's response to Mary's grief in the here and now of the image is thus fueled by her anamnesis, or, more precisely, by a call to the viewer to reconstruct what might have been Mary's own anamnesis. Key components of the image invite the beholder to imagine that Mary is remembering the birth of her child, as well as moments when she held the child tenderly in her arms. The placement of the adult child between Mary's legs is a remarkably explicit reference to the birth of Christ, and has none of the sentimentality of most Christmastime "Nativity" scenes, where the birthing process has already finished, and the newborn lies swaddled in a manger somewhere in Mary's vicinity.

Something roughly comparable to the twelfth-century Nerezi fresco would be Michelangelo's often imitated mid-sixteenth-century *Pietà* drawn for the poet Vittoria Colonna.[60] Here, too, Mary grieves, her eyes turned upward and her arms spread wide in an orans gesture of resignation. By virtue of this gesture, however, Mary is not holding or supporting her son's body the way she does in Nerezi, or in conventional Western *Pietàs* for that matter.[61] But, below the overhang of her ample breasts, and emerging in frontal presentation *from between her legs*, is the naked, semi-vertical, majestic corpse of her son Jesus. As in the Nerezi fresco, Mary's anamnesis is suggested by the birth imagery. There is much else happening in the Michelangelo drawing, of course.[62] The point here is to show that the same visual device can facilitate (the representation of) Mary's anamnesis in very different art-historical contexts.

Anamnesis is a familiar component of representations of the early stages of Mary's mourning. By comparison with prolepsis, anamnesis seems ordinary, necessary, almost trite. Prolepsis is sexier. Mary's proleptic knowledge of her son's future death has an aura of mystery, or a hint of conspiracy in what is to come. There is none of that in anamnesis. When Mary begins to mourn by reminiscing about the child her son once was, what was once to come has already come into existence, and closure begins.

*

Some visual representations of the annunciation show a fully formed Christ child descending from God the Father in heaven downward toward Mary – as if it were not up to Mary to do the work of conceiving, gestating, and giving birth to Jesus. In some of these theologically incorrect images, the child is already bearing his cross (e.g., the Mérode triptych of 1425), so that Mary receives proleptic knowledge of what will become of her son at a very early stage. Other instances of such prolepsis include images of an apparently depressed, distant Mary holding the child in her arms, but with the instruments of Christ's passion on the reverse (e.g., the twelfth-century Vladimir Mother of God). There also exist texts in which the Christ child himself traumatizes Mary by informing her of his future suffering and death on the cross (e.g., a fourteenth-century English nativity lament).

The opposite of prolepsis is anamnesis, where Mary sees the past rather than the future. Many images and texts that place Mary at the scene of the crucifixion enable her to think about her son as the child she once held in her arms. In some of the *Pietàs*, for example, the dead Christ is reduced to child-like proportions, as if he were still alive. In the Digby mystery *Burial of Christ* (late-fifteenth-century), Mary repeatedly recalls breastfeeding the son who now lies dead on her lap. In such works, it is possible for Mary to indulge in a wishful denial of her son's death, even as she begins the work of mourning.

Notes

1 See: Robb 1936, 523–526; Schiller 1966–1991, vol. 1, 55–57.
2 Schiller 1966–1991, vol. 1, fig. 101.
3 Schiller 1966–1991, vol. 1, fig. 102.
4 Robb 1936, fig. 14; Schiller 1966–1991, vol. 1, fig. 104 (cf. fig. 103).
5 Robb 1936, fig. 29; Schiller 1966–1991, vol. 1, fig. 113; Lane 1984, 40, fig. 25 (cf. 44, fig. 27); Acres 2006, figs. 1, 6.
6 Robb 1936, fig. 39; Schiller 1966–1991, vol. 1, fig. 114.
7 O'Reilly 1992, 197, referring to plate 16 (= fig. 538 in Schiller 1966–1991, vol. 2).
8 Füglister 1964, fig. XVIII.
9 *Biblia pauperum* 1987, 50.
10 Tanner, ed. 1990, vol. I, 50–51.
11 Grimoüard 1872–1875, vol. IV, 112. The author notes (113) that representations of a fully formed infant Christ approaching his mother had been harshly condemned by Saint Antoninus of Florence (*Summa historialis*, 1491), Johannes Molanus (*De picturis et imaginibus sacris*, 1570), and Juan Interián de Ayala (*Pictor christianus*, 1730).
12 Tanner, ed. 1990, vol. I, 86.
13 There is a reference to "both births" of Christ in the "Profession of Faith" made at the Eleventh Synod of Toledo in 676. See: Denzinger 2012, 186 (no. 536). The first "birth" is a fantasy about God the Father begetting Christ long before Christ was born from Mary. See my work in progress: "Three Levels of Couvade in the History of the Christian Church."
14 Among the many sources that reproduce both sides of this icon are: Acheimastou-Potamianou, ed. 1988, plates 9, 10 (in color), with commentary by M. Chatzidakis; Evans and Wixom 1997, 125, cat. no. 72 (in color), with commentary by Annemarie Weyl Carr; Vassilaki, ed. 2000, 484–485, cat. no. 83 (in color), with commentary by Euthymios Tsigaridas.
15 Carr 1995, 121.
16 Cf. Belting 1981, 143 ff.
17 Pallas 1965, 91–95; Belting 1981, 162; 1994 (1990), 262.
18 Belting 1980, 6.
19 Pentcheva 2006, 114–117, and figs. 83–84.
20 Baltoyanni 2000, 152, and figs. 91–92.
21 Vassilaki, ed. 2000, cat. no. 64 (with commentary by Myrtali Acheimastou-Potamianou).
22 Baltoyanni 1994, 160 and figs. 71–72.
23 Evans, ed. 2004, cat. no. 98 (with commentary by Euthymios N. Tsigaridas).
24 Rancour-Laferriere 2005, fig. 27.
25 Rancour-Laferriere 2005, 269–273, 297–303.

26 Pallas 1965, 101.
27 Garrison 1949, nos. 240–241, 243–245, 247, 272–273.
28 Essen 1968, cat. no. 263; Füglister 1964, fig. I. See also Van Ausdall (2012, 560) on fourteenth-century diptychs that "pair the Virgin and Child with a Crucifixion in the other wing."
29 Boespflug 2012, 76–80; figs. II.10, II.12.
30 Belting 1994, 290.
31 Ševčenko 1991a, 439.
32 Kondakov 1911 (1910), 153.
33 Kondakov 1911 (1910), 141, fig. 94.
34 Rancour-Laferriere 2005, fig. 26.
35 There is much disagreement on what images should be termed *Eleousa* (Tatić-Djurić 1976), and in the larger art-historical picture the Passion Madonna images appeared centuries later than the *Eleousa*.
36 For quotations from the last three strophes, see: Maas and Trypanis 1963, 15–16, as translated by M. Carpenter in: Romanos the Melodist 1970–1973, vol. I, 20–21 (Mary's assertion in the first strophe that her son is God may be found in the Greek, p. 10; in the English, p. 15).
37 See: Vines 2010.
38 Brown, ed. 1924, 74 (no. 56); cf. Davies, ed. 1964, 114 (no. 38); Greene, ed. 1977 (1935), 94 (no. 149).
39 Vines 2010, 216.
40 A "devotee for Christ," according to Davies, ed. 1964, 323.
41 For a particularly brutal lullaby along these lines, see the fifteenth-century lyric with the (surely ironic) title, "Jesus comforts his mother," in: Davies, ed., 1964, 197–198 (no. 102).
42 As Vines comments on another version of this Nativity lyric, "the reader is unable to discern whether the promise of Christ's resurrection and eventual reunion with his mother . . . allays her mourning at all" (2010, 217). Not all of the early English nativity lyrics that feature proleptic knowledge of the passion and resurrection make it clear that Mary possesses this knowledge. For example, in a fifteenth-century lyric quoted by Kenney (2012, 29–30), we read that, "The blyssfull chyld was borne, / To were a crown of thorne," but only the lyric persona (and of course the omniscient Christ child) knows this, and in any case Mary ("My dere modyre") does not respond.
43 See: Rancour-Laferriere 2005, 288; Ryan 1999, 298–300; Fedotov 1991 (1935), 50 ff., 129–130. Ryan observes that *Son Bogoroditsy* is "the most commonly found text amulet in Russia," and that it is "probably of medieval Latin origin" (1999, 298).
44 Bezsonov 1861–1864, vol. 2, part 6, 184.
45 Bezsonov 1861–1864, vol. 2, part 6, 190.
46 Bezsonov 1861–1864, vol. 2, part 6, 190–191.
47 Georgii Petrovich Fedotov is explicit about the element of prolepsis in the folkloric Russian "Dream of the Mother of God." He writes: "all of the sufferings of Christ are endured proleptically by the Mother of God [*perezhivaiutsia proleptícheski Bogoroditsei*]" (Fedotov 1991 [1935], 42).
48 Pinder 1920, 152; translation by Dronke, ed., trans. 1994, 233.
49 Pinder 1920, 157 (quoting Suso's German vernacular). English translation: Suso 1953, 121.

50 Furnivall 1965 (1882), 195 (lines 718–720), 196 (lines 745–746), 197 (lines 772–773), 197 (lines 788–789). Cf. Reiners-Ernst 1939, 71–72; Woolf 1968, 260 (similar imagery in the first stanza of the lament *Listyns, lordyngus, to my tale*), and 263–265.

51 Panofsky 1927, 266, 268.

52 Swarzenski 1935, 142.

53 Mâle 1931, 125 (illustrated by fig. 68, from a Latin manuscript of the early fifteenth century).

54 Emminghaus 1972, 452 (or *mit dem kindhaft kleinen Schmerzensmann* – Vetter 1958–1959, 55, and figs. 28, 29).

55 Berliner 1956, 111 (fig. 12). Cf. Vetter 1958–1959, 55 (fig. 25).

56 Ziegler 1992.

57 A count derived from the (relevant, unrepeated, and sufficiently clear) 119 plates at the end of Ziegler's book. Ziegler herself speaks of the "contrast of scale" in many Pietà images (p. 165), but does not quantify this contrast empirically.

58 Belting 1980, fig. 1, 11; see Weitzmann 1961 on the origin of such imagery.

59 Kalavrezou 2000a, 43 (emphasis added; cf. Kalavrezou 2005, 106–107).

60 Steinberg 1970, fig. 175.

61 Steinberg 1970, 268–269.

62 Steinberg 1970, 265–270. On the break with late medieval iconography and drama of the Passion in this work, see: Nagel 2000, 184–185.

12 Theologizing Mary at the Foot of the Cross

Mary's Theologically Correct Rejoicing in the Later Medieval Period

The Roman Catholic version of Mary is such an idealized figure that it is easy to forget the theological party line about her need to be redeemed by her son. Indeed, she was the "first of the redeemed," as is so often asserted by theologians.[1] According to Ubertino of Casale (1259–ca.1330), for example, "the Blessed Virgin was the first-born of the redemption of her Son; and he came more to redeem her than any other creature."[2] And it is not only asserted by theologians. As Christ rather bluntly informs his mother from the cross, in a thirteenth-century English lyric:

> *"Moder, now I shall thee telle,*
> *Yef* [if] *I ne deye thou gost to helle:*
> *I thole ded* [suffer death] *for thine sake."*[3]

Only after her son's death had been accomplished was Mary ready for her many post-biblical exaltations – immaculate conception, assumption into heaven, queen of this, queen of that.

According to Jaroslav Pelikan, the theological "consensus" in the West by the twelfth–thirteenth centuries was that "Mary had been saved by Christ, so that, while she lamented his death because he was her Son, she welcomed it because he was her Savior."[4] And well she should have "welcomed" her son's death, if thereby he was actually going to save her, except that: (1) welcoming one's own son's death does seem a bit unmotherly; (2) there is not a shred of scriptural evidence that Mary knew anything about her son's mission to "save" or to "redeem" her; and (3) in the history of Christianity, there is not an abundance of representations of Mary's welcoming attitude toward her son's death.

Nevertheless, there do exist some such representations. From the visual arts, for example, there is what in German is termed *das freudvolle Vesperbild* (roughly, "joyful Pietà"). This rare image type is examined in an equally rare 1939 book of the same title by Elisabeth Reiners-Ernst. The first four plates of the book constitute four different views of one particular Pietà, sculpted from wood and originating from Switzerland in around 1300.[5] Mary tenderly holds the body of her adult child on her lap. The wounded body appears slightly diminished in scale, the lower part horizontal on Mary's lap, the upper part lifted somewhat by Mary's right hand. The head of Jesus, still crowned in thorns, is stiffly erect. Mary's head, by contrast, is slightly tilted downward toward her son, and there is an unmistakable smile on her face. It is a gentle, soft smile, but it is a smile.

According to Reiners-Ernst, the overall composition of this work conveys an impression of harmonious spiritual balance: "Spirit [*Geist*], not feeling is represented here; consciousness, not gloom [*Hindämmern*]; possession, not parting." A certain "discipline of the spirit" is evident in the entire work, "from its external construction to the knowing smile of the mother."[6] Such a configuration, notes Reiners-Ernst, could not be retained as art-historical time passed, and the type of the Pietà lost its transcendental religious essence, evolving toward the naturalistic expression of emotions connected with pain, suffering, and death.[7] In other words, the smile was lost because the artists (or sponsors) involved in the creation of such imagery gravitated toward the depiction of normal mourning.

One ordinarily thinks of the Pietà, after all, as an image representing a mother's grief as she contemplates the body of her son, which has recently been taken down from the cross and which she now holds on her lap.[8] A smiling Pietà, by contrast, must represent something else. That atypical "knowing smile," as Reiners-Ernst puts it, could be the smile of theological correctness. Mary is glad to have been saved (and perhaps, into the bargain, she is glad that all of humankind has been saved).

Another theologically correct hypothesis is that Mary smiles at the sight of her dead son because she "knows" he will rise from the dead on the third day. That would be a straightforward denial of his death and would fit in with the tradition, beginning at least as early as Odo of Ourscamp (d. 1171), that Mary was the only one who kept the faith in her son's death-defying divinity during the *triduum mortis*.[9]

Regardless of whether such hypotheses are correct from a theological viewpoint, they are scripturally groundless and psychologically delusional.

In medieval liturgical-devotional works as well, there are some unusual examples of Mary's rejoicing over the crucifixion of her son. The Meersseman collection contains a variant on an original prayer attributed to Philippe de Grève in which Mary is urged to rejoice (*Gaude . . .*), not only for having nursed and otherwise cared for her child, and for having witnessed the miracles he worked as an adult, but also for having grieved as he was dying (or dead) on the cross (*Gaude, quia in cruce moriendo doluisti*) and having placed him in the tomb (*Gaude, quia in sepulcro posuisti*).[10] Rachel Fulton points to a late-eleventh-century Bavarian prayer that consists of a series of salutations to Mary, one of them calling for her to rejoice (*Gaude . . .*) at having given birth to a king who would be crucified.[11]

But, generally speaking, as Fulton rightly observes, in the later medieval texts, "the Crucifixion would more typically be counted among Mary's Sorrows."[12]

André Wilmart quotes the meditations of the Cistercian Étienne de Salley (= Stephen of Sawley, d. 1252) on the 15 "joys" of Mary, one of which (the eleventh *gaudium*) is her actually beholding her dear son hanging on the cross: *Gaude, gloriosissima dei genitrix et sanctissima uirgo semper Maria, que piis oculis* ***conspexisti dilectissimum filium tuum in cruce pendentem***.[13] Compare this with the enumeration of the seven "sadnesses" of Mary by Philippe de Maizières (d. 1405), one of which (the fifth *tristicia*) utilizes a vocabulary almost identical to that of the "joy" just quoted: *Quintam tristiciam, mater dulcissima, tunc habuisti, quando* ***dilectissimum filium tuum in cruce pendentem conspexisti***.[14] The second of these contrasting texts of course represents the medieval norm – and the psychologically normal. The first is probably another failed attempt to express the "knowing" mother Mary's pride over what she thinks her daring son accomplishes by dying voluntarily before her very eyes, namely, the redemption or the salvation of sinful humankind.

Even in the realm of medieval theology per se, it is difficult to find assertions that Mary "welcomed" (Pelikan) her son's death. It is true that all human beings – including Mary – were supposed by most medieval theologians to have been "saved" by the crucifixion of Mary's son, as Pelikan observes. Mary's personal need for salvation (or redemption) would theoretically have been a motive in "welcoming" the death of her son. The doctrine of Mary's foreordained Immaculate Conception would not be made official until 1854 in the Roman Catholic West (the bull *Ineffabilis Deus* of Pope Pius IX), and in any case even this doctrine did not prevent Catholic theologians from continuing to assert that Mary needed salvation or redemption as much as the rest of us.[15]

But, it is difficult to find theologians asserting that Mary both "welcomed" and "lamented" her son's death, as Pelikan says. Baldwin of Ford and Ralph the Ardent (Radulfus Ardens) are mentioned by Pelikan.[16] The renegade Dominican preacher Girolamo Savonarola (d. 1498) might also be mentioned in this context, as he asserted in 1496 that Mary was both "happy and sad [*lieta e triste*]" while following her son to his death.[17]

Sandro Sticca points to Albertus Magnus (d. 1280), a major philosopher and theologian of his time. According to Sticca, Albertus affirmed that, "the Virgin experienced a natural *sorrow* in her participation in the sufferings of her Son and at the same time a supernatural *joy* in her complete fidelity to the immolation of Christ for the redemption of the world,"[18] although there is no explicit reference to her own personal need for redemption. Sticca quotes from *De laude beatae Mariae virginis*, which, apparently, is among the many works falsely attributed to Albertus. In this case, we may say, however, that it was some "Pseudo-Albertus" who claimed that, "just as our Lord simultaneously experienced the greatest joy and the greatest sorrow, so too our Lady simultaneously experienced the greatest compassion for, and the greatest rejoicing with him [*summam congratulationem*]." This joy seems to have been ascribed to Mary on the basis of the usual theological rationalization of Christ's death, for "Pseudo-Albertus" writes that Mary understood her son's violent death in redemptive terms (*ut medium in redemptionem humani generis*), thereby causing in her the greatest pleasure (*summam delectationem*).[19] In other words, Mary seems to have been joyful to the extent that she truly *believed* her son was effecting the redemption of humankind (including herself as logically included, and others on the basis of her supposedly altruistic attitude).

Another theologian, the Catalan mariophile Ramon Llull (d. 1316), tries to capture (or create) the meaning of Mary's contradictory feelings in a somewhat different way. He devotes a chapter to the topic of "compassion" in his *Libre de sancta Maria* (ca.1290). Llull believed that Mary understood that her son died of his own volition in order to honor God and in order to make it possible for humankind to be created anew.[20] Mary could not but share her son's plan, for, whatever it pleased him to do also pleased her. Mary's compassion for her son's suffering was also perfect, however. Therefore, even as she rejoiced at what he was accomplishing by dying on the cross, she was simultaneously suffering with him in intense pain and sorrow. Her joy and her pain were equal, and somehow one did not cancel out the other.[21] Psychologically speaking, Llull is describing ambivalence grounded in strong empathic and sympathizing capabilities. Mary was perfectly attuned to both the grandiosity and the suffering of her son. This binarity is strangely bleak, simple, and lacking in theological sophistication. It is even more contrived than the few other known attempts to make Mary rejoice over what her son is supposed to have accomplished at Golgotha.

Mary's "Loving Consent" to Her Son's Crucifixion in the Twentieth Century

Fast-forward to the twentieth-century Catholic context, and the accompaniment to Mary's sorrow is not joy but consent. The rationale for consent derives from Mary's initial *fiat* to the announcing angel. Correct theology seems to have learned something from the representations of Mary's prolepsis in poetry, the visual arts, and other areas of the imagination.

In 1968, the prominent mariologist René Laurentin wrote that, "the Mother of Jesus did not yet know the future; she had only some imperfect notion that Jesus was to return to his Father by ways full of mystery and sorrow for her." Yet, "some imperfect notion" is a notion nonetheless, and eventually it gets perfected in the form of a premonition of doom, for later in his treatise Laurentin is more explicit about Mary's attitude:

> At the foot of the cross as at the Annunciation, Mary's activity was essentially a *consent* in which her faith and love are involved. In the Incarnation it was consent to life – this human life which she gives to

> her Son; in the Redemption, it is consent to death – this human death that Christ had to suffer (Lk. 24:46) in order to redeem the world. But these two acts of consent were in reality only one and the same consent: the *fiat* of the Annunciation (Lk. 1:38) [which] bore unconditionally and irrevocably on everything that was going to be accomplished [*le* fiat *de l'Annonciation (Lc 1, 38), qui portait inconditionnellement et irrévocablement sur tout ce qui allait s'accomplir*].[22]

This parallelism of consents – the first to life, the second to death – seems irresistible. In scripture, however, there is only one consent, and that is Mary's *fiat* at the annunciation.

Even Catholic theologians without a particularly mariological bent perceived a connection between Mary's attitude before the birth of Jesus and her acceptance of some ill-defined future horror. For example, in his magisterial 1977 study *The Birth of the Messiah*, Raymond E. Brown writes at length about Mary's words in Luke's Magnificat, including her implicit glorification of the poor and the downtrodden, and her self-identification as a "slavewoman." The Magnificat, Brown avers, "anticipates the Lucan Jesus in preaching that wealth and power are not real values at all since they have no standing in God's sight." What does have standing, of course, is *the cross*, which is "not an easy message." Brown refers to Luke 14:27: "Whoever does not carry the cross and follow me cannot be my disciple." But Mary is the model disciple, even the "first disciple," according to Brown and many other theologians since Augustine, as we have seen. In effect, then, "Luke has begun to introduce the offense of the cross into the good news proclaimed by Gabriel," and we should not be surprised that "some of the offense of the cross rubbed off on Mary."[23]

How "rubbed off" Brown does not say. But, he seems to mean that Mary might have picked up some of her son's moral masochism and, therefore, have been as accepting of his crucifixion as he was.

Lumen Gentium, a document issued by the Second Vatican Council, also suggests that Mary had some awareness of what would happen in the future and states explicitly that she gave her consent to what happened at Golgotha:

> The blessed Virgin made progress in her pilgrimage of faith, and maintained faithfully her union with the Son right up to the cross where, in keeping with the divine plan, she stood (see Jn 19, 25), suffering very profoundly with her only begotten son, and associated herself with a mother's heart with his sacrifice, lovingly consenting to the immolation of the victim that had been born from her [*victimae de se genitae immolationi amanter consentiens*].[24]

This message from Vatican II regarding Mary's thoughts and feelings at the foot of the cross is best understood as a mass deviation from scripture: not an isolated theologian, and not the pope alone, but a large collective of religious leaders from the top tiers of the Roman Catholic hierarchy composed and approved of these words about Mary.

In accordance with beliefs held at least since the Council of Trent,[25] Christ's sacrifice of himself on "the altar of the cross" could be taken for granted by participants at Vatican II. But, the promulgators of *Lumen Gentium* are saying something more. They affirm that Mary is also, in some sense, participating in the sacrificial immolation performed at Golgotha. But, they do not further clarify what the nature of that participation was. Who, for example, might have asked Mary to consent to such an act? Did Mary volunteer to consent on her own, without being asked? Was Mary's consent required, or was it optional? These questions are not raised. Instead, there are repeated assertions of the "predestination" of Mary, which essentially cancel Mary's ability to make choices, including the choice to consent. The result is a (by definition) theologically correct but conceptually incoherent statement about Mary's "loving consent" to her son's immolation at Golgotha.

Hans Urs von Balthasar: Mary's Son as a Sadist at Golgotha

A modern and truly original attempt to theologize the relationship of Mary and her son at the crucifixion is offered by the late Hans Urs von Balthasar.[26] Despite its originality, moreover, this attempt may be viewed as correct from the viewpoint of Roman Catholic theology. That is because von Balthasar achieved official recognition of the correctness of his theological *oeuvre* near the end of his life. In 1984, he received the Paul VI prize for theology. Pope John Paul II named him a cardinal in 1988, but von Balthasar died just two days before the ceremony at which he would have taken up that position. At the funeral, Cardinal Joseph Ratzinger (the future Pope Benedict XVI) explained the meaning of the pope's elevation of von Balthasar to the cardinalate: "no longer only private individuals but the Church itself, in its official responsibility, tells us that he is right in what he teaches of the faith."[27]

Von Balthasar's analysis is grounded on an honest recognition of Jesus' estrangement from his family and, in particular, from his mother. For example, Jesus humiliates Mary and her other children for failing to believe in Jesus: "when he [Jesus] refused to see his family when they came to visit him, describing those who heard his word in faith as his 'brother, and sister, and mother' (Mt 12:50), a sword must have pierced his Mother's heart."[28] The sword image (borrowed from Simeon's speech at Luke 2:35) is merely a metaphor, of course. But the metaphor is meant to represent Mary's real psychological pain, and the pain is being inflicted by her own real son, Jesus. This sword, moreover, cannot be a sword of compassion (*gladius compassionis*), for Jesus is not suffering and dying on the cross in this biblical scene, and there is no reason for Mary to be compassionate. The sword must, instead, be the sword of unbelief (*infidelitatis gladius*) that Origen had proposed (above, pp. 39–41) as an interpretation of Simeon's prophecy. Mary *does not believe in* that Jesus whose family is the unreal, metaphorical family of his followers. More precisely, in von Balthasar's view, Mary is not yet a believer at this particular juncture, for otherwise her heart would not have been "pierced" by the words her son spoke.

Von Balthasar understands that Jesus places greater value on the metaphorical family of his followers than on his real family members. But, this differential evaluation is actually part of a plan to inflict pain on Mary. According to von Balthasar, Jesus is making a conscious effort to give Mary "constant training in the naked faith":

> People are astonished and embarrassed by the way in which Jesus treats his Mother, whom he addresses both in Cana and at the Cross only as "woman." He himself is the first one to wield the sword that must pierce her [*Er selber ist es, der als erster das Schwert handhabt, das sie durchbohren muß*]. But how else would she have become ready to stand by the Cross, where not only her Son's earthly failure, but also his abandonment [*Verlassenheit*] by the God who sends him is revealed. She must finally say Yes [*ja zu sagen*] to this, too, because she consented a priori to her child's whole destiny [*sie doch von vornherein dem ganzen Schicksal ihres Kindes zugestimmt hat*]. And as if to fill her bitter chalice to the brim, the dying Son expressly abandons his Mother [*verläßt der sterbende Sohn noch ausdrücklich seine Mutter*], withdrawing from her and foisting on her another son: "Woman, behold your son."
>
> . . . just as the Son is abandoned by the Father, so, too, he abandons his Mother, so that the two of them may be united in a common abandonment [*auf daß beide in einer gemeinsamen Verlassenheit geeint seien*]. Only thus does she become inwardly ready to take on ecclesial motherhood toward all of Jesus' new brothers and sisters.[29]

Clearly, von Balthasar believes that a strong element of aggression is directed at the mother by the son on the cross, for he depicts the crucifixion as the final and essential test of endurance for Mary, as one last round of "training in the naked faith." Jesus himself, wielding the sword which Simeon had said was bound to pierce Mary's soul, delivers multiple blows to his mother:

1 Jesus addresses Mary with the contemptuous term "woman."
2 Jesus obliges Mary to "say Yes" to the "earthly failure" of his life.
3 Jesus obliges Mary to "say Yes" to God's abandonment of him.
4 Jesus "foists" a substitute son on Mary.
5 Jesus "abandons" Mary by dying in her presence.
6 Jesus obliges Mary to "say Yes" to his death (i.e., his abandonment of her).

Von Balthasar does not seem to mind that his Jesus is doing all this. If Jesus is suffering on the cross, then Mary ought to be suffering too. In an allusion to the "cup" Jesus felt obliged to accept in Gethsemane (Mark 14:36, 39; Matthew 26:39, 42, 44), von Balthasar writes that Mary too was drinking from a "bitter chalice." What fills this chalice to the brim, according to von Balthasar, is Mary's loss of her son, which she is supposed to experience as "abandonment" (*Verlassenheit*) by him. The scriptural subtexts here may be found in the crucifixion narrations of the two gospels where Jesus – in a reprise of Psalm 22:1 – cries out from the cross: "My God, my God, why have you forsaken me?" (Matthew 27:46; cf. Mark 15:34). Hence, just as it pains Jesus mightily to be abandoned by the Father, so, too, must Mary suffer intensely when she is abandoned by her son.

According to von Balthasar, Jesus and Mary are "united in a common abandonment." This is a curious and perverse commonality, however, especially for a nonbeliever. Jesus only loses an imagined, substitute father, that is, his "Father" in heaven, who is *abba* for him. But, Mary loses her – decidedly real – son. Jesus and Mary may be "united" insofar as they are both abandoned, but in such a union Jesus is depicted as victimizing his mother Mary by abandoning her, whereas Mary victimizes no one by abandonment. Mary is harmless in this respect, whereas Jesus commits an act of premeditated aggression. He does not just die in the presence of his mother, but rather *he dies on his mother*. His death is more like the suicide of someone very close than an ordinary death.

Von Balthasar thinks it was a good thing for Mary to have had to "say Yes" to such treatment from her son, for otherwise she would not have become "inwardly ready to take on ecclesial motherhood toward all of Jesus' new brothers and sisters." This is an implicit reference to the somewhat tenuous tradition of Mary as "Mother of the Church" (*Mater Ecclesiae*), and to the then-recent official bestowal of that title on Mary by Pope Paul VI at the culmination of the third session of Vatican II in 1964.[30]

The reference to Mary's "ecclesial motherhood" is also a way for von Balthasar to imply that Mary had somehow agreed – despite the acknowledged psychological strain in relations with Jesus – to mother the metaphorical family that Jesus had struggled to form around himself. Here, however, theologian von Balthasar (along with Pope Paul VI and many of the conciliar fathers at Vatican II) goes far beyond the evidence in canonical scripture. There, the adult Jesus had no help whatsoever from his real mother Mary in forming the metaphorical or substitute family that would eventually become the Church. Mary was not even a member of that community, let alone its "mother," until after Jesus had died, risen, and ascended. After one modest post-ascension appearance of "Mary the mother of Jesus" among members of the early Christian community in Acts (1:14), she is never explicitly mentioned again in scripture. Surely there would have to have been further references to her if, as von Balthasar asserts, her son on the cross had not only managed to insert her into "the apostolic Church," but, in so doing, had also "giv[en] the Church her center or apex."[31] The remaining 27 chapters of Acts detail the works of Peter, Saul/Paul, Stephen, Philip,

Barnabas, and various others, and make passing reference to numerous minor figures – including a certain "Mary, the mother of John whose other name was Mark" (12:12) – but there is no more mention of "Mary the mother of Jesus."

Von Balthasar is hardly alone in extracting so much marian material from so little scriptural evidence, but his picture of an extremely aggressive, even a cruel and sadistic, Jesus on the cross is refreshingly blunt and original and is supported at least by the considerable body of biblical evidence for strained relations between the adult Jesus and his mother. It would be tempting to add, as well, the historical evidence for the lifelong psychological pain Jesus himself must have been enduring because of his illegitimacy (above, I suggested that Jesus' words from the cross were essentially a reproach against Mary, blaming her for his fatherless status).[32] But, von Balthasar is not interested in either the historical Jesus or the historical Mary. His enterprise is strictly theological. It is also devoid of explicit psychological interpretations, although Jesus' sadistic cruelty is nevertheless evident in the portrait von Balthasar paints of Jesus at Golgotha.

In earlier eras, the terrible psychological pain Mary must have felt in beholding the sufferings and death of her son on the cross had often been contrasted with the *absence of pain* in her giving birth to Jesus. Bernard of Clairvaux, for example, raised a rhetorical question about the burning bush (Exodus 3:1 ff.): "what did it signify if not Mary giving birth and yet not suffering the pangs of birth?"[33] Bernard was certainly aware of the more traditional reading of the burning bush (as signifying the perpetual virginity of Mary – see above, p. 75), and so his question made sense only if he understood the absence of damage to the hymen during the process of giving birth (i.e., virginity *in partu*) as resulting in the absence of "pangs of birth." Bernard's student, Amadeus of Lausanne, also said as much in one of his homilies in praise of Mary: the mother of Jesus gave birth "without pain," as "she suffered no tearing at his birth."[34] Neither author seems willing to consider the possibility that some other factor, such as uterine contractions or insufficient cervical dilation, might be responsible for the pain ordinarily experienced by a woman during childbirth. On the other hand, both theologians were probably ignorant of such basics as the uterine musculature or the cervix, and they could not have been aware of the many other potential factors contributing to the pain of childbirth now known to modern medicine.

In any case, regardless of one's views on the causality of childbirth pain, the idea that Mary gave birth painlessly had been affirmed long before Bernard and Amadeus, and long afterward would be repeated. The idea is voiced in the apocryphal *Odes of Solomon*, as well as in the writings of Ephrem the Syrian, Gregory of Nyssa, Theophilus of Alexandria, John of Damascus, Andrew of Crete, Cosmos of Maiuma, George of Nicomedia, Maximus the Confessor, Hugh of Saint Victor, Anthony of Padua, Richard of Saint Laurent, Albertus Magnus, Saint Bonaventure, and many others.[35] Even Nestorius, who had resisted honoring Mary with the title *theotokos*, believed Mary was exempt from the words of condemnation spoken by the Lord to the fallen Eve: "I will greatly increase your pangs in childbearing; in pain you shall bring forth children" (Genesis 3:16).[36]

By the twentieth century, mariophile Pope Pius XII seemed to take it for granted that Mary was exempt from the pain of giving birth, as when he quoted an eighth-century authority – John of Damascus – in his 1950 bull *Munificentissimus Deus*:

> It was fitting that she, who had seen her Son upon the Cross and who had thereby received into her heart *the sword of sorrow which she had escaped in the act of giving birth to Him*, should look upon Him as He sits with the Father.[37]

What is interesting in this particular formulation (widely accepted by mariophile theologians) is the supposed connection between the painlessness of giving birth to her son Jesus and the great psychological pain at having to behold this son suffering and dying on the cross. But, the connection has no basis in the New Testament. Indeed, there is nothing to connect, for there is no description of how Mary experienced childbirth in the infancy narratives of Matthew and Luke, nor is anything said about Mary's reaction to the death of her son in the one gospel, of John, where she is present at the crucifixion. Theologians simply assume that Mary is the exception to the rule dictated by God in Genesis 3:16 ("in pain you shall bring forth children"), and they link this unmotivated assumption to the entirely reasonable assumption that what happened at Golgotha must have given Mary great pain.

This linkage, seemingly gratuitous, does have a certain logic: if Mary escaped the usual pangs of birth while Jesus was being born, then perhaps it is not so terrible that she had to stand by the cross and experience the psychological pain of watching her son suffer and die. But then, along comes von Balthasar, who, bypassing Mary's supposed escape from childbirth pain, seems to say: No, the pain Mary endured at Golgotha (and even on several occasions before Golgotha) was indeed terrible, but it was also a good thing for her and was essential for the early formation of the church. It does not matter that Jesus was cruel to his mother. What matters is that Mary received "constant training in the naked faith," and that this "training" made her ready for her central "ecclesial" role. For von Balthasar, Golgotha is the last stage in a kind of leadership boot camp designed to kick the sentimental, bodily mother out of Mary, and to form in her an "ecclesial" mother of the coming church militant.

Mary herself neither resists nor stands by passively in the face of such "training," but, according to von Balthasar, actively "says Yes" to everything, including the death of her son (that is, to the son's "abandonment" of her). That a mother's consent should even be required in this matter might seem odd (and may have seemed odd to many readers of the document *Lumen Gentium* produced by Vatican II, as noted earlier). But, von Balthasar is flying high in the theological stratosphere, rather than operating on a commonsense level, when he writes a chapter titled "The Dimensions of the Marian Yes" (*Die Dimensionen des marianischen Jaworts*).[38] In the opening paragraph of this chapter, von Balthasar refers first to Mary's *fiat* at the annunciation, then to Abraham's willingness to kill his own son at God's request (Genesis 22), and finally turns to Mary's agreement to let her son die. In the first two instances, there was a choice to be made, and von Balthasar clearly assumes that a choice was available as well to Mary as she stood by the cross. Here, her faith was being tested for the umpteenth time and, as ever, she goes along. Von Balthasar writes: "she must give back to God her Son, the Son of the fulfillment, in darkness of faith that she cannot comprehend or penetrate."[39]

Why *must* she give back to God her son, that is, agree to let Jesus die on the cross? It is not that Jesus will die anyway, with or without Mary's agreement. Rather, according to von Balthasar, it is something that binds her from the past – namely, her initial Yes, her *fiat* to the archangel Gabriel – that moves her. Mary must say Yes by the cross "because," as von Balthasar affirms, "she consented a priori to her child's whole destiny."[40] Von Balthasar is obviously unfamiliar with the various texts where Mary *questions* the sadistic trickery that God had perpetrated through this Gabriel (above, pp. 187–189).

The child's *whole* destiny from the start (*von vornherein*) is quite a burden for von Balthasar to be dumping on Mary's shoulders. Could Mary have had the slightest idea about the "whole destiny" of her child back then, at the start? If so, would Mary not thereby have refused to consent to the violent death that was part and parcel of that "whole destiny?" The burden that Mary would have to have been carrying ever since the annunciation would have amounted to this: with her *fiat* to Gabriel, Mary had "consented" in principle to anything that would happen, including that very crucifixion that God the Father would inflict in sadistic fashion on Mary's nonresisting son.

Von Balthasar's thinking is in line with the "loving consent" theory of *Lumen Gentium* (but perhaps without the "loving"). Von Balthasar's divine Jesus may sadistically mistreat his mother with repeated testing of her faith to the very end of his earthly days, but her initial *Jawort*, with its unfortunate connotations of future complicity in the mistreatment of her own child (i.e., her priestly offering of him as victim – see below), makes this end possible in von Balthasar's interpretation.

*

From the later medieval period come some theologically correct interpretations of Mary at the foot of the cross that suggest, not only that Mary was "saved" by her son's death, but also that she rejoiced over it. Medieval German images termed "the joyful *Pietà*" (starting from around 1300) depict Mary with a happy smile on her face. Some Latin devotional works of the time urge Mary to rejoice (*Gaude . . .*) at having beheld her son hanging from the cross. These ideas contradict the psychologically more normal and abundant phenomena of marian lamentation. Some, such as Girolamo Savonarola in the fifteenth century, found Mary ambivalent, both "happy and sad" as she followed her son to his death. In the twentieth century (in the document *Lumen Gentium* issued by Vatican II), Catholic theologians returned to this fraught issue, asserting that Mary gave her "loving consent" to the death of her son at Golgotha.

By far the most radical interpretation in the twentieth century of what went on between Jesus and Mary at Golgotha was advanced by Hans Urs von Balthasar, who painted a picture of Mary being subjected to sadistic psychological cruelty by her son. Jesus not only refers to his mother with the contemptuous term "woman," but he also obliges her to "say yes" to the "earthly failure" of his life, he "abandons" her by dying in her presence, and furthermore he obliges her to "say yes" to his death. As a result of this (and other manifestations of his) "training" of his mother, Mary supposedly becomes worthy of her subsequent role as "Mother of the Church." Von Balthasar makes all of Mary's "Yes"-saying follow from her initial "Yes" at the annunciation, which is to say that von Balthasar's Mary is represented as being at least partially responsible for her son's crucifixion.

Notes

1 Laurentin 1991 (1968), 241.
2 As quoted by O'Carroll 2000 (1982), 348.
3 Davies, ed. 1964, 87.
4 Pelikan 1971–1989, vol. 3, 169 ("and the Savior of the world," adds Pelikan to this sentence later [1996, 126]).
5 For more examples of an (arguably) joyful Pietà, see: Reiners-Ernst 1939, figs. 12–14, 19–20; Schiller 1966–1991, vol. 2, figs. 622–623 (= Reiners-Ernst 1939, figs. 1–4), 629 (?); Vetter 1958–1959, 58, fig. 28.
6 Reiners-Ernst 1939, 4.
7 Reiners-Ernst 1939, 6.
8 For general surveys of the Pietà type, see: Schiller 1966–1991, vol. 2, 192–195; Emminghaus 1972; Schawe 1993 (with rich bibliography). See also the fine study of the Pietà and the Beguines in the southern Low Countries by Ziegler (1992).
9 See: Laurentin 1952–1953, vol. I, 138–139; Laurentin 1991 (1968), 111–112, n. 18; De Lubac 1986 (1953), 339, nn. 128, 129.
10 Meersseman 1958–1960, vol. II, 171–172 (the fourteenth-century variant; cf. the discussion of the origin of this text, 40–41, which probably needs to be reformulated in light of the fact that Chancellor Philip of Paris [d. 1236] was not Philippe de Grève, a cleric who died around 1222 and who apparently left no writings [see: Dronke 1987, 565]).
11 Fulton 2002, 231; Barré 1963, 276.
12 Fulton 2002, 232.

13 Wilmart 1971 (1932), 352 (emphasis added). Cf. Vetter 1958–1959, 56, where this very passage is quoted in connection with the analysis of the "Joyful Pietà" by Reiners-Ernst (1939, 66).
14 Wilmart 1971 (1932), 534 (emphasis added).
15 For example: De Lubac 1986 (1953), 334–335. C. Dillenschneider's idea of Mary's *prérédemption priviligiée* (1951, 134) is mentioned by de Lubac (335, n. 109) in this connection.
16 Pelikan 1971–1989, vol. 3, 169.
17 As quoted and translated by: Nagel 2000, 38; 226, n.25.
18 Sticca 1988, 26.
19 As quoted by Korošak 1954, 522, n. 18.
20 Llull's understanding of the Incarnation and the Redemption as a cosmic new creation was rather unusual in comparison with other theologies being offered in the medieval West. The idealization and aggrandizement of Mary is extreme, and the mysticism of Llull's formulations can sometimes be impenetrable. See the informative Introduction to Llull 2005 by Fernando Domínguez Reboiras and Blanca Garí.
21 In the Latin, we read: *Cum ergo tanta passio, et tantus dolor, et tanta complacentia essent in ea, nec alterum istorum alterum minuebat* (Llull 2003, 203; cf. Llull 2005, 302–303). See also Sticca's analysis of "the coexistence of *dolor* and *gaudium* in the soul of Mary at the moment of the act of redemption" in the writings of Llull (1988, 27–29).
22 Laurentin 1991 (1968), 33, 236; 1968, 141.
23 Brown 1993 (1977), 364.
24 Tanner, ed. 1990, vol. II, 894.
25 Denzinger 2012, 417 (no. 1740), 418 (no. 1743).
26 The following remarks are by no means intended to be an adequate overall commentary on von Balthasar's dense, labyrinthine, and – for some – even offensive mariology. The most expansive and scholarly version is to be found in the third volume of von Balthasar's *Theo-Drama* (1992 [1978], 283–360). For useful commentaries, see: Johnson 2003, 57–60; Gardner 2004; Murphy 2007 (with bibliography).
27 See: O'Donnell 1996, 39–40. Ratzinger's remarks are quoted from the Wikipedia website on Hans Urs von Balthasar (1905–1988): https://en.wikipedia.org/wiki/Hans_Urs_von_Balthasar (accessed August 29, 2015).
28 Von Balthasar 1992 (1978), 330.
29 Von Balthasar in: Ratzinger and von Balthasar 2005 (1997), 109–110 (German original in: Ratzinger and von Balthasar 1980, 55–56).
30 See: René Laurentin's discussion of the sometimes tense meetings of delegates at Vatican II on this matter (1965, 8–50); the entry "Mother of the Church" in O'Carroll 2000 (1982), 251–253; O'Donnell 1996, 292 (second col.); O'Malley 2008, 245–246; Murphy 2007 (on von Balthasar's "ecclesial mariology").
31 Von Balthasar in: Ratzinger and von Balthasar 2005 (1997), 110.
32 See above, pp. 136–138.
33 Bernard of Clairvaux and Amadeus of Lausanne 1979, 18.
34 Bernard of Clairvaux and Amadeus of Lausanne 1979, 88. Amadeus refers to the virginal conception as another reason why Mary gave birth painlessly (mistakenly assuming that any other mode of conception would have involved sexual pleasure – "lust," "delight" – and would therefore have required punishment in the form of pain during childbirth; Bernard makes the same assumption – see p. 38 of the same volume).

35 See: Hirn 1957 (1909), 355 ff.; Jugie 1949, 627; the entry "Virginity in Partu" in O'Carroll 2000 (1982), 361–362; Reynolds 2012–, 87–90 (some medieval theologians in the West), 260–262 (various Eastern Fathers). For an overview in the Byzantine context, see: Custer 2006. On theology and iconography of Mary's "childbirth" on Calvary in the medieval West, see: Neff 1998.

36 Miegge 1955, 111.

37 *Papal Teachings: Our Lady* 1961, 309 (emphasis added).

38 Von Balthasar in: Ratzinger and von Balthasar 2005 (1997), 104–107 (German original in: Ratzinger and von Balthasar 1980, 48–52).

39 Von Balthasar in: Ratzinger and von Balthasar 2005 (1997), 104.

40 Von Balthasar in: Ratzinger and von Balthasar 2005 (1997), 109.

13 Mary of the Eucharist

Mary's Child in the Host

One way to bring Christ more convincingly to the altar of the eucharist was to bring his mother there too. In the medieval West, transubstantiationalist theologians (including those *avant la lettre*) tended to link the eucharistic elements with Mary. For example, Paschasius Radbertus (ca.790–865) repeatedly characterized the reality of Christ's eucharistic body specifically in terms of the maternal origin of that body. Christ's flesh (*caro*), which Christ said he would give "for the life of the world" (John 6:51), and which "is still offered today," is "none other, plainly, than that born of Mary [*non alia plane, quam quae nata est de Maria*], and suffered on the cross, and rose from the tomb."[1] Lanfranc of Bec (d. 1089), famous for rebutting Berengar's anti-literalist view of the eucharist, also affirmed the maternal origin of what was "on the Lord's table": "it may truly be said, that what is received is the same body that was assumed from the Virgin [*ipsum corpus quod de Virgine sumptum est nos sumere*]."[2] Particularly enthusiastic in this matter was Peter Damian (d. 1072) who, in a sermon on Mary's nativity, depicted the essential connection between Mary's body and the eucharistic body of Christ as follows:

> O blessed are the breasts [*beata ubera* – cf. Luke 11:27] which, still young and tender, pour milk into the lips/mouth of the little boy, nourishing the food of angels and of human beings! They express a scanty liquid, and yet they refresh the creator of the world! He who, by the power of his virtue subdues the storms of the seas, who furnishes the impulse for the flow of unfailing waters, who irrigates dry land with innumerable fountains everywhere – awaits those rare drops of milk from the virginal breast. Liquid flows from the breasts of the Virgin and is transformed into the flesh of the Savior. This, my esteemed brothers, this I ask, consider how much we are indebted to this most blessed mother of God, and how many thanks we owe to her (after God) concerning our redemption. For that same body of Christ [*Illud . . . corpus Christi*] which the most blessed Virgin brought forth, which she caressed at her bosom, wrapped in swaddling clothes, and nurtured

> with motherly care: that same body, I say, and none other [*illud inquam . . . non aliud*], we now receive [*nunc . . . percipimus*] without any doubt from the sacred altar, and likewise his blood which we drink in the sacrament of our redemption. This the Catholic faith holds, and this the holy church faithfully teaches.[3]

One could almost conclude from this paean to Mary's maternal body that Mary herself had rushed the sacrificial offering of her freshly weaned child straight to the "sacred altar" of Peter's local church. But no, Peter Damian is only dressing up the distant past with hyperbolic rhetoric in order to make a point about the eucharist in his own day: what "we now receive . . . from the sacred altar" *is* "that same body of Christ which the most blessed Virgin brought forth." Peter suggests that there exists an absolute identity between what the priest produces at the altar and what Mary produced centuries ago, namely, the physical Christ.[4] Eventually, that identity would be guaranteed by the church under the rubrics of "transubstantiation" and "real presence."

As word spread about the communion host being literally the body of Christ sacrificed upon the altar at mass, stories about the appearance of the Christ *child* in that host were beginning to be told. Starting from the eleventh and twelfth centuries in various sectors of the Roman Catholic West, these stories were recorded in sermons (especially Corpus Christi sermons), collections of *exempla* and tales (including marian tales), tracts on miracles, and so on. Some typical narrative sequences are as follows:

- During mass, the priest consecrates the host, then raises it with both hands above his head (the "elevation"), whereupon a child appears in his hands.
- A doubter in the real presence of Christ in the host experiences a miraculous vision of the Christ child in the host and, as a consequence, becomes a believer in the real presence.
- A Jew enters a church and sees a mutilated child in place of the host. The Jew converts to Christianity.
- A baby is found in a tree at the spot where a consecrated host had previously been placed.
- A child sees the priest at the altar eating another child and becomes afraid of the priest.
- A nun takes a host to her living quarters, and the host becomes a beautiful baby.
- The host on the altar turns into the Christ child and then comes down from the altar.
- A Jew attempts to chop up or otherwise desecrate a consecrated host, which bleeds, and then a child appears.
- A woman who had regularly seen the Christ child in the priest's hands at mass during her youth no longer sees the child after getting married.

These are just schematizations of some stories selected from the large and variegated corpus known to modern scholars.[5] Such stories were so popular and pervasive that even professional theologians felt obliged to deal with them. Thomas Aquinas, for example, acknowledged that miraculous changes could occur in certain properties of the sacrament of the eucharist that were the visible "accidents" (as opposed to the unseeable "substance"), "so that flesh, or blood, or a child, is seen," but that, "this is not deception, because it is done *to represent the truth*, namely, to show by this miraculous apparition that Christ's body and blood are truly in this sacrament" (*Summa theologiae*, Part 3, question 76, article 8).[6]

In some cases, visual depictions were made for the stories.[7] The stories were also exploited in dramatic works, most notably the *Croxton Play of the Sacrament*.[8] The corresponding visual representations in Eastern Orthodoxy should also be mentioned here, such as images of a living Christ child (naked or semi-naked, often adultomorphic, with cruciferous nimbus) lying on a paten (*diskos*) that is placed next to or on top of the eucharistic chalice, or seemingly floating on the surface of the (usually) red liquid in the chalice (see Figure 13.1). This overall configuration is termed *Amnos* (Lamb) in Greek, or *Agnets Bozhii* (Lamb of God – see John 1:29) in Russian, and probably goes back to the twelfth century.[9]

The numerous texts and images that represent the bread of the eucharist as a child only sometimes involve Mary directly. But, it is always understood that the child is Mary's child, and Mary herself occasionally

Figure 13.1 *Amnos* (Lamb) lying on a paten near the eucharistic chalice, Serbian monastery of Hilandar, Mount Athos, beginning of the fourteenth century (Vloberg 1946, 51).

Figure 13.2 Mary as priest at the altar of eucharistic sacrifice. *Confrérie du Puy Notre Dame d'Amiens*, 1474 (Durand 1911, plate 9).

participates in the action represented. An example is an image created for the *Confrérie du Puy Notre Dame d'Amiens* in 1474 (see Figure 13.2). Mary stands at an altar while propping upright the body of her child in a chalice placed on the altar of eucharistic sacrifice. Here, as Jeffrey F. Hamburger observes, Mary is functioning as a priest.[10] The poetic text accompanying the image characterizes Mary as "the chalice chosen for divine sacrifice" (*calice eslut au divin sacrifice*). The Christ child's eyes seem to be closed, and his nimbus is not yet cruciferous. He appears to submit meekly to whatever it is that his mother is doing to him. No liquid is visible in the chalice. The child's blood has not yet been spilled for the sacrifice (to speak in transubstantiationalist terms).

One Western category of tales about the child in the host (but with Byzantine origins) has a distinctly anti-Jewish message. Here, too, Mary participates in the action represented. Miri Rubin, who has conducted some revealing investigations of the eucharist in late medieval culture,[11] examines this particular category at the beginning of her book, *Gentile Tales: The Narrative Assault on Late Medieval Jews*. To paraphrase the tales in this category examined by Rubin, a typical sequence runs as follows:

> A Jewish boy happens to be attending mass with Christians. In the church the boy sees a beautiful woman at the altar enthroned with her child (or he sees a picture of her enthroned with her child). The Jewish boy receives communion along with the Christians. Then he leaves the church, returns home, and tells his parents about the pleasant experience he has just had. The Jewish father becomes enraged and throws the boy into an oven or a furnace. As the boy burns in the fire, his distraught mother calls for help. Eventually some Christians come running. They pull the boy out of the flames and, to their astonishment, they find that the boy is alive and unharmed. He explains to them that the same fine woman he had seen in the church had also protected him from the devouring flames (in many versions the cruel Jewish father is then killed by the Christians, while the mother and child are converted to Christianity).[12]

Thus is Mary's linkage with the eucharist enhanced, Christian belief glorified, and Judaism denigrated. As for the child in the host, the Jewish boy sometimes reports (naively) on this. For example, a child – who resembles the one in the picture of the nice woman with her child – is divided up and handed out to the communicants, including to the Jewish boy, who receives his piece of "raw flesh" from the priest and takes it home (Honorius of Autun, early twelfth century). Or, the Jewish boy says that the nice woman who was with him in the hot oven was the mother of the child being divided among the people in church (William of Malmesbury, before 1141).[13] Of course, we know that the body of the Christ child is not literally present in the host, nor is it divided up there into parts, for the eucharist is just a metaphor. But, the naive Jewish child does not know that, nor do the implicitly transubstantiationalist Christians who cooked up these tales.

It is tempting to ask: if Mary could save the Jewish boy from the flames, then why could she not save her own child from being "divided" and fed to the Christians who cannibalized this child? The theologically correct answer is that her (adult) son had already established the sacrament of the eucharist at the last supper, when he had resolved voluntarily to submit to crucifixion, and the eucharist itself is a reenactment of that voluntary sacrifice. Mary is obliged to conform – retrospectively – to the redemptive plan of her divine son. Still, some members of the medieval audience must have noticed that, whereas one of the two children in these tales is rescued, the other is not.

As a rule, in the medieval lore about Mary, she saves a great variety of potential victims. This is obvious from Frederic Tubach's erudite compilation, *Index Exemplorum*, where the "Virgin, Blessed":

- saves denounced monk (5136);
- saves dying monk from demons (5137);
- saves falsely accused murderess (5138);
- saves [many] from drowning (5139);
- saves incestuous man (5140);
- saves novice from hell fire (5141);
- saves orphan girl (5142);
- saves prior (5143);
- saves run-away nun (5144);
- saves soul of peasant (5145);
- saves unjustly condemned man (5146).[14]

But, this powerful goddess could not – or would not – save her own son (literally) from sacrificial death on the cross or save him (metaphorically) from eucharistic sacrifice at the altar in any of the tales indexed by Tubach.

There is one atypical example of Mary going to the trouble of rescuing the host (her son) from a hot oven:

> 2685. *Host tested in oven.* A woman, prompted by the devil to test the Eucharist, brings it home in a napkin and then tries to bake it in the oven; she hears a boy's voice calling his mother, and sees the Virgin taking the Christ Child out of the oven. In remorse, she is about to hang herself, but the Virgin bids her trust in Christ's mercy.[15]

Here, however, the rescue of the host is incidental to the moral of the tale: with Mary's intercession, her son will be merciful to the woman who has yielded to the devil's wiles.

There is also a rare example of Mary at least expressing sympathy for her child in an abused host. It involves an alleged host desecration by a gang of Jews in Deggendorf in 1337. In a poetic retelling from about 1500, a child appears when one Jew pierces the host; the child again appears when another Jew attacks the host with an axe; and a child appears when yet another Jew puts the host in his mouth – whereupon Mary finally cries out, "You false, blind Jews, how you have tortured my beloved son!"[16] This outburst, however, has the effect of drawing the attention of watchmen to the dastardly behavior of the Jews, which in turn leads to a pogrom against local Jews. Mary's momentary outburst is not effective as an intervention on behalf of her son, nor could it have been effective. Just as Christ had never intervened on behalf of himself on Golgotha, so too Mary was in no position to intervene *effectively* on behalf of her son, for, according to orthodox Christian belief, he had already willed his own humiliation and death. Mary's words cannot and must not save her child in the host from abuse by allegedly deicidal Jews. And, as for those non-fictitious Jews who died in the resulting real-life pogrom – that was just the usual medieval riot against

Christ killers.[17] There, too, Mary obviously would not have been able to intervene effectively. To my knowledge, there are no tales or exempla of either Mary or her son attempting to intervene in a pogrom against Jews.

It is interesting that, if some person in all these stories should happen to appear in, or to emerge out of, the eucharistic host, it is always the Christ child. This would seem to make sense, for the consecrated bread and wine are intended to represent in some way the sacrificed body and blood of Christ. As Leah Sinanoglou Marcus observes, commentators on such miracles cited them "as proof that the Mass is an actual re-sacrifice of the body and blood of Christ."[18] But still, why specifically the body and blood of the Christ child? These miraculous apparitions or manifestations of Christ are true christophanies, but why are they specifically paedochristophanies (to coin a term)? Even as a practical matter, the Christ child, though he would have been smaller than the adult Christ, would still not have been small enough to fit (non-miraculously) into something the size of a communion host. However, this child would have been small enough to be placed upon an altar, and there are quite ancient texts (and later, images) that indicate an equivalence of the manger in Bethlehem with an altar, as we will see (below, pp. 257–260).

All four canonical gospels tell a story of the *adult* Christ's voluntary sacrifice on the cross. A human child – as human – would not be capable of dying a voluntary, self-sacrificial death. Only a responsible adult could make the necessary arrangements for such a death. This would be true of the eucharistic reenactment of that death on the altar as well, for the Fourth Lateran Council of 1215 affirmed, not only that the body and blood of Christ were present on the altar in the forms of bread and wine, but that this Christ was both priest and sacrificial victim there (*ipse sacerdos et sacrificium*).[19] If it is difficult to imagine a human child dying a self-sacrificial death, it is even more difficult to imagine a truly human child who is already mature enough to have become the priest capable of making that sacrifice.

Of course, if the immature child – the toddler?, the infant?, the fetus?, the embryo?, the fertilized zygote? – is already believed to be "God," then anything goes. For example, the adult-like baby Jesus is able to lecture his mother about his future crucifixion in the medieval English lyric quoted above. But, does that prolepsis not detract from the very kenosis of God, that is, God's emptying himself of his divine form in condescending to become truly human (Philippians 2:5–8)? Did not God the Word *become* human flesh (John 1:14)? There is nothing in canonical New Testament scripture to indicate that God, in becoming human, was also altering the normal pattern of early childhood development, which makes it impossible for a child to take responsibility for its own death. To assert that a human child (*qua* child) might bear that responsibility is to blame the child victim. Child victims cannot be blamed for their victimization. Adult victims, too, may sometimes be unjustifiably blamed, but there are also cases where blaming an adult is justified – for example, where an adult victim is actually responsible for his or her own death. Among them are suicidal moral masochists, including the adult Jesus Christ, but not including the child Jesus.

So, the question remains: why the prevalence of visions and stories about a child in the host? Why paedochristophanies rather than simple christophanies? Where is the *appeal* of such visions to those who experienced them, and to those who heard and read stories about them?

Part of the answer must lie in the appeal of little children generally. When a toddler appears in a room full of adults, normally everyone's attention turns temporarily to the child. The rounded facial features, the small high voice, the "cute" little mouth, the miniature bodily features generally – all attract pleasantly condescending comments from the adults (especially the women) in the room. Of particular relevance are the child's small size and other features that give an impression of helplessness, weakness, and especially innocence.

A small child is, above all, automatically innocent – as innocent as the many children in and around Bethlehem who were slaughtered instead of the Christ child by Herod's killers in the so-called "massacre of the innocents" (Matthew 2:16). It is simply taken for granted that a small child is innocent, whereas one can never be quite certain about an adult. Christ sacrificed on the cross was allegedly innocent of whatever crime he was allegedly accused of, but he was an adult. Better (more convincing), then, to have him appear in the form of a child in eucharistic iterations of the original sacrifice.

For some historians, this idea of a child's inherent emotional appeal may sound anachronistic. Medieval attitudes toward children did not *necessarily* match attitudes that are taken for granted in the twenty-first century. However, although many aspects of the history of childhood involve change (e.g., mortality rates, types of diet, educational practices, and so on), there is no reason to believe that medieval adults (especially mothers) were indifferent to their own children or were incapable of bonding emotionally with them. The now abundant studies of childhood in the Middle Ages demonstrate that children held emotional value for the adults around them.[20] Indeed, some of the evidence for this view has been culled precisely from medieval representations of Mary and her child in such diverse sources as folklore, literary works, paintings, theological writings, and so on. For example, Ronald G. Kecks points to increasingly realistic depictions of mother-and-child interaction in madonnas created for private devotion in late medieval Florence. By the fifteenth century, Mary may be fondly caressing or tickling her child in these images, and the two may be seen in a mutual embrace of great emotional intensity (as in the famous marble relief of Donatello – *Madonna Pazzi* – where mother and child press their foreheads together and look into each other's eyes.[21] Albrecht Classen draws our attention to Konrad von Fussesbrunne's *Die Kindheit Jesu* (ca.1200), with its "astoundingly intimate images of the Christ child at the bosom of his mother, the Virgin Mary, playing in the bath tub, and of the mother kissing her child."[22] I should add, of course, that numerous other examples of the emotional value of Mary's child for his mother in Western medieval representations have already been discussed at length in earlier portions of this book, as well as in many of the sources I have cited.

The dramatic increase in attention directed toward mother Mary herself, starting in the twelfth century in the West, meant that increased attention was by definition being given to Mary's child – *qua* child – as well. Any new sermons or theological treatises dealing with Mary's role in the incarnation of God, for example, would not have neglected the conception and birth of the child. As new marian hymns in Latin and in the vernaculars were created, singers and reciters found new opportunities to praise Mary as, for instance, the kind of mother who would breastfeed her own child. At a time when visual images of Mary were proliferating, most of them, of course, included Mary's winsome child. Even texts and images of the passion often featured the mother's reminiscences about her child. As we have seen repeatedly in this book, Bethlehem was often brought to Golgotha.

All of these factors would have increased the likelihood of an association between the eucharist and the Christ child, not the adult Christ. With growing belief in transubstantiation acting as a catalyst, miraculous visions of (and stories about) this child appearing in the host would become common. Even the priests officiating at the sacrifice of the mass had a stake in the child who occasionally replaced the host in their hands.

"Birth Done Better"

"Mother of the Eucharist" is a title for Mary that goes back at least to the spiritual writer Jean Gerson (1363–1429). Taking transubstantiation as a given, and certainly aware of the tradition of the Christ child in the eucharistic host, Gerson can address Mary as the mother of this child: *Tu mater es eucharistiae*.[23] In a poem to Mary, Gerson requests the eucharistic bread from her: "Give me your bread which makes the heart whole and purifies the soul: this unleavened bread which, drawn from human nature, repairs that nature."[24] Of course, one normally receives the unleavened bread of the eucharist from the hands of a priest, but here tacit acknowledgment is being made of the eucharist's human source, which is Mary.

The words of consecration uttered by the priest – particularly the formula *Hoc est corpus meum* – effected (and for many still effect) the transubstantiation of the bread into the body of Christ. In the twentieth century, theologian Henri de Lubac quotes a famous medieval exclamation (pre-dating Gerson) about the priest's performance of transubstantiation as a reiteration of the incarnation:

> The spiritual maternity of the Church . . . includes that power over the Eucharist by the exercise of which the Church, we may say, carries

> out a sort of maternal function with regard to Christ himself. Hence those comparisons, sometimes rather daring, between our Lady and the priest. . . . It was natural enough to consider, after the gift of life in baptism, and that of the Word in the preaching that gives birth to faith, the sacramental sentence [*Hoc est corpus meum*] that makes present the body of Christ, as did Mary's *fiat* at Nazareth. From the twelfth century onward we repeatedly come across the exclamation: "O truly to be venerated is the dignity of priests, for in their hands, as in the womb of the Virgin, Christ is incarnated anew [*O veneranda sacerdotum dignitas, in quorum manibus Dei Filius, velut in utero Virginis incarnatur*]."[25]

The *O veneranda* exclamation is also quoted by art scholar Leo Steinberg in his essay on Michelangelo's *Pietàs*. Steinberg, unlike De Lubac, is not threatened by the idea that priests may be imitating Mary. Instead, he tries to understand the psychology of the process. He is apparently the first to have discerned the specific psychological mechanism operating in the mind of the individual priest who consecrated the communion host: "A priest for whom the transubstantiation of the Host was absolute reality might indeed have experienced a sense of identification with the Virgin birthgiver."[26] In retrospect, such identification may not seem to be theologically relevant, but Steinberg is suggesting that it was psychologically real. Steinberg implies, moreover, that the motivational basis of the priest's identification with Mary was the appeal of Mary's birth-giving power.

Psychoanalytic scholars have made analogous claims about the mind of today's priest who celebrates the sacrifice of the mass. As the celebrant is a man, and as women are prohibited from joining the (still) all-male club of the priesthood, then the central ritual of the club could be based on envy of some uniquely female function. Psychoanalytic folklorist Alan Dundes writes that the eucharist entails "male usurpation of the female nurturant role," and that it is "a purely male ritual involving the imitation of female nurturance."[27] Clinical psychoanalyst Naomi Janowitz asserts that eucharistic sacrifice, like sacrifice traditions across cultures generally, gives men an opportunity to play the envied role of "nursing mother," feeding the congregation "sacred food" in the form of "the bread and wine of the Eucharist."[28]

Freud had taken a rather different approach to the eucharist in *Totem and Taboo* (1913). He speculated that, "in the Christian myth the original sin was one against God the Father," namely, "the murder of the father." Christ took it upon himself to make amends for this crime, for he "redeemed mankind from the burden of original sin by the sacrifice of his own life." The result, however, was a power realignment, as well as the establishment of "Christian Eucharist":

> The very deed in which the son offered the greatest possible atonement to the father brought him at the same time to the attainment

> of his wishes *against* the father. He himself became God, beside, or more correctly, in place of, the father. A son-religion displaced the father-religion. As a sign of this substitution the ancient totem meal was revived in the form of communion, in which the company of brothers consumed the flesh and blood of the son – no longer the father – obtained sanctity thereby and identified themselves with him.[29]

Unfortunately, Freud cites no passage from Christian scripture to support this. Why speak of some "ancient totem meal," when Christ's institution of the eucharist at the so-called "last supper" is made explicit in the three synoptics (Matthew 26:26–30; Mark 14:22–26; Luke 22:14–20), and earlier as well in Paul's first letter to the Corinthians (11:23–26)? Also, the relationship of "son" and "father" in Freud's hypothesis bears no resemblance to any Christian doctrine about the relationship of God the Son with God the Father.[30]

What may be taken seriously in Freud's formulation is his all-male cast of characters: "father" ("Father"), "son," and "brothers." Very likely, Freud had in mind what eventually became the norm in Roman Catholicism – that is, the all-male priesthood. What the priests of this "son-religion" actually (believed they) did on a regular basis was consume "the flesh and blood of the son"; that is, they reenacted the sacrifice of God the Son in the sacrament of the eucharist.

In a wider context, the Roman Catholic sacrifice of the mass is not atypical, and perhaps this is where Freud was on to something. As it turns out, sacrifice traditions in cultures from various locations and historical periods tend to be the exclusive province of men. In her book on this subject, feminist scholar Nancy Jay examines in detail a variety of sacrificial practices – Greek (classical Athenian), ancient Israelite, Roman Catholic, Hawaiian, Ashanti (southern Ghana and adjacent areas), Tallensi (Gold Coast), Lugbara (Uganda), and Nuer (Sudan). According to Jay, there is a reason why sacrifice traditions are exclusively male. She writes of the "many vivid metaphors in which sacrifice is opposed to childbirth as birth done better, under deliberate purposeful control, and on a more exalted level than ordinary mothers do it."[31] "In the West African city of Benin," for example, "before the many occasions of human sacrifice, all women were driven out of the city by the priests, who masqueraded as pregnant women themselves during the sacrifice."[32]

Jay devotes a chapter of her book to Christian sacrifice, particularly as it pertains to the Roman Catholic priesthood:

> Celibacy became an ideal for the priesthood, much later a requirement. Celibate women, transcending their own profane nature, could be classified up one supernatural hierarchical rank, as male. Wrote Jerome, "As long as woman is for birth and children she is as different from man as body is from soul. But when she wishes to serve Christ more than

> the world, then she will cease to be a woman and will be called man" – *vir*, as in "virile," not *homo*. . . . In the sixth century, the Council of Auxerre banned women from receiving the host in an uncovered hand lest they profane the sacred victim; later still, only priests could handle the host or drink the wine.[33]

Jay's analysis concentrates on the social structure of the Catholic priesthood, not on what individual priests do (and have done, for centuries). Jay does not consider the question of how the Catholic priesthood's "exclusive sacrificing power"[34] might be construed by individual Catholics. How, for example, can the priest's routine sacrificial activity be understood as "birth done better"[35] – to quote the theoretical formula in Jay's Introduction? What is there about the male priest's daily performance of the sacrifice of the mass that may be compared in any way with a woman's ability to give birth?

Transubstantiation as the Priest's Couvade

Transubstantiation comes to mind here, but Jay pays no attention to it in this connection.[36] What Jay does instead is focus on the lineage and power of *bishops*, which go back to the early stages of Christian apostolic succession: "Only bishops have the power to generate descendants in this genealogical line; priests, who cannot ordain, are immature members of the apostolic descent system."[37]

It is true that ordinary priests cannot ordain. Perhaps it is also true that episcopal lineages have indeed been a response to "having-been-born-of-woman," and are valued as "birth done better" by bishops themselves (one would have to ask them). But, all priests, not just bishops, perform the sacrifice of the mass and are members of the Roman Catholic sacrifice tradition. Ordained priests are the ones who effect transubstantiation by uttering the words of consecration over bread and wine. What could be more extraordinary (for believers) than transubstantiation, when compared with ordinary childbirth?

In order to perform the eucharistic ritual, the priest first has to don the appropriate "vestments."[38] In the thirteenth century, these were located in the church sacristy, the meaning of which was explained by William of Durand in his *Rationale divinorum officiorum*:

> The sacristy – the place where the sacred vessels are stored, or the place where the priest puts on the sacred vestments – signifies the womb of the most blessed Mary, in which Christ clothed himself with the sacred vestment of his flesh [*uterum sacratissime Marie significat in quo Christus se sacra ueste carnis uestiuit*]. The priest processes to the people from the place where he put on his vestments because Christ, proceeding from the womb of the virgin Mary, came into the world.[39]

William understood that the priest, when performing the sacrifice of the mass, acted *in persona Christi*,[40] so that, like Christ, the priest first had to be "born." After that, the priest eventually made his way to the place of sacrifice wearing the vestments, much as Christ had come to the place of *his* sacrifice at Golgotha wearing almost nothing but the "vestment of his flesh," which, as William says, he had obtained in the womb from his mother Mary.

In drawing this parallel of vestment images, I wish to remind the reader of the implicit equivalence of the flesh of Christ with the flesh of Mary (*Caro enim Jesu caro est Mariae* – above, p. 60). If the priest put on his vestments in a place representing the place (the womb of Mary) where Christ had put on "the vestment of his flesh," then the vestments worn by the priest represented the flesh of Mary as much as they represented the vestment of Christ's flesh, for the vestment of Christ's flesh was itself derived exclusively (i.e., without a carnal father) from, and hence was equivalent to, the flesh of Mary. Consequently, the priest was performing the sacrifice of the mass as much *in persona Mariae* as he was *in persona Christi* (this parallel will have implications with respect to the issue of whether Mary was a priest, as we will see below).

The priest's actions were – and largely still are – as follows: Wearing his complicated and colorful long gown of various overlapping vestments, which would suggest transvestism or a transgender issue (outside the liturgical context), and holding the eucharistic host with loving care in his hands, the biologically male priest pronounced his magical words and – presto! – Jesus Christ was born in the place where before there was only a wafer of bread.[41] This is still the case in the Roman Catholic church. Any priest – whether he is the local parish priest, a bishop, a cardinal, or indeed the pope himself – performs this sacrificial ritual in basically the same way. Women clergy cannot do it. This has been so since well before Trent[42] and continues to be so after Vatican II. The transubstantiationalist eucharist is – among other things – childbirth for otherwise male priests.

Such childbirth is only a wishful metaphor, of course, like the eucharist generally. But, it satisfies Jay's characterization of male sacrificing as "birth done better," for the male priest performs it without having to gain sexual access to a woman's body for assistance (although donning what appears to be a woman's attire is of some psychological assistance). The "birth done better" in this case is not a natural birth but a birth made possible primarily with the supernatural intervention invoked by the priest's words of consecration: *Hoc est corpus meum*. It is performed, as Jay says of sacrifice generally, "under deliberate purposeful control, and on a more exalted level than ordinary mothers do it."[43] Indeed, for believers, there has never been anything "more exalted" than what takes place at a church altar during the sacrifice of the mass. The person who is "born" in the hands of the priest is not just any child, but is one's savior. The person who is sacrificed at the hands of the priest is also that savior, who is again volunteering to be sacrificed, just as he had at Golgotha.

Of course, what the men who became priests were doing (and still do) was done (and is still done) repeatedly, whereas it sufficed for a woman named Mary to utter her *fiat* just once, and the incarnation of God was accomplished. God had already become human in Mary's womb, and so it is no wonder that Mary has always been an admired model for priests. But, occasionally, we find something else besides admiration in their views of Mary, something that creates what Laurentin calls *conflit des grandeurs*.

For example, Saint Bernardino of Siena (1380–1444), after an inept apology to *Virgo amorosa et benedicta* for what he is about to say, goes ahead and says it anyway:

> The power [*potestas*] of the priest exceeds [*excedit*] the power of the Virgin in four ways: first, in brevity [*brevitate*]; second, in grandeur [*maioritate*]; third, in immortality [*immortalitate*]; fourth, in reiterability [*replicabilitate*].[44]

This solemn crescendo of increasingly multisyllabic rhyming ablatives[45] brings us with bated breath to Bernardino's explanation of himself. By brevity, Bernardino means the merely five words of consecration (*Hoc est enim corpus meum*) needed by the priest to open heaven's gate and bring the Lord down to the altar, whereas Mary had to speak a total of eight words (*ecce ancilla Domini fiat mihi secundum verbum tuum* – Luke 1:38) in order to bring the Lord down to our level (as if Mary had been speaking Latin!). By grandeur, Bernardino means that the Christ held in the priest's hands at the altar is the great one who rules high above in heaven, not the tiny, just-conceived Christ in Mary's womb. By immortality, he is saying that, "on the altar [Christ] is impassible and is endowed with immortality," but when in Mary's womb Christ is merely mortal. Finally, by reiterability, Bernardino is observing that, "every time the priest, in accordance with church rite, consecrates the Body of Christ, the Son of God descends from heaven," whereas, even if Mary had uttered her words of consent "thousands of times," still, the Son of God would not have become flesh each time.[46]

There is something gratuitous about what Bernardino says. If the anonymous *O veneranda* exclamation had been a gentle metaphor in praise of priests, without any denigration of Mary, Bernardino's odious comparisons and forced literalism heap undeserved praise on priests while transforming Mary into a historical accident. The seemingly scholastic precision of his sarcasm masks a sense of personal deficiency, a sense of himself as a priest who is inferior to Mary. It would seem that Saint Bernardino of Siena is envious of the woman who, alone – not only of her sex but of all humankind – gave birth to God.

There are some old behavioral-psychological terms that may be usefully applied to what priests do at the sacrificial altar. In the ethnographic and anthropological literature, we find reports on a wide variety of male pregnancy rituals and male birthing rituals that have been gathered from pre-modern societies. These practices go under the rubric of *couvade* (from the obsolete French word meaning "a brooding and hatching"; cf. modern French *couver*). An example would be the Black Carib practice (in the former British Honduras) where a male – during his wife's pregnancy – experienced daytime sleepiness or fatigue, food cravings, fever, toothache, and other symptoms that his pregnant wife was also likely to experience.[47] In the modern medical context, *couvade syndrome* refers to such symptoms in the expectant father as nausea, abdominal bloating, abdominal pain, headaches, anxiety, and toothache, which manifest themselves while the wife is pregnant or giving birth.[48] In the literature on so-called *womb envy* in males (or uterus envy, pregnancy envy, parturition envy, and so on), the phenomenon of couvade has usually been cited as an important form of evidence.[49]

I propose that the male priest's performance of transubstantiating the eucharistic host into Mary's child be viewed as a culture-specific form of couvade. Womb envy may also be involved, but it is not often encountered (and it seems to have negative overtones, as when Bernardino made his itemized comparison of the priest with Mary). Couvade is generally an affectively positive phenomenon. It is empathic, not remote. It is not necessarily conscious.

Some of the stories and visions concerning a *child in the host* (above, pp. 228 ff.) make it particularly obvious that the celebrant at the sacrifice of the mass can himself experience the transubstantiation as couvade. Here, for example, is what happened to a certain Cistercian monk, Gotteschalk of Volmarstein, as narrated in the collection of exempla titled *Dialogus Miraculorum* by Caesarius of Heisterbach (d. ca.1240):

> When he was before a certain private altar on Christmas day [*in die Natalis Domini*] filled with devotion and shedding many tears, as he was wont, and had begun as usual, to wit, "Unto us a son is born," and the transubstantiation had taken place ["*Puer natus est nobis,*" *factaque esset transsubstantiatio*], forthwith he found in his hands and saw with his eyes no longer the appearance of bread, but a most glorious infant [*sed infantem pulcherrimum*], indeed, Him who is most beautiful compared with the sons of men on whom also angels desire to look. Kindled with His love and transported with His wondrous beauty, he embraced Him and kissed Him. Being afraid that any delay might upset the others who were there, he laid thc Beloved on a corporal and he took again the sacramental form in order that the mass might be accomplished.[50]

In this case, the miraculous "birth" of the Christ child occurs, not just on any day, but literally on Christmas day, the feast of the birth of Christ. Any "pregnancy" antecedent to the birth is not represented here, although Caesarius does tell of another priest who was so filled with devotion as he was going to the altar to celebrate mass that it seemed that his belly was going to burst (*ut venter eius dirumpi videatur*).[51] As for our Gotteschalk, it should be noted that the "most glorious infant" does not appear in his hands until "the transubstantiation had taken place," which is to say that it is understood that the words uttered by Gotteschalk caused Mary's child to appear. All reports (that I am aware of) about a child in the host involve a host that has already been consecrated by the celebrant of the mass. It is the celebrant (priest) who determines when Mary's child is "born" anew in the host.

Of course, the words that were ordinarily understood to effect the transubstantiation did not always bring about an actual appearance of a child in the host to someone in the vicinity – that is, they did not always trigger a miracle. Or, rather, they did not always make Christ really visible. It was believed that the words made Christ really present (the "real presence") – which was a miracle in itself, according to some medieval thinkers.[52] For a child to be *seen* in the host as well was, therefore, doubly miraculous.[53] There was no better proof that transubstantiation had taken place than a paedochristophany.

Although the transubstantiation of the host may be interpreted as the metaphorical "birth" of the Christ child in the hands of a male "mother," the real mother of Christ was not necessarily forgotten. In some of the reports about a child in the host, Mary's presence is explicit, as we have seen earlier. Here is another example, from Caesarius of Heisterbach:

> One day when this [priest] Adolphus was celebrating mass and before the "Agnus Dei" had lifted up the host to break it, he saw the virgin in the host itself, sitting upon a throne and holding the infant to her breast [*in ipsa hostia virginem in sede residere infantemque in sinu servare contemplatus est*]. Wishing to know what was on the other side, as soon as he turned to the host he saw a lamb [*agnum*] in it and when he again turned, he saw in it, as if through a glass, Christ hanging on the cross with bent head [*Christum in cruce pendentem capite inclinato*]. When he saw this, the priest was terrified and stood for a long time thinking whether he ought to stop there, or finish the office. When he had appeased the Lord with his tears, the sacrament took again its former appearance and he completed the mass.[54]

Here, what Adolphus has "given birth to" in his hands – just as the enthroned virgin Mary once gave birth to in reality – is not only the infant in the host, but also the sacrificial victim that infant would become, symbolically (the lamb) or literally (Christ on the cross). Earlier in the narration of the miracle, we are told that Adolphus is a "sinner" who often has "doubts about this sacrament," so here he has been caught out by the elaborate, guilt-inducing miracle he conjured, and repents with tears. Only by believing in the words of transubstantiation does Adolphus understand that it was wrong to doubt the effectiveness of his couvade. For he sees that a child is "born" in his hands, the same child Mary is now holding in his vision of her together with her child, and the same child who will go on to be the Christ adult sacrificed on the cross, which he also sees in his vision.

This miraculous series of events exemplifies Nancy Jay's idea of a sacrifice tradition as "birth done better," for the visions of the sacrificial lamb and of Christ's sacrifice on the cross follow the vision of the child Mary has *recently given birth to*, enabling Adolphus to believe that he is not only repeating that childbirth but going on to administer, *in addition*, an iteration of the life-giving sacrifice of the adult Christ. Here, it is worth recalling that the eucharistic sacrifice that Adolphus performs at the altar would be defined as the same sacrifice that Christ made on the cross ("the victim is one and the same: the same now offers himself through the ministry of priests who then offered himself on the Cross").[55]

A Gaelic (fifteenth-century?) variant of the conversion of a doubting celebrant is summarized by Peter O'Dwyer:

> A monk, who was very devoted to Mary, was doubtful about Christ's presence in the Eucharist. One day, as he was saying Mass, the host left his hands and he did not know where it went. He wept and prayed to Mary to help him as he had sinned (by doubt). Mary came with her Child in her bosom. She told him that this was the Person he had blessed on the table a little while earlier. He saw the Child on the altar. He stretched out his hands to reach Him and He was changed into bread as it had been before. He believed – his lack of faith being aided by Mary.[56]

Here, Mary is present with her child already born. The monk only needs to hear Mary's words of assurance in order to believe that he too had "given birth to" the Christ child by having "blessed" the host on the altar, so that the child miraculously appears. The monk's couvade has been effective. The child then turns back into the host, and presumably the monk can then finish "saying Mass."

Friedrich Sunder (1254–1328), who was Chaplain at the convent of Engelthal, succeeded in giving a more properly mystical or spiritual birth to Mary's child from his "soul" on a regular basis. This was accomplished with the personal intervention of Mary. The Middle High German of an anonymous biography (*Gnaden-vita*) of Sunder is here translated by Annette Volfing:

> He had the habit, when he wanted to receive the body of the lord in the mass [*vnsers herren lichnam . . . jn der mesß*], that he would then very often ask our lady to ask her dear child to be born spiritually from his soul. This did indeed happen frequently.[57]

The completed eucharistic transubstantiation is implicit in the reference to what is already Christ's "body" as it exists "in the mass." That is, this priest would have to have uttered the formula, *Hoc est enim corpus meum*, in addition to having received the assistance of Mary in this "spiritual" birth.

Even more graphically maternal imagery is utilized in a mystical conversation Sunder has with the Christ child, here translated by Leonard P. Hindsley. Christ says:

> "Now I have come and am now spiritually born from you. Now I have two mothers: Mary who is my bodily mother, and you, my beloved soul, are my spiritual mother. I have nourished you with myself [Sunder has ingested the bread and wine], now you should nourish me spiritually. Give me, lord, your right breast so that I can suck from it and be fed spiritually."[58]

This remarkable series of images might be characterized as an extended case of couvade. The male priest imagines, not only giving birth to the Christ child, but breastfeeding the child as well. It goes without saying that the model for such fantasizing is Mary herself, who originally gave birth to and then breastfed the Christ child. On a subsequent visit to Sunder, Mary confirms this, saying: "He [Christ] is your Child spiritually and mine corporeally. He was born to you three times on Christmas once at each Mass."[59]

After these occasional medieval stories about the miraculous or mystical couvade of priests, we encounter a sophisticated post-medieval theological and spiritual literature that represents Mary as a supreme role model for priests. This literature propagandizes, in part, what may be termed an intellectualized form of couvade. The so-called French school (*École Française*)[60] of the seventeenth century is famous for this. For the priests in this movement, Mary hovers over them as they perform their task of transubstantiation at the eucharistic altar. Mary is their queen, they depend on her, they try to conform themselves spiritually to her. René Laurentin quotes some of their statements, which clearly convey a sense of imitating Mary's role in the incarnation:

> O Mary, our queen and queen of priests, grant to all who have the holy calling that they see you in the sacred functions [which they perform] and that, when handling Jesus at the altar [*maniant Jésus a l'autel*], they imitate [*ils imitent*] the reverence and the singular piety . . . with which you gave birth and placed your little Jesus in the crib, and touched him with your chaste hands, kissed and embraced him a thousand times.
>
> (François Bourgoing, 1585–1662)

> The Holy Virgin joined as a participant in the power of the eternal Father in order to engender his Word [*pour engendrer son Verbe*]. . . . The priest is likewise called upon to share the power of the eternal Father to engender his Son [*d'engendrer son Fils*].
>
> (Pierre de Bérulle, 1575–1629)

> The Holy Virgin conceived Our Lord, she carried him in her womb, she gave birth [*a donné naissance*] to him, she carried him in her arms, she nourished him with her milk. Likewise the mouth of the priests (so to speak) gives birth [*donne . . . naissance*] every day to Jesus Christ.
>
> (Jean de Neercassel, 1623–1686)

> Priests are called the image of the Virgin because, through her as through them, Christ is formed, is given to the faithful, and is immolated [*Sacerdotes* ***Virginis Matris imago*** *dicuntur quia sicut per eam, sic per ipsos Christus formatur, datur fidelibus et immolatur*].
>
> (Saint John Eudes, 1601–1680)[61]

Saint John Eudes even thought of himself as married to Mary, going so far as to wear a ring that signified his "mystical" marriage contract.[62] We may recall that, in ordinary couvade – as opposed to the extraordinary couvade of priests – a man's performance depends on the fact that he is married to the woman who is giving birth.

By the end of the twentieth century, Roman Catholic priests were still carrying on their tradition of eucharistic couvade, imitating Mary's essential function of giving birth to Christ. Some mariophiles were still referring to Mary with Gerson's title, "Mother of the Eucharist" – for example, the very popular marian "fundamentalist"[63] priest Don Stefano Gobbi (1930–2011). In what Gobbi terms his "interior locutions," Mary speaks in the first person to priests, who are her "beloved sons." On Christmas Eve of 1977, Mary says to some priests: "You have received a power which makes you very much like your heavenly Mother." That "power" is the ability to give birth to a son, and not just any son, but Mary's own son: "When you celebrate Holy Mass, *you too beget my Son*."[64] On August 6, 1986, Mary says:

> "Look at Jesus as He loves, works, prays, suffers, and immolates Himself, from his descent into my virginal womb to his ascent upon the Cross, in this [is] his unceasing priestly action, so that you may understand that I am above all Mother of Jesus, the Priest.
>
> "*I am therefore also true Mother of the Most Blessed Eucharist.* Not because I beget Him again to this mysterious reality upon the altar. *That task is reserved only to you, my beloved sons!* Nevertheless, it is a task which assimilates you very closely to my maternal function because you also, during Holy Mass and by means of the words of consecration, truly beget my Son. For me, the cold manger of a poor and bare cave received Him; for you, it is now the cold stone of an altar which welcomes Him. But you also, as I, give birth to my Son."[65]

One could hardly ask for more explicit statements of the priest's couvadish imitation of Mary. Mary is made to say so, of course. But it is a priest – Gobbi himself – who creates such "interior locutions."

O veneranda indeed is the dignity of Roman Catholicism's transubstantiationalist priests! Mary the woman brought forth the body of Christ in childbirth. Christ's priestly successors (and not merely members of the common priesthood of the faithful), on countless occasions down the centuries, have brought forth – and to this day for many still bring forth – that same body of Christ to which Mary gave birth. As long as transubstantiation is essential to the eucharist, the priest's couvade will never be done.[66]

*

The most important sacramental manifestation of the relationship between Mary and her son is the eucharist. In the eleventh century, Peter Damian wrote that the "body" of the child that Mary "brought forth" and "nurtured with motherly care" was "none other" than the "body" that members of the congregation receive "from the sacred altar." This idea was developed by several other theologians and led to an extensive folklore about a "child in the host," it being understood that the child was Christ.

The Catholic priest who officiated at the eucharistic altar was said by some to be repeating an act that Mary had already accomplished in the incarnation of her son. What the priest wore on this occasion was a complicated arrangement of "vestments" that resembled a woman's attire, and that would have suggested the priest's transvestism (outside the liturgical context). The key performative utterance made by the priest during his celebration of the mass effected the transubstantiation of the host that he held in his hands: *Hoc est corpus meum*. With these magical words the priest gave birth metaphorically to Mary's child.

The priest's performance at the altar is best interpreted as an imitation of what a pregnant woman does. Anthropologists would recognize it as an instance of *couvade*. Some of the medieval miracle tales (e.g., in the thirteenth-century collection of Caesarius of Heisterbach) go one step further, with a child *literally* replacing the host held in the priest's hands; in at least two cases, Mary herself is present with the priest (in his imagination) at the altar. There are also various post-medieval writings in which the priest is said to imitate Mary's birth-giving in some more mystical-spiritual sense.

Notes

1 Paschasius Radbertus 1969, 15. Cf. Laurentin 1952–1953, vol. 1, 38 (n. 19); Macy 1984, 27, 146 (n. 37); Rubin 1991, 22, 142.

2 Lanfranc of Bec 1854, col. 430; as translated by Fulton 2002, 136. Lanfranc qualifies what he has just said by adding (again, Fulton's translation) that what is received is the same with respect to "essence," "character," and "power" of its "true nature," but not with respect to "outward appearance" (*species*). In other words, it just looks different. For two recantations made by the much persecuted Berengar, see: Denzinger 2012, 234 (no. 690), 237 (no. 700).

3 Peter Damian 1983, 267. Cf. Laurentin 1952–1953, vol. 1, 115–116.

4 Modern scholars have understood that Peter Damian finds the origin of the eucharistic body of Christ in the body of Mary. For example, Miri Rubin writes that Peter stressed the idea "that one incarnation created the precedent for another, the very body which was once in Mary's womb was the one placed on the altar" (Rubin 1991, 22).

5 Relevant to the theme of "the child in the host" from a folkloristic perspective are the following categories from Tubach 1981 (1969): nos. 2689c (*Host transformed into Christ Child*), 2644 (*Host and toad*), 2648 (*Host burns priest's hand*), 2661 (*Host hidden in tree*), 2685 (*Host tested in oven*), 1001 (*Christ, eating of, confuses child*), 1019 (*Christ-child and love of young girl*), 1027 (*Christ-child not seen after marriage*), 1030 (*Christ-child reveals Real Presence*), 1042 (*Christians eating bloody child*). For a particularly large corpus of miracle accounts relating to the eucharist, see: Caesarius of Heisterbach 1929, vol. 2, 103–169; Caesarius of Heisterbach 1966 (1851), vol. 2, 164–217. See also: Dumoutet 1926, 70; Browe 1938, 100–111 (the section titled "Verwandlungen in das Jesuskind"); Marcus 1999 (1938), 176; Vloberg 1946, 185 ff.; Marcus 2012 (1973), 4–6, 10, 12; Hsia 1988, 55–56; Bynum 1991, 130, 348 (n. 39 – sources on women visionaries who saw the Christ child in the host); Rubin 1991, 113–124, 143, 344 (cf. also the section titled "The Child in the Host," 135–139); Despres 1996; Price 2003, 26–31; Rubin 2004 (1999), 9, 10, 11, 12, 23–25, 35–36, 77, 84, 130, 141, 149, 155–157, 179, 190; Cohen 2007, 103–109; Williams Boyarin 2010, 65; Kenney 2012, 49–58; Gertsman 2012, 73–77; Merback 2012, 35, 101, 121 (and plate 7), 134, 270, 293–294 (Christ child appears when Jews desecrate host).

6 Thomas Aquinas 2012, vol. 20, 230. Of course, much more could be said about this. See, for example: Bynum 2007, 88–89, and the references cited there.

7 Dumoutet 1926, 65; Brillant 1947 (1934), 167; Vloberg 1946, 185; Rubin 1991, 117 (fig. 5); Gertsman 2012, 74 (fig. 3.4), 76 (fig. 3.5); Merback 2012, plate 7.

8 Marcus 2012 (1973), 12–13.

9 See: Vloberg 1946, 51–55; Filatov 1996, 5–6 (and fig. 1); Onasch and Schnieper 1997 (1995), 137; Tradigo 2006 (2004), 117. More images ("Agnets Bozhii") are to be found on Russian Yandex: https://yandex.com/images/search?text=агнец+божий (accessed September 2, 2015). For Greek ("Amnos tou theou"), see: www.google.com/search?lr=&newwindow=1&biw=1131&bih=560&tbm=isch&sa=1&q=%CE%AC%CE%BC%CE%BD%CE%BF%CF%82+%CF%84%CE%BF%CF%85+%CE%B8%CE%B5%CE%BF%CF%8D&oq=%CE%AC%CE%BC%CE%BD%CE%BF%CF%82+%CF%84%CE%BF%CF%85+%CE%B8%CE%B5%CE%BF%CF%8D&gs_l=img.3...187951.1967 (accessed September 3, 2015).

10 Hamburger 2011, 13, n. 32, commenting on: Durand 1911, plate 9.

11 See especially: Rubin 1991.

12 See: Rubin 2004 (1999), 7–24 (source texts in various languages, with extensive documentation); cf. Despres 1996 (the anti-Judaic theme of the "child in the oven" in fourteenth-century English devotional manuscripts); Tubach 1981 (1969), no. 2041 (lists numerous variants); Williams Boyarin 2010, 64 ff. (cf. Williams Boyarin, ed., trans. 2015, 32–35 [Middle English text of "The Jewish Boy of Bourges"], 70–75 [Middle English text "Hou a Iew putte his sone in a brennyngge ovene . . ."]).

13 Rubin 2004 (1999), 10, and nn. 14 and 20 (p. 202).

14 Tubach 1981 (1969), 388–389.

15 Tubach 1981 (1969), 211.

16 As translated by Rubin 2004 (1999), 179 (I have simplified somewhat the sequence of desecratory acts).
17 For an account closer to the historical reality of what happened in Deggendorf in 1337, see: Merback 2012, 33–37.
18 Marcus 2012 (1973), 3.
19 Tanner, ed. 1990, vol. I, 230.
20 See, for example, the surveys by: Petroff 2004; Classen 2005.
21 Kecks 1988, 52–57 (and the images discussed there; fig. 34 is the *Madonna Pazzi*). Cf. also Classen 2005, 33–34.
22 Classen 2005, 35.
23 From Gerson's ninth tract on the Magnificat. See: Gerson 1960–1973, vol. 8, 413 (and 454); cf. Ellington 2001, 139.
24 As quoted by: Ellington 2001, 139.
25 De Lubac 1986 (1953), 330–331. The *O veneranda* exclamation dates to about the twelfth century. See: Laurentin 1952–1953, vol. I, 43, n. 41 (where there is also information on the apocryphal attribution to Saint Augustine, and on some of the numerous textual sources).
26 Steinberg 1970, 285.
27 Dundes 1991 (1989), 354.
28 Janowitz 2008, 120.
29 Freud 1953 (1913), 154.
30 I detect a mild (and well-justified) protest against Christian supersessionism in Freud's idea of a "son-religion" displacing "the father-religion."
31 Jay 1992, xxiv.
32 Jay 1992, xxiv.
33 Jay 1992, 117.
34 Jay 1992, 117.
35 Jay 1992, xxiv.
36 Transubstantiation is mentioned in passing by Jay 1992, 4, 118, 166, n. 6.
37 Jay 1992, 118.
38 See: Pierce 2006 (a diachronic overview); Reynolds 1989 (the medieval period).
39 Durand 2007, 21; Durand 1995, 23 (I, 1, 38). Cf. Van Ausdall 2012, 612.
40 Cf. Thomas Aquinas 2012, vol. 20, 317–324 (*Summa theologiae*, Part IIIa, Question 82, articles 1, 3, 5); Denzinger 2012, 341 (no. 1321), 888 (no. 4153).
41 For a forthright commentary on the magical nature of the priest's formulaic words of consecration over the bread and wine, see: Carroll 1992, 9–11.
42 To be more precise, this has been so since at least the early thirteenth century, when, according to Gary Macy (2012, 368), "Ordination became, in effect, a ritual that granted a male (and only a male) an irreversible right to preside over the Eucharist." And, presiding over the eucharist at that time (i.e., at the time of the Fourth Lateran Council of 1215) meant being able to pronounce the words that effected the "transubstantiation" of the bread and wine into the body and blood of Jesus Christ (Tanner, ed. 1990, vol. I, 230).
43 Jay 1992, xxiv.
44 *Quadragesimale de Christiana religione*, sermon 20, in: Bernardino of Siena 1950–1965, vol. 1, 250 (cf. Laurentin 1952–1953, vol. 1, 117).
45 Laurentin 1952–1953, vol. 1, 118, n. 62 (Laurentin notes that Bernadino's sermons are full of such linguistic devices).
46 Bernardino of Siena 1950–1965, vol. 1, 250–251.
47 Munroe et al. 1973, 56–57.

48 For a psychoanalytic and sociobiological overview, see: Rancour-Laferriere 1992 (1985), 362–384. See also: Trethowan and Conlon 1965; Brennan et al. 2007.
49 See, for example: Rancour-Laferriere 1992 (1985), 369 ff.; Bayne 2011, 154.
50 Caesarius of Heisterbach 1966 (1851), vol. 2, 168, as translated in: Caesarius of Heisterbach 1929, vol. 2, 108–109.
51 Caesarius of Heisterbach 1966 (1851), vol. 2, 189. In other words, as Bynum puts it, the priest "swelled up," becoming "pregnant with Christ" (1987, 257) – a clear case of couvade.
52 "Hugh of St Victor called the sacrament [eucharist] *miraculum*, Stephen of Autun said the change was *miraculosa*" (Ward 1987, 15).
53 Writing about the "flood of miracle stories," Ward states: "Such stories could even be called 'counter-miracles', as they break through the miraculous surface of illusion to a representation of the substance that lies behind the unchanged appearance." Or: "miracles of this kind are an inversion of the central miracle of transubstantiation, though they claimed to affirm it" (Ward 1987, 15, 16).
54 Caesarius of Heisterbach 1966 (1851), 169, as translated in: Caesarius of Heisterbach 1929, vol. 2, 110.
55 Denzinger 2012, 418, no. 1743. Cf. Thomas Aquinas 2012, vol. 20, 333–334 (*Summa theologiae*, Part 3, Question 83, article 1).
56 O'Dwyer 1988, 165.
57 As quoted by Volfing 2012, 48.
58 As quoted by Hindsley 1998, 106.
59 As quoted by Hindsley 1998, 108.
60 For historical analysis, see: Laurentin 1952–1953, vol. I, 278–282, 341–385, 434–442. See also the entries on Bérulle, Olier, and John Eudes in: O'Carroll 2000 (1982), 79–80, 272–273, 201–202, resp.
61 Laurentin 1952–1953, vol. 1, 343, 373, 346 (n. 22), 359 (n. 82), resp.
62 Laurentin 1952–1953, vol. 1, 360.
63 See: Kohle 1997, 67, 80–83.
64 Gobbi 1998, 176.
65 Gobbi 1998, 472.
66 This last assertion may be thought of as a special case of the more general proposition I have made elsewhere: "A man's couvade is never done" (Rancour-Laferriere 1992 [1985], 377–384).

14 Mary the Priest

Mary as Sacrificial Altar

An early step in bringing Mary to the altar of the sacrifice of her son was to represent her as the altar itself, to personify it, that is, as Christ's mother. This was done in both the Orthodox East and the Roman Catholic West. For example, the entry *Autel* in Laurentin's list of *Titres de la Vierge* points to both Greek and Latin sources.[1]

The popular thirteenth-century *Legenda Aurea* of Jacobus de Voragine tells a tale of how, on the day of Christ's birth, the prophetic Sibyl showed the Roman emperor Octavius an image in the sky of "a most beautiful virgin holding a child in her lap," while at the same time the emperor heard a voice say to him, "This is the altar of Heaven" (*Haec est ara coeli*).[2] In the fourteenth-century *Speculum humanae salvationis*, attributed to Ludolf of Saxony, Mary is the "most beautiful altar" (*beatissima mensa*) through whom the sacrificial food is brought to us. In his *Vita Jesu Christi*, of about 1325, Ludolf also refers to Mary as an "altar" (*mensa*, literally "table").[3]

Medieval hymnography provides further examples, as can be seen from a search of G. G. Meersseman's "Mariological Glossary" under the relevant entries, *ara*, *altare*, and *mensa*. Thus, in a prosaic reworking (ca.890) of a hymn by Fortunatus, Gondacrus of Reims exclaims to Mary that she is "the altar of the rising god [*Ara dei assurgens*]!"[4] A Grusspsalter (ca.1300) by Columba de Vinchio praises Mary with the words:

> *Salve, dei baiula, templum sanctitatis.*
> *Tu altare aureum summe maiestatis.*[5]
> Hail, carrier of God, temple of sanctity.
> You are the golden altar of highest majesty.

A certain Bishop Christopher of Vienna translates a line from a variant of the Greek Akathistos into Latin (ca.800) as follows:

> *Ave, mensa gestans abundantiam propitiationum.*[6]
> Hail, table bearing an abundance of propitiation.

Propitiation is precisely what Mary's son would be offering to God the Father – but directly from the altar of the cross (*ara crucis*), not distally from the "altar" of Mary.

Analogous conceptualizations had already existed in the Orthodox East. For example, in his seventh-century *Life of the Virgin*, Maximus the Confessor places "the table of the bread of life" right alongside "the urn holding the divine manna" in his enumeration of many titles praising Mary.[7] These particular titles honor Mary because "bread of life" (John 6:35, 48) and "divine manna" ("I am the living bread that came down from heaven" – 6:51) are eucharistic designations of Mary's son, Christ. The word "table" was probably *trapeza* in the original Greek of Maximus (only an Old Georgian translation survives, but the passage alludes to Hebrews 9:2, where the Greek word is *trapeza*, and the Georgian word used here is the one that normally renders that Greek word).[8]

Apart from its literal meaning, in patristic Greek, *trapeza* could refer to the Last Supper, the eucharist, and the Christian altar, but it was also applied in symbolic or poetic fashion to Mary.[9] The marian usage of *trapeza* can be found, for example, in some eighth-century Greek homilies. In a homily on the nativity of Mary, Andrew of Crete speaks of the "holy table" (*trapezan hagian*) as a prefiguration of Mary, and further on he apostrophizes Mary as follows:

> Hail, altar [*thusiastērion*], on which the living Lamb, Christ, is mystically offered as a whole burnt offering! The divinely mystical table [*hē theomustos trapeza*] of holy activity that is beyond the [human] mind, on which [lies] Christ, the Bread from heaven, who, as the Lamb above all [others] has been sacrificed as an offering and living, sacrificial victim, giving life to those that partake of him![10]

Similarly, in a homily on Mary's entrance into the temple as a little girl, accompanied by her parents, Patriarch Germanos of Constantinople imagines that Mary will become an altar:

> You were recognized as the most shining horns of the spiritual temple of the new covenant, holding at your own breasts the sanctified and divinely inaugurated, most rational altar of the holy, sacrificial victim [*to tou hierou sfagiou . . . logikōtaton thusiastērion*]. You, unless it is to speak a little of things that would come later, were also recognized as the cherubim revolving in a most mystical way around the place of propitiation [*hilastērion*] in your nursing of the Priest who guides the universe.[11]

In a footnote to this passage by the translator (Mary B. Cunningham), it is stated that the cherubim who circle around the altar in the Jewish temple are allegorical representatives of Mary's parents, who hover solicitously around their daughter, and that here "the Theotokos represents the altar, or place of propitiation."[12] This interpretation is supported in the next section of the homily, where Germanos first urges the veneration of Mary as *trapeza*, and then emphasizes the importance of this image by repeating and embellishing it: "it has been expressed in a wealth of symbols that you have been designated as a most rational and unblemished table [*trapezan . . . logikōtatēn kai amolunton*]!"[13]

Andrew of Crete and Germanos of Constantinople obviously hold Mary in high regard. A part of their idealization of her is their portrayal of her as a sacrificial table or altar of propitiation. Mary should be *honored* to be so magnificent and so significant an altar. But have they thought through the implications? Who is being slaughtered on that altar? And why should the great self-sacrifice of the victim reflect so well upon the mother of that victim?

Figure 14.1 Jan van Eyck, Lucca *Madonna*. Frankfurt, Städelsches Kunstinstitut (Lane 1984, 12).

Occasionally, one may find visual representations of Mary as a sacrificial altar. In the late-medieval West, the elevated position and adornment of Mary's body in identifiably ecclesiastical surroundings can give the impression of a church altar upon which the Christ child is placed. An example of this is the Lucca *Madonna* (Figure 14.1) of Jan van Eyck (d. 1441), where, according to Barbara G. Lane:

> Mary's rigidly horizontal lap resembles the flat surface of a table. On it, she holds the nursing infant stiffly, on a white piece of cloth. The Christ Child sits on Mary's shelf-like lap as the wafer of the Host rests on the white corporal, on the altar, during Mass. Jan has interpreted the Virgin as the altar of Christ.[14]

The breastfeeding Mary is here the "living altar" where the eucharistic "living bread" (again, John 6:51) of the future – now still only a child – is himself obliged to feed.[15]

Mary's exposed breast itself may also be read as a eucharistic offering in such an image, as Caroline Walker Bynum writes: "both baby and breast are the eucharist, presented to us. The two foods are assimilated."[16] I would add that the assimilation in this case is not merely theological (that is, there being no earthly father, Christ's flesh is "assumed" from and is identical to Mary's flesh, as we have seen), but that it is also configurational – that is, it is represented by the way Mary holds her child. For, with her left hand, Mary lifts her *naked right breast* up into the Christ child's mouth, while, with her right hand, she presses tightly with her fingertips up against the *naked right side* of the child, leaving noticeable semi-horizontal creases (scratches?), in precisely the place where the adult Christ on the cross will be opened with the spear tip. As milk flows from Mary's right breast, blood will flow from the crucified Christ's right side. Christ will give of himself as Mary gave of herself.

Mary as Sacrificial Oven

Another early Netherlandish painting that presents to the viewer both a eucharistic breast and a eucharistic Christ child is the famous *Madonna and Child before a Fire Screen* (attributed to Robert Campin, d. 1444; see Figure 14.2). In front of the round, halo-like firescreen sits Mary, who readies one large, round breast for the chubby-faced Christ child. The child's head is placed directly in front of the other breast. The hearth behind Mary, its flames emerging above the firescreen, has been interpreted in terms of the sacrificial burning of an animal from the herd upon an altar (what used to be called in English a "holocaust"), as in Leviticus 1:13:

> Then the priest shall offer the whole and turn it into smoke on the altar; it is a burnt offering, an offering by fire of pleasing odor to the Lord [in the Vulgate Latin: *et oblata omnia adolebit sacerdos super altare in holocaustum et odorem suavissimum Domino*].

Figure 14.2 Robert Campin, *Madonna and Child before a Fire Screen*. London, The National Gallery (Lane 1984, frontispiece).

Carra O'Meara writes of the Firescreen Madonna:

> The hearth floor, though invisible, would be located where the tiles of the floor meet the rear wall on a line that is traceable along the front of the seat of the bench, across the Virgin's lap, and above her left arm. Thus the Virgin supports the Child as the hearth holds the fire, and Mary literally becomes "the hearth of the virginal womb."[17]

As O'Meara explains, the last phrase here is a reference to a passage in the *Summa theologiae*, where Thomas Aquinas is proposing figurative (i.e., prefigurative) meanings of various sacrificial practices under the old Law:

> In the matter of sacrifices the Law had in view the poverty of the offerers; so that those who could not have a four-footed animal at their disposal, might at least offer a bird; and that he who could not have a bird might at least offer bread; and that if a man had not even bread he might offer flour or ears of corn.

> The figurative cause is that the bread signifies Christ Who is the *living bread* (John 6:41, 51). He was indeed an ear of corn, as it were, during the state of the law of nature, in the faith of the patriarchs; He was like flour in the doctrine of the Law of the prophets; and He was like perfect bread after He had taken human nature; baked in the fire, i.e., formed by the Holy Spirit in the oven of the virginal womb [*in clibano uteri virginalis*]; baked again in a pan by the toils which He suffered in the world; and consumed by fire on the cross as on a gridiron.[18]

From this, it is clear that the hearth in Campin's painting could also be understood as that which bakes a grain offering (not only that which roasts an animal from the herd). O'Meara refers to an annunciation image in a thirteenth-century *Bible moralisée*, where Mary receives her baby directly from the announcing angel. In an adjacent image, Jews place sacrificial loaves into an oven. In O'Meara's translation, the inscription reads: "Jews placing unleavened bread into the oven to bake in the fire signifies God placing his son in the virginal womb."[19]

The idea of Christ the "living bread" being placed to "bake" in the "oven" of Mary's womb was a medieval commonplace. Bynum points out that medieval physiological theory drew on Galen's ideas about conception and gestation: "according to Galen, the mother was the oven or vessel in which the fetus cooked, and her body fed the growing child, providing its matter as it matured"[20] If the Christ fetus had once been "cooked" in Mary's womb, now the eucharistic Christ bread could be "baked" in Mary's "oven." An early English carol of the eucharist makes use of this metaphor:

> In virgyne Mary this brede was bake
> Whenne Criste of her manhoode did take,
> Fre of alle synne mankyende to make;
> Ete ye it so ye be [not dede.][21]

In both readings of the Firescreen Madonna – burnt animal offering, baked grain offering – Mary would appear to be a priest who is engaged in offering her child as a sacrifice. "In this painting," Bynum writes, "Mary not only offers her breast; she also presents her baby, as if he were bread fresh from the oven. Mary is assimilated to Christ and celebrant."[22] By "celebrant," Bynum means the male priest who officiates at the eucharistic sacrifice of the mass and who pronounces the magical words – *Hoc est corpus meum* – over the round wafer of bread. Bynum adds, "we should not be surprised to find paintings that depict Mary as priest."[23] Indeed, there are the more obvious artistic images of Mary standing at an altar, or handling a chalice, or wearing priestly vestments, or making priestly gestures, or distributing communion hosts to the faithful, and so on, which go back to the late medieval period.[24] But, Mary of the Firescreen Madonna is already a priest as well. She is offering her "freshly baked" child victim to the viewer, who knows what is going to become of that child, and on whose behalf that child will eventually suffer and die.

Mary and Her Sacrificial Manger

Before proceeding any further in this exploration of Mary as a priest, it might be a good idea to consider one special consequence of the fact that Mary gave birth to Christ before she could be a priest at the altar of his sacrificial death.

Many Christian thinkers have been inclined to draw a parallel between the tomb in which Jesus was buried before he rose from the dead and the uneared womb in which he lived before he was born. As Swedish scholar Yrjö Hirn wrote in 1909: "The Virgin, indeed, enclosed in her body the same contents as the grave."[25] This is a topic too large to be explored in any detail here. Saint Augustine was succinct and to the point regarding the parallel. In his Tractate 120 on John's gospel, he quotes John (19:41): "Now there was a garden in the place where he [Jesus] was crucified, and in the garden there was a new tomb in which no one had ever been laid." Augustine then comments: "As in the womb of the Virgin Mary no one was conceived before Him, and no one after Him, so in this [tomb] there was no one buried before Him, and no one after Him."[26] If we simply strip the fantasy of Mary's virginity from this formulation, the result turns out to be the common fate of humankind: anyone born is *fated* to die, and exiting the womb *means* eventually entering the tomb. A Google search for the phrase "born to die" yields 13.1 million results.[27]

To suggest that Mary gave birth to Jesus so that Jesus could die is meaningless – in the sense that every mother giving birth to a child so that the child can die is meaningless. To argue, however, that Mary *gave birth* to Jesus so that he could save all of humankind specifically *when he died on the cross* is implicit in much of mariological thinking, and sometimes is even explicit in the claims of marian sacerdotalists, as we will see.

Ordinarily, it would be a priest who places the bread and wine of the eucharist on the altar during the sacrifice of the mass, and it would be the priest who consecrates the eucharistic elements and officiates in a reenactment of the sacrifice of Christ over the altar. There is even evidence that alleged relics of the manger (*praesepe*) in Bethlehem were brought to Rome in the seventh century, reassembled, and later utilized as an altar in the church now known as Santa Maria Maggiore. Karl Young writes that this reassembled manger served as:

> the veritable altar upon which the pope laid the consecrated *Corpus Christi* when he celebrated his annual Mass in this church on the vigil of Christmas. Thus the altar became in every sense the *praesepe Christi*, and in numerous examples of medieval plastic art the Child Himself may be seen lying upon the altar-table.[28]

Theologians and preachers had already been taking an interest in this matter. In the Orthodox East, John Chrysostom, for example, wrote about the altar as a "spiritual manger [*fatnēs pneumatikēs*]."[29] In patristic Greek, it was possible to utilize the word *trapeza* (the word for a table or an altar) in reference to the manger in Bethlehem.[30] As for the Roman Catholic West, already with Augustine there are hints of an equation of the eucharistic food on the altar with the babe in the manger – for example: "Placed in a manger, He became our food [*cibus noster*]";[31] and:

> He lies in the manger as the Food of the faithful beasts of burden [*fidelium cibaria jumentorum*]. For it had been foretold through the Prophet [Isaiah 1:3], *the ox knoweth his owner, and the ass his master's crib*. . . . Let us go to the crib, let us eat our Food [*cibaria manducemus*].[32]

In the Christmas liturgy of the Gregorian Sacramentary, we read: "And He [God the Father] made Him, who is the bread of the angels in the manger of the church [*Panis est angelorum in praesepi Ecclesiae*], be food for the faithful creatures [*cibum fecit esse fidelium animalium*]."[33] Gregory also writes: "He is also for good reasons born in Bethlehem, for Bethlehem means House of Bread [*domus panis*]. He is namely the one who says: 'I am the living bread [*panis vivus*] which came down from heaven' [John 6:51]."[34] Walafrid Strabo (d. 849) characterizes the newborn child as "having been placed in the manger, that is, the body of Christ on the altar [*positus in praesepio, id est corpus Christi super altare*]."[35] Toward the end of a sermon on the nativity, Aelred of Rievaulx (d. 1166) states simply, "The manger in Bethlehem is the altar of the church."[36]

The theological equivalence of manger and altar having been established in written texts, it behooved religious artists to follow suit. At the very beginning of his life, Christ was to be represented as a victim (*doit apparaître sous l'aspect d'une victime*), according to art historian Émile Mâle.[37] Furthermore, the mother of the victim had to be brought into the picture. An apparent side effect of this reconceptualization of the manger as an altar was to include Mary in the scene of eucharistic sacrifice. Where there is an infant, the mother cannot be far behind. However, once Mary was present at the eucharistic scene, the issue of her priestly participation in the sacrifice was raised and, with time, gained a life of its own.

In many nativity scenes depicted in sculptures, stained-glass windows, painted panels, and illuminated manuscripts from twelfth- to thirteenth-century France, the newborn Christ child appears, not in a manger per se, but on an elevated, flat surface that bears an unmistakable resemblance to an altar in a church.[38] Mary reclines somewhere apart from or below the altar, and makes no physical contact with her child. Mâle comments that, "in this scene . . . there is nothing tender or, one could almost say, nothing human."[39] This is a bit of an exaggeration, for occasionally the mother does look in the direction of her swaddled child, or even reaches toward the child in a gesture of blessing, as in a stained-glass window at Chartres.[40] In other cases, however, Mary deliberately turns away from her child.[41] This is striking (*nous frappe*, says Grimoüard).[42] Mary seems to signal that this little package left upon the altar of sacrifice represents the completion of her task.

A thirteenth-century French manuscript illustration from the Vatican offers a particularly chilling example (see Figure 14.3).[43] Having just given birth, and having placed her little Christ child upon the manger/altar above, Mary is now reclining on her birthing bed. She looks upward toward her child and points at him with her right hand, while holding an open palm toward him with her left. She seems to be making an *offering* of the child. Joseph, too, looks upward – into the higher register of the image. We, the viewers, also look upward, and what we see just above the manger/altar is the adult Christ already crucified upon his cross. His head hangs downward as if looking in the direction of his mother, but his eyes are closed in death. To Christ's right is Mary, to his left is John – a standard configuration for an image of the crucifixion. Mary clasps her hands together in seemingly ostentatious piety. She does not even look at her dead son. Instead, she appears to be looking backwards with hesitation, or doubt. *What* has she done?

Figure 14.3 Copy of a thirteenth-century French manuscript illustration from the Vatican (Broussolle 1903, 10, fig. 8).

The viewer who notices the physical basis of the cross will be able to answer this question. The central beam of the cross is a continuation of the column to which the manger/altar with the Christ child is attached, and which originates ultimately at some point veiled by the garment covering Mary's nakedness. In other words, the base of the image's central column coincides approximately with Mary's womb.

Mâle comments, "the tree of the cross grows out of the very altar [*l'arbre de la croix sort de l'autel même*] upon which the infant is lying: the symbolism here is right in plain sight."[44] Christ, it seems, has flown out of the womb and onto the manger/altar, and from there he has landed on the cross. This vertical trajectory, however, can also be viewed in terms of marian agency: Mary has hurled her child from the womb to the manger/altar, and from there her gesture of oblation propels him onto the cross. Any hesitancy and doubt in her visage and in her pious pose by the cross suggest horror: can it be that she is responsible for the sacrifice of her son (infanticide) and her God (deicide)?

The southern tympanum of the west façade at Chartres shows multiple marian altars in a vertical arrangement, the first of which is the manger. The swaddled child is first placed upon the table above Mary's birthing bed. Adolf Katzenellenbogen comments: "the manger of the Child is transformed into an altar-like table with a very precise sacramental [i.e., eucharistic] meaning."[45] Originally, the ox and the ass (now lost) were also there, feeding at the manger containing the Christ child in accordance with the sermon where Gregory says: "The new-born babe lies in the manger to refresh all the faithful, namely the holy animals, with the grain of His flesh [*carnis suae frumento reficeret*]."[46] No sooner is her child born, it seems, than Mary has passed him up to an altar/manger for consumption by the faithful.

The artistic tradition of connecting the manger of the nativity with an altar of sacrifice was not limited to France. Barbara Lane offers a nuanced analysis of several works in this tradition from early Netherlandish painting (fifteenth century), including Hugo van der Goes's Berlin *Nativity* and the *Nativity* of Geertgen tot Sint Jans in London.[47] As a less sophisticated but telling illustration of the same theme, Lane points to a fourteenth-century German panel in Munich, where Mary and Joseph pray before the swaddled Christ child in his manger, as the traditional ox and ass look down at the child in the hay.[48] What is decidedly untraditional about this manger is that it sits upon a high church altar. The manger has been "raised" to a sacrificial level.

The New Eve as Priest

Another way to represent Mary as a priest was to counterpose her positive action in the history of salvation to the negative action of her predecessor Eve. There is, for example, the famous miniature created by Berthold Furtmeyr (see Figure 14.4) for the missal of Salzburg Archbishop Bernhard

Figure 14.4 Detail of a miniature created by Berthold Furtmeyr for the missal of Salzburg Archbishop Bernhard von Rohr (ca.1481; Guldan 1966, frontispiece).

von Rohr (ca.1481).[49] At the center of this picture is a single tree that divides the picture roughly into two halves. The tree is topped with a crown of dense green foliage containing numerous round white flowers, suggesting the shape of communion hosts, as well as some fruits ripening from green to red. Also visible in the foliage are a human skull (death's head) on the tree's left and a cross upon which is nailed Christ's body – that is, a crucifix – on the tree's right. Adam sits stark naked at the base of the tree trunk, and a serpent – originating suggestively from Adam's midsection – winds up the trunk and offers a fruit to the naked Eve, who passes it to some people accompanying her (including a demonic skeletal figure) on the left side of the tree. Mary, meantime, stands fully clothed opposite Eve on the other side of the tree. She is the New Eve. She reaches up to pick the round white objects from near the foot of her son's cross in the foliage and presents these edible little metaphors of his crucified body to faithful communicants (accompanied by an angel) near her.[50]

Here, then, we have a single, symmetrically designed tree, its own left side being understood as the overall type for its antitype on its own right side. In other words, what once happened on its left side when humankind fell into sin prefigures (by contrast) what is happening on its right side, where humanity is being redeemed by Christ on the cross, and Mary is handing out to congregants the eucharistic "fruit" of this redemption.

The foregrounded figure of Mary is quite striking. What she does seems to be even more important than what her son had done on his little cross. Art historian Maurice Vloberg, referring to some analogous images that also show Mary offering the eucharist, wrote:

> These compositions aim to remind us that the Virgin is at the origin of the immense beneficial effect of eucharistic bread, since from her was born the body substantially the same as [when] under the sacramental species [*le Corps substantiellement le même sous les espèces sacramentelles*]."[51]

In all such images, transubstantiation is a given. Mary is handing out little clones of her son's sacrificed body, just as male priests did (and still do) at the holy sacrifice of the mass. As Jennifer O'Reilly observes, "she [Mary] administers, *priest-like*, to the faithful souls kneeling beside her."[52]

More problematical from a theological viewpoint is the idea that Mary might *originally* have played a sacerdotal role by offering up her son as a sacrifice at Golgotha, that is, at the very site of the crucifixion. Furtmeyr's famous little painting does not illustrate this very well, however, for the crucifix in the foliage above Mary is a rather trite miniature within the larger and strikingly executed miniature that was intended to illustrate the feast of Corpus Christi. At most, the placement of the crucifix amid the host-like flowers that Mary is distributing to the faithful suggests that she is willing to hand over a substitute (albeit transubstantiated) for the body of her son to carnivorous Christians. The issue of what role she played in getting her son up onto that cross in the first place is avoided. Note that, ultimately, *Eve* is held responsible for initiating the Fall that led to the crucifixion of one of her progeny, for she was first to bite the fruit offered by the serpent. But, she is many generations distant in time from Mary's son, and is separated from Mary and her crucified son by the implied central vertical axis of the painting.

Mary's actual participation in the sacrifice of her son on the cross is not avoided in a specific example of a type of imagery known as the Living Cross, where the vertical beam of the cross provides the axis of symmetry. Such a cross is characterized as "living" because one (or more) of its four ends takes the shape of an arm engaged in an activity connected with Christ's death on the cross. For our purposes, the activities typical of the arms at the two ends of the horizontal beam are relevant: to the right of the crucified Christ (from Christ's own viewpoint), the arm is reaching down to crown or otherwise honor *Ecclesia* (the Christian church personified as a woman); to Christ's left, the arm is vengefully slashing, stabbing, or humiliating *Synagoga* below (the Jewish faith personified as a woman). The supersessionist message of the Living Cross is obvious.

A specific example is a woodcut[53] from Bavarian (or Austrian) territory (ca.1465). It shows, not only *Ecclesia* holding a eucharistic chalice to collect the blood spurting from the crucified Christ's right side, but also Mary herself, a little further back and down to her son's right (see Figure 14.5).[54] She stands near a small tree of life, the foliage of which contains 11 vaguely round, host-like (eucharistic) fruits. She gestures toward the central Living Cross with her upraised left hand, which holds a small crucifix. Perhaps that crucifix is one of the 12 fruits (Revelation 22:2), her divine son, "the living bread" (John 6:51) that she has just picked from the tree of life.[55]

Directly opposite Mary – the New Eve – on the left side of the central Living Cross is Eve, who stands by a similarly small tree of knowledge, its trunk wound round with the serpent, and its crown filled with somewhat skull-like fruits. Under her arm, Eve holds one of the fruits from the tree, which is definitely a death's head. Above the tree of knowledge, in a position symmetrically opposite *Ecclesia*, is the blindfolded figure of *Synagoga*, whose head is being stabbed by the left arm of the Living Cross. Overall, the picture places some rather ordinary type–antitype images in mirror

Figure 14.5 German woodcut, Pavia, ca.1465 (Füglister 1964, plate 9).

positions with respect to the vertical axis of the Living Cross: Eve versus Mary, *Synagoga* versus *Ecclesia*, and forbidden fruit versus communion host.

From a marian perspective, the action to the blood-spurting Christ's right is noteworthy. Above Mary, who holds up the little crucifix in her left hand while standing beside the host-laden tree of life, there is a banderole that has her declare that she knew well the fruit of her womb (*di frucht des leibs hab ich wol erkant*).[56] This could refer either to her son on the crucifix she is holding and/or to her son hanging on the central Living Cross, toward whom she appears to be pointing. Either way, the viewer's overall impression is that Mary knows what she is doing, experiences no regret, and certainly does not lament the humiliation, suffering, and death of her son, which has taken place before her very eyes. Rather, she must approve of these horrors, for otherwise she would have shown at least some slight sign of emotion with respect to her son – as opposed to making an intercessory gesture of protecting two strangers under her cloak with her right arm while proudly holding the crucifix up with her left. In a word, on behalf of strangers, *Mary appears to have offered up her son in sacrifice.*

As the viewer's gaze moves from this potentially sacerdotalized Mary to the central, large image of the copiously bleeding Christ, we see that a gruesome (and non-eucharistic) sacrifice is indeed in progress. God the Father looks down with approval from above, but he too does not participate directly. The victim, like a sacrificed Passover lamb, is being bled, and is perhaps already dead. His blood, having been collected in the (anachronistic and non-biblical) chalice held by *Ecclesia*, will presumably be ready later for consumption – an unthinkable act for *Synagoga*, but a normal practice for late medieval Christians who, centuries after the murder depicted at the center of the picture, would consume metaphorical blood – that is, wine – from the chalice. Mary's role in all of this is belied by her peripheral position in the picture. In fact, her position is symmetrical with – and just as important as – that of Eve on the opposite side of the picture. As the New Eve, Mary makes possible the redemption of humankind from the Fall – itself made possible by Eve. By holding high the relatively small tree/cross upon which her dead son hangs, she effectively proclaims her sacerdotal responsibility for what has happened to her son on the large cross at the center of the picture. She hails the son she "knew well" in her womb, and who is now where he belongs.

Sacerdotalist Mariology

Saint Bernard of Clairvaux seems to have originated the idea of Mary making an "active offering"[57] of her son at the presentation in the temple (Luke 2:22–38). Michael O'Carroll translates the key passage in a sermon where Bernard addresses Mary:

> Offer, O consecrated Virgin, your Son and present to the Lord the blessed fruit of your womb. Offer, for the reconciliation of all of us, this

holy victim, this victim pleasing to God [*hostiam sanctam, Deo placentem*]. God the Father will most willingly receive this new and most precious victim [*novam et pretiosissimam hostiam*], of whom he himself said, "This is my beloved son, in whom I am well pleased" (Mt 3:17).

Bernard continues:

> This offering, brethren, does not appear painful; no sooner is the victim presented to the Lord than it is ransomed with some birds and borne away at once. But the day will come when he will be offered not in the Temple, nor in Simeon's arms, but outside the city between the arms of the Cross. The day will come when he will not be ransomed by the blood of another, but when he himself will ransom others by his own blood. For it is he whom God the Father has sent to be the ransom (*redemptionem*) of his people. That will be the evening sacrifice; today's is the morning sacrifice. This is more joyous, that fuller; this is offered at the time of birth, that in the fullness of age. To one and the other can be applied what the prophet announced: "He offered himself because he willed it" [Isaiah 53:7, Vulgate: *Oblatus est, quia ipse voluit*; cf. John 10:17–18].[58]

This sequence of two offerings, remarks Laurentin, creates the impression that the offering of the child victim at the presentation in the temple is a *prélude* to the offering of the same victim (but now an adult) at Golgotha. There is also the temptation to conclude that, as Mary made the first offering in the temple, she too must have made the last offering at Golgotha.[59] In other words (though Laurentin does not say this explicitly), Mary must have been a priest from the start, and her victim (*hostia*)[60] must have been the same – her own son – from start to finish.

Strictly speaking, Bernard's text is not quite amenable to such a reading, at least according to Laurentin. Bernard does not actually call Mary *sacerdos* (priest) in either the first case or the second case. Also, Bernard names Mary as the one who makes the offering of the victim in the first case, but not in the second case, where – in a scripturally based spirit of true Christian masochism – the victim offers himself.

Actually, according to Bernard, the victim offered himself in *both* cases. The only difference is that the victim was the Christ child in the first case and the Christ adult in the second case. Christ was God in both developmental stages of ontogeny, after all. That being so, however, one has to wonder why Bernard made such a fuss about *Mary* offering her child victim in the temple to begin with. Was he just unable to control his mariophile enthusiasm in the first case? Bernard is famous for this outburst. We do not know why he tempered his enthusiasm in the second case. Perhaps he experienced a moment of silent compassion for both the mother and the son in that sordid affair at Golgotha.

For, there is a strand of mariology – or a "theological malaise," as Laurentin puts it[61] – that gives Mary a remarkably proactive role in the crucifixion of her son. It seems that Mary is not just an obedient "slave-woman of the Lord" who "consents" to the murder of her son. Nor is she the merely human mother of a divine son who separates from her, and then goes on to redeem humankind on his own by voluntarily offering *himself* up as a sacrifice on the cross. Rather, Mary is an active, "sacerdotal" participant herself in the redemptive event at Golgotha, which is to say that she participates as a *priest* who *offers* her own son as a *sacrifice*. Those who believe this about Mary may be termed "sacerdotalists."

The church Fathers had little to say about Mary as a priest, whereas, in the medieval West, there were a few tentative theological forays in this area, such as the passage by Saint Bernard just examined. With time, some theologians started taking explicitly sacerdotalist positions. An important figure was the Spanish Jesuit Ferdinand Quirino (Chirino) de Salazar (1576–1646).[62] In Salazar's *Expositio in Proverbia Salomonis* (1619), we read:

> Therefore, though the Virgin by prayer and by pouring out petitions contributed something to our salvation, that assuredly, in my opinion, is not enough to justify calling her cause of our salvation, its author or mediatress, as is clear of others who also prayed and poured out petitions. What clearly brought the Virgin to this glory and made her a collaborator [*cooperatricem*] and helper with Christ was that joining her will in association with the will of Christ she offered him who was hers to us and for us [*illum nobis et pro nobis obtulit, qui vere suus erat*] for which reason . . . the Virgin especially bound God and men to herself, for she so greatly pleased God by this free offering of her son [*quia Deo tantopere placuit hac voluntaria filii sui oblatione*] that in a manner singular and proper to herself she obtained life and salvation for the human race.[63]

Salazar writes about Mary's sacrifice of her son without excluding the coexistence and simultaneity of that sacrifice with the grandiose son's own morally masochistic sacrifice of himself. In scholastic terms, Mary's merit is admittedly *de congruo*, whereas her son's is *de condigno*. Yet, her accomplishment rests on more than the congruence of her will with that of her son. She was just as much a priest at Golgotha as her son was:

> In this also the Blessed Virgin fulfilled the office of priest [*sacerdotis munus peregit*] in that showing her will in all things conform to the will of her Son she offered and sacrificed him on the altar of the Cross as did Christ himself [*illum in ara crucis non secus obtulit ac sacrificavit, quam seipsum Christus*].[64]

If Christ sacrificed himself literally, Mary sacrificed him literally as well. It could be said that Christ and Mary were co-priests in this affair.

She *offered and sacrificed* her son. Salazar gives Mary a very active, even aggressive role. According to Laurentin, Salazar has a deplorable tendency to "materialize" the role of Mary, insinuating that Mary was not satisfied to accept her son's death passively, but actively sent him to his death, immolated him, sacrificed him, and so on (*multipliant les termes latines*).[65] Mary seems to have treated Jesus as a mere object (*la chose de Marie*), to have become even his executioner (*le bourreau de Jésus*).[66]

Not that Mary's son would have resisted. Salazar writes:

> If *per impossibile* the will of Christ the Lord had not been expressed, the will of the Mother would have been sufficient to interpret the will of the Son, for the Son could have been thought to will what the Mother willed [*filius velle putaretur quod mater voluit*].[67]

In other words, for the sake of humankind, the mother's wish that her son Christ die would actually have sufficed, and Christ, obedient to his mother, would freely have accepted death (*le Christ obéissant à sa mère ait librement accepté la mort*, in Laurentin's translation of Salazar).[68]

In order for Salazar to come up with such a bizarre hypothetical situation, he would have to have been thinking that Mary had interpreted the grandiosity of her son as real grandeur. But, that is not a particularly unusual belief for a Christian to hold about Mary's son (and it can safely be assumed that our Laurentin himself holds this belief, namely, that Jesus was God, the savior of humankind). But, Salazar's Mary would *also* have to have been grandiose, thinking that only she and her son knew what was the right thing to do for all of humankind. Here, Salazar conjured up a very interesting case of *folie à deux*. Only this double madness of Mary and her son would have freed Mary of the compunctions – the revulsion, the horror – a mother would ordinarily have had about murdering her son. To this, Salazar needed only to add a dash of omnipotent thinking to Mary's diagnostic chart. That way, Mary would have been in a position to exercise remote control over both her son and his murderers, and she would then successfully have caused her son's sacrificial death through a sheer act of will.

Salazar was a very influential figure in the history of marian sacerdotalism, and the imprint of his fantasies can be detected in works that were penned centuries later. For example, Pierre Jeanjacquot, writing in 1868, states:

> The Blessed Virgin shares with our Divine Saviour this two-fold quality of Victim and Priest. As then He could say that He sacrificed His own life, because He gave it up and placed it in the power of His murderers; so we may say with all truth of the Blessed Virgin, that she herself sacrificed the Divine Victim, by the perfect union of her will with that of Jesus Christ in that immolation, and with a view to that immolation.

Mary is not acquitted of murder in such a formulation. She looks like an accessory to the crime, or at least guilty of the assisted suicide of a man whose terminal illness is psychological rather than physical. The "perfect union" of the will of Mary with the will of her suicidal son not only erases the boundary between mother and son in the act of immolation, but places co-responsibility for the act upon her shoulders (unless one grants that she herself is deluded and, therefore, not responsible):

> Our Lord made His death dependent up to the last moment [*jusqu'au dernier instant*] upon the will and consent of the Blessed Virgin. For if He was a Priest because He offered and immolated Himself, in such a sense that, but for His will to suffer and sacrifice Himself, His murderers would have had no power over Him, it must have been the same with regard to His Mother to make her to be a Priest like Him and with Him.[69]

Here, Laurentin balks (as he did with some of Salazar's formulations): Jeanjacquot's "hypothesis" is clever, but unverifiable.[70] It is all too clear that Mary is either a filicide or a delusional co-participant in the sacrifice at Golgotha.

Mary as Coredeemer

The notion that Mary turned over (or could theoretically have turned over) her son as a sacrifice to his murderers is related to – but not necessarily the same as – the idea that she was a *coredeemer* along with him. Unfortunately, there are myriad meanings of this term (or of its cognates in various languages) when applied to Mary.[71] Generally speaking, there is an inclination to ascribe "coredemptive" attributes to Mary when her seemingly compassionate involvement in the events on Golgotha is foregrounded. But Mary may be "coredemptive" for other reasons as well.

Sandro Sticca devotes an entire chapter to "Mary as Co-Redemptrix" in his book on marian lamentation (*planctus Mariae*) in medieval drama of the passion, and thereby implies that the intense compassion expressed by Mary for her suffering and dying son in her laments helps to qualify her as the coredeemer, alongside Christ the redeemer on Golgotha. Sticca does *not*, however, attribute a sacerdotal function to Mary's participation (even if some of his theological sources do assume a sacerdotalist premise).[72]

The same may be said of Rachel Fulton's interpretations of several medieval sources, such as: Arnold of Bonneval's depiction of "an (almost) equal role for Mary in the work of human redemption"; "Mary's identity with Christ in his pain" in the *Quis dabit* meditation; and the foregrounding of "the *mysterium* of Mary's corporeal identity with her son" in William of Newburgh's commentary on the Song of Songs.[73] There is no suggestion of an explicitly sacerdotal role for Mary in any of these engaging interpretations by Fulton.

Representations of Mary's coredemptive potential have also been detected in the visual arts. Quite striking are images of a type of double intercession in which Mary exposes her right breast to the adult Christ, who, in turn, exposes the lance wound in his right side to God the Father. Such an intercession is "double" in this case insofar as the prayers of the faithful reach the highest instance (God the Father) after passing through the two mediators, Mary and her son Christ. An example is the double intercession at the Cloisters in New York (a Florentine painting attributed to Lorenzo Monaco, from before 1402: see Figure 14.6).

In this work, some small figures are kneeling in prayer. A large Mary, extending her protective hand over them, says to Christ: "Dearest son, because of the milk that I gave you, have mercy on them." Christ, in turn, says to the Father above, "My father, let those be saved for whom you wished me to suffer the Passion."[74] This pair of requests is enhanced by

Figure 14.6 Intercession of Christ and the Virgin, attributed to Lorenzo Monaco, before 1402. Cloisters, New York (Barnet and Wu 2005, 120, fig. 84).

the artist's use of color. Mary is clothed in a white robe (corresponding to the milk she fed to the Christ child), and the adult Christ appears in a red garment (corresponding to the blood he shed for humankind). According to Beth Williamson, such a pairing not only suggests a comparison of Mary's breast with Christ's wound, or her milk with his blood, but also gives the breastfeeding Mary "a share in the blood-sacrifice of Christ's Crucifixion, and makes her Co-redemptrix." To support her interpretation, Williamson refers to the medieval notion that a woman's blood gives rise to the child in her womb, as well as the idea that breast milk results from the transformation of blood within a woman's body during pregnancy and nursing (see above, p. 120, n. 65). The latter idea is particularly relevant to this type of double intercession imagery. It is not only Mary's compassion on Golgotha that is coredemptive, for "the milk is to be understood as identical with the blood of Christ and therefore gains some salvatory aspect in its own right."[75] Again, however, there is no explicit suggestion that Mary's coredemptive role in this sort of image entails a sacerdotal role for Mary as well.

These examples (and many more could be adduced) of Mary's supposedly coredemptive role at Golgotha have no basis whatsoever in canonical New Testament scripture. They also contradict principles advanced by some theologians at a relatively early stage in the development of Christianity, notably Saint Ambrose, who wrote that perhaps Mary "thought that by her death also she might add something to the public weal. But Jesus did not need a helper for the redemption of all, Who saved all without a helper."[76] If anything, Mary needed her son to redeem *her* along with all the rest of humankind, as has been pointed out repeatedly in this book.[77] How could one who needed to be redeemed also be the coredeemer?

These are interesting complications. But, marian coredemptionists, like marian sacerdotalists, have moved on. Whole new worlds of interpretation have opened up. Marian coredemptionism is a *fait accompli* in the history of mariology. What is done is done, and what is done also happens to be of considerable psychological interest.

In the present context, which is an analysis of Mary's role as a priest at Golgotha, the question that naturally comes up is this: what is the difference between Mary the coredeemer and Mary the priest? Unfortunately, there is no clear answer to this question, for there is considerable overlapping of her roles in the many contexts where such a question could come up. In many cases, however, Mary's coredemptive role appears to be more basic and explicit, whereas the sacerdotal role (if it is present at all) is optional, or only implicit. If, for example, Mary is said to suffer an intensely compassionate pain for her son as he suffers and dies in pain on the cross, and if Mary's compassionate suffering by itself is said to qualify her as coredeemer along with her suffering and dying son the redeemer, then no claim up to that point is being made about Mary being a priest. If, however, Mary is said, in addition, *to offer either her bodily self and/or her bodily son as a sacrifice to God,* then an additional claim is being made that Mary is a priest at Golgotha. Words such as "priest," "priestly," "sacerdotal," and so on, may not necessarily be utilized, but a sacerdotalist claim is being made nonetheless.

Consider, for example, two key statements by Arnold of Bonneval (a contemporary of Saint Bernard) that are often quoted in support of the idea of Mary's coredemption. The first is in Part 3 of his treatise *de septem verbis Domini in cruce*, where Arnold writes: "in that tabernacle you could see two altars: one in the heart of Mary, the other in the body of Christ. Christ immolated his flesh, Mary her soul [*Christus carnem, Maria immolabat animam*]." Here, the imagery of two "altars" is nicely symmetrical, with coordinated immolations taking place. The argument appears to be coredemptionist, with Mary playing a subordinate role, not making a bodily offering of herself to be sacrificed. In her enthusiasm, however, Mary wishes also to participate more fully in the sacrifice – that is, "with the Lord Jesus, to consummate the mystery of our Redemption, through her mortal body." Now the argument is moving in a sacerdotalist direction, and so Arnold feels obliged to intervene, noting that what Mary wishes to do "was the exclusive task of the High Priest [*sed hoc solius summi sacerdotis privilegium erat*; cf. Hebrews 9:11–12], to bring, that is, the offering of his own blood to the sanctuary, and he could not let anyone else participate in this dignity."[78] In this first statement by Arnold, it is clear that he rejects a sacerdotal role for Mary.[79]

A second key statement is to be found in Arnold's booklet *de laudibus Beatae Mariae Virginis*:

> There was one single will of Christ and Mary, both together offered one holocaust to God; she in the blood of her heart, he in the blood of his flesh [*erat una Christi et Mariae voluntas, unumque holocaustum ambo pariter offerebant Deo: haec in sanguine cordis, hic in sanguine carnis*].[80]

Again, we have a pairing, this time of the mother's "blood" with the son's "blood." Arnold's coredemptionist drift is clear in the "single will" of mother and son (and elsewhere in Arnold's phraseology as well).[81] But, the "one holocaust," insofar as it included, not only the "blood" of the mother, but also the "blood" of the son, was going too far. Without saying so, Arnold has given Mary a sacerdotal role.

Of course, "the blood of her heart" could only have been the metaphorical "blood" of Mary's metaphorical "heart." Indeed, if the "blood" Mary shed had been anything other than metaphorical, then she would have died along with her son on Golgotha. But, Mary did not die there. Christ did. As Laurentin writes, borrowing a Latin phrase from Arnold, "Mary, who was not crucified in any material sense, was crucified by sympathy: *concrucifigebatur affectu*."[82]

Nevertheless, in his second statement, Arnold says that the metaphorical "blood" of Mary, together with the real "blood" of Christ, constituted "one holocaust," jointly offered to God by virtue of the "one single will" of son *and* mother. From this, it follows that part of the "one holocaust" (the real part, not only the metaphorical part) offered to God by the mother was the son himself. There is a category error here, a forced mixing of the real with the metaphorical. But, by virtue of this mixing, the real blood of the son ends up being included in the efficacious bloody mixture offered by Mary, so that it is possible to say – as Jean Galot does, without recognizing the problem – that "what Mary offers is her Son [*ce que Marie offre, c'est son Fils*], and her offering is presented by the Christ to the Father."[83]

There is another problem as well. In his second statement, Arnold seems to be operating under the presupposition that Mary possessed some kind of *right* over the literal "blood" of her son. To state the problem in terms of a modern moral issue, Arnold's Mary thinks and acts as though her child is still a fetus, and believes that she has a rightful choice to decide whether or not the fetus should be aborted. Of course, Christ on the cross was not a fetus, but an adult, and there is no biblical evidence whatsoever about what Mary was doing or thinking on Golgotha. Arnold of Bonneval is only imagining what Mary may have been doing or thinking there, and he does presuppose that Mary possessed some right to be offering to God the literal "blood" of his and her son.[84]

Granted, Mary's right had to be subordinate to the right Christ himself had over his own "blood." Christ had veto power, as it were. Furthermore, if Christ had not offered himself up for sacrifice in the first place, Mary could not even have made her offering. But Christ did, and so Mary did. There were two priests. Jointly, they offered to God the "one holocaust" of Christ's real "blood" mixed with Mary's metaphorical "blood." Christ the "High Priest" died, while Mary the subordinate priest survived.

Arnold of Bonneval is torn. To judge from the two statements considered here, Arnold wants Mary to play as important a role as possible in her son's crucifixion, without making her a priest. In the first case, she is explicitly denied a priestly role; in the second, she is implicitly granted the role of priest. So, was Arnold's Mary a priest or was she not a priest? Apparently, Arnold never did resolve his ambivalent attitude toward the idea of Mary being a priest (nor did many mariophile theologians resolve this ambivalence right down to the twentieth century). But, as Laurentin points out, Arnold did give theologians an innovative ensemble of concepts and terms for explicating both the coredemption and the priesthood of Mary.[85]

Marian Sacerdotalism in the Papal Magisterium

The heyday of marian sacerdotalism was reached in the late nineteenth and early twentieth centuries. But, then came papal interventions against the sacerdotalist movement. The marian title *Virgo Sacerdos* was suppressed by the papal magisterium around 1913–1914, which just happened to be a time when the title *Corredemptrix* was beginning to achieve legitimacy.[86] In 1916, during the rule of Benedict XV, a decree was published forbidding images of the "Virgin-Priest," and in 1927 devotion to this particular version of Mary was officially deemed to be unacceptable.[87]

These incidents slowed – but did not halt – sacerdotalism among Roman Catholic mariophiles. Indeed, there were clear sacerdotalist tendencies among the popes themselves, before, during, and after the early decades of the twentieth century.

Some of the papal statements give the impression that Mary knew all along what would happen to her son, as if the son was a calf being fattened up for slaughter, and as if the mother was knowingly involved in the preparation for the sacrifice. In his encyclical *Iucunda semper* of 1894, Pope Leo XIII writes:

> In the Garden of Gethsemani, where Jesus undergoes His agony, in the judgment hall, where He is scourged, crowned with thorns, condemned to death, we do not find Mary. But she knew beforehand all these agonies; she knew and saw them [*talia vero iamdiu habet cognita et perspecta*]. When she professed herself the handmaid of the Lord for the mother's office, and when, at the foot of the altar, she offered up her whole self with her Child Jesus – then and thereafter she took her part in the painful expiation offered by her Son for the sins of the world.[88]

Saint Peter's successor goes on to say that, "it was before the eyes of Mary that the divine Sacrifice for which she had borne and nurtured the Victim [*victimam de se generosa aluerat*] was to be finished."[89]

Pope Pius X was also an enthusiastic supporter of a sacerdotalized Mother of God. In his encyclical *Ad diem illum* (1904), he asserts that Mary prepared and offered up a sacrificial victim in Jesus:

> It was not only the glory of the Mother of God [*Deiparae*] to have presented to God the Only-Begotten who was to be born of human members the material by which he was prepared as a Victim [*hostia*] for the salvation of mankind, but hers also the office of tending and nourishing that Victim, and at the appointed time of offering Him at the altar [*verum etiam officium eiusdem hostiae custodiendae nutriendaeque, atque adeo, stato tempore, sistendae ad aram*].[90]

The syntax may be a bit convoluted here, with its initial allusion to Saint Bede,[91] but Mary's direct role in the eventual death of her son is conveyed in stark, even shocking terms. What would motivate an ordinary peasant mother from Galilee to nourish and care for her child specifically for the purpose of offering up that child as a sacrificial "Victim" at some "appointed time"? Even if the conversation with the archangel Gabriel recorded in Luke's gospel had actually taken place, it did *not* include long-term plans for making the child a sacrificial "Victim" upon some "altar" at some "appointed time." Not that such terminology is new, for we have found plenty of precedents in mariophile theology from earlier centuries. But here, the marian sacerdotalist ideas emanate from the highest ecclesiastical level. This is the same pope who (in 1906) gave official approval to the prayer ending with the words, "Mary, Virgin Priest, pray for us."[92]

Pope Benedict XV, in his apostolic letter *Inter Sodalicia* of 1918, avoids the characterization of Mary as a mother who appears to be fattening up her son for the slaughter. Instead, he introduces the language of immolation. He writes that Mary not only turned Jesus over to the killers, but contributed to the redemption of humankind by immolating him insofar as this was possible for her (*quantum ad se pertinebat, Filium immolavit*).[93] This seems to tone down the blatant marian sacerdotalism of Pius X. But still, to "immolate" means to offer up specifically for sacrificial slaughter, or even to participate in the slaughter, no matter the qualification. Such is precisely what Laurentin had objected to in Salazar's vocabulary.

Insofar as some form of the verb *offero* is utilized, the language of sacerdotalist papal documents has Mary "offering [up]" her son to his murderers. The perfect tense form *obtulit* is utilized, for example in the encyclical *Mystici Corporis Christi* of Pope Pius XII (1943), where Mary is said to have offered up in holocaust, not only her son, but also her mother's rights and her mother's love to the eternal Father on Golgotha (*una cum maternorum iurium maternique amoris sui holocausto . . . Aeterno Patri* ***obtulit***).[94] Some form of this verb had also been utilized earlier, for example by Leo XIII (1894; *Mater . . . Filium ipsa suum ultro* ***obtulit*** *Divinae Justitiae*), and by Pius XI (1928; *quae . . . apud crucem hostiam* ***obtulerit***), as can be seen in a convenient list compiled by Laurentin.[95] The verb also raises its ugly head in more recent papal marian discourse – for example, in this comment by John Paul II in his 1995 encyclical *Evangelium Vitae*: "'Standing by the cross of Jesus' (Jn 19:25), Mary shares in the gift which the Son makes of himself: she offers Jesus [*Iesum* ***offert***]."[96] Here, John Paul II, like other sacerdotalist popes, is being influenced by the famous sermon on the presentation in the temple by Bernard of Clairvaux ("Offer your son, sacred virgin . . .").[97]

Continuing his sentence in *Evangelium Vitae*, the Polish pope emphasizes Mary's active role with respect to her seemingly passive son. She "gives him over [*tradit illum*], and begets him to the end for our sake [*semel in sempiternum eum generat pro nobis*]."[98] "Begets" him indeed! Here, Mary's oblation seems already to have been made at the annunciation, as when the pope continues, "The 'yes' spoken on the day of the Annunciation reaches full maturity on the day of the Cross [*Illud 'fiat' Annuntiationis die prolatum plene maturescit Crucis die*]."[99] Apparently, the pope grants that the "yes" spoken by a 12-year-old girl on the day of the annunciation was *im*mature. Yet, that "yes" begat her son "to the end for our sake," which is to say that it was an unbreakable commitment to sacrifice him "on the day of the Cross." It seems that the best that a marian sacerdotalist such as John Paul II can do is to misconstrue the distal "yes" of the annunciation and, having done so, give believers to understand that Mary was a co-priest together with her son, the other priest, on the cross. There were two priests at Golgotha.

The Polish pope's thinking about what happened at Golgotha is replicated in his thinking about the eucharist. For example, in an Angelus address delivered on the Feast of Corpus Christi, June 5, 1983, John Paul II speaks of Mary's presence in the eucharist as follows:

> Every Eucharist is a memorial of that Sacrifice and that Passover that restored life to the world; every Mass puts us in intimate communion with her, the Mother, whose sacrifice "becomes present" just as the sacrifice of her Son "becomes present" at the words of consecration of bread and wine pronounced by the priest.[100]

Note that the pope speaks here of Mary's "sacrifice," and not only in the eucharist. According to Arthur Burton Calkins, the pope's thesis is "that Mary's sacrifice becomes present in the Mass just as her Son's sacrifice becomes present. This is true, above all, precisely because Jesus *is* Mary's sacrifice; she offered him in sacrifice on Calvary to the Father for us."[101] Without saying so, Calkins has here discerned the pope's sacerdotalist position, for the pope does say of Mary that "*she offered him* [Jesus] and she offered herself to the Father."[102] This is more than a statement about Mary's coredemption. It is a statement about Mary's priesthood at Golgotha.

Feminist Considerations

Here, we might ask: what about the male priest who officiates at the sacrifice of the mass, the one who reenacts what had happened at Golgotha? Is he impersonating Mary as well as Christ? If he is acting *in persona Christi* (as is so often said), can he also be acting *in persona Mariae*? Indeed, he must be, if the covertly sacerdotalist logic of John Paul II is right. Mary is present at the eucharistic altar. She is again sacrificing her son, just as she had sacrificed him *in ara crucis*. A male priest is doing this in her stead.

As I have noted earlier (p. 240), the priest's "vestments," worn on the occasion of celebrating the sacrifice of the mass, resemble a woman's attire. The Catholic priest at the eucharistic altar is a socially sanctioned cross-dresser. In addition, some priests also show signs of couvade in their priestly activities at the altar, as has been discussed earlier. These phenomena have come into existence because there is no other way of bringing the maternal figure of Mary to the altar – short of ordaining women to the priesthood.

It is well known that women have traditionally not been permitted to enter the Catholic priesthood, although the theological and doctrinal correctness of this form of prejudicial discrimination against women has been challenged.[103] Precisely here is where a feminist mariology might be relevant. The fact that the scriptural Mary was no feminist (discussed earlier in this book) is not really relevant here. There were no feminists in the first century. What is relevant is the absence of women priests in the twenty-first-century Catholic Church.

Toward the end of a book titled *God's Mother, Eve's Advocate: A Marian Narrative of Women's Salvation*, theologian Tina Beattie laments the absence of women priests in the Roman Catholic Church hierarchy. She suggests that the Catholic priesthood needs to be reconceived and enlarged in such a way as to include symbolic representation of Mary's giving birth to Christ, along with the already existing symbolic representation of Christ's sacrificial death on the cross. Beattie believes that, "Mary exercises a maternal form of priesthood, equal to but different from the sacrificial priesthood of Christ." A scriptural indication of this equality between priestly modes is the oft-noted voluntary acceptance of roles by both parties, with Mary speaking to the announcing angel at Luke 1:38 ("let what you have said be done to me"), and Christ speaking to the Father in Gethsemane at Luke 22:42 ("let your will be done, not mine"). According to Beattie:

> Christ echoes Mary's words of self-consecration in Gethsemane, thus completing the cycle of birth and death into which God became incarnate. There can be no death without birth, and no incarnation without a mother. The mother is the priest of creation who consecrates birth, fecundity and new life. Mary's priesthood reflects the active, salvific dimension of her role in the incarnation.[104]

For Beattie, the Roman Catholic mass ought to be reshaped in such a fashion as to permit meaningful officiation by either a female or a male priest (or perhaps both?), and to open up a new system of performative rituals, together with a new palette of symbols appropriate for conveying both maternal and sacrificial meanings. Clearly, the mass would no longer be what has traditionally been termed "the holy sacrifice of the mass."

Or rather, it would be that plus something else, which would somehow have to fit with what is already in place. Beattie's proposal is intriguing, but short on detail. It is clear from her proposal, however, that she does not advocate exclusion, so that a male priest would not be excluded from representing "the maternal priesthood of Mary," and, conversely, a female priest would not be excluded from representing "the sacrificial priesthood of Christ."[105]

Is Tina Beattie's proposal feasible? In principle, it ought to be as feasible as the many already accomplished juxtapositions of maternal and sacrificial imagery in other areas. In the visual arts, for example, we have seen numerous examples of the meaningful placement of a nativity scene or an image of Mary breastfeeding the Christ child right alongside (or on the reverse side of) an image of a bloodied adult Christ hanging from the cross. Or, as we know from René Laurentin's massive historical study, *Marie, l'Église et le sacerdoce* (1952–1953), there have been numerous theologians and mystics who represent Mary as actively sacrificing the son she gave birth to.

The psychological problem with previous intimations of a marian priesthood is that the mother of one's God appears to be a murderer. If women were to become Catholic priests as Beattie suggests, and especially if women priests were not to be excluded from performing "the sacrificial priesthood of Christ," then their performance might also be perceived by the faithful as a shocking criminal act. Furthermore, such a perception would be fostered among the faithful generally, not just among a few museum-goers, or lovers of medieval poetry, or theologians.

We know that marian sacerdotalism has been controversial in the distant past, and it is clear that it has offended Christian sensibilities in the more recent past. For example, Protestant church historian Giovanni Micgge writes about a large banner displayed at a gathering of Roman Catholic mariophiles in 1946:

> She [Mary] knows beforehand the sacrifice that is to crown her and accepts it, suffering with Him [Jesus] and dying with Him spiritually at the foot of the cross. The *labarum* of the Marian congress of La Salette, dedicated to Mary, co-redemptress, represents her erect, stretched out [across] the body of the crucified, slightly lower than Him, her arms extended under His and partly supporting His in the gesture of offering. Jesus dies leaning His head upon that of His mother, who dies spiritually with Him, *offering Him to death.* Mary's face is serene and piteous; Christ's face is disfigured with pain. It is clear that *He is the victim offered up and she is the officiating priest.* And the dying body of Jesus is almost completely hidden by the monastic dress of the sorrowful Mother. What symbols![106]

What symbols indeed. A schematic rendering of the *grande bannière* of the 1946 Marian National Congress, held in Grenoble and La Salette, is featured on the cover of the proceedings of that congress (see Figure 14.7). The cover logo is clearer than the poor-quality photographs of the actual *grande bannière.*[107] As Miegge notes, the banner image is simultaneously sacerdotal and coredemptive. Although the stated theme of the 1946 congress is *Marie Corédemptrice*, it is obvious that the congress banner represents a sacerdotal Mary as well – this despite the near-absence of any scholarly consideration of Mary as a priest in the actual conference proceedings.[108]

Catholic feminist scholar Elizabeth A. Johnson relates a story she heard from a Mexican woman:

> During a basic Christian community prayer meeting in Oaxaca, southern Mexico, Sabina Lopez de Hernandez reflected with the group on her strong reaction to a recent sermon. The gospel reading had depicted Mary at the foot of the cross. The priest said that she stood there in accord with God's will, *freely offering up her son for the salvation of the world.* As a mother, Sabina found this abhorrent. A mother, even a woman of faith, wants her

Figure 14.7 Cover of the proceedings of the 1946 Marian National Congress held in Grenoble and La Salette (Congrès Marial National 1948).

> child to live, not to be killed. Did the others not think so? They did. This preacher did not understand a mother's heart. The prayerful discussion turned toward the idea that the God of life passionately abhors people killing or hurting each other. The violence of the cross is not what is salvific in and of itself. The long-standing idea that Mary willingly joined in a divine plan for the suffering of her son was rejected.[109]

These examples of anti-sacerdotalist abhorrence speak for themselves. At an altar where, as Tina Beattie suggests, a priest might exercise both Mary's maternal priesthood and Christ's sacrificial priesthood, there is a risk of establishing (or enhancing an already existing) perceptual or associative linkage between mothering the Christ child and sacrificing that child. If women were to be ordained along with men, and if a reformed mass were to include both maternal and sacrificial priesthoods, would the faithful then be given to understand that Mary herself endangered – and continues to endanger under the cover of eucharistic ritual – the life of the very son to whom she gave – and continues to give – life? I believe that the faithful would indeed notice this connection between mothering Christ and killing Christ, and that they would leave the church in droves if something were not done to exclude any hint of such a connection in a reformed mass.

Women's ordination to the Catholic priesthood has long been blocked by the all-male church hierarchy.[110] But, in a world where some Protestant denominations already have women ministers, and some branches of Judaism already have women rabbis, the absence of women priests in Roman Catholicism is beginning to look odd. To my knowledge, however, the issue of a central woman figure sacrificing her own child does not come up in the relevant Protestant denominations or branches of Judaism. This may mean that the real hindrance to the ordination of women to the priesthood is not (or not only) old-fashioned misogyny, but the continuing prominence of the *sacrifice of Mary's son* in the Roman Catholic mass.

Curiously enough, there is a sense of the word "priest" that might actually describe what Mary is supposed to have done at Golgotha, but without implicating her in her son's sacrifice. I am thinking of the old notion of the "common priesthood of the faithful," which was explicitly promulgated at Vatican II and which is distinct from the "ministerial or hierarchical priesthood."[111] Of the faithful, it is stated: "When they take part in the eucharistic sacrifice, the source and the culmination of all Christian life, they offer to God the divine victim and themselves along with him."[112] By "themselves" is apparently meant the ordinary pieties of prayer, reception of the sacraments, self-denial, and active charity.[113] If ordinary believers "offer" the victim and themselves in this fashion, then surely the extraordinary Mary must have offered the victim and herself in at least this sense as well. Colman E. O'Neill writes: "There is a perfect analogy between her [Mary's] cooperation in the sacrifice of Calvary and the participation of the faithful in the Mass."[114] Like the faithful at mass who "can adopt the eucharistic Victim as the sign, made sacrificial by the celebrant, of their own self-offering," so at the foot of the cross Mary "was able to adopt the Victim as the sacrificial sign of her own self-offering."[115]

But, surely, Mary must have accomplished much more than what this lowest common denominator of the faithful accomplish daily in offering the eucharistic victim as a "sign" of "self-offering." For O'Neill, one particular attribute of Mary stands out: "She alone is Co-redemptrix."[116] Here, then, is another example of the possibility of Mary being the coredeemer, without being a priest: "Our Lady is not a priest. She could not make Calvary a sacrifice and she cannot make the Mass a sacrifice. Christ did the first, the ordained priest as Christ's minister does the second."[117]

We are left, then, with a coredeemer at Calvary (Golgotha) who co-offered her son along with offering herself, but who did not perform the actual sacrifice of herself or her son. Making an offering, even co-offering the first and principal victim, was not the same thing as sacrificing the victim. Christ alone performed the sacrifice on Golgotha. He was the first and principal Christian priest, and Mary's presence with him there made her just another member of the "priesthood of the faithful," even if she was awarded the title of coredeemer as well.

This watered-down version of Mary's priesthood, like the sacerdotalist version, has no basis whatsoever in canonical New Testament scripture. Needless to say, it would not be acceptable to traditional marian sacerdotalists. However, there may be some way to integrate it with Tina Beattie's proposal for reforming the priesthood. There is something to be said for the principle of women having an equal right to join the ranks of the Catholic priesthood. One needs only to be a humanist to understand the inherent virtue of gender equality.

*

Textual sources from both the Orthodox East and the Catholic West have represented Mary as a sacrificial altar (Greek: *trapeza*, *thusiastērion*; Latin: *ara*, *altare*, *mensa*), as have some visual images (e.g., works by Jan van Eyck and Rogier van der Weyden). Mary was also a sacrificial "oven" in which Christ the "living bread" was placed to "bake" (e.g., a late-fifteenth-century English carol). Especially widespread since Augustine has been the equivalence of the Christ child on a manger in Bethlehem to the edible (eucharistic) Christ on a church altar. It seems that, from the very beginning of his life, Christ was being represented as a sacrificial victim, as Émile Mâle observed about certain medieval visual images where Mary has coldly deposited her newborn child on an elevated, altar-like manger.

All of this sacrificial imagery would eventually result in explicit representations of Mary as a priest. Early in the seventeenth century, Ferdinand Quirino de Salazar wrote of Mary that, "she offered and sacrificed him [Christ] on the altar of the cross, as did Christ himself." Mary's co-priesthood here should not be confused with the psychologically more comprehensible idea that Mary coredeemed humankind with her son at Golgotha. Both ideas imply considerable grandiosity on Mary's part, but, in the history of such representations, a coredemptive Mary is more likely to demonstrate compassion for her son than is a sacerdotal Mary.

By the late nineteenth century, an intensely mariophile papal magisterium was displaying sacerdotalist tendencies, but, around 1913–1914, the popular title *Virgo Sacerdos* was suppressed. Nevertheless, the twentieth-century papacy kept issuing implicit endorsements of Mary's priestly role. Feminists who have lobbied for the ordination of women to the priesthood would not be likely to support such endorsements, for in them the mother of one's God appears to be actively participating in a ritual murder.

Notes

1 Laurentin 1952–1953, vol. II, 214.
2 De Voragine 1850, 44; de Voragine 1993 (1850), vol. 1, 40 (and cf. Lane 1984, 21).
3 Lutz and Perdrizet, eds. 1907–1909, vol. 1, 12; and Ludolf of Saxony 1878, vol. 1, 22; both are quoted and translated in: Lane 1984, 20–23, 37 (nn. 29–30).
4 Meersseman 1958–1960, vol. 1, 141.
5 Meersseman 1958–1960, vol. 2, 110.
6 Meersseman 1958–1960, vol. 1, 108.
7 Maximus the Confessor 2012, 45.
8 I thank Stephen J. Shoemaker for this information (email of August 26, 2013).
9 Lampe 1961, 1399–1400 (see A4c, A6 for the marian usages).
10 Andrew of Crete 2008, 127, 136; Andrew of Crete 1860, cols. 868, 880.
11 Germanos of Constantinople 2008, 155; Germanos of Constantinople 1860b, col. 301.
12 Germanos of Constantinople 2008, 155, n. 59.
13 Germanos of Constantinople 2008, 156; Germanos of Constantinople 1860b, col. 304. In other works as well, Germanos utilizes imagery in this same vein – for example, "the golden altar for the burnt offerings," and "table, through which we who were starved of the bread of life have been filled beyond measure" (Cunningham 2008, 242, 255). One of the Latin examples of the representation of Mary as a table (*mensa*) quoted above came from Bishop Christopher's translation of a variant of the Akathistos attributed to Germanos. Not surprisingly, the original Greek word there as well is *trapeza* (Meersseman 1958–1960, vol. 1, 109 [54]; so also in the original Akathistos, Peltomaa 2001, 7 [5:11]). There is some indication that the Byzantine Greek notion of Mary as an altar reached Orthodox Rus' as well (Veselovskii 1881, 19 [Church Slavonic *prĕstol"*, *trapjeza svętaja*]; cf. Toporkov 1985, 239, n. 71). Some of the Old Testament background for marian table/altar imagery includes: Exodus 25:17–18, 23–30; 30:1–10; Leviticus 16:14; 24:5–9 (cf. Robert 1949, 27).
14 Lane 1984, 16. Lane interprets other images of Mary as an altar, such as: van Eyck's Dresden Triptych, *Madonna of Canon van der Paele*, and *Madonna of Chancellor Rolin*; Rogier van der Weyden's *Augustus and the Tiburtine Sibyl*; Petrus Christus' *Madonna with Saints Jerome and Francis* (Lane 1984, 16–25).
15 See: Lane 1984, 21 (and nn. 24–26, p. 37); Bynum 1991, 103 (and n. 65, p. 340).
16 Bynum 1991, 103.
17 O'Meara 1981, 83.
18 *Summa Theologiae, Prima Secundae*, question 102, article 3. See: Thomas Aquinas 2012, vol. 16, 326–327.
19 O'Meara 1981, 79.
20 Bynum 1991, 100.
21 Greene, ed. 1977 (1935), 194, no. 318 (a carol by the prolific Franciscan James Ryman, ca.1492); cf. Rubin 1991, 145; Kenney 2012, 54–55.
22 Bynum 1991, 103 (and n. 66, p. 340); cf. Williamson 2004, 390, 392.
23 Bynum 1991, 103 (and nn. 67, 68, p. 340), 219 (fig. 6.12).
24 Durand 1911, plate 9; Vloberg 1946, 262, 269–290; Guldan 1966, frontispiece, and discussion, p. 142 (cf. O'Reilly 1992, 193–196); Cardile 1984; Lane 1984, 71; Lechner 1993a; Heilbronner 2007–2008; Hamburger 2011, 12–13.
25 Hirn 1957 (1909), 337.
26 *Nicene and Post-Nicene Fathers* (first series), vol. VII, 435.

27 Google search of May 9, 2015.

28 Young 1962 (1933), vol. II, 25; cf. Marcus 2012 (1973), 8. For a wide-ranging historical study of the manger as altar, see: Kenney 2012.

29 As quoted by Kenney 2012, 47, from: Chrysostom 1860a, col. 79.

30 Lampe 1961, 1399 (under usages A3, A4c).

31 Augustine of Hippo 1841a, col. 1006, as translated in Augustine of Hippo 1952b, 100; cf. Kenney 2012, 48.

32 Augustine of Hippo 1841b, col. 1008, as translated in Augustine of Hippo 1952b, 104; cf. Kenney 2012, 48; Tubach 1981 (1969), no. 3558, *Ox and ass worship Christ-Child.*

33 Gregory the Great 1849a, col. 31D, as translated by Lane 1984, 53.

34 Gregory the Great 1849b, col. 1104A, as translated by Katzenellenbogen 1959, 12; cf. Marcus 2012 (1973), 6–7; Lane 1984, 53.

35 Walafrid Strabo 1852, col. 896C, with translation by Lane 1984, 53 (modified, DR-L).

36 Aelred of Rievaulx 1855, col. 227, as translated by Marcus 2012 (1973), 7.

37 Mâle 1925, 188.

38 Mâle lists some examples (1925, 188–189, n. 3). More images of the nativity in which the manger resembles an altar are to be found in Broussolle 1903, 3 (fig. 1), 8 (fig. 6), 9 (fig. 7), 10 (fig. 8).

39 Mâle 1925, 188.

40 For example, Fassler 2010, fig. 12.3 (Chartres, center lancet, panel 3, west façade). Cf. Mâle 1928, 109 (fig. 97).

41 For example: Grimoüard 1872–1875, vol. IV, 134, fig. 16 (thirteenth-century reliquary panel from the Vatican Museum); Mâle 1925, 188, fig. 98 (thirteenth-century Latin manuscript).

42 Grimoüard 1872–1875, vol. IV, 134.

43 Broussolle 1903, 10 (fig. 8), with commentary, p. 37; cf. Mâle 1925, 188, n. 2.

44 Mâle 1925, 188.

45 Katzenellenbogen 1959, 8 (see his fig. 10).

46 As translated by Katzenellenbogen 1959, 12, from Gregory the Great 1849b, col. 1104A.

47 Lane 1984, 50–60 (figs. 31, 38).

48 Lane 1984, fig. 32.

49 Guldan 1966, frontispiece, and discussion, p. 142; cf. O'Reilly 1992, 193–196.

50 For some related examples, see: Guldan 1966, figs. 152–159, as well as the informative discussion there of the art-historical and theological complexities of medieval arboreal symmetry (136–143). Cf. the analyses of symmetrical tree/cross configurations in: Füglister 1964; O'Reilly 1992, 180–201; Schreckenberg 1996, 31–66.

51 Vloberg 1946, 285.

52 O'Reilly 1992, 193 (emphasis added). In some of her visions, the mystic Saint Veronica Giuliani received communion from the hands of Mary. See: Perillo 2007, 262–266.

53 Füglister 1964, fig. IX; Guldan 1966, fig. 154.

54 Mary herself (in addition to *Ecclesia*) is depicted together with the tree of life in some other Living Cross images. See: Füglister 1964, figs. X, XII, XXIV, XXVI.

55 Guldan 1966, 138.

56 Füglister 1964, 41. Thanks to Livia Rosman for assistance in deciphering this banderole.

57 O'Carroll 2000 (1982), 292.

58 Bernard of Clairvaux 2004b, 280 (this portion of the sermon is nearly identical to the text in *Patrologia Latina* 183, col. 370 CD), as translated in: O'Carroll 2000 (1982), 292–293.
59 Laurentin 1952–1953, vol. I, 142–143.
60 The use of "victim," not "host" for *hostia* is appropriate here, because the context is not eucharistic, and because the English word "host" in the sense of a victim for sacrifice became obsolete after about 1653 (*Oxford English Dictionary* 1991, vol. VII, 417).
61 Laurentin 1947.
62 Laurentin 1952–1953, vol. I, 232–304.
63 Quoted in Dos Santos 1962, 55–56; translation from O'Carroll 2000 (1982), 317.
64 Quoted in Dos Santos 1962, 60; translation from O'Carroll 2000 (1982), 317; cf. Laurentin 1952–1953, vol. I, 252.
65 The Latin verbs that Salazar typically utilizes to depict what Mary does to her son on behalf of humankind include: *offere, sacrificare, mactare, immolare, litare* (see diagram in: Laurentin 1952–1953, vol. I, 247).
66 Laurentin 1952–1953, vol. I, 245–246.
67 Quoted in Dos Santos 1962, 52, n. 63; translation (modified) from O'Carroll 2000 (1982), 317.
68 Laurentin 1952–1953, vol. I, 246.
69 Jeanjacquot 1871 (1868), 99–100; Pourrat 1949, 814; Laurentin 1952–1953, vol. I, 402.
70 Laurentin 1952–1953, vol. I, 402.
71 The Latin *coredemptrix* (*conredemptrix, corredemptrix*) is normally rendered as *corédemptrice* (French), *corredentora* (Spanish), *corredentrice* (Italian), *Miterlöserin* (German). In the West, the concept goes back at least to the early sixteenth century. In the Orthodox East, the concept of a coredeemer is generally absent (apparently no Greek equivalent of the term exists; Russian *соискупительница* [*soiskupitel'nitsa*] is a somewhat artificial-sounding rendition of the Roman Catholic mariological term). Useful scholarly and theological sources on the coredemption (or lack thereof) by Mary include: Druwé 1949; Laurentin 1951 (a valuable historical survey); Dillenschneider 1951; Boyer 1952; Von Simson 1953 (striking similarity of a swooning Mary's bodily attitude to Christ's body as it is being taken down from the cross helps the viewer understand that she is *co-redemptrix*) Carroll 1955, 35–40; Galot 1957; Carol 1957 ("final decision" on question of Mary's coredemption is up to the Supreme Pontiff, not theologians or historians); Bonano 1957 (Mary's own death after her son's death on the cross is coredemptive); Alastruey 1963–1964 (1952), vol. II, 138–152; Miegge 1955, 155–177; Graef 2009 (1963–1965), 371–378, 396–397; Hunt 1964 (ecumenical aspects of Mary's coredemption); Laurentin 1965, 102–107 (why the topic was skirted at Vatican II); Roschini 1969, vol. II, 116–198; Finkenzeller 1992; entry on "Redemption" in O'Carroll 2000 (1982), 305–309; Miravalle 1996; Calkins 1996; Keeler 2003; Galot 2005; Hauke 2007; Calkins 2007, 2008; Dillard 2009 (invents an amusing "Marian mathematics" to rebut the thesis of Mary's coredemption); Stephen J. Shoemaker's Introduction to Maximus the Confessor 2012, 25–35; Reynolds 2012–, 107–151 (on Mary's "remote co-operation"); 246–292 (on Mary's "immediate co-redemption"). Current advocacy for papal recognition of Mary's coredemptive role may be read on the web: www.fifth mariandogma.com (accessed September 15, 2015).
72 Sticca 1988, 19–30.
73 Fulton 2002, 425, 427, 457.

74 As translated from an Italian vernacular by Barnet and Wu 2005, 120.

75 Williamson 2000, 50. Visual representations of this type of double intercession may be linked to the writings of Arnold of Bonneval (Perdrizet 1908, 251–252; Laurentin 1952–1953, vol. I, 148). For various late-medieval texts in which Mary pleads on behalf of sinners by exposing her breast(s) to God (either the Father or the Son), see: Perdrizet 1908, 237–252. See also: Panofsky 1927 (esp. 283–292); Meiss 1954 (historical study of the Cloisters picture); Koepplin 1970; Thomas 1974, 240–242; an analysis of the Cloisters picture by Luciano Bellosi, in Tartuferi and Parenti, eds. 2006, 161–166; Miles 2008, 8, and plate 2; Boespflug 2012, index entry "Intercession (Double)," 445.

76 *Nicene and Post-Nicene Fathers* (second series), vol. 10, 473. Cf. Laurentin 1952–1953, vol. I, 150.

77 See also: Laurentin 1952–1953, vol. I, 150.

78 Arnold of Bonneval 1854a, col. 1694B, C, as translated by Reynolds 2012–, 275.

79 Laurentin 1952–1953, vol. I, 150–151 (and nn. 63–67).

80 Arnold of Bonneval 1854b, col. 1727A, as translated by O'Carroll 2000 (1982), 51.

81 Laurentin 1952–1953, vol. I, 146 ff., especially the second paragraph of p. 153.

82 Laurentin 1952–1953, vol. I, 151.

83 Galot 2005, 175.

84 Neither Laurentin nor Galot addresses Arnold's violation of this presupposition in the "one holocaust" statement.

85 Laurentin 1952–1953, vol. I, 153.

86 See: Laurentin 1951, 425. For a detailed study of the attitude of the teaching church and of the Holy See toward the priesthood of Mary in the period 1872–1916, see: Laurentin 1952–1953, vol. I, 509–537.

87 See especially: *Acta Apostolicae Sedis* (1916, vol. 8, p. 146). Cf. Laurentin 1948, 165–169; Lécuyer 1954, 80–81; O'Carroll 2000 (1982), 122, 293–294.

88 *Papal Teachings: Our Lady* 1961, 126–127; *Acta Sanctae Sedis* (vol. 27, p. 178).

89 *Papal Teachings: Our Lady* 1961, 127; *Acta Sanctae Sedis* (vol. 27, p. 178).

90 *Papal Teachings: Our Lady* 1961, 172; *Acta Sanctae Sedis* (vol. 36, p. 453). Compare this pope's letter *Ubere cum fructu* of 1911, where it is asserted that, "in the presence and under the very gaze of Mary . . . the divine sacrifice of our redemption was consummated; she took part in it by giving to the world and nourishing the divine Victim" (*Papal Teachings: Our Lady* 1961, 186).

91 Keeler 2003, 276.

92 O'Carroll 2000 (1982), 293.

93 *Papal Teachings: Our Lady* 1961, 194; *Acta Apostolicae Sedis* (vol. 10, p. 182).

94 *Acta Apostolicae Sedis* (vol. 35, p. 247, emphasis added); *Papal Teachings: Our Lady* 1961, 253; cf. Laurentin 1991 (1968), 240, n. 5.

95 Laurentin 1948, 161–162 (n. 3, emphasis added).

96 *Acta Apostolicae Sedis* (vol. 87, p. 520) as translated in: John Paul II 2001 (1996), 761 (emphasis added).

97 See: above, pp. 264–265; Calkins 1996, 135 (where John Paul II quotes Bernard in a catechesis of October 25, 1995).

98 *Acta Apostolicae Sedis* (vol. 87, p. 520), as translated in: John Paul II 2001 (1996), 761; cf. Calkins 1996, 137.

99 *Acta Apostolicae Sedis* (vol. 87, p. 520), as translated in: John Paul II 2001 (1996), 761.

100 As quoted by Calkins (2007, 25) from the weekly edition in English of *L'Osservatore Romano*, no. 788, June 13, 1983, p. 2.

101 Calkins 2007, 25.
102 *L'Osservatore Romano*, no. 788, June 13, 1983, p. 2 (emphasis added).
103 See, for example: Raming 2004 (1976); Macy 2007.
104 Beattie 2002 (1999), 205.
105 Beattie 2002 (1999), 205.
106 Miegge 1955, 179 (emphasis added).
107 Congrès Marial National 1948, opposite pp. 7, 14.
108 The exceptions. The Servite priest Augustin.-M. Lépicier writes of Mary heroically offering her son *sur l'autel de la Croix*, and refers to Saint Lawrence Justinian's characterization of Mary as *Vierge-prêtre*; M. Moreton, speaking to seminarians, refers to the hymn about *Virgo Sacerdos* (Congrès Marial National 1948, 175, 176, 302, resp.).
109 Johnson 2003, 8 (emphasis added).
110 Beattie believes that "the male fear of women" has been the primary obstacle blocking both the inclusion of women in the Catholic priesthood and the formal recognition of Mary's priesthood. See: Beattie 2002 (1999), 198–206.
111 *Lumen Gentium* pars. 10, 11, 34 in: Tanner, ed. 1990, vol. 2, 856–857, 877. See also the entry "Priesthood," in O'Donnell 1996, 386–388 (with rich bibliography).
112 Tanner, ed. 1990, vol. 2, par. 11, 857.
113 Tanner, ed. 1990, vol. 2, par. 10, 857.
114 O'Neill 1991, 222–223; cf. Calkins 1996, 135.
115 O'Neill 1991, 223–224.
116 O'Neill 1991, 227.
117 O'Neill 1991, 227.

15 Our Lady of the Good Death

The Virgin will wait; she will not be angry; she knows her power; we all come back to her in the end. – Henry Adams[1]

Death and the True Body in the Host

One of the finest poetical-musical compositions linking the eucharist to Mary is the dark – but sublime – hymn, *Ave verum corpus.* Its author is anonymous, and the precise time of origin is unknown. Already by the beginning of the fourteenth century, it was being sung. It became most widely known as a hymn to be sung during the mass at the elevation of the host, and could also have been recited silently as a preparation for receiving communion. Nowadays, it is best known as the exquisite choral composition by Mozart. Of the available variants, Dreves and Blume offer the following:

Ave, verum corpus natum
Ex Maria virgine,
Vere passum, immolatum
In cruce pro homine,
Cuius latus perforatum
Vero fluxit sanguine,
Esto nobis praegustatum
Mortis in examine
O dulcis, o pie,
O fili Mariae.
Hail, true body, born
Of the Virgin Mary,
You who truly suffered and was immolated
On the cross for humankind,
You whose pierced side
Flowed with true blood,
May you be for us a foretaste
Of the ordeal of death
O sweet, O holy,
O son of Mary.[2]

The eucharistic essence of this work is clear from the start. The "true body" that is "born" in the first line must be the communion host, for it would hardly have been necessary to assert that the body that Mary originally gave birth to was the "true" body of her son. That was already obvious. The hymn takes for granted what Mary accomplished centuries ago, and transubstantiation is a given. As Maurice Vloberg says of the opening distich, "the Eucharist renews the Incarnation, it causes the same Christ, born of the Virgin Mary, to be reborn in the form of Bread [*elle fait renaître sous la forme du Pain le même Christ né de la Vierge Marie*]."[3] Such words are in the spirit of the oft-repeated *O veneranda* exclamation, and they reflect as well the beliefs of mariophile eucharistic literalists such as Peter Damian and others, discussed earlier.

Although *Ave verum corpus* is clearly a hymn to the eucharist, one might be forgiven for thinking that it is also about Mary.[4] Christ the host/victim is not even named, although the poem's lyric persona does hail the host/victim at the beginning of the poem (*Ave, verum corpus*), and does call out to the host/victim with a vocative form (*O fili*) at the end. By contrast, the mother of the host/victim is actually named with a proper noun (*Maria*) – and that twice, once in the opening distich, and once in the closing distich.

From a structural viewpoint, it may be said that the hymn is framed, or enclosed, by the explicit references to Mary. This leaves an impression that the unnamed, eucharistic Christ is still Mary's charge, still "held" by her after having been born of her (as in the folk motif of a "child in the host"). Yet, at the same time, the person who is in fact holding the *verum corpus* in his hands is not even mentioned in the hymn – namely, the priest. It is the priest, after all, who effects the "conversion" (Aquinas) of bread and wine into the "true body" and "true blood" of Christ. One might ask: is *verum corpus natum ex Maria virgine*, or is *verum corpus natum ex . . . sacerdote*? Indeed, is it possible that these two figures – *virgo* and *sacerdos* – are even the same person? As we have seen, that would eventually become a serious question in the history of mariology.

For the late-medieval time being, however, the correct view expressed by the poem was that the "true body" in the eucharist was the same body to which Mary gave birth. That body was also the one that later "truly suffered" and shed "true blood" while hanging from the cross. By consuming the eucharistic version of the body and blood of Christ, believers obtained a "foretaste" of the ordeal of death – captured with impressive emotional force in the English translation of Edward Caswall:

> Suffer us to taste of Thee,
> In our life's last agony.[5]

This is, of course, the same ordeal that calls for Mary's intercession in the second part of the Hail Mary (*Ave Maria*), which, by the middle of the sixteenth century, was complete in the form familiar to Catholics today:

> Sancta Maria,
> Mater Dei,
> Ora pro nobis peccatoribus,
> Nunc et in hora mortis nostrae.
> Amen.
> Holy Mary,
> mother of God,
> pray for us sinners,
> Now and at the hour of our death.
> Amen.[6]

Both the second part of *Ave Maria* and the final lines of *Ave verum corpus* focus attention on the believer's own mortality. Both also bring Mary to the scene of death. In both works, the frightening task of facing death is made at least somewhat easier by an imagined maternal presence. Like us, Mary's son was mortal. But, after he died, he rose from the dead. There is hope.

Unlike *Ave Maria*, there is no explicit request for intercession in *Ave verum corpus*. Mary is just "there," she is implicitly available in our time of need, without our having to say so. Indeed, her merely lexical presence in the final invocation of her unnamed son – *O . . . fili Mariae* – serves quite well enough to signify our desperate need for the son's mother, not only the son himself, at the hour of death.

The "foretaste" of death in *Ave verum corpus* was not only gustatory, but also horrifyingly visual. The cross of Christ, with its suggestively vertical dimension, comes to mind. Jesus said, "And I, when I am *lifted up* from the earth, will draw all people to myself" (John 12:32), and the gospel writer immediately adds: "He said this to indicate the kind of death he was to die" (12:33). So too the host, the eucharistic metaphor for the true body of Christ, was *elevated* by the priest. Hearing the choir commence singing *Ave verum corpus* right at the moment of the elevation must have been an especially poignant reminder of death. As Dumoutet suggests in this connection, one of the effects promised to those who viewed the elevated host must have been *une très spéciale assistance à l'heure suprême.*[7]

A poignant example of how important *Ave verum corpus* could be for devout believers, even in our own day, is offered by the late Pope John Paul II. In his encyclical *Ecclesia de Eucharistia*, the Polish pope expresses a profound emotional attachment to the eucharist. Well known lines from *Ave verum corpus* serve as a vehicle for conveying what the pope felt on this occasion:

> Allow me, dear brothers and sisters, to share with deep emotion, as a means of accompanying and strengthening your faith, my own testimony of faith in the Most Holy Eucharist. *Ave verum corpus natum de Maria Virgine, vere passum, immolatum, in cruce pro homine!* Here is the Church's treasure, the heart of the world, the pledge of the fulfillment [*pignus metae*] for which each man and woman, even unconsciously, yearns.

Why, exactly, is the eucharist a "treasure," or "the heart of the world"? What "pledge" is made by the eucharistic representation of Christ's crucifixion, the "fulfillment" of which believers yearn for?

These questions are answered by what the pope sees in the eucharistic elements:

> Each day my faith has been able to recognize in the consecrated bread and wine the divine Wayfarer [*divinum Peregrinatorem agnovit*] who joined the two disciples on the road to Emmaus and opened their eyes to the light and their hearts to new hope (cf. Lk 24:13–35).[8]

This "divine Wayfarer" was of course an apparition of the newly risen Christ. If, day after day, over many decades, Karol Wojtyla could contemplate the lifeless eucharistic elements and see in them, not only a dead Christ on the cross, but also a resurrected Christ on the road to Emmaus, then he must have been a most optimistic and credulous man. For the "Wayfarer" in question was the one who had made a "pledge" to the disciples before he was crucified: "Those who eat my flesh and drink my blood have eternal life, and I will raise them up on the last day" (John 6:54). This simple recipe for immortality is "the Church's treasure, the heart of the world," and, more importantly, it is the "pledge" that the pope believed would be fulfilled at the end of time.

Mary, who, according to the pope, received the eucharist after her son died, enters this picture as the one for whom the "pledge" has been already fulfilled:

> Gazing upon Mary, we come to know *the transforming power present in the Eucharist.* In her we see the world renewed in love. Contemplating her, assumed body and soul into heaven, we see opening up before us those "new heavens" and that "new earth" [Revelation 21:1] which will appear at the second coming of Christ.[9]

In the case of Christ, reports of his resurrection followed not long after the crucifixion. In the case of ordinary mortals (*except Mary*), resurrection would have to wait until some point in the future. As for living Christian believers, they are still waiting. Deceased believers, including the good Pope John Paul II, are no longer troubled by the issue of resurrection – or any other issue.[10]

Marian Societies of the Good Death

Ave verum corpus is a pungent reminder of death, its final invocation also reminding believers of their potential recourse in the face of death. The second part of the Hail Mary prayer is more explicit, bringing Mary right to the deathbed of the individual believer ("at the hour of our death"). Of all the saints, Mary was in fact the one most likely (after the celestial court) to receive explicit or implicit requests for intercession at the hour of death. There were many poems, prayers, hymns, and other texts on this theme.[11] In the West, after Trent, however, it was the Hail Mary (multiplied many times over in recitation of the rosary) that became the most popular vehicle of all for requesting a last chance at eternal life – that is, an opportunity to experience a *good death*.

Consider a document from the middle of the twentieth century. A certificate registering the membership of one Madame Leopold Langlois in the Association de Notre-Dame de la Bonne Mort (Charlemagne, Assomption County, Province of Quebec) is dated March 6, 1949. Had Madame wished to register for "first degree" membership in the Association, she would only have to have signed up, without having to satisfy any other requirements. The certificate states that Madame has registered for "second degree" membership. This means that every morning and evening she is to recite three Hail Marys, along with the invocation, "Our Lady of the Good Death, pray for us" (300 days indulgence each time, a plenary indulgence once a month). Had she signed up for "third degree" membership, she would have obliged herself to say the three morning and evening Hail Marys, plus perform an examination of conscience every evening, as well as perform a *petite récollection et préparation à la mort chaque mois* (plenary indulgence), preferably on the last Saturday (a marian holiday) of each month.[12] What the two highest degrees of membership in the Association have in common is repeated recitation of the Hail Mary prayer, with its key request for Mary's intercession "at the hour of our death."

"Our Lady of the Good Death" is not a well-known marian title. To my knowledge, there is no prefiguration of her in the Christian Old Testament. She is not known in the world of Eastern Orthodoxy. Properly speaking, she is a Roman Catholic invention, a distant offshoot of the "Good Death" (*Bona Mors*) confraternity founded in 1648 by Jesuit general Vincenzo Carafa (1585–1649).[13]

In principle, any Christian sinner who believes that Mary can intercede with her son on the sinner's behalf already has implicit awareness of Our Lady of the Good Death. That awareness comes close to being explicit at the end of the Hail Mary prayer. So, too, in wishes expressed by some Catholics imagining how they would like to die. A sample of Catholic testamentary records from sixteenth-century Paris shows that people wanted marian intercession above all when their lives came to an end.[14] Eighteenth-century testators in Nice wished for intercession by Mary (often termed *l'Immacolata* locally) in the overwhelming majority of cases.[15] In nineteenth-century Bahia, Brazil, testators also preferred Mary over other saints.[16]

The idea that Mary can facilitate a "good death" caught on in primarily French-speaking areas of the Catholic world. However, there are other parts of the world where Our Lady of the Good Death has had and still has a presence. In post-communist Poland, there exists a Society of the Mother of God, Patron of the Good Death (*Stowarzyszenie Matki Bożej Patronki*

Dobrej Śmierci).[17] Portuguese-speaking Catholics have a history of familiarity with *Nossa Senhora da Boa Morte*. In Portugal, brotherhoods of Our Lady of the Good Death go back to the seventeenth century. In Brazil, this cult figure is best known from various locales in the province of Bahia. In the town of Cachoeira, for example, there was a lay sisterhood "of the Good Death," which celebrated the death (assumption) of Mary with mourning, processions with images of Mary, dancing, and food for a week in mid-August (August 15 being the official Catholic feast of Mary's death, which, had it really been her "assumption" into heaven, would have been a "good death" indeed).[18] Oral history suggests that this organization was originally a group of African women freed from slavery, probably dating from the early nineteenth century.[19] In the provincial capital of Salvador, the story is similar and is well documented for the nineteenth century. In August, as João José Reis relates, it was the custom for some brotherhoods and convents in Salvador to commemorate Our Lady of the Good Death. At one of these – organized by a black confraternity – a procession would carry "the dead Lady's [Mary's] bier" from a church to a convent, and back. Afterwards, "a huge banquet was held, with plenty of food, wine, and liqueurs to accompany the Virgin's wake."[20]

Confraternities of *Notre Dame de la bonne mort* were established in various places in nineteenth-century France, for example in: Le Puy (1824), Orsinval (1857), and Clermont-Ferrand (1864).[21] A black madonna dating to the second half of the twelfth century in the cathedral of Clermont-Ferrand is called *Notre-Dame de la Bonne Mort*.[22] Of considerable historical significance in France was the founding, in 1865, of the Association de Notre-Dame de la Bonne Mort in Tinchebray (in Orne, Normandy). The Tinchebray association received formal papal approval (with indulgences) from Benedict XV in his apostolic letter *Inter sodalicia* of March 22, 1918: "The choosing and invoking of Our Lady of Sorrows as patroness of a happy death [*Virgo Perdolens bonae mortis Patrona*] is in full conformity with Catholic Doctrine and with the pious sentiment of the Church."[23] Appended to the pope's letter is the Latin novena prayer *Recordare* entreating Mary to grant the supplicant assistance in achieving a good death. This prayer includes the line:

> *Nostra Domina a bona morte, ora pro nobis.*[24]
> Our Lady of the Good Death, pray for us.

Also appended to the apostolic letter is a *rhythmus* "in honor of Our Lady of the Good Death." Clearly, Pope Benedict XV was a supporter of the cult of Our Lady of the Good Death.

Tinchebray was a pilgrimage destination for French civilians during the German occupation of France in World War II.[25] The work of the Tinchebray association continued until recently. At one point, 6,000 readers subscribed to the association's journal, *Espérance et vie* (formerly *Bulletin de Notre-Dame de la Bonne-Mort*).[26] Publication of the journal appears to have ceased in 2002.[27] A letter of June 15, 2015 to the last known address of the association was returned to me unopened.

Mary at One's Deathbed, and After

Why would the presence of Mary at one's deathbed make for a "good death"? The theologically correct answer (but with paltry biblical foundation) is that Mary has special access to her son and is naturally inclined to intercede with him on behalf of the individual Christian. Both Mary and her son, moreover, have already conquered death – she by her assumption into heaven, he by his resurrection and ascension into heaven. What better recourse could a believer seek than Christianity's two successfully deified humans?

Of course, Mary had not been able to save her own son from death on the cross. But, to judge from what we have seen of the abundant post-biblical passion narratives, poetry, dramaturgy, visual arts, and other ways of representing the crucifixion (but excluding the writings of marian sacerdotalists), Mary certainly would have *wished* that such a terrible fate had not befallen her son, and she would have *tried* to save him if that had been possible. Nevertheless, there is a fundamental contrast between what Our Lady of the Good Death supposedly can do for believing mortals who are about to die, and what Mary could *not* do for her dying son. Simple mortals have long needed Mary's help in dying, but Jesus Christ, thank you, managed death on his own.

All adult believers understand at some level that death is inevitable, and that the result of death is a corpse. And besides, even Mary (non-biblically) and Jesus (biblically) died before their deaths were canceled by subsequent denialist theologies. Ordinary mortals, in any case, are obliged to die. But, orthodox theology holds that something of the individual mortal does not go into the ground with the corpse, and continues to live forever. This immortal something is called the *soul*, which may be thought of as a reified denial of the body's death. Here is where Mary can be of assistance in facilitating a "good death" for the believer.

Mary is not particularly interested in preventing physical death from happening, but believers hope that the "Mother of Mercy" will nevertheless be inclined to intercede with her divine son on their behalf. It is especially important that Mary intercede on behalf of one who is about to die – that is, one who may be burdened with sins that could ultimately block the way to heaven. That, after all, is the meaning of the final words of supplication in the Hail Mary prayer: "pray for us, *sinners*, now and *at the hour of our death*." If Mary intervenes at a time close enough to death that it would be extremely unlikely for the sinner then to commit a (mortal) sin, and if (as has long been commonly believed) her son is inclined to grant her wish and forgive the sinner, then the sinner will be able to die in peace, knowing that his or her *soul* will have been saved from eternal perdition in a place called hell.[28]

True, the sinner's soul may be obliged to spend some time in a place (or a state) of suffering and deprivation that Catholics call purgatory, before being allowed to enter, body and soul, into heaven after the general resurrection and the final judgment.[29] But, Mary's timely intercession will have saved the sinner, who ultimately ends up in heaven. If this was not clear from the above-quoted comments made by Pope Benedict XV in 1918 regarding the Tinchebray Association of Our Lady of the Good Death, then the apostolic letter *Explorata res est* of Pope Pius XI (1923) clinched the matter in categorical fashion:

> He will not taste death forever, who in his dying moments has recourse to the Blessed Virgin Mary [*neque enim is mortem oppetat sempiternam, cui Beatissima Virgo, praesertim in discrimine ultimo, adfuerit*].[30]

Such is the mariophile Catholic's idea of a happy death. Ordinary atheists may not be impressed by such wishful thinking, but today's clinical psychologists and psychoanalysts certainly ought to be aware of this thinking when dealing with Catholic patients who face end-of-life issues.

As for the dead themselves, they (except those already in heaven) cannot pray – to Mary or to anyone else. But, some of the living faithful have believed that Mary can intercede even on behalf of the dead. For example, a few have expressed the view that Mary will be able to save those already condemned by her son to burn forever in hell at the final judgement.[31] Some others have believed that Mary has an ability to intercede on behalf of those deceased who are merely burning in the flames of purgatory. For example, Frederick William Faber (1814–1863) composed a hymn on this theme titled "The Queen of Purgatory," which opens:

> O turn to Jesus, Mother! turn,
> And call Him by His tenderest names;
> Pray for the Holy Souls that burn
> This hour amid the cleansing flames.[32]

Since the seventeenth century, there have been scattered references to Mary as "Our Lady of Suffrage," that is, a version of Mary who intercedes specifically for members of the church who are suffering in purgatory.[33] Even here, however, theological works about Mary's ability to intercede on behalf of the dead in purgatory have been rather sparse, and the authenticity of some of them is questionable.[34] Various exempla, other narratives, and a few visual images from the middle–late-medieval period on refer to Mary's intercession for souls in purgatory.[35] There is also the famous apocryphal papal bull declaring that, if any members of the Carmelite Order and its confraternities who satisfied certain requirements during their lifetime went to purgatory upon death, they would be liberated by Mary on the very next Saturday (hence their "Sabbatine Privilege") and brought directly to heaven.[36] In this case, we may say that the usual Christian denial of death is augmented by a narcissistic sense of entitlement specific to Carmelites.

Saint Alphonsus de Liguori

Generally speaking, when it comes to applying for Mary's intercession, by far the most prevalent prayers and practices have concerned intercession on behalf of members of the church militant – that is, on behalf of those who are still alive and struggling against sin here on Earth.

Saint Alphonsus de Liguori (1696–1787) was an ardent mariophile who believed in the importance of gaining Mary's intercession just before death. In a prayer to Mary he wrote: "I am resolved to save my soul. Therefore I place my eternal salvation into your hands and I offer myself to you." The assumption that Alphonsus goes on to make explicit here reflects the pious hope of mariophiles everywhere, but is also theologically questionable: "Speak in my favor: Your Son does whatever you ask of him."[37] The prayer closes:

> Protect me, therefore, my Mother, and obtain for me the pardon of my sins, a love for Jesus, holy perseverance, *a good death*, and heaven at last. It is true that I am undeserving of these favors, but if you ask the Lord for them for me, I will obtain them. Pray then to Jesus for me. O Mary, my Queen, I trust in you. On this hope I rely. In this hope I live and with it I hope to die. Amen.[38]

Another prayer ends in similar fashion:

> Through you I hope to die *a good death*. O my Mother, by the love which you bear to God, I beg you to help me at all times but especially at the last moments of my life. Do not leave me, I pray you, until you see me safe in heaven; blessing you and singing your mercies for all eternity. Amen. So I hope. So may it be.[39]

Alphonsus does not explicitly name Our Lady of the Good Death here, but surely it is she whom he addresses when he calls out, "O my Mother."

It is said that Alphonsus died while holding an image of Mary.[40] On the evidence of his later canonization as a saint, it seems likely that Alphonsus was granted his wish for a good death, and it is certain that he was granted his wish for "heaven at last." However, those for whom canonization is not evidence will understand that Alphonsus is simply dead.

Blessed Daniel Brottier

A booklet from the Association de Notre-Dame de la Bonne Mort in Tinchebray offers a more recent example of a mariophile's hope in the face of death. Father Daniel Brottier (1876–1936, beatified 1984) was famous for his brave service as a French chaplain in World War I, for his missionary work in Senegal, and for his administration of the Auteuil Orphanage in a Paris suburb. On a piece of paper found in Brottier's breviary was the following prayer:

> At the hour of my death, Oh Mary, whom I have invoked so many times, be close by my bed. Be there the way my mother would be there if she were still alive. Perhaps my paralyzed tongue will no longer be able to say your name, but my heart will always repeat it . . . I call you now for this awful moment. Will I be alone, expiring far away from all help? . . . alone without a dear hand to close my eyes? I will die smiling, because you will be there. I hope so. I believe it. I am certain of it.[41]

In this prayer, the final phrases of which bear a certain resemblance to the phraseology of the two prayers of Alphonsus quoted above, Brottier expresses great confidence in Mary. Brottier does accept the fact that he will die. The need to have Mary at his bedside is premised on that acceptance. The specifically maternal nature of the comfort Mary will provide is also openly expressed, for Brottier compares what Mary will do for him with what his mother would have done for him if she were still alive – that is, what his real mother probably had done for him in times of need in the past. Brottier's earliest personal model for what Mary could be was what his own mother was.

The real mother quickly vanishes from the picture, however. A reality check ("if she were still alive") permits the entry of the normal Roman Catholic mother-substitute, Mary, who is also dead, yet very much alive in the belief structure of the Catholic faith. Brottier's call for Mary's help is quite upbeat and positive. The certainty with which the good Father affirms Mary's future arrival at his deathbed reflects the high frequency with which he has repeated his Hail Marys in the past ("whom I have invoked so many times"). It does not matter that he may not be able to speak before he dies, or that he may not be able to close his eyes after he dies. These are merely physical, corporeal matters. His *soul* will have flown away – all the way to heaven, indeed, if the hopes of those who succeeded in getting him beatified are fulfilled by his canonization as a saint.

Daniel Brottier suffered from chronic ill health. He died after a short but painful illness on February 28, 1936, in the Hospital of Saint Joseph in Paris. He was buried at the Chapel of Saint Thérèse in Auteuil on April 5, 1936. As his mother Herminie (*née* Bouthe) had predeceased him, she could not be present at his bedside when he died. As Miryam of Nazareth had died many centuries earlier, she too could not be present with him at his deathbed, although his prayerful wish that his *Marie* be with him at the hour of death may well have been fulfilled in some hallucinatory fashion as he lay dying. We will never know. In any case, he no longer suffers, for he no longer exists.[42]

Father Brottier's attitude toward coming death was structured in an orderly, intellectualized fashion. The man was a priest, a well-educated representative of the Roman Catholic faith as it existed in the first half of the twentieth century. He was certainly aware of the possibility of receiving the "last rites" for the dying – that is, the sacraments of penance, extreme unction (now anointing of the sick), and the eucharist as viaticum ('provision for the final journey'). But Brottier also wanted Mary to be present, not only her son (in eucharistic form). He was a true believer who took out near-total insurance coverage against eternal damnation, not understanding that total annihilation makes such insurance irrelevant.

On the other hand, the thought that Mary would be present at his deathbed was clearly therapeutic for Brottier. Marian therapy can never be denied to Mary's patients, for Mary needs only to be wished into existence for that therapy to be available.

*

Both the late medieval hymn *Ave verum corpus* and the traditional Catholic prayer *Ave Maria* bring a maternal Mary to the scene of the believer's death. This gives the believer an opportunity to ask for Mary's intercession with her son who, after all, escaped death himself by rising from the dead. There are many poems, prayers, and hymns on this theme. Various marian societies of "the good death" came into existence in the post-medieval West (but not in the Orthodox East). "Our Lady of the Good Death" has been venerated at various times in France, Portugal, Brazil, Poland, and elsewhere.

The contrast between what Mary did *not* do in the presence of her dying son and what she *might* do for others who are dying is here explored. At one end of the range of options is extreme credulity, where believers (e.g., Saint Alphonsus de Liguori, the Blessed Daniel Brottier) are absolutely certain that Mary will intervene on their behalf in the final moments. At the other end is atheist realism, where it is recognized that all humans die and remain dead, including Mary the goddess and her son, Jesus the god.

Notes

1 Adams 1986 (1904), 184.
2 Dreves and Blume 1909, vol. II, 218–219; translation adapted from Brittain 1962, 275. For historical information, see: Dumoutet 1926, 61–62, 86; Dumoutet 1932, 169–170, 173–174, 178; Wilmart 1971 (1932), 373, n. 1; 376; 377, n. 1, item #8; 379, n. 1; Jungmann 1951 (1949), vol. II, 216.
3 Vloberg 1946, 269.
4 For example, *Ave verum corpus* is included in the marian devotional collection of Miles, ed. 2001, 82–83.
5 Caswall 1884 (1949), 249.
6 Ayo 1994, 210. On the historical development of the *Ave Maria* prayer, see: Thurston 1953, 90–114; De Marco 1967; O'Carroll 2000 (1982), 165–166; the

entry *Ave Maria* (multiple sections, multiple authors) in *Marienlexikon* (Bäumer and Scheffczyk, eds. 1988–1994, vol. 1, 309–317, with bibliographies); Ayo 1994, 9–12 (a brief but useful historical overview).

7 Dumoutet 1932, 170.

8 John Paul II 2003, 64; *Acta Apostolicae Sedis* (vol. 95, p. 472).

9 John Paul II 2003, 67; *Acta Apostolicae Sedis* (vol. 95, p. 474).

10 For an examination of the psychoanalytic structures supporting a belief in resurrection from the dead, see: Rancour-Laferriere 2011, 121–138.

11 Here are some examples from G. G. Meersseman's rich two-volume compendium (1958–1960):

Ave, pia, hora mortis, da ius, michi prime sortis (I, 189; from a twelfth-century hymn of greeting).

. . . *in hora mortis nostre et in die iudicii cum gloriosissimo filio tuo veni in adiutorium nostrum* (II, 233; from an All Saints litany of the fifteenth century).

In hora mortis, succurre nobis, domina (II, 250; from a Flanders rhyme-litany of the fifteenth century).

From eleventh-century Winchester comes a litany with the invocation, *Sancta Maria, adiuua me in die exitus mei ex hac praesenti uita* (as quoted by Clayton 1990, 111). Those who still pray from the *Little Office of the Blessed Virgin Mary* address Mary with the words, *Tu nos ab hoste protege, / Et mortis hora suscipe* (Keller, ed. 2013, 38, 43, 47, 52, 68).

12 Lessard 1981, 88.

13 McDonnell 1967, 655.

14 Chaunu 1978, 309.

15 Vovelle 1989, 681.

16 Reis 2003 (1991), 209.

17 See: www.apostolstwo.pl/?p=main&what=40 (accessed June 10, 2015).

18 On Mary's death as a model for the right way to die, see: Schreiner 2006 (1996), 474–477.

19 On the practices in Cachoeira see, for example: Roca 2005, 191–197.

20 Reis 2003 (1991), 118.

21 Dates given are dates of ephemera published on the occasion of establishing a confraternity of *Notre Dame de la bonne mort*. These works are listed in OCLC WorldCat: www.worldcat.org/search?qt=worldcat_org_all&q=Notre+Dame+de+la+bonne+mort%2C+Orsinval; www.worldcat.org/search?qt=worldcat_org_all&q=Notre+Dame+de+la+bonne+mort%2C+Le+Puy; www.worldcat.org/search?qt=worldcat_org_all&q=Notre+Dame+de+la+bonne+mort%2C+Clermont-Ferrand (accessed August 26, 2017).

22 Cassagnes-Brouquet 2000, 84, 85 (figure).

23 *Papal Teachings: Our Lady* 1961, 193; *Acta Apostolicae Sedis* (vol. 10, pp. 181–182).

24 *Acta Apostolicae Sedis* (vol. 10, p. 185; cf. vol. 3 [1911], p. 265, where Pope Pius X addresses words of encouragement to the head of the Tinchebray Fathers on the same topic).

25 Bourdin 1992, 488.

26 Estin 1993, 26.

27 To judge from the cessation of entries in the general catalogue of Bibliothèque nationale de France: http://catalogue.bnf.fr/rechercher.do?motRecherche=Bulletin%20de%20Notre-Dame%20de%20la%20Bonne-Mort (accessed August 27, 2017).

28 Many apocrypha, miracle tales, visions, religious images, etc., downplay or skip altogether the intercessory element, giving Mary enormous (and theologically incorrect) power to save sinners on her own. For a very readable overview (with bibliography), see: Warner 1983 (1976), 321–331.

29 For an overview of the notion of purgatory in the Bible and in Catholic theology, see: Cevetello and Bastian, 1967. See also these historical studies: Le Goff 1984 (1981); Cuchet 2005; Pasulka 2015.

30 *Papal Teachings: Our Lady* 1961, 205; *Acta Apostolicae Sedis* (vol. 15, p. 104).

31 Clayton 1990, 253–255 (texts from Anglo-Saxon England).

32 Faber 1862, 164.

33 Cuchet 2005, 92.

34 See, for example: Mother Mary of the Visitation (Mère Marie de la Visitation) 1958.

35 For example: Le Goff 1984 (1981), 177–179, 302–303, 306, 309; Cuchet 2005, 90–95.

36 The spurious bull is *Sacratissimo uti culmine*, allegedly issued by Pope John XXII in 1322. Conditions of the Sabbatine Privilege included wearing the brown scapular, reciting daily the Little Office of the Blessed Virgin Mary, and observing certain fasts. See: the entry "Sabbatine Privilege" in Cross and Livingstone, eds. 1997, 1434; Mother Mary of the Visitation 1958, 899–900; Carroll 1986, 68–70; Carroll 1996, 126; the Wikipedia entry "Sabbatine Privilege" on the Internet at http://en.wikipedia.org/wiki/Sabbatine_Privilege (accessed June 2, 2015).

37 See: Graef 2009 (1963–1965), 336–338.

38 Alphonsus de Liguori 1999, 247 (emphasis added).

39 Alphonsus de Liguori 1999, 248 (emphasis added).

40 See the editorial note in: Alphonsus de Liguori 1999, 241. On the importance of marian images for the dying, see: Schreiner 2006 (1996), 268–270.

41 Translated from: Estin 1993, 27 (ellipses as in the French original).

42 Biographical information about Daniel Brottier has been obtained from these sites: http://en.wikipedia.org/wiki/Daniel_Brottier#cite_note-spiritan-2 and http://spiritanroma.org/world/wwwroot/cssphistmission/D.Brottier%20.html (accessed April 30, 2015).

Bibliography

van Aarde, Andries G. 1997. "Social Identity, Status Envy and Jesus' *Abba*." *Pastoral Psychology* 45, 451–472.

van Aarde, Andries G. 2001. *Fatherless in Galilee: Jesus as Child of God*. Harrisburg, PA: Trinity Press.

Abbott, Walter M., ed. 1966. *The Documents of Vatican II*. New York: Herder & Herder/Association Press.

Abulafia, Anna Sapir. 1998. "Twelfth-Century Christian Expectations of Jewish Conversion: A Case Study of Peter of Blois." *Aschkenas* 8/1, 45–70.

Acheimastou-Potamianou, Myrtali, ed. 1988. *Holy Image, Holy Space: Icons and Frescoes from Greece*, trans. David A. Hardy. Athens: Greek Ministry of Culture, Byzantine Museum of Athens.

Acres, Alfred. 2006. "Porous Subject Matter and Christ's Haunted Infancy." *The Mind's Eye: Art and Theological Argument in the Middle Ages*, ed. Jeffrey F. Hamburger and Anne-Marie Bouché. Princeton, NJ: Princeton University Press, 241–262.

Acta Apostolicae Sedis. 1909–2014. Rome: Typis Vaticanis, 106 vols.

Adams, Henry. 1986 (1904). *Mont Saint Michel and Chartres*. New York: Penguin.

Aelred of Rievaulx, Saint. 1855. "Sermo II in Natali Domini." *Patrologia Latina* (ed. J.-P. Migne) 195, cols. 220–227.

Aelred of Rievaulx, Saint. 1989. *Aelredi Rievallensis Sermones I–XLVI*, ed. Gaetano Raciti (= *Corpus Christianorum, continuatio mediaevalis*, IIA). Turnhout, Belgium: Brepols.

Agouridis, Savvas. 2000. "The Virgin Mary in the Texts of the Gospels." *Mother of God: Representations of the Virgin in Byzantine Art*, ed. Maria Vassilaki. Milan, Italy: Skira, 58–65.

Akafistnik. 2000. Moscow: Danilovskii blagovestnik.

Akafisty presviatoi Bogoroditse, chtomye v razlichnykh nuzhdakh. 1999. Moscow: Danilovskii blagovestnik.

Akhtar, Salman. 2009. *Comprehensive Dictionary of Psychoanalysis*. London: Karnac.

Alain of Lille. 1855. "Compendiosa in Cantica Canticorum ad Laudem Deiparae Virginis Mariae Elucidatio." *Patrologia Latina* (ed. J.-P. Migne) 210, cols. 51–110.

Alastruey, Gregory. 1963–1964 (1952). *The Blessed Virgin Mary*, trans. M. Janet La Giglia. St. Louis, MO: B. Herder, 2 vols.

Albertus Magnus, Saint. 1890–1899. *Opera omnia*, ed. A. Borgnet. Paris: L. Vives, 38 vols.

Alexiou, Margaret. 1975. "The Lament of the Virgin in Byzantine Literature and Modern Greek Folk-Song." *Byzantine & Modern Greek Studies* 1, 111–140.

Alexiou, Margaret. 2002 (1974). *The Ritual Lament in Greek Tradition* (revised by Dimitrios Yatromanolakis and Panagiotis Roilos). Lanham, MD: Rowman & Littlefield.

Allison, Dale C., Jr. 2001. "Matthew." *The Oxford Bible Commentary*, ed. John Barton and John Muddiman. Oxford, UK: Oxford University Press, 844–886.

Allison, Dale C., Jr. 2005. *Resurrecting Jesus: The Earliest Christian Tradition and Its Interpreters*. New York: T & T Clark.

Alphonsus de Liguori, Saint. 1999. *Selected Writings*, ed. Frederick M. Jones. New York: Paulist Press.

Alphonsus de Liguori, Saint. 2012 (1977). *The Glories of Mary*, trans. by "The Translator," revised by Robert A. Coffin. Charlotte, NC: TAN Books.

Altaner, Berthold. 1960 (1958). *Patrology*, trans. Hilda C. Graef. Freiburg, Germany: Herder & Herder.

Altés, Francesc Xavier, Jordi Camps, Josep de C. Laplana, and Montserrat Pagès. 2003. *La imatge de la Mare de Déu de Montserrat*. Barcelona, Spain: Publicacions de l'Abadia de Montserrat.

Amadeus of Lausanne. 1960. *Huit homélies mariales*, ed. G. Bavaud. Paris: Éditions du Cerf.

Ambrose of Milan, Saint. 1845. "De obitu Valentiniani consolatio." *Patrologia Latina* (ed. J.-P. Migne) 16, cols. 1357–1384.

Ambrose of Milan, Saint. 1956–1958. *Traité sur l'Évangile de S. Luc* (= *Sources Chrétiennes*, vols. 45, 52), ed., trans. Gabriel Tissot. Paris: Éditions du Cerf, 2 vols.

American Psychiatric Association. 2013. *Diagnostic and Statistical Manual of Mental Disorders* (fifth ed.). Arlington, VA: American Psychiatric Association.

Anderson, Gordon A., ed., trans. 1981. *Notre-Dame and Related Conductus: Opera Omnia*. Henryville, PA: Institute of Mediaeval Music, vol. 6.

Andrew of Crete. 1860. "In sanctam Nativitatem praesanctae Dominae nostrae Dei Genitricis, semperque virginis Mariae [Oratio IV]." *Patrologia Graeca* (ed. J.-P. Migne) 97, cols. 861–882.

Andrew of Crete. 2008. "On the Holy Nativity of Our Supremely Holy Lady, the Theotokos and Ever-Virgin Mary." *Wider than Heaven: Eighth-Century Homilies on the Mother of God*, trans. Mary B. Cunningham. Crestwood, NY: St. Vladimir's Seminary Press, 123–138.

Angela of Foligno. 1985. *Il libro della beata Angela da Foligno*, ed. Ludger Thier and Abele Calufetti. Rome: Collegio S. Bonaventura.

Angela of Foligno. 1993. *Complete Works*, trans. Paul Lachance. New York: Paulist Press.

Anonymous. 1971. "Pelikan." *Lexikon der christlichen Ikonographie*, ed. Engelbert Kirschbaum. Freiburg, Germany: Herder, vol. 3, 390–392.

Anselm of Canterbury, Saint. 1968 (1938–1961). *Opera omnia*, ed. F. S. Schmitt. Stuttgart-Bad Cannstatt, Germany: Friedrich Frommann, 2 vols.

Anselm of Canterbury, Saint. 1973. *The Prayers and Meditations of St Anselm with the Proslogion*, trans. Benedicta Ward. Harmondsworth, UK: Penguin.

Ante-Nicene Fathers, ed. by Alexander Roberts *et al.* 2004 (1885–1887). Peabody, MA: Hendrickson, 10 vols.

Apuleius. 1989. *Metamorphoses*, trans. J. Arthur Hanson. Cambridge, MA: Harvard University Press (Loeb Classical Library 44, 453), 2 vols.

Archibald, Elizabeth. 2001. *Incest and the Medieval Imagination*. Oxford, UK: Oxford University Press.

Arlow, Jacob A. 1964. "The Madonna's Conception through the Eyes." *Psychoanalytic Study of Society* 3, 13–25.

Arnold of Bonneval. 1854a. "Tractatus de septem verbis Domini in cruce." *Patrologia Latina* (ed. J.-P. Migne) 189, cols. 1677–1726.

Arnold of Bonneval. 1854b. "Libellus de laudibus B. Mariae Virginis." *Patrologia Latina* (ed. J.-P. Migne) 189, cols. 1725–1734.

Atanassova, Antonia. 2008. "Did Cyril of Alexandria Invent Mariology?" *Origins of the Cult of the Virgin Mary*, ed. Chris Maunder. London: Burns & Oates, 105–125.

Athanase d'Alexandrie. 1973. *Sur l'incarnation du Verbe*, trans,. ed. Charles Kannengiesser. Paris: Éditions du Cerf.

Athans, Mary Christine. 2013. *In Quest of the Jewish Mary: The Mother of Jesus in History, Theology, and Spirituality*. Maryknoll, NY: Orbis.

Augustine of Hippo, Saint. 1841a. "Sermo CLXXXIX in Natali Domini." *Patrologia Latina* (ed. J.-P. Migne) 38, cols. 1005–1007.

Augustine of Hippo, Saint. 1841b. "Sermo CXC in Natali Domini." *Patrologia Latina* (ed. J.-P. Migne) 38, cols. 1007–1009.

Augustine of Hippo, Saint. 1841c. "In Epistolam Joannis ad Parthos." *Patrologia Latina* (ed. J.-P. Migne) 35, cols. 1977–2062.

Augustine of Hippo, Saint. 1845a. "Contra Faustum Manichaeum." *Patrologia Latina* (ed. J.-P. Migne) 42, cols. 207–518.

Augustine of Hippo, Saint. 1845b. "In Psalmum XCVIII Enarratio." *Patrologia Latina* (ed. J.-P. Migne) 37, cols. 1258–1271.

Augustine of Hippo, Saint. 1952a. "Sermo habitus in Basilica Restituta die natalis Domini," ed. Cyrille Lambot. *Colligere Fragmenta: Festschrift Alban Dold*, ed. Bonifatius Fischer and Virgil Fiala. Beuron in Hohenzollern, Germany: Beuroner Kunstverlag, 109–112.

Augustine of Hippo, Saint. 1952b. *Sermons for Christmas and Epiphany*, trans. Thomas Comerford Lawler. Westminster, MD: Newman Press.

Augustine of Hippo, Saint. 2007. *Answer to Faustus, a Manichean*, trans. Roland Teske. Hyde Park, NY: New City Press.

Pseudo-Augustine. 1845. "De Assumptione Beatae Mariae Virginis." *Patrologia Latina* (ed. J.-P. Migne) 40, cols. 1141–1148.

Aurenhammer, Hans. 1956. *Die Mariengnadenbilder Wiens und Niederösterreichs in der Barockzeit*. Vienna: Selbstverlag des Österreichischen Museums für Volkskunde.

Averintsev, S. S. 2001. *Sofiia-Logos: Slovar'*. Kiev, Ukraine: Dukh i Litera.

Ayo, Nicholas. 1994. *The Hail Mary: A Verbal Icon of Mary*. Notre Dame, IN: University of Notre Dame Press.

Azarov, A. A. 2002. *Russko-angliiskii slovar' religioznoi leksiki (s tolkovaniiami)*. Moscow: Russo.

von Balthasar, Hans Urs. 1992 (1978). *Theo-Drama: Theological Dramatic Theory*, trans. Graham Harrison. San Francisco, CA: Ignatius Press, vol. 3.

Baltoyanni, Chryssanthi. 1994. *Eikones: Mētēr Theou*. Athens: Adam.

Baltoyanni, Chryssanthi. 2000. "The Mother of God in Portable Icons." *Mother of God: Representations of the Virgin in Byzantine Art*, ed. Maria Vassilaki. Milan, Italy: Skira, 139–153.

Barker, Margaret. 2010. "The Images of Mary in the Litany of Loreto." *Usus Antiquior* 1 (2), 110–131.

Barker, Margaret. 2011. "Wisdom Imagery and the Mother of God." *The Cult of the Mother of God in Byzantium: Texts and Images*, ed. Leslie Brubaker and Mary B. Cunningham. Burlington, VT: Ashgate Publishing, 91–108.

Barnet, Peter, and Nancy Wu. 2005. *The Cloisters: Medieval Art and Architecture*. New York/New Haven, CT: Metropolitan Museum of Art/Yale University Press.

Barnstone, Willis. 2009. *The Restored New Testament: A New Translation with Commentary, Including the Gnostic Gospels Thomas, Mary, and Judas*. New York: W. W. Norton.

Barré, H. 1952. "Le 'Planctus Mariae' attribué à Saint Bernard." *Revue d'ascétique et de mystique* 28, 243–266.

Barré, H. 1963. *Prières anciennes de l'occident à la Mère du Sauveur: Des origines à Saint Anselme*. Paris: P. Lethielleux.

Bartholomaeus Anglicus. 1964 (1601). *De genuinis rerum coelestium, terrestrium et inferarum Proprietatibus*. Frankfurt, Germany: Minerva.

Basadonna, G., and G. Santarelli. 1997. *Litanie Lauretane*. Città del Vaticano: Libreria Editrice Vaticana.

Bastero, Juan Luis. 2006 (1995). *Mary, Mother of the Redeemer: A Mariology Textbook*, trans. Michael Adams and Philip Griffin. Portland, OR: Four Courts Press.

Bauer, Walter. 1957 (1952). *A Greek–English Lexicon of the New Testament and Other Early Christian Literature*, translation and adaptation by William F. Arndt and F. Wilbur Gingrich. Chicago, IL: University of Chicago Press.

Baumer, Christoph. 1977. "Die Schreinmadonna." *Marian Library Studies* (New Series) 9, 237–272.

Bäumer, Remigius, and Leo Scheffczyk, eds. 1988–1994. *Marienlexikon*. St. Ottilien, Germany: EOS, 6 vols.

Baun, Jane. 2004. "Discussing Mary's Humanity in Medieval Byzantium." *The Church and Mary*, ed. R. N. Swanson. Woodbridge, UK: Boydell Press, 63–72.

Bayne, Emma. 2011. "Womb Envy: The Cause of Misogyny and Even Male Achievement?" *Women's Studies International Forum* 34, 151–160.

Bearsley, Patrick J. 1980. "Mary the Perfect Disciple: A Paradigm for Mariology." *Theological Studies* 41, 461–504.

Beattie, Tina. 2002 (1999). *God's Mother, Eve's Advocate: A Marian Narrative of Women's Salvation*. New York: Continuum.

Beinert, Wolfgang A. 1991. "The Relatives of Jesus." *New Testament Apocrypha*, ed. Wilhelm Schneemelcher, trans. R. M. Wilson. Louisville, KY: Westminster John Knox Press, vol. 1, 470–488.

Beinert, Wolfgang, and Heinrich Petri, eds. 1996–1997. *Handbuch der Marienkunde*. Regensburg, Germany: Friedrich Pustet, 2 vols.

Beit-Hallahmi, Benjamin. 1996. *Psychoanalytic Studies of Religion: A Critical Assessment and Annotated Bibliography*. Westport, CT: Greenwood Press.

Beit-Hallahmi, Benjamin. 2010. "Mapping the Imagination: Heroes, Gods, and Oedipal Triumphs." *Psychoanalysis and Theism: Critical Reflections on the Grünbaum Thesis*, ed. Benjamin Beit-Hallahmi. Lanham, MD: Jason Aronson, 155–181.

Bell, Richard H. 1994. *Provoked to Jealousy: The Origin and Purpose of the Jealousy Motif in Romans 9–11*. Tübingen, Germany: J. C. B. Mohr (Paul Siebeck).

Bell, Rudolph M. 1985. *Holy Anorexia*. Chicago, IL: University of Chicago Press.

Belting, Hans. 1980. "An Image and Its Function in the Liturgy: The Man of Sorrows in Byzantium." *Dumbarton Oaks Papers* 34, 1–16.

Belting, Hans. 1981. *Das Bild und sein Publikum im Mittelalter: Form und Funktion früher Bildtafeln der Passion*. Berlin: Gebr. Mann.

Belting, Hans. 1994 (1990). *Likeness and Presence: A History of the Image before the Era of Art*, trans. Edmund Jephcott. Chicago, IL: University of Chicago Press.

Ben-Chorin, Schalom. 1971. *Mutter Mirjam: Maria in jüdischer Sicht*. Munich, Germany: Paul List.

Ben-Chorin, Schalom. 1983 (1971). "A Jewish View of the Mother of Jesus," trans. T. L. Westow. *Mary in the Churches*, ed. Hans Küng and Jürgen Moltmann. Edinburgh/New York: T & T Clark/Seabury Press, 12–16.

Benko, Stephen. 2004 (1993). *The Virgin Goddess: Studies in the Pagan and Christian Roots of Mariology*. Leiden, Netherlands: Brill.

Bennett, J. A. W. 1982. *Poetry of the Passion: Studies in Twelve Centuries of English Verse*. Oxford, UK: Clarendon Press.

Bergmann, Martin S. 1988. "The Transformation of Ritual Infanticide in the Jewish and Christian Religions with Reference to Anti-Semitism." *Fantasy, Myth, and Reality: Essays in Honor of Jacob A. Arlow, M. D.*, ed. Harold P. Blum, Yale Kramer, Arlene K. Richards, and Arnold D. Richards. Madison, CT: International Universities Press, 233–257.

Bergmann, Martin S. 1992. *In the Shadow of Moloch: The Sacrifice of Children and Its Impact on Western Religions*. New York: Columbia University Press.

Berliner, Rudolf. 1956. "Bemerkungen zu einigen Darstellungen des Erlösers als Schmerzensmann." *Das Münster* 9, 97–117.

Bernard of Clairvaux. 2004a. *Sermons pour l'année. I.1 (Avent et Vigile de Noël)*, ed. J. Leclercq, H. Rochais, and Ch. H. Talbot, trans. Marie-Imelda Huille (= *Sources Chrétiennes* No. 480). Paris: Éditions du Cerf.

Bernard of Clairvaux. 2004b. *Sermons pour l'année. I.2 (De Noël à la Purification de la Vierge)*, ed. J. Leclercq, H. Rochais, and Ch. H. Talbot, trans. Marie-Imelda Huille (= *Sources Chrétiennes* No. 481). Paris: Éditions du Cerf.

Bernard of Clairvaux and Amadeus of Lausanne. 1979. *Magnificat: Homilies in Praise of the Blessed Virgin Mary*, trans. Marie-Bernard Saïda and Grace Perigo. Kalamazoo, MI: Cistercian Publications.

Bernardino of Siena, Saint. 1950–1965. *Opera omnia*. Florence, Italy: Quaracchi, 9 vols.

Bernt, G. 1993. "Planctus. 1. Lateinische Tradition." *Marienlexikon*, ed. Remigius Bäumer and Leo Scheffczyk. St. Ottilien, Germany: EOS, vol. 5, 247–248.

Berruti, Paolo, ed. 2006. *Madonna del Latte: la sacralità umanizzata*. Florence, Italy: Edizioni Polistampa.

Berry, R. J. 1996. "The Virgin Birth of Christ." *Science and Christian Belief* 8, 101–110.

Bestul, Thomas H. 1996. *Texts of the Passion: Latin Devotional Literature and Medieval Society*. Philadelphia, PA: University of Pennsylvania Press.

Bezsonov, P. 1861–1864. *Kaleki perekhozhie: sbornik stikhov*. Moscow, 2 vols.

Biale, David. 2007. *Blood and Belief: The Circulation of a Symbol between Jews and Christians*. Berkeley, CA: University of California Press.

Biblia pauperum, trans., comm. Avril Henry. 1987. Ithaca, NY: Cornell University Press.

Bisconti, Fabrizio. 1996. "La Madonna di Priscilla: Interventi di restauro ed ipotesi sulla dinamica decorativa." *Rivista di archeologia cristiana* 72, 7–34.

Bobkov, K. V. and E. V. Shevtsov. 1996. *Simvol i dukhovnyi opyt pravoslaviia*. Moscow: IZAN.

Boespflug, François. 1984. *Dieu dans l'art: Sollicitudini Nostrae de Benoît XIV (1745) et l'affaire Crescence de Kaufbeuren.* Paris: Éditions du Cerf.

Boespflug, François. 2012. *Dieu dans l'art à la fin du Moyen Âge.* Geneva, Switzerland: Droz.

Boff, Leonardo. 1982. *A Ave-Maria, o feminino e o Espírito Santo.* Petrópolis, Brazil: Vozes.

Boff, Leonardo. 1989 (1979). *The Maternal Face of God: The Feminine and Its Religious Expressions*, trans. Robert R. Barr and John W. Diercksmeier. London: Collins.

Bolman, Elizabeth S. 2005. "The Enigmatic Coptic Galaktotrophousa and the Cult of the Virgin Mary in Egypt." *Images of the Mother of God: Perceptions of the Theotokos in Byzantium*, ed. Maria Vassilaki. Aldershot, UK: Ashgate Publishing, 13–22.

Bonani, Gian Paolo, and Serena Baldassarre Bonani. 1995. *Maria Lactans.* Rome: Edizioni Marianum.

Bonano, Salvatore J. 1957. "Our Lady's Alleged Immortality '*de jure*' and '*de facto*'." *Marian Studies* 8, 24–57.

Bonaventure, Saint. 1868a. "Meditationes vitae Christi." *Opera omnia.* Paris: L. Vives, vol. 12, 509–630.

Bonaventure, Saint. 1868b. "Lignum Vitae." *Opera omnia.* Paris: L. Vives, vol. 12, 67–84.

Bonaventure, Saint. 1960. "The Tree of Life." *The Works of Bonaventure*, trans. José de Vinck. Paterson, NJ: St. Anthony Guild Press, vol. I, 95–144.

Bonaventure, Saint. 2000 (1260–1263). "The Major Legend of Saint Francis." *Francis of Assisi: Early Documents*, ed. Regis J. Armstrong, J. A. Wayne Hellmann, and William J. Short. New York: New City Press, vol. II, 525–683.

Bonnefoy, John F. 1957. "The Predestination of Our Blessed Lady." *Mariology*, ed. Juniper B. Carol. Milwaukee, WI: Bruce, vol. 2, 154–176.

Book of Akathists to Our Saviour, the Mother of God, and Various Saints. 1994. Jordanville, NY: Holy Trinity Monastery.

Borgeaud, Philippe. 2004 (1996). *Mother of the Gods: From Cybele to the Virgin Mary*, trans. Lysa Hochroth. Baltimore, MD: Johns Hopkins University Press.

Bornstein, Daniel E. 1993. *The Bianchi of 1399: Popular Devotion in Late Medieval Italy.* Ithaca, NY: Cornell University Press.

Boskovits, Miklós, and Angelo Tartuferi, eds. 2003. *Cataloghi della Galleria dell'Accademia di Firenze: Dipinti, volume primo, Dal Duecento a Giovanni da Milano.* Florence, Italy: Giunti/Firenze Musei.

Boskovits, Miklós, and Daniela Parenti, eds. 2010. *Cataloghi della Galleria dell'Accademia di Firenze: Dipinti, volume secondo, Il tardo Trecento, dalla Tradizione Orcagnesca agli Esordi del Gotico Internazionale.* Florence, Italy: Giunti/Firenze Musei.

Boss, Sarah Jane. 2000. *Empress and Handmaid: On Nature and Gender in the Cult of the Virgin Mary.* London: Cassell.

Boss, Sarah Jane. 2007a. "The Development of the Virgin's Cult in the High Middle Ages." *Mary: The Complete Resource*, ed. Sarah Jane Boss. Oxford, UK: Oxford University Press, 149–172.

Boss, Sarah Jane. 2007b. "The Development of the Doctrine of Mary's Immaculate Conception." *Mary: The Complete Resource*, ed. Sarah Jane Boss. Oxford, UK: Oxford University Press, 207–235.

Bourassé, Jean Jacques. 1866. *Summa aurea de laudibus Beatissimae Virginis Mariae, Dei Genitricis sine labe conceptae*, ed. J.-P. Migne. Paris, 13 vols.

Bourdin, Gérard. 1992. "Aspects de la piété populaire dans l'Orne 1940–1944." *Cahier des Annales de Normandie* 24, 481–496.

Bouyer, Louis. 1965 (1957). *The Seat of Wisdom: An Essay on the Place of the Virgin Mary in Christian Theology*, trans. A. V. Littledale. Chicago, IL: Henry Regnery Company.

Bovon, François. 2002. *Luke 1: A Commentary on the Gospel of Luke 1:1—9:50*, trans. Christine M. Thomas. Minneapolis, MN: Fortress Press.

Bowlby, John. 1973. *Separation: Anxiety and Anger* (= *Attachment and Loss*, vol. II). New York: Basic Books.

Boyer, Charles. 1952. "Réflexions sur la corédemption de Marie." *Alma Socia Christi. Acta Congressus Mariologici-Mariani Romae Anno Sancto MCML Celebrati*. Rome: Academia Mariana/Officium Libri Catholici, vol. II, 1–12.

Boynton, Susan. 2004. "From the Lament of Rachel to the Lament of Mary: A Transformation in the History of Drama and Spirituality." *Signs of Change: Transformations of Christian Traditions and their Representation in the Arts, 1000–2000*, ed. Nils Holger Petersen, Claus Clüver, and Nicolas Bell. Amsterdam: Rodopi, 319–340.

Brading, D. A. 2001. *Mexican Phoenix. Our Lady of Guadalupe: Image and Tradition across Five Centuries*. Cambridge, UK: Cambridge University Press.

Brankin, Patrick. 2002. *Bilingual Ritual of Hispanic Popular Catholicism*. New Hope, KY: New Hope Publications.

Brennan, Arthur, Susan Ayers, Hafez Ahmed, and Sylvie Marshall-Lucette. 2007. "A Critical Review of the Couvade Syndrome: The Pregnant Male." *Journal of Reproductive and Infant Psychology* 25 (3), 173–189.

Bretzke, James T. 2013. *Consecrated Phrases: A Latin Theological Dictionary*. Collegeville, MN: Liturgical Press.

Brillant, Maurice, ed. 1947 (1934). *Eucharistia: encyclopédie populaire sur l'Eucharistie*. Paris: Librairie Bloud et Gay.

Brittain, Frederick. 1962. *The Penguin Book of Latin Verse*. Baltimore, MD: Penguin.

Brock, Sebastian. 1993. "Planctus, Syrische Tradition." *Marienlexikon*, ed. Remigius Bäumer and Leo Scheffczyk. St. Ottilien, Germany: EOS, vol. 5, 249–250.

Brock, Sebastian, ed., trans. 1994. *Bride of Light: Hymns on Mary from the Syriac Churches*. Baker Hill, Kerala, India: St. Ephrem Ecumenical Research Institute (SEERI).

de Broglie, Guy. 1946. "L'Église, nouvelle Ève, née du Sacré-Coeur." *Nouvelle revue théologique* 68 (1), 3–25.

Broussolle, J.-C. 1903. *Le Christ de la Légende Dorée*. Paris: Maison de la Bonne Presse.

Browe, Peter. 1938. *Die eucharistischen Wunder des Mittelalters*. Wrocław, Poland: Müller & Seiffert.

Brown, Carleton, ed. 1924. *Religious Lyrics of the XIVth Century*. Oxford, UK: Clarendon Press.

Brown, Carleton, ed. 1939. *Religious Lyrics of the XVth Century*. Oxford, UK: Clarendon Press.

Brown, Peter. 2008 (1988). *The Body and Society: Men, Women, and Sexual Renunciation in Early Christianity*. New York: Columbia University Press.

Brown, Raymond E. 1966–1970. *The Gospel According to John*. Garden City, NY: Doubleday, 2 vols.

Brown, Raymond E. 1993 (1977). *The Birth of the Messiah: A Commentary on the Infancy Narratives in the Gospels of Matthew and Luke*. New Haven, CT: Yale University Press.

Brown, Raymond E. 1994. *The Death of the Messiah: From Gethsemane to the Grave*. New York: Doubleday, 2 vols.

Brown, Raymond E., Karl P. Donfried, Joseph A. Fitzmyer, and John Reumann, eds. 1978. *Mary in the New Testament: A Collaborative Assessment by Protestant and Roman Catholic Scholars*. New York: Paulist Press.

Buby, Bertrand. 1981–1982. "Research on the Biblical Approach and the Method of Exegesis Appearing in the Greek Homiletic Texts of the Late Fourth and Early Fifth Centuries, Emphasizing the Incarnation Especially the Nativity and Mary's Place within It." *Marian Library Studies* (New Series) 13–14, 223–394.

Buby, Bertrand. 1994–1996. *Mary of Galilee: A Trilogy of Marian Studies*. New York: Alba House, 3 vols.

Budge, E. A. Wallis. 1915. *Miscellaneous Coptic Texts in the Dialect of Upper Egypt*. London: British Museum, Part I (Coptic); Part II (English).

Bulgakov, Sergii. 1927. *Kupina neopalimaia: Opyt dogmaticheskago istolkovaniia nekotorykh chert v pravoslavnom pochitanii Bogomateri*. Paris: YMCA Press.

Bulgakov, Sergii. 1931. *Ikona i ikonopochitanie: Dogmaticheskii ocherk*. Paris: YMCA Press.

Bulgakov, Sergius [Sergii]. 1937. *The Wisdom of God: A Brief Summary of Sophiology*, trans. Patrick Thompson, O. Fielding Clarke, and Xenia Braikevitch. New York: Paisley Press.

Bulgakov, Sergius [Sergii]. 2008 (1933). *The Lamb of God*, trans. Boris Jakim. Grand Rapids, MI: William B. Eerdmans.

Buono, A. 1997. "Saturday of Our Lady." *Dictionary of Mary*. Totowa, NJ: Catholic Book Publishing, 416–418.

Burghardt, Walter J. 1955. "Mary in Western Patristic Thought." *Mariology*, ed. Juniper B. Carol. Milwaukee, WI: Bruce, vol. 1, 109–155.

Burghardt, Walter J. 1957. "The Testimony of the Patristic Age Concerning Mary's Death." *Marian Studies* 8, 58–99.

Bynum, Caroline Walker. 1982. *Jesus as Mother: Studies in the Spirituality of the High Middle Ages*. Berkeley, CA: University of California Press.

Bynum, Caroline Walker. 1987. *Holy Feast and Holy Fast: The Religious Significance of Food to Medieval Women*. Berkeley, CA: University of California Press.

Bynum, Caroline Walker. 1991. *Fragmentation and Redemption: Essays on Gender and the Human Body in Medieval Religion*. New York: Zone Books.

Bynum, Caroline Walker. 1995. *The Resurrection of the Body in Western Christianity, 200–1336*. New York: Columbia University Press.

Bynum, Caroline Walker. 2006. "Seeing and Seeing Beyond: The Mass of St. Gregory in the Fifteenth Century." *The Mind's Eye: Art and Theological Argument in the Middle Ages*, ed. Jeffrey F. Hamburger and Anne-Marie Bouché. Princeton, NJ: Princeton University Press, 208–240.

Bynum, Caroline Walker. 2007. *Wonderful Blood: Theology and Practice in Late Medieval Northern Germany and Beyond*. Philadelphia, PA: University of Pennsylvania Press.

Bynum, Caroline Walker. 2011. *Christian Materiality: An Essay on Religion in Late Medieval Europe*. New York: Zone Books.

Caesarius of Heisterbach. 1929. *The Dialogue on Miracles*, trans. H. von E. Scott and C. C. Swinton Bland. London: George Routledge, 2 vols.

Caesarius of Heisterbach. 1966 (1851). *Dialogus miraculorum*. Ridgewood, NJ: Gregg Press (reprint of Cologne edition, ed. J. Strange), 2 vols.

Calkins, Arthur Burton. 1996. "Pope John Paul II's Teaching on Marian Coredemption." *Mary: Coredemptrix, Mediatrix, Advocate. Theological Foundations II: Papal, Pneumatological, Ecumenical*, ed. Mark I. Miravalle. Santa Barbara, CA: Queenship Publishing, 113–147.

Calkins, Arthur Burton. 2007. "Mary's Presence in the Mass According to Pope John Paul II." *Mary at the Foot of the Cross VI: Marian Coredemption in the Eucharistic Mystery*. New Bedford, MA: Academy of the Immaculate, 11–38.

Calkins, Arthur Burton. 2008. "The Relation of Coredemption to the Concept of Redemption in the Magisterium." *Mary at the Foot of the Cross VIII: Coredemption as Key to a Correct Understanding of Redemption, and Recent Attempts to Redefine Redemption Contrary to the Belief of the Church*. New Bedford, MA: Academy of the Immaculate, 11–55.

Cameron, Averil. 2000. "The Early Cult of the Virgin." *Mother of God: Representations of the Virgin in Byzantine Art*, ed. Maria Vassilaki. Milan, Italy: Skira, 3–15.

Cameron, Averil. 2004. "The Cult of the Virgin in Late Antiquity: Religious Development and Myth-Making." *The Church and Mary*, ed. R. N. Swanson. Woodbridge, UK: Boydell Press, 1–21.

von Campenhausen, Hans. 1964 (1962). *The Virgin Birth in the Theology of the Ancient Church*, trans. Frank Clarke. London: SCM Press.

Capps, Donald. 2000. *Jesus: A Psychological Biography*. St. Louis, MO: Chalice Press.

Capps, Donald. 2002a. "A Summary of *Jesus*." *Pastoral Psychology* 50, 391–400.

Capps, Donald. 2002b. "Response to Ellens, Miller, and Anderson." *Pastoral Psychology* 50, 425–446.

Cardile, Paul Y. 1984. "Mary as Priest: Mary's Sacerdotal Position in the Visual Arts." *Arte cristiana* 72, 199–208.

Carol, Juniper B. 1957. "Our Lady's Coredemption." *Mariology*, ed. Juniper B. Carol. Milwaukee, WI: Bruce, vol. 2, 377–425.

Carr, Annemarie Weyl. 1995. "Originality and the Icon: The Panel Painted Icon." *Originality in Byzantine Literature, Art and Music*, ed. A. R. Littlewood. Oxford, UK: Oxbow Books, 115–124.

Carreres, Joan. 1988. *Guia para visitar los santuarios marianos de Cataluña*. Madrid: Ediciones Encuentro.

Carroll, Eamon R. 1955. "Mary in the Documents of the Magisterium." *Mariology*, ed. Juniper B. Carol. Milwaukee, WI: Bruce, vol. 1, 1–50.

Carroll, Michael P. 1986. *The Cult of the Virgin Mary: Psychological Origins*. Princeton, NJ: Princeton University Press.

Carroll, Michael P. 1989. *Catholic Cults and Devotions: A Psychological Inquiry*. Kingston, ON/Montreal, QC: McGill-Queen's University Press.

Carroll, Michael P. 1992. *Madonnas that Maim: Popular Catholicism in Italy since the Fifteenth Century*. Baltimore, MD: Johns Hopkins University Press.

Carroll, Michael P. 1996. *Veiled Threats: The Logic of Popular Catholicism in Italy*. Baltimore, MD: Johns Hopkins University Press.

Carveth, Donald L. 2013. *The Still Small Voice: Psychoanalytic Reflections on Guilt and Conscience*. London: Karnac.

Casagrande, Dominicus. 1974. *Enchiridion Marianum biblicum patristicum*. Rome: Cor Unum.

Cassagnes-Brouquet, Sophie. 2000. *Vierges Noires*. Rodez, France: Éditions du Rouergue.

Caswall, Edward. 1884 (1849). *Lyra Catholica*. London: Granville Mansions.

Catechism of the Catholic Church, 2nd edition. 2000 (1997). Washington, DC: United States Catholic Conference.

Catta, Étienne. 1961. "*Sedes Sapientiae*." *Maria: Études sur la Sainte Vierge*, ed. Hubert du Manoir. Paris: Beauchesne, vol. VI, 689–866.

de Cavlibvs, Iohannis. 1997. *Meditaciones vite Christi, olim S. Bonauenturo attributae*, ed. M. Stallings-Taney. Turnhout, Belgium: Brepols.

Celsus. 1987. *On the True Doctrine: A Discourse Against the Christians*, trans. R. Joseph Hoffmann. New York: Oxford University Press.

Cevetello, J. F. X., and R. J. Bastian. 1967. "Purgatory." *New Catholic Encyclopedia*. New York: McGraw-Hill, vol. 11, 1034–1039.

Chapman, David W. 2010 (2008). *Ancient Jewish and Christian Perceptions of Crucifixion*. Grand Rapids, MI: Baker Academic.

Chatzidakis, Manolis. 1962. *Icônes de Saint-Georges des Grecs et de la collection de l'Institut*. Venice, Italy: Neri Pozza.

Chatzidakis, Manolis, and Dimitrios Sofianos. 1990. *The Great Meteoron: History and Art/To Megalo Meteōro: Istoria kai Technē*, trans. Alexandra Doumas. Athens: Interamerican.

Chaunu, Pierre. 1978. *La mort à Paris: XVIe, XVIIe, et XVIIIe siècles*. Paris: Fayard.

Chidester, David. 2000. *Christianity: A Global History*. New York: HarperCollins.

Chrysostom, John. 1860a. "Homiliae XC in Matthaeum." *Patrologia Graeca* (ed. J.-P. Migne) 57, cols. 13–472.

Chrysostom, John. 1860b. "Homiliae XXXIV in Epistolam ad Hebraeos." *Patrologia Graeca* (ed. J.-P. Migne) 63, cols. 9–236.

Clark, Elizabeth A. 1999. *Reading Renunciation: Asceticism and Scripture in Early Christianity*. Princeton, NJ: Princeton University Press.

Classen, Albrecht. 2005. "Philippe Ariès and the Consequences: History of Childhood, Family Relations, and Personal Emotions. Where Do We Stand Today?" *Childhood in the Middle Ages and the Renaissance: The Results of a Paradigm Shift in the History of Mentality*, ed. Albrecht Classen. Berlin: Walter de Gruyter, 1–65.

Clayton, Mary. 1990. *The Cult of the Virgin Mary in Anglo-Saxon England*. Cambridge, UK: Cambridge University Press.

Clendenin, Daniel B. 2003 (1994). *Eastern Orthodox Christianity: A Western Perspective*. Grand Rapids, MI: Baker Academic.

Coathalem, Hervé. 1954 (1939). *Le parallelisme entre la sainte Vierge et l'église dans la tradition latine jusqu'à la fin du XIIe siècle*. Rome: apud aedes Universitatis Gregorianae.

Cohen, Jeremy. 2007. *Christ Killers: The Jews and the Passion from the Bible to the Big Screen*. Oxford, UK: Oxford University Press.

Collins, Adela Yarbro. 1999. "The Worship of Jesus and the Imperial Cult." *The Jewish Roots of Christological Monotheism*, ed. Carey C. Newman, James R. Davila, and Gladys S. Lewis. Leiden, Netherlands: Brill, 234–257.

Collins, Kristen M. 2006. "Visual Piety and Institutional Identity at Sinai." *Holy Image, Hallowed Ground: Icons from Sinai*, ed. Robert S. Nelson and Kristen M. Collins. Los Angeles, CA: J. Paul Getty Museum, 95–119.

Congar, Yves. 1950. "Incidence ecclésiologique d'un thème de dévotion mariale." *Mélanges de science religieuse* 7, 277–292.

Congar, Yves. 1954. "Marie et l'Église dans la pensée patristique." *Revue des sciences philosophiques et théologiques* 38, 3–38.

Congar, Yves. 1974 (?). "Modèle monastique et modèle sacerdotal en Occident de Grégoire VII (1073–1085) à Innocent III (1198)." *Études de civilisation médiévale (IXe – XIIe siècles). Mélanges offerts à Edmond-René Labande.* Poitiers, France: C. É. S. C. M., 153–160.

Congrès Marial National. 1948. *Marie Corédemptrice. 1846–1946, Centenaire de l'apparition. Ve Congrès Marial National, Grenoble-La Salette.* Lyons, France: Editions et Imp. du Sud-Est.

Constable, Giles. 1995. *Three Studies in Medieval Religious and Social Thought.* Cambridge, UK: Cambridge University Press.

Constas, Nicholas. 2003. *Proclus of Constantinople and the Cult of the Virgin in Late Antiquity: Homilies 1–5, Texts and Translations.* Leiden, Netherlands: Brill.

Constitutiones, Decreta, Declarationes, Cura et Studio Secretariae Generalis Concilii Oecumenici Vaticani II. 1966. Rome: Typis Polyglottis Vaticanis.

Corcoran, C. J. 1967. "Glorified Body." *New Catholic Encyclopedia.* New York: McGraw-Hill, vol. 6, 512–513.

Cormack, Robin. 2000a. "The Mother of God in Apse Mosaics." *Mother of God: Representations of the Virgin in Byzantine Art*, ed. Maria Vassilaki. Milan, Italy: Skira, 91–105.

Cormack, Robin. 2000b. "The Mother of God in the Mosaics of Hagia Sophia in Constantinople." *Mother of God: Representations of the Virgin in Byzantine Art*, ed. Maria Vassilaki. Milan, Italy: Skira, 107–123.

Courtois, Christine A. 2010. *Healing the Incest Wound: Adult Survivors in Therapy.* New York: W. W. Norton.

Crashaw, Richard. 1974 (1970). *The Complete Poetry of Richard Crashaw*, ed. George Walton Williams. New York: W. W. Norton.

Cross, F. L., and E. A. Livingstone, eds. 1997. *The Oxford Dictionary of the Christian Church*, 3rd ed. Oxford, UK: Oxford University Press.

Crossan, John Dominic. 1991. *The Historical Jesus: The Life of a Mediterranean Jewish Peasant.* New York: HarperCollins.

Crossan, John Dominic. 1994. *Jesus: A Revolutionary Biography.* New York: HarperCollins.

Crossan, John Dominic. 1996. *Who Killed Jesus? Exposing the Roots of Anti-Semitism in the Gospel Story of the Death of Jesus.* San Francisco, CA: HarperCollins.

Crossan, John Dominic. 2005 (2003). "Virgin Mother or Bastard Child?" *A Feminist Companion to Mariology*, ed. Amy-Jill Levine and Maria Mayo Robbins. Cleveland, OH: Pilgrim Press, 37–55.

Crossan, John Dominic, and Jonathan L. Reed. 2004. *In Search of Paul: How Jesus's Apostle Opposed Rome's Empire with God's Kingdom.* New York: HarperCollins.

Cuchet, Guillaume. 2005. *Le crépuscule du purgatoire.* Paris: Armand Colin.

Cunningham, Mary B. 2008. *Wider than Heaven: Eighth-Century Homilies on the Mother of God.* Crestwood, NY: St. Vladimir's Seminary Press.

Custer, John S. 2006. "The Virgin's Birth Pangs: A Johannine Image in Byzantine Hymnography." *Marianum* 68, 417–436.

Cutler, Anthony. 1987. "The Cult of the Galaktotrophousa in Byzantium and Italy." *Jahrbuch der österreichischen Byzantinistik* 37, 335–350.

Cyprian, Saint. 1971. *De Lapsis; and De Ecclesiae Catholicae Unitate*, text and trans. Maurice Bévenot. Oxford, UK: Oxford University Press.

Cyril of Alexandria. 1859. "Epistola I. Cyrilli ad monachos Aegypti." *Patrologia Graeca* (ed. J.-P. Migne) 77, cols. 9–40.

Czarnowus, Anna. 2010. "Mary, Motherhood, and Theatricality in the Old Polish *Listen, Dear Brothers* and Chaucer's *Man of Law's Tale*." *Laments for the Lost in Medieval Literature*, ed. Jane Tolmie and M. J. Toswell. Turnhout, Belgium: Brepols, 129–147.

Dal', Vladimir. 1984 (1862). *Poslovitsy russkogo naroda*. Moscow: Khudozhestvennaia literatura, 2 vols.

Daley, Brian E. 1998. *On the Dormition of Mary: Early Patristic Homilies*. Crestwood, NY: St. Vladimir's Seminary Press.

Daley, Brian E. 2001. "'At the Hour of our Death': Mary's Dormition and Christian Dying in Late Patristic and Early Byzantine Literature." *Dumbarton Oaks Papers* 55, 71–89.

Daly, Robert J. 2009. *Sacrifice Unveiled: The True Meaning of Christian Sacrifice*. London: T & T Clark.

Daniélou, J. 1949. "Le Culte Marial et le Paganisme." *Maria: Études sur la Sainte Vierge*, ed. Hubert du Manoir. Paris: Beauchesne, vol. I, 159–181.

Daniélou, J. 1950. *Sacramentum futuri: Études sur les origines de la typologie biblique*. Paris: Beauchesne.

Dante Alighieri. 1939. *The Divine Comedy: III, Paradiso*, trans. John D. Sinclair. New York: Oxford University Press.

Davies, R. T., ed. 1964. *Medieval English Lyrics: A Critical Anthology*. Evanston, IL: Northwestern University Press.

Deiss, Lucien. 1972 (1958). *Mary, Daughter of Sion*, trans. Barbara T. Blair. Collegeville, MN: Liturgical Press.

Denzinger, Heinrich. 2012. *Compendium of Creeds, Definitions, and Declarations on Matters of Faith and Morals* (*Enchiridion symbolorum definitionun et declarationum de rebus fidei et morum*), 43rd bilingual ed., Robert Fastiggi and Anne Englund Nash, eds. for English version. San Francisco, CA: Ignatius Press.

Despres, Denise L. 1996. "Mary of the Eucharist: Cultic Anti-Judaism in Some Fourteenth-Century English Devotional Manuscripts." *From Witness to Witchcraft: Jews and Judaism in Medieval Christian Thought*, ed. Jeremy Cohen. Wiesbaden, Germany: Harrassowitz, 375–401.

Dewez, Léon, and Albert van Iterson. 1956. "La lactation de saint Bernard. Légende et iconographie." *Cîteaux in de Nederlanden* 7 (3), 165–189.

Dillard, Peter S. 2009. *The Truth about Mary: A Theological and Philosophical Evaluation of the Proposed Fifth Marian Dogma*. Eugene, OR: Wipf & Stock.

Dillenschneider, Clément. 1951. *Le mystère de la corédemption mariale*. Paris: J. Vrin.

Dio Cassius. 1924. *Roman History, Books LVI–LX*, trans. Earnest Cary. Cambridge, MA: Harvard University Press (Loeb Classical Library 175).

Dionysius of Halicarnassus. 1937. *The Roman Antiquities, vol. I*, trans. Earnest Cary and Edward Spelman. Cambridge, MA: Harvard University Press (Loeb Classical Library [unnumbered]).

Dobrov, Gregory W. 1994. "A Dialogue with Death: Ritual Lament and the Θρηνος Θεοτόκου of Romanos Melodos." *Greek, Roman and Byzantine Studies* 35, 385–405.

Dodd, C. H. 1961. *The Parables of the Kingdom*. New York: Charles Scribner's.

Doolan, Aegidius. 1952. "'Ab Aeterno Ordinata Sum'." *Alma Socia Christi. Acta Congressus Mariologici-Mariani Romae Anno Sancto MCML Celebrati*. Rome: Academia Mariana/Officium Libri Catholici, vol. 3, 21–26.

Dorenskaia, I. 1999. *Molitvy ko Presviatoi Bogoroditse pred chudotvornymi ikonami Eia*. Moscow: Eleon.

Drandaki, Anastasia. 2002. *Greek Icons, 14th–18th Century: The Rena Andreadis Collection*, trans. John Avgherinos. Milan, Italy: Skira.

Dreves, Guido Maria, and Clemens Blume. 1909. *Ein Jahrtausend Lateinischer Hymnendichtung*. Leipzig, Germany: O. R. Reisland, 2 vols.

Dronke, Peter. 1987. "The Lyrical Compositions of Philip the Chancellor." *Studi Medievali* (3rd series) 28, 563–592.

Dronke, Peter. 1992. *Intellectuals and Poets in Medieval Europe*. Rome: Edizioni di Storia e Letteratura.

Dronke, Peter, ed., trans. 1994. *Nine Medieval Latin Plays*. Cambridge, UK: Cambridge University Press.

Dronke, Peter. 1996 (1968). *The Medieval Lyric*. Cambridge, UK: D. S. Brewer.

Druwé, E. 1949. "La médiation universelle de Marie." *Maria: Études sur la Sainte Vierge*, ed. Hubert du Manoir. Paris: Beauchesne, vol. I, 417–572.

Dückers, Rob, and Ruud Priem, eds. 2009. *The Hours of Catherine of Cleves: Devotion, Demons and Daily Life in the Fifteenth Century*. New York: Abrams.

Duffy, Eamon. 1988. "Mater Dolorosa, Mater Misericordiae." *New Blackfriars* 69, 210–227.

Dumoutet, Édouard. 1926. *Le Désir de voir l'hostie et les origines de la dévotion au Saint-Sacrement*. Paris: Gabriel Beauchesne.

Dumoutet, Édouard. 1932. *Le Christ selon la chair et la vie liturgique au moyen-âge*. Paris: Gabriel Beauchesne.

Dundes, Alan. 1980. *Interpreting Folklore*. Bloomington, IN: Indiana University Press.

Dundes, Alan. 1991 (1989). "The Ritual Murder or Blood Libel Legend: A Study of Anti-Semitic Victimization through Projective Inversion." *The Blood Libel Legend: A Casebook in Anti-Semitic Folklore*, ed. Alan Dundes. Madison, WI: University of Wisconsin Press, 336–376

Dunn, James D. G. 1996 (1989). *Christology in the Making: A New Testament Inquiry into the Origins of the Doctrine of the Incarnation*. Grand Rapids, MI: William B. Eerdmans.

Dunnill, John. 2013. *Sacrifice and the Body: Biblical Anthropology and Christian Understanding*. Burlington, VT: Ashgate.

Dünzl, Franz. 2007 (2006). *A Brief History of the Doctrine of the Trinity in the Early Church*, trans. by John Bowden. London: T & T Clark.

Dupeux, Cécile. 1991. "La lactation de Saint Bernard de Clairvaux. Genèse et évolution d'une image." *L'Image et la production du sacré*, ed. Françoise Dunand, Jean-Michel Spieser, and Jean Wirth. Paris: Méridiens Klincksieck, 165–193.

Durand, Georges. 1911. *Tableaux et chants royaux de la Confrérie du Puy Notre Dame d'Amiens reproduits en 1517 pour Louise de Savoie, duchesse d'Angoulême (Bibliothèque Nationale, ms. français 145)*. Paris: Librairie Picard.

Durand, Guillame. 1995. *Guillemi Duranti Rationale Divinorum Officiorum I–IV*, ed. A. Davril and T. M. Thibodeau (= *Corpus Christianorum, continuatio medievalis* 140). Turnhout, Belgium: Brepols.

Durand, Guillame. 2007. *The Rationale Divinorum Officiorum of William Durand of Mende: A New Translation of the Prologue and Book One*, trans., ed. Timothy M. Thibodeau. New York: Columbia University Press.

Dürig, W. 1992. "Lauretanische Litanei." *Marienlexikon*, ed. Remigius Bäumer and Leo Scheffczyk. St. Ottilien, Germany: EOS, vol. 4, 33–42.

Ehrman, Bart D. 2014. *How Jesus Became God: The Exaltation of a Jewish Preacher from Galilee*. New York: HarperCollins.

Ellington, Donna Spivey. 2001. *From Sacred Body to Angelic Soul: Understanding Mary in Late Medieval and Early Modern Europe*. Washington, DC: Catholic University of America Press.

Elliott, J. K. 1993. *The Apocryphal New Testament: A Collection of Apocryphal Christian Literature in an English Translation*. Oxford, UK: Oxford University Press.

Elliott, J. K. 2008. "Mary in the Apocryphal New Testament." *Origins of the Cult of the Virgin Mary*, ed. Chris Maunder. London: Burns & Oates, 57–70.

Emminghaus, J. H. 1972. "Vesperbild." *Lexikon der christlichen Ikonographie*, ed. Engelbert Kirschbaum. Freiburg, Germany: Herder, vol. 4, 450–456.

Ephrem the Syrian. 1989. *Hymns*, trans. Kathleen E. McVey. New York: Paulist Press.

van Esbroeck, Michel. 1995. *Aux origines de la Dormition de la Vierge: Études historiques sur les traditions orientales*. Brookfield, VT: Ashgate.

van Esbroeck, Michel. 2005. "The Virgin as the True Ark of the Covenant." *Images of the Mother of God: Perceptions of the Theotokos in Byzantium*, ed. Maria Vassilaki. Aldershot: Ashgate, 63–68.

Essen (Diocese). 1968. *Marienbild in Rheinland und Westfalen*. Essen, Germany: Gemeinnütziger Verein Villa Hügel.

Estin, Colette. 1993. *Contes et fêtes de la mort*. Paris: Beauchesne.

Evans, Helen C., ed. 2004. *Byzantium: Faith and Power (1261–1557)*. New York/ New Haven, CT: Metropolitan Museum of Art/Yale University Press.

Evans, Helen C., and William D. Wixom, eds. 1997. *The Glory of Byzantium: Art and Culture of the Middle Byzantine Era, A. D. 843–1261*. New York: Metropolitan Museum of Art.

Faber, Frederick William. 1862. *Hymns*. London: Burns & Oates.

Fallon, Nicole. 2012. "The Christ Child in the Tree: The Motif in the Thirteenth-Century Wood-of-the-Cross Legends and Arthurian Romances." *The Christ Child in Medieval Culture: Alpha es et O!*, ed. Mary Dzon and Theresa M. Kenney. Toronto, ON: University of Toronto Press, 92–114.

Farmer, Hugh. 1957. "The Meditations of the Monk of Farne." *Analecta Monastica* 4, 141–245.

Fasmer, Maks. 1986–1987 (1950–1958). *Etimologicheskii slovar' russkogo iazyka*. Moscow: Progress, 4 vols.

Fassler, Margot E. 2010. *The Virgin of Chartres: Making History through Liturgy and the Arts*. New Haven, CT: Yale University Press.

Fastenrath, E., and F. Tschochner 1991. "Königtum Mariens." *Marienlexikon*, ed. Remigius Bäumer and Leo Scheffczyk. St. Ottilien, Germany: EOS, vol. 3, 589–596.

Fastiggi, Robert. 2007. "Mary and the Eucharist in St. Louis de Montfort." *Mary at the Foot of the Cross VI: Marian Coredemption in the Eucharistic Mystery*. New Bedford, MA: Academy of the Immaculate, 287–299.

Faustus of Riez. 1891. *Favsti Reiensis Praeter Sermones Psevdo-Evsebianos Opera*, ed. Augustus Engelbrecht. Prague: F. Tempsky.

Favez, Charles. 1937. *La consolation latine chrétienne*. Paris: Librairie philosophique J. Vrin.

Fedotov, G. 1991 (1935). *Stikhi dukhovnye (Russkaia narodnaia vera po dukhovnym stikham)*. Moscow: Progress-Gnosis.

Fein, Susanna Greer. 1998. *Moral Love Songs and Laments*. Kalamazoo, MI: Medieval Institute Publications.

Feuillet, A. 1981. *Jésus et sa Mère: d'après les récits Lucaniens de l'enfance et d'après Saint Jean*. Paris: J. Gabalda.

Fiene, Donald M. 1989. "What Is the Appearance of Divine Sophia?" *Slavic Review* 48, 449–476.

Filatov, V. V. 1996. *Kratkii ikonopisnyi illiustrirovannyi slovar'*. Moscow: Prosveshchenie.

Filimonov, Sergii, ed. 2000. *Polnyi pravoslavnyi molitvoslov na vsiakuiu potrebu*. St. Petersburg, Russia: Obshchestvo Sviatitelia Vasiliia Velikogo.

Finkenzeller, J. 1992. "Miterlöserin." *Marienlexikon*, ed. Remigius Bäumer and Leo Scheffczyk. St. Ottilien, Germany: EOS, vol. 4, 484–486.

Finlan, Stephen. 2009. *The Family Metaphor in Jesus' Teaching: Gospel and Ethics*. Eugene, OR: Wipf & Stock.

Finlan, Stephen, and Vladimir Kharlamov, eds. 2006. *Theōsis: Deification in Christian Theology*. Eugene, OR: Pickwick.

Fitzmyer, Joseph A. 1989. *Luke the Theologian: Aspects of His Teaching*. New York: Paulist Press.

Fitzmyer, Joseph A. 2008. *First Corinthians: A New Translation with Introduction and Commentary*. New Haven, CT: Yale University Press.

Flora, Holly. 2012. "Women Wielding Knives: The Circumcision of Christ by His Mother in an Illustrated Manuscript of the *Meditationes vitae Christi* (Paris, Bibliothèque nationale de France ital. 115)." *The Christ Child in Medieval Culture: Alpha es et O!*, ed. Mary Dzon and Theresa M. Kenney. Toronto, ON: University of Toronto Press, 145–166.

Florensky, Pavel. 1997 (1914). *The Pillar and Ground of the Truth: An Essay in Orthodox Theodicy in Twelve Letters*, trans. Boris Jakim. Princeton, NJ: Princeton University Press.

Flusser, David. 1986 (1985). "Mary and Israel." *Mary: Images of the Mother of Jesus in Jewish and Christian Perspective*, trans. Xavier John Seubert. Philadelphia, PA: Fortress Press, 7–16.

Flusser, David. 1991. "Jesus, His Ancestry, and the Commandment of Love." *Jesus' Jewishness: Exploring the Place of Jesus within Early Judaism*, ed. James H. Charlesworth. New York: Crossroad, 153–176.

Flusser, David. 2001. *Jesus*. Jerusalem: Hebrew University Magnes Press.

Forsyth, Ilene H. 1972. *The Throne of Wisdom: Wood Sculptures of the Madonna in Romanesque France*. Princeton, NJ: Princeton University Press.

Franklin, Eric. 2001. "Luke." *The Oxford Bible Commentary*, ed. John Barton and John Muddiman. Oxford, UK: Oxford University Press, 922–959.

Freud, Sigmund. 1953 (1913). "Totem and Taboo." *Standard Edition of the Complete Psychological Works of Sigmund Freud*, translated under direction of J. Strachey. London: Hogarth Press, vol. 13, 1–162.

Freud, Sigmund. 1957 (1917). "Mourning and Melancholia." *Standard Edition of the Complete Psychological Works of Sigmund Freud*, translated under direction of J. Strachey. London: Hogarth Press, vol. 14, 239–258.

Freud, Sigmund. 1958 (1911). "Great is Diana of the Ephesians." *Standard Edition of the Complete Psychological Works of Sigmund Freud*, translated under direction of J. Strachey. London: Hogarth Press, vol. 12, 342–344.

Freud, Sigmund. 1959 (1926). "Inhibitions, Symptoms and Anxiety." *Standard Edition of the Complete Psychological Works of Sigmund Freud*, translated under direction of J. Strachey. London: Hogarth Press, vol. 20, 75–175.

Frey, Winfried. 2001. "'der vngetruen Iudden rat disz hertzleit geraden hat': Die Mutter Jesu in deutschsprachigen Passionsspielen." *Maria – Tochter Sion? Mariologie, Marienfrömmigkeit und Judenfeindschaft*, ed. Johannes Heil and Rainer Kampling. Paderborn, Germany: Ferdinand Schöningh, 139–162.

Füglister, Robert L. 1964. *Das Lebende Kreuz: Ikonographisch-ikonologische Untersuchung der Herkunft und Entwicklung einer spätmittelalterlichen Bildidee und ihrer Verwurzelung im Wort*. Einsiedeln, Switzerland: Benziger.

Fulton, Rachel. 2002. *From Judgment to Passion: Devotion to Christ and the Virgin Mary, 800–1200*. New York: Columbia University Press.

Funk, Robert W., and the Jesus Seminar. 1998. *The Acts of Jesus: The Search for the Authentic Deeds of Jesus*. New York: HarperCollins.

Furnivall, F. J., ed. 1965 (1882). *The Digby Mysteries (= New Shakspere Society Publications, Series VII, No. 1)*. Vaduz: Kraus.

Galavaris, George P. 1959. "The Mother of God, 'Stabbed with a Knife'." *Dumbarton Oaks Papers* 13, 229–234.

Galot, Jean. 1957. "La plus ancienne affirmation de la corédemption mariale." *Recherches de science religieuse* 45, 187–208.

Galot, Jean. 2005. *Marie, mère et corédemptrice*. Paris: Éditions Parole et Silence.

Gambero, Luigi. 1999 (1991). *Mary and the Fathers of the Church: The Blessed Virgin Mary in Patristic Thought*, trans. Thomas Buffer. San Francisco, CA: Ignatius Press.

Gardner, Lucy. 2004. "Balthasar and the Figure of Mary." *The Cambridge Companion to Hans Urs von Balthasar*, ed. Edward T. Oakes and David Moss. Cambridge, UK: Cambridge University Press, 64–78.

Garrison, Edward B. 1949. *Italian Romanesque Panel Painting: An Illustrated Index*. Florence, Italy: L. S. Olschki.

Gaventa, Beverly Roberts. 2002. "'Standing Near the Cross': Mary and the Crucifixion of Jesus." *Blessed One: Protestant Perspectives on Mary*, ed. Beverly Roberts Gaventa and Cynthia L. Rigby. Louisville, KY: Westminster John Knox Press, 47–56.

Gaventa, Beverly Roberts. 2004. "'Nothing Will Be Impossible with God': Mary as the Mother of Believers." *Mary, Mother of God*, ed. Carl E. Braaten and Robert W. Jenson. Grand Rapids, MI: William B. Eerdmans, 19–35.

Gebara, Ivone, and Maria Clara Bingemer. 1989 (1987). *Mary: Mother of God, Mother of the Poor*, trans. Phillip Berryman. Maryknoll, NY: Orbis Books.

Gelin, Albert. 1964 (1953). *The Poor of Yahweh*, tr. Kathryn Sullivan. Collegeville, PA: Liturgical Press.

Germanos of Constantinople. 1860a. "In Dormitionem B. Mariae III." *Patrologia Graeca* (ed. J.-P. Migne) 98, cols. 359–372.

Germanos of Constantinople. 1860b. "In Praesentationem Sanctissimae Deiparae I." *Patrologia Graeca* (ed. J.-P. Migne) 98, cols. 291–310.

Germanos of Constantinople. 1998. "An Encomium on the Holy and Venerable Dormition of Our Most Glorious Lady, the Mother of God and Ever-Virgin Mary." *On the Dormition of Mary: Early Patristic Homilies*, trans. Brian E. Daley. Crestwood, NY: St. Vladimir's Seminary Press, 169–181.

Germanos of Constantinople. 2008. "On the Entrance [into the Temple] of the Supremely Holy Theotokos." *Wider than Heaven: Eighth-Century Homilies on the Mother of God*, trans. Mary B. Cunningham. Crestwood, NY: St. Vladimir's Seminary Press, 145–162.

Gerson, Jean. 1960–1973. *Oeuvres complètes*, ed. Palémon Glorieux. Paris: Desclée, 10 vols.

Gertsman, Elina. 2012. "Signs of Death: The Sacrificial Christ Child in Late-Medieval Art." *The Christ Child in Medieval Culture: Alpha es et O!*, ed. Mary Dzon and Theresa M. Kenney. Toronto, ON: University of Toronto Press, 66–91.

Gil, Rosa Maria, and Carmen Inoa Vazquez. 1996. *The Maria Paradox: How Latinas Can Merge Old World Traditions with New World Self-Esteem*. New York: G. P. Putnam's.

Gilmore, David D., ed. 1987. *Honor and Shame and the Unity of the Mediterranean*. Arlington, VA: American Anthropological Association.

Glossa Ordinaria. 1852. *Patrologia Latina* (ed. J.-P. Migne) 113 (cols. 67–1316)–114 (cols. 9–752).

Gobbi, Don Stefano. 1998. *To the Priests, Our Lady's Beloved Sons*. Toronto, ON: The Marian Movement of Priests.

Le Goff, Jacques. 1984 (1981). *The Birth of Purgatory*, trans. Arthur Goldhammer. Chicago, IL: University of Chicago Press.

Goodich, Michael. 1975. "Bartholomaeus Anglicus on Child-Rearing." *History of Childhood Quarterly* 3, 75–84.

Gougaud, Louis. 1925. *Dévotions et pratiques ascétiques du moyen age*. Paris: Desclée, de Brouwer.

Gounelle, Rémi. 2008. *Les recensions byzantines de l'Évangile de Nicodème*. Turnhout, Belgium: Brepols.

Gradel, Ittai. 2002. *Emperor Worship and Roman Religion*. Oxford, UK: Oxford University Press.

Graef, Hilda. 2009 (1963–1965). *Mary: A History of Doctrine and Devotion*. Notre Dame, IN: Ave Maria Press.

Gray, Douglas. 1963. "The Five Wounds of Our Lord." *Notes and Queries* 10 (1), 50–51, 83–89, 127–134, 163–168.

Grayzel, Solomon. 1991 (1962). "The Papal Bull *Sicut Judeis*." *Essential Papers on Judaism and Christianity in Conflict: From Late Antiquity to the Reformation*, ed. Jeremy Cohen. New York: New York University Press, 231–259.

The Greek New Testament, ed. Barbara Aland, Kurt Aland, Johannes Karavidopoulos, Carlo M. Martini, and Bruce M. Metzger. 2001. Stuttgart, Germany: Deutsche Bibelgesellschaft.

Green, Joel B. 2002. "Blessed Is She Who Believed: Mary, Curious Exemplar in Luke's Narrative." *Blessed One: Protestant Perspectives on Mary*, ed. Beverly

Roberts Gaventa and Cynthia L. Rigby. Louisville, KY: Westminster John Knox Press, 9–20.

Greene, Richard Leighton, ed. 1977 (1935). *The Early English Carols*. Oxford, UK: Oxford University Press.

Gregori, Mina. 1994. *Paintings in the Uffizi & Pitti Galleries*, trans. C. H. Murphy and H. D. Fernandez. Boston, MA: Little, Brown.

Gregory of Nazianzus, Saint. 1969. *La Passion du Christ: tragédie* [*Christos Paschōn*], ed., trans. André Tuilier. Paris: Les Éditions du Cerf.

Gregory the Great, Saint. 1849a. "Liber Sacramentorum cum variis praefationibus et supplementis." *Patrologia Latina* (ed. J.-P. Migne) 78, cols. 9–636.

Gregory the Great, Saint. 1849b. "Homilia VIII, in die Natalis Domini." *Patrologia Latina* (ed. J.-P. Migne) 76, cols. 1103–1105.

Grimoüard de Saint-Laurent, Henri-Julien. 1872–1875. *Guide de l'art chrétien: études d'esthétique et d'iconographie*. Paris: Librairie Archéologique de Didron, 6 vols.

Grintz, Yehoshua M. 1972. "Ark of the Covenant." *Encyclopaedia Judaica*. Jerusalem: Keter, vol. 3, 459–466.

Grünbaum, Adolf. 2010 (1993). "Psychoanalysis and Theism." *Psychoanalysis and Theism: Critical Reflections on the Grünbaum Thesis*, ed. Benjamin Beit-Hallahmi. Lanham, MD: Jason Aronson, 3–41.

Guldan, Ernst. 1966. *Eva und Maria: Eine Antithese als Bildmotiv*. Graz, Austria: Hermann Böhlaus Nachf.

Gutiérrez, Gustavo. 1988 (1971). *A Theology of Liberation: History, Politics, and Salvation*, trans. Caridad Inda and John Eagleson. Maryknoll, NY: Orbis.

Hahn, Scott, ed. 2009. *Catholic Bible Dictionary*. New York: Doubleday.

Hallebeek, Jan. 2007. "Papal Prohibitions Midway between Rigor and Laxity. On the Issue of Depicting the Holy Trinity." *Iconoclasm and Iconoclash: Struggle for Religious Identity*, eds. Willem van Asselt, Paul van Geest, Daniela Müller, and Theo Salemink. Leiden, Netherlands: Brill, 353–383.

Hamburger, Jeffrey F. 2011. "Bloody Mary: Traces of the *Peplum Cruentatum* in Prague – and in Strasbourg?" *Image, Memory and Devotion: Liber Amicorum Paul Crossley*, ed. Zoë Opačić and Achim Timmermann. Turnhout, Belgium: Brepols, 1–34.

Hapgood, Isabel Florence. 1922. *Service Book of the Holy Orthodox-Catholic Apostolic Church*. New York: Association Press.

Hatfield, Rab. 1990. "The Tree of Life and the Holy Cross: Franciscan Spirituality in the Trecento and the Quattrocento." *Christianity and the Renaissance: Image and Religious Imagination in the Quattrocento*, ed. Timothy Verdon and John Henderson. Syracuse, NY: Syracuse University Press, 132–160.

Hauke, Manfred. 1993. "Priestertum. I. Dogmatik." *Marienlexikon*, ed. Remigius Bäumer and Leo Scheffczyk. St. Ottilien, Germany: EOS, vol. 5, 314–317.

Hauke, Manfred. 2007. "Die Lehre von der 'Miterlöserin' im geschichtlichen Durchblick. Von den biblischen Ursprüngen bis zu Papst Benedikt XVI." *Sedes Sapientiae. Mariologisches Jahrbuch* 11 (1), 17–64.

Hebert, A. G. 1950. "The Virgin Mary as the Daughter of Zion." *Theology* 53, 403–410.

Heil, Johannes, and Rainer Kampling, eds. 2001. *Maria – Tochter Sion? Mariologie, Marienfrömmigkeit und Judenfeindschaft*. Paderborn, Germany: Ferdinand Schöningh.

Heilbronner, Tim. 2007–2008. "The Wooden 'Chasuble Madonnas' from Ger, Ix, Targasona and Talló," *Locvs Amoenvs* 9, 31–50.

Hengel, Martin. 1977 (1976). *Crucifixion in the Ancient World and the Folly of the Message of the Cross*, trans. John Bowden. Philadelphia, PA: Fortress Press.

Heretz, Leonid. 2008. *Russia on the Eve of Modernity: Popular Religion and Traditional Culture under the Last Tsars*. Cambridge, UK: Cambridge University Press.

Hesbert, René Jean, ed. 1952. *Le prosaire de la Sainte-Chapelle: manuscrit du chapitre de Saint-Nicolas de Bari (vers 1250)* (= *Monumenta musicae sacrae* 1). Mâcon, France: Protat Frères.

Hickey, Emily, trans. 1916. "Lignum vitae quaerimus." *Irish Monthly* 44 (514), 225–226.

Hindsley, Leonard P. 1998. *The Mystics of Engelthal: Writings from a Medieval Monastery*. New York: St. Martin's Press.

Hirn, Yrjö. 1957 (1909). *The Sacred Shrine: A Study of the Poetry and Art of the Catholic Church*. Boston, MA: Beacon Press.

Honorius Augustodunensis. 1854. "Sigillum Beatae Mariae ubi Exponuntur Cantica Canticorum." *Patrologia Latina* (ed. J.-P. Migne) 172, cols. 495–518.

Honorius Augustodunensis. 1991. *The Seal of Blessed Mary*, trans. Amelia Carr. Toronto, ON: Peregrina.

Hood, Ralph W., Ronald J. Morris, and P. J. Watson. 1991. "Male Commitment to the Cult of the Virgin Mary and the Passion of Christ as a Function of Early Maternal Bonding." *International Journal for the Psychology of Religion* 1, 221–231.

Hopkins, Brooke. 2001 (1989). "Jesus and Object Use: A Winnicottian Account of the Resurrection Myth." *Freud and Freudians on Religion: A Reader*, ed. Donald Capps. New Haven, CT: Yale University Press, 230–240.

van der Horst, P. W. 1999. "God (II) Θεός." *Dictionary of Deities and Demons in the Bible*, ed. Karel van der Toorn, Bob Becking, and Pieter W. van der Horst. Leiden, Netherlands/Grand Rapids, MI: Brill/William B. Eerdmans, 365–369.

van der Horst, P. W. 2005 (1994–1995). "Sex, Birth, Purity and Asceticism in the Protevangelium Jacobi." *A Feminist Companion to Mariology*, ed. Amy-Jill Levine and Maria Mayo Robbins. Cleveland, OH: Pilgrim Press, 56–66.

Hsia, R. Po-chia. 1988. *The Myth of Ritual Murder: Jews and Magic in Reformation Germany*. New Haven, CT: Yale University Press.

Hunt, Priscilla. 2009. "The Wisdom Iconography of Light: The Genesis, Meaning and Iconographic Realization of a Symbol." *Byzantinoslavica* 67, 55–118.

Hunt, Robert E. 1964. "Our Lady's Coredemption as an Ecumenical Problem." *Marian Studies* (2nd series) 15, 48–86.

Huot, Sylvia. 1997. *Allegorical Play in the Old French Motet: The Sacred and the Profane in Thirteenth-Century Polyphony*. Stanford, CA: Stanford University Press.

Iacopone da Todi. 1953. *Laudi, Trattato e Detti*. Florence, Italy: Felice le Monnier.

"Index in Mariana SS. Patrum Occidentalis Ecclesiae." *Patrologia Latina* (ed. J.-P. Migne) 219 (1862), cols. 493–528.

Irénée de Lyon. 1969. *Contre les hérésies, Livre V*, ed. A. Rousseau, L. Doutreleau, and C. Mercier, vol. II (= *Sources Chrétiennes*, no. 153). Paris: Éditions du Cerf.

Jacobs-Malina, Diane. 1993. *Beyond Patriarchy: The Images of Family in Jesus*. New York: Paulist Press.

Jacopone da Todi. 1982. *The Lauds*, trans. Serge and Elizabeth Hughes. New York: Paulist Press.

James, E. O. 1959. *The Cult of the Mother-Goddess: An Archaeological and Documentary Study*. London: Thames & Hudson.

Janowitz, Naomi H. 2008. "Envy of Maternal Functions in Sacrifice Rituals." *Jealousy and Envy: New Views about Two Powerful Feelings*, ed. Léon Wurmser and Heidrun Jarass. New York: Analytic Press, 117–128.

Jay, Nancy. 1992. *Throughout Your Generations Forever: Sacrifice, Religion, and Paternity*. Chicago, IL: University of Chicago Press.

Jeanjacquot, Pierre. 1871 (1868). *Simple Explanations Concerning the Co-Operation of the Most Holy Virgin in the Work of Redemption, and Concerning Her Quality of Mother of Christians* (anonymous translation from the French). London: John Philp.

Jenkins, Philip. 2010. *Jesus Wars: How Four Patriarchs, Three Queens, and Two Emperors Decided What Christians Would Believe for the Next 1,500 Years*. New York: HarperCollins.

Jenson, Robert W. 2004. "A Space for God." *Mary, Mother of God*, ed. Carl E. Braaten and Robert W. Jenson. Grand Rapids, MI: William B. Eerdmans, 49–57.

The Jewish Annotated New Testament: New Revised Standard Version Bible Translation, ed. Amy-Jill Levine and Marc Zvi Brettler. 2011. Oxford, UK: Oxford University Press.

The Jewish Study Bible, ed. Adele Berlin and Marc Zvi Brettler. 2004. Oxford, UK: Oxford University Press.

John of Damascus. 1988. *Die Schriften des Johannes von Damaskos*, ed. Bonifatius Kotter. Berlin: Walter de Gruyter, vol. 5.

John of Damascus. 1998a. "On the Dormition of the Holy Mother of God." *On the Dormition of Mary: Early Patristic Homilies*, trans. Brian E. Daley. Crestwood, NY: St. Vladimir's Seminary Press, 183–201.

John of Damascus. 1998b. "On the Holy and Glorious Dormition and Transformation of Our Lady Mary, Mother of God and Ever-Virgin." *On the Dormition of Mary: Early Patristic Homilies*, trans. Brian E. Daley. Crestwood, NY: St. Vladimir's Seminary Press, 203–230.

John of Damascus. 1998c. "A Discourse on the Dormition of Our Lady, the Mother of God." *On the Dormition of Mary: Early Patristic Homilies*, trans. Brian E. Daley. Crestwood, NY: St. Vladimir's Seminary Press, 231–239.

John of Damascus. 2008. "An Oration on the Nativity of the Holy Theotokos Mary." *Wider than Heaven: Eighth-Century Homilies on the Mother of God*, trans. Mary B. Cunningham. Crestwood, NY: St. Vladimir's Seminary Press, 53–70.

John Paul II, Saint. 2001 (1996). *The Encyclicals of John Paul II*, ed. J. Michael Miller. Huntington, IN: Our Sunday Visitor.

John Paul II, Saint. 2003. *On the Eucharist/Ecclesia de Eucharistia*. Washington, DC: United States Conference of Catholic Bishops.

Johnson, E. Elizabeth. 2002. "'Who Is My Mother?' Family Values in the Gospel of Mark." *Blessed One: Protestant Perspectives on Mary*, ed. Beverly Roberts Gaventa and Cynthia L. Rigby. Louisville, KY: Westminster John Knox Press, 32–46.

Johnson, Elizabeth A. 2003. *Truly Our Sister: A Theology of Mary in the Communion of Saints*. New York: Continuum.

Jones, Ernest. 1964 (1914). "The Madonna's Conception through the Ear: A Contribution to the Relation between Aesthetics and Religion." *Essays in Applied Psychoanalysis*. New York: International Universities Press, vol. 2, 266–357.

Jouassard, G. 1949. "Marie à travers la Patristique: Maternité divine, Virginité, Sainteté." *Maria: Études sur la Sainte Vierge*, ed. Hubert du Manoir. Paris: Beauchesne, vol. 1, 69–157.

Jugie, Martin. 1944. *La Mort et l'assomption de la Sainte Vierge: Étude historico-doctrinale*. Vatican City: Biblioteca Apostolica Vaticana.

Jugie, Martin. 1949. "Assomption de la Sainte Vierge." *Maria: Études sur la Sainte Vierge*, ed. Hubert du Manoir. Paris: Beauchesne, vol. 1, 619–658.

Jungmann, Joseph A. 1951 (1949). *The Mass of the Roman Rite: Its Origins and Development (Missarum Sollemnia)*, trans. Francis A. Brunner. Notre Dame, IN: Ave Maria Press, 2 vols.

Justin Martyr. 2006. *Apologie pour les Chrétiens*, ed., trans. Charles Munier (= *Sources Chrétiennes* no. 507). Paris: Éditions du Cerf.

Kalavrezou, Ioli. 1990. "Images of the Mother: When the Virgin Mary Became *Meter Theou*." *Dumbarton Oaks Papers* 44, 165–172.

Kalavrezou, Ioli. 2000a. "The Maternal Side of the Virgin." *Mother of God: Representations of the Virgin in Byzantine Art*, ed. Maria Vassilaki. Milan, Italy: Skira, 41–45.

Kalavrezou, Ioli. 2000b. "The Mother of God in Steatite." *Mother of God: Representations of the Virgin in Byzantine Art*, ed. Maria Vassilaki. Milan, Italy: Skira, 185–193.

Kalavrezou, Ioli. 2005. "Exchanging Embrace: The Body of Salvation." *Images of the Mother of God: Perceptions of the Theotokos in Byzantium*, ed. Maria Vassilaki. Aldershot, UK: Ashgate, 103–115.

Kallis, Anastasios. 2000. *Die Göttliche Liturgie der Orthodoxen Kirche: Deutsch – Griechisch – Kirchenslawisch*. Münster, Germany: Theophano.

Kasper, Walter, editor-in-chief. 1993–2001. *Lexikon für Theologie und Kirche*. Freiburg im Breisgau, Germany: Herder, 11 vols.

Kaspersen, Søren. 2004. "Wall-Paintings and Devotion: The Impact of Late Medieval Piety on Danish Murals." *Images of Cult and Devotion: Function and Reception of Christian Images in Medieval and Post-Medieval Europe*, eds. Søren Kaspersen and Ulla Haastrup. Copenhagen: Museum Tusculanum Press, 183–214.

Katzenellenbogen, Adolf. 1959. *The Sculptural Programs of Chartres Cathedral: Christ, Mary, Ecclesia*. Baltimore, MD: Johns Hopkins Press.

Katzew, Ilona. 2011. "'Remedo de la ya muerta América': The Construction of Festive Rites in Colonial Mexico." *Contested Visions in the Spanish Colonial World*, ed. Ilona Katzew. Los Angeles, CA/New Haven, CT: Los Angeles County Museum of Art/Yale University Press, 150–175.

Kearns, Cleo McNelly. 2008. *The Virgin Mary, Monotheism, and Sacrifice*. Cambridge, UK: Cambridge University Press.

Kecks, Ronald G. 1988. *Madonna und Kind: Das häusliche Andachtsbild im Florenz des 15. Jahrhunderts*. Berlin: Gebr. Mann.

Keel, Pamela K., and Kelly L. Klump. 2003. "Are Eating Disorders Culture-Bound Syndromes? Implications for Conceptualizing their Etiology." *Psychological Bulletin* 129 (5), 747–769.

Keeler, Elizabeth Marie. 2003. "The Mystery of Our Lady's Cooperation in Our Redemption as Seen in the Fathers of Benedictine Monasticism from the VI to the XII Century." *Mary at the Foot of the Cross – III: Mater Unitatis. Acts of the Third International Symposium on Marian Coredemption*, ed. Franciscans of the Immaculate. New Bedford, MA: Academy of the Immaculate, 259–294.

Kehrein, Joseph. 1873. *Lateinische Sequenzen des Mittelalters aus Handschriften und Drucken*. Mainz, Germany: Florian Kupferberg.

Keller, Theo, ed.(?). 2013. *The Little Office of the Blessed Virgin Mary*. London: Baronius Press.

Kelly, J. N. D. 1975. *Jerome: His Life, Writings, Controversies*. London: Duckworth.

Kenney, Theresa. 2012. "The Manger as Calvary and Altar in the Middle English Nativity Lyric." *The Christ Child in Medieval Culture: Alpha es et O!*, ed. Mary Dzon and Theresa M. Kenney. Toronto, ON: University of Toronto Press, 29–65.

Kertzer, David I. 2002 (2001). *The Popes against the Jews: The Vatican's Role in the Rise of Modern Anti-Semitism*. New York: Random House.

Kessler, Edward. 2011. "Mary – The Jewish Mother." *Irish Theological Quarterly* 76 (3), 211–223.

Kessler, Herbert L. 2000. *Spiritual Seeing: Picturing God's Invisibility in Medieval Art*. Philadelphia, PA: University of Pennsylvania Press.

Khitrowo, Sofiia Petrovna, ed., trans. 1966 (1889). *Itinéraires russes en orient*. Osnabrück, Germany: Otto Zeller.

Kirschbaum, Engelbert, and Wolfgang Braunfels, eds. 1968–1976. *Lexikon der christlichen Ikonographie*. Freiburg, Germany: Herder, 8 vols.

Klapisch-Zuber, Christiane. 1985. *Women, Family, and Ritual in Renaissance Italy*, trans. Lydia Cochrane. Chicago, IL: University of Chicago Press.

Klein, Melanie. 1994 (1940). "Mourning and Its Relation to Manic-Depressive States." *Essential Papers on Object Loss*, ed. Rita V. Frankiel. New York: New York University Press, 95–122.

Koepplin, D. 1970. "Interzession: Mariä und Christi vor Gottvater." *Lexikon der christlichen Ikonographie*, ed. Engelbert Kirschbaum. Freiburg, Germany: Herder, vol. 2, 346–352.

Kohle, Hubert. 1997. "XIII. Fundamentalistische Marienbewegungen." *Handbuch der Marienkunde*, ed. Wolfgang Beinert and Heinrich Petri. Regensburg, Germany: Friedrich Pustet, vol. 2, 60–106.

Kondakov, Nikodim P. 1911 (1910). *Ikonografiia Bogomateri: Sviazi grecheskoi i russkoi ikonopisi s ital'ianskoiu zhivopis'iu rannego Vozrozhdeniia*. St. Petersburg, Russia: Tovarishchestvo R. Golike i A. Vil'borg.

Kondakov, Nikodim P. 1998 (1914–1915). *Ikonografiia Bogomateri*. Moscow: Palomnik, 2 vols.

De Koninck, Charles. 1943. *Ego Sapientia . . . La sagesse qui est Marie*. Quebec: Éditions de l'Université Laval.

Kornblatt, Judith Deutsch. 2009. *Divine Sophia: The Wisdom Writings of Vladimir Solovyov*. Ithaca, NY: Cornell University Press.

Korošak, Bruno. 1954. *Mariologia S. Alberti Magni eiusque coaequalium*. Rome: Academia Mariana Internationalis.

Kozyrev, A. P. 1995. "Sofiologiia." *Russkaia filosofiia. Slovar'*, ed. M. A. Maslin. Moscow: Respublika, 465–469.

Kreitzer, Beth. 2004. *Reforming Mary: Changing Images of the Virgin Mary in Lutheran Sermons of the Sixteenth Century*. Oxford, UK: Oxford University Press.

Kugler, Robert A. 2010. "Priests." *The Eerdmans Dictionary of Early Judaism*, ed. John J. Collins and Daniel C. Harlow. Grand Rapids, MI: William B. Eerdmans, 1096–1099.

Küppers, Leonhard, ed. 1974. *Die Gottesmutter: Marienbild in Rheinland und in Westfalen*. Recklinghausen, Germany: Aurel Bongers, vol. II.

Ladis, Andrew. 1982. *Taddeo Gaddi: Critical Reappraisal and Catalogue Raisonné*. Columbia, MO: University of Missouri Press.

Laing, R. D. 1976. *The Facts of Life*. New York: Pantheon Books.

Lambot, Cyrille. 1952. "L'authenticité du sermon 369 de S. Augustin pour la fête de Noël." *Colligere Fragmenta: Festschrift Alban Dold*, ed. Bonifatius Fischer and Virgil Fiala. Beuron in Hohenzollern, Germany: Beuroner Kunstverlag, 103–112.

Lampe, G. W. H., ed. 1961. *A Patristic Greek Lexicon*. Oxford, UK: Oxford University Press.

Lampen, Willibrordus. 1946. "'Pie Pelicane, Iesu Domine'." *Antonianum* 21, 68–92.

Lane, Barbara G. 1984. *The Altar and the Altarpiece: Sacramental Themes in Early Netherlandish Painting*. New York: Harper & Row.

Lanfranc of Bec. 1854. "Liber de corpore et sanguine Domini adversus Berengarium Turonensem." *Patrologia Latina* (ed. J.-P. Migne) 150, cols. 407–442.

Langener, Lucia. 1996. *Isis lactans – Maria lactans: Untersuchungen zur koptischen Ikonographie*. Altenberge, Germany: Oros.

Lasareff, Victor. 1938. "Studies in the Iconography of the Virgin." *Art Bulletin* 20, 26–65.

Laurentin, René. 1947. "Essai sur un malaise théologique: Marie et le sacerdoce." *Nouvelle revue théologique* 69, 271–283.

Laurentin, René. 1948. "Le problème du sacerdoce marial devant le Magistere." *Marianum* 10, 160–178.

Laurentin, René. 1951. "Le titre de Corédemptrice: Étude historique." *Marianum* 13, 396–452.

Laurentin, René. 1952–1953. *Marie, l'Église et le sacerdoce*. Paris: Nouvelles Éditions Latines, 2 vols.

Laurentin, René. 1965. *La Vierge au Concile*. Paris: P. Lethielleux.

Laurentin, René. 1968. *Court traité sur la Vierge Marie*. Paris: P. Lethielleux.

Laurentin, René. 1991 (1968). *A Short Treatise on the Virgin Mary*, trans. Charles Neumann. Washington, NJ: AMI Press.

Laurentin, René. 2009. *Court traité sur la Vierge Marie, sixième édition refondue et mise à jour. Postface: L'après-Concile et l'avenir de Marie dans l'Église*. Paris: François-Xavier de Guibert.

Laurentin, René, and Patrick Sbalchiero, eds. 2007. *Dictionnaire des "apparitions" de la Vierge Marie: Inventaire des origines à nos jours, méthodologie, bilan interdisciplinaire, prospective*. Paris: Fayard.

LaVerdiere, Eugene. 1996. *The Eucharist in the New Testament and the Early Church*. Collegeville, MN: Liturgical Press.

Lazarev, V. N. 1994 (1983). *Russkaia ikonopis' ot istokov do nachala XVI veka*. Moscow: Iskusstvo.

Lechner, G. M. 1981. *Maria Gravida: Zum Schwangerschaftsmotiv in der bildenden Kunst*. Munich, Germany/Zürich, Switzerland: Schnell & Steiner.

Lechner, G. M. 1993a. "Priestertum. II. Kunstgeschichte." *Marienlexikon*, ed. Remigius Bäumer and Leo Scheffczyk. St. Ottilien, Germany: EOS, vol. 5, 317–318.

Lechner, G. M. 1993b. "Platyteramonstranzen." *Marienlexikon*, ed. Remigius Bäumer and Leo Scheffczyk. St. Ottilien, Germany: EOS, vol. 5, 253–255.

Lechner, G. M. 1994a. "*Sedes sapientiae* (Thron Salomos)." *Marienlexikon*, ed. Remigius Bäumer and Leo Scheffczyk. St. Ottilien, Germany: EOS, vol. 6, 113–118.

Lechner, G. M. 1994b. "Schreinmadonna (oder Klappmadonna, franz. 'Vierge ouvrante')." *Marienlexikon*, ed. Remigius Bäumer and Leo Scheffczyk. St. Ottilien, Germany: EOS, vol. 6, 72–75.

Lechner, G. M. 1997. "Marienverehrung und Bildende Kunst." *Handbuch der Marienkunde*, ed. Wolfgang Beinert and Heinrich Petri. Regensburg, Germany: Friedrich Pustet, vol. 2, 109–172.

Leclercq, Henri. 1932. "Marie, mère de Dieu." *Dictionnaire d'archéologie chrétienne et de liturgie*, ed. Fernand Cabrol and Henri Leclercq. Paris: Librairie Letouzey et Ané, vol. 10 (2), cols. 1982–2043.

Lécuyer, Joseph. 1954. "La Vierge Marie et la formation sacerdotale dans la tradition de l'École Bérullienne." *Maria: Études sur la Sainte Vierge*, ed. Hubert du Manoir. Paris: Beauchesne, vol. III, 73–93.

Lederer, Wolfgang. 1968. *The Fear of Women*. New York: Harcourt Brace Jovanovich.

Ledit, Joseph. 1976. *Marie dans la liturgie de Byzance*. Paris: Éditions Beauchesne.

Lefebvre, Dom Gaspar. 1956. *Saint Andrew Daily Missal*. Saint Paul, MN: E. M. Lohmann.

Lessard, Pierre. 1981. *Les petites images dévotes: Leur utilisation traditionnelle au Québec*. Quebec: Les Presses de l'Université Laval.

Levenson, Jon D. 1993. *The Death and Resurrection of the Beloved Son: The Transformation of Child Sacrifice in Judaism and Christianity*. New Haven, CT: Yale University Press.

Levy, Ian Christopher, Gary Macy, and Kristen Van Ausdall, eds. 2012. *A Companion to the Eucharist in the Middle Ages*. Leiden, Netherlands: Brill.

The Liber Usualis, with Introduction and Rubrics in English, ed. Benedictines of Solesmes. 1952. Tournai, Belgium: Desclée.

Lifshits, L. I. 1987. *Monumental'naia zhivopis' Novgoroda XIV–XV vekov*. Moscow: Iskusstvo.

Lifshits, L. I., and A. M. Lukashov. 2000. *Sofiia Premudrost' Bozhiia: Vystavka russkoi ikonopisi XIII–XIX vekov iz sobranii muzeev Rossii*. Moscow: Radunitsa.

Limberis, Vasiliki. 1994. *Divine Heiress: The Virgin Mary and the Creation of Christian Constantinople*. London: Routledge.

Llull, Ramon. 2003. *Opera Latina*. Turnhout, Belgium: Brepols, vol. 28, 49–52.

Llull, Ramon. 2005. *Das Buch über die heilige Maria (Libre de sancta Maria): Katalanisch-deutsch*, trans. Elisenda Padrós Wolff. Stuttgart-Bad Cannstatt, Germany: Friedrich Frommann.

Llywelyn, Dorian. 2010. *Toward a Catholic Theology of Nationality*. Lanham, MD: Rowman & Littlefield.

Loewen, Peter. 2008. "Portrayals of the *Vita Christi* in the Medieval German *Marienklage*: Signs of Franciscan Exegesis and Rhetoric in Drama and Music." *Comparative Drama* 42, 315–345.

Longère, Jean, ed. 2003. *Marie, fille d'Israël, fille de Sion*. Paris: Médiaspaul.

Lossky, Vladimir. 1985 (1967). *In the Image and Likeness of God*, ed. John H. Erickson and Thomas E. Bird. Crestwood, NY: St Vladimir's Seminary Press.

Loverdou-Tsigarida, Katia. 2000. "The Mother of God in Sculpture." *Mother of God: Representations of the Virgin in Byzantine Art*, ed. Maria Vassilaki. Milan, Italy: Skira, 237–249.

de Lubac, Henri. 1982 (1971). *The Motherhood of the Church*, trans. Sr. Sergia Englund. San Francisco, CA: Ignatius Press.

de Lubac, Henri. 1986 (1953). *The Splendor of the Church*, trans. Michael Mason. San Francisco, CA: Ignatius Press.

Lüdemann, Gerd. 1995. *What Really Happened to Jesus: A Historical Approach to the Resurrection*, tr. John Bowden. Louisville, KY: Westminster John Knox Press.

Lüdemann, Gerd. 1998 (1997). *Virgin Birth? The Real Story of Mary and her Son Jesus*, trans. John Bowden. Harrisburg, PA: Trinity Press International.

Lüdemann, Gerd. 2004. *The Resurrection of Christ: A Historical Inquiry*. Amherst, NY: Prometheus Books.

Ludolf of Saxony. 1878. *Vita Jesu Christi*, ed. L. M. Rigollot. Paris: Apud Victorem Palmé, 4 vols.

Ludolf of Saxony. 1887. *Vita Christi: The Hours of the Passion*, trans. Henry James Coleridge. London: Burns & Oates.

Lutz, Jules, and Paul Perdrizet. 1907–1909. *Speculum humanae salvationis*. Leipzig, Germany: La librairie C. Beck, 2 vols.

Lyonnet, S. 1939. "ΧΑΙΡΕ ΚΕΧΑΡΙΤΩΜΕΝΗ." *Biblica* 20, 131–141.

Maas, Paul, and C. A. Trypanis, eds. 1963. *Sancti Romani Melodi Cantica. Cantica Genuina*. Oxford, UK: Oxford University Press.

Maas-Ewerd, Th. 1994. "*Sub tuum praesidium*." *Marienlexikon*, ed. Remigius Bäumer and Leo Scheffczyk. St. Ottilien, Germany: EOS, vol. 6, 327–328.

MacGregor, Alistair. 2008. "Candlemas: A Festival of Roman Origin." *Origins of the Cult of the Virgin Mary*, ed. Chris Maunder. London: Burns & Oates, 137–153.

Macy, Gary. 1984. *The Theologies of the Eucharist in the Early Scholastic Period: A Study of the Salvific Function of the Sacrament According to the Theologians c. 1080–c. 1220*. Oxford, UK: Oxford University Press.

Macy, Gary. 1999. *Treasures from the Storeroom: Medieval Religion and the Eucharist*. Collegeville, MN: Liturgical Press.

Macy, Gary. 2007. *The Hidden History of Women's Ordination: Female Clergy in the Medieval West*. Oxford, UK: Oxford University Press.

Macy, Gary. 2012. "Theology of the Eucharist in the High Middle Ages." *A Companion to the Eucharist in the Middle Ages*, eds. Ian Christopher Levy, Gary Macy, and Kristen Van Ausdall. Leiden, Netherlands: Brill, 365–398.

Maguire, Henry. 1977. "The Depiction of Sorrow in Middle Byzantine Art." *Dumbarton Oaks Papers* 31, 123–174.

Maguire, Henry. 1981. *Art and Eloquence in Byzantium*. Princeton, NJ: Princeton University Press.

Mâle, Émile. 1925. *L'Art religieux du XIIIe siècle en France*. Paris: Librairie Armand Colin.

Mâle, Émile. 1928. *L'Art religieux du XIIe siècle en France*. Paris: Librairie Armand Colin.

Mâle, Émile. 1931. *L'Art religieux de la fin du moyen âge en France*. Paris: Librairie Armand Colin.

Mango, Cyril. 2000. "Constantinople as Theotokoupolis." *Mother of God: Representations of the Virgin in Byzantine Art*, ed. Maria Vassilaki. Milan, Italy: Skira, 16–25.

du Manoir, Hubert, ed. 1949–1971. *Maria: Études sur la Sainte Vierge*. Paris: Beauchesne, 8 vols.

de Marco, A. A. 1967. "Hail Mary." *New Catholic Encyclopedia*. New York: McGraw-Hill, vol. 6, 898.

Marcus, Jacob Rader. 1999 (1938). *The Jew in the Medieval World. A Source Book: 315–1791.* Cincinnati, OH: Hebrew Union College Press.

Marcus, Leah Sinanoglou. 2012 (1973). "The Christ Child as Sacrifice: A Medieval Tradition and the English Cycle Plays." *The Christ Child in Medieval Culture: Alpha es et O!*, ed. Mary Dzon and Theresa M. Kenney. Toronto, ON: University of Toronto Press, 3–28.

Margry, Peter Jan. 2009. "Paradoxes of Marian Apparitional Contestation: Networks, Ideology, Gender, and the Lady of All Nations." *Moved by Mary: The Power of Pilgrimage in the Modern World*, ed. Anna-Karina Hermkens, Willy Jansen, and Catrien Notermans. Burlington, VT: Ashgate, 183–199.

Marx, C. W. 1994. "The *Quis dabit* of Oglerius de Tridino, Monk and Abbot of Locedio." *Journal of Medieval Latin* 4, 118–129.

Mary in the Church: A Selection of Teaching Documents. 2003. Washington, DC: United States Conference of Catholic Bishops.

Mathews, Thomas F., and Norman Muller. 2005. "Isis and Mary in Early Icons." *Images of the Mother of God: Perceptions of the Theotokos in Byzantium*, ed. Maria Vassilaki. Aldershot: Ashgate, 3–11.

Maunder, Chris. 2008. "Origins of the Cult of the Virgin Mary in the New Testament." *Origins of the Cult of the Virgin Mary*, ed. Chris Maunder. London: Burns & Oates, 23–39.

Maunder, Chris. 2016. *Our Lady of the Nations: Apparitions of Mary in Twentieth-Century Catholic Europe*. Oxford, UK: Oxford University Press.

Maximus the Confessor. 2012. *The Life of the Virgin*, trans. by Stephen J. Shoemaker. New Haven, CT: Yale University Press.

McDonnell, M. 1967. "Bona Mors Confraternity." *New Catholic Encyclopedia*. New York: McGraw-Hill Book Company, vol. 2, 655.

McElvaney, William K. 1998. *Eating and Drinking at the Welcome Table: The Holy Supper for All People*. St. Louis, MO: Chalice Press.

McGuckin, John A. 2004 (1994). *St. Cyril of Alexandria: The Christological Controversy, Its History, Theology, and Texts*. Crestwood, NY: St Vladimir's Seminary Press.

McGuckin, John A. 2008. "The Early Cult of Mary and Inter-Religious Contexts in the Fifth-Century Church." *Origins of the Cult of the Virgin Mary*, ed. Chris Maunder. London: Burns & Oates, 1–22.

McGuckin, John A. 2011 (2008). *The Orthodox Church: An Introduction to Its History, Doctrine, and Spiritual Culture*. Malden, MA: Wiley-Blackwell.

McHugh, John. 1975. *The Mother of Jesus in the New Testament*. Garden City, NY: Doubleday.

McLaughlin, Mary Martin. 1974. "Survivors and Surrogates: Children and Parents from the Ninth to the Thirteenth Centuries." *The History of Childhood*, ed. Lloyd deMause. New York: Psychohistory Press, 101–181.

McNamer, Sarah. 2010. *Affective Meditation and the Invention of Medieval Compassion*. Philadelphia, PA: University of Pennsylvania Press.

Meersseman, G. G. 1958–1960. *Der Hymnos Akathistos im Abendland*. Fribourg, Switzerland, Germany: Universitätsverlag Freiburg Schweiz, 2 vols.

Meier, John P. 1991. *A Marginal Jew: Rethinking the Historical Jesus*. New York: Doubleday, vol. 1.

Meiss, Millard. 1936. "The Madonna of Humility." *Art Bulletin* 18, 435–464.

Meiss, Millard. 1945. "Light as Form and Symbol in Some Fifteenth-Century Paintings." *Art Bulletin* 27 (3), 175–181.

Meiss, Millard. 1951. *Painting in Florence and Siena after the Black Death: The Arts, Religion, and Society in the Mid-Fourteenth Century*. Princeton, NJ: Princeton University Press.

Meiss, Millard. 1954. "An Early Altarpiece from the Cathedral of Florence." *Metropolitan Museum of Art Bulletin* 12 (10), 302–317.

Mellinkoff, Ruth. 1970. *The Horned Moses in Medieval Art and Thought*. Berkeley, CA: University of California Press.

Mēnaion tou Augoustou. 1982. Athens, vol. 8.

Merback, Mitchell B. 2012. *Pilgrimage and Pogrom: Violence, Memory, and Visual Culture at the Host-Miracle Shrines of Germany and Austria*. Chicago, IL: University of Chicago Press.

Meyendorff, John. 1987. "Wisdom – Sophia: Contrasting Approaches to a Complex Theme." *Dumbarton Oaks Papers* 41, 391–401.

Middlemore, Merell P. 1953 (1941). *The Nursing Couple*. London: Cassell.

Miegge, Giovanni. 1955. *The Virgin Mary: The Roman Catholic Marian Doctrine*, trans. Waldo Smith. Philadelphia, PA: Westminster Press.

Mielke, U. 1972. "*Sapientia* (Sophia, Weisheit)." *Lexikon der christlichen Ikonographie*, ed. Engelbert Kirschbaum. Freiburg, Germany: Herder, vol. 4, 39–43.

Miles, M. M., ed. 2001. *Maiden and Mother: Prayers, Hymns, Songs and Devotions to Honour the Blessed Virgin Mary throughout the Year*. San Francisco, CA: Ignatius Press.

Miles, Margaret R. 2008. *A Complex Delight: The Secularization of the Breast, 1350–1750*. Berkeley, CA: University of California Press.

Miller, John W. 1997. *Jesus at Thirty: A Psychological and Historical Portrait*. Minneapolis, MN: Fortress Press.

Miller, Robert J., ed. 1994. *The Complete Gospels: Annotated Scholars Version*. San Francisco, CA: HarperCollins.

Mimouni, Simon Claude. 1995. *Dormition et assomption de Marie. Histoire des traditions anciennes*. Paris: Beauchesne.

Miravalle, Mark I. 1996. "The *Whole Truth about Mary*, Ecumenism, and the Year 2000." *Mary: Coredemptrix, Mediatrix, Advocate. Theological Foundations II: Papal, Pneumatological, Ecumenical*, ed. Mark I. Miravalle. Santa Barbara, CA: Queenship, 3–55.

The Mirror of Salvation (Speculum humanae salvationis): An Edition of British Library Blockbook G. 11784, trans., comm. Albert C. Labriola and John W. Smeltz. 2002. Pittsburgh, PA: Duquesne University Press.

Modestus of Jerusalem. 1860. "Encomium in Dormitionem Sanctissimae Dominae Nostrae Deiparae Semperque Virginis Mariae." *Patrologia Graeca* (ed. J.-P. Migne) 86, cols. 3277–3312.

Modestus of Jerusalem. 1998. "An Encomium on the Dormition of Our Most Holy Lady, Mary, Mother of God and Ever-Virgin." *On the Dormition of Mary: Early Patristic Homilies*, trans. Brian E. Daley. Crestwood, NY: St. Vladimir's Seminary Press, 83–102.

Moldenke, Harold N., and Alma L. Moldenke. 1986 (1952). *Plants of the Bible*. New York: Dover.

The Monk of Farne. 1961. *The Meditations of a Fourteenth Century Monk*, ed. Hugh Farmer. London: Darton, Longman & Todd.

Monks, Peter Rolfe. 1990. *The Brussels Horloge de Sapience: Iconography and Text of Brussels, Bibliothèque Royale, MS. IV 111*. Leiden, Netherlands: E. J. Brill.

de Montfort, Louis Marie. 1966. *Oeuvres complètes*. Paris: Éditions du Seuil.
de Montfort, Louis Marie. 1988. *God Alone: The Collected Writings of St. Louis Marie de Montfort*. Bay Shore, NY: Montfort.
Moore, Burness E., and Bernard D. Fine, eds. 1990. *Psychoanalytic Terms and Concepts*. New Haven, CT: American Psychoanalytic Association/Yale University Press.
Morin, G., ed. 1930. *Sancti Augustini Sermones post Maurinos reperti* (= *Miscellanea Agostiniana*, vol. 1). Rome: Typis Polyglottis Vaticanis.
Morinay, J. 1994. "Beatitudes." *Jesus Living in Mary: Handbook of the Spirituality of St. Louis Marie de Montfort*. Bay Shore, NY: Montfort, 57–66.
Mother Mary and Archimandrite Kallistos Ware. 1969. *The Festal Menaion*. London: Faber & Faber.
Mother Mary of the Visitation (Mère Marie de la Visitation). 1958. "Marie et le Purgatoire." *Maria: Études sur la Sainte Vierge*, ed. Hubert du Manoir. Paris: Beauchesne, vol. 5, 887–921.
Moxnes, Halvor. 2003. *Putting Jesus in His Place: A Radical Vision of Household and Kingdom*. Louisville, KY: Westminster John Knox Press.
Muir, Lynette R. 1995. *The Biblical Drama of Medieval Europe*. Cambridge, UK: Cambridge University Press.
Müller, Hans Wolfgang. 1963. "Isis mit dem Horuskinde: Ein Beitrag zur Ikonographie der Stillenden Gottesmutter im hellenistischen und römischen Ägypten." *Münchner Jahrbuch der bildenden Kunst* (series 3), vol. 14, 7–38.
Munroe, Robert L., Ruth H. Munroe, and John W. M. Whiting. 1973. "The Couvade: A Psychological Analysis." *Ethos* 1, 30–74.
Murphy, Francesca. 2007. "Immaculate Mary: The Ecclesial Mariology of Hans Urs von Balthasar." *Mary: The Complete Resource*, ed. Sarah Jane Boss. Oxford, UK: Oxford University Press, 300–313.
Murray, Robert. 2004 (1975). *Symbols of Church and Kingdom: A Study in Early Syriac Tradition*. London: T & T Clark.
Nagel, Alexander. 2000. *Michelangelo and the Reform of Art*. Cambridge, UK: Cambridge University Press.
Neale, John. 1852. *Sequentiae ex Missalibus Germanicis, Anglicis, Gallicis, Aliisque Medii Aevi, Collectae*. London: J. G. Parker.
Neff, Amy. 1998. "The Pain of *Compassio*: Mary's Labor at the Foot of the Cross." *Art Bulletin* 80 (2), 254–273.
Nelson, Robert S., and Kristen M. Collins, eds. 2006. *Holy Image, Hallowed Ground: Icons from Sinai*. Los Angeles, CA: J. Paul Getty Museum.
Neusner, Jacob. 2001 (1991). *Jews and Christians: The Myth of a Common Tradition*. Binghamton, NY: Global.
The New Oxford Annotated Bible, 4th edition, ed. Michael D. Coogan. 2010. Oxford, UK: Oxford University Press.
Newman, Barbara. 1987. *Sister of Wisdom: St. Hildegard's Theology of the Feminine*. Berkeley, CA: University of California Press.
Newman, Barbara. 2003. *God and the Goddesses: Vision, Poetry, and Belief in the Middle Ages*. Philadelphia, PA: University of Pennsylvania Press.
Newton, John, and Benjamin Durham, eds. 2013. *The Roman Breviary in English and Latin*. London: Baronius Press, 3 vols.
Neyrey, Jerome H. 1990. "Maid and Mother in Art and Literature." *Biblical Theology Bulletin* 20 (1), 65–75.
Nicene and Post-Nicene Fathers (first series), ed. Philip Schaff. 1991 (1886–1890). Edinburgh: T & T Clark, 14 vols.

Nicene and Post-Nicene Fathers (second series) ed. Philip Schaff and Henry Wace. 2004 (1890–1900). Peabody, MA: Hendrickson, 14 vols.

Nicolaïdès, Andréas. 1996. "L'église de la Panagia Arakiotissa à Lagoudéra, Chypre: Etude iconographique des fresques de 1192." *Dumbarton Oaks Papers* 50, 1–137.

Nikolakopoulos, K. 1991. "Kosmas v. Majum." *Marienlexikon*, ed. Remigius Bäumer and Leo Scheffczyk. St. Ottilien, Germany: EOS, vol. 3, 650–651.

Nitz, G. 1988. "Arbor Virginis." *Marienlexikon*, ed. Remigius Bäumer and Leo Scheffczyk. St. Ottilien, Germany: EOS, vol. 1, 219–220.

Nitz, G. 1992. "Lebensbaum." *Marienlexikon*, ed. Remigius Bäumer and Leo Scheffczyk. St. Ottilien, Germany: EOS, vol. 4, 53–54.

Norman, Diana. 1999. *Siena and the Virgin: Art and Politics in a Late Medieval City State*. New Haven, CT: Yale University Press.

The N-Town Plays, ed. Douglas Sugano and Victor I. Scherb. Kalamazoo, MI: Medieval Institute.

O'Carroll, Michael. 2000 (1982). *Theotokos: A Theological Encyclopedia of the Blessed Virgin Mary*. Eugene, OR: Wipf & Stock.

Ocker, Christopher. 1998. "Ritual Murder and the Subjectivity of Christ: A Choice in Medieval Christianity." *Harvard Theological Review* 91, 153–192.

O'Donnell, Christopher. 1996. *Ecclesia: A Theological Encyclopedia of the Church*. Collegeville, MN: The Liturgical Press.

O'Dwyer, Peter. 1988. *Mary: A History of Devotion in Ireland*. Dublin: Four Courts Press.

Offner, Richard, and Miklós Boskovits. 1987. "Pacino di Bonaguida." *A Critical and Historical Corpus of Florentine Painting: The Fourteenth Century* (section III, vol. II). Florence, Italy: Giunti Barbèra, 82–121.

Ogier of Locedio. 2006. *In Praise of God's Holy Mother. On Our Lord's Words to His Disciples at the Last Supper*, trans. D. Martin Jenni. Kalamazoo, MI: Cistercian.

O'Malley, John W. 2008. *What Happened at Vatican II*. Cambridge, MA: Harvard University Press.

O'Meara, Carra Ferguson. 1981. "'In the Hearth of the Virginal Womb': The Iconography of the Holocaust in Late Medieval Art." *Art Bulletin* 63, 75–88.

Onasch, Konrad. 1961. *Ikonen*. Gütersloh, Germany: Gerd Mohn.

Onasch, Konrad, and Annemarie Schnieper. 1997 (1995). *Icons: The Fascination and the Reality*, trans. Daniel G. Conklin. New York: Riverside.

O'Neill, Colman E. (revised by Romanus Cessario). 1991. *Meeting Christ in the Sacraments*. New York: Alba House.

O'Reilly, Jennifer. 1992. "The Trees of Eden in Mediaeval Iconography." *A Walk in the Garden: Biblical, Iconographical and Literary Images of Eden*, ed. Paul Morris and Deborah Sawyer. Sheffield, UK: Sheffield Academic Press, 167–204.

Origène. 1998 (1962). *Homélies sur S. Luc*, ed. M. Rauer, intro., trans., notes Henri Crouzel, François Fournier, and Pierre Périchon, resp. (= *Sources chrétiennes* vol. 87). Paris: Éditions du Cerf.

Orsi, Robert A. 2001. "The Many Names of the Mother of God." *Divine Mirrors: The Virgin Mary in the Visual Arts*, ed. Melissa R. Katz. New York: Oxford University Press, 3–18.

Orsi, Robert A. 2010 (1985). *The Madonna of 115th Street: Faith and Community in Italian Harlem, 1880–1950*. New Haven, CT: Yale University Press.

van Os, Bas. 2011. *Psychological Analyses and the Historical Jesus: New Ways to Explore Christian Origins* (= *Library of New Testament Studies* vol. 432). London: T & T Clark.

van Os, H. W. 1970. "Krönung Mariens." *Lexikon der christlichen Ikonographie*, ed. Engelbert Kirschbaum. Freiburg, Germany: Herder, vol. 2, 671–676.

Ouspensky, Leonid, and Vladimir Lossky. 1982. *The Meaning of Icons*, trans. G. E. H. Palmer and E. Kadloubovsky. Crestwood, NY: St Vladimir's Seminary Press.

The Oxford English Dictionary, 2nd ed. 1991. Oxford, UK: Clarendon Press, 20 vols.

Pallas, Demetrios I. 1965. *Die Passion und Bestattung Christi in Byzanz. Der Ritus – Das Bild.* Munich, Germany: Institut für Byzantinistik und neugriechische Philologie der Universität München.

Panella, D. A. 1967. "Proto-Evangelium." *New Catholic Encyclopedia.* New York: McGraw-Hill, vol. 11, 910–911.

Pankeev, Ivan. 2001. *Presviataia Bogoroditsa: Chudotvornye ikony i molitvy v zhiteiskikh nuzhdakh.* Moscow: Olma-Press.

Panofsky, Erwin. 1927. "'Imago Pietatis': Ein Beitrag zur Typengeschichte des 'Schmerzensmanns' und der 'Maria Mediatrix'." *Festschrift für Max J. Friedländer zum 60. Geburtstage.* Leipzig, Germany: E. A. Seemann, 261–308.

Papal Teachings: Our Lady, ed. Benedictine Monks of Solesmes, trans. Daughters of Saint Paul. 1961. Boston, MA: St. Paul.

Parish, Helen. 2010. *Clerical Celibacy in the West: c. 1100–1700.* Burlington, VT: Ashgate.

Parlby, Geri. 2007. "The Origins of Marian Art: The Evolution of Marian Imagery in the Western Church until AD 431." *Mary: The Complete Resource*, ed. Sarah Jane Boss. Oxford, UK: Oxford University Press, 106–129.

Parlby, Geri. 2008. "The Origins of Marian Art in the Catacombs and the Problems of Identification." *Origins of the Cult of the Virgin Mary*, ed. Chris Maunder. London: Burns & Oates, 41–56.

Paschasius Radbertus. 1969. *De corpore et sanguine Domini*, ed. Bede Paulus (= *Corpus Christianorum, continuatio medievalis* 16). Turnhout, Belgium: Brepols.

Pasulka, Diana Walsh. 2015. *Heaven Can Wait: Purgatory in Catholic Devotional and Popular Culture.* Oxford, UK: Oxford University Press.

Pelikan, Jaroslav. 1971–1989. *The Christian Tradition: A History of the Development of Doctrine.* Chicago, IL: University of Chicago Press, 5 vols.

Pelikan, Jaroslav. 1996. *Mary through the Centuries: Her Place in the History of Culture.* New Haven, CT: Yale University Press.

Pelikan, Jaroslav. 2004. "*Most* Generations Shall Call Me Blessed: An Essay in Aid of a Grammar of Liturgy." *Mary, Mother of God*, ed. Carl E. Braaten and Robert W. Jenson. Grand Rapids, MI: William B. Eerdmans, 1–18.

Peltomaa, Leena Mari. 2001. *The Image of the Virgin Mary in the Akathistos Hymn.* Leiden, Netherlands: Brill.

Pentcheva, Bissera V. 2006. *Icons and Power: The Mother of God in Byzantium.* University Park, PA: Pennsylvania State University Press.

Peppard, Michael. 2011. *The Son of God in the Roman World: Divine Sonship in Its Social and Political Context.* Oxford, UK: Oxford University Press.

Perdrizet, Paul. 1908. *La Vierge de Miséricorde: étude d'un thème iconographique.* Paris: A. Fontemoing.

Perillo, Maria Francesca. 2007. "Mary Coredemptrix and the Eucharist in the Mystical Experience of St. Veronica Giuliani." *Mary at the Foot of the Cross VI: Marian Coredemption in the Eucharistic Mystery.* New Bedford, MA: Academy of the Immaculate, 221–284.

Pérouas, Louis. 1982 (1973). *A Way to Wisdom: Louis Marie Grignion de Montfort and His Beliefs*, trans. Daughters of Wisdom, Montfort Missionaries. n.p.

Perreau-Saussine, Emile. 2012 (2011). *Catholicism and Democracy: An Essay in the History of Political Thought*, trans. Richard Rex. Princeton, NJ: Princeton University Press.

Perry, Nicholas and Loreto Echeverría. 1988. *Under the Heel of Mary*. London: Routledge.

Peter Comestor (Hildebertus Cenomanensi). 1854. "In festo Assumptionis Beatae Mariae, et de laudibus ejus, sermo primus." *Patrologia Latina* (ed. J.-P. Migne) 171, cols. 627–631.

Peter Damian. 1983. *Sancti Petri Damiani Sermones*, ed. Giovanni Lucchesi (= *Corpus Christianorum, continuatio mediaevalis* LVII). Turnhout, Belgium: Brepols.

Petroff, Elizabeth A. 2004. "Childhood and Child-Rearing in the Middle Ages." *Women in the Middle Ages: An Encyclopedia*, ed. Katharina M. Wilson and Nadia Margolis. Westport, CT: Greenwood Press, vol. I, 170–179.

Philip of Harvengt. 1855. "Commentaria in Cantica Canticorum." *Patrologia Latina* (ed. J.-P. Migne) 203, cols. 181–490.

Philippart, Guy. 1996. "Le récit miraculaire marial dans l'Occident médiéval." *Marie. Le culte de la Vierge dans la société médiévale*, ed. Dominique Iogna-Prat, Éric Palazzo, Daniel Russo. Paris: Beauchesne, 563–589.

Pierce, Joanne M. 2006. "Vestments and Objects." *The Oxford History of Christian Worship*, ed. Geoffrey Wainwright and Karen B. Westerfield Tucker. Oxford, UK: Oxford University Press, 841–857.

Pinder, Wilhelm. 1920. "Die dichterische Wurzel der Pietà." *Repertorium für Kunstwissenschaft* 42, 145–163.

Pitarakis, Brigitte. 2006. *Les croix-reliquaires pectorales byzantines en bronze*. Paris: Editions A. et J. Picard.

Pius XII, Pope. 1995. *Selected Encyclicals and Addresses*. Harrison, NY: Roman Catholic Books.

Plumpe, Joseph C. 1943. *Mater Ecclesia: An Inquiry into the Concept of the Church as Mother in Early Christianity*. Washington, DC: Catholic University of America Press.

Plutarch. 1936. *Moralia, V*, trans. Frank Cole Babbitt. Cambridge, MA: Harvard University Press (Loeb Classical Library 306).

Poole, Stafford. 1995. *Our Lady of Guadalupe: The Origins and Sources of a Mexican National Symbol, 1531–1797*. Tucson, AZ: University of Arizona Press.

Poselianin, Evgenii. 1911. *Bogomater': Polnoe illiustrirovannoe opisanie Eia zemnoi zhizni i posviashchennykh Eia imeni chudotvornykh ikon*. St. Petersburg, Russia: P. P. Soikin.

de la Potterie, Ignace. 1985–1991. "La venue de Marie à Éphese d'après le témoignage du Concile de 431." *Marian Library Studies* 17–23, 218–235.

Pourrat, M. P. 1949. "Marie et le sacerdoce." *Maria: Études sur la Sainte Vierge*, ed. Hubert du Manoir. Paris: Beauchesne, vol. I, 801–824.

Price, Merrall Llewelyn. 2003. *Consuming Passions: The Uses of Cannibalism in Late Medieval and Early Modern Europe*. London: Routledge.

Price, Richard. 2007. "Theotokos: The Title and Its Significance in Doctrine and Devotion." *Mary: The Complete Resource*, ed. Sarah Jane Boss. Oxford, UK: Oxford University Press, 56–73.

Purtle, Carol J. 1982. *The Marian Paintings of Jan van Eyck*. Princeton, NJ: Princeton University Press.

Raby, F. J. E. 1953 (1927). *A History of Christian-Latin Poetry from the Beginnings to the Close of the Middle Ages*. Oxford, UK: Oxford University Press.

Radler, Gudrun. 1990. *Die Schreinmadonna "Vierge Ouvrante": von den bernhardinischen Anfängen bis zur Frauenmystik im Deutschordensland; mit beschreibendem Katalog*. Frankfurt, Germany: Kunstgeschichtliches Institut der Johann Wolfgang Goethe-Universität.

Ragusa, Isa, and Rosalie B. Green, trans., ed. 1961. *Meditations on the Life of Christ: An Illustrated Manuscript of the Fourteenth Century*. Princeton, NJ: Princeton University Press.

Rakić, Svetlana. 2006. "The Representations of the Virgin on Cretan Icons in Serbian Churches in Bosnia-Herzegovina." *Serbian Studies* 20, 57–93.

Raming, Ida. 2004 (1976). *The Priestly Office of Women: God's Gift to a Renewed Church*, tr. Bernard Cooke and Gary Macy. Lanham, MD: Scarecrow Press.

Rancour-Laferriere, Daniel. 1992 (1985). *Signs of the Flesh: An Essay on the Evolution of Hominid Sexuality*. Bloomington, IN: Indiana University Press.

Rancour-Laferriere, Daniel. 1995. *The Slave Soul of Russia: Moral Masochism and the Cult of Suffering*. New York: New York University Press.

Rancour-Laferriere, Daniel. 2000. *Russian Nationalism from an Interdisciplinary Perspective: Imagining Russia*. Lewiston, NY: Edwin Mellen Press.

Rancour-Laferriere, Daniel. 2001. "Psychoanalytic Remarks on Russian Icons of the Mother of God," *Journal of European Psychoanalysis* 12–13, 65–78.

Rancour-Laferriere, Daniel. 2003. "The Moral Masochism at the Heart of Christianity: Evidence from Russian Orthodox Iconography and Icon Veneration." *Journal for the Psychoanalysis of Culture and Society* 8, 12–22.

Rancour-Laferriere, Daniel. 2005. *The Joy of All Who Sorrow: Icons of the Mother of God in Russia/Traditsiia pochitaniia ikon Bogomateri v Rossii glazami amerikanskogo psikhoanalitika* (bilingual edition). Moscow: Ladomir.

Rancour-Laferriere, Daniel. 2008. "From Death to Resurrection: The Case of Jesus." *Clio's Psyche* 15 (3), 146–148.

Rancour-Laferriere, Daniel. 2011. *The Sign of the Cross: From Golgotha to Genocide*. New Brunswick, NJ: Transaction.

Rancour-Laferriere, Daniel. 2014. "Pope Pius XII, the Dogma of Mary's Assumption, and the Holocaust." *Clio's Psyche* 21 (1), 28–32.

Rancour-Laferriere, Daniel. Forthcoming. "Three Levels of Couvade in the History of the Christian Church."

Ransel, David L. 1991. "Infant-Care Cultures in the Russian Empire." *Russia's Women: Accomodation, Resistance, Transformation*, ed. Barbara Evans Clements, Barbara Alpern Engel, and Christine D. Worobec. Berkeley, CA: University of California Press, 113–132.

Ratzinger, Joseph. 1983 (1977). *Daughter Zion: Meditations on the Church's Marian Belief*, trans. John M. McDermott. San Francisco, CA: Ignatius Press.

Ratzinger, Joseph. 2007. *Jesus of Nazareth: From the Baptism in the Jordan to the Transfiguration*, trans. Adrian J. Walker. New York: Doubleday.

Ratzinger, Joseph, and Hans Urs von Balthasar. 2005 (1997). *Mary: The Church at the Source*, trans. Adrian Walker. San Francisco, CA: Ignatius Press.

Ratzinger, Joseph, and Hans Urs von Balthasar. 1980. *Maria – Kirche im Ursprung*. Freiburg, Germany: Herder.

Raymond of Capua. 2011 (1960). *The Life of St. Catherine of Siena*, trans. George Lamb. Charlotte, NC: TAN Books.

Reijners, G. Q. 1965. *The Terminology of the Holy Cross in Early Christian Literature as Based upon Old Testament Typology*. Nijmegen, Netherlands: Dekker & van de Vegt.

Reiners-Ernst, Elisabeth. 1939. *Das freudvolle Vesperbild und die Anfänge der Pietà-Vorstellung*. Munich, Germany: Neuer Filser.

Reis, João José. 2003 (1991). *Death Is a Festival: Funeral Rites and Rebellion in Nineteenth-Century Brazil*, trans. H. Sabrina Gledhill. Chapel Hill, NC: University of North Carolina Press.

Remensnyder, Amy G. 2014. *La Conquistadora: The Virgin Mary at War and Peace in the Old and New Worlds*. Oxford, UK: Oxford University Press.

Reynolds, Brian K. 2012–. *Gateway to Heaven: Marian Doctrine and Devotion, Image and Typology in the Patristic and Medieval Periods*. Hyde Park, NY: New City Press, vol. 1.

Reynolds, Roger E. 1989. "Vestments, Liturgical." *Dictionary of the Middle Ages*, ed. Joseph R. Strayer. New York: Charles Scribner's, vol. 12, 397–404.

Riabov, O. V. 2001. *"Matushka-Rus'": Opyt gendernogo analiza poiskov natsional'noi identichnosti Rossii v otechestvennoi i zapadnoi istoriosofii*. Moscow: Ladomir.

Rimmele, Marius. 2006. "Die Schreinmadonna: Bild – Körper – Matrix." *Bild und Körper im Mittelalter*, ed. Kristin Marek, Raphaèle Preisinger, Marius Rimmele, and Katrin Kärcher. Munich, Germany: Wilhelm Fink, 41–59.

Robb, David M. 1936. "The Iconography of the Annunciation in the Fourteenth and Fifteenth Centuries." *Art Bulletin* 18, 480–526.

Robert, A. 1949. "La Sainte Vierge dans l'Ancien Testament." *Maria: Études sur la Sainte Vierge*, ed. Hubert du Manoir. Paris: Beauchesne, vol. I, 23–39.

Robinson, Forbes. 1896. "Coptic Apocryphal Gospels." *Texts and Studies. Contributions to Biblical and Patristic Literature*, vol. 4, no. 2. Cambridge, UK: Cambridge University Press.

Robson, Janet. 2011. "Assisi, Rome and the *Miracle of the Crib at Greccio*." *Image, Memory and Devotion: Liber Amicorum Paul Crossley*, ed. Zoë Opačić and Achim Timmermann. Turnhout, Belgium: Brepols, 145–155.

Roca, Roger Sansi. 2005. "Catholic Saints, African Gods, Black Masks and White Heads: Tracing the History of Some Religious Festivals in Bahia." *Portuguese Studies* 21, 182–200.

Romanos the Melodist. 1970–1973. *Kontakia of Romanos, Byzantine Melodist*, trans., annot. Marjorie Carpenter. Columbia, MO: University of Missouri Press, 2 vols.

Romanos the Melodist. 1995. *Kontakia: On the Life of Christ*, trans. Ephrem Lash. San Francisco, CA: HarperCollins.

Ronig, Franz. 1956. "Zwei Bilder der stillenden Muttergottes in einer Handschrift des trierer Bistumsarchivs." *Archiv für mittelrheinische Kirchengeschichte* 8, 362–370.

Ronig, Franz. 1974. "Zum theologischen Gehalt des Bildes der stillenden Muttergottes." *Die Gottesmutter: Marienbild in Rheinland und in Westfalen*, ed. Leonhard Küppers. Recklinghausen, Germany: Aurel Bongers, vol. 1, 197–214.

Roschini, G.-M. 1949. "Royauté de Marie." *Maria: Études sur la Sainte Vierge*, ed. Hubert du Manoir. Paris: Beauchesne, vol. I, 601–618.

Roschini, G.-M. 1969. *Maria Santissima nella Storia della Salvezza*. Rome: Tipografia Editrice M. Pisani, 4 vols.

Ross, James Bruce. 1974. "The Middle-Class Child in Urban Italy, Fourteenth to Early Sixteenth Century." *The History of Childhood*, ed. Lloyd deMause. New York: Psychohistory Press, 183–228.

Rosso, S. 1986. "Sabato." *Nuovo dizionario di mariologia*, ed. Stefano De Fiores and Salvatore Meo. Turin, Italy: Edizioni Paoline, 1216–1228.

Rowe, Nina. 2011. *The Jew, the Cathedral, and the Medieval City: Synagoga and Ecclesia in the Thirteenth Century*. Cambridge, UK: Cambridge University Press.

Rubin, Miri. 1991. *Corpus Christi: The Eucharist in Late Medieval Culture*. Cambridge, UK: Cambridge University Press.

Rubin, Miri. 2004 (1999). *Gentile Tales: The Narrative Assault on Late Medieval Jews*. Philadelphia, PA: University of Pennsylvania Press.

Rubin, Miri. 2009. *Mother of God: A History of the Virgin Mary*. New Haven, CT: Yale University Press.

Ruether, Rosemary Radford. 1977. *Mary – The Feminine Face of the Church*. Philadelphia, PA: Westminster Press.

Ruether, Rosemary Radford. 1993 (1983). *Sexism and God-Talk: Toward a Feminist Theology*. Boston, MA: Beacon Press.

Ruether, Rosemary Radford. 2005. *Goddesses and the Divine Feminine: A Western Religious History*. Berkeley, CA: University of California Press.

Russell, Norman. 2004. *The Doctrine of Deification in the Greek Patristic Tradition*. Oxford, UK: Oxford University Press.

Ryan, Edward A. 1961. "Devotion to Our Lady in the United States." *Mariology*, ed. Juniper B. Carol. Milwaukee, WI: Bruce, vol. 3, 353–381.

Ryan, W. F. 1999. *The Bathhouse at Midnight: An Historical Survey of Magic and Divination in Russia*. University Park, PA.: Pennsylvania State University Press.

Salaville, S. 1949. "Marie dans la Liturgie byzantine ou gréco-slave." *Maria: Études sur la Sainte Vierge*, ed. Hubert du Manoir. Paris: Beauchesne, vol. I, 247–326.

Salzer, Anselm. 1893. *Die Sinnbilder und Beiworte Mariens in der deutschen Literatur und lateinischen Hymnenpoesie des Mittelalters*. Linz, Austria: Hofbuchdruckerei Jos. Feichtingers Erben.

Sánchez Cantón, F. J. 1948. *Nacimiento e infancia de Cristo*. Madrid: Biblioteca de Autores Cristianos.

Sanders, E. P. 1993. *The Historical Figure of Jesus*. London: Penguin.

Dos Santos, José. 1962. "A doutrina do sacerdocio mariano segundo Fernando Q. de Salazar, S. I. (sec. XVII)." *Maria et Ecclesia: Acta Congressus Mariologici-Mariani in Civitate Lourdes Anno 1958 Celebrati* 7, 39–79.

Sawicki, Marianne. 1994. *Seeing the Lord: Resurrection and Early Christian Practices*. Minneapolis, MN: Fortress Press.

Saxl, F. 1942. "A Spiritual Encyclopaedia of the Later Middle Ages." *Journal of the Warburg & Courtauld Institutes* 5, 82–142.

Schaberg, Jane. 2005 (1997). "Feminist Interpretations of the Infancy Narrative of Matthew." *A Feminist Companion to Mariology*, ed. Amy-Jill Levine and Maria Mayo Robbins. Cleveland, OH: Pilgrim Press, 15–36.

Schaberg, Jane. 2006 (1987). *The Illegitimacy of Jesus: A Feminist Theological Interpretation of the Infancy Narratives*. Sheffield, UK: Sheffield Phoenix Press.

Schäfer, Peter. 2007. *Jesus in the Talmud*. Princeton, NJ: Princeton University Press.

Schäfer, Peter, Michael Meerson, and Yaacov Deutsch, eds. 2011. *Toledot Yeshu ("The Life Story of Jesus") Revisited*. Tübingen, Germany: Mohr Siebeck.

Schawe, M. 1993. "Pietà." *Marienlexikon*, ed. Remigius Bäumer and Leo Scheffczyk. St. Ottilien, Germany: EOS, vol. 5, 218–222.

Schildenberger, J. 1967. "Bundeslade." *Lexikon der Marienkunde*, eds. Konrad Algermissen, Ludwig Böer, Georg Englhardt, Carl Feckes, Michael Schmaus, and Julius Tyciak. Regensburg, Germany: Friedrich Pustet, vol. I, 1001–1003.

Schildenberger, J. 1989. "Dornbusch, brennender." *Marienlexikon*, ed. Remigius Bäumer and Leo Scheffczyk. St. Ottilien, Germany: EOS, vol. 2, 224–225.

Schiller, Gertrud. 1966–1991. *Ikonographie der christlichen Kunst*. Gütersloh, Germany: Gütersloher Verlagshaus Gerd Mohn, 5 vols.

Schmidt, Firmin M. 1957. "The Universal Queenship of Mary." *Mariology*, ed. Juniper B. Carol. Milwaukee, WI: Bruce, vol. 2, 493–549.

Schmitt, Jean-Claude. 2006. "L'Exception corporelle: à propos de l'Assomption de Marie." *The Mind's Eye: Art and Theological Argument in the Middle Ages*, ed. Jeffrey F. Hamburger and Anne-Marie Bouché. Princeton, NJ: Princeton University Press, 151–185.

Schmuck, N. 1993. "Passionsmadonna." *Marienlexikon*, ed. Remigius Bäumer and Leo Scheffczyk. St. Ottilien, Germany: EOS, vol. 5, 117–118.

Schneemelcher, Wilhelm, ed. 1991–1992. *New Testament Apocrypha*, ed., trans. R. M. Wilson. Louisville, KY: Westminster John Knox Press, 2 vols.

Schneider, G. 1991 (1981)a. "Μαρία, ας /Μαριάμ. *Maria/Mariam*. Mary." *Exegetical Dictionary of the New Testament*, ed. Horst Balz and Gerhard Schneider. Grand Rapids, MI: William B. Eerdmans, vol. 2, 386–389.

Schneider, G. 1991 (1981)b. "'Ιησους, ου. *Iēsous*. Jesus." *Exegetical Dictionary of the New Testament*, ed. Horst Balz and Gerhard Schneider. Grand Rapids, MI: William B. Eerdmans, vol. 2, 180–184.

Schreckenberg, Heinz. 1996. *The Jews in Christian Art: An Illustrated History*. New York: Continuum.

Schreiner, Klaus. 2006 (1996). *Maria: Jungfrau, Mutter, Herrscherin*. Cologne, Germany: Anaconda.

Schröder, Karl, ed. 1871. *Der Nonnen von Engelthal Büchlein von der Genaden Überlast*. Tübingen, Germany: Bibliothek des litterarischen Vereins in Stuttgart.

Schuler, Carol M. 1992. "The Seven Sorrows of the Virgin: Popular Culture and Cultic Imagery in Pre-Reformation Europe." *Simiolus: Netherlands Quarterly for the History of Art* 21, 5–28.

Schüssler Fiorenza, Elisabeth. 1994. *Jesus: Miriam's Child, Sophia's Prophet. Critical Issues in Feminist Christology*. New York: Continuum.

Sciacca, Christine. 2012. "Pacino di Bonaguida and His Workshop." *Florence at the Dawn of the Renaissance: Painting and Illumination, 1300–1350*, ed. Christine Sciacca. Los Angeles, CA: Getty, 285–303.

Sciacca, Christine, ed. 2012. *Florence at the Dawn of the Renaissance: Painting and Illumination, 1300–1350*. Los Angeles, CA: Getty.

Scott, Martin. 1992. *Sophia and the Johannine Jesus*. Sheffield, UK: Sheffield Academic Press.

Scourfield, J. H. D. 1993. *Consoling Heliodorus: A Commentary on Jerome, Letter 60*. Oxford, UK: Oxford University Press.

Semmelroth, Otto. 1963 (1950). *Mary, Archetype of the Church*, trans. Maria von Eroes and John Devlin. New York: Sheed & Ward.

Ševčenko, Nancy Patterson. 1991a. "Christ Anapeson." *The Oxford Dictionary of Byzantium*, ed. Alexander P. Kazhdan. Oxford, UK: Oxford University Press, vol. 1, 439.

Ševčenko, Nancy Patterson. 1991b. "Virgin of the Passion." *The Oxford Dictionary of Byzantium*, ed. Alexander P. Kazhdan. Oxford, UK: Oxford University Press, vol. 3, 2176.

Ševčenko, Nancy Patterson. 1991c. "Virgin Nikopoios." *The Oxford Dictionary of Byzantium*, ed. Alexander P. Kazhdan. Oxford, UK: Oxford University Press, vol. 3, 2176.

Ševčenko, Nancy Patterson. 1991d. "Virgin Blachernitissa." *The Oxford Dictionary of Byzantium*, ed. Alexander P. Kazhdan. Oxford, UK: Oxford University Press, vol. 3, 2170–2171.

Ševčenko, Nancy Patterson. 1991e. "Virgin Hodegetria." *The Oxford Dictionary of Byzantium*, ed. Alexander P. Kazhdan. Oxford, UK: Oxford University Press, vol. 3, 2172–2173.

Shahar, Shulamith. 1990. *Childhood in the Middle Ages*, trans. Chaya Galai. London: Routledge.

Shapiro, Fred R., ed. 2006. *The Yale Book of Quotations*. New Haven, CT: Yale University Press.

Sheingorn, Pamela. 2004 (1990). "Appropriating the Holy Kinship: Gender and Family History." *Medieval Families: Perspectives on Marriage, Household, and Children*, ed. Carol Neel. Toronto, ON: University of Toronto Press/Medieval Academy of America, 273–301.

Shengold, Leonard. 1989. *Soul Murder: The Effects of Childhood Abuse and Deprivation*. New York: Fawcett Columbine.

Shevzov, Vera. 2004. *Russian Orthodoxy on the Eve of Revolution*. Oxford, UK: Oxford University Press.

Shevzov, Vera. 2007. "Scripting the Gaze: Liturgy, Homilies, and the Kazan Icon of the Mother of God in Late Imperial Russia." *Sacred Stories: Religion and Spirituality in Modern Russia*, ed. Mark D. Steinberg and Heather J. Coleman. Bloomington, IN: Indiana University Press, 61–92.

Shoemaker, Stephen J. 2004. *Ancient Traditions of the Virgin Mary's Dormition and Assumption*. Oxford, UK: Oxford University Press.

Shoemaker, Stephen J. 2005. "The Virgin Mary in the Ministry of Jesus and the Early Church According to the Earliest *Life of the Virgin*." *Harvard Theological Review* 98, 441–467.

Shoemaker, Stephen J. 2007. "Marian Liturgies and Devotion in Early Christianity." *Mary: The Complete Resource*, ed. Sarah Jane Boss. Oxford, UK: Oxford University Press, 130–145.

Shoemaker, Stephen J. 2008. "The Cult of the Virgin in the Fourth Century: A Fresh Look at Some Old and New Sources." *Origins of the Cult of the Virgin Mary*, ed. Chris Maunder. London: Burns & Oates, 71–87.

Shoemaker, Stephen J. 2011a. "Mary at the Cross, East and West: Maternal Compassion and Affective Piety in the Earliest *Life of the Virgin* and the High Middle Ages." *Journal of Theological Studies* 62, 570–606.

Shoemaker, Stephen J. 2011b. "A Mother's Passion: Mary at the Crucifixion and Resurrection in the Earliest *Life of the Virgin* and its Influence on George of Nikomedeia's Passion Homilies." *The Cult of the Mother of God in Byzantium: Texts and Images*, ed. Leslie Brubaker and Mary B. Cunningham. Burlington, VT: Ashgate Publishing, 53–67.

Simon, Marcel. 1986 (1964). *Verus Israel: A Study of the Relations between Christians and Jews in the Roman Empire (135–425)*, trans. H. McKeating. Oxford, UK: Oxford University Press.

Simonsohn, Shlomo. 1988. *The Apostolic See and the Jews. Documents: 492–1404*. Toronto, ON: Pontifical Institute of Mediaeval Studies.

Simonsohn, Shlomo. 1991. *The Apostolic See and the Jews. History*. Toronto, ON: Pontifical Institute of Mediaeval Studies.

von Simson, Otto G. 1953. "*Compassio* and *Co-redemptio* in Roger van der Weyden's *Descent from the Cross*." *Art Bulletin* 35, 9–16.

Skazaniia o zemnoi zhizni presviatoi Bogoroditsy. n. d. (reprint of 1904 edition). Moscow: Peresvet.

Smirnov, S. 1914. *Drevne-russkii dukhovnik: issledovanie po istorii tserkovnogo byta*. Moscow: Sinodal'naia tipografiia.

Smith, M. Q. 1968. "Dornbusch, brennender." *Lexikon der christlichen Ikonographie*, ed. Engelbert Kirschbaum. Freiburg, Germany: Herder, vol. 1, 510–511.

Snessoreva, Sofiia. 1999 (1898). *Zemnaia zhizn' Presviatoi Bogoroditsy i opisanie sviatykh chudotvornykh ee ikon*. Iaroslavl', Russia: Verkhniaia Volga.

Socias, James. 2011. *Daily Roman Missal, Complete with Readings in One Volume*. Woodridge, IL: Midwest Theological Forum.

Sonet, Jean. 1956. *Répertoire d'incipit de prières en ancien français*. Geneva, Switzerland: Librairie E. Droz.

Soulen, R. Kendall. 2005. "Supersessionism." *A Dictionary of Jewish–Christian Relations*, ed. Edward Kessler and Neil Wenborn. Cambridge, UK: Cambridge University Press, 413–414.

Southern, R. W. 1953. *The Making of the Middle Ages*. New Haven, CT: Yale University Press.

Spier, Jeffrey. 2007. *Picturing the Bible: The Earliest Christian Art*. New Haven, CT/ Fort Worth, TX: Yale University Press/Kimbell Art Museum.

Spretnak, Charlene. 2004. *Missing Mary: The Queen of Heaven and Her Re-Emergence in the Modern Church*. New York: Palgrave Macmillan.

Sri, Edward. 2005. *Queen Mother: A Biblical Theology of Mary's Queenship*. Steubenville, OH: Emmaus Road.

Stylianopoulos, Theodore. 1998. "Justin Martyr (d. ca. 165)." *Encyclopedia of Early Christianity*, ed. Everett Ferguson. New York: Garland, 647–650.

Steenberg, M. C. 2004. "The Role of Mary as Co-recapitulator in St Irenaeus of Lyons." *Vigiliae Christianae* 58, 117–137.

Steinberg, Leo. 1970. "The Metaphors of Love and Birth in Michelangelo's *Pietàs*." *Studies in Erotic Art*, ed. Theodore Bowie and Cornelia V. Christenson. New York: Basic Books, 231–336.

Stern, Jean. 1980. *La Salette. Documents authentiques: dossier chronologique intégral, septembre 1846 – début mars 1847*, vol. I. [Paris]: Desclée de Brouwer.

Stevens, Evelyn P. 1973. "*Marianismo*: The Other Face of *Machismo* in Latin America." *Female and Male in Latin America: Essays*, ed. Ann Pescatello. Pittsburgh, PA: University of Pittsburgh Press, 89–101.

Stevens, John. 1986. *Words and Music in the Middle Ages: Song, Narrative, Dance and Drama, 1050–1350*. Cambridge, UK: Cambridge University Press.

Sticca, Sandro. 1988. *The Planctus Mariae in the Dramatic Tradition of the Middle Ages*, trans. Joseph R. Berrigan. Athens, GA: University of Georgia Press.

Suetonius. 1998. *Lives of the Caesars*, trans. J. C. Rolfe. Cambridge, MA: Harvard University Press (Loeb Classical Library 31).

Suso, Henry. 1953. *Little Book of Eternal Wisdom and Little Book of Truth*, trans. James M. Clark. New York: Harper & Brothers.

Suso, Henry. 1994. *Wisdom's Watch upon the Hours*, trans. Edmund Colledge. Washington, DC: Catholic University of America Press.

Swarzenski, H. 1935. "Quellen zum deutschen Andachtsbild." *Zeitschrift für Kunstgeschichte* 4, 141–144.

Sweeney, Jon M. 2006. *Strange Heaven: The Virgin Mary as Woman, Mother, Disciple, and Advocate*. Brewster, MA: Paraclete Press.

Szövérffy, Joseph. 1966. "'Crux Fidelis . . .': Prolegomena to a History of the Holy Cross Hymns." *Traditio* 22, 1–41.

Szövérffy, Joseph. 1976. *Hymns of the Holy Cross: An Annotated Edition with Introduction*. Leiden, Netherlands: Classical Folia Editions.

Szövérffy, Joseph. 1985a. *Marianische Motivik der Hymnen*. Leiden, Netherlands: Classical Folia Editions.

Szövérffy, Joseph. 1985b. *A Concise History of Medieval Latin Hymnody: Religious Lyrics between Antiquity and Humanism*. Leiden, Netherlands: Classical Folia Editions/E. J. Brill.

Talbert, Charles H. 2002. *Reading Luke: A Literary and Theological Commentary*. Mâcon, France: Smyth & Helwys.

Talbot, Alice-Mary. 1991. "Hodegon Monastery." *The Oxford Dictionary of Byzantium*, ed. Alexander P. Kazhdan. Oxford, UK: Oxford University Press, vol. 2, 939.

Tanner, Norman P., ed. 1990. *Decrees of the Ecumenical Councils*. London/ Washington, DC: Sheed & Ward/Georgetown University Press, 2 vols.

Tappolet, Walter. 1962. *Das Marienlob der Reformatoren*. Tübingen, Germany: Katzmann.

Tartuferi, Angelo, and Daniela Parenti, eds. 2006. *Lorenzo Monaco dalla tradizione Giottesca al Rinascimento*. Florence, Italy: Giunti Editore.

Tatić-Djurić, Mirjana. 1976. "Eleousa. A la recherche du type iconographique." *Jahrbuch der österreichischen Byzantinistik* 25, 259–267.

Tavard, George H. 1996. *The Thousand Faces of the Virgin Mary*. Collegeville, MN: Liturgical Press.

Terrier, Jean. 2002 (1635). *Portraicts des S S Vertus de la Vierge contemplées par feue S. A. S. M. Isabelle Clere Eugenie Infante d'Espagne*, facsimile edition, introd. Cordula van Wyhe. Glasgow, UK: University of Glasgow.

Tertullian, Quintus Septimius Florens. 1844. "Liber de Oratione." *Patrologia Latina* (ed. J.-P. Migne) 1, 1143–1196.

Thérel, Marie-Louise. 1979–1980. "'LA FEMME A LA COUPE'. Marie, l'Église et l'Eucharistie dans l'iconographie du Moyen-Age." *Études Mariales: Bulletin de la Société Française d'Études Mariales* 36–37, 81–92.

Thomas, Alois. 1970. "Maria die Weinrebe." *Kurtrierisches Jahrbuch* 10, 30–55.

Thomas, Alois. 1974. "Schutzmantelmaria." *Die Gottesmutter: Marienbild in Rheinland und in Westfalen*, ed. Leonhard Küppers. Recklinghausen, Germany: Aurel Bongers, vol. 1, 227–242.

Thomas, Alois. 1981 (1936). *Die Darstellung Christi in der Kelter: eine theologische und kulturhistorische Studie, zugleich ein Beitrag zur Geschichte und Volkskunde des Weinbaus*. Düsseldorf, Germany: Schwann.

Thomas Aquinas, Saint. 1969. *Summa Theologiae, Volume 51 (3a. 27–30), Our Lady*, trans., ed. Thomas R. Heath. Cambridge, UK: Cambridge University Press.

Thomas Aquinas, Saint. 2012. *Summa Theologiae*, trans. Laurence Shapcote, eds. John Mortensen and Enrique Alarcón. Lander, WY: Aquinas Institute for the Study of Sacred Doctrine, 8 vols (= vols. 13–20 of "Latin/English Edition of the Works of St. Thomas Aquinas").

Thornton, T. C. G. 1972. "Trees, Gibbets, and Crosses." *Journal of Theological Studies* 23, 130–131.

Thurian, Max. 1968. *Marie: mère du Seigneur, figure de l'Église*. Taizé, France: Les Presses de Taizé.

Thurston, Herbert. 1953. *Familiar Prayers: Their Origin and History*. London: Burns Oates.

Tillyard, H. J. W. 1949. *The Hymns of the Octoechus*, Part II (= *Monumenta Musicae Byzantinae, Transcripta*, vol. V). Copenhagen: Ejnar Munksgaard.

Tóibín, Colm. 2012. *The Testament of Mary*. New York: Scribner.

Toporkov, A. L. 1985. "Proiskhozhdenie elementov zastol'nogo etiketa u slavian." *Etnicheskie stereotipy povedeniia*, ed. A. K. Baiburin. Leningrad, Russia: Nauka, 223–242.

Toscani, Bernard, ed. 1979. *Le laude dei Bianchi*. Florence, Italy: Libreria Editrica Fiorentina.

Towl, Elizabeth. 2010. "'Son, dey þou nat without þy modyre': The Landscape of Suffering in *The Lamentacioun of Oure Lady*." *Laments for the Lost in Medieval Literature*, ed. Jane Tolmie and M. J. Toswell. Turnhout, Belgium: Brepols, 243–263

The Towneley Plays, ed. Martin Stevens and A. C. Cawley. 1994. Oxford, UK: Oxford University Press, 2 vols.

Trachtenberg, Joshua. 1983 (1943). *The Devil and the Jews: The Medieval Conception of the Jew and Its Relation to Modern Antisemitism*. Philadelphia, PA: Jewish Publication Society.

Tradigo, Alfredo. 2006 (2004). *Icons and Saints of the Eastern Orthodox Church*, trans. Stephen Sartarelli. Los Angeles, CA: J. Paul Getty Museum.

Tran Tam Tinh, V. 1973. *Isis Lactans: Corpus des monuments gréco-romains d'Isis allaitant Harpocrate*. Leiden, Netherlands: E. J. Brill.

Trebilco, Paul. 1994. "Asia." *The Book of Acts in Its Graeco-Roman Setting*, ed. David W. J. Gill and Conrad Gempf. Grand Rapids, MI/Carlisle, UK: William B. Eerdmans/Paternoster Press, 291–362.

Trethowan, W. H., and M. F. Conlon 1965. "The Couvade Syndrome." *British Journal of Psychiatry* 111, 57–66.

Triod' postnaia. 1992. Moscow: Izdanie Moskovskoi Patriarkhii, 2 vols.

Triōdion katanuktikon. 1983. Athens: Phōs.

Tromp, S. 1932. "De Nativitate Ecclesiae ex Corde Iesu in Cruce." *Gregorianum* 13, 489–527.

Tsironis, Niki. 2011. "Emotion and the Senses in Marian Homilies of the Middle Byzantine Period." *The Cult of the Mother of God in Byzantium: Texts and Images*, ed. Leslie Brubaker and Mary B. Cunningham. Burlington, VT: Ashgate, 179–196.

Tubach, Frederic C. 1981 (1969). *Index Exemplorum: A Handbook of Medieval Religious Tales* (= *Folklore Fellows Communications*, no. 204). Helsinki: Academia Scientiarum Fennica.

Tzvetkova-Ivanova, Christina. 2000. "The Virgin Mary of the Burning Bush: From Text to Image." *Rutgers Art Review* 18, 7–26.

Uryga, Jan. 2001. *Nigdym ja ciebie, ludu, nie rzuciła: Rok Polski z Maryją*. Włocławek, Poland: Wydawnictwo Duszpasterstwa Rolników.

Uspenskii, B. A. 1996–1997. *Izbrannye trudy*. Moscow: Iazyki Russkoi Kul'tury, 3 vols.

Uspenskii, Leonid. 1989. *Bogoslovie ikony Pravoslavnoi Tserkvi*. Paris: Izdatel'stvo Zapadno-Evropeiskogo Ekzarkhata/Moskovskii Patriarkhat.
de Vaan, Michiel. 2008. *Etymological Dictionary of Latin and the Other Italic Languages*. Leiden, Netherlands: Brill.
Valliere, Paul. 2000. *Modern Russian Theology: Bukharev, Soloviev, Bulgakov. Orthodox Theology in a New Key*. Grand Rapids, MI: William B. Eerdmans.
Van Ausdall, Kristen. 2012. "Art and Eucharist in the Late Middle Ages." *A Companion to the Eucharist in the Middle Ages*, eds. Ian Christopher Levy, Gary Macy, and Kristen Van Ausdall. Leiden, Netherlands: Brill, 541–617.
Vassilaki, Maria, ed. 2000. *Mother of God: Representations of the Virgin in Byzantine Art*. Milan, Italy: Skira.
Vassilaki, Maria, ed. 2005. *Images of the Mother of God: Perceptions of the Theotokos in Byzantium*. Burlington, VT: Ashgate.
Verdier, Philippe. 1980. *Le couronnement de la Vierge: Les origines et les premiers développements d'un thème iconographique*. Montréal, QC/Paris: Institut d'études médiévales Albert-le-Grand/Librairie J. Vrin.
Verdon, Timothy. 2005 (2004). *Mary in Western Art*. Manchester, VT: Hudson Hills Press.
Vermes, Geza. 1993. *The Religion of Jesus the Jew*. Minneapolis, MN: Fortress Press.
Vermes, Geza. 2000. *The Changing Faces of Jesus*. London: Allen Lane/Penguin Press.
Vermes, Geza. 2003 (1983). *Jesus in His Jewish Context*. Minneapolis, MN: Fortress Press.
Vermes, Geza. 2006. *The Nativity: History and Legend*. New York: Doubleday.
Veselovskii, A. N. 1881. *Razyskaniia v oblasti russkago dukhovnago stikha*, parts III–V. St. Petersburg, Russia: Imperatorskaia Akademiia Nauk.
Vetter, E. M. 1958–1959. "Mulier Amicta Sole und Mater Salvatoris." *Münchner Jahrbuch der bildenden Kunst* (ser. 3) 9–10, 32–71.
Vetter, E. M. 1967. "Dornbusch, Brennender. II. Ikonographie." *Lexikon der Marienkunde*, eds. Konrad Algermissen, Ludwig Böer, Georg Englhardt, Carl Feckes, Michael Schmaus, and Julius Tyciak. Regensburg, Germany: Friedrich Pustet, vol. I, 1431–1433.
Viladesau, Richard. 2006. *The Beauty of the Cross: The Passion of Christ in Theology and the Arts, from the Catacombs to the Eve of the Renaissance*. Oxford, UK: Oxford University Press.
Villers, Caroline, Robert Gibbs, Rebecca Hellen, and Annette King. 2000. "Simone dei Crocefissi's 'Dream of the Virgin' in the Society of Antiquaries, London." *Burlington Magazine* 142 (1169), 481–486.
Vines, Amy N. 2010. "Lullaby as Lament: Learning to Mourn in Middle English Nativity Lyrics." *Laments for the Lost in Medieval Literature*, ed. Jane Tolmie and M. J. Toswell. Turnhout, Belgium: Brepols, 201–223.
Vinnikov, Viacheslav. 2000. *Ia poveril ot rozhden'ia v Bogoroditsyn pokrov*. Moscow: Rusaki.
Virgil. 1999. *Eclogues. Georgics. Aeneid I–VI*, trans. H. Rushton Fairclough, rev. G. P. Goold. Cambridge, MA: Harvard University Press (Loeb Classical Library 63).
De Visscher, Eva. 2007. "Marian Devotion in the Latin West in the Later Middle Ages." *Mary: The Complete Resource*, ed. Sarah Jane Boss. Oxford, UK: Oxford University Press, 177–203.
Vloberg, Maurice. 1946. *L'Eucharistie dans l'art*. Paris: B. Arthaud.
Vloberg, Maurice. 1954. *La Vierge et l'Enfant dans l'art français*. Paris: B. Arthaud.

Volfing, Annette. 2012. "Ever-Growing Desire: Spiritual Pregnancy in Hadewijch and in Middle High German Mystics." *Desire in Dante and the Middle Ages*, ed. Manuele Gragnolati, Tristan Kay, Elena Lombardi, and Francesca Southerden. London: Modern Humanities Research Association & Maney, 45–57.

de Voragine, Jacobus. 1850. *Jacobi a Voragine Legenda aurea vulgo Historia lombardica dicta/ad optimorum librorum fidem recensuit Th. Graesse*. Leipzig, Germany: Impensis Librariae Arnoldianae.

de Voragine, Jacobus. 1993 (1850). *The Golden Legend: Readings on the Saints*, trans. William Granger Ryan. Princeton, NJ: Princeton University Press, 2 vols.

Vovelle, Michel. 1989. "Nice, frontière du baroquisme au siècle des Lumières." *Annales du Midi: revue archéologique, historique et philologique de la France méridionale* 2 (1), 677–688.

Walafrid Strabo. 1852. "Expositio in Evangelium Lucae." *Patrologia Latina* (ed. J.-P. Migne) 114, cols. 893–904.

Waller, Gary. 2011. *The Virgin Mary in Late Medieval and Early Modern English Literature and Popular Culture*. Cambridge, UK: Cambridge University Press.

Walsh, Peter G., ed, trans. 2012. *One Hundred Latin Hymns: Ambrose to Aquinas*. Cambridge, MA: Harvard University Press.

Ward, Benedicta. 1987. *Miracles and the Medieval Mind: Theory, Record and Event, 1000–1215*. Philadelphia, PA: University of Pennsylvania Press.

Warner, Marina. 1983 (1976). *Alone of All Her Sex: The Myth and the Cult of the Virgin Mary*. New York: Random House.

Waszink, J. H. 2010. *Quinti Septimi Florentis Tertulliani De Anima*. Leiden, Netherlands: Brill.

Weber, Annette. 2001. "'. . . Maria die ist juden veind.' Antijüdische Mariendarstellungen in der Kunst des 13.–15. Jahrhunderts." *Maria – Tochter Sion? Mariologie, Marienfrömmigkeit und Judenfeindschaft*, ed. Johannes Heil and Rainer Kampling. Paderborn, Germany: Ferdinand Schöningh, 69–91.

Weber, Annette. 2008. "New Attitudes towards the Jews in the Era of Reformation and Counter-Reformation: The Patronage of Bishop Echter von Mespelbrunn." *Beyond the Yellow Badge. Anti-Judaism and Antisemitism in Medieval and Early Modern Visual Culture*, ed. Mitchell B. Merback. Leiden, Netherlands: Brill, 347–369.

Wechssler, Eduard. 1893. *Die romanischen Marienklage: ein Beitrag zur Geschichte des Dramas im Mittelalter*. Halle, Germany: E. Karras.

Weis, Adolf. 1985. *Die Madonna Platytera: Entwurf für ein Christentum als Bildoffenbarung anhand der Geschichte eines Madonnenthemas*. Königstein im Taunus, Germany: Karl Robert Langewiesche Nachfolger Hans Köster.

Weitzmann, Kurt. 1961. "The Origin of the Threnos." *Essays in Honor of Erwin Panofsky*, ed. Millard Meiss. New York: New York University Press, vol. I, 476–490.

Weitzmann, Kurt. 1978. *The Icon: Holy Images – Sixth to Fourteenth Century*. New York: George Braziller.

Wenger, Antoine. 1955. *L'Assomption de la T. S. Vierge dans la tradition byzantine du VIe au Xe siècle: études et documents*. Paris: Institut français d'études byzantines.

Werblowsky, R. J. Zwi, and Geoffrey Wigoder, eds. 1997. *The Oxford Dictionary of the Jewish Religion*. Oxford, UK: Oxford University Press.

Westermann, Claus. 1986. *Am Anfang: 1. Mose (Genesis)*. Neukirchen-Vluyn, Germany: Neukirchener.

William of Newburgh. 1960. *Explanatio sacri epithalamii in matrem sponsi*, ed. John C. Gorman. Fribourg, Switzerland: University Press (= *Spicilegium Friburgense* 6).

Williams, Paul. 2007. "The English Reformers and the Blessed Virgin Mary." *Mary: The Complete Resource*, ed. Sarah Jane Boss. Oxford, UK: Oxford University Press, 238–255.

Williams Boyarin, Adrienne. 2010. *Miracles of the Virgin in Medieval England: Law and Jewishness in Marian Legends*. Cambridge, UK: D. S. Brewer.

Williams Boyarin, Adrienne, ed., trans. 2015. *Miracles of the Virgin in Middle English*. Peterborough, ON: Broadview Press.

Williamson, Beth. 1998. "The Virgin *Lactans* as Second Eve: Image of the *Salvatrix*." *Studies in Iconography* 19, 105–138.

Williamson, Beth. 2000. "The Cloisters Double Intercession: The Virgin as Co-Redemptrix." *Apollo* 152 (November), 48–54.

Williamson, Beth. 2004. "Altarpieces, Liturgy, and Devotion." *Speculum* 79, 341–406.

Williamson, Beth. 2009. *The Madonna of Humility: Development, Dissemination & Reception, c. 1340–1400*. Woodbridge, UK: Boydell Press.

Wills, Garry. 2013. *Why Priests? A Failed Tradition*. New York: Viking.

Wilmart, André. 1971 (1932). *Auteurs spirituels et textes dévots du moyen age latin: Études d'histoire littéraire*. Paris: Études Augustiniennes.

Wilpert, Josef (Giuseppe). 1903. *Roma sotterranea: Le pitture delle catacombe romane*. Rome: Desclée, Lefebvre, 2 vols.

Winnicott, D. W. 1990 (1971). *Playing and Reality*. London: Routledge.

Witherington, Ben. 1994. *Jesus the Sage: The Pilgrimage of Wisdom*. Minneapolis, MN: Fortress Press.

Witt, R. E. 1971. *Isis in the Graeco-Roman World*. London: Thames & Hudson.

Wittkemper, K. 1967. "Dreifaltigkeit. I. Dogmatik." *Lexikon der Marienkunde*, eds. Konrad Algermissen, Ludwig Böer, Georg Englhardt, Carl Feckes, Michael Schmaus, and Julius Tyciak. Regensburg, Germany: Friedrich Pustet, vol. I, 1444–1453.

Wolf, Hubert. 2010 (2008). *Pope and Devil: The Vatican's Archives and the Third Reich*, trans. Kenneth Kronenberg. Cambridge, MA: Harvard University Press.

Woolf, Rosemary. 1968. *The English Religious Lyric in the Middle Ages*. London: Oxford University Press.

Worrell, William H. 1923. *The Coptic Manuscripts in the Freer Collection*. New York: Macmillan.

Wright, D. F. 2004. "From 'God-Bearer' to 'Mother of God' in the Later Fathers." *The Church and Mary*, ed. R. N. Swanson. Woodbridge, UK: Boydell Press, 22–30.

Yalom, Marilyn. 1997. *A History of the Breast*. New York: Ballantine Books.

Yeager, Peter. 1981. "The Dispute between Mary and the Cross: Debate Poems of the Passion." *Christianity & Literature* 30 (3), 53–69.

Young, Karl. 1962 (1933). *The Drama of the Medieval Church*. London: Oxford University Press, 2 vols.

Yuval, Israel Jacob. 2006 (2000). *Two Nations in Your Womb: Perceptions of Jews and Christians in Late Antiquity and the Middle Ages*, trans. Barbara Harshav and Jonathan Chipman. Berkeley, CA: University of California Press.

Załęcki, Marian. 1976. "Theology of a Marian Shrine: Our Lady of Częstochowa." *Marian Library Studies* (New Series) 8, 37–315.

Zerón-Medina, Fausto. 1995. *Felicidad de México: Centenario de la Coronación de María Señora de Guadalupe*. Mexico City: Editorial Clío.

Zervos, George Themelis. 2005. "Christmas with Salome." *A Feminist Companion to Mariology*, ed. Amy-Jill Levine and Maria Mayo Robbins. Cleveland, OH: Pilgrim Press, 77–98.

Ziegenaus, A. 1991. "Jungfräulichkeit. II. Dogmatik." *Marienlexikon*, ed. Remigius Bäumer and Leo Scheffczyk. St. Ottilien, Germany: EOS, vol. 3, 469–481.

Ziegler, Joanna E. 1992. *Sculpture of Compassion: The Pietà and the Beguines in the Southern Low Countries, c. 1300–c. 1600*. Brussels: Institut Historique Belge de Rome.

Zimdars-Swartz, Sandra L. 1992 (1991). *Encountering Mary: Visions of Mary from La Salette to Medjugorje*. New York: Avon Books.

Zoras, G. 1956. *Vyzantinē poiēsis*. Athens: J. N. Zacharopoulos.

Index of Biblical References

Subject Index